Lecture Notes in Computer Science 12015

More information about this series at http://www.springer.com/series/7409

Troy McDaniel · Stefano Berretti ·
Igor D. D. Curcio · Anup Basu (Eds.)

Smart Multimedia

Second International Conference, ICSM 2019
San Diego, CA, USA, December 16–18, 2019
Revised Selected Papers

 Springer

Editors
Troy McDaniel
Arizona State University
Mesa, AZ, USA

Igor D. D. Curcio (iD)
Nokia Technologies
Tampere, Finland

Stefano Berretti (iD)
University of Florence
Florence, Italy

Anup Basu
University of Alberta
Edmonton, AB, Canada

ISSN 0302-9743   ISSN 1611-3349   (electronic)
Lecture Notes in Computer Science
ISBN 978-3-030-54406-5   ISBN 978-3-030-54407-2   (eBook)
https://doi.org/10.1007/978-3-030-54407-2

LNCS Sublibrary: SL3 – Information Systems and Applications, incl. Internet/Web, and HCI

This Springer imprint is published by the registered company Springer Nature Switzerland AG
The registered company address is: Gewerbestrasse 11, 6330 Cham, Switzerland

Preface

Welcome to the proceedings of the Second International Conference on Smart Multimedia. The idea behind this conference originated from the need for bringing together smart algorithm design and various multimedia technologies ranging from smart sensing to haptics. We organized this conference with only one track to facilitate exchanges between researchers from various communities (e.g., deep learning, signal processing, haptics, computer vision, robotics, and medical multimedia processing) who are focusing on different topics. We hope this will help initiate new interdisciplinary collaborations and accelerate projects that need expertise in multiple disciplines.

In the long term, we would like to go beyond collecting big data, and using such data for learning, to understanding what smartness really means and how many animals in nature can learn and generalize from a limited number of examples.

In our second conference we received around 100 submissions. However, only around 30% could be accepted in the regular tracks due to limited space. In addition, two excellent tutorials covering the topics of "Haptics for Smart Multimedia" and "Domain Adaptation for Computer Vision" were included. Papers in the conference were organized into 14 sessions plus invited talks and tutorials, and the Springer LNCS proceedings containing the papers are arranged following these sessions into 9 topics. The topics in the proceedings include, among others: Smart Multimedia Beyond the Visible Spectrum; Smart Multimedia for Citizen-Centered Smart Living; Haptics and Applications; Multimedia in Medicine; 3D mesh and Depth Image Processing; 3D Perception; Video Applications; Machine Learning; and Smart Social and Connected Household Products. These areas cover a broad range of disciplines in the wider field of Smart Multimedia.

We thank several donors to the conference on Smart Multimedia whose gifts have not only assisted in covering the cost of organizing the conference, but have also made the variety of social events possible.

June 2020

Troy McDaniel
Stefano Berretti
Igor D. D. Curcio
Anup Basu

Organization

General Chairs

S. Panchanathan	Arizona State University, USA
A. Leleve	INSA Lyon, France
A. Basu	University of Alberta, Canada

Program Chairs

S. Berretti	University of Florence, Italy
M. Daoudi	IMT Lille, France

Area Chairs

N. Thirion-Moreau	SeaTech, France
W. Pedrycz	University of Alberta, Canada
J. Wu	University of Windsor, Canada

Industrial/Short Papers Chairs

G.-M. Su	Dolby, USA
H. Azari	Microsoft, USA
A. El-Saddik	University of Ottawa, Canada
T. Wang	SAS, USA
L. Cheng	University of Alberta, Canada

Special Sessions Chairs

T. McDaniel	Arizona State University, USA
P. Atrey	University of Albany, USA

Special Sessions Assistant

S. Soltaninejad	University of Alberta, USA

Tutorial Chair

H. Venkateswara	Arizona State University, USA

Registration Chair

Y.-P. Huang	Taipei Tech, Taiwan

Publicity Chairs

J. Zhou	Griffith University, Australia
L. Gu	NII, Japan
A. Liew	Griffith University, Australia
Q. Tian	University of Texas, USA

Finance Chair

L. Ying	Together Inc., USA

Submissions Chairs

C. Zhao	University of Alberta, Canada
S. Mukherjee	University of Alberta, Canada

Web Chair

X. Sun	University of Alberta, Canada

Advisors

E. Moreau	SeaTech, France
I. Cheng	University of Alberta, Canada

ICSM 2019 Program Committee

K. Abed-Meraim	Université d'Orléans, France
D. Aouada	University of Luxembourg, Luxembourg
S. Beauchemin	University of Western Ontario, Canada
C. Bhatt	FxPal, USA
F. Bouchara	University of Toulon, France
M. Brubaker	University of Toronto, Canada
V. Charvillat	The National Institute of Electrical Engineering, Electronics, Computer Science, Fluid Mechanics & Telecommunications and Networks, France
C. T. Y. Chet	Institute for Infocomm Research, Singapore
F. Denis	Aix-Marseille Université, France
C. Ferrari	University of Florence, Italy
L. Fillatre	UNS, CNRS, France
D. Fofi	University of Bourgogne Franche-Comté (UBFC), France
O. Garcia-Panella	Ramon Llull University, Spain
H. Ghennioui	Université Sidi Mohamed Ben Abdellah, Morocco
C. Grana	University of Modena and Reggio Emilia, Italy
A. Jepson	University of Toronto, Canada

J. Zhang   University of Technology Sydney, Australia
G. Zhao   University of Oulu, Finland
X. Zabulis   ICS-Forth, Greece
P. Zanuttigh   University of Padova, Italy
R. Zimmermann   National University of Singapore, Singapore

Contents

Multimedia in Medicine

Haptics and Applications

Smart Multimedia Beyond the Visible Spectrum

3D and Image Processing

Smart Social and Connected Household Products

Short Paper

3D Mesh and Depth Image Processing

Fused Geometry Augmented Images
for Analyzing Textured Mesh

Bilal Taha[1], Munawar Hayat[2] (ID), Stefano Berretti[3](✉)(ID),
and Naoufel Werghi[4](ID)

[1] University of Toronto, Toronto, ON, Canada
bilal.taha@mail.utoronto.ca
[2] University of Canberra, Canberra, Australia
munawar.hayat@canberra.edu.au
[3] University of Florence, Florence, Italy
stefano.berretti@unifi.it
[4] Khalifa University, Abu Dhabi, UAE
Naoufel.Werghi@ku.ac.ae

Abstract. In this paper, we propose a novel multi-modal mesh surface representation fusing texture and geometric data. Our approach defines an inverse mapping between different geometric descriptors computed on the mesh surface or its down-sampled version, and the corresponding 2D texture image of the mesh, allowing the construction of fused geometrically augmented images. This new fused modality enables us to learn feature representations from 3D data in a highly efficient manner by simply employing standard convolutional neural networks in a transfer-learning mode. In contrast to existing methods, the proposed approach is both computationally and memory efficient, preserves intrinsic geometric information and learns highly discriminative feature representation by effectively fusing shape and texture information at data level. The efficacy of our approach is demonstrated for the tasks of facial action unit detection, expression classification, and skin lesion classification, showing competitive performance with state of the art methods.

Keywords: Image representation · Mesh surface analysis · Surface classification · Learned features

1 Introduction

Compared to 2D photometric images, 3D data provides more information and is invariant to illumination, out-of-plane rotations and color variations, in addition to geometric cues, which enable better separation of the object of interest from its background. Despite being more promising and information-rich, the focus of previous research on representing 3D data has been to carefully design hand-crafted methods of feature description. While automatically learned feature representations in terms of activations of a trained deep neural network have

© Springer Nature Switzerland AG 2020
T. McDaniel et al. (Eds.): ICSM 2019, LNCS 12015, pp. 3–12, 2020.
https://doi.org/10.1007/978-3-030-54407-2_1

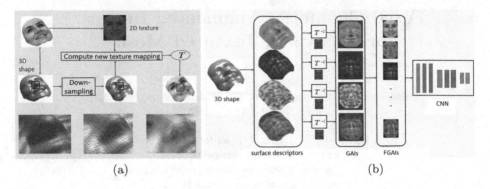

(a)   (b)

Fig. 1. Method overview: (a) Computation of a texture mapping transformation $\mathcal{T}$ between the down-sampled mesh of the face and its texture image, both derived from the original face model. (b) A variety of geometric descriptors are computed on the down-sampled face mesh surface. These are mapped to the texture 2D image using the inverse texture mapping function $\mathcal{T}^{-1}$. From the constructed *geometry-augmented images* (GAIs), we derive combinations of image triplets arranged into three-channel images. These latter *fused geometry-augmented images* (FGAIs) are used with different CNN models.

shown their superiority on a number of tasks using 2D RGB images, learning generic shape representations from surface data is still in its infancy.

In this paper, we propose an original approach to extend the application of deep learning solutions to 3D data given in the form of triangular meshes. This is obtained by developing on the idea of establishing a mapping between the 3D mesh domain and the 2D image domain. Existing mapping solutions directly generate 2D photometric images by flattening the 3D model to the image plane, or representing it by different 2D views. But, in doing so, descriptors are computed on the 2D generated images, thus losing most of the real geometry of the 3D shape. Different from previous works, we propose to directly capture the geometric information from 3D mesh surface in terms of a set of local geometric descriptors. The extracted geometric information is then fused in our proposed geometrically augmented 2D images, which can efficiently be used in conjunction with state-of-the-art CNN models. Moreover, our method makes it possible to compute the geometric descriptors on a down-sampled version of the mesh-model allowing a considerable gain in efficiency without compromising the performance. We showcase the effectiveness of our new paradigm on two applications: face recognition and classification of skin cancer.

Li *et al.* [9] is the closest work to our proposed solution. However, our method presents two fundamental differences. First, their method separately encoded texture and geometric information, and dedicates a sub-network to each descriptor. Afterwards, the related output features go into a subsequent feature-level fusion network. In contrast, in our approach, the texture and the geometric information are fused at the data level by mapping the geometric descriptors onto texture images, then rendering multiple three-channel images, which are fed as input to the CNN model. Second, their geometry maps are obtained by computing the geometric attributes on the face mesh model, then displaying and saving them as 2D images. In our method, we rather establish a correspondence between geometric descriptors computed on 3D triangular facets of the mesh and pixels in the texture image. Specifically, in our case, geometric attributes are computed on the mesh at each triangle facet, and then mapped to their corresponding pixels in the texture image using the newly proposed scheme. Third, our method is computationally more-efficient as we compute the geometric attributes on a compressed facial mesh surface. With respect to the conformal mapping method proposed by Kittler *et al.* [6], our method presents three fundamental differences. First, in [6], the mapping is performed fitting a generic 3D morphable face model (3DMM) to the 2D face image, whereas in our solution we map each face model of a subject to its corresponding 2D face image. Second, the geometric information mapped from the 3DMM to the 2D image is given by the point coordinates, which are just an estimate of the actual values, obtained from the 3DMM by landmark-based model fitting. In our work, instead, we map the actual point coordinates, in addition to other varieties of shape descriptors, from each face model to its corresponding image. Third, in terms of scope, while the work in [6] deals with 2D face recognition, our work extends to any 3D textured mesh surface. In [21], similarly to [6], a 3DMM is fit to a 2D image, but for face image frontalization purposes. The face alignment method employs a cascaded CNN to handle the self-occlusions. Finally, in [16], a spherical parameterization of the mesh manifold is performed allowing a two-dimensional structure that can be treated by conventional CNNs.

In the next section, we elaborate on our proposed scheme. Afterwards, in Sect. 3, we describe the experiments validating our proposed method, then we terminate by concluding remarks in Sect. 4.

2   3D Learned Feature Representation

As shown in the block diagram of Fig. 1, our proposed framework jointly exploits the 3D shape and 2D texture information. First, we perform a down-sampling on the facial surface derived from the full 3D face model. Subsequently, we compute the new texture mapping transformation T between the texture image and the compressed mesh. Afterward, we extract a group of local shape descriptors that include *mean* and *Gaussian* curvature (H, K), *shape index* (SI), and the *local-depth* (LD). These local descriptors can be computed efficiently and complement each other by encoding different shape information. We also consider the *gray-level* (GL) of the original 2D texture image associated to the mesh. A novel scheme is then proposed to map the extracted geometric descriptors onto 2D textured images, using the inverse of the texture mapping transform T. We dubbed these images *Geometry Augmented Images* (GAIs). It is relevant to note here that we assume the existence of a 2D texture image, which is in correspondence with the triangulated mesh via standard texture-mapping. In this respect, our solution can also be regarded as a multi-modal 2D+3D solution, where the

2D texture data is required to enable the mapping, and also constitutes an additional feature that can be early fused with the 3D data in a straightforward way. Here, triplets of GAIs originated from the 3D-to-2D descriptors mapping are then fused to generate multiple three-channel images. We dubbed these images *Fused Geometry Augmented Images* (FGAIs). The FGAIs are used as input to a CNN network to generate, through their output activations, a highly discriminative feature representation to be used in the subsequent classification stage. To the best of our knowledge, we are the first to propose such 2D and 3D information fusion for textured-geometric data analysis.

Given a triangular mesh originated from a surface, we project the mesh vertices onto the plane spanned by the main orientation of the surface. This yields the depth function $z = f(x, y)$ defined on the scattered set of vertices. The function is then interpolated and re-computed over a regular grid constructed by a uniform down-sampling of order k. The 2D Delaunay triangulation computed over the achieved regular points produces a set of uniform triangular facets. We complete them with interpolated z coordinate to obtain a 3D down-sampled regular mesh (Fig. 1(a)). A sub-sampling of step k produces approximately a compression ratio of k for both the facets and the vertices. As the original 3D mesh has an associated texture image, the mapping between the mesh and the texture image is established by the usual texture mapping approach, where the vertices of each triangle (facet) on the mesh are mapped to three points (*i.e.*, pixels) in the image. However, the projection and the re-sampling step break such correspondence. Therefore, in the next stage, we reconstruct a new texture mapping between the 2D face image and the newly re-sampled mesh vertices. For each vertex in the re-sampled mesh, we use its nearest neighbor in the original mesh, computed in the previous stage, to obtain the corresponding pixel in the original image via the texture mapping information in the original face scan. This new obtained texture mapping transformation ($\mathcal{T}$ in Fig. 1) between the original image and the new re-sampled facial mesh allows us to map descriptors computed on the facial surface, at any given mesh resolution, to a 2D *geometry-augmented image* (GAI), which encodes the surface descriptor as pixel values in a 2D image. In order to keep consistent correspondence between the texture information and the geometric descriptors, we down-sample the original texture images to bring it at the same resolution of its GAI counterpart. We do this as follows: we take the vertices of each facet in the down-sampled facial mesh, and we compute, using $\mathcal{T}^{-1}$ their corresponding pixels in the original image. These three pixels form a triangle in the original image; we assign to all pixels that are confined in that triangle the average of their gray-level values (Fig. 2(a)(b)(c)). Figure 2(d) depicts the GAIs obtained by mapping the LD descriptor computed on the original mesh and its down-sampled counterpart, at a compressed ratio of 3.5.

After mapping the extracted local geometric descriptors onto the 2D textured images, we encode the shape information with the help of a compact 2D matrix. As we extract four local geometric descriptors, the shape information is represented by their corresponding three 2D GAIs, to which we add the gray level

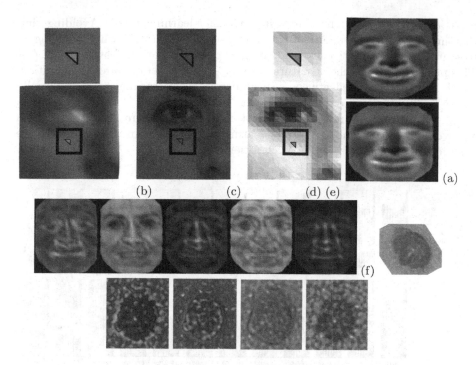

Fig. 2. (a) A triangular facet in a down-sampled face mesh; (b) The texture mapping associates the vertices of the facet in (a) to three pixels in the texture image forming a triangle; (c) All the pixels confined in the triangle in (b) are assigned their mean gray level; (d) GAIs obtained by 2D mapping of the LD descriptor computed on the original mesh (top) and its down-sampled version (bottom); (e) FGAIs generated for a sample face with the combination H-LD-SI, H-GL-SI, K-H-SI, GL-LD-SI, K-H-LD; (f) a textured lesion surface and its FGAIs images GL-SI-LD, H-GL-LD, H-K-GL, and K-GL-SI.

image. We propose to fuse the shape information in terms of multiple descriptors by selecting three descriptors at once. This results in ten three-channel *Fused Geometry Augmented images* (FGAIs). Each FGAI realizes a sort of early fusion between the descriptors. For example, an FGAI can be a combination of the three K, SI and GL GAIs, and thus labelled with K-SI-GL. Figure 2(e)(f) depicts some FGAI examples related to face and a skin lesion.

The proposed FGAIs constitute a data-fusion scheme, as opposed to feature-level scheme, where the fusion operates on the features derived from the input images. Here, a CNN can act as feature extractor to each GAI type, and the derived features can be fed at fusion layer, which output goes to a fully connected layer followed by an SVM or softmax classifier. This feature-level fusion architecture was adopted by Li *et al.* [9]. We believe that our data-fusion approach will be more advantageous for three main reasons: *(i)* low-level fusion performs better than higher-level counterparts [12]; *(ii)* Our data-fusion allows us to utilize

pre-trained powerful architectures in a transfer-learning mode. Avoiding thus
the time demanding training of CNNs created from scratch, while allowing us
to gain from the effectiveness and the generality of learned features [11]; *(iii)*
This proposed fusion scheme naturally brings-in the effect of data augmentation,
which has proved its effectiveness in numerous deep learning tasks, especially
where limited training data are available. Therefore, we employed the FGAIs in
a transfer-learning approach using two standard architectures, the AlexNet and
Vgg-vd16, in a reuse mode, whereby features extracted from these networks are
used in conjunction with an SVM classifier.

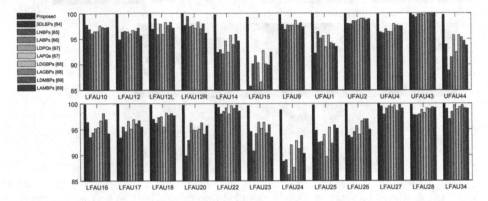

Fig. 3. Bosphorus dataset: AU detection measured as AuC for each of the 24 AUs.
Results for 12 AUs are reported in the upper plot, and for the rest in the lower one
(notation: LF and UF stay, respectively, for lower- and upper-face; R and L indicate the
left and right part of the face). Comparison includes the following state-of-the-art methods: 3DLBPs [4], LNBPs [14], LABPs [13], LDPQs [10], LAPQs [10], LDGBPs [20],
LAGBPs [20], LDMBPs [17], LAMBPs [17].

3   Experiments

We demonstrated the effectiveness of our representation paradigm on three tasks:
facial expression recognition, action unit (AU) detection, and skin cancer classification, using respectively, the Bosphorus 3D face database [15], the Binghamton
University 4D Facial Expression database (BU-4DFE) [19], and the Dermofit
dataset[1]. First, we conducted an ablative analysis experimentation that aims to
compare the performance of the different variants in terms of the FGAI combination, the CNN layer used to derive the output features, and the down-sampled
data versus the original data. Because of the limited space, we just report the best
variant obtained for each dataset, namely, AlexNet-Conv4, H-GL-SI, AlexNet-
Conv4, H-LD-SI, and Vgg-vd16-Conv5$_3$ H-GL-LD for Bosphorus, BU-4DE and

---

[1] https://licensing.eri.ed.ac.uk/i/software/dermofit-image-library.html.

Dermofit, respectively. Note that for the Dermofit, we augmented and normalized the data using the same protocol reported in [5].

For AU classification, we compared our results with a number of existing methods, adopting the same protocol (*i.e.*, 5-fold cross validation, $3,838$ AU scans of 105 subjects). Figure 3 shows the AuC results for each AU individually, obtained with our proposed method, using the combination (H-GL-SI), together with the state-of-the-art methods. Computing the average AuC on all the AUs, it can be observed that our proposed feature representation scheme achieves the highest score of 99.79%, outperforming the current state-of-the art AuC of 97.2%, which is scored by the Depth Gabor Binary Patterns (LDGBP) feature proposed in [13].

For facial expression recognition, we adopted the same experimentation protocol reported in the recent state-of-the-art methods [7–9, 18] (10-cross validation, expression scans collected from 60 subjects, randomly selected from 65 individuals). Results obtained with the H-GL-SI are reported in Table 1. For both original and compressed face scans our method outperforms the current state-of-the-art solutions by a significant margin of 18%/13% and 17%/12% for the learned features of the AlexNet and the Vgg-vd16, respectively.

Table 1. Comparison with the state-of-the-art on the Bosphorus dataset using the following configuration: FGAI H-GL-SI.

Method	Accuracy
MS-LNPs [15]	75.83
GSR [16]	77.50
iPar-CLR [17]	79.72
DF-CNN svm [1]	80.28
Original-AlexNet	**98.27**
Compressed-AlexNet	**93.29**
Original-Vgg-vd16	**98.16**
Compressed-Vgg-vd16	**92.38**

On BU-4DFE, we experimented our proposed method in a static mode, whereby we recognized the expression in each frame. We considered seven classes, *i.e.*, the neutral expression plus the six other expressions. Classification has been obtained using 5-fold cross validation, which makes our setting quite comparable to [3] and [1]. Table 2 reports results obtained with our method together with competitive state-of-the-art solutions. Note that the first method in [3] employs geometric and HOG descriptors with a standard random forest classifier, while the second uses geometric descriptors and CNN features with the neural forest classifier. We notice that our proposed method outperforms the state-of-the-art solutions by a large margin of 17% and 15% for the AlexNet and the Vgg-vd16 versions, respectively.

Table 2. Comparison with the state-of-the-art on the BU-4DFE dataset using the following configuration: FGAI H-LD-SI.

Method	Accuracy
Abd EI Meguid et al. [19]	73.10
Dapogny et al. [18]-1	72.80
Dapogny et al. [18]-2	74.00
Compressed-AlexNet	**91.34**
Compressed-Vgg-vd16	**89.81**

Table 3. Comparison with the state-of-the-art on the Dermofit dataset using the following configuration: FGAI H-GL-LD.

Method	5 classes	2 classes
[2]	75.1	92.7
[5]	85.8	94.8
Compressed-AlexNet	**88.7**	**96.2**
Compressed-Vgg-vd16	**88.9**	**97.3**

The dermofit dataset comprehends 10 lesion categories, named as AK, BCC, ML, SCC, SK, IEC, PYO, VSC, DF and MEL. However, we found that only five classes (AK, BCC, ML, SCC, SK) contain complete 3D images counterparts. Therefore, we focused our experimentation on these 5 classes, as in [2] and [5]. They also adopted a 2-class classification, namely, cancer (ML, SK), and potential risk lesion class (BCC, SCC, AK). In both problems, they adopted 3-fold cross validation. Results obtained with our method together with those reported in [2] and [5] are compiled in Table 3, whereby we can notice that our variant compressed-Vgg-vd16 achieves the best score with an accuracy of 88.9% and 97.32% for the 5 classes and the 2 classes, respectively.

4   Conclusion

We proposed a novel scheme, which maps the geometric information from 3D meshes onto 2D textured images, providing a mechanism to simultaneously represent geometric attributes from the mesh-model alongside with the texture information. The proposed mapped geometric information can be employed in conjunction with a CNN for jointly learning 2D and 3D information fusion at the data level, while providing a highly discriminative representation. Compared to existing learned feature representation schemes for 3D data, the proposed method is both memory and computation efficient as it does not resort to expensive tensor-based or multi-view inputs. The effectiveness of our representation has been demonstrated on three different surface classification tasks, showing a neat boost in the performance when compared to competitive methods.

Acknowledgment. This work is supported by a research fund from Cyber-Physical Systems Center (C2PS), Khalifa University, UAE.

References

1. Abd El Meguid, M.K., et al.: Fully automated recognition of spontaneous facial expressions in videos using random forest classifiers. IEEE Trans. Affect. Comput. **5**(2), 141–154 (2014). https://doi.org/10.1109/TAFFC.2014.2317711
2. Ballerini, L., et al.: A color and texture based hierarchical K-NN approach to the classification of non-melanoma skin lesions. In: Celebi, M., Schaefer, G. (eds.) Color Medical Image Analysis, vol. 6, pp. 63–86. Springer, Dordrecht (2015). https://doi.org/10.1007/978-94-007-5389-1_4
3. Dapogny, A., et al.: Investigating deep neural forests for facial expression recognition. In: IEEE International Conference on Automatic Face and Gesture Recognition (FG), pp. 629–633, May 2018
4. Huang, Y., et al.: Combining statistics of geometrical and correlative features for 3D face recognition (2006)
5. Kawahara, J., et al.: Deep features to classify skin lesions. In: International Symposium on Biomedical Imaging (2016)
6. Kittler, J., et al.: Conformal mapping of a 3D face representation onto a 2D image for CNN based face recognition. In: International Conference on Biometrics, pp. 146–155 (2018)
7. Li, H., et al.: 3d facial expression recognition via multiple kernel learning of multi-scale local normal patterns. In: ICPR, pp. 2577–2580 (2012)
8. Li, H., et al.: An efficient multimodal 2D + 3D feature-based approach to automatic facial expression recognition. Comput. Vis. Image Underst. **140**(Suppl. C), 83–92 (2015)
9. Li, H., et al.: Multimodal 2D+3D facial expression recognition with deep fusion convolutional neural network. IEEE Trans. Multimed. **19**(12), 2816–2831 (2017). https://doi.org/10.1109/TMM.2017.2713408
10. Ojansivu, V., Heikkilä, J.: Blur insensitive texture classification using local phase quantization. In: Elmoataz, A., Lezoray, O., Nouboud, F., Mammass, D. (eds.) ICISP 2008. LNCS, vol. 5099, pp. 236–243. Springer, Heidelberg (2008). https://doi.org/10.1007/978-3-540-69905-7_27
11. Razavian, S., et al.: CNN features off-the-shelf: an astounding baseline for recognition. In: IEEE Conference on Computer Vision and Pattern Recognition Workshops (CVPRW), pp. 806–813 (2014)
12. Ross, A., Jain, A.K.: Information fusion in biometrics. Pattern Recogn. Lett. **24**, 2115–2125 (2003)
13. Sandbach, G., et al.: Binary pattern analysis for 3D facial action unit detection. In: British Machine Vision Conference (BMVC), pp. 119.1–119.12. BMVA Press, September 2012
14. Sandbach, G., et al.: Local normal binary patterns for 3D facial action unit detection. In: IEEE International Conference on Image Processing (ICIP), pp. 1813–1816, September 2012
15. Savran, A., Alyüz, N., Dibeklioğlu, H., Çeliktutan, O., Gökberk, B., Sankur, B., Akarun, L.: Bosphorus database for 3D face analysis. In: Schouten, B., Juul, N.C., Drygajlo, A., Tistarelli, M. (eds.) BioID 2008. LNCS, vol. 5372, pp. 47–56. Springer, Heidelberg (2008). https://doi.org/10.1007/978-3-540-89991-4_6

16. Sinha, A., Bai, J., Ramani, K.: Deep learning 3D shape surfaces using geometry images. In: Leibe, B., Matas, J., Sebe, N., Welling, M. (eds.) ECCV 2016. LNCS, vol. 9910, pp. 223–240. Springer, Cham (2016). https://doi.org/10.1007/978-3-319-46466-4_14
17. Yang, M., et al.: Monogenic binary pattern (MBP): a novel feature extraction and representation model for face recognition. In: International Conference on Pattern Recognition, pp. 2680–2683 (2010)
18. Yang, X., et al.: Automatic 3D facial expression recognition using geometric scattering representation. In: IEEE International Conference and Workshops on Automatic Face and Gesture Recognition (FG), vol. 1, pp. 1–6, May 2015
19. Yin, L., et al.: A high-resolution 3D dynamic facial expression database. In: IEEE Conference on Face and Gesture Recognition (FG), pp. 1–6, September 2008
20. Zhang, W., et al.: Local gabor binary pattern histogram sequence (LGBPHS): a novel non-statistical model for face representation and recognition. In: IEEE International Conference on Computer Vision (ICCV), vol. 1, pp. 786–791, October 2005
21. Zhu, X., et al.: Face alignment across large poses: a 3D solution. In: IEEE Conference on Computer Vision and Pattern Recognition (CVPR), pp. 146–155, June 2016

Textureless Object Recognition Using an RGB-D Sensor

Gabriel Lugo[1(✉)], Nasim Hajari[1], Ashley Reddy[2], and Irene Cheng[1]

[1] Multimedia Research Centre, University of Alberta, Edmonton, AB, Canada
{lugobust,hajari,locheng}@ualberta.ca
[2] Rational Robotics, Edmonton, AB, Canada
ashley@rationalrobotics.com

Abstract. Object recognition is a significant task in an industrial assembly line, where a robotic arm should pick a small, textureless, and mostly homogeneous object to place it in its designated location. Despite all the recent advancements in object recognition, the problem still remains challenging for textureless industrial parts with similar shapes. In this paper, we propose an effective and real-time system using a single RGB-D camera to recognize the industrial objects placed at arbitrary viewing direction around the vertical axis. First, we segment the region of interest using an improved watershed segmentation approach. Then, we extract low-level geometrical features. Finally, we train five models and compare their accuracy based on different rotation strategies. Our experimental results highlight the efficiency as well as real-time suitability of our approach.

Keywords: Textureless objects · Object recognition · Robotics

1 Introduction

Shape recognition plays a significant role in manufacturing and production processes. These applications usually require a robotic system to perform precise commonplace tasks such as pick-and-place or object inspection. Several challenges can arise through this process [30] which lead to applying different computer vision and shape analysis techniques. However, even the mentioned techniques cannot solve the industrial application's challenges effectively as the industrial parts are usually textureless, similar and homogeneous.

Shape analysis techniques have been widely studied and can be divided into two main classes: shape representation and shape description methods. A shape representation method is a graph where the important attributes of the shape are preserved. On the other hand, shape description methods provide a shape descriptor, commonly called feature vector, represented by numerical data. A good shape descriptor should quantify the shape effectively as well as represent essential properties, *i.e.*, identifiability, affine invariance, noise resistance, occultation invariance and so on [44]. Shape recognition, in the machine learning

© Springer Nature Switzerland AG 2020
T. McDaniel et al. (Eds.): ICSM 2019, LNCS 12015, pp. 13–27, 2020.
https://doi.org/10.1007/978-3-030-54407-2_2

paradigm, generally consists of two well-known stages called training and evaluation. In the training stage, a number of samples are collected and then processed to determine a set of characteristics that can accurately and uniquely represent each object. Once the feature set is obtained, one can proceed to train a model that allows separating the features and therefore be able to distinguish between the different classes of the objects. The major challenge is designing a recognition system with real-time capabilities, robust against occlusions, illumination variations, and noisy environments. Industrial objects are usually textureless (*e.g.*, made of aluminum material), small and homogeneous, and therefore, extracting a representative and unique feature set is even more challenging. That is why current object recognition algorithms often fail to recognize industrial parts.

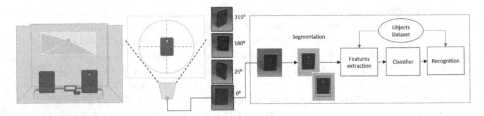

Fig. 1. An illustration of our object recognition framework: (Left) A 48×48 cm² box, where multiple objects are placed on the electric motorized 360° rotating turntable. Three different objects are shown in this example. (Center) We used the Intel RealSense D415 sensor and its field of view FOV (H × V × D with range of 69.4° × 42.5° × 77° +/− 3°) to capture the entire experimental scene. Four different views with rotation 0°, 25°, 180°, and 315° of an example object are shown. (Right) Our object recognition processing pipeline.

In this paper, we propose a real-time object recognition system for industrial assembly applications. We simulate such an industrial application scenario by using small plastic objects with similar shapes. We place these objects at the top of an electric turntable to create different viewing perspectives, as shown in Fig. 1. Although we use an RGB-D sensor, only optical data is needed for our object recognition. We have four representative objects and capture their images from arbitrary orientation around the y-axis (with respect to the camera). A segmentation process is applied to locate the objects in the image. The second step is extracting an adaptive and compact representation of essential RGB characteristics. Note that although we use the term RGB, color is not needed as a feature in our analysis. Finally, we apply different machine learning algorithms to train our object recognition model. The rest of the paper is structured as follows. Section 2 briefly reviews the related work on object recognition. Section 3 presents the different stages of the processing pipeline. Section 4 investigates the performance of different machine learning algorithms. Section 5 shows the experimental results, and finally, Section 6 concludes the paper.

2   Relate Work

The original object detection methods were based on shape descriptors. Several shape descriptors have been proposed by researchers. They can be categorized into two groups: region based and contour based descriptors depending on pixel values or curvature information [11].

Shape matrix [13], Zernike moments [6], convex hull [10], moment-based descriptors [24], and media axis features [19] are some region based shape descriptors that have been proposed in the literature. Moment based descriptors are very popular among them. It is shown that they are usually concise, computational cost effective, robust and easy to compute, as well as invariant to scaling, rotation, and translation of the object. However, it is difficult to correlate higher order moments with the shape's salient features due to the global nature of these methods [6]. The media axis features are robust to noise, but are computationally expensive due to their capability to reduce information redundancy.

Some of the proposed contour based shape descriptors are harmonic shape representation [31], Fourier descriptors [46], Wavelet descriptors [9], chain code [14], curvature scale space (CSC) descriptors [29], spectral descriptors [8] and boundary moments [42]. Fourier and Wavelet descriptors are stable over noise in the spectral domain, while chain code is sensitive to noise. CSC descriptors capture the maximal contour known as the object's CSC contour. This approach is robust to noise, changes in scale and orientation of objects, but does not always produce results consistent with the human visual system [1,45].

Visual recognition is another key factor used to improve the accuracy of object detection and recognition. Techniques such as histogram of oriented gradient (HOG) [25], local ternary patterns (LTP) [7], local binary patterns (LBP) [36], scale invariant feature transform (SIFT) [12], binary robust independent elementary features (BRIEF) [5], speed-up robust features (SURF) [43], and oriented fast and rotated brief (ORB) [40] have been proposed over the years. However, these techniques still have insufficiencies. For example, various images of a specific object may appear profoundly different due to changes in the orientation of the object and lighting conditions [28]. SIFT and ORB are robust descriptors that facilitate the object recognition. Although SIFT is slower than ORB, it is more stable. Both SIFT and ORB are suitable for real-time applications. However, these methods rely on textural patterns, and if the objects do not have enough textural information, like most of the industrial robotic automation and machine shop applications, they will fail to detect objects accurately.

In order to improve the accuracy of traditional object detection methods, people later combined machine learning techniques with shape descriptors [18,39]. Many machine learning algorithms, such as support vector machine (SVM) [22], decision trees (DT) [35], linear discriminant analysis (LDA) [2], Naive Bayes (NB) [15], random forest (RF) [4], learning vector quantization (LVQ) [27], k-means [20] and k-medians [26] have been tested and showed their efficiencies in solving classification problems.

Others object recognition approaches like LINE2D [23] and their variants, examine a template of sparse points across a gradient map. These approaches capture the target shape directly without extracting the edges. The trade-off is a high false positive rate due to the lack of edge connectivity information in the object recognition process.

More recently, Artificial Neural Networks (ANN) gain popularity in solving computer vision problems [32]. Current approaches for object detection are based on bounding boxes, reconstruction of features in each detected bounding box, and high-quality classifiers. These approaches are driven by the success of region proposal methods and region-based convolutional neural networks (R-CNNs) [17]. Fast R-CNN [16] and Region Proposal Network (RPN) + Fast R-CNN [38] are more effective and accurate than original region-based CNNs. Despite their advancements, these methods are still computationally intensive. Therefore, an embedded system, even with high-end hardware, is unable to perform the recognition tasks in real-time.

The usefulness of robust baseline systems, such as Faster R-CNN, Fully Convolutional Network (FCN), and YOLO9000 [37] frameworks, improved the object detection and semantic segmentation rapidly. These methods are conceptually intuitive and offer flexibility and robustness. They also provide fast training and inference time. A novel method called Mask R-CNN [21], extends Faster R-CNN by adding a branch for predicting segmentation masks on each Region of Interest (RoI), in parallel with the existing branch for classification and bounding box regression. The mask branch is a small FCN applied to each RoI, predicting a segmentation mask in a pixel-to-pixel manner. Mask R-CNN is simple to implement and train, given the Faster R-CNN framework, which facilitates a wide range of flexible architecture designs. The mask branch enables a fast system and practical experimentation. However, a major limitation of these deep learning-based approaches is the demand of numerous representative training samples for high accuracy performance [34].

3   Proposed Method

Although our processing pipeline consists of a number of steps, as shown in Fig. 1, our object recognition framework has two major components: object detection and object recognition. During object detection, the RGB input image is transformed initially into grayscale image. Then, the image is segmented into background and foreground regions using a watershed segmentation approach. Morphological operations are applied later to remove noise. For object recognition, we train several models to predict the different object classes based on a set of features extracted from the segmented regions.

3.1   Data Acquisition

We use an Intel RealSense D415 camera for image acquisition. This sensor uses an optical image sensor to capture regular RGB images and stereo vision to calculate depth. The camera offers high RGB-D resolution capabilities and is very light and easy to use in industrial environments. We fix the camera with a

Fig. 2. Experimental setup in a controlled environment.

tripod in front of an automatic turntable in this experiment. The camera must be placed with a minimum distance of 20 cm from the scene according to the sensor specifications. The electric 360° rotating turntable is used to capture 2D images of each object from different viewing directions. Note that the objects are plastic rigid with no texture. However, any objects with matt material can be used. The setup is arranged in an enclosed environment to control the illumination condition. Figure 2 shows our experimental setup.

3.2 Dataset

In order to match the design of manufactured parts, we use the Prusa i3 3D printer to print 3D industrial parts. We create 4 small plastic objects using the same material and without texture attributes. Two of the objects are very similar in shape, which makes the recognition very challenging. To create our database, each object is rotated 360° on the y-axis and captured with a refresh rate of 30 fps. The resolution of the images in the database is 640 × 360. Since our application is for the pick-and-place assembly line of small parts, our system should be robust toward translation and y-axis rotation changes. Therefore, in our test scenes, we placed the objects in random viewpoints with respect to the camera.

3.3 Segmentation

The objective of segmentation is to select the target object(s) in the RGB data stream. We apply the watershed transformation technique by Meyer *et al.* [3], which is a morphological algorithm for image segmentation. The algorithm groups the pixels in an image based on their intensity similarity. It uses gray values of the input image, which is interpreted as a topographic surface. The sequential "flooding" of the surface minima of the pixel intensities, partitions the gradient image into watershed lines and catchment basins. The watershed transformation produces closed object contours at low computational cost compared to other more sophisticated vision-based segmentation techniques.

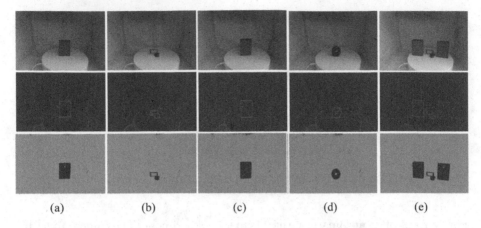

(a)   (b)   (c)   (d)   (e)

Fig. 3. Top row: shows different scenes with single and multiple objects. Middle row: shows images after applying the morphological Sobel operator. Bottom row: shows the segmentation of the objects using our modified watershed algorithm. The first (a), second (b) and (c–d) columns, represent object A, object C, object B, and object D respectively. The last column (e) shows a scene with objects A, B and C randomly placed.

In practice, this traditional transformation often leads to over-segmentation due to noise in the data. We use the marker-based watershed approach, where the watershed transformation floods the elevation image, starting from the markers. This solves the problem of over segmentation. However, it is necessary to pre-process the optical image to determine the catchment basins of these markers. The marker regions are pixels that we can label unambiguously as either object or background. Markers are found at the two extreme parts of the gray value histogram. A good choice of the elevation map is critical for segmentation, and we use the gradient amplitude to generate the elevation map. This technique works best if the foreground and background histograms are distinctive. Otherwise, choosing useful markers for background and foreground can be challenging.

We apply the simple and fast sobel operator to compute the amplitude of the gradient in the optical image. The sobel filter uses two 3×3 kernels: One for changes in the horizontal direction, and one for changes in the vertical direction. The two kernels are convolved with the original image to measure an approximation of the derivatives. Even if the markers in the background are not well distributed, the barriers in the elevation map are high enough for these markers to flood the entire background. After that, small holes are removed with mathematical morphological operations. Using these regions, we apply the classical marker-based watershed transformation to detect the objects in the image. As shown in Fig. 3, our approach provides good quality object segmentation with a low computational cost. After successful segmentation of the ROI, different features for each segmented region are extracted to uniquely characterize each object.

3.4 Feature Extraction

The extracted feature set should represent different characteristics of each object correctly and uniquely, even from different viewing direction. This is especially important for similar objects with minimal variations. Even dissimilar objects can be quite alike from one direction but will show distinctive characteristics from another direction. To achieve this goal, we extract different shape related features such as area, contour, corners, and other geometrical characteristics.

Below is an overview of the pixel and region properties deployed for feature extraction:

- Area: This computes the total number of pixels in the labeled region:

$$Area = \sum_{x=1}^{m} \sum_{y=1}^{n} f(x,y) \tag{1}$$

  where f is the pixel label in a two-dimensional space, m and n represent the pixel count along the x and y axis respectively.
- Bounding box: The smallest rectangle containing the labelled region after the segmentation stage, denoted by the vector $[x, y, w, h]$, where x and y are the coordinates of the center of mass of the labelled region, w and h are width and height of the bounding box respectively.
- Eccentricity: The eccentricity of the ellipse that has the same second-moments as the labelled region. Eccentricity is the ratio of the focal distance (distance between focal points) divided by the major axis. The value is in the interval (0, 1). When it is 0, the ellipse becomes a circle.

$$Eccentricity = \left(\frac{\max \sum_{x=1}^{m} f(x,:)}{\min \sum_{y=1}^{m} f(:,y)} \right) \tag{2}$$

- Extent: Extent is the ratio of pixels in the labelled region to pixels in the total bounding box.

$$Extent = (\frac{Area}{Area\ of\ Bounding\ box}) \tag{3}$$

- Orientation: This is the angle, ranging from $-\pi/2$ to $+\pi/2$ counter-clockwise, between the 0th axis (rows) and the major axis of the ellipse, that has the same second moments as the labelled region.
- Perimeter: We approximate the contour of an object by measuring the line through the centres of border pixels using a 4-connectivity.
- Solidity: It is measured as the ratio of the area of an object to the area of a convex hull of the object.
- Hu Moments: Moment invariants have been a classical approach for object recognition during the last decades. These invariant moments were firstly presented in the pattern recognition community by Hu [24], who employed the results of the theory of algebraic invariants and derived the seven important

invariants to rotation of objects in 2D images. A two-dimensional $(p+q)th$ order moment is described as follow:

$$m_{pq} = \int_{-\infty}^{\infty} \int_{-\infty}^{\infty} x^p y^q g(x,y) dx dy \tag{4}$$

For a given image $g(x,y)$, the moments of all orders exist if the image is represented by a piecewise continuous bounded function. The moment sequence m_{pq} is uniquely determined by $g(x,y)$; and conversely, $g(x,y)$ is also uniquely determined by the moment sequence m_{pq}. The invariant features can be found using central moments, which are defined as follow:

$$\mu_{pq} = \int_{-\infty}^{\infty} \int_{-\infty}^{\infty} (x - \bar{x})^p (y - \bar{y})^q f(x,y) dx dy \tag{5}$$

Where $\bar{x} = \frac{m_{10}}{m_{00}}$ and $\bar{y} = \frac{m_{01}}{m_{00}}$, represent the centroid of the image $f(x,y)$. The centroid moment μ_{pq} is computed using the centroid of the image which is equivalent to m_{pq}, whose center has been shifted to coincide with its centroid. The normalized central moments are defined as follow:

$$\eta_{pq} = \frac{\mu_{pq}}{\mu_{00}^\gamma}, \ \gamma = (p+q+2)/2, \ p+q = 2, 3, ...,) \tag{6}$$

Based on normalized central moments, the seven moment invariants used are:

$$\phi_1 = \eta_{20} + \eta_{02}$$
$$\phi_2 = (\eta_{20} - \eta_{02})^2 + 4\eta_{11}^2$$
$$\phi_3 = (\eta_{30} - 3\eta_{12})^2 + (3\eta_{21} - \mu_{03})^2$$
$$\phi_4 = (\eta_{30} + 3\eta_{12})^2 + (3\eta_{21} + \mu_{03})^2$$
$$\phi_5 = (\eta_{30} - 3\eta_{12})(\eta_{30} + \eta_{12})[(\eta_{30} + \eta_{12})^2 - 3(\eta_{21} + \eta_{03})^2]$$
$$+3(\eta_{21} - \eta_{03})(\eta_{21} + \eta_{03})[3(\eta_{30} + \eta_{12})^2 - (\eta_{21} + \eta_{03})^2]$$
$$\phi_6 = (\eta_{20} - \eta_{02})[(\eta_{30} + \eta_{12})^2 - (\eta_{21} + \eta_{03})^2] + 4\eta_{11}(\eta_{30} + \eta_{12})(\eta_{21} + \eta_{03})$$
$$\phi_7 = (3\eta_{21} - \eta_{03})(\eta_{30} + \eta_{12})[(\eta_{30} + \eta_{12})^2 - 3(\eta_{21} + \eta_{03})^2]$$
$$-(\eta_{30} - 3\eta_{12})(\eta_{21} + \eta_{03})[3(\eta_{30} + \eta_{12})^2 - (\eta_{21} + \eta_{03})^2]$$

These seven moment invariants have useful properties, which are robust under image scaling, translation and rotation.

– Filled area: Describes the number of pixels in the labelled region with all the holes filled.

4   Classification

We automatically detect objects using the proposed detection and segmentation method. Features are extracted from the segmented regions. Five supervised

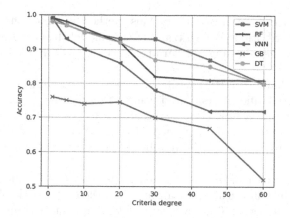

Fig. 4. Comparison of different classifiers (SVM, RF, KNN, GB and DT) using different rotation strategies.

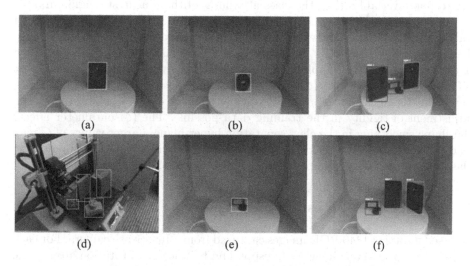

Fig. 5. Examples of object recognition: our method can handle single (a, b and e) or multiple objects in scenes (c, f). The bounding box around the object indicates that the target object is labelled correctly. (d) A different configuration background.

machine learning algorithms, namely K-Nearest Neighbor (KNN), Decision Tree (DT), Random Forest (RF), Naive Bayes (NB), and Support Vector Machines (SVM) are used for classification. We also analyze and compare the performance of these algorithms as shown in Fig. 4. NB is a supervised learning algorithm, which applies Bayes' theorem with the naive assumption of strong conditional independence between every pair of features. This method makes use of all the variables in the feature vector X and analyses them independently as they are uniformly independent of each other. The Gaussian Naive Bayes method is the easiest to work with as it only needs to estimate the mean μ and the standard deviation σ from the training vector. This method assumes that features follow a normal distribution. Before training this model, feature normalization is applied to normalize the range of variables, reduce over-fitting, and accelerate the training time.

On the other hand, the RF classifier consists of a combination of tree classifiers, where each classifier is generated using a random vector sampled independently from the input vector. Each tree casts a unit vote and the majority votes determine the label (class) of the input vector. In order to implement RF [4], two parameters need to be set up: the number of trees and the number of features in each split.

The KNN approach is a non-parametric approach [41], that was used in the early 1970s in statistical applications. The theory behind KNN is that in the calibration dataset, it finds a group of k samples that are nearest to the unknown samples (*e.g.*based on distance functions). From these k samples, the label (class) of unknown samples are determined by calculating the average of the response variables (i.e., the class attributes of the k nearest neighbours).

Knorn *et al.* [33] discussed that the Radial Basis Function (RBF) kernel for the SVM classifier shows an efficient performance in numerous problems. Therefore, we use the RBF kernel for our SVM classification. There are two parameters to set when applying the SVM classifier with RBF kernel: the cost (C) and the kernel width (ζ). The C parameter decides the acceptable number of misclassification for a non-separable training dataset, which makes the adjustment of rigidity in the training data possible. The (ζ) parameter affects the shape smoothing in the class separation hyper-plane. Larger values of C may lead to over-fitting, whereas increasing the ζ value will affect the shape of the class separation hyper-plane, and thus affect the classification accuracy.

5   Experimental Results and Analysis

We used a total of 1440 RGB images captured from a RealSense camera. For each object we captured 360 images corresponding to 1 degree of rotation around the y-axis. The original resolution of each image was 1280×720. We down-sampled to a resolution of 640×360 and converted the RGB into grayscale images. The decrease in resolution saved the segmentation time by 60%. Segmentation was subsequently carried out using the watershed algorithm with markers discussed in Sect. 3.3. It was observed that this algorithm can efficiently segment the textureless objects without losing important properties and unique characteristics of each object. We also performed another experiment to detect objects using shape descriptors such as SURF, ORB and SIFT. However, these methods cannot detect the objects correctly due to the lack of texture information.

The challenge in object recognition is when the objects have similar shapes. In our database, object A and object B are similar in height and width, except that object A, as can be seen in Fig. 3, has a hole in the middle, which is a significant characteristic. Depending on the viewing angles, the two objects are almost identical and they only have a small difference in corners and thickness.

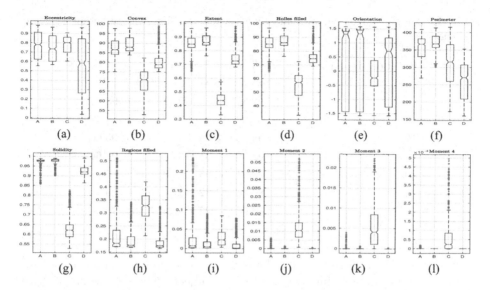

Fig. 6. The box plots of 12 example features representing objects A, B, C and D: (a) eccentricity of the ellipse, (b) convex hull, (c) extent region, (d) holes-filled region, (e) the orientation of region, (f) perimeter, (g) solidity, (h) regions filled in the bounding box, (i–l) and the first four Hu invariant moments.

Therefore, segmenting the entire object precisely as a single part is crucial to get all the required features in the region. Objects C and D have very different characteristics comparing to objects A and B, and they can easily be distinguished.

After detecting ROI, the features are extracted. Figure 6 shows how the statistical characteristics distribution of each object differs as the viewing perspective changes along the 360° rotation. Some obvious observations can be found in the box plots relating to the holes-filled region of every object. The medians of this feature for the two similar objects (A and B) are close to each other, with approximately a difference of 2 units, in comparison with object C, which also has a different distribution. As for eccentricity, the medians of objects A, B, and C are between 0.7 to 0.81, while object D is below 0.6 with a wide dispersion of values. Likewise, object D has its perimeter distribution below the average of the other objects, which means that it has good characteristics to distinguish itself. On the other hand, some objects show a high difference in extent, hole-filled, and solidity features. Object C's boxes are observed lower than the other boxes (A, B and D) in all cases, which indicates that these features enable good differentiation of object C in the training stage. However, the challenge is to determine the features that can distinguish objects A and B, which have very similar attributes. In most of the features, the respective boxes of objects A and B share similar behaviours but not exactly the same. A feature in which the difference between these two objects can be observed is the convex hull, in which the median of object A is around 86, unlike object B which is around 87. Both have a compact distribution and the same variation appears in most

Table 1. Comparison of different machine learning models with different rotation strategies.

Rotation step in degree (°)	Classifier Accuracy (%)				
	SVM	RF	KNN	GB	DT
1	99.37	99.29	99.01	76.15	98.11
5	97.36	98.53	93.42	75.89	97.30
10	95.96	96.68	90.87	74.63	95.66
20	93.56	92.31	86.31	74.11	92.64
30	93.21	82.95	78.63	70.74	87.52
45	87.30	81.32	72.31	67.96	85.30
60	80.98	81.23	72.54	52.32	79.41

other features. We believe that the characteristics distribution at each angle of rotation is significant and different among the 4 objects. For the learning of these characteristics, we trained and evaluated 5 supervised machine learning models. To evaluate these models, different training was carried out using 7 different rotation strategies, which differ by the size of the rotation step. A rotation step of 1°, results in capturing 360 images for each object. For a rotation step of 5°, 72 images are captured for each object. The idea is to compare the robustness of each machine learning model towards rotation. Figure 5 shows an example of classification results using different test scenes with single and multiple objects.

Table 1 and Fig. 4 present the comparison results, which show that the SVM model outperforms all other classifiers with 99.37% accuracy when the rotation step is 1°. When using a step of 5°, Random Forest (RF) has the best accuracy followed by SVM. As the rotation step increases, it is understandable that the classifiers reduce their accuracy because significant features are missed in between rotation steps and thus omitted in the training. When using a rotation step of 10°, RF continues maintaining the best classification, but for the rotation steps of 20°, 30°, 45° and 60°, SVM outperformed all others. There is always a trade-off between time performance and accuracy. It is interesting to see that SVM can obtain over 93% accuracy even with a rotation step of 30°. Concerning the performance time, the SVM model takes a few seconds (~34) for training, and the average processing time for each frame during the testing takes ~115 ms. This also reflects the effectiveness of our object recognition system.

6 Conclusion

We presented a real-time object recognition system to identify small textureless objects similar to those used in industrial applications. We extracted geometrical features from segmented regions, and then trained different classifiers to predict the object's class. The experimental results demonstrated that our approach can distinguish between very similar objects and is suitable for real-time robotics applications. In future, we will use depth information to estimate the 6d pose of the object, and to handle occlusion. Also, we will expand our dataset by incorporating more industrial assembly parts.

References

1. Abbasi, S., Mokhtarian, F., Kittler, J.: Enhancing css-based shape retrieval for objects with shallow concavities. Image Vis. Comput. **18**(3), 199–211 (2000)
2. Balakrishnama, S., Ganapathiraju, A.: Linear discriminant analysis-a brief tutorial. Inst. Signal Inf. Process. **18**, 1–8 (1998)
3. Beucher, S., Meyer, F.: The morphological approach to segmentation: the watershed transformation. Math. Morphol. Image Process. **34**, 433–433 (1992). Optical Engineering-New York-Marcel Dekker Incorporated-
4. Breiman, L.: Random forests. Mach. Learn. **45**(1), 5–32 (2001)
5. Calonder, M., Lepetit, V., Strecha, C., Fua, P.: BRIEF: binary robust independent elementary features. In: Daniilidis, K., Maragos, P., Paragios, N. (eds.) ECCV 2010. LNCS, vol. 6314, pp. 778–792. Springer, Heidelberg (2010). https://doi.org/10.1007/978-3-642-15561-1_56
6. Celebi, M.E., Aslandogan, Y.A.: A comparative study of three moment-based shape descriptors. In: International Conference on Information Technology: Coding and Computing (ITCC'05)-Volume II, vol. 1, pp. 788–793. IEEE (2005)
7. Cevikalp, H., Triggs, B.: Efficient object detection using cascades of nearest convex model classifiers. In: 2012 IEEE Conference on Computer Vision and Pattern Recognition (CVPR), pp. 3138–3145. IEEE (2012)
8. Chen, Y.W., Chen, Y.Q.: Invariant description and retrieval of planar shapes using radon composite features. IEEE Trans. Signal Process. **56**(10), 4762–4771 (2008)
9. Chuang, G.H., Kuo, C.C.: Wavelet descriptor of planar curves: theory and applications. IEEE Trans. Image Process. **5**(1), 56–70 (1996)
10. Davies, E.: Machine Vision: Theory, Algorithms, Practicalities. Academic Press, Cambridge (1997)
11. Ding, W., Wang, X., Liu, H., Hu, B.: An empirical study of shape recognition in ensemble learning context. In: 2018 International Conference on Wavelet Analysis and Pattern Recognition (ICWAPR), pp. 256–261. IEEE (2018)
12. Feng, Y., An, X., Liu, X.: The application of scale invariant feature transform fused with shape model in the human face recognition. In: 2016 IEEE Advanced Information Management, Communicates, Electronic and Automation Control Conference (IMCEC), pp. 1716–1720. IEEE (2016)
13. Flusser, J.: Invariant shape description and measure of object similarity. In: 1992 International Conference on Image Processing and its Applications, pp. 139–142. IET (1992)
14. Freeman, H.: On the encoding of arbitrary geometric configurations. IRE Trans. Electron. Comput. **2**, 260–268 (1961)
15. Friedman, N., Geiger, D., Goldszmidt, M.: Bayesian network classifiers. Mach. Learn. **29**(2–3), 131–163 (1997)
16. Girshick, R.: Fast r-cnn. In: Proceedings of the IEEE International Conference on Computer Vision, pp. 1440–1448 (2015)
17. Girshick, R., Donahue, J., Darrell, T., Malik, J.: Rich feature hierarchies for accurate object detection and semantic segmentation. In: Proceedings of the IEEE Conference on Computer Vision and Pattern Recognition, pp. 580–587 (2014)

18. Girshick, R., Donahue, J., Darrell, T., Malik, J.: Region-based convolutional networks for accurate object detection and segmentation. IEEE Trans. Pattern Anal. Mach. Intell. **38**(1), 142–158 (2015)
19. Guru, D., Nagendraswamy, H.: Symbolic representation of two-dimensional shapes. Pattern Recogn. Lett. **28**(1), 144–155 (2007)
20. Hartigan, J.A., Wong, M.A.: Algorithm as 136: a k-means clustering algorithm. J. Roy. Stat. Soc. Ser. C (Appl. Stat.) **28**(1), 100–108 (1979)
21. He, K., Gkioxari, G., Dollár, P., Girshick, R.: Mask r-cnn. In: Proceedings of the IEEE International Conference on Computer Vision, pp. 2961–2969 (2017)
22. Hearst, M.A., Dumais, S.T., Osuna, E., Platt, J., Scholkopf, B.: Support vector machines. IEEE Intell. Syst. Appl. **13**(4), 18–28 (1998)
23. Hinterstoisser, S., Holzer, S., Cagniart, C., Ilic, S., Konolige, K., Navab, N., Lepetit, V.: Multimodal templates for real-time detection of texture-less objects in heavily cluttered scenes. In: 2011 International Conference on Computer Vision, pp. 858–865. IEEE (2011)
24. Hu, M.K.: Visual pattern recognition by moment invariants. IRE Trans. Inf. Theory **8**(2), 179–187 (1962)
25. Huang, C., Huang, J.: A fast hog descriptor using lookup table and integral image (2017). arXiv preprint arXiv:1703.06256
26. Jain, A.K., Dubes, R.C.: Algorithms for Clustering Data. Prentice-Hall, Upper Saddle River (1988)
27. Kohonen, T.: Learning vector quantization. In: Self-Organizing Maps, pp. 175–189. Springer (1995). https://doi.org/10.1007/978-3-642-97610-0_6
28. Kortli, Y., Jridi, M., Al Falou, A., Atri, M.: A comparative study of CFs, LBP, HOG, SIFT, SURF, and BRIEF for security and face recognition (2018)
29. Kpalma, K., Ronsin, J.: Multiscale contour description for pattern recognition. Pattern Recogn. Lett. **27**(13), 1545–1559 (2006)
30. Kurnianggoro, L., Jo, K.H., et al.: A survey of 2d shape representation: methods, evaluations, and future research directions. Neurocomputing **300**, 1–16 (2018)
31. Lee, S.M., Abbott, A.L., Clark, N.A., Araman, P.A.: A shape representation for planar curves by shape signature harmonic embedding. In: 2006 IEEE Computer Society Conference on Computer Vision and Pattern Recognition (CVPR 2006), vol. 2, pp. 1940–1947. IEEE (2006)
32. Liang, M., Hu, X.: Recurrent convolutional neural network for object recognition. In: Proceedings of the IEEE Conference on Computer Vision and Pattern Recognition, pp. 3367–3375 (2015)
33. Mountrakis, G., Im, J., Ogole, C.: Support vector machines in remote sensing: a review. ISPRS J. Photogram. Rem. Sens. **66**(3), 247–259 (2011)
34. Pham, T.T., Do, T.T., Sünderhauf, N., Reid, I.: Scenecut: joint geometric and object segmentation for indoor scenes. In: 2018 IEEE International Conference on Robotics and Automation (ICRA), pp. 1–9. IEEE (2018)
35. Quinlan, J.R.: Induction of decision trees. Mach. Learn. **1**(1), 81–106 (1986)
36. Rahim, M.A., Azam, M.S., Hossain, N., Islam, M.R.: Face recognition using local binary patterns (lbp). Glob. J. Comput. Sci. Technol. (2013)
37. Redmon, J., Farhadi, A.: Yolo9000: better, faster, stronger. In: Proceedings of the IEEE Conference on Computer Vision and Pattern Recognition, pp. 7263–7271 (2017)
38. Ren, S., He, K., Girshick, R., Sun, J.: Faster r-cnn: towards real-time object detection with region proposal networks. IEEE Trans. Pattern Anal. Mach. Intell. **6**, 1137–1149 (2017)

39. Ren, Z., Gao, S., Chia, L.T., Tsang, I.W.H.: Region-based saliency detection and its application in object recognition. IEEE Trans. Circ. Syst. Video Technol. **24**(5), 769–779 (2013)
40. Rublee, E., Rabaud, V., Konolige, K., Bradski, G.R.: Orb: an efficient alternative to sift or surf. In: ICCV, vol. 11, p. 2. Citeseer (2011)
41. Smith, B.L., Williams, B.M., Oswald, R.K.: Comparison of parametric and non-parametric models for traffic flow forecasting. Transp. Res. Part C Emerg. Technol. **10**(4), 303–321 (2002)
42. Sonka, M., Hlavac, V., Boyle, R.: Image Processing, Analysis, and Machine Vision. Cengage Learning, Boston (2014)
43. Verma, R., Kaur, R.: Enhanced character recognition using surf feature and neural network technique. IJCSIT Int. J. Comput. Sci. Inf. Technol. **5**(4), 5565–5570 (2014)
44. Yang, M.: Extraction d'attributs et mesures de similarité basées sur la forme. Ph.D. thesis, INSA de Rennes (2008)
45. Yang, M., Kpalma, K., Ronsin, J.: Scale-controlled area difference shape descriptor. In: Document Recognition and Retrieval XIV, vol. 6500, p. 650003. International Society for Optics and Photonics (2007)
46. Zhang, D., Lu, G.: A comparative study of curvature scale space and fourier descriptors for shape-based image retrieval. J. Vis. Commun. Image Representation **14**(1), 39–57 (2003)

CSIOR: An Ordered Structured Resampling of Mesh Surfaces

Claudio Tortorici[1], Mohamed Riahi[1], Stefano Berretti[2], and Naoufel Werghi[1(✉)]

[1] Khalifa University, Abu Dhabi, UAE
{claudio.tortorici,naoufel.werghi}@ku.ac.ae
[2] University of Florence, Florence, Italy
stefano.berretti@unifi.it

Abstract. Triangular mesh is one of the most popular 3D modalities which usage spans a wide variety of application in computer vision, computer graphics and multimedia. Raw mesh surfaces generated by 3D scanning devices often suffer from mesh irregularity and also lacks the implicit ordered structure that characterizes 2D images. Therefore they are not suitable to be processed as such, especially for applications requiring fine surface analysis tasks. In this paper, we propose CSIOR, a novel mesh regularization technique exhibiting novel capabilities including a quasi-equilateral triangle tessellation, and structured and ordered tessellation that can accommodate non-convex shaped surfaces, implicit generation of iso-geodesic contours and preservation of the geometric texture on the mesh surface. We evidence the superiority of our technique over current methods through a series of experiments performed on a variety of geometric textured surfaces.

Keywords: CSIOR · Triangular mesh · Mesh resampling · Ordered mesh · Shape analysis

1 Introduction

The last decade has witnessed an abundance of 3D digitizers usage as well as substantial developments in techniques for analyzing and interpreting 3-D shapes. Shape digitalization is the process of encoding the shape of an object into a discrete format amenable to computing purposes. Surface tessellation is the backbone of this process, whereby the surface is encoded by a group of stitched polygons, most commonly triangles, that cover the whole surface. A triangular mesh is characterized by its simplicity and flexibility. Contrary to other polygons, the triangle is the only polygon in which the vertices are guaranteed to be coplanar. This made triangular mesh the format most supported by graphics software and hardware. Triangular meshes are used animation, simulation training, architecture, medical and natural sciences, and many other applications. Typically, 3D scanners produce clouds of irregularly distributed 3D points that

© Springer Nature Switzerland AG 2020
T. McDaniel et al. (Eds.): ICSM 2019, LNCS 12015, pp. 28–41, 2020.
https://doi.org/10.1007/978-3-030-54407-2_3

have to be connected in order to produce the triangular mesh approximation of the surface. But, due to the irregular disposition of points in 3D, triangles are likely to be irregular, *i.e.*, they show a large variability in size and shape.

This flexibility in adapting the size and shape of the facets to the sampled points may help to save memory using larger facets in less informative regions of the surface (*e.g.*, flat one), and smaller facets in regions where finer details should be accounted for. However, proceeding in this way shows a clear limitation when descriptors of the surface (*i.e.*, curvature, mesh-HOG, mesh-LBP, *etc.*) are computed from the vertex positions and facet areas. Indeed, these descriptors are the natural extension of their 2D counterpart defined on a regular grid of pixels in the image domain, and applying them to an irregularly faceted mesh, drastically impairs the outcomes. Also, the advances in the surface scanning technology lead the proliferation of large datasets of objects exhibiting 3D relief patterns. Examples include knitted fabrics, artworks' patterns, artists' styles, rock types or engravings. The style of these patterns does not depend on the overall structure of the shape. They are rather characterized by some form of repeatability across the surface so that they can be regarded as the 3D geometric equivalent of textures in 2D images. For this category of objects, mesh regularization should preserve the integrity of the 3D relief patterns which represent the information of interest in these objects. In another side, the most widely adopted data structure format for storing a triangular mesh is the face-vertex format, which encompasses two arrays. The first array stores the coordinates of the vertices, while in the second, each element corresponds to one facet and contains pointers to the three vertices that form that facet, i.e., the indexes of the three vertices in the first array. This simple triangular mesh representation embeds a major drawback, namely, the lack of an intrinsic ordered structure that allows the facets in the mesh to be browsed systematically. Indeed, the storing of the facets in the facet array is usually arbitrary and does not follow any particular arrangement. This makes the processing of triangular mesh more complex compared with other intrinsically ordered shape modalities such as 2D and range images. In the literature, this problem has been addressed using either planar or spherical surface parameterization by mapping the mesh surface to either a plane or sphere. Planar parameterization suffers from parameterization discontinuities. Apart from its heavy computational cost, spherical surface parameterization is rather more suitable for shape modeling tasks (e.g., texture and mesh reduction) rather than shape analysis [1].

The above considerations evidence the need of mesh pre-processing tools ensuring: 1) a mesh regularization, 2) preservation of the geometric texture on the surface, and 3) mesh ordering. The benefit of a tool meeting these requirements is two-fold: *i)* It prevents or reduce the dependence of a surface descriptor from irregular tessellations, *ii)* It allows the deployment of analysis tool requiring and ordered structure (e.g. convolution) on the mesh manifold.

In this paper, we propose a novel mesh resampling approach that meets the above requirements, unifying mesh regularization and mesh ordering. The proposed algorithm called *Circle-Surface Intersection Ordered Resampling*

(CSIOR), generates a mesh composed by quasi-equilateral triangles which are *globally ordered* with respect to a seed point in a polar fashion. To the best of our knowledge, our algorithm is the first of its kind, capable of generating a uniform mesh tessellation while exhibiting a global ordered structure.

The rest of the paper is organized as follows: In Sect. 2, we report the most relevant state of the art resampling approaches. In Sect. 3, we describe our method and its features. Then, in Sect. 4, we assess our methods and compare it with other competitive techniques. Finally, we terminate the paper with concluding remarks and future work in Sect. 5.

2   Related Work

In the Computer Graphics literature, several methods do exist for mesh resampling and regularization [2–5], with some of them available in common mesh editing tools. However, such tools often require several trials to get the desired quality of the resulting models; besides, they do not provide a straightforward way to obtain a regular mesh that preserves, at the same time, the geometric texture of the surface with sufficient accuracy. The capability of an algorithm to preserve the geometric texture, like bas-relief, is attractive for the computer-aided design community [6], but just a few methods can be used to that aim.

In [7], Peyrè and Cohen proposed a greedy algorithm based on geodesic distance, which iteratively selects equidistant points (landmarks) on the mesh. Starting from a seed landmark, first, the geodesic distance is computed to all the other points on the mesh; then, the farthest point is selected as the next landmark, and the process is iterated by computing the geodesic distance between any point and all the previously selected landmarks. The process stops when a predefined number N of landmarks is reached. In a final step, these landmarks are used to divide the mesh into a set of N non-overlapping regions by clustering each point to its closest landmark. The centroids of these regions are connected to generate a new mesh. According to the authors' claim, on large meshes (more than 500,000 vertices) their technique speeds up the computation by over one order of magnitude in comparison to classical remeshing and parameterization methods [7]. However, the final mesh is more a down-sampled version of the original mesh than a resampled one, being the vertices selected to generate the new mesh a subset of the original set of vertices. Also, even increasing the number of landmarks, we verified the technique does not preserve the geometric texture, although it well preserves the shape of the original mesh. One possibility to overcome the down-sampling problem that limits the number of resampled vertices to the original point cloud is to augment the number of vertices in the original mesh by mesh subdivision. Using this additional step, we were able to obtain a more fine-grained resampled mesh compared to the original one, but losing geometric texture information. In [8], Xu *et al.* proposed a shape regularization technique, which is specifically designed to cope with mesh irregularities and artifacts introduced by 3D scanners as part of their work on optical projection of tomography scanning. In this technique, Principal Component Analysis

(PCA) is used to detect the two main axes of the shape and generate a 2D grid. The original point cloud is projected on the 2D grid, and a kernel density estimation is computed at each projected point to evaluate the number of points projected on a certain area of the 2D grid. After defining the contour of the point cloud on the grid according to the density function estimation, a 2D mesh is generated within these contours. Finally, Thin-Plate Splines are used to smoothly interpolate the points and map the 2D mesh grid to the original cloud of point in the 3D space.

Werghi *et al.* [9,10] followed a similar idea and used 2D projection for resampling quasi-planar surfaces. The technique consists of three steps: *a)* projection, *b)* regularization, and *c)* restoring. In *a)*, PCA is used to determine the two main axes of the shape that define a 2D plane of projection; the third dimension of the shape is then projected to this plane. In *b)*, a uniform 2D grid of points is generated at the desired spatial resolution; points are then triangulated using Delaunay function. In the last step *c)*, the points on the grid are projected back to the mesh surface using interpolation, while keeping their triangulation. Although, it is possible to constrain the triangle to be equilateral the projection step may hardly affect the mesh tessellation. This is emphasized for meshes that show three large PCA eigenvalues, or sudden variation in the overall shape. In [11], Delingette *et al.* proposed a reconstruction approach, which uses deformable simplex meshes. First, the simplex mesh is initialized, either automatically or manually, then the model is modified by creating holes or increasing its genus. Finally, the distance between the mesh and the data is minimized, preserving the data topology. Similarly, McInerney *et al.* [12] analyzed the use of deformable models in medical applications. An isotropic remeshing of arbitrary genus surfaces was proposed by Surazhsky *et al.* in [13]. This solution first generates vertices by simplification and refinement of the original mesh; then, it performs vertex partitioning using an area relaxation method. The approach proposed by Kunert *et al.* in [14], uses a variant that combines the analysis of an isotropic information and error estimation using the so-called Hessian strategy. We conclude mentioning two relevant work by Kokkinos *et al.* [15], and Werghi *et al.* [16] on local ordering of mesh manifolds. In the first, Kokkinos *et al.* proposed ISC, a descriptors for 3D shapes, which generalize the polar sampling of the image domain to surfaces in 3D space. The descriptor is constructed over a polar grid which is determined by iso-geodesic contour. However, the points over these contours have to be ordered with respect to a reference ray in a subsequent stage. In [16], Werghi *et al.*, exploited the facet connectivity to linearly determine ordered rings of facets (ORF). The ORF construction starts with adjacent facets to a central facet and linearly derives an ordered ring filling the gap between the adjacent facets. The advantage of this process is that can be repeated for multiple radii to get multiple rings, thus extending the coverage of the ordered area. Since at each ring the first facet is aligned to the same axis, the local ordered structure can be used as a local polar grid. However, the algorithm requires a quasi-regular mesh in order to be deployed effectively.

3   Circle-Surface Intersection Ordered Resampling (CSIOR)

Our goal here is to design a mesh tessellation algorithm, capable of producing an *ordered equilateral triangular mesh, i.e.,* a mesh with equilateral facets ordered with respect to a seed point. We also want to keep as much as possible the geometric texture of the surface. To this end, we start by observing that the simplest geometry that can contain a close set of equilateral triangles is the *hexagon.* Such hexagon shape can be "propagated" adding a new layer of equilateral triangles of the same size e (as shown in Fig. 1(a)). We can demonstrate that the number of facets at each ring follows the arithmetic progression $\sharp E(\ell) = 6(2\ell - 1)$, where ℓ is the ring number.

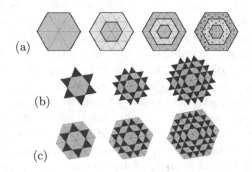

Fig. 1. (a) The first hexagon of six equilateral triangular facets on the first image. Then, on the second and third image, *rings* of equilateral triangles that form a close set of facets, "propagate" the hexagon shape following the arithmetic progression $\sharp E(\ell) = 6(2\ell - 1)$ as shown in the last image. (b, c) CSIOR algorithm: from left to right, three consecutive iterations of the algorithm are shown. (b) reports the result of the Circle-Surface Intersection step, while in (c) the outcome of the Facet Connection step is illustrated. *FacetIn* and *FacetOut* are displayed in light blue and blue, respectively. (Color figure online)

Referring to Fig. 1(a), the CSIOR algorithm operates as follows: An initialization step is performed at first to define the starting set of six facets, forming the hexagon. These facets, dubbed *FacetIn* share the same seed vertex, and oriented inward with respect to that starting seed vertex. The seed vertex is best chosen at the center of the mesh surface. Starting from the initial set of *FacetIn*, the process evolves iteratively in two steps, *Circle-Surface Intersection:* generates new facets from the previous ring of facets while propagating the order of the previous ring (Fig. 1(b)) *Step 2: Facets Connection:* Connects the facets obtained at the first step, keeping the hexagon arithmetic progression and the facets ordering (Fig. 1(c)).

Algorithm 1. CSIOR Algorithm

1: **Initialize:**
       $FacetIn \leftarrow$ First Hexagon, $SampledMesh \leftarrow FacetIn$
2: **repeat**
3:     $FacetOut \leftarrow []$
4:     **for** fin in $FacetIn$ **do**
5:         $fout \leftarrow$ CIRCLEINTERSECTION(fin)
6:         $FacetOut \leftarrow FacetOut + fout$
7:     **end for**
8:     $FacetIn \leftarrow []$
9:     **for** $fout$ in $FacetOut$ **do**
10:         **if** $fout$ and $fout + 1$ consecutive facets **then**
11:             $fin \leftarrow$ CONNECT($fout, fout + 1$)
12:             $FacetIn \leftarrow FacetIn + fin$
13:         **end if**
14:     **end for**
15:     $SampledMesh \leftarrow SampledMesh + FacetIn + FacetOut$
16: **until** Mesh fully resampled

The initial hexagon, or set of $FacetIn$ is generated as follows: (a) Firstly, the neighborhood region of the seed point is defined, then (b) PCA is performed to obtain the main plane of this region; (c) six equidistant points of a circle of radius l – set a priori as the desired equilateral triangle edge length – that relies on that plane are selected, then (d) projected on the mesh surface with respect to the least principal component. Finally, (e) the six points are connected with the seed vertex, generating a hexagon composed of six ordered (clockwise or anti-clockwise) equilateral triangular facets as shown in the top-left of Fig. 2. In the following, we will describe Step 1 and Step 2.

Step 1: Circle-Surface Intersection: The circle intersection procedure aims to determine new vertices that lay on the original mesh surface while forming equilateral triangles with the surrounding vertices of the new mesh. It is based on the idea that a circle centered on the external edge of a $FacetIn$ and orthogonal to it, will intersect the original mesh, unless it is located at the mesh boundaries. The facets, generated by CIRCLE INTERSECTION in Algorithm 1, are called $FacetOut$, as they go outward with respect to the seed hexagon. As shown in Fig. 2, for each $FacetIn$ a circle is defined by the $FacetIn$ external edge $\overrightarrow{e}$ as normal, and a point C corresponding to the midpoint of edge $\overrightarrow{e}$. The procedure seeks for the intersection between such circle and a facet of the original mesh manifold. The intersection determines the new vertex, equidistant to the vertices of $\overrightarrow{e}$, and therefore the new $FacetOut$ is constructed. We can show that the intersection is obtained by solving a second order equation. The detected point is not part of the set of vertices in the original mesh; however, it inherits all its preserving its shape local properties while generating an equilateral triangle, $FacetOut$, with the extremities of $\overrightarrow{e}$.

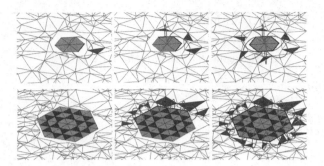

Fig. 2. Circle intersection procedure (step 1. Each external edge of the hexagon (highlighted in bold black) is used as normal of the plane that holds the red circle. The intersecting facet is colored in yellow, showing the intersecting point in black. In the first the circle intersection after initialization, while in the second row the process after three iterations. *FacetIn* are painted in cyan, while *FacetOut* in blue. (Color figure online)

Step 2: Facets Connection: At the end of the first step, a new set of unconnected *FacetOut* is obtained. The second step aims to connect consecutive *FacetOut* (*i.e.*, obtained in Step 1, while keeping the arithmetic progression of the number the facets across the rings, and the facets ordering. In order to explain the connection procedure, we refer to the concept of *valence*. The valance $\mathcal{V}(v)$ of a vertex v on the mesh is defined as the number of connected edges to that vertex, however from now on we will refer to $\mathcal{V}(v)$ as the number of facets connected to the vertex v. To connect the *FacetOut* two key factors have to be taken into account: *i)* At each iteration, the number of facets of the new ring increases by twelve according to the arithmetic progression. Since the number of *FacetOut* is equal to the number of *FacetIn* at the previous ring, the additional twelve facets will be added to the new set of *FacetIn* at the new ring. This new set of *FacetIn* will be the base for constructing the subsequent ring (see Fig. 3); *ii)* A property of the ring of facets is that vertices of *FacetOut*, which belong to the external edges of the outer hexagon have valence $\mathcal{V} = 5$, while those that correspond to the six corners of the hexagon have valence 4. The rightmost image of Fig. 3 depicts the facets on the hexagon edge ($\mathcal{V} = 5$) and those on the hexagon corners ($\mathcal{V} = 4$) in white and yellow, respectively.

Fig. 3. Facets Connection procedure: the newly obtained *FacetIn* (in green). From left to right, the process at the first and third iteration. The rightmost image highlights in yellow the connection between two *FacetOut* sharing a vertex with $\mathcal{V}(v) = 4$, and in white those with $\mathcal{V}(v) = 5$. (Color figure online)

Given these assumptions, we can distinguish three cases: *a)* Two *FacetOut* share a vertex v with valence $\mathcal{V}(v) = 5$; in this case a new *FacetIn* that connect v with the outer vertices of the two *FacetOut* will be added; *b)* Two *FacetOut* share a vertex v with valence $\mathcal{V}(v) = 4$; in this case, v corresponds to one of the hexagon corners, thus two *FacetIn* are required to "fill in the gap" between the consecutive *FacetOut*. *c)* The two *FacetOut* do not have any vertex in common; in this latter case, the two *FacetOut* are not consecutive. This situation occurs at the original mesh boundaries, no connections are hence required.

The first and the third case are trivial; in the second case, instead, a new point needs to be added to the mesh. To maintain the equilateral property of the resampled mesh, the new point can be obtained tracing a line $\overrightarrow{t}$ passing through v and $pMid = \frac{pOut_1 + pOut_2}{2}$, the mid point between the outer vertices of the two *FacetOut*. Then, the point at distance l from v on the line $\overrightarrow{t}$ is connected to the two couple $\langle v, pOut_1 \rangle$ and $\langle v, pOut_2 \rangle$, respectively, generating the two new *FacetIn*. The procedure is illustrated in Fig. 3, with the different valence cases shown on the right. The Algorithmic representation of the above is depicted in Algorithm 2.

3.1   Algorithm Properties

Compared with the state of the art resampling techniques, CSIOR is distinguished by the following properties: **Ordered Mesh:** CSIOR returns a regular, quasi-equilateral, mesh manifold which is ordered in polar fashion with respect to the seed point, by propagating the ordering scheme of the initial hexagon. The Circle-Surface Intersection step described in Step 1, generates a list of *FacetOut*;

Algorithm 2. Step 2: Facets Connection

Input: The set of *FacetOut* obtained with CIRCLE INTERSECTION
Output: A new set of *FacetIn*

```
 1: for fout in FacetOut do
 2:     if fout and fout + 1 consecutive facets then
 3:         v ← shared vertex of fout and fout + 1
 4:         pOut₁ ← outer vertex of fout
 5:         pOut₂ ← outer vertex of fout + 1
 6:         if 𝒱(v) == 5 then
 7:             F ← Connect ⟨v, pOut₁, pOut₂⟩
 8:             FacetIn ← F
 9:         else if 𝒱(v) < 5 then
10:             pMid ← new point between pOut₁ and pOut₂
11:             F₁ ← Connect ⟨v, pOut₁, pMid⟩
12:             F₂ ← Connect ⟨v, pMid, pOut₂⟩
13:             FacetIn ← {F₁, F₂}
14:         end if
15:     end if
16: end for
```

---

these are derived by the set of *FacetIn* of the previous hexagon ring, thus inheriting their order. The Facet connection in Step 2 completes the new ring by generating *FacetIn* between each couple of consecutive *FacetOut*, thus obtaining a complete ordered ring of facets interleaving *FacetOut* and *FacetIn*. **Continuous ordering over Mesh Boundaries:** As the Facet Connection step derives its order from the set of *FacetOut*, it is capable of generating ordered rings that propagate even beyond the mesh boundaries. Figure 4(a) illustrates this robust aspect whereby we can observe that the progression of the hexagonal ring does not stop at the mesh boundaries but continues until the whole surface is covered. More interestingly, is that the ordering aspect of the triangular facets is still maintained across the discontinuous rings as it can be noticed in Fig. 4(b). This property makes our algorithm and its structured order aspect capable of accommodating non-convex shapes. **Iso-Geodesic approximation** The hexagon-shaped rings, obtained at each iteration of the algorithm, maintain a constant thickness. These rings form a sequence of iso-geodesic contours approximations centered at the seed vertex (see Fig. 4(c, d)) **Facets Normals Coherency:** The facets of a mesh manifold may not be coherently oriented, in fact, contiguous facets may show opposite normals orientations as illustrated in Fig. 4(e). Normals are important features often used for local shape analysis. To employ them properly, mesh manifolds require some additional pre-processing

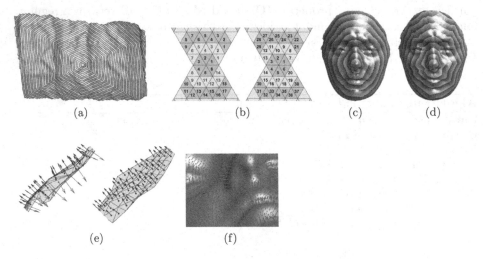

(a)   (b)   (c)   (d)

(e)   (f)

Fig. 4. (a) The ordered ring propagation over mesh boundaries. (b) the ordering over a not-convex shape, showing the ring-wise ordering and the global ordering, respectively on the left and the right image. (c) the actual iso-geodesic circles from the seed point. (d) the iso-geodesic approximation obtained with CSIOR ordered structure. (e) an example of facets orientation inconsistency (on the left) and the resampled region using CSIOR with the correct facets normals orientation (on the right); opposite orientations are shown in different colors. (f) a resampled surface with the facet normals coherently pointing outwards with respect to the surface. (Color figure online)

to re-orient their facets coherently. On the contrary, CSIOR intrinsically propagates the facets normals orientation (*i.e.*, inward or outward with respect to the object surface.) of the seed hexagon across the constructed rings making all the facets pointing at the same orientation.

4   Experimentation

We compared our proposed CSIOR re-sampling method with the *Geodesic Resampling* (GR) method of Peyrè and Cohen [7], the *Spline Resampling* (SR) method by Xu *et al.* [8] and the *Projection Resampling* (PR) approach by Werghi *et al.* [9,10] as introduced in Sect. 2. For the mesh tessellation evaluation, we adopted four criteria: (i) the ratio between the standard deviation and the mean of the mesh edge length $\frac{\sigma_e}{\bar{e}}$, (ii) the ratio between the standard deviation and the mean of the facet area $\frac{\sigma_A}{\bar{A}}$ (iii) the mesh tessellation quality measure proposed in [16], and (iv) the distribution of the triangles' angles. The metric proposed in [16] measures the mesh regularity as the normalized difference $\Delta_r = \frac{\eta_r - \tilde{\eta}_r}{\tilde{\eta}_r}$ between the ideal Ordered Ring Facets (ORF) sequence $\tilde{\eta}_r = [12, 24, 36, ..., 12r]$ and the actual one η_r at each facet, where r is the number of concentric rings in the ORF. For this metric, we set $r = 3$. The three first metrics are listed for all the tested approaches in Table 1(a) The distribution of the angles is used to assess to what extent the facets have an equilateral triangle shape. This last criterion is reported in Fig. 5 for the different methods. The distribution considers angles multiple of 5, *i.e.*, $5, 10, 15 ...$, and a tolerance of ± 2. We can clearly notice that the distribution of our method presents a peak centered at around $60°$, largely outperforming the other methods.

From the results, our method got the best tessellation quality score in three criteria out of the four. With respect to the geometric texture preservation, our method outperforms [8] and scores a bit less than [7]. These results indicate that our method achieves the best trade-off between the quality of tessellation and the preservation of the geometric texture. The SR method in [8] obtains good tessellation, but substantially fails in terms of texture preservation (see the third mesh instance image in Fig. 5, and also it is the most demanding in terms of computational time. The method in [7], on the contrary, is capable of maintaining the texture information to a reasonable extent, but the final mesh is more a down-sampled version of the original one and showing non-regular tessellation. Also, it computes geodesic distance N times, resulting in an $O(N^2 \log N)$ complexity, being N the number of triangular facets. The projection re-sampling solution [9], instead, is quite efficient, running in $O(N \log N)$, while preserving to a large extent the geometric texture. However, though it is possible to constrain the triangles to be equilateral, the projection step may hardly affect the mesh tessellation. This is emphasized for meshes that show three large PCA eigenvalues and instances showing sudden variation in the overall shape. Our proposed approach has $O(F \cdot k)$ complexity, where F is the number of facets on the regularized mesh (which depends on the edge length l) and k is the number

Table 1. (a) Tessellation quality comparison: The first two rows report the ratio between standard deviation and mean for edge length and facet area, while in the third row, we report the facets propagation regularity. In all the cases, values for the original mesh, three state-of-the-art methods, and our proposed approach are reported. The lower the value the better the performance. (b) Texture and shape preservation analysis: Hausdorff distance and ICP error for three state-of-art methods and our proposed approach compared with the original meshes. (c) Overall comparison of the four methods.

Evaluation method	Original	GR [7]	SR [8]	PR [9]	CSIOR
Edge Length ratio	0.421	0.233	0.394	0.669	**0.103**
Facet Area ratio	0.670	0.314	0.340	0.494	**0.165**
Propagation regularity	0.222	0.153	**0.001**	0.002	0.009

(a)

Evaluation Method	GR [7]	SR [8]	PR [9]	CSIOR
Hausdorff	1.860	4.668	4.112	**1.576**
ICP error	**0.449**	0.672	0.509	0.509

(b)

Step	GR [7]	SR [8]	PR [9]	CSIOR
Regular tessellation	X	✓	✓*	✓
Texture preservation	✓	X	✓	✓
Projection independent	✓	X	X	✓
Re-sampled facet control	X	X	X	✓
Ordered structure	X	X	X	✓
Complexity	$N^2 \log N$	-	$N \log N$	$F \cdot k$

* only in case of quasi-planar surfaces   (c)

of facets on the original mesh to seek for the Circle-Surface Intersection. So far, our algorithm is the only one capable of producing an ordered mesh.

Measuring the geometric texture preservation is a much harder task as it requires a framework for geometric texture retrieval robust to strong shape deformation. Since this is a quite new topic and it goes well beyond the scope of this assessment, in Table 1(b) we present two point-to-point distances to measure the closeness of the re-sampled mesh with respect to the original one. The table shows the Hausdorff distance and the error obtained with the Iterative Closest Point (ICP) registration to evaluate geometric texture and shape preservation. The experiment has been computed on a set of samples of the SHREC'17 dataset, track on "Retrieval of surfaces with similar relief patterns" [17], selecting the most challenging surfaces and evaluating multiple patches. From Table 1(b), we can see that our method produces the least Hausdorff distance evidencing the best preservation of the geometric texture. The same is noticed for the ICP error, except with [7] that shows the least error. This is explained by the fact that in [7], the new vertices of the re-sampled mesh are actually a subset of the original ones.

Table 1(c) summarizes the comparison between the four methods. On the left of Fig. 5, we show one example of a mesh surface processed with the four methods.

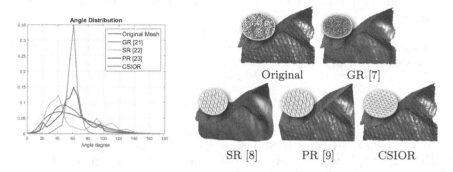

Fig. 5. Left: Angle distribution in degrees for the original mesh, three state-of-the-art methods and our proposed CSIOR. The distributions are normalized with respect to the number of angles. Right: Comparison of the geometric texture and tessellation quality of the four methods when applied to the mesh on the left.

Fig. 6. From left: an example of a grid of facets extracted from the ordered hexagon rings. A grid of facets extracted from a real surface and a zoomed portion. Images, derived from that grid, showing local descriptors computed on the mesh, namely: the local depth, the mean curvature, and the shape index. The last image shows the three previous descriptors mapped to the RGB channels.

5   Conclusion

In this paper, we have proposed a new mesh-resampling method which goes beyond the classic objective of mesh regularization as in previous methods. In addition to mesh regularization our method exhibits the unprecedented capacity of generating structured and globally ordered mesh, ensuring coherent facets normals orientation across the mesh surface, and implicitly providing concentric rings approximating iso-geodesic contours. Compared with the state of art methods our approach demonstrated superior performance in terms of mesh regularity and preservation of geometric structure on the surface while keeping a competitive computational complexity. The regular and ordered mesh of our method allows to automatically extract grid-like structures from the mesh surface, and derive images of descriptors computed on the mesh (see Fig. 6) and exploit them in mesh surface analysis. We believe that this is an unprecedented representation tool for mesh surface that would allow approaching mesh surface analysis and interpretation with 2D tools. This aspect is part of our current and future research.

Acknowledgment. This work is supported by a research fund from Cyber-Physical Systems Center (C2PS), Khalifa University, UAE.

References

1. Hormann, K., Lévy, B., Sheffer, A.: Mesh parameterization: theory and practice. In: Proceedings SIGGRAPH, Singapore, Asia, 2018. ACM (2008)
2. Kazhdan, M., Hoppe, H.: Screened Poisson surface reconstruction. ACM Trans. Graph. (ToG) **32**(3), 29 (2013)
3. Pietroni, N., Tarini, M., Cignoni, P.: Almost isometric mesh parameterization through abstract domains. IEEE Trans. Visual Comput. Graphics **16**(4), 621–635 (2010)
4. Chen, Z., et al.: Point cloud resampling using centroidal Voronoi tessellation methods. Comput. Aided Des. **102**, 12–21 (2018)
5. Bischoff, S., Kobbelt, L.: Teaching meshes, subdivision and multiresolution techniques. Comput. Aided Des. **36**(14), 1483–1500 (2004)
6. Bian, Z., Hu, S.: Preserving detailed features in digital bas-relief making. Comput. Aided Geom. Des. **28**(4), 245–256 (2011)
7. Peyré, G., Cohen, L.D.: Geodesic remeshing using front propagation. Int. J. Comput. Vision **69**(1), 145 (2006). https://doi.org/10.1007/s11263-006-6859-3
8. Xu, Q., et al.: Correlations between the morphology of sonic hedgehog expression domains and embryonic craniofacial shape. Evol. Biol. **42**(3), 379–386 (2015). https://doi.org/10.1007/s11692-015-9321-z
9. Werghi, N., Tortorici, C., Berretti, S., Del Bimbo, A.: Representing 3D texture on mesh manifolds for retrieval and recognition applications. In: IEEE Conference on Computer Vision and Pattern Recognition (CVPR), June 2015, pp. 2521–2530. IEEE (2015)
10. Tortorici, C., Werghi, N., Berretti, S.: Boosting 3D LBP-based face recognition by fusing shape and texture descriptors on the mesh. In: IEEE International Conference on Image Processing (ICIP), September 2015, pp. 2670–2674. IEEE (2015)
11. Delingette, H.: General object reconstruction based on simplex meshes. Int. J. Comput. Vision **32**(2), 111–146 (1999). https://doi.org/10.1023/A:1008157432188
12. McInerney, T., Terzopoulos, D.: Deformable models in medical image analysis. In: Mathematical Methods in Biomedical Image Analysis, pp. 171–180. IEEE (1996)
13. Surazhsky, V., Alliez, P., Gotsman, C.: Isotropic remeshing of surfaces: a local parameterization approach. Ph.D. thesis, INRIA (2003)
14. Kunert, G.: Toward anisotropic mesh construction and error estimation in the finite element method. Numer. Methods Partial Differ. Equ. Int. J. **18**(5), 625–648 (2002)
15. Kokkinos, I., Bronstein, M.M., Litman, R., Bronstein, A.M.: Intrinsic shape context descriptors for deformable shapes. In: 2012 IEEE Conference on Computer Vision and Pattern Recognition, June 2012, pp. 159–166. IEEE (2012)

16. Werghi, N., Rahayem, M., Kjellander, J.: An ordered topological representation of 3D triangular mesh facial surface: concept and applications. EURASIP J. Adv. Signal Process. **2012**(1), 144 (2012). https://doi.org/10.1186/1687-6180-2012-144
17. Biasotti, S., et al.: Shrec'17 track: retrieval of surfaces with similar relief patterns, April 2017

Image Understanding

Background Subtraction by Difference Clustering

Xuanyi Wu[1], Xin Gao[1], Chenqiu Zhao[1(✉)], Jiangzheng Wu[2], and Anup Basu[1]

[1] Department of Computing Science, University of Alberta, Edmonton, Canada
`zhao.chenqiu@ualberta.ca`
[2] Huawei Technologies Co., Ltd., Shenzhen, China

Abstract. Previous approaches to background subtraction typically considered the problem as a classification of pixels over time. We frame the problem as clustering the difference vectors between pixels in the current frame and in the background image set, and present a novel background subtraction method called Difference Clustering. This not only saves computational time, but also achieves high Pr and Fm values for accuracy. In particular, the difference between the current frame and the background image set is extracted using the quartile method for clustering. Compared to traditional k-means model to generate k clusters, our quartile method needs only 2 clusters. Moreover, traditional k-means clustering models need to update the means until convergence, which is time-consuming. In contrast, our quartile method finds the final means directly to reduce the numbers of iterations and computational time, resulting in a real-time algorithm. Experiments on several videos from standard benchmarks demonstrate that our proposed approach achieves promising results compared to several previous methods.

1   Introduction

As a fundamental research topic in computer vision, background subtraction has attracted significant attention from researchers. However, due to the diversity and complexity of natural scenes, it is still a challenging problem. There are two main categories for background subtraction models, traditional and supervised. Basic models, statistical models [16], cluster models and estimation models [16] are different types of traditional models. K-means model, codebook model [17] and basic sequential clustering [18] are built for cluster models. However, all of them require a long time to classify the foreground and background. Therefore, we focus on developing an effective method for background subtraction which can be widely used in different situations.

Background subtraction is a technique to separate the foreground of videos from the static background scene. When applied to videos obtained from complex scenes, such as objects with shadows and dynamic backgrounds, it becomes a challenging problem. Fortunately, the variations in pixel observations resulting from different factors have different patterns, which can be used to classify these

T. McDaniel et al. (Eds.): ICSM 2019, LNCS 12015, pp. 45–56, 2020.
https://doi.org/10.1007/978-3-030-54407-2_4

pixels into foreground or background. Based on this observation, we propose clustering the differences directly for background subtraction, as shown in Fig. 1, to introduce a novel difference clustering method.

In difference clustering, the subtraction result between the current frame and a set of background images is used to represent the differences. Then, a quality method is proposed to cluster the difference for background subtraction. The contributions of this paper are: difference clustering needs only two clusters and the clustering is done in one iteration. It is different from the traditional k-means algorithm [4] and the genetic k-means algorithm [5], which need several iterations until convergence. Difference clustering saves significant computational time. Also, the result of difference clustering has a relatively high value in Pr (Precision) and Fm (F-measure) compared to other unsupervised background subtraction methods. Our difference clustering method is a very practical and competitive method in background subtraction suitable for real-time video analysis.

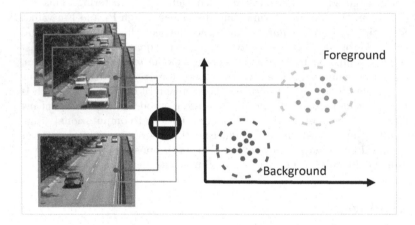

Fig. 1. Illustration of the proposed approach. The differences between the current frame and a set of background images are clustered for background subtraction.

2   Related Work

Background subtraction methods are divided into two categories, which are traditional background subtraction methods and supervised machine learning algorithms.

In traditional background subtraction methods, the algorithms can be grouped into single-feature algorithms and multi-feature algorithms. Single-feature algorithms are methods that only deal with a single feature, like spectral features, spatial features, and temporal features [2].

■ Spectral algorithms focus on color features. The Gaussian Mixture Model (GMM) proposed by Stauffer and Grimson is an example [3]. This method simply models the values of a particular pixel as a mixture of Gaussians. Some models are classified as background models based on the persistence and the variance of the GMMs [3]. In GMM, pixels are assumed to be independent of each other, and the spatial information is thus completely ignored. By contrast, in the proposed approach, the differences in the spatial domain are used for clustering.

■ Spatial algorithms focus on texture features and edge features. For a texture-feature model, local binary pattern (LBP) is frequently used. A binary number is calculated for each pixel by thresholding all its neighbors, within a circle of radius R centered at that pixel. The best matching LBP histogram is used to update the background model [1]. Motion-assisted spatiotemporal clustering of low-rank (MSCL) is an example of the edge-feature model. MSCL is a method starting with a set of detected frames, which is subtracted with a motionless frame to avoid redundant information. Then, a binary mask is created based on the result of the subtraction, computed using motion-aware cross-correlation, which is a calculation of the central correlation including pixels exhibiting motion [9], to avoid being affected by lighting conditions.

■ Temporal algorithms focus on motion features. The background objects, such as the shadows of tress and the waves in water, can be subtracted using false positive detection. False-positive detection can detect areas frame-by-frame to find the motion changes or compare areas in each frame with that in a reference frame. Intersection over Union (IOU) values are used to estimate among all detection responses from the previous frame, to eliminate the size of data from the detection and demonstrate effectiveness [26].

Since single-feature algorithms only focus on one of the features for background subtraction, each of these has limitations. Therefore, multi-feature algorithms combine single-feature algorithms in order to overcome the shortcomings. One of the implementations integrates similarity measures for different features. Chiranjeevi and Sengupta came up with a fuzzy aggregation measure. Sugeno and Choquet integrals are used to get fuzzy similarities. Some implementations use global constant-valued weight, some have designed specific similarity models for specific features, some use a uniform similarity model, which means that we can fit any kind of feature into this model [2].

In both single-feature and multi-feature algorithms, some traditional models like basic models, statistical models [16], cluster models and estimation models [16] are widely used. In the basic model, they model the background image using average, median or histogram analysis over time [16]. Statistical models include Gaussian models, subspace learning models and vector models [16]. In estimation models, the background is estimated using a Wiener like filter, Kalman filter, Correntropy filter, and Chebychev filter [16]. Cluster models include the k-means model, codebook model, and basic sequential clustering [16]. K-means is the most widely used clustering model, and can be used for building other clustering models like the codebook model [24].

Supervised machine learning algorithms include deep learning algorithms that are used in background subtraction. Many machine learning algorithms achieve a higher score, and more accurate results [6] compared to traditional methods. Following are some background subtraction methods using supervised machine learning algorithms:

- Convolutional neural networks (CNN) is an important class of neural networks. They contains multiple layers of linear and non-linear operations that can learn simultaneously [8]. Based on CNNs, Foreground Segmentation Networks (FgSegNet) provide two implementations for background subtraction. They are multi-scale segmentation architecture FgSegNet_M and FgSegNet_S.

- Bayesian generative adversarial networks (BSGAN) is a Bayesian formulation, which is created by a deep learning method with generative adversarial networks (GANs) [10]. BSGAN creates background models using every pixel from several frames, which are ordered by time. The result works well in dealing with moving objects in the background, lighting changes and distraction shadows [11].

- The Cascade CNN model is created with a small number of example data, since the background and foreground moving objects appear repeatedly in some of the frames. The outline of foreground objects is defined from a small set of frames. Cascade CNN does not require a large number of segment frames, because its training and generation of images are on the same video. It also detects moving objects on each frame independently, and does not require a background model [9].

3   Proposed Method

Computer Vision based methods can be applied to various kinds of problems. For example, Wang et al. proposed vision-based hand gesture recognition methods [27]; Liu, Cheng and Basu proposed a synthetic vision assisted real-time runway detection for infrared aerial images [28]. Both of them achieved good results.

Our method for background subtraction is a vision-based method as well. The flow chart of the proposed approach is shown in Fig. 2, with four steps excluding the image sequence capture and foreground mask generation. The first step is difference vector extraction, followed by clustering of these differences for background subtraction including the quartile method and the k-nearest neighbor method. Finally, the foreground image generated by the last step is improved by morphological filtering.

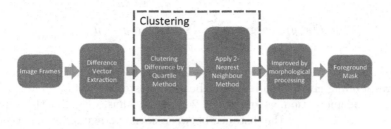

Fig. 2. Flow chart of the proposed approach.

3.1 Difference Clustering

The difference between the current and historical frames is used for clustering. To extract the representation of the historical frames, several frames are randomly selected from the previous image sequence. Assume the image frames to be $\{I_1, I_2, \cdots, I_t\}$, where t represents time. Then, a random permutation $G = \{g_1, g_2, \cdots g_N\} = \{g_i | i \in [1 \ N]\}$ is utilized for selecting the historical frames. The selection procedure can be described as follows:

$$\mathcal{I}^s = \{I_i^s | i \in G, I_i^s \in \mathcal{I} = \{I_1, I_2, \cdots, I_t\}\}, G = \{g_j | j \in [1 \ N]\} \qquad (1)$$

where $\mathcal{I}$ is the representation of the image frames captured from the camera, G is the set of random permutation for sampling and $\mathcal{I}^s$ is the set of frames after sampling. During the experiments, 100 frames are randomly selected without any scaling operation.

After sampling, the representations of historical frames are captured, which is used to extract differences for clustering. A difference is extracted from the average difference between the current frame and every frame in the sampled image sequence, in which the absolute value is used as the difference measure. Mathematically, this can be represented as:

$$D(x, y) = \frac{1}{N} \sum_{i=0}^{N} |I_i^s(x, y) - I_t(x, y)| \qquad (2)$$

where (x, y) is the locations of pixels, $I_t(x, y)$ is the current frame, $I_i^s(x, y)$ is the set of sample frames and N is the number of sample frames.

3.2 Difference Clustering with 2-Nearest Neighbours

In the k-means algorithm, we use the average of each cluster in each iteration (except for the first iteration). However, it is highly likely that the calculated mean is not in the cluster. By using the k-nearest neighbour algorithm, we can get the point in the cluster which is closest to the calculated mean as the mean for that iteration. This is a supervised algorithm and improves the k-means algorithm, which is described as follows:

$$\mathcal{F}(x,y) = \operatorname*{argmin}_{S} \sum_{i=1}^{k} \sum_{x,y \in S_i} ||D(x,y) - \mu_i||^2 \qquad (3)$$

where μ_i denotes the center of the clusters, $D(x,y)$ represents the pixels among the corresponding clusters and S describes the cluster we need.

In our implementation, we only need 2 clusters. Thus, we call it the 2-nearest neighbor method. We get the distance between each average difference vector to the origin $[0, 0, 0]$. If the distance is small, then the change between the current and the 100 corresponding pixels in the basic matrix is small. Thus, the pixel belongs to the background. Otherwise, it belongs to the foreground. So, to distinguish foreground from background, we only need 2 clusters. We decided to make some improvements to the 2-nearest neighbour method. We use quartiles to find the two means directly before clustering in order to decrease the computational time. As we find the 2 means directly, we only need one iteration to get the outcome. In the quartile method, the ordinary data is sorted in ascending order and then divided into 4 equal subgroups [7]. In [25], the research on periventricular hemorrhage detection used a similar binary classification. The authors considered the largest 5% of the data to be outliers. So they applied the k-means algorithm on the remaining 95% of the data and achieved good results. Considering the largest 5% data to be outliers as well, we tried the following quartile model in Table 1:

Table 1. Quartile design

Min	5%	Q1	45%	Medium	45%	Q3	5%	Max

However, we found that this model is still not accurate for our experiments. According to the average difference of RGB values for each pixel in this frame we calculated previously, we can plot them using 3D coordinates, as shown in Fig. 3:

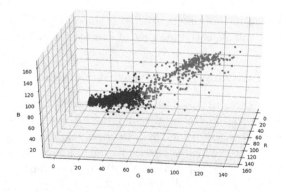

Fig. 3. 3D plot of the average difference of RGB value for each pixel.

From the plot we find that we do not have outliers in the first group, as the distance cannot be negative. The closer the distance is to 0, the higher the probability that it is a background pixel. Also, we find that if we drop the last 5%, we will loose some useful data, as not all of them are outliers. After several tests, we decide to use Q1 = 0 and Q3 = 99%. The remaining 1% is considered to be outliers (Table 2).

Table 2. Quatile design

Min	0%	Q1	49.5%	Medium	49.5%	Q3	1%	Max

There are many methods applying k-means algorithm like traditional k-means algorithm [4] and genetic k-means algorithm [5]. In those algorithms, we need to separate the data into several clusters, recalculate each cluster's centers, and repeat the clustering until the function does not change [5]. This approach is relatively time-consuming. Our difference clustering method uses a supervised algorithm, the k-nearest neighbour algorithm, instead of the k-means algorithm. Furthermore, we only need two clusters and the clustering is done in one iteration.

As we mentioned above, if the magnitude of the vector is small, the pixel goes to the background group, otherwise it goes to the foreground group. As a result we only need 2 clusters. Traditional k-means algorithm and genetic k-means algorithm need to update the centers using several iterations until convergence, this takes a long time. In our implementation, we apply the quartile method to get the 2-nearest neighbor algorithm completed in only one iteration. We noticed that since we only need 2 clusters, we can find the boundaries of the data and cluster the data based on the two boundaries. The quartile method can help us remove potential outliers so that we can get more reliable boundary values.

3.3   Erosion and Dilation

After computing the binary mask, we find that there is still some noise. So, we use erosion and dilation to improve our output. Erosion can remove distinct pixels in the output. Dilation can add pixels to the boundary of objects in an image. We applied the opening method to improve the quality of our image, where opening means an erosion following a dilation.

$$\mathcal{M}(x,y) = g(\sum_{n=y-R}^{y+R} \sum_{m=x-R}^{x+R} \mathcal{F}(m,n) \cap 1, T) \tag{4}$$

where $\mathcal{F}(m,n)$ denotes the foreground mask before morphological processing, R is the range of processing and $g(x,y)$ is a piecewise function:

$$g(x,y) = \begin{cases} 1, & x < y \\ 0, & otherwise \end{cases}, \tag{5}$$

4 Experiments

In this section, the experimental results for every method we used in background subtraction is presented. In the proposed approach, although the differences between the background image and the current frame are captured from a temporal sequence, all these differences from the spatial domain are used for clustering. This is the reason why we compared the proposed approach with GraphCutDiff, SSO-BS, and M-Distance, since all of them are related to spatial information.

4.1 Time Complexity

Both the k-means [4,5] and k-nearest neighbor [22] algorithms use iterations which are time-consuming. These algorithms separate the data into several clusters, and iteratively recalculate the center of each cluster until the calculation converges. Such a procedure usually takes tens or even hundreds of iterations, which is too expensive to be used in real applications. To address this problem, we propose the quartile method which needs only one iteration. The purpose of the iteration is to try to find the correct cluster centers. We assume that the foreground object and background scene differ considerably. This led us to seek the boundaries of the data to determine suitable cluster centers corresponding to the foreground and background. After this, the difference between the current pixel and the background representation can be easily clustered into the foreground or background, in only one iteration.

The qualitative comparison between our quartile algorithm and the traditional k-nearest neighbor is shown in Fig. 4. Following is a comparison of the outputs. The left one uses the ordinary k-nearest neighbor algorithm and updates the means and re-clusters for 20 iterations. This takes around 57 s to process one frame. The right one uses boundary values obtained by the quartile method as the final means and applies the 2-nearest neighbor algorithm; this takes only 4 s for each frame.

As shown in Fig. 4, our method used less time but gets a more precise output.

Fig. 4. Traditional K-Nearest neighbour (left) and quartile (right).

4.2   Quantitative and Qualitative Evaluation

The proposed approach is evaluated using several videos from the CDnet2014 [6] benchmark. The Re (Recall), Pr (Precision) and Fm (F-measure) metrics are used to compare the proposed approach with GraphCutDiff [20], SSO-BS [21] and M-Distance [23]. Mathematically, these metrics are:

$$Re = \frac{TP}{TP + FN}, Pr = \frac{TP}{TP + FP}, Fm = \frac{2 \times Pr \times Re}{Pr + Re},$$

where TP and FP are True Positive and False Positive. Here, positive means foreground, while negative refers to the background. True means correct detection, while False denotes incorrect. Thus, TP indicates that the result of the detection is foreground and it is the same as the ground-truth.

The quantitative and qualitative evaluation of the proposed approach is shown in Table 3 and Fig. 5. In particular, several challenging videos includ-

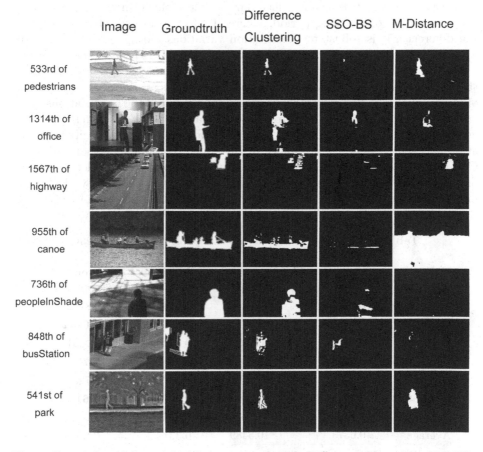

Fig. 5. From left to right: original frame, ground truth, Difference Clustering, SSO-BS, M-Distance.

ing pedestrians, office, highway, canoe, peopleInShade, busStation and park are selected from the CDNet dataset [6], due to the limitation of our computational resources. Furthermore, these videos are selected from different categories for a comprehensive evaluation of the proposed approach. Highway and Office comes from the baseline category, while Canoe is selected from the category dynamic background.

As shown in the Table 3, the proposed approach achieves the highest average Fm value compared to other algorithms. Therefore, it is fair to say that the proposed approach generates promising results, and the qualitative results shown in Fig. 5 show the same as well. In the video pedestrians, the main challenges is the intensity of the illumination as shown in the Fig. 5. For this kind of video, the relative gradient change between neighborhood pixels has high robustness. It is the main reason why GraphCutDiff [20] and the proposed approach have good performance. Since the proposed approach is based on difference clustering, the differences captured from pixels are compared with each other for their final clusters. In the video office, the challenge comes from the illumination changes during the movement of people. Since our difference clustering model considers the information over a long period, where 100 frames are selected to capture the difference, it is robust to illumination variations during the time interval compared to other methods. A similar situation also occurs in the video highway.

In the video canoe, the main challenge is the dynamic background, in which the pixels of the background have repeated variations. However, the variation of pixels' observations have obvious differences compared to the variations generated by moving objects. The proposed approach clusters the differences and works well in this condition. By contrast, M-Distance [23] cannot classify the variation and achieves poor performance in this video. For similar reasons, Graph-CutDiff [20] and SSO-BS [21] also work poorly for this video. The video peopleIn-Shade and busStation belong to the category Shadow. The shadow of objects in these videos is the main challenge, since the variations generated by different

Table 3. Comparison with two recently published methods [23]

Video	GraphCutDiff [20]	SSO-BS [21]	M-Distance [23]	Proposed approach
Pedestrians	**0.9259**	0.8283	0.6159	0.8702
Office	0.3513	0.2725	0.4654	**0.6552**
Highway	**0.9033**	0.6838	0.2735	0.6331
Canoe	0.1194	0.2327	0.1557	**0.7791**
PeopleInShade	**0.7472**	0.6999	0.4375	0.7269
BusStation	0.5915	0.4904	0.3378	**0.6122**
Park	**0.8222**	0.6350	0.0328	0.6110
Average	0.6373	0.5489	0.3312	**0.6982**

factors have differences for various objects. The proposed approach works well in these videos. The final video selected for evaluation is the video park.

5 Conclusion

We proposed the difference clustering method for various backgrounds in this paper. Unlike the traditional k-means algorithms, we used a new idea for clustering. We started by analyzing the differences between the current frame and 100 randomly generated frames to get the average difference. To cluster the average difference, 2 clusters were required. Furthermore, since we only needed two clusters, the two boundary values could be used as the two means of the two clusters. We applied the quartile method to remove the potential outliers to get the boundary values. Then, we applied the 2-nearest neighbor algorithm to cluster in only one iteration. This modification saved us about 92% of the computational time. Compared to other unsupervised background subtraction methods, the Fm (F-measure) values are still relatively high. Our difference clustering method is very practical and competitive for real-time video background subtraction.

References

1. Heikkila, M., et al.: A texture-based method for modeling the background and detecting moving objects. IEEE Trans. Pattern Anal. Mach. Intell. **28**(4), 657–662 (2006)
2. Yang, D., et al.: Background modeling by stability of adaptive features in complex scenes. IEEE Trans. Image Process. **27**(3), 1112–1125 (2018)
3. Stauffer, C., et al.: Adaptive background mixture models for real-time tracking. In: 1999 IEEE Computer Society Conference on Computer Vision and Pattern Recognition (Cat. No PR00149) (1999)
4. Butler, D., et al.: Real-time adaptive foreground/background segmentation. EURASIP J. Adv. Sig. Process. **2005**(14), 841926 (2005)
5. Xiuman, D., et al.: Moving target detection based on genetic k-means algorithm. In: 2011 IEEE 13th International Conference on Communication Technology, pp. 819–822. IEEE, September 2011
6. Goyette, N., et al.: Changedetection. net: a new change detection benchmark dataset. In: 2012 IEEE Computer Society Conference on Computer Vision and Pattern Recognition Workshops, pp. 1–8. IEEE, June 2012
7. Lim, L.A., et al.: Foreground segmentation using convolutional neural networks for multiscale feature encoding. Pattern Recogn. Lett. **112**, 256–262 (2018)
8. Sun, B., Saenko, K.: Deep CORAL: correlation alignment for deep domain adaptation. In: Hua, G., Jégou, H. (eds.) ECCV 2016. LNCS, vol. 9915, pp. 443–450. Springer, Cham (2016). https://doi.org/10.1007/978-3-319-49409-8_35
9. Mahmood, A., et al.: Exploiting transitivity of correlation for fast template matching. IEEE Trans. Image Process. **19**(8), 2190–2200 (2010)
10. Saatci, Y., et al.: Bayesian gan. In: Advances in Neural Information Processing Systems, pp. 3622–3631 (2017)

11. Wang, Y., et al.: Interactive deep learning method for segmenting moving objects. Pattern Recogn. Lett. **96**, 66–75 (2017)
12. Braham, M., et al.: Semantic background subtraction. In: 2017 IEEE International Conference on Image Processing (ICIP), pp. 4552–4556. IEEE, September 2017
13. Bianco, S., et al.: Combination of video change detection algorithms by genetic programming. IEEE Trans. Evol. Comput. **21**(6), 914–928 (2017)
14. Isik, S., et al.: SWCD: a sliding window and self-regulated learning-based background updating method for change detection in videos. J. Electron. Imaging **27**(2), 023002 (2018)
15. Lee, S., et al.: WisenetMD: motion detection using dynamic background region analysis. Symmetry **11**(5), 621 (2019)
16. Bouwmans, T.: Traditional and recent approaches in background modeling for foreground detection: an overview. Comput. Sci. Rev. **11**, 31–66 (2014)
17. Kim, K., et al.: Background modeling and subtraction by codebook construction. In: 2004 International Conference on Image Processing, 2004. ICIP 2004, vol. 5, pp. 3061–3064. IEEE, October 2004
18. Xiao, M., et al.: A background reconstruction for dynamic scenes. In: 2006 9th International Conference on Information Fusion, pp. 1–7. IEEE, July 2006
19. Chang, R., et al.: A novel content based image retrieval system using K-means/KNN with feature extraction. Comput. Sci. Inf. Syst. **9**(4), 1645–1661 (2012)
20. Miron, A., et al.: Change detection based on graph cuts. In: 2015 International Conference on Systems, Signals and Image Processing (IWSSIP), pp. 273–276. IEEE, September 2015
21. Sehairi, K., et al.: Comparative study of motion detection methods for video surveillance systems. J. Electron. Imaging **26**(2), 023025 (2017)
22. Keller, J., et al.: A fuzzy k-nearest neighbor algorithm. IEEE Trans. Syst. Man Cybern. **4**, 580–585 (1985)
23. Benezeth, Y., et al.: Comparative study of background subtraction algorithms. J. Electr. Imaging **19**(3), 033003 (2010)
24. Zhu, B., Gao, W., Wu, X., Yu, R.: A heterogeneous image fusion algorithm based on LLC coding. In: Basu, A., Berretti, S. (eds.) ICSM 2018. LNCS, vol. 11010, pp. 134–144. Springer, Cham (2018). https://doi.org/10.1007/978-3-030-04375-9_12
25. Mukherjee, S., Cheng, I., Basu, A.: Atlas-free method of periventricular hemorrhage detection from preterm infants' T1 MR images. In: Basu, A., Berretti, S. (eds.) ICSM 2018. LNCS, vol. 11010, pp. 157–168. Springer, Cham (2018). https://doi.org/10.1007/978-3-030-04375-9_14
26. Nigam, J., Sharma, K., Rameshan, R.M.: Detection-based online multi-target tracking via adaptive subspace learning. In: Basu, A., Berretti, S. (eds.) ICSM 2018. LNCS, vol. 11010, pp. 285–295. Springer, Cham (2018). https://doi.org/10.1007/978-3-030-04375-9_24
27. Wang, T., et al.: A survey on vision-based hand gesture recognition. In: Basu, A., Berretti, S. (eds.) ICSM 2018. LNCS, vol. 11010, pp. 219–231. Springer, Cham (2018). https://doi.org/10.1007/978-3-030-04375-9_19
28. Liu, C., Cheng, I., Basu, A.: Synthetic vision assisted real-time runway detection for infrared aerial images. In: Basu, A., Berretti, S. (eds.) ICSM 2018. LNCS, vol. 11010, pp. 274–281. Springer, Cham (2018). https://doi.org/10.1007/978-3-030-04375-9_23

Semantic Learning for Image Compression (SLIC)

Kushal Mahalingaiah, Harsh Sharma, Priyanka Kaplish, and Irene Cheng[✉]

University of Alberta, Edmonton, Canada
{hosahall,hsharma,kaplish,locheng}@ualberta.ca

Abstract. Image compression is an ever-evolving problem with different approaches coming into prominence at different times. Data analysts are still contemplating about the best approach with compression ratio, visual quality and complexity of the architecture as the main criteria of evaluation. Most recent one is the advancements in machine learning and its applications on image classification. Researchers are currently exploring the possibility of using this advanced computing power to enhance the quality of images with the availability of large datasets. Here, we present a deep learning Convolutional neural network (CNN) implemented and trained for image recognition and image processing tasks, to understand semantics of an image. We achieve higher visual quality in lossy compression by increasing the complexity of an encoder by a slight margin to generate semantic maps of image. The semantic maps are tailored to make the encoder content-aware for a given image. In the proposed work, we present a novel architecture developed specifically for image compression, which generates a semantic map for salient regions so that they can be encoded at higher quality as compared to background regions. Experiments are conducted on the Kodak PhotoCD dataset and the results are compared with other state-of-the-art models. Results of the conducted experiment reveal an increase in compression ratio by more than 17% compared to the referred state-of-the-art model while maintaining the visual quality.

Keywords: Image compression · Deep learning · Semantic maps

1 Introduction

Image compression is the process of optimizing image size in such a way that it takes less memory without compromising much on the quality of the image. There are two ways in which compression can be achieved - lossy and lossless compression. In lossless compression, file size is reduced without any loss in the original quality. However in lossy compression, image compression is achieved with some loss in quality compared to the original image.

Recent advances in artificial Neural Networks have paved the way for major breakthroughs in image compression. Neural Networks can be used to optimize the tradeoff between the amount of distortion and compression ratio.

© Springer Nature Switzerland AG 2020
T. McDaniel et al. (Eds.): ICSM 2019, LNCS 12015, pp. 57–66, 2020.
https://doi.org/10.1007/978-3-030-54407-2_5

In this work, we propose a lossy compression approach developed using a CNN based model. We integrate our model with the most popular lossy compression scheme, Joint Photographic Experts group, commonly known as JPEG, to produce visually appealing image with a smaller filesize.

The efficiency of JPEG compression is based on the spatial frequency, or concentration of detail, of the image. Areas in the image with low frequency are compressed more than areas with higher frequency. This characteristic of JPEG along with our approach helps us outperform standard JPEG in terms of compression while preserving the latent semantics in the compressed image.

The rest of the paper is organized as follows: Sect. 2 includes the conducted literature review, Sect. 3 details the architecture of the proposed work, Sect. 4 illustrates the results of the experiments on the proposed model, Sects. 5, and 6 provide concluding remarks and areas of improvement in future work respectively.

2   Related Work

The idea of semantic segmentation for image compression has been explored since the 1990s [12], however due to unavailability of good segmentation techniques the approach was not used widely. The feature extraction, transfer learning capabilities of CNNs and ability to classify images by their most prominent object have helped in semantic image understanding and with recent advancements in deep learning and cheaper hardware, there are several works that leverage CNN for image compression, [2,3,7,8,10]. Akbari et al. in [2] used multiple networks for segmentation whereas, Prakash et al. in [8] developed 3D feature maps using a modified VGG-16 network [11].

Autoencoders can also be used for flexible lossy compression algorithms. Depending on the situation, encoders and decoders of different computational complexity are required. When sending data from a server to a mobile device, it is desirable to pair a powerful encoder with a less complex decoder, but the requirements are reversed when sending data in the other direction. In [13], Theis et al. implement lossy image compression with the help of autoencoders. The authors use common convolutional neural networks (LeCun et al. 1998) for the encoder and the decoder of the compressive autoencoder. Zhao and Liao also use autoencoders for image compression in [14]. This implementation is capable of implicitly optimizing the bitrate without the use of an entropy estimator. The encoder maps the original image to a latent representation z which are then mapped to compressed presentation of the image z'. Finally, the decoder attempts to reconstruct the original image from the information in z'.

Generative adversarial networks (GANs) have emerged as a popular technique for learning generative models for intractable distributions in an unsupervised manner. The use of GAN is still being explored as a viable option for image compression. Santurkar et al. in [9] and Agustsson, et al. in [1] have used GAN, however, there is still a lot of scope for improvement.

3 Proposed Approach

The basic flow diagram for our approach is shown in Fig. 1 and details are discussed in subsections below.

Fig. 1. Basic flow diagram of the developed approach

3.1 Model Details

The two most common convolutional networks used for image classification are the VGG architecture and the ResNet architecture. For developing our model, we have considered the VGG-19 and the ResNet-50 architectures. Since these models have been originally developed for classification, we had to modify them to suit our needs. Our modifications are developed on top of the Class Activation Mapping (CAM) approach described in [15]. The modified model for ResNet-50 (our final proposed approach) is shown in Fig. 2.

We have removed the average pooling, flattening and the final connected layers and replaced them with three new layers, a 2D convolutional layer followed by a 2-D depthwise convolution and finally another convolutional layer. This replacement helps us to identify the regions of interests in the image, details of which are provided in the next subsection.

3.2 Extracting Regions of Interests

Region of Interest (ROI) based compression is achieved by detecting the image content and obtaining a corresponding saliency map, which provides the means for quantifying the relevance of different image regions. CAM, proposed by Zhou et al. [15], enables the localization of discriminative image regions. The network consists of repeated convolutional and pooling layers, followed by a Global Average Pooling (GAP) layer. GAP is performed on the feature maps from the convolutional layer preceding the GAP layer and the resulting vector is fed into the softmax layer, which outputs the predicted class. Each node in the GAP layer corresponds to a specific feature map, whereas the weights connecting the GAP layer to the softmax layer encode the contribution of each feature map (the detected visual pattern) to the predicted class. The detected patterns that are

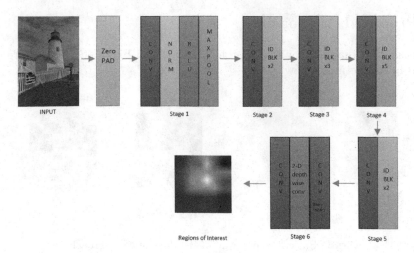

Fig. 2. Modified ResNet-50 architecture

more relevant to the predicted class are given more weight. To obtain the CAM, the weights of the output layer are projected back to the last convolutional layer and a weighted sum of the feature maps is calculated. The obtained heatmap indicates the importance of different image regions and highlights the discriminative regions that are used by the network to identify a particular class. Due to the CAM method maximizing the posterior probability of the class, the generated heatmap emphasizes only one discriminative region, i.e. the highest-scoring class.

Class activation maps (CAMs) and multi-structure region of interest (MS-ROI) maps are able to represent arbitrary shapes, capture object silhouettes and produce soft borders around objects. The resulting saliency maps are more coherent and therefore better suited for their incorporation into a compression scheme. The proposed work is a MS-ROI based model, which is a variation of CAM, the main difference or upgrade is the ability to detect multiple salient image regions unlike CAMs.

For the MS-ROI model, the architecture of the CAM model is modified in order to obtain heatmaps that allow for the localization of multiple regions of interest. Instead of using argmax to find the index of the element with the maximum value (most probable class), argsort is used to obtain sorted activations from the index of the element with the lowest value to the index of the element with the highest value. Rather than picking only the highest-scoring class (top-1 prediction) to obtain the top-k information, we pick the five highest-scoring classes (top-5 predictions) and take their weighted sum, while discarding the less probable classes. The final localization is expressed as a heatmap, where the colour-coding scheme, which consists of a range of cold and warm colours (from blue to red), identifies the importance of individual salient and non-salient regions.

As mentioned earlier, we used both VGG and ResNet architectures for our research, however, the model developed using the VGG-19 network generated poor heatmaps as the model returned too many high scoring classes. This resulted in the failure of localization of multiple regions of interest in the compressed image. As shown in Fig. 3, the results for our final proposed model, using ResNet-50, were better than the VGG-16 model used in [8] and lot better than the developed VGG-19 model. The proposed model performed better argsort for the activations, making it more capable to localize features.

3.3 Training and Testing

As mentioned earlier, we considered both VGG-19 and ResNet-50 architectures during our research. We trained both the modified networks on the Caltech-256 dataset [4] for 200 epochs with a learning rate of 0.001 and a batch size of 32. To speed up the training, we used Numpy and stored all the images in memory instead of reading them individually during training. The training graphs for VGG19 and ResNet50 are shown in Fig. 4 and 5, respectively.

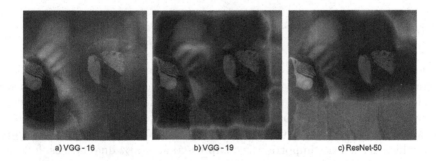

a) VGG - 16   b) VGG - 19   c) ResNet-50

Fig. 3. Heatmaps generated using various CNN models

The Caltech-256 dataset was chosen because the classes in this dataset cover most real world objects that occur in images and the categories are also not deeply divided in subdomains, which would be irrelevant for our purpose. The sufficiently large number of categories also make it possible to train the network on a more readily available hardware.

For the testing and comparison, we used the Kodak PhotoCD Dataset along with random natural images captured using the camera on Google Pixel 3.

3.4 Integration with JPEG

The JPEG architecture consists of two parts - an encoder and a decoder. The encoder divides the image into 8 × 8 blocks and applies DCT to obtain coefficients which are then stored using a variable bit length encoding scheme. The

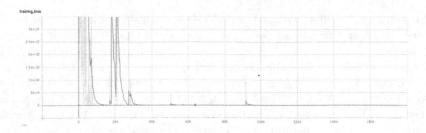

Fig. 4. Training loss for VGG-19

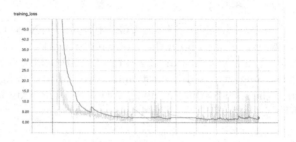

Fig. 5. Training loss for ResNet-50

decoder performs the inverse operations when the image is displayed. We have integrated our model with an off the shelf JPEG encoder/decoder architecture.

Once the regions of interests in an image are identified, we use a discrete percentile based technique to divide image into 4 compression regions - 0–20 percentile, 20–60 percentile, 60–90 percentile and 90–100 percentile. The first region which is the least important is compressed at a 60% quality loss, followed by a 40% and a 20% loss. The most relevant details are compressed with the best quality with only a 10% loss over the regular JPEG compression.

4   Results

We evaluated our model using both qualitative as well as quantitative measures. For qualitative analysis we compared the visual quality with the standard JPEG compressed image and also analyzed the heatmaps generated by VGG-16, used in [8] and ResNet-50, our approach. The results for 5 images from our testing dataset are shown in Fig. 6. As visible, our approach captures more details than the VGG-16 architecture. In scenarios like image 2 and 4 in Fig. 6 our network was able to detect areas of interests with better accuracy than VGG-16 and in cases where there is no definite focus area, image 3 and 5 the regions identified are equivalent. The visual quality of the images for both the networks is comparable with our approach producing better results in several test cases.

For quantitative measurement of the performance of our approach, we calculated the following metrics

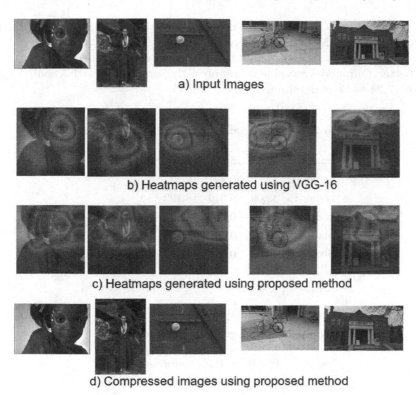

a) Input Images

b) Heatmaps generated using VGG-16

c) Heatmaps generated using proposed method

d) Compressed images using proposed method

Fig. 6. Qualitative results and comparison of proposed approach with VGG-16

- **Peak Signal to Noise Ratio (PSNR)**, calculated usually in logarithmic (dB) scale, is a metric used to measure the quality of any reconstructed, restored or corrupted image with respect to its reference or ground truth image. Higher the PSNR, better the image quality.
- **Structural Similarity Index Measurement (SSIM)**, is a full reference metric based on an initial uncompressed image as reference. SSIM index is a decimal value between -1 and 1, and value 1 is only reachable in the case of two identical sets of data.
- **Compression Ratio**, is the ratio of size of the original uncompressed image to the compressed image

We calculated all the three values for all the images from our testing dataset and for the Kodak dataset. The value for the images shown in Fig. 6 are listed in Tables 1 and 2, for VGG 16 and ResNet-50 respectively.

As illustrated in the table, compression ratio achieved by the proposed model is better than the state-of-the-art. Compression ratio of the output images is 17.29% more than VGG-16 accompanied by only a 1.99% decrease in PSNR and a 2.59% decrease in SSIM. With the increased compression ratio and the slight decrease in PSNR and SSIM, the visual quality of the compressed images is not compromised. Our approach works exceptionally well for images of higher resolution. For a 20 MP image, where the standard JPEG encoder was able to attain a compression ratio of 4.65, our semantically compressed image was 3.7 times better. Our model was able to compress the same image with a compression ratio of 17.24 while maintaining a SSIM of 0.85.

Table 1. Results for images from Fig. 6 for VGG-16

Image	PSNR	SSIM	Compression ratio
kodak-02	32.855	0.891	18.33
kodak-15	33.09	0.919	18.123
kodak-18	30.29	0.908	14.525
pixel-03	29.041	0.839	11.894
pixel-05	30.39	0.91	11.944

Table 2. Results for images from Fig. 6 for our approach

Image	PSNR	SSIM	Compression Ratio
kodak-02	32.175	0.875	21.763
kodak-15	32.348	0.907	21.043
kodak-18	29.521	0.894	16.791
pixel-03	28.246	0.811	14.185
pixel-05	29.376	0.892	13.944

5   Conclusion

Current lossy image compression standards like JPEG and JPEG2000 achieve remarkable compression ratio however, as seen in Fig. 7, the visual quality has a scope for improvement. We have presented a model which can achieve compression ratios better than JPEG while maintaining a similar level of visual quality. Our model can detect multiple objects at any scale and this information can be used for performing variable-quality image compression for varying resolutions. Though the compression is more profound for images of higher resolution, it can be used for images of any size and resolution. The current drawback of our model include the large amount of time to compress images of high resolutions and minor degradation of quality for images with no definite region of interests.

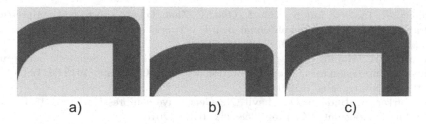

a)   b)   c)

Fig. 7. Image quality comparison a) PNG b) JPG c) Our approach

6 Future Work

As we mentioned earlier, image compression is still an ever-evolving research problem. The results achieved by our model outperform JPEG, however, there are several research areas related to this work which can be pursued. Real time performance for compression of higher size or resolution images is still a work in progress. Video compression using machine learning, for a streaming service, has a constraint of slower execution speed of the model. Image compression using semantic analysis can be implemented with GAN to produce better quality results as GAN are found to be more effective at image classification tasks. Also, a similar approach of detecting key features to compress can be extended for audio, text and other types of files. Deploying the compression library on a public server for public use is also another task in pipeline. The current model is computationally heavy due to the complexity of the network used. With use of a less complex model like MobileNet [5] or SqueezeNet [6], the architecture can be extended for compression on mobile devices as well.

References

1. Agustsson, E., Tschannen, M., Mentzer, F., Timofte, R., Gool, L.V.: Generative adversarial networks for extreme learned image compression. CoRR abs/1804.02958 (2018). http://arxiv.org/abs/1804.02958
2. Akbari, M., Liang, J., Han, J.: DSSLIC: deep semantic segmentation-based layered image compression. In: ICASSP 2019–2019 IEEE International Conference on Acoustics, Speech and Signal Processing (ICASSP), pp. 2042–2046. IEEE (2019)
3. Cai, C., Chen, L., Zhang, X., Gao, Z.: Efficient variable rate image compression with multi-scale decomposition network. IEEE Trans. Circuits Syst. Video Technol. (2018)
4. Griffin, G., Holub, A., Perona, P.: Caltech-256 object category dataset. Technical report, 7694, California Institute of Technology (2007). http://authors.library.caltech.edu/7694
5. Howard, A.G., et al.: MobileNets: efficient convolutional neural networks for mobile vision applications. CoRR abs/1704.04861 (2017). http://arxiv.org/abs/1704.04861
6. Iandola, F.N., Moskewicz, M.W., Ashraf, K., Han, S., Dally, W.J., Keutzer, K.: SqueezeNet: Alexnet-level accuracy with 50x fewer parameters and <1mb model size. CoRR abs/1602.07360 (2016). http://arxiv.org/abs/1602.07360

7. Jiang, F., Tao, W., Liu, S., Ren, J., Guo, X., Zhao, D.: An end-to-end compression framework based on convolutional neural networks. IEEE Trans. Circuits Syst. Video Technol. **28**(10), 3007–3018 (2017)
8. Prakash, A., Moran, N., Garber, S., DiLillo, A., Storer, J.A.: Semantic perceptual image compression using deep convolution networks. CoRR abs/1612.08712 (2016). http://arxiv.org/abs/1612.08712
9. Santurkar, S., Budden, D., Shavit, N.: Generative compression. In: 2018 Picture Coding Symposium (PCS), pp. 258–262. IEEE (2018)
10. Selimović, A., Meden, B., Peer, P., Hladnik, A.: Analysis of content-aware image compression with VGG16. In: 2018 IEEE International Work Conference on Bioinspired Intelligence (IWOBI), pp. 1–7. IEEE (2018)
11. Simonyan, K., Zisserman, A.: Very deep convolutional networks for large-scale image recognition. arXiv preprint arXiv:1409.1556 (2014)
12. Talluri, R., Oehler, K., Barmon, T., Courtney, J.D., Das, A., Liao, J.: A robust, scalable, object-based video compression technique for very low bit-rate coding. IEEE Trans. Circuits Syst. Video Technol. **7**(1), 221–233 (1997)
13. Theis, L., Shi, W., Cunningham, A., Huszár, F.: Lossy image compression with compressive autoencoders. arXiv preprint arXiv:1703.00395 (2017)
14. Zhao, H., Liao, P.: CAE-ADMM: implicit bitrate optimization via ADMM-based pruning in compressive autoencoders. CoRR abs/1901.07196 (2019). http://arxiv.org/abs/1901.07196
15. Zhou, B., Khosla, A., Lapedriza, A., Oliva, A., Torralba, A.: Learning deep features for discriminative localization. In: Proceedings of the IEEE Conference on Computer Vision and Pattern Recognition, pp. 2921–2929 (2016)

Background Subtraction Based on Principal Motion for a Freely Moving Camera

Yingnan Ma[1], Guanfang Dong[1], Chenqiu Zhao[1(✉)], Anup Basu[1], and Zhengjiang Wu[2]

[1] Department of Computing Science, University of Alberta, Edmonton, Canada
chenqiu1@ualberta.ca
[2] Huawei Technologies Co., Ltd, Shenzhen, China

Abstract. As a fundamental research topic of computer vision, background subtraction technology can be implemented in many applications. This problem becomes even more challenging once the videos are obtained with a moving camera. To solve the challenging task, we analyze the principal motion of pixels for subtracting background in videos obtained from freely moving cameras. In particular, the optical flow is captured for the representation of motion for pixels. Moreover, assuming that the background motion should be the principal part, Robust Principal Components Analysis (RPCA) is utilized for subtracting the background of videos obtained from freely moving cameras, in which both angle and magnitude of the optical flow are utilized for the analysis of motion. Finally, super-pixels are utilized to compensate for the defects produced by inaccuracies in optical flow, where a double threshold strategy is proposed to integrate the foreground results captured from the angle as well as the magnitude. Experiments based on several videos from standard benchmark datasets illustrate that the proposed method achieves promising performance compared to the state-of-the-art.

1 Introduction

Background Subtraction is a popular problem in computer vision [1–3], used as a pre-processing procedure in a large number of high-level applications like traffic monitoring [4] or activity recognition [5]. Traditionally, background subtraction assumes that videos are obtained from a stationary camera. However, with increasing numbers of freely moving cameras, such as on mobile phones, more and more applications require the background subtraction methods to work for freely moving cameras. This makes the problem even more challenging. Although many methods have been presented, there are still few approaches that produce promising results, since the entire background moves due to camera motion. In this paper, Robust Principal Component Analysis (RPCA) is utilized to analyze the motion of video background, and a novel subtracting background approach for freely moving camera is proposed.

© Springer Nature Switzerland AG 2020
T. McDaniel et al. (Eds.): ICSM 2019, LNCS 12015, pp. 67–78, 2020.
https://doi.org/10.1007/978-3-030-54407-2_6

The main challenge of subtracting background for a freely moving camera comes from the camera motion, which makes every pixel of the scene move. To handle this challenge, we assume that the background motion is the principal part of the motion in the scene. Therefore, the motion of pixels in the background implies linear correlations, which is reasonably described as a low-rank matrix. Robust Principal Components Analysis (RPCA) is naturally selected for the decomposition of the motion representation to capture the low-rank matrix. In particular, the motion is represented by optical flow, and the Robust Principal Components Analysis is used for the decomposition of background motion and foreground objects, as shown in Fig. 1.

In our proposed method, the optical flow is captured for the description of the motion of pixels. Then, Robust Principal Components Analysis is used for the extraction of background motion. In particular, the optical flow is converted into the angle and the magnitude of motion for the subtraction of the background scene. However, the optical flow itself includes several defects. To enhance the accuracy and the efficiency, the neighborhood information between pixels is utilized. We first segment the current frame into several super-pixels. Super-pixels takes the statistic of pixels' label as the final label of the super-pixels. Benefiting from the utilization of RPCA as well as the consideration of the neighborhood information implied in the super-pixels, the proposed approach can work with the video obtained by freely moving the camera in complex scenes. Our proposed approach can be summarized as below:

1. We assume the background motion of scenes is represented by a low-rank matrix, and RPCA is utilized for the decomposition of background motion for subtracting the background.
2. For the compensation of defects produced during the generation of the optical flows, we consider the neighborhood information and use super-pixels to improve the accuracy of the proposed approach.

Fig. 1. Demonstration of the proposed approach, the motion of pixels is represented by the optical flow, and Robust Principal Component is proposed to decompose the background motion and foreground motion.

2   Related Work

In recent years, different methods and algorithms have been designed to solve the subtracting background with a freely moving camera. Background subtraction can be involved in medical research [1] and person authentication applications [6]. Based on previous research, the optical flow is a popular method designed to solve background subtraction with a freely moving camera. Specifically, the optical flow can be described as patterns between two frames. Note that the optical flow can be recognised as sparse optical flow and dense optical flow. For dense optical flow, every pixel in an image needs to be considered for calculating the magnitude and angle changes. Conversely, sparse optical flow only needs to consider the feature points in an image. To utilize the advantages of the optical flow, we can use the dense optical flow to detect the foreground object. Several methods can be utilized to calculate the optical flow. Zhou and Zhang [7] suggested that the optical flow can be calculated by Lucas-Kanada's gradient-based method because it has been shown to be the most accurate and computationally efficient.

Barron [8] firstly computed the velocities. Then, they constrained 2D velocity by the second-order differential method. Finally, they produce an estimate of the optical flow by combining local estimation of the component velocity and 2D velocity.

The optical flow can be combined with other methods. Employing particle trajectory is a popular method to detect moving objects. Particle trajectory can reveal a particle's movement procedure [9]. By computing the optical flow, a particle trajectory that involves finding dense trajectories can be captured.

After obtaining the particle trajectory, the motion of objects [10] can be reliably differentiated from objects at rest at sparse locations using geometric constraints, such as the rank constraint for orthographic cameras, or the fundamental polynomial constraint for projective cameras. After obtaining a fine foreground, [10] we can build the foreground and background models. In addition, Otsu's threshold selection method [11] can also help to obtain a fine foreground.

In addition to the particle trajectory, the optical flow can also be combined with the Gaussian Mixture Model (GMM). According to Ren et al. [12], the spatial distribution of Gaussian allows each background pixel to be modeled temporally and spatially. However, it is still necessary to update GMM parameters in each iteration for better performance. To deal with this problem, we obtain a flat Gaussian model to handle the moving objects. For background, we obtain a narrow Gaussian model instead. With the help of these two models, better results can be obtained.

Detecting moving objects can also be solved by [13] Bayesian low-rank estimation. Different from the above methods, this algorithm utilizes a hierarchical Bayesian model, which can obtain a low-rank matrix for further analyzing moving procedure.

Similar to the hierarchical Bayesian method, high-efficiency video coding (HEVC) method [14] is also focusing on analyzing low-rank estimation. HEVC method firstly generates a global motion vector based on low-rank value. Then it utilizes the motion background coding tree units (MBCTUs) to iteratively update the background reference pictures.

Another popular method used to detect moving objects is analyzing the texture of a video. M. Heikkila, and M. Pietikainen [15] used a modified local binary pattern as the texture operator. By calculating the histograms over a circular region of each pixel, they modeled pixels as a group of adaptive local binary pattern (LBP) histograms, which can be further solved by [16] center-surround computations.

Deep learning can also solve the background subtraction problem for a freely moving camera. Instead of formulating the representation of the background, we can achieve the goal by implementing the convolutional neural network (CNN). Zhao [17] solved the background subtraction by using a Deep Pixel Distribution Learning (DPDL) model. By implementing the DPDL model, the distribution of observations could be obtained. They represented the distribution of past observations by Random Permutation of Temporal Pixels (RPoTP) [17]. With the use of pixel-wise representation, enough RPoTP features could be promised, which lays a solid foundation for the analyzing steps. After obtaining the distribution, they learned the distribution using a neural net. They implemented CNN to recognize the foreground and the background. With the use of random permutation, the framework could be designed to focus on the distribution of observations [17].

3   Proposed Method

In this section, we explained the details of our proposed approach. The flow chart of the proposed method is shown in Fig. 2.

3.1   Optical Flow Extraction

The first step of our method is the extraction of the optical flow, which describes the motion of pixels. The optical flow is captured from two frames captured at different times. Assume that $\mathcal{I} = \{I_1, I_2, \cdots, I_N\} = \{I_i(m,n)|i \in [1\ N]\}$ are the continuous frames of video, where i represents the frame index, and (m,n) represents the location of each pixel. Following camera motion, pixel no longer maintains their positions, and the optical flow can be utilized to describe the motion of pixels' positions as follows:

$$
\begin{aligned}
V_{i+1} &= \underset{v}{\arg\min} |I_i \bigotimes v - I_{i+1}|_1, \\
&= \underset{v}{\arg\min} \sum_{m,n} |I_i(m + v_m(m,n), n + v_n(m,n)) - I_{i+1}(m,n)|_1
\end{aligned}
\tag{1}
$$

where V_{i+1} is the optical flow matrix which have two dimensions representing the m and n components of the motion vector for a pixel. The dense optical flow algorithm [18] is utilized to capture the optical flow. It utilizes a polynomial

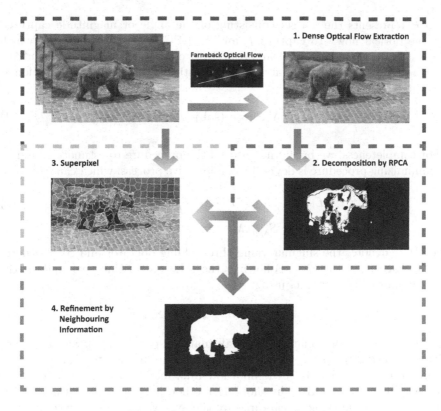

Fig. 2. Proposed method flowchart

expansion to approximate the neighborhoods for a robust evaluation of pixel displacement, which is shown as follows:

$$R(p) = p^T M p + v^T p + s \tag{2}$$

where M represents a symmetric matrix, v and s represent a vector and a scalar separately.

3.2   Motion Decomposition by RPCA

The optical flow is utilized to describe the motion of pixels, which generates a motion matrix to be decomposed by Robust Principal Component Analysis (RPCA). RPCA decomposes the motion into two components, a low-rank component and a sparse component. Since the motions of pixels in the background come from the camera motion, there is a linear correlation among these motions. Thus, the background motion is considered to be a low-rank component (L) of the entire pixels' motion. In contrast, the motion of moving objects is considered to be a sparse matrix (S). Mathematically, the decomposition can be shown as:

$$F = L + S \tag{3}$$

where F represents the matrix consisting of the angle or magnitude captured from the optical flow. To capture L and S, RPCA [19–21] is utilized, which focuses on minimizing the nuclear norm $\|L\|_*$ of the low-rank matrix and the $\ell1$-norm $\|S\|_1$ of the sparse matrix. Mathematically, the objective function is represented as:

$$\underset{L,S}{\arg\min} \; \|L\|_* + \lambda\|S\|_1 \quad (\text{subject to } F = L + S) \tag{4}$$

For completeness, we briefly introduced the procedure to estimate L and S. The minimizing procedure is devised as an iterative process, which can be shown as:

$$L_{k+1} = \mathcal{D}_{1/\mu}(M - S_k + \mu^{-1}G_k) \tag{5}$$

$$S_{k+1} = \mathcal{S}_{\lambda/\mu}(M - L_k + \mu^{-1}G_k) \tag{6}$$

where $\mathcal{D}_{1/\mu}$ denotes the singular value thresholding operator and $\mathcal{S}_{\lambda/\mu}$ denotes the shrinkage operator [22]. Following the ALM algorithm, we update the Lagrange multiplier matrix G using:

$$G_{k+1} = G_k + \mu(M - L_{k+1} - S_{k+1}). \tag{7}$$

With the iterations of updating low-rank matrix, sparse matrix and Lagrange multiplier matrix, the penalty function can converge to some tolerance or reach maximum iterations, in which the final low-rank matrix and sparse matrix are captured. Then, an adaptive thresholding method is applied to distinguish the background. The threshold is captured by the average of the sparse component as follows:

$$\mathcal{M}(x,y) = f(|S(x,y) - \frac{1}{N}\sum_{\forall x,y} S(x,y)|_1, P) \quad N = x \times y \tag{8}$$

where S denotes the sparse component representing the moving objects; x, y are the indexes of pixel location; P is the user input threshold parameter; and $f(m, n)$ is a piecewise function shown as follows:

$$f(m,n) = \begin{cases} 255 & m > n \\ 0 & m < n \end{cases} \tag{9}$$

3.3   Integration of Foreground Masks

The angle feature and the magnitude feature of the optical flow generate foreground masks independently, which include their corresponding detects. To integrate them, a double thresholding method is proposed. In Sect. 3.2, we generate the general mask equation $\mathcal{M}$ by averaging the sparse component. Because the optical flow includes the angle feature and the magnitude feature, the input sparse component of the equation can be either angle matrix or magnitude matrix. We denote the foreground masks generated by the angle matrix and magnitude matrix to be $\mathcal{M}_{ang}(x, y)$ and $\mathcal{M}_{mag}(x, y)$ respectively; x, y are denoted as pixel positions. The double thresholding strategy is proposed to replace several parts of $\mathcal{M}_{ang}$ by $\mathcal{M}_{mag}$, in which the foreground rates θ_{ang} of the $\mathcal{M}_{ang}(x, y)$ is compared with two thresholds, T_s and T_l. Foreground rates θ_{ang} is calculated based on the angle-feature mask, which is equal to the number of foreground pixels divided by the total number of pixels. The extraction of the foreground rates θ_{ang} is the given by:

$$\theta_{ang} = \frac{\sum\limits_{y=1}^{R} \sum\limits_{x=1}^{C} \mathcal{M}_{ang}(x, y) \cap 255}{||\mathcal{M}_{ang}(x, y)||_1} \tag{10}$$

where R, C denote the resolution of image. When the foreground rate θ_{ang} is smaller than T_s, we assume that the moving object is too small to be detected by the magnitude features. Therefore, $\mathcal{M}_{ang}$ is directly used as the final foreground mask. If the rate θ_{ang} is larger than T_s but smaller than T_l, the pixels are recognized as foreground. However, when the rate θ_{ang} is larger than T_l, it means the foreground represents a greater part of the scene. In this case, the common parts of $\mathcal{M}_{ang}(x, y)$ and $\mathcal{M}_{mag}(x, y)$ is used in the final foreground. Mathematically, the double thresholding can be shown as:

$$\mathcal{M}_{fin} = \begin{cases} \mathcal{M}_{ang}(x, y) \cup \mathcal{M}_{mag}(x, y), & if \quad \theta_{ang} < T_{small} \\ \mathcal{M}_{ang}, & if \quad T_{small} < \theta_{ang} < T_{large} \\ \mathcal{M}_{ang}(x, y) \cap \mathcal{M}_{mag}(x, y), & if \quad \theta_{ang} > T_{large} \end{cases} \tag{11}$$

where $\mathcal{M}_{fin}$ denotes the final foreground mask.

Unfortunately, $\mathcal{M}_{fin}$ includes noise, which can be refined by super-pixels. The super-pixels are captured under different scales, in which the density of super-pixels is different. For each super-pixel, if the foreground ratio of the super-pixel is larger than an adaptive threshold, we will label this whole super-pixel as temporary foreground. We denote this ratio threshold as T_s. For each frame, we generate super-pixels under different scale cases. If a pixel is labeled as temporary foreground in the adaptive number of cases, we take this pixel as foreground in our final output. This adaptive number of cases is denoted as T_f.

In a particular scale, the statistic of pixels in a super-pixel is used to label the super-pixel. Therefore, there are several foreground images $\mathcal{M}_i(x, y)$ captured from different scales, which is shown as:

$$\mathcal{M}_i(x, y) = g\left(\frac{\sum\limits_{r,c \in Sp_i} \mathcal{M}_{fin}(r, c) \cap 255}{||Sp_i||}, T_s\right), \quad x, y \in Sp_i \tag{12}$$

where r, c represent the indices of pixels in a particular super-pixel; T_s is the threshold to label the super-pixel and Sp_i denotes a super-pixel. Finally, these foreground results is used as the outcome of the proposed approach:

$$\mathcal{F}_g(x,y) = g(\frac{\sum\limits_{i=1}^{S} M_i(x,y)}{S}, T_f) \tag{13}$$

where S represents the scale number. $\mathcal{F}_g(x,y)$ is the outcome of our proposed approach.

4   Experimental Results

4.1   Dataset and Evaluation Metrics

In this section, evaluation experiments are proposed to demonstrate the performance of our approach. During the experiments, videos from the Freiburg-Berkeley Motion Segmentation Dataset (FBMS-59) is utilized for evaluation. The FBMS dataset [23] is a challenging dataset, in which all of the videos are obtained by freely moving cameras. We use the *bear02*, *meerkats01* and *lion02* videos for the evaluation experiments.

During evaluation experiments, we utilize Recall (Re), Precision (Pr), and F-Measure (Fm) metrics. These are computed as:

$$Re = \frac{TP}{TP+FN}, Pr = \frac{TP}{TP+FP}, Fm = \frac{2 \cdot Pr \cdot Re}{Pr+Re}$$

where TP represents the same parts of black areas between the ground truth and the foreground binary mask; FP represents the same parts between the ground truth black area and the foreground binary mask white area; and TN represents the same parts of the white areas between the ground truth and the foreground binary mask.

4.2   Comparison Experiments

In order demonstrating the performance of our proposed method, we make comparisons with PCA Angle, RPCA Angle, RPCA Magnitude and Revised RPCA. The quantitative and qualitative results are shown in Table 1 and Fig. 3 separately.

Table 1. Accuracy table

Video	PCA Angle	RPCA Angle	RPCA Mag.	RPCA Revised	RPCA SP.
bear02	0.4104	0.4596	0.4546	0.5473	**0.6835**
meerkats01	0.1141	0.5257	0.4041	0.4299	**0.6498**
lion02	0.2046	0.4619	0.4308	0.4813	**0.5810**

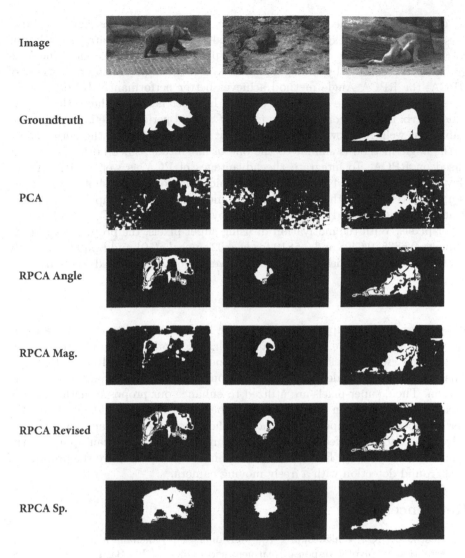

Fig. 3. Comparison of results

In the PCA Angle method, the low-rank matrix and the sparse matrix are iteratively updated until convergence of the objective function. The overall performance of the angle method is not promising; $bear02$, $meerkats01$ and $lion02$ achieve 0.4104, 0.1141 and 0.2046 separately in the Fm metric, due to the complexity of natural scenes as well as the camera motion. The reason for this poor performance is that the method fails when the moving object has a similar motion as the camera. Moreover, the scaling transformation also invalidates the methods based on the angle of motion.

Compared with the PCA method, the RPCA method has better robustness. Similarly, the background is considered as the low-rank matrix as well, due to the correlation between the motion of pixels in the background. The foreground is represented by the sparse matrix. Benefitting from the robustness of RPCA, the RPCA Angle method achieves better performance. Unfortunately, the angle features have their own defects. In order handling these, the magnitude matrix is also decomposed by the RPCA, and performance is shown in the Table 1 as well. As shown in the Table 1, it is reasonable that the performance of the angle method is similar to the one of magnitude, since both of these are based on RPCA. To integrate the advantages of PCA as well as RPCA, the Revised RPCA method is proposed, in which the double thresholding strategy is applied. Therefore, the Revised RPCA method obviously improves accuracy. Finally, the foreground mask generated by the Revised RPCA is refined by super-pixels. With the motivation of using super-pixels, the proposed approach achieves 0.6835, 0.6498 and 0.5810 for *bear*02, *meerkats*01 and *lion*02 separately in the Fm metrics, which prove the effectiveness of the proposed method.

5   Conclusion

We proposed a novel approach to solve the background subtraction for a freely moving camera. In the proposed approach, the motion is represented by the optical flow, which consists of the angle and magnitude, and Robust Principle Analysis is utilized to decompose the motion of moving objects and background motion. Then, super-pixels are utilized to enhance our proposed method. Comparison experiments on the video from a benchmark dataset demonstrates the performance of the proposed approach. Although the proposed approach did not solve the problem perfectly, it proposed a new method that can approach the solution in a new way. This can be utilized in the future to solve the problem of background detection with a freely moving camera.

References

1. Heath, C.D.C., Venkateswara, H., McDaniel, T., Panchanathan, S.: Detecting attention in pivotal response treatment video probes. In: Basu, A., Berretti, S. (eds.) ICSM 2018. LNCS, vol. 11010, pp. 248–259. Springer, Cham (2018). https://doi.org/10.1007/978-3-030-04375-9_21
2. Soltaninejad, S., Cheng, I., Basu, A.: Towards the identification of Parkinson's disease using only T1 MR images. In: Basu, A., Berretti, S. (eds.) ICSM 2018. LNCS, vol. 11010, pp. 145–156. Springer, Cham (2018). https://doi.org/10.1007/978-3-030-04375-9_13
3. Yang, J., Tong, L., Faraji, M., Basu, A.: IVUS-net: an intravascular ultrasound segmentation network. In: Basu, A., Berretti, S. (eds.) ICSM 2018. LNCS, vol. 11010, pp. 367–377. Springer, Cham (2018). https://doi.org/10.1007/978-3-030-04375-9_31
4. Friedman, N., Russell, S.: Image segmentation in video sequences: a probabilistic approach. In: Proceedings of the Thirteenth Conference on Uncertainty in Artificial Intelligence, pp. 175–181. Morgan Kaufmann Publishers Inc., August 1997

5. Bobick, A.F., Johnson, A.Y.: Gait recognition using static, activity-specific parameters. In: Proceedings of the 2001 IEEE Computer Society Conference on Computer Vision and Pattern Recognition, CVPR 2001, vol. 1, p. I. IEEE (2001)
6. Chiu, L.-W., Hsieh, J.-W., Lai, C.-R., Chiang, H.-F., Cheng, S.-C., Fan, K.-C.: Person authentication by air-writing using 3D sensor and time order stroke context. In: Basu, A., Berretti, S. (eds.) ICSM 2018. LNCS, vol. 11010, pp. 260–273. Springer, Cham (2018). https://doi.org/10.1007/978-3-030-04375-9_22
7. Zhou, D., Zhang, H.: Modified GMM background modeling and optical flow for detection of moving objects. In: 2005 IEEE International Conference on Systems, Man and Cybernetics, vol. 3, pp. 2224–2229. IEEE, October 2005
8. Barron, J.L., Fleet, D.J., Beauchemin, S.S.: Performance of optical flow techniques. Int. J. Comput. Vision 12(1), 43–77 (1994)
9. Wu, Y., He, X., Nguyen, T.Q.: Moving object detection with a freely moving camera via background motion subtraction. IEEE Trans. Circuits Syst. Video Technol. 27(2), 236–248 (2017)
10. Sheikh, Y., Javed, O., Kanade, T.: Background subtraction for freely moving cameras. In: 2009 IEEE 12th International Conference on Computer Vision, pp. 1219–1225. IEEE, September 2009
11. Liu, C., Cheng, I., Basu, A.: Synthetic vision assisted real-time runway detection for infrared aerial images. In: Basu, A., Berretti, S. (eds.) ICSM 2018. LNCS, vol. 11010, pp. 274–281. Springer, Cham (2018). https://doi.org/10.1007/978-3-030-04375-9_23
12. Ren, Y., Chua, C.S., Ho, Y.K.: Motion detection with nonstationary background. Mach. Vis. Appl. 13(5–6), 332–343 (2003)
13. Chengcheng, L., Lei, Y., Shihui, H., Hong, S.: Background subtraction with moving cameras via Bayesian low-rank estimation. In: 2016 IEEE 13th International Conference on Signal Processing (ICSP), pp. 133–137. IEEE, November 2016
14. Wang, G., Li, B., Zhang, Y., Yang, J.: Background modeling and referencing for moving cameras-captured surveillance video coding in HEVC. IEEE Trans. Multimedia 20(11), 2921–2934 (2018)
15. Heikkila, M., Pietikainen, M.: A texture-based method for modeling the background and detecting moving objects. IEEE Trans. Pattern Anal. Mach. Intell. 28(4), 657–662 (2006)
16. Mahadevan, V., Vasconcelos, N.: Background subtraction in highly dynamic scenes. In: IEEE Conference on Computer Vision and Pattern Recognition, CVPR 2008, pp. 1–6. IEEE, June 2008
17. Zhao, C., Cham, T.L., Ren, X., Cai, J., Zhu, H.: Background subtraction based on deep pixel distribution learning. In: 2018 IEEE International Conference on Multimedia and Expo (ICME), pp. 1–6. IEEE, July 2018
18. Farnebäck, G.: Two-frame motion estimation based on polynomial expansion. In: Bigun, J., Gustavsson, T. (eds.) SCIA 2003. LNCS, vol. 2749, pp. 363–370. Springer, Heidelberg (2003). https://doi.org/10.1007/3-540-45103-X_50
19. Yuan, X., Yang, J.: Sparse and low-rank matrix decomposition via alternating direction methods, 12, 2 (2009). Preprint
20. Guyon, C., Bouwmans, T., Zahzah, E.H.: Robust principal component analysis for background subtraction: systematic evaluation and comparative analysis. In: Principal Component Analysis. IntechOpen (2012)

21. Lin, Z., Chen, M., Wu, L., Ma, Y.: The augmented lagrange multiplier method for exact recovery of corrupted low-rank matrices, UIUC Technical report (2009)
22. CandЁs, E.J., Li, X., Ma, Y., Wright, J.: Robust principal component analysis? J. ACM (JACM) **58**(3), 11 (2011)
23. Brox, T., Malik, J.: Object segmentation by long term analysis of point trajectories. In: Daniilidis, K., Maragos, P., Paragios, N. (eds.) ECCV 2010. LNCS, vol. 6315, pp. 282–295. Springer, Heidelberg (2010). https://doi.org/10.1007/978-3-642-15555-0_21

Miscellaneous

Ontology Based Framework for Tactile Internet Applications

Hikmat Adhami[(✉)], Mohammad Al Ja'afreh, and Abdulmotaleb El Saddik

School of Electrical Engineering and Computer Science (EECS),
University of Ottawa, Ottawa, Canada
{hadha068,jaafreh,elsaddik}@uottawa.ca

Abstract. In the past decade, auditory and visual multimedia have reached an advanced quality level which is characteristically referred to as high definition (HD) and beyond. On the contrary, technical solutions addressing the sense of touch, which are typically referred to as haptic technology, have not yet received the same level of attention and evolution. With the emergence of the 5G mobile networks and the Tactile Internet, the haptic modality will be part of our daily usage and thus both tactile and kinesthetic information and their deployment solutions will gain significantly in relevance to stakeholders from academic and industrial domains. In this context, we extended our previous Service Oriented Development of Haptics Ontology (SODHO) to address the relationship between 5G network applications and their main key performance indicators (KPIs). In addition, our fully unified and lightweight ontology was built using the SUMO model according to which the vocabulary and classes that describe human-haptic system interaction were formalized, providing a formal categorization of the haptics domain in regular multimedia Tactile Internet applications.

Keywords: Ontology · Tactile Internet · 5G · Haptics · OWL

1 Introduction

Tactile Internet is the future communication system that enables the communication of the human sense of touch and actuation in a real time. The main technical requirements which define Tactile Internet are: extremely low latency, high availability, reliability and security [2]. Latency is considered the main challenge in making Tactile Internet available, and is defined as the time measured from the instant of sending haptic signal till receiving the response [3]. The network which could support haptic communications, must ensure all the requirements for a certain Tactile Internet application. Different applications are offered by Tactile Internet, like teleoperation (depicted in Fig. 1), online gaming, remote surgery operations, and mixed augmented reality. Because of the sensitivity and accuracy of these applications, the round trip time must be reduced as much as possible.

Nowadays, Tactile Internet is in its infancy deployment phase worldwide. For this reason, and because of the growing need of its applications, we investigated in a previous

© Springer Nature Switzerland AG 2020
T. McDaniel et al. (Eds.): ICSM 2019, LNCS 12015, pp. 81–86, 2020.
https://doi.org/10.1007/978-3-030-54407-2_7

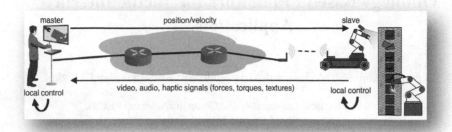

Fig. 1. An example of the tactile internet application

work [4], the feasibility of these applications on the existing and deployed networks infrastructures, such as: Wi-Fi, WiMAX, 3G and 4G. The outcome of our research confirmed that the evolutionary 5G is highly recommended to perform most of Tactile Internet applications. In this paper, we proposed an ontology to automatically relate the future Tactile Internet applications to their KPIs. This can be very beneficial, for instance to the network controller, to dynamically optimize the communication channel needed to satisfy the Quality of service to those applications.

2 Methodology

In this work, the major part is dedicated to find the most suitable network type for the Tactile Internet applications based on their natures and requirements. Therefore, we used Protégé which is an OWL Web Ontology Language emulator to infer [1], from the obtained results, the adequate network type to be used for a specific application of Tactile Internet.

2.1 Relationship Between 5G Applications and Their Requirements

The work in Adhami *et al.* [4] discussed the performance evaluation for each deployed type of network. Now we are able to make a relationship between a list of future applications and their requirements by referring to available current network backbones. To this end, we tried to use Protégé in order to create the suitable links between different classes of applications and KPIs, in addition to classes which represent networks.

2.2 Ontology Description

5G is developed to solve 3 modern-day problems [7]:

Ultra-low latency: latency is measured by sending a packet that is returned to the sender; the round-trip time is considered the latency.
A massive number of devices communicate with the same access point.
Ultra-high throughput: throughput is the rate at which messages are delivered successfully.

Therefore, 5G KPIs are divided into 3 classes (Fig. 2):

uRLLC: ultra-Reliable Low Latency Communication
mBB: enhanced mobile BroadBand
mMTC: massive Machine Type Communication

These are 3 subclasses of the class KPI in the proposed ontology.

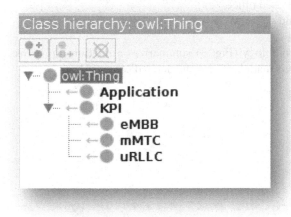

Fig. 2. Main KPIs classes

New Applications are classified based on their requirements: like low latency, high data consumption and multiple devices (i.e. Tactile Internet applications).
Individuals of the Class "Application" are directly linked to the KPIs mentioned earlier by the relation: "requires" in the proposed ontology.

Some of the KPIs which we mentioned in our Ontology are listed below:

- Latency
- Data rate
- Reliability
- Availability
- Data utilized per frame
- Connection density (User/Km^2)
- Traffic density (Gbps/Km^2)
- Communication range
- Mobility
- Download rate
- Upload rate

The main applications among those mentioned in the Ontology are listed below:

- Tactile Internet/Augmented reality
- Remote automated parking
- Moving hotspots
- Cloud services
- Smart office
- Device remote controlling
- Disaster alert
- Healthcare
- Airplanes connectivity
- Wireless Cloud-Based office
- Media on Demand

The following ontology (Fig. 3) summarizes a relationship between 5G network applications and their main key performance indicators [5].

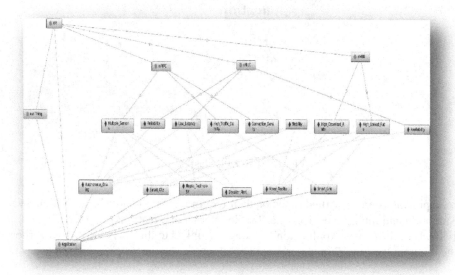

Fig. 3. Ontograph that represents 5G applications and their related KPIs

By selecting any application, we get the list of its required KPIs, as seen in the following Fig. 4.

2.3 Preliminary Results

At the beginning, two main classes were created (Class1: Applications and Class2: KPIs). KPIs have subclasses where each class contains individuals (each individual represents a range of values or specific value of related KPI). In data properties, some variables are created where each one defines an individual inside each class. After defining an individual (application in this case), we select the class which it is related to. And the relation is also selected to highlight the KPIs that it requires (by using the already defined relation in object properties: REQUIRES).

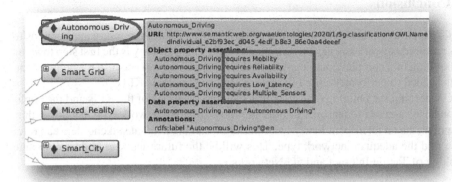

Fig. 4. Ontology: a way of representing data

After that, applications were classified due to their requirements, grouped into three network types: 5G, 4G & 3G. Now, any application in specific network subclass relates to an individual value of the needed KPIs.

Finally, the full ontology is created, and now, the necessary list of requirements and the Network type which may cover these preconditions are clearly shown for each type of application.

We can see below (Fig. 5), the ontology which lists all available applications for each network type, and links us to specific KPIs.

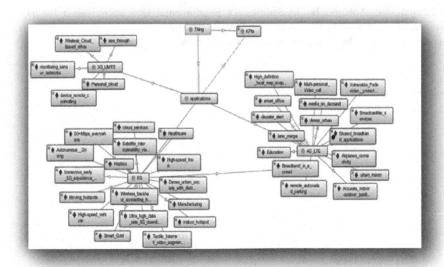

Fig. 5. Ontology which links a 5G application to the specific KPI

3 Conclusion

In this paper, we presented a preliminary ontology that relates the future applications to their required network key performance indicators. This ontology is the first step towards the building of a complete ontology that links 5G applications (because we believe that, 5G is needed to perform Tactile Internet applications) to their KPIs.

Concerning the Ontology, by changing the classifications of the KPIs and the applications, we can use the reasoner to infer the most suitable network type. By doing this, we will create an intelligent Fuzzy Information System (FIS) that stakeholders can refer to, to find the adequate network type. This will be the future work to build a complete ontology of Tactile Internet and 5G Networks.

References

1. Adhami, H., El Saddik, A.: SODHO: service oriented development of haptics ontology. In: HAVE (2014)
2. Antonakoglou, K., Xu, X., Steinbach, E., Mahmoodi, T., Dohler, M.: Towards haptic communications over the 5G tactile internet. IEEE Commun. Surv. Tutor. **20**(4), 3034–3059 (2018). https://doi.org/10.1109/comst.2018.2851452
3. Aijaz, A., Dohler, M., Aghvami, A.H., Friderikos, V., Frodigh, M.: Realizing the tactile internet: haptic communications over next generation 5G cellular networks. IEEE Wirel. Commun. **24**(2), 82–89 (2017)
4. Adhami, H., Al Ja'afreh, M., El Saddik, A.: Can we deploy tactile internet applications over Wi-Fi, 3G and WiMAX: a comparative study based on riverbed modeler. In: HAVE (2019)
5. Scenarios, requirements and KPIs for 5G mobile and wireless system. ICT-317669 METIS Project
6. Al Ja'afreh, M., Adhami, H., El Saddik, A.: Experimental QoS optimization for haptic communication over the tactile internet. In: HAVE (2018)
7. Huawei Learning Website. http://learning.huawei.com/en

Potential of Deep Features for Opinion-Unaware, Distortion-Unaware, No-Reference Image Quality Assessment

Subhayan Mukherjee[1]($\boxtimes$) (ID), Giuseppe Valenzise[2], and Irene Cheng[1] (ID)

[1] University of Alberta, Edmonton, AB T6G 2R3, Canada
{mukherje,locheng}@ualberta.ca
[2] CNRS - CentraleSupelec - Université Paris-Sud, 91192 Gif-sur-Yvette Cedex, France
giuseppe.valenzise@l2s.centralesupelec.fr

Abstract. Image Quality Assessment algorithms predict a quality score for a pristine or distorted input image, such that it correlates with human opinion. Traditional methods required a non-distorted "reference" version of the input image to compare with, in order to predict this score. However, recent "No-reference" methods circumvent this requirement by modelling the distribution of clean image features, thereby making them more suitable for practical use. However, majority of such methods either use hand-crafted features or require training on human opinion scores (supervised learning), which are difficult to obtain and standardise. We explore the possibility of using deep features instead, particularly, the encoded (bottleneck) feature maps of a Convolutional Autoencoder neural network architecture. Also, we do not train the network on subjective scores (unsupervised learning). The primary requirements for an IQA method are monotonic increase in predicted scores with increasing degree of input image distortion, and consistent ranking of images with the same distortion type and content, but different distortion levels. Quantitative experiments using the Pearson, Kendall and Spearman correlation scores on a diverse set of images show that our proposed method meets the above requirements better than the state-of-art method (which uses hand-crafted features) for three types of distortions: blurring, noise and compression artefacts. This demonstrates the potential for future research in this relatively unexplored sub-area within IQA.

Keywords: Image quality assessment · Opinion unaware · Distortion unaware · No reference · Deep learning

1 Introduction

Before the invention of digital cameras and other consumer grade digital imaging devices, the capture of images was quite limited. The time from capture to

---

Supported by NSERC Discovery Grant and DND Supplement.

T. McDaniel et al. (Eds.): ICSM 2019, LNCS 12015, pp. 87–95, 2020.
https://doi.org/10.1007/978-3-030-54407-2_8

visualization was significant as in case of film cameras, we had to develop the photos in a dark room with chemical solutions. However, nowadays, with the advent of digital photography, coupled with the explosion in bandwidth of transmission channels like the Internet and social media, a tremendous volume of images are being captured and shared. Curating this huge volume of visual data that is being captured, stored, transmitted and viewed is a challenging task. Transmission of visual content occupies a large amount of Internet bandwidth. To meet the in-time transmission constraints limited by hardware resources, images and videos are usually processed and compressed before transmission and storage. Quality reductions happen as a trade-off between limited hardware resources and visual fidelity. Thus, automatic quality assessment methods are desirable to estimate the human-perceived quality measure, to replace subjective human perception. The distortions can be wide and varied; A common type of distortion is noise. Noise affects images captured using all types of sensors (optical or otherwise) and can even get injected into the image signal during transmission, for example through a telecommunications channel like television. The image quality research domain has focused on quality assessment of natural images and videos, since that is the dominant form of images we deal with everyday.

Existing IQA methods can be classified into three categories, based on the amount of the information that is available to the method: Full-Reference (FR), Reduced-Reference (RR), and No-Reference (NR) methods [10]. FR quality assessment requires both access to the distorted images or videos as well as the clean references. RR utilizes the limited information, depending on the actual situation, regarding the reference, rather than the full reference itself, together with the distorted images. NR approaches usually perform automatic quality assessment of the images or videos using only the distorted sources. We focus specifically on the No-Reference quality assessment of images. We can draw a parallel with the Human Visual System (HVS) which has the ability to distinguish between natural and distorted scenes based on few visual memories learned while the human brain processes visual information in various ways. Most NR-IQA algorithms follow the two step process (1) feature extraction and (2) quality prediction [15]. The schematic diagram of the same is shown in Fig. 1.

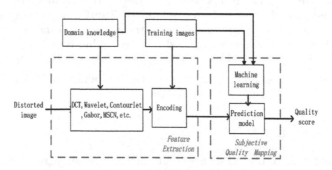

Fig. 1. General framework of NR-IQA algorithms.

Recent attempts at image quality assessment aim to mimic the response of the HVS which can mask certain artefacts depending on the location of the artefact in the image and the surrounding image content, brightness, contrast, etc. Such "perceptual" methods can be categorized into different classes based on availability of subjective rating scores for the distorted images, and knowledge about the type of possible distortions. Of those, we are interested in the specific case where the subjective rating scores are unavailable (opinion-unaware/OU) and the type of distortions is unknown (distortion-unaware or 'general'). Convolutional Neural Networks (CNNs) have been successfully used in different computer vision tasks, including style transfer, image generation, etc. Internal activations of deep convolutional networks, trained on high-level image classification tasks, have been found to be useful for natural feature representation, and are used to mimic human perception. In this work, we propose perceptual quality assessment using such "deep" features, and objectively evaluate its effectiveness.

1.1 Summary of Contributions

IQA has already been a quite active research area for several decades; Thus, our contribution is focused to a very specific sub-area (which has not received much attention) at the intersection of the following paradigms:

1. Using deep instead of hand-crafted features for image representation.
2. Using non-parametric instead of parametric approach to fit the distribution of pristine image features, and compare it to that of query image features.
3. Using unsupervised instead of supervised learning, thus removing the dependence on manual labelling (subjective scores) to train the IQA model.

The rest of the paper is organized as follows: Sect. 2 summarizes related IQA research. Section 3 describes how proposed method design differs from existing ones. Section 4 presents experimental results. Section 5 concludes the paper.

2 Background and Related Work

IQA methods may be broadly classified as reference or no-reference ("NR/blind") [10]. In simple terms, all the reference-based methods try to estimate some form of *distance* between the reference ("clean") image and the input/query image. The larger the distance, the greater the distortion score. No-reference methods predict the image quality based on the distorted image itself, without the need of a reference image. Most NR-IQA algorithms follow the two step process (1) feature extraction and (2) quality prediction [15]. NR-IQA algorithms are further categorized as (a) distortion-specific and (b) general/universal. The former assumes that the distortion-type is known, and employ distortion model(s) to predict one or more types of distortions in the image like noise, blur, blocking, ringing etc. to estimate its overall visual quality. The latter broadly assumes that natural scenes contain repeating patterns with a definite set of statistical properties called Natural Scene Statistics (NSS) in the spatial [8] or transformed [13] domain, and distortions to natural images distort these properties in measurable ways. Researchers also explored more effective ways to characterize structural and contrast distortions by modelling the gradient magnitudes of natural images as Weibull distribution, in the works popularized as (IL)NIQE [9,16].

For score prediction, a popular approach is to fit the joint distribution of the feature vector and the associated opinion scores to a subset of the training data [13]. In this case, the score prediction amounts to maximizing the probability of opinion score of test data, given the test data feature vector. Other approaches quantify the distance in sparse feature space between reference and distorted images [12] in a manner that is both opinion-unaware and distortion-unaware. More recent works are based on machine learning, and extend to High Dynamic Range (HDR) images [5], though for this method the training is opinion-aware.

Very recent methods in the opinion/distortion unaware domain use (IL)NIQE features, but consider activations in pre-trained deep neural networks to select salient patches. They assign more weight to scores from those patches over others during score aggregation [17]. (IL)NIQE features can also reliably predict quality of multi-spectral images [18]. Few methods even tread the boundaries of opinion (un-)awareness and/or (no-)reference [6,11]. But even they do not operate at the intersection of paradigms outlined in Sect. 1.1, which motivates our research.

3   Proposed Method

Below, we briefly outline how the proposed method's functionality as visualised in Fig. 3 conforms to the intersection of paradigms outlined in Sect. 1.1:

3.1   Deep Features for Image Representation

We use the local normalization non-linearity inspired by local gain control behaviors in biological visual systems in the 256-channel end-to-end compression architecture [2]. The CNN architecture used in the proposed method is shown in Fig. 2. The analysis transform block progressively down-samples the input image patch by a factor of 4, 2, 2 respectively, and uses the forward Generalized Divisive Normalization activation [2] for all except the last layer. The synthesis transform block progressively up-samples the output of the analysis transform block by a factor of 2, 2, 4 respectively, and uses the *inverse* Generalized Divisive Normalization activation [2] for all except the last layer. However, contrary to the authors in [2], our aim is not image compression; Hence, we remove the rate-distortion term from the loss function and re-train the network on the DIV2K dataset [1,4]. Random, overlapping 256×256 random patches are extracted from each 2 K resolution color image. All patches are aggregated and shuffled into batches of 32 patches. Thus, the training is completely unsupervised, and does not use any subjective scores. Note that the CNN in Fig. 2 is used for feature extraction, but not score prediction, thereby making our proposed method opinion-*unaware*.

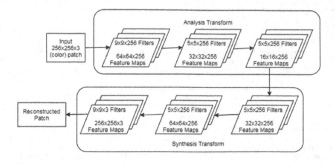

Fig. 2. Architecture of CNN used as feature extractor.

3.2 Non-parametric Modelling of Feature Distribution

We use Kernel Density Estimation with Epanechnikov kernels to model any arbitrary-shaped distribution of the features in the encoded layer of the auto-encoder architecture (output of analysis transform block), for building the natural model. This choice was motivated by experiments which showed that the distribution of those features do not conform well to any well-known distribution. This is unlike other NR-IQA methods which mostly fit different types of parametric distributions to hand-crafted features for training and testing. The benefit of using a non-parametric approach is that we need very little information about the underlying distribution. In such scenarios, we cannot properly specify a parametric model. Thus, we can think of non-parametric models as much "broader" than parametric ones. Specifically, the kernel density estimator model usually just assumes that the probability density function of the *true* distribution from which the data are sampled satisfies 'smoothness' conditions like continuity or differentiability. Equation 1 describes a kernel density estimator fitted to n observations $X_1, ..., X_n$, where h (positive, chosen empirically) is the *bandwidth*, and K is the function representing the kernel, such that it outputs only positive values which sum (integrate) to 1 over the set of all observations (real numbers).

$$\hat{f}_n(x) = \frac{1}{nh} \sum_{i=1}^{n} K\left(\frac{X_i - x}{h}\right) \tag{1}$$

3.3 Opinion-and Distortion-Unaware Training and Score Prediction

After opinion-unaware training of the natural model, we predict the score for any given input image by comparing its distribution of encoded features with those of the natural model, using KL-Divergence. Thus, neither the training nor the testing phase uses any subjective scores or prior knowledge of any expected type(s) of distortions, making the proposed method opinion-and-distortion-*unaware*.

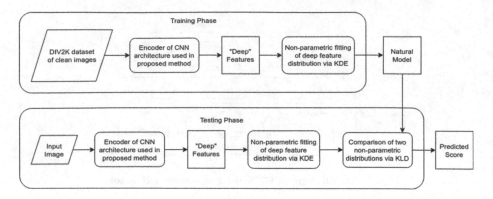

Fig. 3. Architecture of proposed method.

4   Results

4.1   Dataset

Two primary requirements for an IQA method [7] are monotonicity (monotonic increase in predicted scores with increasing degree of input image distortion), and consistency (consistent ranking of images with the same distortion type and content, but different distortion levels). To evaluate the same for our proposed method and compare against other state-of-the-art methods, we randomly selected 20 images from the General-100 dataset [3] and distorted them with five different levels of each of (Gaussian) blurring, (AWGN) noise and (JPEG-2000) compression artefacts. Thus, our test dataset had $20 \times (1 \text{ clean} + 15 \text{ distorted}) = 20 \times 16 = 320$ images.

4.2   Context of Comparison with State-of-Art NR-IQA Methods

We compare the proposed method with three state-of-art methods that operate under similar as well as relaxed constraints. As explained earlier, the proposed method is both opinion-unaware (OU) and distortion-unaware (DU) and we first compare it against another "(OU, DU)" method, NIQE [9]. Next, we compare with an opinion-*aware*, distortion-unaware "(OA, DU)" method, BRISQUE [8]. Lastly, we compare against an opinion-unaware, distortion-*aware* "(OU, DA)" method, PIQE [14]. Understandably, NIQE has similar constraints as proposed method, whereas BRISQUE and PIQE operate under relaxed constraints. Thus, it is easier for the last two methods to perform better than our proposed method, because they have more information available to them, although their application scenarios are much more limited than the proposed method, as explained earlier. To remind the reader, OA methods like BRISQUE require supervised training on subjective scores which are difficult to obtain and standardize, and suffers from generalization concerns. DA methods like PIQE have unpredictable performance for (combinations of) distortion types they haven not been designed to detect.

4.3 Comparison Metrics

Pearson (Eq. 2), Kendall (Eq. 3) and Spearman (Eq. 4) correlation of predicted quality scores with distortion levels (0 through 5) were calculated. The average over all images and distortion types for all methods are reported in Table 1.

Pearson's correlation coefficient ρ_P measures the linear relationship between two variables X and Y, which have standard deviations σ_x and σ_y respectively, and co-variance $cov(X, Y)$. ρ_P can have a maximum value of $+1$ denoting perfect positive relationship and a minimum value of -1 denoting perfect negative relationship between X and Y, while a value of 0 indicates no relationship.

$$\rho_P = \frac{cov(X, Y)}{\sigma_x \sigma_y} \tag{2}$$

Kendall's correlation coefficient τ quantifies the degree of monotone relationship between two *ranked* variables X and Y, each having n observations. Total number of possible pairings of observations from two variables is $\binom{n}{2} = \frac{n(n-1)}{2}$. In some of those pairs, the order in which the observations are ranked are same for both variables ("concordant pairs", c) and in other pairs, the order in which the observations are ranked are different for both variables ("discordant pairs", d) such that $n = c + d$ and $S = c - d$ in Eq. 3. It follows that when $c = n$ and $d = 0$, $\tau = +1$ (perfect positive correlation), when $c = 0$ and $d = n$, $\tau = -1$ (perfect negative correlation), and when $c = d$, $\tau = 0$ (no correlation).

$$\tau = \frac{c - d}{c + d} = \frac{S}{\binom{n}{2}} = \frac{2S}{n(n - 1)} \tag{3}$$

Spearman's correlation coefficient ρ_S measures the relationship between n observations of two *ranked* variables X and Y, where d_i is the pairwise difference of the variables' ranks. A value of $+1$ denotes perfect positive correlation, -1 indicates perfect negative correlation, and a 0 value indicates no correlation.

$$\rho_S = 1 - \frac{6 \sum d_i^2}{n(n^2 - 1)} \tag{4}$$

Table 1. Performance comparison of proposed method with state-of-art NR-IQA methods operating under similar (NIQE) and relaxed constraints (BRISQUE and PIQE).

Method (constraints)	Pearson score	Kendall score	Spearman score	Time (sec.)
Proposed (OU, DU)	0.91	0.88	0.92	42.91
NIQE [9] (OU, DU)	0.85	0.85	0.89	0.04
BRISQUE [8] (OA, DU)	0.78	0.68	0.75	0.04
PIQE [14] (OU, DA)	0.89	0.90	0.94	0.06

Table 1 shows better correlation scores for proposed method against a state-of-art method operating under similar constraints (NIQE), and even one which operates under relaxed constraints (BRISQUE). Another type of relaxed constraint method (PIQE) performs slightly better for distortions types it has been designed to detect. However, the proposed method's execution time is significantly higher than all compared methods, and thus it has room for improvement.

5   Conclusion and Future Work

We proposed a no-reference IQA method in an otherwise unexplored intersection of paradigms. We showed how biologically inspired activation in CNN layers can encode image patches in a reduced dimension, that captures the degree of distortion in the patch, without training on subjective opinion scores or assumption about possible distortion types. We showed via objective evaluation, the superior performance of our proposed method over the state-of-art. The next stage of our research will focus on improving the execution time of our proposed method, as well as further validating our proposed method on much larger datasets.

References

1. Agustsson, E., Timofte, R.: Ntire 2017 challenge on single image super-resolution: dataset and study. In: The IEEE Conference on Computer Vision and Pattern Recognition (CVPR) Workshops, July 2017
2. Ballé, J., Laparra, V., Simoncelli, E.P.: End-to-end optimized image compression. In: International Conference on Learning Representations (ICLR 2017), Toulon, France, April 2017. http://arxiv.org/abs/1611.01704
3. Dong, C., Loy, C.C., Tang, X.: Accelerating the super-resolution convolutional neural network. In: Leibe, B., Matas, J., Sebe, N., Welling, M. (eds.) ECCV 2016. LNCS, vol. 9906, pp. 391–407. Springer, Cham (2016). https://doi.org/10.1007/978-3-319-46475-6_25
4. Ignatov, A., et al.: PIRM challenge on perceptual image enhancement on smartphones: report. In: Leal-Taixé, L., Roth, S. (eds.) ECCV 2018. LNCS, vol. 11133, pp. 315–333. Springer, Cham (2019). https://doi.org/10.1007/978-3-030-11021-5_20
5. Kottayil, N.K., Valenzise, G., Dufaux, F., Cheng, I.: Blind quality estimation by disentangling perceptual and noisy features in high dynamic range images. IEEE Trans. Image Process. **27**(3), 1512–1525 (2018)
6. Lin, K.Y., Wang, G.: Hallucinated-IQA: no-reference image quality assessment via adversarial learning. In: The IEEE Conference on Computer Vision and Pattern Recognition (CVPR), June 2018
7. Ma, K., et al.: Waterloo exploration database: new challenges for image quality assessment models. IEEE Trans. Image Process. **26**(2), 1004–1016 (2017)
8. Mittal, A., Moorthy, A.K., Bovik, A.C.: No-reference image quality assessment in the spatial domain. IEEE Trans. Image Process. **21**(12), 4695–4708 (2012)
9. Mittal, A., Soundararajan, R., Bovik, A.C.: Making a "completely blind" image quality analyzer. IEEE Signal Process. Lett. **20**(3), 209–212 (2013)
10. Mittal, A., Moorthy, A.K., Bovik, A.C.: No-reference approaches to image and video quality assessment. In: Multimedia Quality of Experience (QoE), pp. 99–121. Wiley, November 2015

11. Pan, D., Shi, P., Hou, M., Ying, Z., Fu, S., Zhang, Y.: Blind predicting similar quality map for image quality assessment. In: The IEEE Conference on Computer Vision and Pattern Recognition (CVPR), June 2018

12. Priya, K.V.S.N.L.M., Channappayya, S.S.: A novel sparsity-inspired blind image quality assessment algorithm. In: 2014 IEEE Global Conference on Signal and Information Processing (GlobalSIP), pp. 984–988, December 2014

13. Saad, M.A., Bovik, A.C., Charrier, C.: A DCT statistics-based blind image quality index. IEEE Signal Process. Lett. **17**(6), 583–586 (2010)

14. Venkatanath, N., Praneeth, D., Maruthi Chandrasekhar, Bh., Channappayya, S.S., Medasani, S.S.: Blind image quality evaluation using perception based features. In: 2015 Twenty First National Conference on Communications (NCC), pp. 1–6, February 2015

15. Xu, S., Jiang, S., Min, W.: No-reference/blind image quality assessment: a survey. IETE Tech. Rev. **34**(3), 223–245 (2016)

16. Zhang, L., Zhang, L., Bovik, A.C.: A feature-enriched completely blind image quality evaluator. IEEE Trans. Image Process. **24**(8), 2579–2591 (2015)

17. Zhang, Z., Wang, H., Liu, S., Durrani, T.: Deep activation pooling for blind image quality assessment. Appl. Sci. **8**(4), 478 (2018)

18. Zhou, B., Shao, F., Meng, X., Fu, R., Ho, Y.: No-reference quality assessment for pansharpened images via opinion-unaware learning. IEEE Access **7**, 40388–40401 (2019)

Non-invasive Lactate Threshold Estimation Using Machine Learning

Hawazin Faiz Badawi[1]([✉]) [iD], Fedwa Laamarti[1] [iD], Ken Brunet[2], Ed McNeely[2], and Abdulmotaleb El Saddik[1] [iD]

[1] Multimedia Communications Research Lab, University of Ottawa, Ottawa, ON, Canada
lhbada049@uottawa.ca
[2] Peak Centre for Human Performance, Ottawa, ON, Canada

Abstract. The Lactate threshold (LT) has gained special attention in the sport world and is considered one of the potential indicators to evaluate individual performance in different sports. Traditionally, measuring LT requires frequent collection of blood samples from individuals under specific spatiotemporal conditions. This procedure causes discomfort to individuals besides test related cost. In this paper, we propose a non-invasive model to estimate LT using a machine learning (ML) algorithm as a step towards eliminating the need of blood sample collection and facilitating non-invasive performance test. We train and test this model on a 100-subject dataset, which we constructed in collaboration with Peak Center for Human Performance. We also propose a method to fill the missing values in this dataset, which contains the collected data of real life incremental running tests performed at this Centre. We also shed the light on the correlation between demographic data and the LT occurrence and hence help determine the factors affecting LT estimation as a vital sign in the sport world. Applying a multi-layer perceptron (MLP) algorithm on the constructed dataset provided the best correlation coefficient of 0.7983 compared with the LT ground truth scores. Using different combinations of demographic data in conjunction with heart rate (HR) and speed in the training and testing provided various correlation coefficients, which are also presented in this paper.

Keywords: Lactate threshold · Machine learning · MLP · Non-invasive · Sport

1 Introduction

Lactate formation plays a critical role in health and well-being since it appears in the blood stream with any physical movement [1]. It is produced and consumed by the skeletal muscles but when the produced amount surpasses the consumed amount, lactate threshold occurs [1]. Besides, research has been conducted to increase physical activity level [2] and to improve sport training [3]. In the sport field, many indicators are utilized by coaches, training centers and organizations to evaluate individuals (athletes and non-athletes) performance. LT is one of the accurate indicators of individuals' level of endurance [4]. It is defined as "A point at which blood lactate begins to increase above

© Springer Nature Switzerland AG 2020
T. McDaniel et al. (Eds.): ICSM 2019, LNCS 12015, pp. 96–104, 2020.
https://doi.org/10.1007/978-3-030-54407-2_9

resting values during a graded exercise challenge" [5]. For athletes, LT helps to determine the overall performance level in a specific sport such as running and swimming and thus facilitates the prescription of recommended training routine [4]. For non-athletes, it helps to make individuals more aware of their state of health and well-being and to encourage them to be more physically active. Traditionally, LT measurement requires frequent collection of blood samples during the test, under specific spatiotemporal conditions. This procedure causes discomfort to individuals, besides the test related cost. Thus, developing a non-invasive method to estimate LT helps to overcome these obstacles. In this paper, we propose a non-invasive ML model to estimate LT, applied on a dataset constructed using data from real life tests.

The rest of this paper is organized as follows. Section 2 presents related work. Section 3 discusses the proposed ML model to predict LT non-invasively by elaborating on dataset construction, used algorithm and achieved results. The results are further discussed in Sect. 4 and compared to literature. Section 5 concludes the paper and presents areas of future work.

2   Related Work

To minimize invasive methods cost and discomfort, several studies utilize various physiological features, tests, and sensors for estimating LT non-invasively. Heart rate [6–9] and peripheral capillary oxygen saturation (spo2) [10] are examples of physiological features used in literature to estimate LT. One of the earliest attempts in this regard is the research in [11], in which authors attempt to utilize respiratory gas exchange as a non-invasive method to estimate LT. Researchers in [12] used two tests: incremental maximal running test, which is conducted in University of Montreal Track Test, UMTT, and constant velocity test (CVT) to assess maximal lactate steady state (MLSS) in a non-invasive way to prescribe endurance training for team sport players. Authors in [13] used microwave sensors for real-time non-invasive monitoring of blood lactate. The results show that the electromagnetic wave sensors represent a good alternative for invasive blood sampling. The authors highlighted the benefits of this non-invasive method in hospital and sport environments. In hospital, the benefits consisted of reducing infection risks, increasing measurement frequency, and intervening in a proper time. Enhancing athletes training and prescribing effective training regimes are some of this method's benefits in sport. Besides, artificial intelligence (AI) has potential to help in sport and physical well-being [14]. The proposed AI-virtual trainer system for training prescription [15] is an example of AI utilization in sport field. Research in [16] also discussed how computational intelligence can be utilized in sports. It focused on the importance of developing intelligent systems that enhance athletic measurements such as LT. Reviewing literature shows one paper using ML to detect LT value in a non-invasive method [17] in which a neural network model is used for heart rate - work rate relationship. This work estimates lactate for soccer players only and lacks generalization to other populations of athletes and non-athletes. We found that there is a lack in non-invasive methods for LT estimation, and thus in this paper, we aim to contribute a ML model towards this goal.

3   Non-invasive Lactate Threshold Estimation: Proposed Model

This section presents information on the proposed dataset, the proposed ML model and the achieved results.

3.1   Dataset Description

We constructed the dataset used in this paper from collected data of real life incremental running tests performed at Peak Center for Human Performance [18]. The information about the incremental running test known as fitness assessment test at this centre is found in [19]. It contains data of 100 subjects: 51 male and 49 female (mean age, 35.88 years) both athletes and non-athletes. The demographic data for each subject including age, gender, height in cm, and weight in pound are collected. In addition, speed (km/h) and HR (bpm) are noted during each stage of the test. These features are the predictor variables of the proposed ML model whereas the LT point determined by the coach(es), who are domain experts, for each subject is used as the ground truth scores for the conducted experiments. Our dataset consists of a diverse population sample in terms of athletic background (if any) such as running, biking and kayaking besides other demographic differences attempting to ensure the applicability of our findings to a large population. A description of the demographic features of all 100 subjects is shown in Table 1.

Table 1. Subjects demographic features.

Term	Minimum	Maximum	Mean ($\pm$) Std. Dev.
Age	11	64	35.88 ($\pm$) 14.432
Height	147	188.5	170.801 ($\pm$) 8.498
Weight	85.5	257	160.57 ($\pm$) 31.126

3.2   Data Preprocessing

In order to fill the missing values in the dataset due to the different fitness levels for subjects, we checked the available "speed" and "HR" values throughout the ten stages, where the tenth stage is the highest reached stage by subjects in this dataset. Since the "speed" feature is incremented by 1 in each stage, we filled its missing values accordingly. For missing "HR" values, we identified whether the missing values occurred before or after the stage in which the LT occurred. Thus, the average "HR" is calculated if the missing value is before that stage, according to formula (1). However, if the missing "HR" value is after the lactate stage then only the previous available "HR" values are used to calculate the missing one according to formula (2) as shown in the following:

$$HR = (HR_{s-1} + HR_{s+1})/2 \tag{1}$$

$$HR = (HR_{s-1}) - (HR_{s-2}) + (HR_{s-1}) \tag{2}$$

Where:

HR_{s-1} and HR_{s+1} are the HR values in the immediate previous and following stages to the current stage, whereas HR_{s-2} is the HR value in the stage before the immediate previous stage of the current stage.

Checking the final dataset demonstrated the occurrence of LT, according to coach(es) decision, in between the second and the seventh stages for the majority (95%). For the remaining subjects, who have the highest endurance level, the LT occurs as follows: stage 8 (2%), stage 9 (2%) and stage 10 (1%). LT occurrence is not expected in the first stage since it is the following stage after the warm up session. The diversity of our dataset applies not only to the demographic data, but also to the starting stage "speed" value for each subject, which is related to the subject's fitness level. It is a result of having a random sample containing athletes and non-athletes who performed the test for various purposes. Such diversity serves as a comparison criteria between the proposed non-invasive ML model in this paper and the one proposed in [17], towards proposing a generalized non-invasive ML model for LT prediction as discussed in Sect. 4.

3.3 LT Prediction Model and Results

Estimating LT is a regression problem, hence, we applied a MLP, on the dataset discussed above. According to [20], MLP is "a network of simple neurons called perceptrons. The basic concept of a single perceptron was introduced by Rosenblatt in 1958. The perceptron computes a single output from multiple real-valued inputs by forming a linear combination according to its input weights" [20]. MLP aims to learn to model the correlation/dependencies between inputs and outputs by training on a set of input-output pairs focusing on minimizing errors [21]. MLP is a feed forward network that "mainly involved in two motions, a constant back and forth" [21]. The forward pass involves moving from the input layer through the hidden layers to the output layer that made a correlation decision, which is measured against the ground truth label [21]. The backward pass involves moving backwards using back propagation to minimize error [21]. The above-mentioned description highlights the convenience of MLP for the nature of the addressed problem in this paper and justifies our choice. Figure 1 shows an overview of the proposed model in this paper. It is generated using the visualization feature in Weka platform [22].

To avoid overfitting, we chose 10 folds cross-validation for training and testing using the stages from second to seventh according to the occurrence of LT discussed above. Considering our dataset diversity as mentioned above, we were able to conduct several experiments to test the correlation between the LT and the demographic data used individually or combined to evaluate their effect on LT prediction. The results are shown in Table 2. The highest correlation score using single demographic data is achieved when "Height" feature is used, resulting in a correlation coefficient of 0.7381, which suggests the positive correlation between "Height" and LT. In dual combinations, the pair ("Age" and "Gender") provided the best correlation coefficient of 0.8135 whereas in the triple combinations the ("Age", "Height" and "Weight") provided the best correlation coefficient of 0.7901 compared to other pairs and triples correlation scores respectively. Implementing the experiment including all demographic features in addition to the "HR" and "Speed" features from the second to the seventh stages provide the best correlation

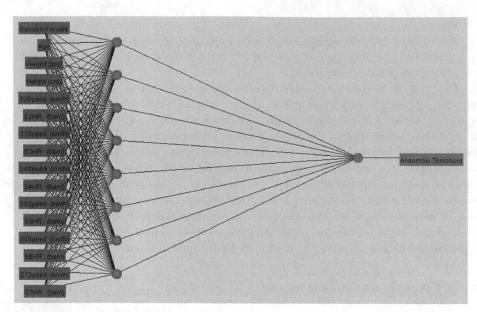

Fig. 1. An overview of the proposed model for non-invasive LT estimation using MLP, generated by Weka [22].

Table 2. Achieved correlation coefficient by applying MLP on different demographic data combinations beside other features

No.	Age	Gender	Height	Weight	HR$_{(s2-s7)}$	Speed $_{(s2-s7)}$	Correlation
1	✗	✗	✗	✗	✓	✓	0.6801
2	✓	✗	✗	✗	✓	✓	0.6666
3	✗	✓	✗	✗	✓	✓	0.6204
4	✗	✗	✓	✗	✓	✓	0.7318
5	✗	✗	✗	✓	✓	✓	0.6717
6	✓	✓	✗	✗	✓	✓	0.8135
7	✓	✗	✓	✗	✓	✓	0.0806
8	✓	✗	✗	✓	✓	✓	0.803
9	✗	✓	✓	✗	✓	✓	0.6565
10	✗	✓	✗	✓	✓	✓	0.7569
11	✗	✗	✓	✓	✓	✓	0.6906
12	✓	✓	✓	✗	✓	✓	0.6029
13	✓	✓	✗	✓	✓	✓	0.7532
14	✓	✗	✓	✓	✓	✓	0.7901
15	✗	✓	✓	✓	✓	✓	0.6548
16	✓	✓	✓	✓	✓	✓	0.7983

Table 3. Examples of the ground truth scores and the predicted LT scores using the proposed model

Subject	Actual LT score	Predicted LT score
1	10.5	10.302
2	9.25	12.234
3	7.5	7.728
4	10.75	12.591
5	8.6	8.83
6	8.8	8.026
7	9.8	10.297
8	6.1	5.41
9	6.5	5.664
10	9.3	9.134

score (0.7983) using the LT ground truth scores. Table 3 shows ten examples of the ground truth scores and the predicted LT scores.

4 Discussion

The findings shown in Table 2 suggest the effect of demographic data on the LT prediction non-invasively. Based on our observations while conducting the experiments, we found that the correlation to LT of the physical features "Age", "Gender", "Height" and "Weight", respectively is (0.6666), (0.6204), (0.7318) and (0.6717) when training and testing the noninvasive model using single demographic data besides other HR and speed features. However, in case of using demographic features in pairs besides other HR and speed features, the least correlation coefficient among pairs occurs in the case of using "Age" and "Height" pair (0.0806%).The decision of using the data between the second and the seventh stages has been made after conducting several experiments using the data in all ten stages, and the data between the second and the tenth stages, as well as the data between the second and the seventh stages. The resulted coefficient correlation scores are (0.7148), (0.7179), and (0.7983) respectively. In addition to correlation score improvement, removing the last three stages data, which represents 5% of the LT ground truth scores, will help to minimize the number of input features towards enhancing model reliability and generalization.

Table 4 shows the comparison criteria between the proposed system in this paper including the constructed dataset and the ML model, and the work in [17] which is, to the best of our knowledge, the only work we found in literature that uses ML to predict LT non-invasively. This table demonstrates the potential of our proposed system as a new step towards estimating LT non-invasively on a large target population. Starting with the dataset, research in [17] used a dataset constructed by conducting a controlled experiment on soccer players exclusively whereas the proposed dataset in this paper was constructed by selecting a random sample from real life tests data. Participants in [17] are all male soccer players whereas subjects in the proposed dataset are male and female who perform different physical activities and sports. The minimum age in the proposed dataset is 11 and the maximum is 64 with average (35.88 ± 14.432) whereas it is (21.6 ± 4.5) in [17], and thus the proposed dataset covers a wider age range compared to the one in [17]. The "Weight" feature in the proposed dataset is also diverse compared to the dataset in [17] (72.3 ± 8.1), since players share a common weight range. The same applies in exhaustion speed and HR for soccer players compared to the diverse values for these features in the proposed dataset. "Height" is the only diverse feature in both datasets but to a lesser extent in [17]. Hence, our model emanates from a more diverse sample population in terms of fitness level, athletic background and demographic data, which represent some of the affecting factors on LT estimation.

Table 4. Comparison between the proposed system and the system in [17]

Comparison criteria	Our model	Non-invasive model in [17]
Sport diversity	✓	×
Gender diversity	✓	×
Age diversity	✓	×
Weight diversity	✓	×
Height diversity	✓	✓
Exhaustion speed diversity	✓	×
Sport diversity	✓	×
Exhaustion HR diversity	✓	×
ML algorithm	MLP	MLP
Correlation score	0.7983	0.875

5   Conclusion and Future Work

In this paper, we proposed a ML model to estimate LT non-invasively. We train and test this model on a 100-subject dataset that we constructed using real life tests data collected at Peak Center for Human Performance in Ottawa, Canada. We also proposed a method to fill the missing values in this dataset considering the stage at which LT occurs. We achieved the best correlation scores of 0.7983 compared to the ground truth obtained from domain experts. As a future work, we plan to expand the dataset and further investigate the affecting factors on LT prediction. We also plan to use different machine learning models for training and testing the dataset in order to minimize the number of input features towards building a general non-invasive model to predict LT.

References

1. Myers, J., Ashley, E.: Dangerous curves: a perspective on exercise, lactate, and the anaerobic threshold. Chest **111**(3), 787–795 (1997)
2. Badawi, H.F., Dong, H., El Saddik, A.: Mobile cloud-based physical activity advisory system using biofeedback sensors. Future Gener. Comput. Syst. **66**, 59–70 (2017)
3. Lamaarti, F., Arafsha, F., Hafidh, B., El Saddik, A.: Automated athlete haptic training system for soccer sprinting. In: Proceedings - 2nd International Conference on Multimedia Information Processing and Retrieval, MIPR 2019, pp. 303–309 (2019)
4. Faude, O., Kindermann, W., Meyer, T.: Lactate threshold concepts: how valid are they? Sports Med. **39**(6), 469–490 (2009)
5. Hall, M.M., Rajasekaran, S., Thomsen, T.W., Peterson, A.R.: Lactate: friend or foe. PM R **8**(3), S8–S15 (2016)
6. Nascimento, E.M.F., Kiss, M.A.P.D.M., Santos, T.M., Lambert, M., Pires, F.O.: Determination of lactate thresholds in maximal running test by heart rate variability data set. Asian J. Sports Med. **8**(3), e58480 (2017)
7. Marques-Neto, S.R., Santos, E.L., Maior, A.S., Neto, G.A.M.: Analysis of heart rate deflection points to predict the anaerobic threshold by a computerized method. J. Strength Cond. Res. **26**(7), 1967–1974 (2012)
8. Simões, R.P., Mendes, R.G., Castello-Simões, V., Catai, A.M., Arena, R., Borghi-Silva, A.: Use of heart rate variability to estimate lactate threshold in coronary artery disease patients during resistance exercise. J. Sports Sci. Med. **15**(4), 649–657 (2016)
9. Garcia-Tabar, I., Llodio, I., Sánchez-Medina, L., Ruesta, M., Ibañez, J., Gorostiaga, E.M.: Heart rate-based prediction of fixed blood lactate thresholds in professional team-sport players. J. Strength Cond. Res. **29**(10), 2794–2801 (2015)
10. Nikooie, R., Gharakhanlo, R., Rajabi, H., Bahraminegad, M., Ghafari, A.: Noninvasive determination of anaerobic threshold by monitoring the %SpO2 changes and respiratory gas exchange. J. Strength Cond. Res. **23**(7), 2107–2113 (2009)
11. Wasserman, K., Whipp, B.J., Koyal, S.N., Beaver, W.L.: Anaerobic threshold and respiratory gas exchange during exercise. J. Appl. Physiol. **35**(2), 236–243 (1973)
12. Llodio, I., Garcia-Tabar, I., Sánchez-Medina, L., Ibáñez, J., Gorostiaga, E.M.: Estimation of the maximal lactate steady state in junior soccer players. Int. J. Sports Med. **36**(14), 1142–1148 (2015)
13. Mason, A., et al.: Noninvasive in-situ measurement of blood lactate using microwave sensors. IEEE Trans. Biomed. Eng. **65**(3), 698–705 (2018)
14. Arteaga-Falconi, J.S., et al.: Dtwins: a digital twins ecosystem for health and well-being. IEEE COMSOC MMTC Commun. Front. **14**(2), 39–43 (2019)
15. Henriet, J.: Artificial intelligence-virtual trainer: an educative system based on artificial intelligence and designed to produce varied and consistent training lessons. Proc. Inst. Mech. Eng. Part P: J. Sports Eng. Technol. **231**(2), 110–124 (2017)
16. Fister Jr., I., Ljubič, K., Suganthan, P.N., Perc, M., Fister, I.: Computational intelligence in sports: challenges and opportunities within a new research domain. Appl. Math. Comput. **262**, 178–186 (2015)
17. Erdogan, A., Cetin, C., Goksu, H., Guner, R., Baydar, M.L.: Non-invasive detection of the anaerobic threshold by a neural network model of the heart rate-work rate relationship. Proc. Inst. Mech. Eng. Part P: J. Sports Eng. Technol. **223**(3), 109–115 (2009)
18. Peak Centre For Human Performance. https://www.peakcentre.ca/. Accessed 20 Aug 2019
19. Fitness Assessment. https://www.peakcentre.ca/individual-training/personal-fitness-assessment/. Accessed 20 Aug 2019

20. Multilayer Perceptrons. http://users.ics.aalto.fi/ahonkela/dippa/node41.html. Accessed 12 Sep 2019
21. Nicholson, C.: A beginner's guide to multilayer perceptrons (MLP). https://skymind.ai/wiki/multilayer-perceptron#code. Accessed 12 Sept 2019
22. Witten, I.H., Frank, E., Hall, M.A., Pal, C.J.: Data Mining: Practical Machine Learning Tools and Techniques. Morgan Kaufmann, Burlington (2016)

Smart Multimedia for Citizen-Centered Smart Living

An Interdisciplinary Framework for Citizen-Centered Smart Cities and Smart Living

Sethuraman Panchanathan, Ramin Tadayon$^{(\boxtimes)}$, Troy McDaniel, and Vipanchi Chacham

Arizona State University, Tempe, AZ 85281, USA
{panch,rtadayon,troy.mcdaniel,vchacham}@asu.edu

Abstract. Rapid population growth and urbanization have led to increasing demands for management, healthcare, safety, among many other concerns, resulting in the recent formation and worldwide investment in IoT and ICT-enabled smart cities. Citizen-centric approaches toward the development of research solutions within these smart city environments focus on the citizen, their attributes, values, roles, and responsibilities to improve applicability, accessibility, and public value of technologies. In this work, an integrated and interdisciplinary framework for the implementation of citizen-centric research toward smart cities is proposed. Two example case studies are described as initial proofs of concept for applying the framework in specific areas. The first is a solution for indoor localization and information discovery targeted at citizens who are blind or visually impaired, while the second is the implementation of Virtual Reality (VR) sports stadium attendance within a smart stadium testbed environment. Finally, a new graduate program which integrates multiple disciplines to train the next generation of smart city leaders is presented.

Keywords: Smart cities · Citizen-Centered design · Interdisciplinary research

1 Introduction

As we head deeper into the 21st century, the rise and rapid advancement of ubiquitous and scalable technologies have given imminence to an era of smart cities in modern society. A "smart city" has been defined by Dameri as "a well-defined geographical area" in which modern technologies "cooperate to create benefits for citizens in terms of well-being, inclusion and participation, environmental quality, intelligent development..." and more [1]. Rising citizen populations and population density in cities have tasked governments at all levels with meeting increasingly complex demands for management, resources, healthcare, and security, and smart cities equipped with Information and Communications Technology (ICT) and Internet of Things (IoT) have been proposed to enable greater access to information, smoother and more inclusive transportation, enhanced security and safety, smarter sustainability, better citizen engagement, greater economic prosperity, and a well-connected infrastructure architecture to enable these

© Springer Nature Switzerland AG 2020
T. McDaniel et al. (Eds.): ICSM 2019, LNCS 12015, pp. 107–122, 2020.
https://doi.org/10.1007/978-3-030-54407-2_10

solutions at a city-wide scale [2]. To support these efforts, the government of the United States, with the National Science Foundation's (NSF) support, launched an investment in 2015 of over $160 million in research for smart city development [3].

At the center of a smart city is the citizen, a participant characterized by a set of goals, abilities, responsibilities, needs, and demands that result from that individual's attributes. The goals of smart city development should apply directly toward the citizen, as evidenced within the goals of leading Smart Cities organizations including the globally recognized Smart Cities Council, which advocates for a "people-first" approach toward smart city design which is both inclusive and equitable [4]. Indeed, the effectiveness of any smart city solution can be measured by the public value it is able to generate toward its citizenry [5]. As such, effective technological solutions should be aware of the (often unique) characteristics of the citizens they are intended to serve and should adapt to and learn from the citizen just as the technologically enabled citizen learns from and adapts to technologies. Person-Centered Multimedia Computing (PCMC) is a paradigm of multimedia design focused on centering the process around the individual "person" and using adaptive design characteristics to serve the needs of the broader public [6]. The paradigm of citizen-centered design further characterizes the "person" as a "citizen" and calls upon technology to take into additional account the roles played by that citizen within a population and the resulting demands on smart city design.

Under this new perspective, smart city technologies and solutions may benefit from a citizen-centric focus, but how can such a strategy be successfully implemented? NSF's Smart and Connected Communities program [7] has emphasized the need for a cross-directorate approach, wherein the focus expands beyond technology to include communities, societies and other factors [8]. This suggests that an approach which incorporates multiple disciplines of expertise, which together combine to yield solutions which are effective in advancing each of these areas, is the most impactful method of addressing the smart cities problem. Based on these findings, this work proposes an interdisciplinary framework for the design, development and deployment of citizen-centered solutions for smart cities. Details of the disciplines emphasized in this framework and their related contributions to smart city development are introduced in Sect. 2. In Sect. 3, two case studies demonstrating initial proofs of concept for the application of citizen-centric design in the areas of indoor localization and sports stadiums are presented with a discussion of preliminary findings. An overview of the "Citizen-Centered Smart Cities and Smart Living" project, a new graduate program under the National Science Foundation Research Traineeship (NRT), is provided along with the main goals of the project toward applying the proposed interdisciplinary and citizen-centered paradigm. Finally, directions for future work and development of the paradigm are provided.

2 Interdisciplinary Approach

At the city-wide scale, a variety of expertise is required to design useful technological solutions and generate optimum public value from those solutions. For example, solutions considered to be highly effective from a computational accuracy standpoint may be impractical or have a negative impact on communities and populations when viewed from a policy perspective or may be considered unscalable or unsustainable from

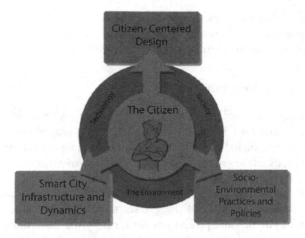

Fig. 1. An overview of the interdisciplinary and citizen-centered smart cities paradigm.

other perspectives. Often, technologies, policies, and practices within the area of smart city research are developed with a focus on a single discipline in isolation and validate themselves under the lens of that discipline alone. As a result, while these research developments are proven successful under the evaluation and validation practices of the respective discipline through which their development was focused, they ultimately fail in practice due to incompatibility with societal standards and many other issues. Furthermore, solutions which fail to recognize the variability of needs among the citizens for which they are developed will ultimately only serve a small portion of the population and generate little value. Hence, interdisciplinarity and citizen-centered design should be considered together.

Recent findings studying smart city implementations support the necessity of interdisciplinarity and citizen-centered focus. A recent study [9] suggests that even for those citizens among smart cities populations with the highest levels of knowledge and awareness of smart city services, there remain serious concerns about the accessibility, safety, utility and efficiency of these services, suggesting that current implementations could benefit from a broader interdisciplinary view of the communities they serve. Other findings have supported this claim and argued for an approach which integrates multiple fields and encompasses the whole of smart city infrastructure [10]. Studies on the inclusivity of smart city implementations including that of Neto and Kofuji [11] find that one-size-fits-all solutions typically fail to meet the needs of significant populations of citizens due to characteristics such as disability and age because they observe citizens as a static and homogeneous entity. To address these challenges, we propose a framework for smart city research that, through specific perspectives and research thrusts, emphasizes both interdisciplinarity and citizen-centeredness.

In this framework, three interdisciplinary perspectives and three research thrusts are identified which together form the basis of more reliable, scalable, effective, and citizen-centric research. These elements, as shown in Fig. 1, include the following:

- **Interdisciplinary Perspectives:** *Technology*, *Society*, and *The Environment*
- **Research Thrusts:** *Citizen-Centered Design*, *Smart City Infrastructure and Dynamics*, and *Socio-Environmental Practices and Policies.*

2.1 Interdisciplinary Perspectives

Technology: Disciplines involved in the development of technological solutions for citizens should consider how IoT and ICT can best be leveraged toward a variety of citizens and landscapes, including adaptivity and flexible interface design to deal with changes in these needs as they occur between citizens and over time.

Society: Societal considerations include whether smart city research can meet the ethical, safety, and cultural standards of the greater society, and whether technological solutions align with policies and procedures set forth by the governing bodies of that society.

The Environment: Smart City solutions may also be evaluated for their sustainability, ecological impact, scalability and applicability within both urban and rural environments and landscapes, as well as the various areas and sectors of smart cities.

2.2 Research Thrusts

Citizen-Centered Design: This research thrust is at the confluence of *Technology*, *Society*, and the *Citizen*. In order to be accepted and generate the greatest levels of public value, solutions should take into account changes in the needs of citizens as they vary by culture, age group, career, transportation methods used, living space (urban versus rural), financial standing, and technological knowledge. These solutions should pay particularly careful attention to citizens with disabilities and those in underrepresented groups.

Smart City Infrastructure and Dynamics: This research thrust is at the confluence of *Technology*, *The Environment*, and the *Citizen*. Research should be aware that Smart Cities are highly connected entities with complex and dynamic architectures and infrastructures. The interplay between these city environments, the citizens within them, and the technologies which connect them is worthy of exploration and evaluation.

Socio-Environmental Practices and Policies: This research thrust is at the confluence of *Society*, *The Environment*, and the *Citizen*. As the technologies implemented within smart city environments become increasingly complex, and the amount of sensitive data and information captured by these technologies become increasingly vast, studies into the viability and feasibility of various solutions from social, ethical environmental and policy perspectives become increasingly critical.

3   Case Studies

To demonstrate some of the considerations of the proposed framework in practice, and the framing of research related to smart cities around the citizen, two example cases of research from the Center for Cognitive Ubiquitous Computing (CUbiC) at Arizona State University are considered. These solutions view the citizen through the lens of disability to generate the technological, societal and environmental considerations of technological solutions in two areas of application: indoor navigation and smart stadium development.

3.1   Indoor Navigation for Citizens with Visual Impairments

Fig. 2. Three screenshots showing various identified objects in a room using the prototype (Color figure online)

Introduction and Related Work: The U.S. Department of Transportation has solidified its interest in smart city technologies and development through an investment in smart transportation systems for the smart cities of the future as one primary component of their Smart City Challenge [12]. Two aspects of this challenge related to transportation are navigation and information discovery. These challenges have been largely addressed in outdoor environments through the development of GPS technology; however, this technology is too imprecise to be used for indoor localization, which warrants the development of a novel approach. To understand the impact of such a system, one must first characterize a smart citizen who faces great levels of challenge in indoor navigation and could benefit from such a technology. Blindness presents exactly such a challenge, affecting approximately 36 million worldwide [13]. Citizens who are blind in indoor smart city environments could benefit from the design of technology to assist in indoor localization, navigation and information discovery; but what type of design would be the most effective for this type of citizen?

To date, many solutions have been developed to aid in indoor localization and navigation. However, existing approaches often either limited in addressing the problem from the various perspectives introduced in Sect. 1 [14], or they are limited in terms of accounting for the needs and demands of citizens who are blind or visually impaired within indoor environments and social contexts [15]. Cydalion Navigation [16] is an example of one such approach, wherein the user equips a camera on the front of his or her chest or stomach and, while moving indoors, the user receives audio cues that assist in ambulation and avoiding obstacles. This approach is limited in that it requires the subject to equip and constantly wear a body camera, which negatively impacts the solution's social acceptability, and makes it more difficult to setup and use independently by a blind individual. Individuals who are blind or visually impaired may hesitate to adopt such an approach because the externally worn camera is not very discreet. Other approaches such as Nvidia's Horus [17] suffer from similar issues, in addition to being highly costly due to the equipment involved. Vision technologies such as the vOICe system [18] allow for a limited amount of information discovery by using audio characteristics to convey the size and distance of objects in the environment, but fail to specify what those objects actually are, which may be of critical interest to the citizen.

Methodology: To address these challenges, a smartphone-based solution was developed which would solve the problem of identifying the objects and obstacles in an indoor space for information discovery and localization while being simple, discreet, easy-to-use, low-cost and socially acceptable for individuals with blindness and visual impairment. This is accomplished by leveraging smart IoT-enabled technologies embedded within an indoor space and communicating with these devices to capture information about the layout and objects present within the room.

The project was developed within the Center for Cognitive Ubiquitous Computing (CUbiC) at Arizona State University. The first step in this process was to convert CUbiC into an IoT-enabled smart indoor space. This was accomplished through partnership with SpotSense, who deployed the SpotSense indoor positioning system [19] within the lab. This system utilizes a combination of Bluetooth beacons, a customized Android SDK, and a REST API to track individuals using the SpotSense smartphone app. The beacons, distributed throughout the space, are detected by the SDK including their identifiers and attached metadata such as room number. This can be used, for example, to determine which room, or which part of a room, the user is currently in by determining the strongest signal strength among the most recently detected beacons, and information which guides the user from room to room can be conveyed to assist in navigating between them. To assist in information discovery, CUbiC also partnered with Intel Corporation, who provided a set of cameras and RFID tags together comprising the Intel Responsive RFID Sensor Platform [20]. A series of H3000 1080p color cameras with 98-degree wide-angle lens were installed around the lab space, capable of reading Ultra High Frequency (UHF) Radio Frequency Identification (RFID) tags to provide information about the various types of objects currently present within a space such as chairs, tables and walls, within a range of 5–15 m at a maximum of 400 tags per second. Beyond informing a user about what objects are present, the Intel sensors can also help to provide more information and characteristics about these objects that may be of pertinence to a user who is blind. For example, the sensors can detect if a chair is empty or occupied, or if a door is open or closed.

Table 1. Survey summary related to indoor nonvisual travel

Survey topic	Results/Examples
Primary method of travel	63% cane, 30% guide dog, 5% sighted/human guide, 1% other
Confidence in local travel	1% not confident, 4% not very confident, 14% somewhat confident, 21% confident, 56% very confident, 3% no answer
Information gathered about the environment (can choose more than one)	90% landmarks, 88% texture change, 85% obstacle avoidance, 70% orienting self in space, 56% echolocation, 3% other
Methods for navigating in structures	Dog finds door, listen for door and elevator, echo and sound of items, feel along wall, texture changes or collision with cane, listening to surroundings, listen for voices in social setting, using directions from human, cardinal directions

To determine the specific needs and challenges encountered by blind individuals in these circumstances, an in-depth survey was previously conducted which asked blind citizens about the challenges and requirements for nonvisual travel. 80 complete responses were obtained. Table 1 summarizes the subset of findings in this survey related to indoor navigation for blind individuals. Most individuals (63%) use a cane for navigating, and nearly 20% of this population are less than confident with travel in local contexts. An issue with using canes alone, or using canes and a guide dog, is that the individual may have difficulty identifying exactly what types of objects comprise the obstacles in the environment, and information about the structure of the indoor environment cannot be known without manually scanning it section by section. The objects in a space such as furniture can be considered "landmarks" in the indoor navigation context, and 90% use these landmarks for orienting and localizing themselves within a space. Avoiding obstacles is listed as another form of information gathered during travel, at 85% prevalence. Methods for navigation also included listening for doors opening and closing (which requires waiting on others to use them), finding the door with a dog (which may be difficult in previously unexplored areas), feeling along the wall (which restricts one to the edges of the space and takes time), and the use of a cane to discover information (which costs time, can be awkward in social situations and often yields incomplete information). Based on these findings, and the requirements for indoor navigation assistance provided in [14, 15], the following requirements were determined for the implementation of the indoor navigation prototype:

- Use of audio, preferably through bone conduction headphones, was deemed acceptable as it was the modality already used by most individuals for getting information about the environment.

- The solution would need to identify the types of objects that were within the environment, so that the user can learn as much about a new room layout as his or her sighted peer after using the app.
- A smartphone app would be useful as it is ubiquitous, utilizes pre-existing technology with no cost overhead, and could communicate with the IoT enabled devices currently distributed in the lab environment.
- By using a phone only, the solution would not incur any extra wearables, setup, socially inacceptable or stand-out appearance on the user.
- The solution should allow the citizen to quickly and efficiently learn about the environment and provide sufficient detail without incurring high cognitive load.

These considerations go beyond the scope of simply developing a technology that enables navigation. By considering the challenge from a technological, social and environmental standpoint, the solution is more cost-effective, practical and socially acceptable than many of the recent approaches which had not taken these factors into account. Furthermore, the process of surveying and identifying challenges, goals and strategies taken by blind citizens ensures that the solution developed can match demands and generate the greatest public value. In this manner, the framework has been implemented and its benefits identified within this application area.

Figure 2 depicts a mock-up of the proposed app. Three screenshots depict various objects and how they would be identified by the app during use, as well as its overall appearance. The initial version of the app will present a top-down map of a chosen room within CUbiC's lab space. To use the app, the user simply loads the map and moves his or her finger around the screen to explore the space. The red dot represents the location of the user's finger within the map as he or she explores the space to determine what obstacles exist and how the room is structured. When the red dot collides with an object or wall, and audio voice is played which describes the type of object (table, chair, door, wall, etc.) the user is currently in contact with. This audio voice plays in a continuous loop until the user's finger leaves contact with that object or wall. The interface is flexible in its usability – an individual can either quickly scan a path to determine if it is clear, or scan the entire space with his or her finger until the full layout is explored and all objects are identified. Characteristics of the objects shown in the room, such as which chairs are occupied, whether the door is open, and more, are also made available through communication between RFID tags attached to the objects in the space and the Intel sensors and platform. Furthermore, which room the user is currently exploring, as well as additional information about the space such as when meetings in the room are scheduled, can be accessed through communication with SpotSense beacons.

Initial Findings and Discussion: In an initial approach toward guiding visitors within CUbiC, an interface was under development with a voice platform to inform the user where objects would be located in a given room. However, it was determined through feedback from prospective users that this type of interaction requires external communication between the citizen and platform which could serve as a distraction in a social environment and can agitate the already prevalent issue that blind citizens face when receiving unwanted attention within these environments. This had inspired the discreet design of the smartphone app currently in place. The same prospective users identified that bone-induction headphones could be used to obtain audio feedback from the app about objects and information discovery while leaving their ears open for communications with the environment and others. Furthermore, it was determined through preliminary testing that a mental map of a space could be formed by drawing out paths starting at the entrance toward various corners and walls present in the space. Finally, prospective users cautioned that repetitive audio loops may be distracting and, in many cases, redundant as the user already knows about an object or obstacle from initial contact on the map. Based on this preliminary feedback, future iterations can adapt modalities and frequency of interaction to the preferences of the user by allowing them to customize these in an options menu.

3.2 Case Study 2: Smart Stadium

Introduction and Related Work: As a second case study, another type of citizen and community is defined for which there is an active and growing population within smart cities: the sports fan. The 'Smart Stadium' is a concept characterized by the equipping of a sports stadium with IoT and ICT in order to transform it into a testing platform for the implementation of these technologies among the sports society which is populated by sports fans of varying age and ability. Under this definition, and through the proposed framework for smart city research, an integrated approach which includes the perspectives of society, technology and the environment, and centers itself on the citizen as a sports attendee, has been established. It is proposed that many of the challenges present in smart cities occur in smart stadiums at a much smaller scale, making them an ideal testbed for research solutions in this space.

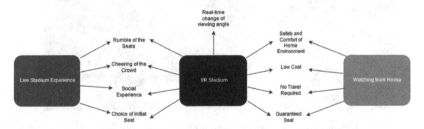

Fig. 3. Merging of advantages of live attendance and home viewing of sports matches in VR.

The modern sports fan treats live sports events as a fully immersive and social experience, which sets it distinctly apart from the act of simply viewing the event from a home television broadcast. Stadiums around the world become increasingly populated as the population of sports fans and their respective communities grow. Attending a live sports event provides a citizen with a highly energetic atmosphere in which the cheering of the crowd and the rumbling of seats all feed into the excitement an attendee feels. These multisensory stimuli often make the overall experience more memorable compared to remote alternatives. However, due to restrictions in the number of stadiums, their location, the number of seats available within a given stadium, and the limitations placed by a single seating location on the citizen's view of a sports match, that citizen is offered a very limited amount of control over his or her experience. Citizens with disabilities are particularly impacted by these limitations as they affect their access to sports events, often requiring them to view the event from home when mobility in crowded environments becomes a factor. Yet, fans viewing from home are even more limited by the field of view of the camera covering the event, over which they have no control.

Fortunately, Virtual Reality (VR) technology is becoming increasingly ubiquitous and commonplace, while becoming increasingly affordable for public use, which has given rise to research interest in the creation of virtual sports attendance experiences. These include immersive or augmented 360° video, which is currently already implemented in many cases. These implementations may utilize VR camera setups which have very high complexity and costly pipelines necessary to generate the VR content. More practical and affordable alternatives have aimed to transform multiple regular video feeds into a surrounding VR experience [21]. Therefore, work at CUbiC aims to leverage these video transformations, as well as IoT sensors and other mechanisms installed within smart stadiums, to present an immersive, multimodal, stadium-like experience to fans. An overview of the advantages of stadium attendance and at-home viewing is given in Fig. 3, along with the benefits of merging the two in a VR environment, wherein the view of the match can be controlled by the fan in real-time.

Fig. 4. Screenshot of VR Stadium experience and headset.

One particularly significant factor relating to the need of smart stadium implementations is the globalization of sport, which has been closely related with international economic, social and cultural relationships. One of the primary platforms showcasing these relationships is the Olympics, which encompasses a significant variety of sports types [22]. The process of globalization has allowed sports which previously only enjoyed local attendance within a city or country to gain a massive global audience which often transcends cultural differences [23]. Such events are primarily enjoyed, in addition to live attendance, through radio, television or live stream broadcasts [24]. Yet it is shown that more immersive experiences improve the presence and level of engagement of a fan with a sport or sport event [25], although currently deployed VR systems such as that of the NBA don't include the multisensory aspects of the experience [26]. To address this issue, we have developed a prototype for a VR stadium experience which seeks to globalize the smart stadium experience, creating a more connected global society around sports events. In addition to global expansion of otherwise locally broadcast sports, this development also seeks to make the stadium attendance experience more accessible for individuals with visual or mobility impairment, and to empower sports fans to control in real-time the angle by which they view a sports event.

Methodology: As in other research endeavors in smart cities research, the first step taken by CUbiC was to obtain access to a local smart stadium as a testing platform. Arizona State University (ASU) has been partnered with Dublin City University (DCU) since 2016 through the Transatlantic Higher Education Partnership, under which the two universities transformed their respective stadia into smart stadia equipped with smart sensing technology provided through support by Intel. At ASU's Sun Devil Stadium, a total of 44 sensor boxes, each containing a microphone, altitude sensor, vibration sensor and Bluetooth for communication, were distributed across the seats in the lower section. CUbiC designed a prototype for VR stadium attendance with the intention of eventually leveraging these sensors for real-time immersive data on sports games.

The implementation of immersive VR stadium attendance not only serves to globalize the live experience, but also to explore strategies for the delivery of multimodal data to best represent a sports event in real-time, as well as strategies for increasing accessibility for a wider variety of fans, particularly those with physical, cognitive or sensory impairment. Public value of this solution will include increased participation and social impact for these populations of citizens. An initial prototype was developed, as shown in Fig. 4, to serve as a multimodal and immersive VR experience which included haptic (touch-based) feedback and crowd-based audio feedback layered on the standard audiovisual feed of a sports broadcast. The prototype was developed in Unity under the SteamVR platform and deployed on an HTC Vive headset and controllers. The software consisted of a 360° sample video of a sports game which was distributed across a skybox to create a surrounding immersion. Through the multiple audio sources present in this environment, a variety of audio stimuli are possible, such as the noise of those sitting to one's left and right in the crowd. When the stadium rumbles at various energy points in the video feed, haptic feedback can be provided to the subject through the use of a specialized chair equipped with an array of vibrotactile motors across the back. These motors mimic the rumble of the stadium to energize the user and provide motivation. While participants view a pre-recorded video stream, this implementation served as a useful prototype and demonstration platform for the proposed project.

Initial Findings and Discussion: A preliminary survey was used to determine, among individuals who had either attended live sports games at Sun Devil Stadium or had watched them at home, what new features would be the most useful and create the greatest experience when using VR to watch sports games. The study was also open to individuals with disabilities in order to help identify the main issues faced by these citizens in enjoying the stadium experience through this prototype. To identify candidate features and characteristics which could be implemented in a VR environment for a highly effective and purposeful spectating experience of stadium sports, the prior experience of those who had already experienced games held in Sun Devil stadium, both live and from home, was necessary. Once these characteristics were identified, the set of cameras, sensors and IoT-enabled technology within the stadium could be analyzed to determine how they could operate in conjunction to one another to achieve these goals within the VR viewing experience. Both the experiences of sports fans who had attended ASU Sun Devil sports games live within the stadium itself, as well as the experience of those who had seen the games from their home or other remote viewing platforms, were necessary as it was the aim of this research to address the challenges faced by each type of audience; hence, both populations of sports fans were targeted as subjects for the survey. Another perspective that was of importance in this research was that of individuals with disabilities, specifically the challenges resulting from these disabilities on the experience of attending or viewing a match; therefore, this population was also open and encouraged to participate and contribute to the need-finding process.

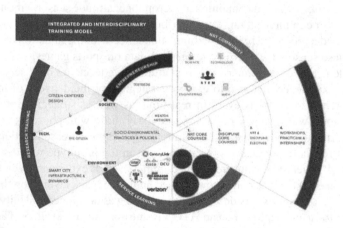

Fig. 5. NRT project integrated and interdisciplinary training model.

The study was initially presented in [27]. Seven participants volunteered to complete the survey. To summarize, traffic, difficulties with seating and crowd congestion were considered the most common issues with in-person sports game attendance, in addition to the occasional difficulty with properly viewing the game from one's seat. Blind individuals required the accompaniment of sighted individuals to convey visual information from both a safety and accessibility perspective and an enjoyment perspective. The greatest frustration when watching from home was the lack of energy and immersion and the lack of in-stadium experiences including a marching band performance. The social aspects of stadium experiences were greatly emphasized, while the advantage of comfort, avoidance of traffic and increased sense of control over the sound and visuals were touted from an at-home standpoint. Other desirable features of the VR stadium experience included instant access to replays, the ability to instantly switch between views of a stadium, player point-of-view, greater access to real-time match statistics, and augmented reality elements. Participants indicated a positive reaction to the proposed technology and a high likelihood of attending more sports matches if they were shown in VR. Challenges included dizziness due to long-term exposure to VR as well as the display quality of current VR headsets. Through these need-finding exercises and the development of a prototype, we have gathered the requirements for an effective solution by examining the VR stadium and VR sports experience as a multidisciplinary challenge, and focusing the exploration of this challenge on the citizen.

4 ASU's NRT Graduate Program

The proposed framework, as presented above, is currently under implementation through a newly-formed five-year graduate program funded by the National Science Foundation Research Traineeship (NRT). The grant, entitled "Citizen-Centered Smart Cities and Smart Living," brings together multiple schools and disciplines across Arizona State University with the shared vision of training a future generation of graduate students to become lead researchers, scientists, entrepreneurs, engineers and policy makers for Smart City development under the integrated and interdisciplinary focus on the environmental, technological and societal aspects of citizen-centered solutions. This experience includes integrative research that transcends boundaries and includes experiences such as internships and service-learning experiences in collaboration with industry partners such as Intel, Adidas, Cisco, Verizon, City of Tempe, among many others. The program specifically targets and recruits students with disabilities in line with the understanding that these citizens are part of often-neglected communities in Smart Cities with limited accessibility and limited opportunity for citizen engagement.

The program employs an integrated *education-research-practice* model that provides interdisciplinary training and education to students through a curriculum consisting of cross-disciplinary courses, highly immersive internships and service learning, joint multidisciplinary research projects, training for entrepreneurship and the development of professional communication. This integrated and interdisciplinary training model is shown in Fig. 5 and includes six complementary components: *research training, curriculum training, applied learning, service learning, entrepreneurship,* and *teamwork.* The six core disciplines of Computer Science (CSE), Public Affairs (PAF), Civil, Environmental, and Sustainable Engineering (CEE), Applied Engineering Programs (EGR), Human and Social Dimensions of Science and Technology (HSD), and Mechanical & Aerospace Engineering (MAE) combine to form the multidisciplinary core of expertise central to developing effective research through this project. Components include: **Research Training:** Trainees lead interdisciplinary research projects united with the NRT community under specialization in a common research thrust with a focus on practical solutions made possible by integrating domains of application under the diverse expertise of NRT faculty in the above disciplines. **Curriculum Training:** Trainees complete a set of NRT core courses and electives which prepare them to collaborate with experts among the diverse fields comprising the NRT in addition to completing their own core courses within their discipline. **Applied Learning:** Trainees participate in an applied learning component wherein professional growth is built through annual workshops aimed at communication skills training. Trainees are expected to present and support their research under an interdisciplinary audience which includes fellow NRT trainees and faculty. Furthermore, internships enable trainees to directly interact with government, industry, non-profit and global partnerships, allowing them to build professional networks and career paths as well as gain hands-on experience within real challenges related to smart cities. **Service Learning:** Service learning experiences are research collaborations with NRT partners that allows trainees to make an impact within their community. During these experiences, trainees apply their creativity and skills as well as the principles of integrated and interdisciplinary research, and often involve first-hand interactions with a variety of smart citizen populations in smart cities or smart city testbeds. **Entrepreneurship:** In order to transform research ideas and developments into real-world solutions, it is critical for entrepreneurship to be a part of the lead researcher's repertoire. Hence, a seminar series is developed and maintained by co-PIs and other faculty members to explain the applications and significance of entrepreneurship and entrepreneurial thinking in smart city development. **Teamwork:** Trainees will regularly meet to present and evaluate one another's research, form collaborative research ideas, lend their expertise to other trainees and receive expertise from outside disciplines to boost the effectiveness and quality of their research in return.

5   Conclusion

This work presented an integrated and interdisciplinary framework for the implementation of citizen-centered research for smart cities. Under the three interdisciplinary perspectives of technology, society and the environment, and the three research thrusts of citizen-centered design, smart city infrastructure and dynamics, and socio-environmental practices and policies, high quality and high impact research is emphasized which can yield the highest levels of public value. Two case studies were presented which served as initial and preliminary proofs of concept toward the application of this framework in two specific sub-areas of smart city development, and a five-year NRT project entitled "Citizen-Centered Smart Cities and Smart Living" was described which encompasses all of the principles of effective interdisciplinary smart city research necessary for the development of future leaders in the field.

Acknowledgment. The authors would like to thank Bryan Duarte for his work on the survey for nonvisual travel; Joshua Chang for graphic design assistance; and the National Science Foundation and Arizona State University for their funding support. This material is partially based upon work supported by the NSF under Grant No. 1828010.

References

1. Dameri, R.P.: Searching for Smart City definition: a comprehensive proposal. IJCT **11**, 2544–2551 (2012)
2. Komninos, N.: Intelligent cities: variable geometries of spatial intelligence. Intell. Build. Int. **3**, 172–188 (2011)

3. FACT SHEET: Administration Announces New "Smart Cities" Initiative to Help Communities Tackle Local Challenges and Improve City Services. https://obamawhitehouse.archives. gov/the-press-office/2015/09/14/fact-sheet-administration-announces-new-smart-cities-ini tiative-help

4. Smart Cities Council | White House Commitment: Smart Cities Council Challenge Grants. https://smartcitiescouncil.com/article/white-house-commitment-smart-cities-council-challenge-grants

5. O'Flynn, J.: From new public management to public value: paradigmatic change and managerial implications. Aust. J. Public Adm. **66**, 353–366 (2007)

6. Panchanathan, S., Chakraborty, S., McDaniel, T., Tadayon, R.: Person-centered multimedia computing: a new paradigm inspired by assistive and rehabilitative applications. IEEE Multimedia **23**, 12–19 (2016)

7. SCC | NSF - National Science Foundation. https://www.nsf.gov/cise/scc/

8. Smart and Connected Communities (S&CC) (nsf18520) | NSF - National Science Foundation. https://www.nsf.gov/pubs/2018/nsf18520/nsf18520.htm

9. Lytras, M.D., Visvizi, A.: Who uses smart city services and what to make of it: toward interdisciplinary smart cities research. Sustainability **10**, 1998 (2018). https://doi.org/10.3390/su10061998

10. Ojo, A., Curry, E., Janowski, T.: Designing next generation smart city initiatives - harnessing findings and lessons from a study of ten smart city programs. Tel Aviv. **15** (2014)

11. de Oliveira Neto, J.S., Kofuji, S.T.: Inclusive smart city: an exploratory study. In: Antona, M., Stephanidis, C. (eds.) UAHCI 2016. LNCS, vol. 9738, pp. 456–465. Springer, Cham (2016). https://doi.org/10.1007/978-3-319-40244-4_44

12. Smart City Challenge: Lessons for Building Cities of the Future. https://www.transportation. gov/policy-initiatives/smartcity/smart-city-challenge-lessons-building-cities-future

13. Vision impairment and blindness. https://www.who.int/news-room/fact-sheets/detail/blindn ess-and-visual-impairment

14. Singh, B., Kapoor, M.: A survey of current aids for visually impaired persons. In: International Conference on Internet of Things: Smart Innovation and Usages, pp. 1–5 (2018)

15. Miao, M., Spindler, M., Weber, G.: Requirements of indoor navigation system from blind users. In: Holzinger, A., Simonic, K.-M. (eds.) USAB 2011. LNCS, vol. 7058, pp. 673–679. Springer, Heidelberg (2011). https://doi.org/10.1007/978-3-642-25364-5_48

16. Cydalion. Navigation App for the Blind and Visually Impaired. http://cydalion.com/

17. Wearable Device for Blind People Could be a Life Changer | NVIDIA Blog. https://blogs.nvi dia.com/blog/2016/10/27/wearable-device-for-blind-visually-impaired/

18. The vOICe - New Frontiers in Sensory Substitution. https://www.seeingwithsound.com/

19. SpotSense - Geofencing for iOS. https://spotsense.io/

20. Using Data-Driven Insights to Reinvent the In-Store Experience. https://www.intel.com/con tent/www/us/en/retail/rfid-sensor-platform-retail.html

21. Calagari, K., Elgharib, M., Shirmohammadi, S., Hefeeda, M.: Sports VR content generation from regular camera feeds. In: ACM Multimedia, pp. 699–707 (2017)

22. Pop, C.: The modern olympic games–a globalised cultural and sporting event. Procedia Soc. Behav. Sci. **92**, 728–734 (2013)

23. Lee, B.J., Kim, T.Y.: A study on the birth and globalization of sports originated from each continent. J. Exerc. Rehabil. **12**, 2–9 (2016). https://doi.org/10.12965/jer.150248

24. Beck, D.: Media Representation: Sports. In: The International Encyclopedia of Media Effects. Wiley (2017)

25. Kim, K., Cheong, Y., Kim, H.: The influences of sports viewing conditions on enjoyment from watching televised sports: an analysis of the FIFA world cup audiences in theater vs. home. J. Broadcast. Electron. Media **60**, 389–409 (2016)

26. VR. http://www.nba.com/vr
27. Panchanathan, S., McDaniel, T., Tadayon, R., Rukkila, A., Venkateswara, H.: Smart stadia as Testbeds for smart cities: enriching fan experiences and improving accessibility. In: International Conference on Computing, Networking and Communications, pp. 542–546 (2019)

Implementing Robotic Platforms for Therapies Using Qualitative Factors in Mexico

Pedro Ponce[1]([✉]), Edgar Omar Lopez[2], and Arturo Molina[2]

[1] Tecnologico de Monterrey, Writing Lab, TecLabs, Vicerrectoría de Investigación y Transferencia de Tecnología, 64849 Monterrey, NL, Mexico
`pedro.ponce@tec.mx`
[2] Escuela de Ingeniería y Ciencias, Tecnologico de Monterrey, Ave. Eugenio Garza Sada 2501, 64849 Monterrey, NL, Mexico
`{edlopez,armolina}@tec.mx`

Abstract. In recent years, robotic platforms (RP) have been implemented to assist human beings during therapeutic treatments. As a result, successful experimental cases have been reported around the world. However, there is not enough information about them being implemented in developing countries where nobody is familiar with RPs. Moreover, there are economic, cultural, and technological factors that must be satisfied to provide therapy in rehabilitation centers or hospitals in Mexico. On the other hand, there are several RPs that are directly derivative without including those three factors, so occasionally they do not achieve good results in Mexico resulting in the exclusion of RP from the therapy. Nevertheless, in developing countries, it is urgent to implement successful RPs because the birth and death rates are swiftly incrementing; therefore, RPs could be an excellent alternative for increasing the number of therapies that can be provided at hospitals or rehabilitation centers where there are not enough therapists. As a result, implementing an effective RP in a developing country is related to economic, cultural, and technological factors, which cannot always be measured, to make decisions regarding its design. Therefore, a qualitative analysis that allows the presentation of a general guide to implementing RPs in developing countries such as Mexico is required. To assess the proposed qualitative guide, some RPs were implemented in Mexico City. Moreover, this robotic platform could be adapted for several tasks such as an education platform since this robotic platform could deal with end user needs.

Keywords: Robotic platform · Cultural factor · Technical factor · Economic factor · Therapy · Qualitative guide and educational innovation

1 Introduction

1.1 Robotic Platforms in Mexico

Robotic platforms (RP) that are implemented in developing countries such as Mexico are sometimes designed based on economic factors because the cultural and technological

T. McDaniel et al. (Eds.): ICSM 2019, LNCS 12015, pp. 123–131, 2020.
https://doi.org/10.1007/978-3-030-54407-2_11

factors have already been adapted to the requirements. However, economic, cultural, and technological factors must be integrated into an RP at the beginning of the design process. Moreover, when the RP is implemented, an iterative process for defining the final version of it must take place. On the other hand, in Mexico, there is a strong preference for technology that is considered cheap, reliable, accessible, and easy to use. Besides, the conditions of usability and functionality must be accomplished to reach a successful RP and human–machine interface. Therefore, implementing an RP in Mexico requires some empirical rules that can be followed when it is deployed. These rules will be presented in the succeeding sections of this paper. In addition, there are basic mistakes that must be avoided. For instance, when an RP is designed for children with autism, the first end-user is not a child with autism but the therapist because he or she is the person who approves and assesses the RP. After that, the requirements of the child with autism should be fulfilled. Besides, it is difficult to solve all of the requirements from both sides since the RP budget is usually limited. Moreover, there are cultural factors that need to be included to have a useful RP; those factors also must be incorporated in the initial design of the RP. This paper defines the cultural factors as primary factors that allow the adoption of an RP in a short period of time. For example, when therapists are not familiar with RPs, it is necessary to introduce the RP through technologies that are familiar to them, such as mobile phone applications ("apps"), to provide a first contact with the RP. This additional requirement increments the cost of the RP, but implementing it is essential (Fig. 1).

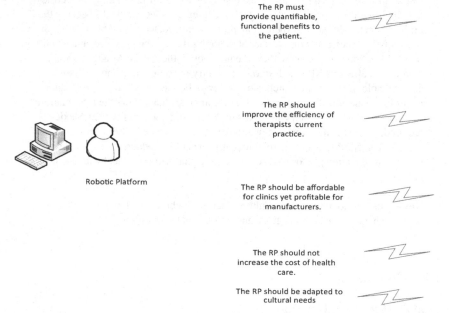

Fig. 1. Economic, cultural, and technological factors for implementing a robotic platform derived from [1].

Consequently, when an RP is implemented in Mexico, one of the main constraints is the cultural factors because they would not directly add value to the therapy. However, if the cultural factors are not included in the RP, they could interrupt its adoption. In general terms, we define qualitative factors as follows:

Cultural factors: They are the qualitative factors that are not directly connected to the technical problem that has been solved. However, they could decide whether the RP is adopted.

Technological factors: They are the qualitative factors that are directly linked to the therapy requirements.

Economic factors: They are the qualitative factors that restrict the design according to the assigned budget.

1.2 Implementing Robotic Platforms

In the beginning, the three qualitative factors have the same hierarchical level, so they should be considered equal in terms of the robotic design. Therefore, the first step is to generate a list of the main requirements of each qualitative factor and try to identify the primary end user. Then, it is necessary to look for overlapping conditions between the requirements of each factor. If overlapping between requirements does not occur, one must consider whether all of them can be fulfilled. If all of them cannot be fulfilled and they are not overlapped, a hierarchical approach should be taken. In the case of Mexico, the first factor that should be fulfilled is the cultural factor; sometimes, this factor is not directly linked with the technological factor. However, if the cultural factor is not fulfilled, the platform will not be adopted. The second and third qualitative factors are the technological and economic factors, respectively. It could be a serious mistake to define the economic factor as the fundamental factor during the design process of an RP. This does not mean that it should not be considered; however, it is not the primary factor.

The robot used in the study helped to provide therapies for children with autism [2]. Table 1 depicts the three main qualitative factors that were included.

Table 1. Qualitative factors

Technological factor	Cultural factor	Economic factor
Pressure sensor for interacting with children	Parents are not familiar with robots	Parents require a low price for adopting the robot
Visual image processing for detecting the distance and facial expressions of children	Therapists do not accept the robot because they prefer to use conventional tools	The therapists require a low cost for adopting the robot
The robot's facial movements for interaction with children	The hospitals are not familiar with using robots	The body of the robot has to be designed using low-cost materials
The robot's body movements for interacting with children	The community is not familiar with robots	The social programs need low-cost robots

The robot had to be designed using these factors. Table 2, therefore, shows the actions taken for each specific factor, based on Table 1.

Table 2. Actions taken according to the qualitative factors

Technological factor	Cultural factor	Economic factor
Pressure sensors were added in the body and face	An application ("app") was designed to familiarize the parents with robots	The robot can be fabricated using a 3D printer, so the manufacturing process is cheap and easy
A video camera was included in the robot	An app was designed to familiarize the therapist with robots	The control algorithms run on a low-cost microprocessor
DC servomotors were included in the face for moving it	To familiarize hospitals, programmed visits using the robot were done	The robot's body is made of low cost materials
DC servomotors were included in the body to enable movement	Some interviews and promotional articles were done	The mass production of the robot is not considered, but a 3D printer can produce it

Figure 2 illustrates the body of the robot, which was generated using a 3D printer. Figure 3 depicts the image processing system using a low-cost video camera.

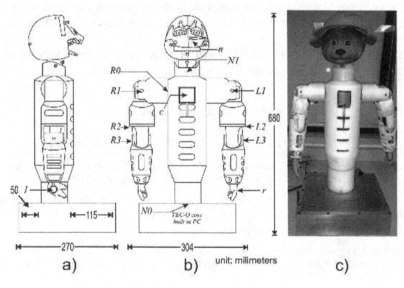

Fig. 2. Robot structure (body).

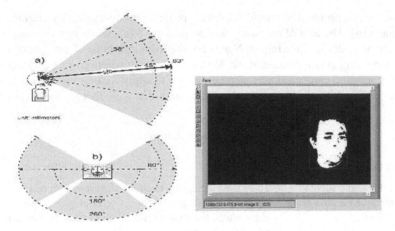

Fig. 3. Low-cost image processing system.

Figure 4 shows the app for mobile devices, which was used to familiarize people with robots. This app helped to connect the parents, therapist, and RP.

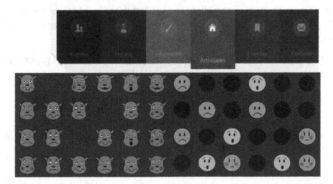

Fig. 4. App for mobile devices.

For this RP, the app was considered the fundamental element for fulfilling the cultural factors and sensors, while the robot's body and signal processing system were considered secondary elements. When the RP was implemented without the app, its adoption rate was quite low. On the other hand, when the app was included with the RP, it allowed familiarization of the end-user with the RP. Consequently, they were more comfortable using the RP and adopted it more easily.

2   Case Studies with Nao

By 2010, the number of older (over 65 years) adults in Mexico had increased to about 7 million people. That number is expected to grow to as many as 28 million people by 2050. This growth is closely related to the number of people diagnosed with dementia in the country, which has an incidence of 4.6 million documented new cases per year [3–5].

To tackle this problem, a multidisciplinary project was developed by engineers and geriatricians [6]. The aim of our study was to provide information to the caregivers of older adults with dementia using the Nao robot (SoftBank Robotics®) and standardized information with general content about dementia [7, 8]. In addition, a direct interaction between robots and caregivers was also performed to apply a caregiver burden test.

Table 3 depicts the three main qualitative factors that were included in the study.

Table 3. Qualitative factors

Technical factor	Cultural factor	Economical factor
Software that could serve as a simple interface for answering questionnaires	There is an increasing need for health specialists to care for older adults, but patients need personal contact	Investment in new technologies is difficult to obtain in public hospitals
How to evaluate caregivers to know how they feel about their sick relatives	Caregivers do not accept robots because they are not used to interacting with technologies	It is necessary to have specialists or engineers in areas of information, communication, and technology (ICT)
Sometimes, older adults have difficulty hearing, owing to some degree of deafness	Specialists are not familiar with using robots	Maintenance of an RP is expensive
Workshops must be given to caregivers and seniors	Geriatric hospitals in Mexico usually do not have advanced technology related to robotics	Social programs need low-cost robots

Figure 5 illustrates the workshop session with older adults. Figure 6 shows the "App for Caregivers" interview.

Fig. 5. Attendees of dementia presentation.

Fig. 6. Bluetooth application for Caregiver Burden Inventory questionnaire.

Table 4 shows the actions performed for each specific factor, based on Table 3.

Table 4. Actions according to qualitative factors

Technical factor	Cultural factor	Economical factor
A Bluetooth application was developed for Android, to be used with the patients so that the robot could ask every question and the person would be able to respond with predefined answers on a dedicated tablet. It also provided the option of repeating the question whenever asked	Thinking about the acceptance and approach of the project, this was divided into two sections. The first one was a spoken. After the session, five individuals from the crowd were chosen to have a private conversation with the robot. This was the second section	Considering the number of workshops that the RP can give, the cost could be viable
The data collected from the Zarit questionnaire [9] is interpreted by the geriatrician. Meanwhile, after the interview, the robot uses a small stage of fuzzy logic to separate the total score of the questions and give a prediagnostic to the patients, dividing them into low, moderate, or high severity. It provides a few tips, if required, depending on the results of each question	We developed a presentation in which the robot could provide people with some knowledge about dementia with relevant information about the illness, its phases, the normal behaviors that people have, and how to react in certain events	Agreements between health institutions and universities and research centers could generate social service projects, for example
Although the threshold of the robot was put to the maximum, such as the volume, occasionally a person had to ask the questions because, ultimately, it was not possible with the robot	Each step of the procedure was completed under the direction of medical experts in the field, and there were prior sessions for familiarization with the robot	The proper use of PRs and the contracting of policies by distributors should be characteristic of these proposals
An oral presentation on dementia and how the relatives should deal with it was given to attendees	Appointments were made with the management of the geriatrician to provide authorization as well as an explanatory brochure and demonstrations of the robot	New RPs must be found that have the necessary fundamental characteristics that the Nao robot presented

One problem surfaced in the question-and-answer portion of the presentation of dementia information to the caregivers, during which they could ask any question to the Nao robot. The physician typed the answers into a computer, and these were received by the robot, which responded to the caregiver. The questions were more about the robot than about the information session, and even when they understood the purpose of the presentation, the caregivers preferred to ask questions about the robot itself. Somehow, this behavior showed that the interest of the audience was in the interaction with the robot and the potential use of it, rather than in the content.

More issues arose during the personal interviews. Two of the subjects did not know the reason for the study, even when it was explained to them by the head physician. One of them had deceased relatives who had suffered the same illness, though they were not able to remember how they felt about it. Another had a high degree of deafness, so he was not able to hear the questions of the robot no matter how many times the question was repeated. Ultimately, one of the students who were part of the project had to ask the questions himself because it was not possible with the robot.

3 Discussion for Expanding This Platform into Educational Applications

When this robotic platform was created, it was designed with a great deal of flexibility in the structure. Thus, the structure could be used for teaching undergraduate students by changing the final application or using it as a final project, and students must deal with a real social project as is presented in [10] in which NAO robots tackle a social integration problem. In addition, this type of application could be expanded to classes that are involved with robotics as shown in [11]. When utilizing this type of real social problem, top technologies for teaching classification systems can be taught such as deep learning [12]. Hence, the theoretical classes could be improved since they have elements that are complemented in laboratory classes [13]. It is important that this platform deal with the end-user needs in education and design, and that the technical targets be defined in order to cover the cultural requirements from teachers, parents, and other people who are involved so that students learn to integrate those requirements into the solution. Hence, designing a robotic platform is an integral strategy process, which requires increased knowledge about qualitative factors such that the proposed platform could be considered as a reference frame for teaching qualitative parts of a design system. As a result, a similar process and structure could be expanded to an educational robotic platform for designing robot solutions to social problems since this also requires the inclusion of cultural, economic, and technological issues that occur during the design of an educational robotic platform. These qualitative factors could be employed to avoid difficult abstract design and methodologies when a robotic platform is implemented in education.

4 Conclusion

When an RP is implemented, several design factors must be considered to achieve the main technical goals. However, there are economic and cultural factors which should also be included. This research demonstrated how those factors affect the design of the platform as well as its adoption.

This work presented clear examples of where the economic and cultural aspects should be considered for complete acceptance of RPs and their potential use. Furthermore, it illustrated how those factors are connected to one another and cannot be disconnected during the design process; if they are disconnected or isolated, the RP would not be useful or accepted.

Acknowledgment. The authors would like to acknowledge the financial and the technical support of Writing Lab, TecLabs, Tecnologico de Monterrey, Mexico, in the production of this work.

References

1. Lum, P., Reinkensmeyer, D., Mahoney, R., Rymer, W.Z., Burgar, C.: Robotic devices for movement therapy after stroke: current status and challenges to clinical acceptance. Top Stroke Rehabil. **8**(4), 40–53 (2002)
2. Ponce, P., Molina, A., Grammatikou, D.: Design based on fuzzy signal detection theory for a semi-autonomous assisting robot in children autism therapy. Comput. Hum. Behav. **55**, 25–42 (2016)
3. de Población, C.N.: Diagnóstico socio-demográfico del envejecimiento en México (2011)
4. Wu, Y.H., Wrobel, J., Cornuet, M., Kerhervé, H., Damnée, S., Rrigaud, A.S.: Acceptance of an assistive robot in older adults: a mixed-method study of human-robot interaction over a 1-month period in the living lab setting. Clin. Interv. Aging **9**, 801–811 (2014)
5. Gutiérrez Robledo, L.M., Cruz, A.: Plan de acción alzheimer y otras demencias México 2014. J. Neurosurg. Sci. **151**, 667–673 (2015)
6. Nava, A., Pérez, M., Lopez-caudana, E.: Use of NAO robot in training of primary care clinicians for treatment of elderly patients. J. Lat. Am. Geriatr. Med. **3**(2), 53–56 (2017)
7. Pérez Martínez, V.T., De La Vega Pazitková, T.: Repercusión de la demencia en los cuidadores primordiales del policlínico "Ana Betancourt". Rev. Cuba. Med. Gen. Integr. **26**(2) (2010)
8. Ferrer, J.G., et al.: La sobrecarga de las cuidadoras de personas dependientes: análisis y propuestas de intervención psicosocial. Población **1**(557), 3–7 (2006)
9. Novak, M.: Application of a multidimensional caregiver burden inventory. Gerontologist **29**(6), 798–803 (1989)
10. Shamsuddin, S., Yussof, H., Ismail, L.I., Mohamed, S., Hanapiah, F.A., Zahari, N.I.: Humanoid robot NAO interacting with autistic children of moderately impaired intelligence to augment communication skills. Procedia Eng. **41**, 1533–1538 (2012)
11. Shin, J.E., Shin, D.H.: Robot as a facilitator in language conversation class. In: Proceedings of the Tenth Annual ACM/IEEE International Conference on Human-Robot Interaction Extended Abstracts, pp. 11–12. ACM, March 2015
12. Albani, D., Youssef, A., Suriani, V., Nardi, D., Bloisi, D.D.: A deep learning approach for object recognition with NAO soccer robots. In: Behnke, S., Sheh, R., Sariel, S., Lee, D.D. (eds.) RoboCup 2016. LNCS (LNAI), vol. 9776, pp. 392–403. Springer, Cham (2017). https://doi.org/10.1007/978-3-319-68792-6_33
13. Chang Herrera, A.N.: Diseño y Simulación de un Robot Articular con seis grados de Libertad utilizando el Toolbox Robotics de Matlab para fortalecer las clases teóricas realizando prácticas de laboratorio con el software presentado en este proyecto. Bachelor's thesis, Quito (2014)

Foveated Haptic Gaze

Bijan Fakhri[1]([✉]), Troy McDaniel[1], Heni Ben Amor[2], Hemanth Venkateswara[1], Abhik Chowdhury[1], and Sethuraman Panchanathan[1]

[1] The Center for Cognitive Ubiquitous Computing, Arizona State University, Tempe, AZ 85281, USA
bfakhri@asu.edu
[2] The Interactive Robotics Lab, Arizona State University, Tempe, AZ 85281, USA
https://cubic.asu.edu/
https://interactive-robotics.engineering.asu.edu/

Abstract. As digital worlds become ubiquitous via video games, simulations, virtual and augmented reality, people with disabilities who cannot access those worlds are becoming increasingly disenfranchised. More often than not the design of these environments focuses on vision, making them inaccessible in whole or in part to people with visual impairments. Accessible games and visual aids have been developed but their lack of prevalence or unintuitive interfaces make them impractical for daily use. To address this gap, we present Foveated Haptic Gaze, a method for conveying visual information via haptics that is intuitive and designed for interacting with real-time 3-dimensional environments. To validate our approach we developed a prototype of the system along with a simplified first-person shooter game. Lastly we present encouraging user study results of both sighted and blind participants using our system to play the game with no visual feedback.

Keywords: Assistive technology · Haptics · Sensory substitution · Video games

1 Introduction

Virtual worlds are becoming ubiquitous as digital technology permeates society, with augmented and virtual reality being the latest and most immersive manifestations. Unfortunately, the visual domain is central to most virtual worlds, making them inaccessible to people with visual impairments. People with visual impairments already face accessiblity hurdles when using technology but virtual worlds remain one of the most inaccessible mediums. Two competing approaches exist to correct this dilemma. Designers of virtual worlds develop the environments with accessibility in mind in the first approach. Secondly, accessiblity engineers develop tools to make existing virtual environments accessible. While the first approach is gaining traction and public awareness, developers of virtual environments seem to have been excused of this responsibility as accessible virtual environments remain extraordinarily scarce. The second approach has the

© Springer Nature Switzerland AG 2020
T. McDaniel et al. (Eds.): ICSM 2019, LNCS 12015, pp. 132–144, 2020.
https://doi.org/10.1007/978-3-030-54407-2_12

potential to affect many existing environments. An example of the effectiveness of the second approach is screenreader technology. Screenreaders made digital text and many of the invaluable capabilities of smartphones accessible to millions of people with visual impairments.

In the same vein, we aim to develop transformative technologies to make virtual worlds as accessible to people with visual impairments as text-based ones. Mimicing the characteristics of the human visual system that make it so well-suited for interacting with 3-dimensional environments, we developed "Foveated Haptic Gaze", an intuitive method for exploring visual environments with the sense of touch. "Foveated Haptic Gaze" makes use of an attentional mechanism similar to foveated vision that allows users to focus on objects while simultaneously allowing for peripheral awareness. This combination gives users the ability to explore an environment in detail while maintaining broader situational awareness, making "Foveated Haptic Gaze" one of the only vision-to-haptic interfaces flexible enough to generalize to the real world.

To validate our approach, we developed a first-person shooter game based on Doom, a working prototype of the Foveated Haptic Gaze system, and performed a user study with both individuals that are sighted and individuals with visual impairments. Seeking to develop an approach that is useful to people with limited or no sighted priors, our user study measured the in-game performance of both populations to understand the effects sighted priors have on our approach. Additionally, we sought to understand any nuances of non-sighted human-computer interaction for 3D visual environments that could inform future approaches.

      (a)   (b)   (c)

Fig. 1. User's hand position determines where they are gazing: (a) Gazing at leftmost plant (b) Gazing at middle plant (c) Gazing at rightmost plant

2   Related Works

2.1   Non-visual Games

Accessiblity in games is becoming more and more popular. It is no longer uncommon to find color-blind friendly settings in games as well as subtitles and other accessibility features. An example of this in the context of virtual reality is See-ingVR, a suite of VR tools for making VR environments more accessible to people with low vision [25]. Truly non-visual video games though have yet to become mainstream. While non-visual video games are few and far between, there does exist a small collection. Some of the first non-visual video games were developed for academic purposes such as the Audio-based Environment Simu-lator (AbES) games. AbES is a software suite designed to improve real world navigation skills for people with blindness [5]. AudioDOOM and AudioZelda [16,20] were developed using AbES. AudioDOOM is one such AbES game that discritized a 3D environment into voxels that a user's avatar (and other enti-ties) can move through via adjacent voxels. Users could interact with entities such as monsters by fighting them when in the same voxel, although no aiming mechanics were involved. After playing the game, children were asked to recreate the virtual environment using legos rendering promising results for the develop-ment of spatial awareness in the virtual world. In AudioZelda, users navigate a college campus collecting items to develop familiarity with the campus' lay-out. A more recent serious game for developing spatial skills is called Hungry Cat [3]. Researchers designed audio cues users could use for interacting with 3-dimensional maps. The learned layouts were confirmed using physical repre-sentations similar to the validation of learned maps in AudioDOOM. Similarly, researchers in [9] developed a completely non-visual 2D game using a haptic chair interface where the objective was to move your avatar to a goal position. This environment though did not rely on audio, users could feel the position of their avatar and the goal on their back using the haptic chair as they navigated the environment.

Non-visual games for commercial and entertainment purposes also exist. One of the most popular audio-only video games was called Papa Sangre and its suc-cessor Papa Sangre 2 [2]. The game was an immersive adventure game based on 3D audio whereby the user navigates solely by listening to their surroundings (you can hear sleeping monsters whom you must not wake by stepping on) and tapping the screen to walk through the world. Sadly the game is no longer avail-able as of this writing. A more recent iPhone app game is an audio-only "End-less Runner" game called FEER [14,18] whereby a user runs across a platform dodging enemies and collecting power-ups. FEER received high praise from the American Foundation for the Blind (AFB) [17]. Timecrest: The Door, is a story game where one's character has the power to control time and their decisions alter the course of the story [6,11]. A Blind Legend is an action-adventure game where you fight with a sword and, similar to Papa Sangre, uses a 3-dimensional sound engine to create realistic and immersive soundscapes [7]. The game has been well received by the community receiving 16,000 ratings with an average of 4.4 stars as of this writing. All of these environments were designed to be used without a visual representations from the ground up. Inversely, there have been a few efforts to make visual environments accessible via assistive technology.

2.2   General Tools for Interacting with Visual Environments

Most famously, Dr. Bach-y-Rita's work on Sensory Substitution showed that after extensive training individuals with blindness were able to interact with visual stimuli via other sensory channels. The first example of this was the Tactile-to-Vision Sensory Substitution (TVSS) system, a dental chair outfitted with actuators a seated person could feel on their back [1,24]. The next generation of these machines used electro-tactile stimulation via a tongue-display-unit [19] to make the device more portable although slightly more intrusive. Less complex, consumer grade devices have also been developed for less serious applications. Researchers Wall and Brewster compared two such devices with traditional raised-paper diagrams to assess their effectiveness in conveying visual information. The devices compared were the VTPlayer, a computer mouse augmented with braille-like pins for providing cutaneous haptic feedback and the WingMan Force Feedback mouse which provides kinesthetic haptic feedback. Researchers found raised paper to be the most effective while the WingMan Force Feedback Mouse and VTPlayer mouse were followed in effectiveness in that order. Wall and Brewster hypothesized that the combination of kinesthetic and cutaneous haptic cues of the raised paper made it most effective in conveying visual information [23].

One of the most exciting developments in this field is the emergence of Computer Vision methods that are useful for interacting with visual environments. The social media giant Facebook already performs automatic image captioning on uploaded images, updating their alt-text dynamically [13]. The explicitly "assistive" apps Google Lookout and Microsoft Seeing AI give users audio descriptions of scenes captured on a user's phone that are intended to aid in understanding their surroundings [4,15]. Lookout alerts the user of the presence of some objects and their relative location while Seeing AI has a more comprehensive toolchest, sporting document reading and illumination descriptions capabilities. While these methods are incredibly encouraging due to the richness of information they provide, their not yet real-time interfaces do not promote intuitive interaction with the visual world. They provide descriptions and summarizations of visual content, which while impressive and useful in some contexts, hinder a user's agency to explore the visual world deliberately.

One such device that encourages active exploration is the Auditory Night Sight [22]. Researchers developed a system whereby eye-tracking technology was employed to control what portion of a depth map was relayed via audio to a user's ears (tone depicted depth values). The concept of directing attention via the eyes is compelling: sighted individuals do this intuitively with gaze. But solely providing point-depth cues does little for scene understanding and peripheral awareness. To be truly useful for interacting with rich visual environments, a device must provide real-time feedback, be intuitive and exploratory in nature, and grant the user agency and focus without sacrificing the expansive situational awareness made possible by natural peripheral vision.

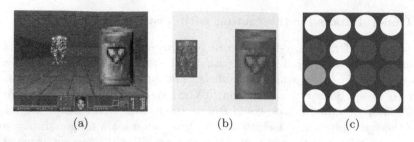

(a)   (b)   (c)

Fig. 2. (a) Original image of room (b) Objects of interest highlighted (c) Corresponding motor array activations

3 Method

Human gaze is characterized by aligning the optical axis of the eye to whatever in the visual field one is interested in. The optical axis also happens to be aligned with the fovea, an area of the retina featuring the highest density of photosentitive receptors [10]. Gazing is thus directing one's visual attention by aligning the most acute portion of the retina with whatever is of interest. The rest of the retina is responsible for peripheral vision, enabling a wide (up to 220° horizontally) spatial awareness in direct spatial relation to one's focus [21]. Thus the human visual system has the capacity for high resolution as well as expansive field-of-view thanks in part to foveated vision.

3.1 Foveated Haptic Gaze

We borrow the concept of foveated vision to develop a biologically inspired haptic implementation called Foveated Haptic Gaze (FHG). In the same way sighted individuals gaze with their eyes by pointing their foveas at objects of interest, using our system individuals with visual impairments can gaze in a visual environment by pointing their hand at objects of interest (an illustration can be seen in Fig. 1). The user wears a purpose built haptic glove (shown in Fig. 5) and when they point their hand at an object, details of the object are haptically conveyed via the glove equiped with vibration motors on the finger tips. This provides an analog to the high-resolution fovea, while a back-mounted haptic display (shown in Fig. 7a) [9] endows the user with peripheral awareness (Haptic Peripheral Vision) of their entire field-of-view. The system thus partitions a user's experience into two channels: one for high-fidelity and one for wide field of view. The back display alerts the user to the presence and coarse location of objects (obstacles, doors, persons, etc) while pointing a hand towards these objects provides the user with finer details of the object, such as the object's identity (e.g. "door", "person", etc). To integrate these two systems so that a user can relate the position of their haptic gaze with their haptic peripheral vision, the system displays the position of their gaze with respect to their field-of-view on the back display. Practically, a user feels on their back where objects

are and where their gaze currently is, moving their hand to align these indicators is essentially gazing at the object. This is akin to noticing an object in your
periphery then gazing at it for more details. To illustrate the effectiveness of our
approach we created a gaming environment with which participants can interact
with rich 3D spatial situations.

3.2   Gaming Environment

The First-Person Shooter (FPS) genre of video games was a natural choice for
testing the system's efficacy because FPSs offer a realistic simulation of the first-
person experience as well as mechanics like aiming and shooting that require keen
visuospatial awareness to play effectively. The game DOOM is one of the most
iconic and modded FPS games in existence, making it our choice for developing
experimental environments using the ViZDoom platform. ViZDoom [12] enabled
us to develop visually rich, low-overhead, and responsive DOOM environments
for use in our experiments. A system that can empower users to effectively play
a game like DOOM has the best chances of generalizing to real-world interactive
visual environments. Figure 3 shows an image of the environment from the first
person perspective.

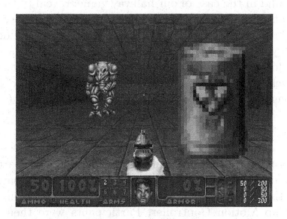

Fig. 3. Doom Environment featuring a "Hell Knight" monster on the left and explosive
barrel on the right.

We designed a level consisting of 10 connected rooms. The player runs
through the rooms encountering monsters and explosive barrels (shown in Fig. 3).
Figure 4 shows a top-down view of the rooms: there are 11 monsters and 5
explosive barrels randomly positioned in the rooms, with more monsters/barrels
occuring in later rooms. The objective is to shoot as many monsters as possible while not shooting the explosive barrels. The player's score is the difference
between the number of monsters killed and the number of explosive barrels
shot: $score = monsters - barrels$. A user willl feel the presence and position of

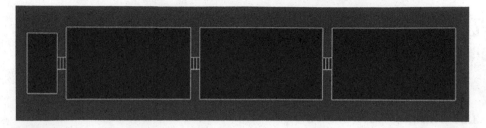

Fig. 4. Bird's eye view of the (abridged) game map used in the study. The full map consisted of 10 interconnected rooms.

monsters or barrels in their field of view on their back via the haptic display. To ascertain whether the objects are monsters or barrels, the user must gaze over the object with their hand.

3.3 System Design

A user wears a glove equiped with a button and vibration motors on the finger tips (shown in Fig. 5). The vibration motors convey information about what the user is gazing at, and in the case of our hallway game, reveal to the user whether they are gazing at a monster or a barrel. The user's hand position is tracked with a Leap Motion Controller, and the 3D coordinates of the hand are mapped onto the field of view of the player's avatar. We extract from the ViZDoom environment the location of obstacles in the avatar's field of view and map this information as well as the user's gaze position onto the haptic display on the user's back. A diagram of the whole system can be seen in Fig. 6.

3.4 Experimental Design

Five participants with visual impairments and ten sighted participants were recruited for the user study. At the beginning of the study, participants were acquainted with the hardware they would be using: haptic display (chair), haptic glove, and Leap Motion Controller. Participants were then introduced to the concept of FHG by performing an introductory exercise that activated the Leap Motion Controller and haptic display only. The participant's hand was tracked and displayed on their back using the haptic display and participants were encouraged to acquaint themselves with the limits of their field of view. The purpose of this exercise was to illustrate the mechanics of the gazing mechanism e.g. moving one's hand to the left moved their gaze to the left on their back. Next they were introduced to the concept of Haptic Peripheral Vision.

Users' avatars were placed in a room in the ViZDoom environment populated by one monster and one explosive barrel on either size of their field of view. The haptic chair relayed the locations of the monster and barrel to them by pulsating on their backs (see Fig. 2c). The location of their gaze was also conveyed by the haptic display via a solid vibration; consequently users learned

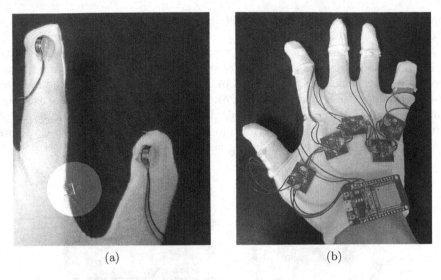

(a)   (b)

Fig. 5. (a) Pancake motors and button (highlighted) on haptic glove (b) Image of the back of the glove with motor driving hardware shown

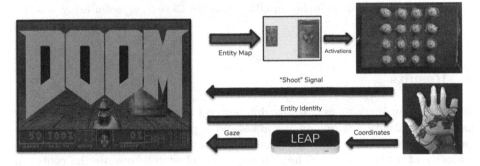

Fig. 6. Diagram of experimental setup. The ViZDoom game engine sends an entity map to the haptic display (red) to be felt by the user. The hand's movements are tracked by the Leap Motion Controller and its position is converted to gaze coordinates on the avatar's field of view. If the gaze intersects with any entities their identity is sent to the glove (blue). If the user presses the trigger button on the glove a shoot signal is sent to the ViZDoom environment and the avatar fires in the direction the user is gazing. (Color figure online)

to gaze towards the objects in the room by aligning the gaze vibrations with the pulsating "entity" vibrations on their back. Upon placing their gaze over one of the entities (monster or barrel), the identity of the entity was conveyed to the user via the glove's vibration motors in a coded manner. Users were instructed to discriminate a "monster pattern" and "barrel" pattern. After exploring the room by gazing over the entities, participants were instructed to shoot both entities. When the barrel is shot it explodes and creates a load explosion sound while shooting the monster results in a triumphant "winning" sound. These are the only audio cues in the whole game other than rhythmic game music.

After this explaination, participants were asked if they were comfortable with the interface and objective and were given the chance to enter the demo room once again, after which the experiment began. Participants entered the hallway game environment described in Sect. 3.2 and illustrated in Fig. 4 to score as many points as possible. Participants were asked to play 7 games (each taking about 1.5 min to complete) and their performance as well as auxiliary metrics (shots fired, hits, misses) were recorded during their gameplay.

(a)   (b)

Fig. 7. (a) Haptic display on office chair (b) Closeup of motor array

4   Results

To assess playability as well as any differences in usability between sighted and users with visual impairments, we measured a player's score throughout every game played. On average, sighted users obtained higher scores although the majority of users with visual impairments also clustered towards the center of the sighted performance distribution shown in Fig. 9a. Both populations saw an initial increase in performance although sighted individuals maintained an upward trajectory slightly longer while participants with visual impairments leveled off sooner. Figure 9b illustrates their performance over time. The theoretical maximum score is 11 as there are 11 monsters to destroy, although their positioning often makes them difficult to destroy due to their brief visibility.

To assess a player's ability to make decisions on-the-fly, they were instructed to avoid shooting explosive barrels, as it would negatively impact one's score. These mistakes as well as good hits and complete misses were recorded on a per-game basis. Players overal made few mistakes, many averaging below one mistake per game (Fig. 8b), indicating that the glove feedback was clear and intuitive: as a ratio of mistakes to good shots (monsters killed), most players stayed below 1/10.

Participants with visual impairments initially missed less than sighted participants, trending upwards throughout the trials eventually ending slightly higher than sighted participants (Fig. 8a). Inversely, sighted participants missed more

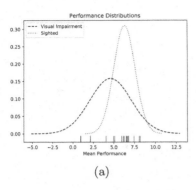
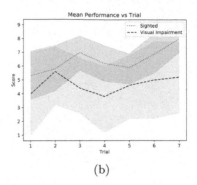

(a)   (b)

Fig. 8. (a) Misses per trial (b) Shots that hit a barrel per trial: mistakes made by participants by shooting an entity they were instructed not to shoot (c) Ratio of enemies killed to explosive barrels (mistakes) over trial. There is a large variance in performance initially for participants with visual impairments that quickly dwindles as the participants learn from their mistakes.

often from games 1 through 5, but during the last two games ended with slightly fewer average misses. These trends imply that participants with visual impairments tended to approach the game more cautiously than sighted individuals, becoming more comfortable as games went on while their sighted counterparts were more cavalier to begin with and reigned in their enthusiasm as the games progressed. This is supported by the total shot counts per trial figure, plotted in Fig. 10b, where it can be seen that sighted participants initially took many more shots than those with visual impairments.

Both sets of participants performed similarly with regards to accuracy (hits over total shots taken per game) as illustrated in Fig. 10a. Players achieved an accuracy between 70–80% during the first 5 games, indicating that the aiming and gazing mechanics of the system were usable for real-time interactions. Interestingly, sighted players' accuracy rose to touch 90% during the last two games, in tandem with their dip in misses (Fig. 8a).

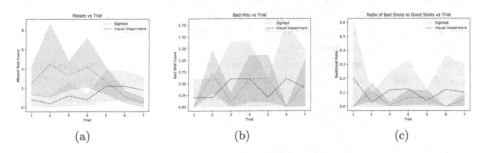

(a)   (b)   (c)

Fig. 9. (a) Normal distribution fit to the performance of both participant populations averaged over all trials (b) Performance over time averaged over participants

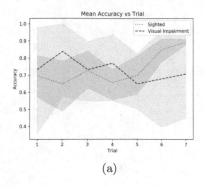
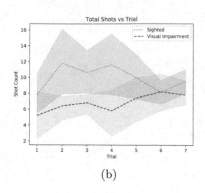

(a)   (b)

Fig. 10. (a) Accuracy over time (hits/shots taken) averaged over all participants in each populaiton (b) Total shots taken per trial, averaged over all participants in each population

5   Conclusion and Future Work

Results from our user study indicated the playability of the Doom game was maintained without vision as most participants were able to achieve respectable performance metrics and accuracies. This was supported by positive subjective user feedback with regards to the system design. Differences in performance between test groups were small, boding well for our approach having only slight sighted usability bias. A more extensive analysis is required to rule out a sighted performance bias and may inform design decisions to make the approach even more intuitive to people without vision. The results also indicate that individuals with visual impairments approached the game more cautiously, becoming less cautious over time while sighted participants approached the game with less caution and became slightly more cautious over time. Consequently, future approaches may benefit from designs that encourage confidence inspiring exploration. Furthermore, the presentation of peripheral vision information (Haptic Peripheral Vision) can likely be improved. The accuracy assessments indicate that foveated gaze feedback worked well, while destroying all 11 monsters remained difficult for both populations, as brief appearances of monsters were sometimes missed. A higher resolution haptic back display or one with wider back coverage such as the HaptWrap [8] may mitigate this by providing more salient peripheral awareness feedback.

For future work, we plan to take a more practical implementation, modifying our system for real-world use. We seek to couple the Foveated Haptic Gaze technology with computer vision techniques and wearable haptic displays such as the HaptWrap to generalize to complex real-world environments.

Awknowledgements. The authors would like to thank Arizona State University and the National Science Foundation for their funding support. This material is partially based upon work supported by the National Science Foundation under Grant No. 1828010.

References

1. Bach-Y-Rita, P., Collins, C.C., Saunders, F.A., White, B., Scadden, L.: Vision substitution by tactile image projection. Nature **221**(5184), 963–964 (1969). https://doi.org/10.1038/221963a0
2. Barry, N.: Papa Sangre - The Videogame With No Video (2011). https://www.wired.com/2011/01/papa-sangre-the-videogame-with-no-video/
3. Chai, C., Lau, B., Pan, Z.: Hungry cat—a serious game for conveying spatial information to the visually impaired. Multimodal Technol. Interact. **3**(1), 12 (2019). https://doi.org/10.3390/mti3010012, http://www.mdpi.com/2414-4088/3/1/12
4. Clary, P.: Lookout: an app to help blind and visually impaired people learn about their surroundings (2018). https://www.blog.google/outreach-initiatives/accessibility/lookout-app-help-blind-and-visually-impaired-people-learn-about-their-surroundings/
5. Connors, E.C., Yazzolino, L.A., Sánchez, J., Merabet, L.B.: Development of an audio-based virtual gaming environment to assist with navigation skills in the blind. J. Vis. Exp. (73) (2013). https://doi.org/10.3791/50272
6. DMNagel: Timecrest: The Door (2017). https://www.applevis.com/apps/ios/games/timecrest-door
7. Dowino: A Blind Legend (2019). https://play.google.com/store/apps/details?id=com.dowino.ABlindLegend
8. Duarte, B., McDaniel, T., Chowdhury, A., Gill, S., Panchanathan, S.: HaptWrap: augmenting non-visual travel via visual-to-tactile mapping of objects in motion. In: ACM Multimedia Workshop on Multimedia for Accessible Human Computer Interfaces. Association for Computing Machinery, Nice (2019)
9. Fakhri, B., Sharma, S., Soni, B., Chowdhury, A.: A low resolution haptic interface for interactive applications. In: HCI International, pp. 1–6 (2019)
10. Hudspeth, A.J., Schwartz, J., Siegelbaum, S., Kandel, E., Jessell, T.: Principles of Neural Science, 5th edn. McGraw-hill, New York (2012). https://doi.org/10.1007/s13398-014-0173-7.2
11. Inc, S.C.: Timecrest: The Door (2015). https://apps.apple.com/za/app/timecrest-the-door/id1027546326
12. Kempka, M., Wydmuch, M., Runc, G., Toczek, J., Jaskowski, W.: ViZDoom: a doom-based AI research platform for visual reinforcement learning. In: IEEE Conference on Computatonal Intelligence and Games, CIG (2017). https://doi.org/10.1109/CIG.2016.7860433, https://arxiv.org/pdf/1605.02097.pdf
13. Metz, C.: Facebook's AI Is Now Automatically Writing Photo Captions (2016). https://www.wired.com/2016/04/facebook-using-ai-write-photo-captions-blind-users/
14. Meyer, I., Mikesch, H.: FEER the Game of Running Blind (2018). http://www.feer.at/index.php/en/home/
15. Microsoft: Seeing AI (2018). https://www.microsoft.com/en-us/ai/seeing-ai
16. Mirsky, S.: Playing by Ear. Sci. Am. **300**(3), 29–29 (2009). https://doi.org/10.1038/scientificamerican0309-29

17. Pauls, J.: FEER: the game of running blind: a game review (2018). https://www.afb.org/aw/19/11/15145
18. Régo, N.: The game of running blind in FEAR (2018). https://coolblindtech.com/the-game-of-running-blind-in-fear/
19. Sampaio, E., Maris, S., Bach-y Rita, P.: Brain plasticity: 'Visual' acuity of blind persons via the tongue. Brain Res. **908**(2), 204–207 (2001). https://doi.org/10.1016/S0006-8993(01)02667-1
20. Sánchez, J., Lumbreras, M.: Virtual environment interaction through 3D audio by blind children. CyberPsychol. Behav. **2**(2), 101–111 (2009). https://doi.org/10.1089/cpb.1999.2.101
21. Szinte, M., Cavanagh, P.: Apparent motion from outside the visual field, retinotopic cortices may register extra-retinal positions. PLoS ONE **7**(10), e47386 (2012). https://doi.org/10.1371/journal.pone.0047386
22. Twardon, L., Koesling, H., Finke, A., Ritter, H.: Gaze-contingent audio-visual substitution for the blind and visually impaired. In: 2013 7th International Conference on Pervasive Computing Technologies for Healthcare and Workshops, pp. 129–136 (2013). https://doi.org/10.4108/pervasivehealth.2013.252018
23. Wall, S.A., Brewster, S.: Sensory substitution using tactile pin arrays: human factors, technology and applications. Sign. Process. **86**(12), 3674–3695 (2006). https://doi.org/10.1016/j.sigpro.2006.02.048
24. White, B.W., Saunders, F.A., Scadden, L., Bach-Y-Rita, P., Collins, C.C.: Seeing with the skin. Percept. Psychophys. **7**(1), 23–27 (1970). https://doi.org/10.3758/BF03210126
25. Zhao, Y., Cutrell, E., Holz, C., Morris, M., Ofek, E., Wilson, A.: SeeingVR: a set of tools to make virtual reality more accessible to people with low vision. In: CHI Conference on Human Factors in Computing Systems Proceedings, p. 14 (2019). https://doi.org/10.1145/3290605.3300341

3D Perception and Applications

Accurate Kidney Segmentation in CT Scans Using Deep Transfer Learning

John Brandon Graham-Knight[3], Kymora Scotland[1], Victor KF. Wong[1],
Abtin Djavadifar[2], Dirk Lange[1], Ben Chew[1], Patricia Lasserre[3],
and Homayoun Najjaran[2(✉)]

[1] The Stone Centre at Vancouver General Hospital, Vancouver, Canada
[2] School of Engineering, University of British Columbia, Vancouver, Canada
homayoun.najjaran@ubc.ca
[3] Department of Computer Science, University of British Columbia, Vancouver,
Canada

Abstract. A competitive model for kidney segmentation in CT scans is trained using the publicly-available KiTS19 dataset. The model performed well against the KiTS19 test dataset, achieving a Sørensen–Dice coefficient of 0.9620 when generating kidney segmentation masks from CT scans. The algorithm employed is U-Net, a common tool used to segment biomedical images of various modalities, including MRI and CT scans. The model is trained using nnU-Net, an open-source framework for training U-Net. To help bring Deep Learning to kidney stone diagnosis and treatment, this promising model is then applied to a dataset developed by the research team, comprised of CT scans from patients who underwent treatment for kidney stones between 2011 and 2014. Despite overall success, the model appears sensitive to changes in features between the two datasets, with some segmentation masks working very well and others unable to correctly separate the kidney from the surrounding anatomy. Improving this model further will enable advanced research in deep learning tools to aid urologists' decision making for best procedure outcomes.

Keywords: Computer vision · Machine learning · Deep learning · Bio-medical imaging · CT scans · Kidney stones · Semantic segmentation

1 Introduction

Ongoing efforts to improve pre-operative surgical decision-making and treatment planning have been aided by recent breakthroughs in the area of computer-aided analysis. The first step in this process is accurate organ segmentation [12,20]. The surgical management of kidney diseases may experience great benefit from the development of successful deep learning techniques for kidney segmentation.

Urolithiasis, or kidney stone disease, is the formation of calcifications within the kidney [18]. When kidney stones become large, obstruction in urine flow

© Springer Nature Switzerland AG 2020
T. McDaniel et al. (Eds.): ICSM 2019, LNCS 12015, pp. 147–157, 2020.
https://doi.org/10.1007/978-3-030-54407-2_13

can occur, causing extreme pain, kidney damage, and an increased risk of end-stage renal failure [1]. Epidemiologically, urolithiasis is a worldwide problem that can affect all groups and ages and is one of the major sources of morbidity globally with lifetime risk and recurrence rates increasing over the past few decades [34]. Urolithiasis currently affects about 12% of the world population at some stage in their lifetime. The relapsing rate of secondary stone formation is estimated to be 10–23% per year, 50% in 5–10 years, and up to 75% in 20 years, with increased rates for patients without medical or surgical treatment [29,37]. Urolithiasis has become progressively recognized as a systemic disorder, being associated with chronic kidney disease, nephrolithiasis-induced bone disease, increased risk of coronary artery disease, hypertension, type 2 diabetes mellitus, and the metabolic syndrome (MS) [37]. The annual expenditure for urolithiasis treatment in the United States now exceeds $5 billion, and investigations into technologies to improve urolithiasis treatment and treatment outcomes is warranted [37].

In the clinical setting, an acute episode of urolithiasis often presents with a sudden onset of cramping and intermittent abdominal and flank pain radiating laterally to the abdomen due to kidney stones traveling down or obstructing the urinary tract. Pain associated with urolithiasis is often accompanied by nausea, vomiting, and malaise; fever and chills may also be present [9]. When an obstruction occurs within the urinary tract due to a stone, the blockage of urine causes pressure within the kidney to increase causing swelling, resulting in hydronephrosis and impairment of kidney function [1]. Kidney stones that cannot be treated with conservative measures (when the patient has uncontrolled pain, when the stone is unlikely to pass spontaneously due to size or if significant hydronephrosis is present [48]) may require surgical intervention by a urologist. The evaluation of imaging is a critical component in the initial diagnosis, potential outcomes, treatment planning and post-treatment surveillance for patients with urolithiasis.

Unenhanced computed tomography (CT) was first introduced for kidney stone imaging in the 1990s and allows for the generation of a three-dimensional image of the stone and the surrounding anatomy. Since its introduction into routine urologic treatment protocols, CT imaging has emerged as the standard for the initial and subsequent evaluation of patients with suspected kidney stones, superseding radiography and intravenous urography due to its high sensitivity and specificity (>95% and >96%, respectively) for the detection of stones, easy availability, faster speed of acquisition and absence of need for administration of intravenous contrast [8,45]. The imaging produced from CT can then be reconstructed into multiple viewing planes, allowing urologists to determine some characteristics of the kidney stone (size, location, orientation, number and appearance of stones), as well as the surrounding anatomy important for surgical considerations. As kidney stones have a markedly different composition compared with renal parenchyma and urine, they absorb considerably more radiation and are easily identifiable without the need for contrast [4]. Preoperative

CT imaging can aid urologists in determining the most logical, safe, and effective treatment method for a given patient.

2 Motivation

Contemporary surgical management of kidney stones largely involves one of three procedures; extracorporeal shock wave lithotripsy (ESWL), ureteroscopy (URS) or percutaneous nephrolithotomy (PCNL). The most effective way to ensure that the patient is rendered stone-free is percutaneous nephrolithomy (PCNL). PCNL attains stone-free rates of up to 95% [10]. PCNL was originally introduced in 1976 by Fernström and Johansson, and has since become one of the main endourological treatment options for the treatment of large kidney stones [36]. As per American Urological Association (AUA) guidelines, PCNL procedures should be offered as first-line therapy for patients with a total renal stone burden > 20 mm, staghorn caliculi, or larger stones within the lower pole as PCNL offers a higher stone-free rate than extracorporeal shockwave lithotripsy (SWL) or ureteroscopy (URS) and is less invasive than open surgery or laparoscopic/robotic assisted procedures [26].

The PCNL surgical intervention involves the creation of a tract from the skin to the kidney through the flank using ultrasound and/or fluoroscopic guidance. Once the tract is in place, it is dilated to a size large enough to admit an endoscope into the kidney. The stone is then removed using a combination of ballistic, ultrasound, and suction techniques [49]. Amongst urologists, the widespread acceptance of preoperative CT imaging prior to a PCNL procedure is due to the ability to define stone burden and distribution, and provides further information regarding collecting system anatomy, position of peri-renal structures and relevant anatomic variants that need to be considered prior to intervention. Furthermore, CT may also be used to predict operative outcomes and, in some instances, stone composition [11,43,51].

Surgically, the procedures of PCNL (the puncture on the kidney, insertion of guidewires, establishment of the percutaneous tract, and the disintegration and removal of stones) are based on the appropriate image guidance provided in CT imaging. However, preoperative imaging inspection currently does not provide a conclusive picture of surgical outcomes. Although Non-contrast CT is the gold standard for the imaging of kidney stones, there are limitations with this type of imaging. The stone location visualized with CT can be described in anatomical terms, however the scans lack the surgical orientation that most urologists prefer [44]. Currently, there are no assistive technologies available to urologists that aid in determining the most suitable surgical modality to employ given a patient's CT scan. We hypothesize that such technologies in the future can aid in a urologist's decision making for best procedure outcomes.

3   Literature Review

3.1   Machine Learning, Deep Learning and the Kidney

To our knowledge, efforts at utilizing deep learning to address the issue of surgical outcome prediction have been seldom presented in peer-reviewed publications. Most of the work done has been in the area of augmented or virtual reality [7]. While there have been several publications using deep learning to address clinical questions involving the kidney, they have largely focused on medical renal disease and more specifically, kidney injury. Many of these studies did not involve kidney segmentation [24,33,47]. A single recent study used kidney segmentation to produce an algorithm for prediction of the glomerular filtration rate, a marker of kidney function [32]. At least one study looked at congenital kidney anomalies using ultrasound as the imaging modality of choice in pediatric patients [53].

The few surgically-focused reviews have largely addressed lesion identification as seen in the work of the Zhang group [52] and later work by other groups concerned itself strictly with identifying carcinoma seen in pediatric renal tumors [31] and adult cancers [2,23] or preoperative planning in cancer patients [50]. The work by Lee and colleagues specifically attempted to differentiate between benign and malignant disease. Non-malignant surgical disease has otherwise been addressed in the work of several groups who have tried to identify polycystic kidneys [19,39].

3.2   Artificial Intelligence Techniques and Urolithiasis

Kidney segmentation is an area of increased interest in the past three years [17,40]. Several groups have directed their efforts at segmentation of CT images [22,27]. The work focused on urolithiasis to date has largely concentrated on developing simulation tools for urology resident training [46] or augmented reality for preoperative planning [30]. Other studies that have been done to date in the area of kidney stones and machine learning have focused thus far on identifying kidney stones on imaging or predicting nephrolithiasis [5,16,21].

With respect to the three most popular techniques for surgical management of kidney stones, there have been recent manuscripts looking at predicting outcomes with shock wave lithotripsy [28,38]. There has been little work done in the areas of ureteroscopy or percutaneous nephrolithotomy.

3.3   Semantic Segmentation

Segmentation is the task of removing unwanted features of an image while retaining desired features. A CT scan contains much information, the entire chest cavity for example, when only a smaller section such as the kidneys is of interest. KiTS19 ([13]) is a 3D semantic segmentation challenge where labels correspond to: 0 - unwanted information; 1 kidney; and, 2, kidney cancer.

Object detection is a simpler task than segmentation, but the two are related. In an object detection task, rather than producing pixel-wise output, a bounding box is defined which contains some region of interest. If an object detection task was applied to Kidney Cancer detection, three bounding boxes might be produced: one containing the right kidney, one containing the left kidney, and one containing the cancerous tissue. Object detection, being a simpler task, is computationally cheaper to perform. It also produces a less useful result, however, since it is not as granular.

The 2017 Kaggle Data Science Bowl (DSB) was won by a team employing a 3D object detector. CT scans were combined into normalized 3D models using traditional CV techniques. Blocks of images were then fed through a neural net to identify probability that such block contained a nodule. The output of this neural network is a sequence of $32 \times 32 \times 32 \times 3$ features, where each feature is a 5-dimensional vector $(\hat{o}, \hat{d}_x, \hat{d}_y, \hat{d}_z, \hat{d}_r)$. $\hat{o}$ represents confidence that this block contains a nodule, and the remaining values represent the centroid and radius of the nodule. The blocks were then processed, without using a neural network, to combine overlapping regions. This provided a tensor of 3-dimensional bounding spheres and probabilities as its output [25]. The same general approach used to win the DSB 2017 was featured recently in a paper on lung cancer screening [3].

Many more competitions have been run with the goal of evaluating medical images. In February 2019, ten data sets were combined into a single challenge called the Medical Segmentation Decathalon [41,42]. In contrast to previous competitions, where task-specific optimisations could provide an edge, the decathalon seeks to provide a more generalisable algorithm.

The winner of the decathalon was nnU-Net [15]. In contrast with other approaches, which sought to improve neural network architecture, Isensee et. al sought to use a well known and relatively simple architecture (U-Net [35], specifically 3D U-Net [6]), but to train it very well.

4 Training the Model

3D U-Net [6] was trained using nnU-Net [15]. Training was done using 5-fold cross validation; to accomplish this, $1/5$ of the training set is withheld for evaluation in each fold. Different samples are held back in each fold. If the training loss and validation loss diverge, it is an indication that the model is overfitting. Training is stopped if there is no improvement in model performance for some time. This is repeated five times, known as folds, with the validation data set changed in each fold. This allows the algorithm to converge to five different critical points, effectively producing five different models. These models are then combined into an ensemble, which is the final result.

It takes many epochs to produce good results when training a fold. In this case, it took approximately 500 epochs for each fold; one fold took nearly 700 epochs. The code for nnU-Net [14] was used on the training data from the 2019 Kidney Tumor Segmentation Challenge [13]. 3-dimensional image segmentation is a computationally heavy task; training of nnU-Net on the KiTS19 data took over two weeks with a single Titan Xp GPU. There have been some attempts to optimize this time. One such optimization is the employment of an object detector before segmentation, which reduces the area of interest. Another optimization is to use U-Net in cascade, which is possible within the nnU-Net framework; the first phase does a coarse segmentation, and the second phase does a finer segmentation. Depending on the features present in the images, cascaded U-Net may not be wise as resolution is lost in the first stage. In this application, only the full-resolution 3D U-Net algorithm was tested. The 2D and 3D-cascaded algorithms were not used.

4.1   Training Results

Fold 1 training results are presented in Fig. 1. The other four folds show similar training results and are not presented here. The blue line indicates training loss and the red line indicates validation loss, which is calculated from the held-back port of the data set for the fold. For loss, lower is better, and the scale is on the left axis. The green line represents the evaluation metric, and in this case it is training to reasonably good results with all folds being above 0.8 and some fold exceeding 0.9; the scale is on the right axis. The folds are combined into an ensemble for final predictions.

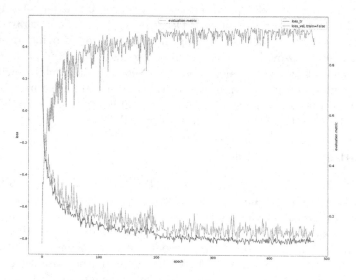

Fig. 1. Training results for fold 1

The trained model was used to predict kidney and tumor segmentations for the 90-image test data set provided by KiTS19. The resulting predictions were submitted to the competition and achieved very promising Dice scores of 0.9620 for Kidney and 0.7839 for Tumor segmentation. This indicates that the model is well trained and should generalize well to similar datasets.

5   Inferencing on Kidney Stones

5.1   Data Set

The data set in use contains information of patients who underwent percutaneous nephrolithotomy at the University of British Columbia from 2011 to 2014 Ethics approval #H14-00475. The current database includes complete information on 153 patients. This encompasses preoperative and postoperative CT data as well patient demographic, co-morbidity and surgical outcome data. CT data includes stone characteristic information. This data set was developed after receiving ethics approval from the Institutional Review Board CREB #H14-00475. This approval is ongoing under a currently running study protocol. CT images were obtained under a separate currently running protocol specifically developed for this project

5.2   Inferencing Results

Inferencing on the full data set of kidney stone CTs produced mixed results. In some cases, the model produced excellent results for kidney segmentation. One such case, and the extracted Kidney mask, is shown in Fig. 2. In many cases, however, the model was unable to interpret the CT scan and produced no segmentation. This is expected in cases where the CT scans differ from those in the source data sets; the model has not been trained on the features necessary to perform the task. One such case is shown in Fig. 3 alongside an example of the Kits19 data which was used in training. Future work will be needed to identify the differences in the scans and make the model robust to support such cases.

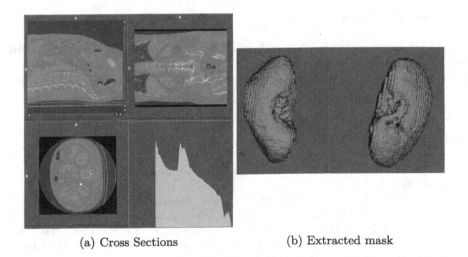

(a) Cross Sections   (b) Extracted mask

Fig. 2. Example cross sections (a) and resulting mask (b) from kidney stone data

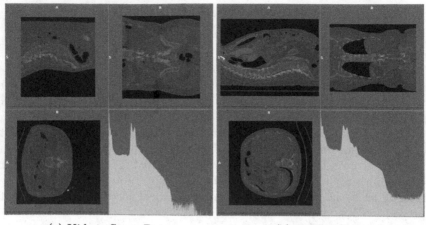

(a) Kidney Stone Data   (b) KiTS19 Data

Fig. 3. Example cross sections of kidney stone data where the model failed (a) and example cross sections of KiTS19 data (b)

6   Conclusion

Accurate kidney segmentation is a necessary requirement for automated identification of kidney abnormalities including tumors and stones. Our transfer learning technique successfully enables the segmentation of kidneys from CT images of kidney stone patients.

7   Future Work

Continued work on inferencing techniques are necessary to achieve successful kidney segmentation in the full kidney stone data set. Ultimately, there will be incorporation of imaging and patient data information into an algorithm useful for preoperative planning and outcomes prediction.

References

1. Alelign, T., Petros, B.: Kidney stone disease: an update on current concepts. Adv. Urol. **2018** (2018)
2. Amir-Khalili, A., Nosrati, M.S., Peyrat, J.-M., Hamarneh, G., Abugharbieh, R.: Uncertainty-encoded augmented reality for robot-assisted partial nephrectomy: a phantom study. In: Liao, H., Linte, C.A., Masamune, K., Peters, T.M., Zheng, G. (eds.) AE-CAI/MIAR -2013. LNCS, vol. 8090, pp. 182–191. Springer, Heidelberg (2013). https://doi.org/10.1007/978-3-642-40843-4_20
3. Ardila, D., et al.: End-to-end lung cancer screening with three-dimensional deep learning on low-dose chest computed tomography. Nat. Med. **25**(6), 954–961 (2019). https://doi.org/10.1038/s41591-019-0447-x

4. Brisbane, W., Bailey, M.R., Sorensen, M.D.: An overview of kidney stone imaging techniques. Nat. Rev. Urol. **13**(11), 654 (2016)
5. Chen, Z., et al.: Development of a personalized diagnostic model for kidney stone disease tailored to acute care by integrating large clinical, demographics and laboratory data: the diagnostic acute care algorithm-kidney stones (daca-ks). BMC Med. Inf. Decis. Mak. **18**(1), 72 (2018). https://doi.org/10.1186/s12911-018-0652-4
6. Çiçek, Ö., Abdulkadir, A., Lienkamp, S.S., Brox, T., Ronneberger, O.: 3D U-Net: learning dense volumetric segmentation from sparse annotation. In: Ourselin, S., Joskowicz, L., Sabuncu, M.R., Unal, G., Wells, W. (eds.) MICCAI 2016. LNCS, vol. 9901, pp. 424–432. Springer, Cham (2016). https://doi.org/10.1007/978-3-319-46723-8_49
7. Detmer, F.J., Hettig, J., Schindele, D., Schostak, M., Hansen, C.: Virtual and augmented reality systems for renal interventions: a systematic review. IEEE Rev. Biomed. Eng. **10**, 78–94 (2017). https://doi.org/10.1109/RBME.2017.2749527
8. Dhar, M., Denstedt, J.D.: Imaging in diagnosis, treatment, and follow-up of stone patients. Adv. Chronic Kidney Dis. **16**(1), 39–47 (2009)
9. Frassetto, L., Kohlstadt, I.: Treatment and prevention of kidney stones: an update. Am. Fami. Physician **84**(11), 1234 (2011)
10. Ganpule, A.P., Vijayakumar, M., Malpani, A., Desai, M.R.: Percutaneous nephrolithotomy (pcnl) a critical review. Int. J. Surg. **36**, 660–664 (2016)
11. Ghani, K.R., Patel, U., Anson, K.: Computed tomography for percutaneous renal access. J. Endourol. **23**(10), 1633–1639 (2009)
12. Gotra, A., et al.: Liver segmentation: indications, techniques and future directions. Insights Imaging **8**(4), 377–392 (2017)
13. Heller, N., et al.: The kits19 challenge data: 300 kidney tumor cases with clinical context, ct semantic segmentations, and surgical outcomes (2019). arXiv preprint arXiv:1904.00445
14. Isensee, F.: nn-unet source code (2019). https://github.com/MIC-DKFZ/nnUNet. Accessed 4 June 2019
15. Isensee, F., Petersen, J., Kohl, S.A., Jäger, P.F., Maier-Hein, K.H.: nnu-net: breaking the spell on successful medical image segmentation (2019). arXiv preprint arXiv:1904.08128
16. Kazemi, Y., Mirroshandel, S.A.: A novel method for predicting kidney stone type using ensemble learning. Artif. Intell. Med. **84**, 117–126 (2018)
17. Khalifa, F., Soliman, A., Elmaghraby, A., Gimel'farb, G., El-Baz, A.: 3d kidney segmentation from abdominal images using spatial-appearance models. Comput. Math. Methods Med. **2017** (2017)
18. Khan, S.R., et al.: Kidney stones. Nat. Rev. Dis. Primers **2**, 16008 (2016)
19. Kline, T.L., et al.: Performance of an artificial multi-observer deep neural network for fully automated segmentation of polycystic kidneys. J. Dig. Imaging **30**(4), 442–448 (2017)
20. Kumar, H., DeSouza, S.V., Petrov, M.S.: Automated pancreas segmentation from computed tomography and magnetic resonance images: a systematic review. Comput. Methods Programs Biomed. **178**, 319–328 (2019)
21. Längkvist, M., Jendeberg, J., Thunberg, P., Loutfi, A., Lidén, M.: Computer aided detection of ureteral stones in thin slice computed tomography volumes using convolutional neural networks. Comput. Biol. Med. **97**, 153–160 (2018)
22. Lee, H.J., et al.: Differentiation of urinary stone and vascular calcifications on non-contrast ct images: an initial experience using computer aided diagnosis. J. Dig. Imaging **23**(3), 268–276 (2010)

23. Lee, H., Hong, H., Kim, J., Jung, D.C.: Deep feature classification of angiomyolipoma without visible fat and renal cell carcinoma in abdominal contrast-enhanced ct images with texture image patches and hand-crafted feature concatenation. Med. Phys. **45**(4), 1550–1561 (2018)
24. Lee, H.C., et al.: Derivation and validation of machine learning approaches to predict acute kidney injury after cardiac surgery. J. Clin. Med. **7**(10), 322 (2018)
25. Liao, F., Liang, M., Li, Z., Hu, X., Song, S.: Evaluate the malignancy of pulmonary nodules using the 3-d deep leaky noisy-or network. IEEE Trans. Neural Netw. Learn. Syst. **30**(11), 3484–3495 (2019)
26. Lingeman, J.E., Siegel, Y.I., Steele, B., Nyhuis, A.W., Woods, J.R.: Management of lower pole nephrolithiasis: a critical analysis. J. Urol. **151**(3), 663–667 (1994)
27. Liu, J., Wang, S., Turkbey, E.B., Linguraru, M.G., Yao, J., Summers, R.M.: Computer-aided detection of renal calculi from noncontrast ct images using tv-flow and mser features. Med. Phys. **42**(1), 144–153 (2015)
28. Mannil, M., von Spiczak, J., Hermanns, T., Poyet, C., Alkadhi, H., Fankhauser, C.D.: Three-dimensional texture analysis with machine learning provides incremental predictive information for successful shock wave lithotripsy in patients with kidney stones. J. Urol. **200**(4), 829–836 (2018)
29. Moe, O.W.: Kidney stones: pathophysiology and medical management. The lancet **367**(9507), 333–344 (2006)
30. Müller, M., et al.: Mobile augmented reality for computer-assisted percutaneous nephrolithotomy. Int. J. Comput. Assist. Radiol. Surg. **8**(4), 663–675 (2013)
31. Müller, S., et al.: Benchmarking wilms' tumor in multisequence mri data: why does current clinical practice fail? which popular segmentation algorithms perform well? J. Med. Imaging **6**(3), 034001 (2019)
32. Park, J., et al.: Measurement of glomerular filtration rate using quantitative spect/ct and deep-learning-based kidney segmentation. Sci. Rep. **9**(1), 4223 (2019)
33. Parreco, J., et al.: Comparing machine learning algorithms for predicting acute kidney injury. Am. Surg. **85**(7), 725–729 (2019)
34. Pearle, M.S., et al.: Prospective, randomized trial comparing shock wave lithotripsy and ureteroscopy for lower pole caliceal calculi 1 cm or less. J. Urol. **173**(6), 2005–2009 (2005)
35. Ronneberger, O., Fischer, P., Brox, T.: U-Net: convolutional networks for biomedical image segmentation. In: Navab, N., Hornegger, J., Wells, W.M., Frangi, A.F. (eds.) MICCAI 2015. LNCS, vol. 9351, pp. 234–241. Springer, Cham (2015). https://doi.org/10.1007/978-3-319-24574-4_28
36. Sabler, I.M., Katafigiotis, I., Gofrit, O.N., Duvdevani, M.: Present indications and techniques of percutaneous nephrolithotomy: what the future holds? Asian J. Urol. **5**(4), 287–294 (2018)
37. Sakhaee, K., Maalouf, N.M., Sinnott, B.: Kidney stones 2012: pathogenesis, diagnosis, and management. J. Clin. Endocrinol. Metab. **97**(6), 1847–1860 (2012)
38. Seckiner, I., Seckiner, S., Sen, H., Bayrak, O., Dogan, K., Erturhan, S.: A neural network-based algorithm for predicting stone-free status after eswl therapy. Int. Braz. J. Urol. **43**(6), 1110–1114 (2017)
39. SharmaK, K., et al.: Automatic segmentation of kidneys using deep learning for total kidney volume quantification in autosomal dominant polycystic kidney disease. Sci. Rep. **7**(1), 2049 (2017)
40. Shehata, M., et al.: 3d kidney segmentation from abdominal diffusion MRI using an appearance-guided deformable boundary. PloS one **13**(7), e0200082 (2018)
41. Simpson, A.L., et al.: A large annotated medical image dataset for the development and evaluation of segmentation algorithms (2019). arXiv preprint arXiv:1902.09063

42. Simpson, A.L., et al.: Medical segmentation decathlon (2019). http://medicaldecathlon.com/. Accessed 12 June 2019
43. Smith, A., et al.: A nephrolithometric nomogram to predict treatment success of percutaneous nephrolithotomy. J. Urol. **190**(1), 149–156 (2013)
44. Smith, A.D.: Smith's Textbook of Endourology. Wiley-Blackwell, Hoboken (2019). 1–119-24135-9, 978-1-119-24135-5
45. Smith, R., Verga, M., McCarthy, S., Rosenfield, A.: Diagnosis of acute flank pain: value of unenhanced helical CT. AJR Am. J. Roentgenol. **166**(1), 97–101 (1996)
46. Tai, Y., et al.: Augmented-reality-driven medical simulation platform for percutaneous nephrolithotomy with cybersecurity awareness. Int. J. Distrib. Sens. Netw. **15**(4), 1550147719840173 (2019)
47. Tomašev, N., et al.: A clinically applicable approach to continuous prediction of future acute kidney injury. Nature **572**(7767), 116 (2019)
48. Türk, C., et al.: Eau guidelines on diagnosis and conservative management of urolithiasis. Eur. Urol. **69**(3), 468–474 (2016)
49. Vrtiska, T.J., et al.: Imaging evaluation and treatment of nephrolithiasis: an update. Minnesota Med. **93**(8), 48 (2010)
50. Wellens, L.M., et al.: Comparison of 3-dimensional and augmented reality kidney models with conventional imaging data in the preoperative assessment of children with wilms tumors. JAMA Netw. Open **2**(4), e192633–e192633 (2019)
51. Wickham, J., Fry, I., Wallace, D.: Computerised tomography localisation of intrarenal calculi prior to nephrolithotomy. Brit. J. Urol. **52**(6), 422–425 (1980)
52. Xia, K.J., Yin, H.S., Zhang, Y.D.: Deep semantic segmentation of kidney and space-occupying lesion area based on scnn and resnet models combined with sift-flow algorithm. J. Med. Syst. **43**(1), 2 (2019)
53. Zheng, Q., Furth, S., Tasian, G., Fan, Y.: Computer-aided diagnosis of congenital abnormalities of the kidney and urinary tract in children based on ultrasound imaging data by integrating texture image features and deep transfer learning image features. J. Pediatr. Urol. **15**(1), 75.e1 (2019)

End to End Robust Point-Cloud Alignment Using Unsupervised Deep Learning

Xuzhan Chen[1,2], Youping Chen[1], and Homayoun Najjaran[2(✉)]

[1] School of Mechanical Science and Engineering,
Huazhong University of Science and Technology, Wuhan, China
[2] School of Engineering, The University of British Columbia, Vancouver, Canada
homayoun.najjaran@ubc.ca

Abstract. The point-cloud alignment methods help robots to map their environment, recognize target objects and estimate rigid-body object poses from the 3D vision sensor data. In this paper, we propose a robust and computationally efficient approach for point-cloud alignment. Unlike the feature descriptor-based pose classifiers or regression methods, the proposed method can process an unordered point cloud by mapping it uniquely onto a particular 2D space determined based on the point cloud from the object. The model training is fully unsupervised and relies on optimizing the projection results based on a loss function. Specifically, the proposed 2D mapping enables the model to recognize objects with a simple linear classifier to increase computational efficiency. Then, the proposed method calculates the object pose in the continuous space rather than classifying the point cloud into discrete pose labels. The experiments and comparison with a well-established descriptor-based point-cloud alignment method show that the proposed method has a good performance and is robust to missing points of the point cloud. The higher performance in recognition and pose estimation precision make the method suitable for industrial robotic and automation applications.

Keywords: Unsupervised learning · Point cloud alignment · Object recognition · Object pose estimation

1 Introduction

Aligning point clouds collected by 3D sensors such as scanning LiDARs and RGB-D cameras to the standard models has potential for frontier robot applications such as object grasping, 3D scene registration, and robot navigation. To successfully align point clouds, the algorithm needs to i) recognize the object from multiple potential candidates, and ii) estimate the rigid body pose from the input point cloud. However, point-cloud alignment is still an open research topic since with a large number of candidate objects there will be a large number of similar and confusing features so that the algorithm needs to be robust to noise and missing points.

In this paper, we focus on the point cloud alignment topic. Typically, the shapes of all candidates are known. Hence, it is reasonable to assume that the CAD models or 3D

© Springer Nature Switzerland AG 2020
T. McDaniel et al. (Eds.): ICSM 2019, LNCS 12015, pp. 158–168, 2020.
https://doi.org/10.1007/978-3-030-54407-2_14

scans of the target objects are given. Our goal is then to recognize the object category and estimate the object pose based on a point cloud, simultaneously.

The intuitive methods to align point cloud builds on the shape descriptors which encode local geometry into a feature vector. Then, the corresponding points are paired based on the feature vector similarity, and the relative 6 degree-of-freedom pose is solved with respect to the rigid body translation determined by point pair matching. One of the problems is that point pairing process requires high-dimension searching, and the search time grows fast with the increasing number of candidate object features. Thus, the point pairing-based method is not well-suited for big data applications. Another problem is that the descriptor- and matching-based point cloud alignment methods highly depend on the quality of the point cloud and repeatable local features. Thus, poor quality point clouds can compromise the performance and leads to incorrect object recognition results. Also, local similarities between different objects can cause difficulties for point-cloud alignment.

Inspired by human recognition i.e., manipulating an object until the most obvious perspective is achieved, this paper introduces Deep Point Cloud Mapping Network (DPC-MN) that is designed as an end-to-end solution to obtain an optimal unique representation for the object point cloud regardless of its pose. Then, the points can be automatically paired based on their unique representation shown in Fig. 1. The DPC-MN point-cloud alignment offer two advantages i) the intra-class differences caused by various poses are omitted so recognition of the object category can be more robust, and ii) pairing is accelerated since the high-dimension searching process is removed.

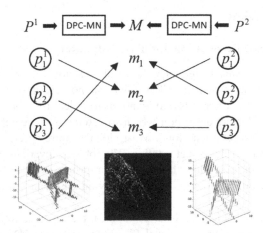

Fig. 1. The DPC-MN model pairs points of the point clouds of an object taken from different poses. P1 and P2 are the point clouds, M is a unique representation of the object, and p is a point in the point cloud.

One of the novelties of the DPC-MN model is that the point-cloud alignment is end-to-end processed by the deep learning technique and fundamentally different from the feature descriptor cascade. Aligning point clouds via the deep learning-based method is also more robust than the descriptor cascade since the feature extraction ability is learned from data instead of using a prior knowledge.

Another novelty is that the DPC-MN model can be trained unsupervised, i.e. the pose labels are not required for pose estimation. Almost similar to reinforcement learning, the proposed method learns a proper action i.e., mapping the point cloud into a unique 2D view. Then, the degree of self-occlusion of the mapping is used as the optimization objective that enables the convergence of the model training. In the end, the performance of the proposed method is also boosted by the use of machine learning and GPU accelerating technique.

The contribution of this paper can be summarized as,

1). The DPC-MN model is proposed. In this way, the point-cloud alignment is end-to-end processed by the deep learning technique and fundamentally different from the feature descriptor cascade.
2). The DPC-MN model can be trained unsupervised, i.e. the pose labels are not required for pose estimation.

The rest of the paper is organized as follows. Section 2 reviews the previous work related to pose estimation based on the 3D data. Section 3 shows the analysis of the deep point cloud mapping network model. In Sect. 4, the proposed model is verified using a 3D shape dataset available online. Section 5 summarizes the concluding remarks of this work.

2 Literature Review

2.1 Descriptor-Based Recognition and Pose Estimation

Descriptors provide a means to quantify the local and global information of the point cloud. Rusu et al. [1] proposed the VFH global shape descriptor which is based on the histogram of the object normals and invariant to object rotation. Aldoma et al. [2] introduced the CVFH feature descriptor which solved the mass center shifting problem by pre-clustering the object point cloud. Most global feature descriptors such as VFH and CVFH are invariant to the object rotation. The rotation invariant property improves recognition accuracy but also blurs the features compromising the object pose estimation. The CVFH is extended to pose estimation by adopting an additional camera roll histogram [2].

In contrast to the global feature descriptors, local feature descriptors emphasize the local geometry of the object surface. Li et al. [3] used a cascade of 3D key point detection, key point description, and key point matching. Their method can align CAD models in the dataset with the point cloud. The cascade is known as the standard framework for pose estimation with local features [4, 5].

One of the most powerful local feature descriptors for pose estimation is the point pair feature (ppf) [6]. Drost et al. [5] proposed the ppf constructed by repeatedly sampling two points from the point cloud and calculating four elements of the feature vector. Each pair of a ppf can estimate a rigid body transformation from the source and the target point cloud, and a voting strategy can be used to find the most likely pose among the calculated poses. Choi et al. [7, 8] extended the idea of ppf to the point-point pair, the point-surface pair, the surface-surface pair, and the color point pair to improve the results. In addition to designing a better feature, Hinterstoisser et al. [9] improved the voting scheme of pose estimation by introducing smart sampling. The ppf methods are dominant among the local feature-based pose estimation methods. However, the computational load of sampling and voting procedures grows fast as the number of object points increases.

2.2 Processing the Raw Point Cloud with Deep Learning

The proposed method offers two key features: i) the model uses raw point clouds, instead of latticing the shape, and ii) it can be trained via unsupervised learning. Neural networks capable of processing raw point clouds have recently drawn a lot of attention. Our previous work [10] proposed a point convolution network which recognizes objects from point cloud via the defined point convolution operation. Qi et al. [11] proposed the PointNet which yields high performance on both the object recognition and segmentation domains. Wang et al. [12] proposed the O-CNN model that leverages on the Oct-tree data structure of the point cloud. Klokov et al. [13] came up with the kd-tree based raw-point network.

However, all of these works [10–13] are based on supervised learning which requires a large labeled dataset and aims to generalize the object recognition to unseen objects within known categories. The proposed method in this paper is based on unsupervised learning which doesn't require labeled dataset to train the model. Furthermore, the proposed method focuses on object pose estimation using neural networks which have received far less coverage in the published literature. Descriptors provide a means to quantify the local and global information of the point cloud. Rusu et al. [1] proposed the VFH global shape descriptor which is based on the histogram of the object normals and invariant to object rotation. In contrast to the global feature descriptors, local feature descriptors emphasize the local geometry of the object surface. Li et al. [3] used a cascade of 3D key point detection, key point description, and key point matching. Their method can align CAD models in the dataset with the point cloud. The cascade is known as the standard framework for pose estimation with local features [4, 5].

One of the most powerful local feature descriptors for pose estimation is the point pair feature (ppf) [6]. Drost et al. [5] proposed the ppf constructed by repeatedly sampling two points from the point cloud and calculating four elements of the feature vector. Each pair of a ppf can estimate a rigid body transformation from the source and the target point cloud, and a voting strategy can be used to find the most likely pose among the calculated poses. Choi et al. [7, 8] extended the idea of ppf to the point-point pair, the point-surface pair, the surface-surface pair, and the color point pair to improve the results.

2.3 Point Cloud Recognition Using Deep Learning

The proposed method offers two key features: i) the model uses raw point clouds, instead of latticing the shape, and ii) it can be trained via unsupervised learning. Neural networks capable of processing raw point clouds have recently drawn a lot of attention. Our previous work [10] proposed a point convolution network which recognizes objects from point cloud via the defined point convolution operation. Qi et al. [11] proposed the

PointNet which yields high performance on both the object recognition and segmentation domains. Wang et al. [12] proposed the O-CNN model that leverages on the Oct-tree data structure of the point cloud. Klokov et al. [13] came up with the kd-tree based raw-point network. However, all of these works [10–13] are based on supervised learning which requires a large labeled dataset and aims to generalize the object recognition to unseen objects within known categories.

3 Method

3.1 Deep Point Cloud Mapping Network Architecture (DPC-MN)

The mapping function g is formulated by the neural network. Given a point cloud P, the mapping function will be invariant to the permutation of P. Inspired by the ideas of NiN [18] and PointNet [11], we adopted a 1×1 convolution kernel to process and extract the features of the point cloud. However, the extracted features are used to generate the mapping matrix instead of classifying the object. The architecture of the DPC-MN is shown in Fig. 2. The network aims to learn an appropriate projection matrix based on the features of the whole point cloud. The average pooling is used to generate the global feature of the point cloud because it is a symmetric operation and invariant to the set order of the point cloud.

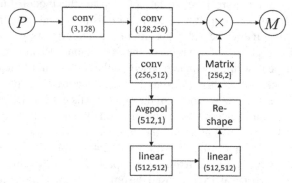

Fig. 2. The architecture of DPC-MN. The 1×1 convolution is noted by conv. (m, n) means the input feature dimension is m and the output feature dimension is n. The linear means the output feature is calculated by a fully connected layer. All layers are activated by the ReLU non-linear function. The Reshape block reshapes the 512-dimension feature into the 256×2 matrix and the mark $\times$ means to multiply the 256 dimensions "point cloud" with the 256×2 matrix. All of the layers are activated by the ReLU non-linear function.

3.2 Loss Function

The goal of the loss function is to map point cloud in different poses into the same 2D representation. In this way, the recognition of point cloud is simplified since the variation caused by the poses is removed. Three principles are designed to obtain the idealized properties of the mapping function: 1) neighborhood points in the point cloud are mapped into a tight area in 2D space, 2) the overlap of mapped shape must be minimum. 3) point clouds in different poses are mapped into the same 2D representation.

The anchor point cloud P_a is the original data collected from the 3D sensor or rendered from the CAD model. Based on the first principle, the positive point cloud P_p is generated by shifting each point in the anchor point cloud P_a within a small random δ. The negative point cloud P_n is generated by shuffling the anchor point cloud P_a so the operation is equivalent to randomly select 2 points for numbers of times. Based on the first and second principles, the function L_m is shown in (1).

$$L_m = \frac{1}{N} \sum \max\left(\left[\varepsilon + \|M_a - M_p\|_2 - \|M_a - M_n\|_2\right], 0\right) \tag{1}$$

where ε is a margin value, and M_a, M_p, M_n are the output generated by applying the proposed DPC-MN to P_a, P_p, and P_n, respectively.

Based on the third principle, the L_p is defined as,

$$L_p = \frac{1}{N} \sum \|M_a - M_i\|_2 \tag{2}$$

The loss function f is,

$$f = L_m(M_a, M_p, M_n) + \lambda \cdot L_p(M_a, M_i) \tag{3}$$

where λ is a hyperparameter that adjusts the weight of Lm and Lp.

3.3 Object Recognition and Pose Estimation

First, the model output M is regularized into a 64×64 2D grid based on the (u, v) values in M. The (u, v) value is rounded into closest integer number and taken as 2D coordinates of the bin in the grid. Then, the value of the bin will accumulate *one unit* for every (u, v) assigning to the bin. Based on the steps, the M can be converted into a 2D grid-based representation. The recognition runs on the 2D grid representation with a linear classifier. The classifier is defined by,

$$y_i = \frac{e^{\sum_{j=1}^{j=k} w_{ij} x_j}}{\sum_i e^{\sum_{j=1}^{j=k} w_{ij} x_j}} \tag{4}$$

where j is the index for the pixel in the 2D grid, i indicates the category, x is the 2D grid representation, and w_{ij} is trainable parameters for the recognition. y_i is the output score for the category i. The linear classifier can be easily trained because of the simple one-layer linear structure.

The pose of the object is calculated by finding the corresponding points in two point clouds. Because the point cloud is an $N \times 3$ matrix, we use left matrix multiplication instead of the standard form. The optimized solution of R is given in (11). The Single

Value Decomposition (SVD) method is used to ensure that R is an orthogonal matrix. The solution is based on the least squares method.

$$\hat{R} = \arg\min(\left\| \hat{S}_{pi} - S_{pi} \right\|_2) = (S_{pj}^T \cdot S_{pj})^{-1} \cdot S_{pj}^T \cdot S_{pi} \tag{5}$$

$$\tilde{R} = U \cdot V^T, where(U, S, V^T) = svd(\hat{R}) \tag{6}$$

4 Experiment Results

A. Experiment Configuration

The whole model ran on a workstation with an Nvidia GTX1070 GPU, E5 CPU, and 27 GB memory. The training and testing CAD models were taken from the ModelNet40 dataset [19]. Firstly, the point cloud is augmented by rotating about x, y, and z axes. The rotation angle is uniformly generated from 0 to $\pi/2$. For training of the network, the angle is incremented by $\pi/24$. For testing of the network, the angle is incremented by $\pi/10$. Thus, the training and testing datasets have no intersections.

The model is optimized by the SGDM solver. The learning rate is 0.001 and the momentum is 0.90. The training batch size is 16 and the maximum training epoch is 300 based on our configuration. The loss weight λ is 0.3. The training time for each epoch was about 380 s, and the model took around 40 epochs to converge.

The input models and the mapped result M for each input model are visualized in Fig. 3(a) and Fig. 3(b), respectively. The view is randomly selected from the test set because the mapped views for objects in different poses are completely identical.

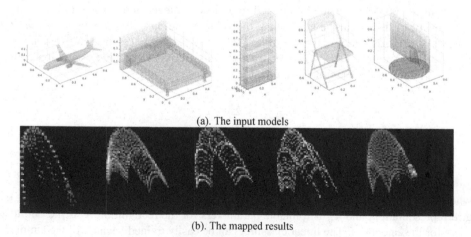

(a). The input models

(b). The mapped results

Fig. 3. The input models and mapped results

4.1   Recognizing Objects from Different Poses

The classifier is trained on the workstation with a GPU accelerator. Because all of the poses are mapped into a unique view, the model took only 2 epochs to converge and the linear classifier took 0.1 s to finish one epoch. Thus, the training time for classification was negligible.

The point cloud sparsity is a common problem for 3D sensors. The point cloud sparsity may be caused by the low resolution of the sensor or the inappropriate measuring distance. The recognition experiment is designed to simulate the sparsity of 3D sensors and verifies the robustness of the recognition algorithm. To simulate the sparsity, 10% to 90% points were randomly selected from the original complete point cloud. Figure 4 shows the downsampling point cloud for a single pose, but downsampling has been applied to the entire test dataset.

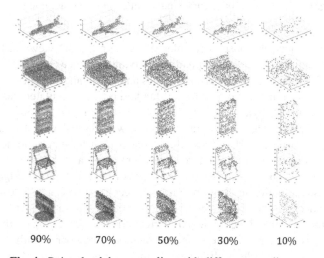

Fig. 4. Point cloud downsampling with different sampling rates

We used the linear classifier that trained on the complete point cloud to process the incomplete data. The classifier is not trained with augmented incomplete data. The proposed method is compared with the Point Pair Feature (PPF)-based point cloud alignment method in Fig. 5. The result shows that the proposed method is remarkably robust to missing points. Even with only 10% of the points, the method can still recognize objects from different poses with acceptable accuracy (more than 80%).

4.2   Estimating Object Poses

The object pose is calculated based on the cascades described in Sect. 3E. For each testing instance, the mapped result M is saved with the input point cloud P as a pair. The input point cloud P for each instance is shuffled to simulate the unordered data collected by 3D sensors.

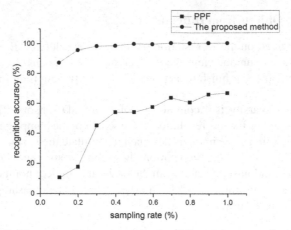

Fig. 5. The recognition accuracy under different downsampling rates

For each test object, the pose is calculated based on the 2D views of the standard pose and the test object. The standard pose refers to the reference (zero) angles, and then the test object can rotate about any arbitrary axes and at any angles. The rotation matrix R which can transform the test object to the standard pose is calculated based on (12).

The accuracy of 3D object poses is quantified by the error of the point cloud alignment. The test object rotates to the standard pose with the calculated rotation matrix R. Then, the nearest neighborhood searching tree is built to match the nearest points between the test object and the standard pose point cloud as the ICP algorithm does. The mean distance is taken as the quantified error of pose estimation. Figure 6 shows the errors of pose estimation in different poses. For each test object, 125 poses are tested as described in Sect. 3. The average error is around 0.1 unit of the object scale which is only 10% compared to the object scale. Alignment error is 1.0 unit means that the object is not successfully recognized. The proposed method is compared with the Point Pair Feature (PPF)-based point cloud alignment method in Fig. 6. The result shows that the proposed method has a better pose estimation precision and is more robust compared to the PPF-based method. Fine tuning algorithms such as ICP can reduce the error with further processing.

A real-world object alignment experiment is conducted to validate that the proposed method can be used in the sensor scanning data. A drill is scanned using a Kinect sensor. The drill model is 3D reconstructed and represented by the point cloud. Then 4 different rigid body poses of the drill is used to validate the method and the drill is scanned by the kinect sensor. The proposed method can automatically align the reconstructed 3D model to the real-world scanning data, shown in Fig. 7.

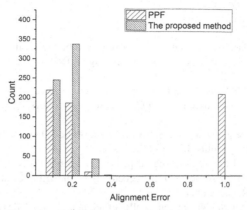

Fig. 6. The error under different poses and categories. The proposed method is compared with the Point Pair Feature (PPF)-based point cloud alignment method in Fig. 6. The result shows that the proposed method has a better pose estimation precision and recognition accuracy. Fine tuning algorithms such as ICP can reduce the error with further processing.

Fig. 7. The real-world experiment on point cloud alignment.

5 Conclusion

In this paper, we proposed a novel idea and an effective method for aligning point clouds and help robot to simultaneously recognize objects and estimate the pose of rigid-body objects. An object in different poses can be mapped into a unique 2D view from its 3D point cloud representation. Based on this idea, the 2D view can dramatically facilitate object recognition and pose estimation performance in terms of efficiency and accuracy. Deep Point Cloud Alignment Network (DPCAN) method is proposed to implement the unique 2D view mapping function. The network can be trained unsupervised by both CAD models and real point clouds of target without the need to labeling the training datasets. The proposed network is verified to be robust against missing points of the test data. Experiments showed that the model has acceptable accuracy and robustly recognize more than 80% of the objects even when only 10% of the points of the point clouds were used. Based on the proposed method, the pose can be calculated continuously instead of estimating the pose at discrete pose labels. The accuracy of the pose estimation is about 10% of the object scale which means the proposed DPCAN is sufficient for many industrial robotic and automation applications

References

1. Rusu, R.B., et al.: Fast 3D recognition and pose using the viewpoint feature histogram. In: 2010 IEEE/RSJ International Conference on Intelligent Robots and Systems (IROS). IEEE (2010)
2. Aldoma, A., et al.: CAD-model recognition and 6DOF pose estimation using 3D cues. In: 2011 IEEE International Conference on Computer Vision Workshops (ICCV Workshops). IEEE 2011
3. Li, Y., et al.: Database-assisted object retrieval for real-time 3D reconstruction. In: Computer Graphics Forum. Wiley Online Library (2015)
4. Malleus, L., et al.: KPPF: keypoint-based point-pair-feature for scalable automatic global registration of large RGB-D scans. In: Proceedings of the IEEE Conference on Computer Vision and Pattern Recognition (2017)
5. Drost, B., et al.: Model globally, match locally: efficient and robust 3D object recognition. In: 2010 IEEE Conference on Computer Vision and Pattern Recognition (CVPR). IEEE (2010)
6. Kiforenko, L., et al.: A performance evaluation of point pair features. Comput. Vis. Image Underst. **166**, 66–80 (2018)
7. Choi, C., et al.: Voting-based pose estimation for robotic assembly using a 3D sensor. In: 2012 IEEE International Conference on Robotics and Automation (ICRA). IEEE (2012)
8. Choi, C., Christensen, H.I.: RGB-D object pose estimation in unstructured environments. Rob. Auton. Syst. **75**, 595–613 (2016)
9. Hinterstoisser, S., Lepetit, V., Rajkumar, N., Konolige, K.: Going further with point pair features. In: Leibe, B., Matas, J., Sebe, N., Welling, M. (eds.) ECCV 2016. LNCS, vol. 9907, pp. 834–848. Springer, Cham (2016). https://doi.org/10.1007/978-3-319-46487-9_51
10. Chen, X., Chen, Y., Najjaran, H.: 3D object classification with point convolution network. In: 2017 IEEE/RSJ International Conference on Intelligent Robots and Systems (IROS). IEEE (2017)
11. Qi, C.R., et al.: Pointnet: deep learning on point sets for 3D classification and segmentation. In: Proceedings of the Computer Vision and Pattern Recognition (CVPR), vol. 1, no. 2, p. 4. IEEE (2017)
12. Wang, P., et al.: O-cnn: Octree-based convolutional neural networks for 3d shape analysis. ACM Trans. Graph. (TOG) **36**(4), 72 (2017)
13. Klokov, R., Lempitsky, V.: Escape from cells: deep kd-networks for the recognition of 3D point cloud models. In: 2017 IEEE International Conference on Computer Vision (ICCV). IEEE (2017)

Homography-Based Vehicle Pose Estimation from a Single Image by Using Machine-Learning for Wheel-Region and Tire-Road Contact Point Detection

Nastaran Radmehr(✉), Mehran Mehrandezh, and Christine Chan

Faculty of Engineering and Applied Science, University of Regina, Regina, SK S4S 0A2, Canada
{nrb191,mehran.mehrandezh,Christine.Chan}@uregina.ca

Abstract. Image-based metric measurement and development of traffic surveillance systems have attracted wide interests within academia and industry for the past decade due to recent advancements in computer vision and the processing power required for machine-learning. Utilization of camera vision is gaining attention in this realm, particularly due to its unobtrusiveness.

The research objective is to develop an image-based photogrammetry system for measuring vehicle lane pose using a single perspective camera with applications in law enforcement and crash-scene investigation. The proposed algorithm comprises of two steps: (1) Developing a Deep-Learning-based technique for identifying/classifying the wheels on a vehicle, as Regions of Interests (ROI), and extracting the tire-road contact point from the image, and (2) using a Homography-based approach to extract metric measurements, such as vehicle pose.

Our proposed method was tested and evaluated on a large number of images taken at different traffic inspection stations under different lighting conditions and weather differentials to demonstrate its efficiency and robustness. Results are promising. This research can pave the way towards automating the task of flagging truck bypass lanes for law enforcement and also for image-based crash-scene investigation

Keywords: Deep learning · Image-based metric measurement · Homography from images · Vehicle lane pose estimation · Wheel region extraction · Tire-road contact point extraction

1 Introduction

Increase in the vehicle population leads to a need for expansion in the novel and cost-effective monitoring and traffic-control technologies. The aim of the Intelligent Transportation Systems (ITSs) research is to integrate electronics, communication, and computer technologies into inspection systems for monitoring traffic conditions so as to enhance road safety and enforce the law.

© Springer Nature Switzerland AG 2020
T. McDaniel et al. (Eds.): ICSM 2019, LNCS 12015, pp. 169–179, 2020.
https://doi.org/10.1007/978-3-030-54407-2_15

Traffic surveillance systems using camera vision have attracted significant attention due to their easy maintenance and high reliability. Vision-based video monitoring systems have been widely investigated within academia and industry, particularly for vehicle detection and classification, [1–3].

The use of image-based metric measurements on vehicles has found its use in a variety of application domains ranging from image-based crash-scene investigation to law enforcement. Much work has been conducted on vehicle detection and pose estimation, and some relevant literature includes [4–10]. However, most of the research work have focused on images taken from the side, the rear, or the front of the vehicle in a structured environment. Furthermore, they typically adopt the conventional image processing techniques to extract physical information, which are hardly robust to lighting and weather differentials.

Iwasaki et al. [4] suggested the background subtraction using fixed cameras. In [6], a side-view wheel-region-extraction method is proposed, which takes into account the distortion in a circular fisheye image. Furthermore, directional- and Sobel-edge detectors are utilized to extract wheel region. Duron-Arellano et al. [10] analyzed the sensitivity in image-based metric measurement for vehicles' wheel base estimation by means of the Pinhole Projection and the Brown-Conrady models. Also, the idea of using multiple cameras for image-based metric measurement has been proposed due to a single camera's limited view, and the lack of depth perception. Yoneyama et al. [11] discussed the three problems of vehicle shadow suppression, occlusion, and night detection situation. They proposed a method in which a 2D joint car-shadow model is deployed for moving cast shadow elimination, while a multi-camera and rear view system are used to deal with the occlusion.

Imaging sensors, utilized for inspecting traffic, are mainly of perspective type and are used in fixed overhead locations. This can provide a wide field of view. However, a major challenge is to extract physical information from perspective images taken at different vantage points. In this study, we tackle this problem and develop a robust method for detecting wheels from an image, and extracting the tire-road contact point within the region of interest in the presence of lens distortion. We propose a method that employs multiple-Homography transformations on the image. A Deep Learning (DL) method is used first for detecting wheels and extracting tire-road contact point from images. This along with the homography-based transformation will provide precise estimations on the relative pose of the vehicles w.r.t to the road line by using only one single perspective camera.

The paper is organized as follows. Section 2 presents an overview of object detection methods using camera vision. Section 3 discusses the structure of homography transformation. Section 4 describes the overall methodology and proposed algorithm for vehicle pose estimation and provides results. Conclusions and future research directions are given in Sect. 5.

2   An Overview of Object Detection Methods Using Camera Vision

Deep learning has empowered almost every facet of computer vision research that involves machine learning. For example, technologies such as image-search engines, localization and mapping, and image segmentation have all been improved dramatically since the latest resurgence in neural networks and deep learning. Similarly, object detection, and in particular, the problem of identification, classification, and localization of objects of interest from the images/videos has made a quantum leap using deep learning. This development can be mainly attributed to the rapid development of high-performance parallel computing systems such as GPUs for treating a large amount of data.

Before the emergence of Convolutional Neural Networks (CNNs) in the field of computer vision, hand-engineered features were used to quantify the contents of an image. The methods used for object detection included: (i) Support Vector Machine (SVM) with Histogram of oriented gradients (HOG) features [12], and (ii) Deformable Parts Models (DPMs) [13], which uses root and part templates to detect bounding boxes. In both methods, a hand-designed algorithm was used to extract features (i.e., shape, color, texture, etc.). The quantified features then served as inputs to the machine learning models.

Till about 2012, approaches for object detection and classification mainly depended on these hand-engineered features. Consequently, defining a set of rules and algorithms correctly to extract good feature was critical for achieving high accuracy. In 2012, Krizhevsky et al. introduced the first large-scale deep convolutional neural network called AlexNet to classify 1.2 million images into 1000 classes. AlexNet outperformed all previous non-deep-learning-based approaches with significant precision reported in the ImageNet Large Scale Visual Recognition Challenge (ILSVRC). This turning point is marked as the dawn of utilizing deep learning in computer vision [14].

Later on, ConvNets started to become the standard approach for general object detection tasks. Girshick et al. [15] proposed Region-based Convolutional Network (R-CNN) for the object classification and localization. This method adopts the selective search approach [16] to extract 2000 region proposals instead of exhaustively searching in an image to extract object locations. Additionally, extracted region proposals for each image are resized to the input size of CNN (AlexNet) and then passed through the ConvNet. The pre-trained CNN acts as a feature extractor and computes features for each region proposals and outputs a 4096-dimensional feature vector for each proposed region. Then, the extracted feature is passed into the Support Vector Machine (SVM) for classifying the object based on a given vector of features. Girshick et al. indicates that CNN is capable of achieving better result than methods such as HOG which relies on low-level features. However, this CNN pipeline is hard to train and needs a huge amount of time and memory as it classifies 2000 region proposals per each image. The method also suffers from test- time latency, which makes it unsuitable for real-time applications. By sharing computation and relying on a Region Proposal Network (RPN) instead of the Selective Search, Fast R-CNN [17] and Faster R-CNN are able to achieve higher accuracies and lower test- time latencies overall. Fast R-CNN and Faster R-CNN [18] achieve 70.0 and 73.2 mAP on the PASCAL VOC 2012 test set respectively. Nevertheless, one of the biggest concerns of the R-CNN family of networks is their test time latency. The networks are incredibly slow, and the fastest version, which is Faster R-CNN, can provide only 5 FPS on a GPU. Instead of having a sequential pipeline of region proposals to localize and classify the object, YOLO [19] treats the overall problem as a regression problem to predict the bounding boxes and class probabilities associated with them by using a single ConvNet. This approach leads to a much lower test- time latency compared to that in others, however, at the cost of leading to a lower accuracy. Nevertheless, YOLO has gone through a number of version improvements. The latest version, i.e., is YOLOv3 [20], performs at par with other state of the art detectors like RetinaNet [21] in terms of accuracy, while being significantly faster, verified under the COCO mAP 50 benchmark tests. Moreover, YOLOV3 surpasses the SSD [22] model and its variants. In this paper, we focus on the third version of object detection algorithm from the YOLO family, which is YOLOV3 [20]. To the best of our knowledge, this is the most promising algorithm by far that requires low computational power while achieving a high enough accuracy.

3   Homography Transformation

Invertible mapping of points and lines on the projective plane is called homography. Considering a point x in one image and x' in another image, projective transformation is a linear transformation on homogeneous 3-vectors [23] (Fig. 1):

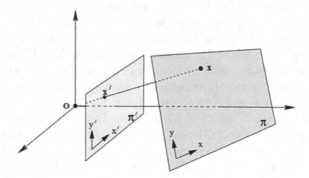

Fig. 1. The projection maps points on one plane to points on another plane.

$$\begin{pmatrix} x'_1 \\ x'_2 \\ x'_3 \end{pmatrix} = \begin{pmatrix} h_{11} & h_{12} & h_{13} \\ h_{21} & h_{22} & h_{23} \\ h_{31} & h_{32} & h_{32} \end{pmatrix} \begin{pmatrix} x_1 \\ x_2 \\ x_3 \end{pmatrix} \tag{1}$$

or in brief,

$$x' = Hx. \tag{2}$$

where H is a 3×3 non-singular homogeneous matrix. The projective transformation has eight degrees of freedom and it projects every line and point into a projectively equivalent line and point, leaving all its projective properties invariant. By assuming a pair of matching points x and x' in the world and the image plane be (x, y) and (x', y') respectively, each point correspondence provides two constraints

$$x' = \frac{x'_1}{x'_3} = \frac{h_{11}x + h_{12}y + h_{13}}{h_{31}x + h_{32}y + h_{33}}, y' = \frac{x'_2}{x'_3} = \frac{h_{21}x + h_{22}y + h_{23}}{h_{31}x + h_{32}y + h_{33}} \tag{3}$$

Or:

$$x'(h_{31}x + h_{32}y + h_{33}) = h_{11}x + h_{12}y + h_{13}$$
$$y'(h_{31}x + h_{32}y + h_{33}) = h_{21}x + h_{22}y + h_{23}.$$

(4)

Therefore, four-point correspondences lead to eight linear equations involving the elements of H. Assuming no three points are collinear, H can be computed uniquely, and it can be then applied to the entire image to undo the effect of perspective distortion on the selected plane. Most homography methods are based on multiple images and they would also require knowledge of the camera's intrinsic parameters and the pose of the plane in advance. In this paper, a calibration-free approach is used to attain an accurate Inverse Perspective Transformation (IPM) of the road, through which a "bird's eye" view of the target road, as well as parallel lanes, are obtained. Perspective correction along with deep learning-based wheel detection is applied to the perspective image to detect the ROI more efficiently. Since the ground and the side are not in the same plane, two separate projective transformations are applied to rectify the side and ground.

4 Proposed Algorithm for Vehicle Pose Estimation and Results

4.1 Extracting Wheel Regina from Images

Wheel region detection is needed in order to be able to extract the point, where wheels touch the road, i.e., tire-road contact point. After finding and extracting all the tire-road contact points visible in the image, then estimating a vehicle's pose w.r.t to the road line can be done using homography.

Perspective imaging in general and lens distortion in particular would make the problem challenging. We combine homography with a unified object detection algorithm, namely YOLOv3 (which is abbreviation for "you only look once") network [20], to detect the wheels on a vehicle, as Regions of Interests (ROI), and their contact points on the road. The algorithm takes perspective images as input, applies homography, and produces a side view of the scene by mapping the pixels to an orthogonal coordinate frame. The result of the ROI extraction is shown in Fig. 2a–b.

a   b

Fig. 2. (a) Original image. (b) Extracted ROI using homography transformation and deep learning.

Once the bounding boxes are found on the image, image processing techniques are applied to extract the tire-road contact point. Finally, without changing the image content, the image is retransformed into the original view.

The following function was utilized to perform geometrical transformation on the side view image and extract the location of tire-road contact point, using the specified matrix.

$$dst(x, y) = src\left(\frac{M_{11}x + M_{12}y + M_{13}}{M_{31}x + M_{32}y + M_{33}}, \frac{M_{21}x + M_{22}y + M_{23}}{M_{31}x + M_{32}y + M_{33}}\right) \quad (5)$$

Where (x, y) denotes the detected wheel contact point using conventional image processing techniques performed on the side-view image and M denotes the perspective transformation matrix. The detected wheel and its contact point with the road in the perspective image is shown in Fig. 3a–b.

a   b

Fig. 3. (a) original image, (b) detected tire-road contact point in the perspective image.

4.2 Training Network

To train the network and to perform the experimental part of our study, we built a traffic inspection imagery dataset and divided that into a training set and a test set. The data set contains 2104 images labeled by experts within the field. The data set contains still images of the trucks driving either too close, too far, or at an angle from the road line. The images are taken at a 1920 × 1080 pixel resolution, by different inspection cameras, and under different lighting and weather conditions. The data set is split randomly into a training set (85%) and a test set (15%). We hand-labeled the bounding box coordinates for our data set by considering the front wheel only. Every image is used as a single image for inference and training.

Concerning hyperparameters in the proposed network, the training was optimized using *stochastic gradient descent* with a momentum measure set to 0.9. The learning rate was set to 0.001 and the weight decay to 0.0005. Network resolution was set at 416 × 416. The batch size was set to 64. The pre-trained convolutional weights, trained on ImageNet from the DarkNet53 model, were used to initialize the parameters and then the network was retrained utilizing the new dataset for a new task. By using those weights as initialization, we could adapt the deep neural network to its highest accuracy.

The configurations of the computer used in this research was: a NVIDIA RTX 2080 Ti machine with 32 GB memory on Ubuntu 18.04, using Intel(R) Xeon(R) W-2125 CPU

@ 4.00 GHz. There are many standard methods to measure the system's performance. In general, the Mean Average Precision (mAP) [24] and Intersection Over Union (IOU) [25] are two choices to measure performance of the object detection. Among these two, mAP is the most commonly used. It indicates mean value of average precisions (AP) for each class, and IOU returns performance as the amount of overlap between the predicted boxes and the ground truth boxes divided by the entire area of union. All the key values such as loss function value, precision, recall, F-score, mAP and average IoU are calculated during training. The training loss moved close to the minimum within the first 2500 iterations (see Fig. 4). To avoid overfitting, the training is stopped after 6000 iterations and updated weights with the highest mAP and IoU are selected for the detection task. The results show that YOLO was able to generate the desired output in all the test cases. Among these, the best result was a mAP of 98.67% and IOU value of 89.10%; which are quite satisfactory. The ROI evaluation results are shown in Table 1.

Table 1. mAP result and valuation metrics of YOLOV3.

Measure	YOLOv3 (test dataset)
TP (True positives)	298
FP (False positives)	0
FN (False negatives)	3
mAP@0.50	98.67%
average IoU	89.10%
Precision	1.00
Recall	0.99
F1-score	0.99

In Table 1:

$$precision = TP / (TP + FP)$$

$$Recall = Sensitivity = TP / (TP + FN) \tag{6}$$

$$F1\ Score = 2 \times ((Recall \times Precision) / (Recall + Precision))$$

Where TP or True Positives, indicates the number of wheels successfully detected by the algorithm. FP or False Positives, indicates the number of non-wheel objects that are falsely detected as wheels. FN or False Negative, indicates the number of wheels that the algorithm failed to recognize as wheels.

4.3 Metric Measurements Using Inverse Perspective Mapping Algorithm

The shape of objects, wheels included, is often distorted under a perspective camera, therefore, a perspective-rectified image is required for applications like image-based

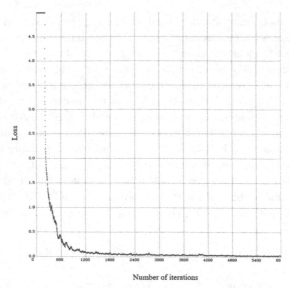

Number of iterations

Fig. 4. Training Loss.

metrology. For instance, as seen in Fig. 5a, the two parallel lines on the side of the road are not parallel in the image, but instead converging to a vanishing point. After detecting the tire-road contact point, extracting metric measurements requires an orthogonal view of the image to obtain photorealistic results.

Inverse Perspective Mapping (IPM) is computed using a non-vehicle image, and applied to the images to correct the geometric shape of objects, particularly wheels, in the image. IPM takes the perspective image as input, applies a homography transformation to that, and produces an orthogonal, but scaled, top-down view of the scene by mapping the pixels to a new 2D-coordinate frame. This view is known as the bird's-eye view. The transformation matrix H obtained from IPM of the non-vehicle image, i.e., an image without vehicle in it, is used to conduct homography on first. The same homography transformation is then utilized on all other images that include vehicles, from which metric measurements and the vehicle's relative pose estimation w.r.t the road line is conducted.

The homography-based mapping results from a road scene in absence of a vehicle is shown in Fig. 5. The real-world measurements from the pavement marking were used for both homography and camera calibration (see Fig. 5b for further details). A representative image that illustrates the results of position estimation of a transport vehicle w.r.t to the road line is shown in Fig. 6.

| a | b |

Fig. 5. (a) Original image with perspective distortion, White lane markings converge at a finite point. (b) Homography-based transformation from perspective to a scaled orthogonal image – a bird's eye view – non vehicle image.

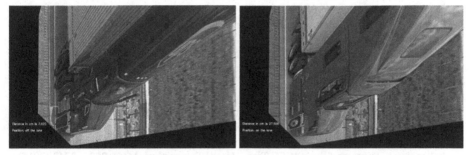

Fig. 6. Results of position estimates using tire-road contact point.

5   Conclusions and Future Research Directions

A Deep Convolutional Neural Network, along with a 2-D projective transformation, were applied to detect the wheels on a vehicle, as the Regions of Interests (ROI). Images collected from different traffic inspection stations were manually annotated and labelled for this purpose. The network's hyper parameters were fine-tuned using training data. By using Inverse Perspective Mapping (IPM), the pixels were mapped to an orthogonal, but scaled, reference frame in which the converging lines are mapped into parallel lines, which defines the homography transformation. This transformation matrix was then used to conduct homography on other images, where vehicles are present, for extracting metric measurements, namely vehicle's relative pose estimation w.r.t the road line.

The algorithm finds the wheel region and the tire-road contact point for all the visible wheels in the image using Deep-Learning, and uses homography transformation to estimate the vehicle's relative pose w.r.t to the road line by using the information embedded on the tire-road contact points. To evaluate how the model would perform for completely new images, we used a new dataset of classified images of vehicles passing through the station, and tested the algorithm on these images. The proposed method can flag vehicles driving either too close, too far, or at an angle from the road line at 92.15% accuracy. The results are promising. Unlike widely-used underground induction loops, as weight-in-motion sensors, implementing the proposed algorithm on images taken by non-contact cameras mounted on fixed locations at the inspection stations will provide continual insight into a road and vehicle scene in a non-intrusive way.

Improving on the quantitative measurements on the distance and angle between the vehicles and side lines of the road using uncalibrated cameras is envisioned as the next step of research.

Acknowledgment. This work was supported by Natural Sciences and Engineering Research Council of Canada (NSERC).

References

1. Hsieh, J.W., Yu, S.H., Chen, Y.S., Hu, W.F.: Automatic traffic surveillance system for vehicle tracking and classification. IEEE Intell. Transp. Syst. Mag. **7**(2), 175–187 (2006)
2. Gupte, S., Masoud, O., Martin, R.F.K., Papanikolopoulos, N.P.: Detection and classification of vehicles. IEEE Trans. Intell. Transp. Syst. **3**(1), 37–47 (2002)
3. Beymer, D., McLauchlan, P., Coifman, B., Malik, J.: A real-time computer vision system for measuring traffic parameters. In: International Conference on Computer Vision Pattern Recognition, pp. 495–501 (1997)
4. Iwasaki, Y., Kurogi, Y.: Real-time robust vehicle detection through the same algorithm both day and night. In: Proceedings 2007 International Conference on Wavelet Analysis Pattern Recognition, ICWAPR 2007, vol. 3, pp. 1008–1014 (2008)
5. Rezaei, M., Terauchi, M., Klette, R.: Robust vehicle detection and distance estimation under challenging lighting conditions. IEEE Trans. Intell. Transp. Syst. **16**(5), 2723–2743 (2015)
6. Hirose, K., Toriu, T., Hama, H.: Robust extraction of wheel region for vehicle position estimation using a circular fisheye camera. In: IIH-MSP 2009, vol. 9, no. 12, p. 55 (2009)
7. Li, S., Meng, Y., Li, W., Qian, H., Xu, Y.: Monocular vision-based vehicle localization aided by fine-grained classification (2018). eprint arXiv:1804.07906, vol. abs/1804.0
8. Wang, C.C.R., Lien, J.J.J.: Automatic vehicle detection using local features - a statistical approach. IEEE Trans. Intell. Transp. Syst. **9**(1), 83–96 (2008)
9. Achler, O., Trivedi, M.M.: Camera based vehicle detection, tracking, and wheel baseline estimation approach. In: IEEE Cat. No. 04TH8749, pp. 743–748 (2005)
10. Duron-Arellano, D., Soto-Lopez, D., Mehrandezh, M.: Image-based wheel-base measurement in vehicles: a sensitivity analysis to depth and camera's intrinsic parameters. In: Arai, K., Bhatia, R., Kapoor, S. (eds.) FTC 2018. AISC, vol. 880, pp. 19–29. Springer, Cham (2019). https://doi.org/10.1007/978-3-030-02686-8_2
11. Yoneyama, A., Yeh, C.H., JayKuo, C.C.: Robust vehicle and traffic information extraction for highway surveillance. EURASIP J. Appl. Signal Process. **2005**(14), 2305–2321 (2005)
12. Surasak, T., Takahiro, I., Cheng, C.H., Wang, C.E., Sheng, P.Y.: Histograms of oriented gradients for human detection. In: 2005 IEEE Computer Society Conference on Computer Vision Pattern Recognition (CVPR 2005), San Diego, CA, USA, pp. 172–176 (2005). https://doi.org/10.1109/cvpr.2005.177
13. Felzenszwalb, P.F., et al.: Object detection with discriminatively trained part-based models. IEEE Trans. Pattern Anal. Mach. Intell. **32**(9), 1627–1645 (2010). ISSN 0162-8828
14. Krizhevsky, A., Sutskever, I., Hinton, G.E.: ImageNet classification with deep convolutional neural networks. In: Proceedings of the 25th International Conference on Neural Information Processing Systems, vol. 1, pp. 1097–1105 (2012)

15. Girshick, R., Donahue, J., Darrell, T., Malik, J.: Rich feature hierarchies for accurate object detection and semantic segmentation. In: Proceedings of IEEE Computer Society Conference on Computer Vision and Pattern Recognition, pp. 580–587 (2014)
16. Uijlings, J.R., Van De Sande, K.E., Gevers, T., Smeulders, A.W.: Selective search for object recognition. Int. J. Comput. Vis. **104**(2), 154–171 (2013)
17. Girshick, R.: Fast R-CNN. In: Proceedings of IEEE International Conference on Computer Vision, vol. 2015, pp. 1440–1448 (2015)
18. Ren, S., He, K., Girshick, R.B., Sun, J.: Faster R-CNN: towards real-time object detection with region proposal networks (2015). CoRR, vol. abs/1506.0
19. Redmon, J., Divvala, S.K., Girshick, R.B., Farhadi, A.: You only look once: unified, real-time object detection. In: IEEE Conference on Computer Vision Pattern Recognition (2016). vol. abs/1506.0
20. Redmon, J., Farhadi, A.: YOLOv3: an incremental improvement (2018). CoRR, vol. abs/1804.0
21. Lin, T.Y., Goyal, P., Girshick, R., He, K., Dollar, P.: Focal loss for dense object detection. In: Proceedings of IEEE International Conference on Computer Vision, vol. 2017-Octob, pp. 2999–3007 (2017)
22. Liu, W., et al.: SSD: single shot multibox detector. In: Leibe, B., Matas, J., Sebe, N., Welling, M. (eds.) ECCV 2016. LNCS, vol. 9905, pp. 21–37. Springer, Cham (2016). https://doi.org/10.1007/978-3-319-46448-0_2
23. Richard Hartley, A.Z.: Multiple View Geometry in Computer Vision. Cambridge University Press, Cambridge (2003)
24. Everingham, M., Van Gool, L., Williams, C.K.I., Winn, J., Zisserman, A.: The pascal visual object classes (VOC) challenge. Int. J. Comput. Vis. **88**(2), 303–338 (2010)
25. Nowozin, S.: Optimal decisions from probabilistic models: the intersection-over-union case. In: Proceedings of IEEE Computer Society Conference on Computer Vision Pattern Recognition, pp. 548–555 (2014)

Video Applications

Using Participatory Design to Create a User Interface for Analyzing Pivotal Response Treatment Video Probes

Corey D. C. Heath$^{(\boxtimes)}$, Tracey Heath, Troy McDaniel, Hemanth Venkateswara, and Sethuraman Panchanathan

Center for Cognitive Ubiquitous Computing, Arizona State University, Tempe, AZ 85287, USA
{corey.heath,tdheath,troy.mcdaniel,hemanthv,panch}@asu.edu

Abstract. Training caregivers in pivotal response treatment (PRT) has been shown to help improve communication skills in children with autism. PRT training programs are implemented by clinicians that provide instruction, modelling, and assessment. Assessments are based on video recordings of the caregivers interacting with their children. Multimodal processing technologies could alleviate the costs involved in analyzing videos and providing performance-based feedback.

Constructing a user interface (UI) for clinicians to view data extracted from PRT videos is an important aspect for creating a feedback system. Including clinicians throughout the design and development process ensures that the application fully meets the user's needs. Currently, automated data collection and analysis is not undertaken in PRT evaluation. In addition to designing an interface, this project seeks to identify meaningful metrics and visual displays that will aid behavior analysts in their assessments. As part of a participatory design paradigm, clinicians evaluated a wireframe, alpha build, and beta build of a UI prototype. Critiques focused on application features, evaluation of automatically collected data, and usability. The prototype was evaluated as being capable of reducing video review time, and affording more opportunities for providing feedback to caregivers.

Keywords: User interface · Participatory design · Pivotal response treatment · Multimodal analysis · Autism spectrum disorder

1 Introduction

Pivotal response treatment (PRT) is a naturalistic applied behavior analysis (ABA) implementation based on incorporating learning objectives into activities that are inherently motivating to an individual [11]. Research on PRT has primarily focused on aiding children with autism spectrum disorder (ASD) to improve social and communications skills, particularly vocalization. PRT sessions aimed at improving a child's communication skills follow a basic procedure. First, the interventionist observes the child to discover an activity the

© Springer Nature Switzerland AG 2020
T. McDaniel et al. (Eds.): ICSM 2019, LNCS 12015, pp. 183–198, 2020.
https://doi.org/10.1007/978-3-030-54407-2_16

child is motivated to participate in. The interventionist then needs to incorporate her/himself into the activity. This affords the interventionist the opportunity to pause the activity to gain the child's attention, and use the continuation of the activity as motivation for compliance. After gaining the child's attention, the interventionist can issue a clear instruction at the vocal level of the child. The child is then expected to respond. If the response is a reasonable attempt given the child's vocal ability, the interventionist immediately allows the child to continue the previous activity as a reward. Utilizing this methodology has been empirically shown to aid in the development of vocal communication skills for children with ASD [12,23].

Training primary caregivers to implement PRT has been the subject of several publications [6,19]. This inherently allows the caregiver to expose the child to PRT methodologies more frequently than relying solely on a behavior analyst. Caregiver-implemented PRT has not only been shown to improve child communication skills, but also has been shown to reduce stress and improve affect in caregivers and children [14,20]. Providing training to caregivers can be challenging, largely due to availability of resources. Resource centers are predominately available in metropolitan areas, leaving rural communities with fewer training options. The time required to attend the training, along with program costs, may also be exclusionary to caregivers. Additionally, after a caregiver attends training, there are limited options to support the continued use of PRT. This is problematic as the caregiver needs to adapt PRT implementation as the child's interest in activities changes, and his or her communication skills grow. A longitudinal study [4] has found a sharp decline in caregiver implementation fidelity in follow up evaluations.

For evaluating fidelity to PRT, video probes of a caregiver interacting with his or her child are recorded and used for the assessment [13]. The video is segmented into one or two minute intervals, and a binary score is assigned to each category based on the presence or absence of the behavior during the interval. The categories focus on the caregiver's actions regarding identifying the activity the child is motivated in, gaining the child's attention, issuing an appropriate instruction, and providing a timely consequence when the child responds.

The utilization of video probes for caregiver assessment provides the opportunity to implement technologies for automated data extraction and analysis that could aid clinicians in training and supporting caregivers learning PRT. Information regarding the interaction between the caregiver and the child can be extracted from the video using multimodal machine learning techniques. This information can also be used to segment the videos with the goal of reducing the time the behavior analyst needs to review the video. This is intended to foster a greater opportunity for clinicians to provide feedback to caregivers, and make long term support more feasible.

Mapping the current manual data collection processes to an automated collection process requires some consideration. Automatically extracted data collection and analysis can be undertaken at a finer level of temporal granularity. This makes it possible to report metrics for smaller intervals than the one to two minutes used in current practice. Additionally, information that is tedious for human collection, such as number of vocal responses, becomes plausible with automated analysis. How the greater level of detail and additional metrics can be utilized by clinicians remains an open question that this project will address.

Ensuring that an application adequately addresses the needs of its target users requires the developers to consult the users frequently. A prototype user interface (UI) for presenting automated PRT data to clinicians was developed on an iterative life cycle consisting of three sprints. The initial design is based on literature review, observations, and conversations with clinicians. The result of this sprint was a wireframe mock of the interface along with examples of extracted data. The second sprint consisted of building an alpha prototype of the UI based on clinician feedback on the wireframe. The UI was evaluated using a think-aloud session with the clinicians. The final sprint improved the UI based on the results of the think-aloud session. The primary objectives for creating this UI are to: elicit information regarding how caregiver and child performance metrics should be displayed; determine what new data metrics can be extracted based on the affordances of automated multimodal analysis; and, develop a UI prototype that could potentially reduce the time required for analyzing PRT implementation and providing feedback based on participatory design methodology.

2   Related Work

2.1   Use of Technology in ABA Training

Exploring how to incorporate technology for training and supporting caregivers is important for aiding treatment discrimination. Research has focused on remote training procedures, predominantly focusing on teleconferencing and video modeling [1,16,17,25]. Teleconferencing approaches have focused on providing real-time instruction using a live video feed. Video modeling training is conducted with offline video materials. These materials present training information and examples of implementation. The materials were accessible at the trainee's leisure and would allow multiple viewings.

The research presented in this paper addresses a different issue from other works incorporating technology for ABA training. Rather than focusing on dissemination of training materials, this project focuses on automated data collection and presentation of a platform for reviewing PRT sessions and providing feedback. In a comprehensive system, this project and the aforementioned training methodologies could be used collectively.

2.2   Agile Development

Agile software development methodologies is based on an iterative delivery of application features. Individual features are designed, implemented, tested, and presented to stakeholders (users and other individuals outside of the development team that are invested in the project) after short development cycles to gain end user feedback quickly and adjust future efforts as needed. Using mockups provides the opportunity to gain feedback on the design layout before undertaking development work. Gaining the perspective of the user on the mockup helps provide insight into the ultimate user experience for the interface [22].

Ideally, stakeholders should be a fundamental contributor to the design and evaluation of the project. Having a co-design process with the stakeholders will aid in ensuring the project requirements are explicit and being addressed as expected [9]. This also helps the project implement a person-centered design, where the application addressed the needs of individuals, as opposed to appealing to a hypothetical 'average' user.

Incorporating the stakeholders can be difficult, as it often requires a willingness on the stakeholders part to invest their time and cooperate over a prolonged period. Often, stakeholders are accommodating in the beginning but become less enthusiastic as time progresses. A recommendation by [22] is to invest more time in the beginning of the process, particularly examining the user's needs and current solutions to problems the speculative project intends to address.

This project was developed with routine interactions with clinicians to examine desired features, evaluate designs, and test implementations. Following the suggestion of [22] the early mockup development was primarily based on conversations with clinicians, evaluation of current tools being utilized, observations of PRT feedback sessions, and video probe evaluations. This was intended to reduce the time investment required from the clinicians in the early stages of the project design and development.

3   Design Process

3.1   Observations

Understanding the needs of a system's users is paramount to the design process. Prior to designing a solution, the principal investigator attended a week long group training program for teaching caregivers PRT, and observed one-on-one training sessions between behavior analysts and a caregiver with her child. This provided the opportunity to learn about the materials, methodologies, and feedback employed by clinicians when training caregivers. Attending these sessions also facilitated conversation with caregivers and clinicians regarding the views on PRT, and the challenges of consistent long-term usage. The observations from these sessions relevant to this project are: performance feedback from clinicians is situated in the context of an activity; evaluating video probes for fidelity was time-consuming; feedback on progression relied on manually gathered data; and, post-treatment feedback and support was minimal. These observations formed the base assumptions utilized for the initial UI design.

During the observed one-on-one sessions, the caregiver practiced implementing PRT with her child in the presence of the clinician. This afforded the clinician the opportunity to provide suggestions and feedback in real time. This benefits the caregiver by helping her situate the feedback into the context of his or her immediate behavior. It allows the caregiver to immediately act on the suggestion.

Commonly, the feedback that was provided started with example. Either the clinician modeled a behavior for the caregiver to emulate, the clinician praised a specific interaction that occurred, or the clinician identified a particular instance where the caregiver acted incorrectly or missed an important opportunity.

Only the adults were present during group sessions. Clinician evaluation during these sessions was conducted using 10-min videos of the adult and child interacting. The videos were reviewed as a group, with the clinician pausing to provide feedback. As with in-person training sessions, this allowed the clinician to isolate specific instances in the video where the feedback was applicable.

Outside of providing face-to-face feedback, scoring video probes is a manual task, requiring a clinician to review the video, evaluate the adult's behaviors in regard to implementation criteria, and identify frequency of child vocalizations. This involves watching the video probe multiple times to ensure proper assessment. For adult implementation, the scores were assessed in minute increments on a binary system reflecting if the adult adequately met the criteria during the interval. The criterium is met if the adult correctly demonstrates the behavior twice during the interval. No data is recorded on the specific action that was taken or where in the interval the actions took place. The scores for each category are tallied and averaged to create a fidelity score percentage. Achieving a score above 80% is considered adequate implementation.

Primarily, utterance frequency is used for child vocal assessment. This is based on a presence or absence value determined by whether or not the child vocalized during a 15-s time period. This can be recorded on whether the utterance was spontaneous or a response to an instruction from the caregiver, however this practice was not observed. The only information collected on the child's vocal attempts were binary indications of an adequate vocal attempt being made.

Upon completing the one-on-one training, the caregiver is presented with a report detailing the treatment and the evaluation metrics from the video probes. This presents a comparison between an assessment of a baseline video probe recorded prior to receiving training, and a post-training probe record on the final day of the course.

After training is concluded, options for continual support are limited. As observed, the process of training and evaluating caregivers is intensive, and centers lack the resource availability for support after training. In interviews, clinicians stated that one of the primary challenges that led caregivers to abandon PRT is an inability to adapt the procedure to new activities and learning objectives. This was also related to the first author during the group course by a participant that was attending the class after previously undertaking the one-on-one training.

3.2   Automated Data Processing and Video Segmentation

The video probes present a challenge for automated data processing and classification. The videos are often recorded using a hand-held camera or mobile device, causing visual instability. Additionally, due the activities that are commonly depicted, the individuals in the frames are often partially or fully occluded.

Audio processing is also challenging, particularly for identifying child vocalizations. The audio recording quality is often dependent on the camera operator's proximity to the dyad, and external noises. Additionally, all child utterances need to be identified. Depending on the vocal ability of the child, the utterance may represent only attempts at speech that may only include individual phonemes.

For the initial research, automated data processing focused on extracting information about the attention state of the child, and identifying the caregiver and child vocalizations. Extracting the attention state of the child follows the methodology described in [8]. The video was processed using OpenPose [3] to detect body and facial landmark points from the individuals in each frame. This data, along with an estimation of the visual focus of the individual, was used to construct a spatio-temporal graph of the dyad in the frame. The data was used to train a support vector machine (SVM) classification model based on three class labels - attentive, inattentive, and shared attention. The labels were based on 30-frame segments, representing approximately one second of the video. The conclusion reached in [8] stated that this method only produced 44% accuracy on individual frames, however an accuracy of 56% is achieved when aggregating samples to assign a label to 30-frame segments.

The audio assessment was based on research presented in [7] using the same video set as [8]. The probe's audio data was processed to extract common features using PyAudioAnalysis [5], and classified as being silence, noise, adult speech or child vocalizations. Two SVM models, one trained to separate speech from noise, and a second for differentiating child and adult vocalizations, were used for the classification tasks. Using this methodology, an overall classification accuracy of 79% was achieved.

Segmenting the videos into semantically meaningful clips was identified as an important feature for utilizing automated processing. This would reduce the amount of time the clinician needed to invest in viewing the video and extracting example clips for situating pointed feedback. These clips were created by first analyzing the audio data to identify when adult and child vocalizations occur. This classification of information was then used to create segments containing adult only speech, child only speech, and both adult and child speech. Based on temporal relationship between the adult and child speech, the child speech could be labeled as either spontaneous or a response. Each of these segments were then classified for the attention state by analyzing the video frame data of the segment and using the most represented label.

3.3   Initial Assumptions and Project Goals

The objective of the project is to explore how data metrics automatically collected from video probes could be used to reduce the amount of time clinicians need to invest to evaluate caregiver PRT implementation, and how an interface can be designed to afford new opportunities for clinicians to provide feedback. This involves not only how the interface can be designed to promote ease-of-use, but also how PRT evaluation procedures can be expanded by new data collection techniques.

Initial assumptions on the design were developed to alleviate the need to view the entire video. Creating the video segments would allow the clinicians to view an annotated storyboard of the video and select the clips they felt were important to view and remark on. Additional information would be provided in accompanying graphs. These graphs were expected to provide a summary of the video, or sections of the video, that could be utilized to gain an understanding of the interactions prior to reviewing the clips. Additional graphs would be made to show the difference between video probes from the same dyad. This was intended to show the progression of the caregiver's PRT implementation fidelity and the child's vocal communications skills.

The data for the graphs was related to the evaluation criteria that clinician manually collected, however at this stage it was not intended to supplant the manual metrics. The data that was thought to be important to track was the overall percentage of each attentive state in the video, the percentage of audio classification throughout the video, the number of adult speeches that occurred with the child that were inattentive or attentive, the number of child spontaneous vocalizations and responses, and the average length of the child's utterances.

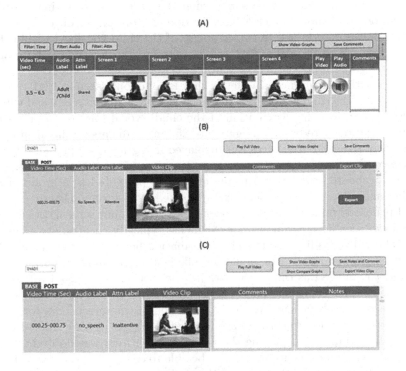

Fig. 1. Depicts the storyboard page throughout the project. (A) is the wireframe mockup, (B) is a screenshot of the alpha build, and (C) is a screenshot of the beta build. Video images were retrieved from [24]

3.4   Sprint 1: Wireframe

The wireframe created for the first sprint consisted of a mock-up of the primary interface page and graphs for visualizing the data extracted from the video. The primary interface page (Fig. 1A) was designed to function as a storyboard depicting an abbreviation of the video, along with controls for launching media players and filtering the gridview based on the video clip labels. Each row of the gridview consists of the time interval, audio label, attention state label, four screen shots from the clip, audio play button, video play button, and a comments section. The screen shots were selected from the clip at evenly spaced intervals. This is intended to show the interaction without the necessity of viewing the full video. The comments field was intended for clinicians to provide feedback to the caregiver based on that specific clip, allowing the feedback to be situated within its context.

Pie charts, bar graphs, and box plots were chosen for displaying data metrics extracted from the videos. The percentage of the video pertaining to specific attention states and audio labels were illustrated in pie charts (Fig. 2). These charts were created to provide a broad overview of the video. In accordance with current procedures of evaluating each minute of the video, bar graphs (Fig. 3) were utilized to show related important vocal utterance scenarios for the child and parent. In particular, these show when the parent is vocalizing based on the attention label and if the child vocalization is spontaneous or a response. A vocalization was determined to be a response if the child vocalized within three seconds after the adult spoke. Bar graphs were created for each minute along with a total graph representing the cumulative data from the video.

Mean length of utterance is a metric that is commonly seen in PRT research as a measure of the child's vocal usage. This was represented as a box and whisker plot (Fig. 4) showing the distribution of the child's vocalizations. At this stage, these vocalization were based on aggregate 250 ms segments as classified by [7]. Frequency of the child utterances was displayed in a grid-based plot showing the presence or absence of at least one vocalization in a 15-s interval (Fig. 5).

The storyboard, graphs, and media clips were presented to a group of four behavior analysts and the design was discussed as a group. Design critiques focused primarily on the storyboard layout. The use of four screenshots for each segment was seen as superfluous. The segments typically encapsulate a few seconds of the video, leading to little new information being provided in each shot. It was stated that a single shot would be sufficient, as the most important information in the image was the toy or activity the dyad were engaged with.

Buttons on the storyboard page were also reorganized. The audio only button was not seen to be beneficial. With the reduction of the screenshots to a single image, it was requested that the image be used to trigger playing the video clip. Additionally, a button for playing the video in its entirety was desired.

The behavior analysts also wanted to be able to easily view the interaction in context. To facilitate this, they wanted the ability to continue watching the video after the clip's ending, as well as view preceding seconds of the video, without

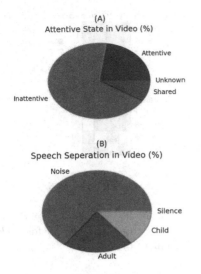

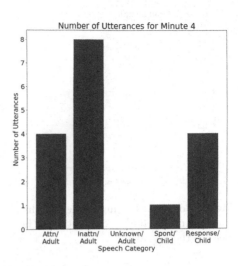

Fig. 2. Example pie charts showing child attentive state and speech separation from video analysis.

Fig. 3. Example bar graph showing the number of vocalizations in a one-minute segment. Shows adult speech based on child attention state, as well as child responses and spontaneous utterances.

having to navigate to a different segment. The ability to save these adjusted clips was also requested.

3.5 Sprint 2: Alpha Prototype

After receiving the feedback from the sprint 1 deliverable session, the UI was developed using a .NET WPF framework. The storyboard page (Fig. 1B) was simplified based on the wireframe feedback. For each segment, an export button was added to the row to allow the clinician to save the video clip. As requested, a button for playing the full video was added to the top of the screen.

An additional page was created for displaying the video segments (Fig. 6A). As requested in the sprint 1 feedback session, this page implemented controls for manually adjusting the clip.

The deliverable session of the alpha prototype was conducted using a think-aloud methodology [15] with the same group of clinicians as the previous session. During the think-aloud, one of the behavior analysts walked through the use of the UI while verbally describing her actions. This provided perspective on the flow of events that could be expected in a typical use-case scenario. She began by viewing the entire video to perform the typical fidelity scoring process, making a note of exemplary interactions. Next, she viewed the graphs, particularly noting the ratio of inattentive versus attentive states. Finally, she examined the video clips, stating she would first look at attentive and shared attention samples, then view inattentive samples. While going through the think-aloud it became

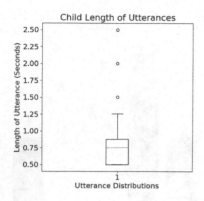

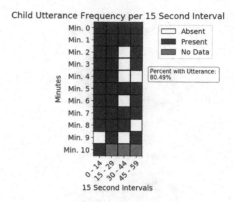

Fig. 4. Box plot showing the length distribution of the child's vocalizations. The mean is the line at 0.75.

Fig. 5. Grid showing the presence or absence of a child vocalization for each 15-s increment of the video.

apparent that clinician's notes not intended to be passed to the parent were an important part of the process and should be accommodated in future designs.

Using the video segment viewing page also elicited areas to improve and expand the UI. During the think-aloud, the clinician viewed the clip and wanted to extend the ending. After updating the segments endpoint, she wanted to return to the start to view the extended clip. This involved viewing the start time displayed in the text box and manually moving the playback pointer to the appropriate spot. This could be improved upon by providing a button to reset the cursor to the beginning.

An additional feature that was requested was the ability to add comments directly to the video in addition to external feedback that pertained to the entire clip. These notes would be intended to further capitalize on situated feedback by displaying the comment for the duration of the video it is applicable to. This will help the feedback recipient to contextualize the information within the specific action.

3.6   Sprint 3: Beta Prototype

For the third sprint, the storyboard page (Fig. 1C) only received minor revisions, including adding an additional clinician's notes field, and adding new buttons to export data and view graphs. The video clip viewing page (Fig. 6B) was updated to include a button to restart the video from the clip start position, and added a grid for creating in-video comments. This grid allows the clinician to input the start and stop time that a comment will appear on the video. The text overlay consists of a dialog box with high transparency to prevent obscuring the video. This can support multiple comments appearing at different times during the video clip.

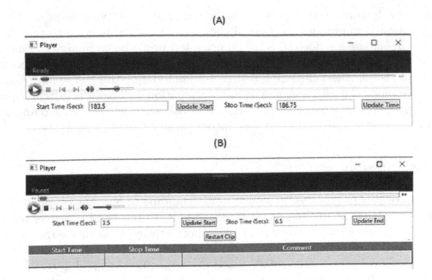

Fig. 6. Screenshots of the video viewer window. (A) represents the alpha build, while (B) is from the beta build. The pane for viewing the video has been reduced.

The beta prototype was evaluated by providing the same group of clinicians as the previous sprints with a downloadable copy of the application. The download package included the program files, data, example results, and a text document containing installation and usage instructions. The clinicians were given 12 days to review the application, and were asked seven questions regarding the usability of the program, the practicality of the information being provided, and desired features not included in the prototype. Only three of the four clinicians provided answers. Due to the small number of evaluating users, responses were not anonymized.

Overall, the clinicians stated that the program was easy to use. The clinicians felt that navigating between videos, launching segments, and viewing graphs was intuitive. The installation process for the prototype required mapping directories to load the data correctly, resulting in unnecessary and confusing installation steps. This would be improved in future iterations by using installers and distributed data storage systems.

The clinicians were excited by the data that was being provided and felt that it would reduce the amount of time necessary for reviewing the videos. They felt that this would aid in the feedback they could present caregivers. Additionally, the ability to add comments directly to the videos was a praised feature. In regard to data, the clinicians stated that the metrics being extracted reflected the majority of what would be useful, and did not have suggestions for additional information that should be collected. It was stated that providing the child's utterance frequency data (Fig. 5) "would reduce the time need to review a video by 10 to 20 min".

No new features were suggested for future implementations, however, there were requested improvements. One of the questions asked referred to the minimum segment size for video clips the clinician felt would be useful. Each clinician stated that 10 to 15 s is the smallest increment they would like to see. In its current state, the smallest clip size is 0.75 s. Accommodating this will require examining sequence classification and result aggregation in future research. Apart from segment size, quality of life improvements, such as providing numerical information on graphs and more descriptive graph titles, were requested.

4   Discussion

The goal of this project was to gain an understanding of how automatically collected data could be utilized in the feedback and evaluation of caregiver implemented PRT sessions. This required looking both at ways to facilitate the current data collection and evaluation process, and how it can be expanded. The current process collects minimal data based on segments of time due to the cost of human evaluation. Automated processing allows for fine granularity of data to be collected that would aid in providing overviews of the videos along with facilitating comparisons between videos. The intended effect would be to provide long term data tracking that could be used to identify progression and indicate when skill acquisition plateaus are encountered. This would aid the clinician in providing encouraging feedback, and indicate when new skills or approaches need to be introduced. Based on the feedback sessions, the data graphs created for the prototype would be useful in accomplishing this goal.

The progression of the user interface illustrated that several of the assumptions that were involved in the initial design did not come to fruition. The goal was to eliminate the need to review the entire video, however, the first action that was taken during the think-aloud was to watch the entire video and perform the traditional evaluation. This is understandable at this stage of the project, as the metrics being automatically collected do not encompass the entirety of the criteria being used for evaluation by clinicians. The segmentation layout and automated collection of the child utterance statistic did eliminate the need for multiple viewings of the video.

An additional assumption that was false regarded the still frames used for the storyboard. It was presumed that the clinicians would benefit from multiple images in order to gain an understanding of the actions undertaken by the dyad in the segment. The clinicians stated that this was unnecessary as the actions could largely be deduced from the visible objects in the frame.

Also regarding the segments, the initial assumption was that isolating speech events would be the preferred method for creating each clip. While this is partially correct, the clinicians each stated that this information alone was inadequate. The group consensus was that clips should be at least 10 to 15 s long, encapsulating the important events. The context leading up to the vocal event, and the consequences after, were valuable for feedback, as well as creating more concrete examples of behaviors.

The two features best received were the frequency of utterance graph and the ability to create customized video clips. The frequency of utterance graph is a full automation of a currently undertaken task. The clinicians saw a direct benefit to this information since it would no longer be needed to be collected by hand. Similarly, the clip controls were seen as valuable for the creation of demonstration and training tools. During the think-aloud session the first comments on how this could be useful were related to creating examples for training and presentations, rather than the effect it would have on reducing the time required for conducting evaluations as intended.

The most important outcome of this project is that it forms the basis for continuing to integrate automated data collection into PRT evaluation. The data being captured in the graphs was based on a conceptualization of what would be important to provide more specific feedback at a reduced human cost. Apart from the utterance frequency metrics, this data was not currently being collected for use in caregiver training. The project provided an opportunity to evaluate how useful this data could be, and the best way it could be presented to clinicians to increase the feedback that can be provide to caregivers.

5   Future Development

This design evaluation for this project was limited to four behavior analysts. This provided adequate insight to develop a prototype, however, the application would benefit from recruiting a broader number of users for future evaluations. The prototype would also need to be expanded to include a persistent back-end for data storage, a distributed architecture for handling the video processing tasks, and a second front-end application for caregivers to upload videos, receive clinician comments, and view automatically extracted performance metrics.

More effort is needed to improve the automated video clip creation and labeling. Based on clinician feedback, the video clips need to be aggregated to a minimum length of 10 to 15 s. Additional research will focus on how to evaluate longer sequences of video data, as well as examine multimodal solutions to identifying periods of attention.

In addition to the current data being extracted, there is the opportunity to provide information regarding the affective state based on video, audio, and lexical data [2,18]. Data on the emotional state of the individuals could provide useful information to the clinician, as well as be important for caregiver self-reflection on depicted activities. This could also provide insight into activities that are particularly motivating for the child.

Examining how this UI could be provided to caregivers also needs to be addressed. Acquisition of knowledge on intervention methods is left solely to the caregiver, requiring him or her to be self-motivated to improve implementation of the techniques. Because of this, the technology should be designed to promote self-regulatory learning [26]. Utilization of the storyboard features presented in this article could aid the learner in evaluating progress on meeting his or her goals. By automatically creating segments of interest, the caregiver could review specific areas of the video that could highlight correct implementations of PRT, while also showing missed opportunities or ineffective behaviors. Reviewing this video immediately after the PRT sessions would help the caregiver situate the feedback in the context of the activity [21]. This provides a framework for self-monitoring and self-evaluation of the caregiver's interaction with his or her child [10]. Automatically collected metrics on the child's responses would also help the caregiver visualize progress and identify periods of stagnation.

6 Conclusions

Following the collaborative design structure in combination with aspects of agile methodology allowed the researchers to gain perspective and pivot the project to meet the clinician's needs as they were identified. The foundation of the project, the initial wireframe, was based solely on observation and research. Although fundamentally useful, it was immediately apparent to the clinicians that it needed to be simplified. Utilizing a think-aloud for the evaluation of the alpha prototype created the opportunity for both the researchers and the clinicians to identify missing key functions and desirable features. The final evaluation of the beta prototype gave the clinicians the opportunity experience how the application could be utilized, and provided important feedback for continuing the project in the future.

Acknowledgements. The authors thank the Southwest Autism Research and Resource Center for their collaboration, and Arizona State University and the National Science Foundation for their funding support. This material is partially based upon work supported by the National Science Foundation under Grant No. 1069125 and 1828010.

References

1. Bagaiolo, L., et al.: Procedures and compliance of a video modeling applied behavior analysis intervention for Brazilian parents of children with autism spectrum disorders. Autism **25**, 603–610 (2017)
2. Bertero, D., et al.: Deep learning of audio and language features for humor prediction. In: LREC (2016)
3. Cao, Z., et al.: Realtime multi-person 2D pose estimation using part affinity fields. In: CVPR (2017)
4. Gengoux, G., et al.: Pivotal response treatment parent training for autism: findings from a 3-month follow-up evaluation. J. Autism Dev. Disord. **45**(9), 2889–2898 (2015)
5. Giannakopoulos, T.: pyAudioAnalysis: an open-source Python library for audio signal analysis. PloS One **10**(12), e0144610 (2015)
6. Hardan, A., et al.: A randomized controlled trial of pivotal response treatment group for parents of children with autism. J. Child Psychol. Psychiatry **56**(8), 884–892 (2015)

7. Heath, C.D.C., McDaniel, T., Venkateswara, H., Panchanathan, S.: Parent and child voice activity detection in pivotal response treatment video probes. In: Zaphiris, P., Ioannou, A. (eds.) HCII 2019. LNCS, vol. 11591, pp. 270–286. Springer, Cham (2019). https://doi.org/10.1007/978-3-030-21817-1_21

8. Heath, C.D.C., Venkateswara, H., McDaniel, T., Panchanathan, S.: Detecting attention in pivotal response treatment video probes. In: Basu, A., Berretti, S. (eds.) ICSM 2018. LNCS, vol. 11010, pp. 248–259. Springer, Cham (2018). https://doi.org/10.1007/978-3-030-04375-9_21

9. Kildea, J., et al.: Design and development of a person-centered patient portal using participatory stakeholder co-design. J. Med. Internet Res. **21**, 2 (2019)

10. Kitsantas, A., Kavussanu, M.: Acquisition of sport knowledge and skill. In: Handbook of Self-regulation of Learning and Performance, pp. 217–233 (2011)

11. Koegel, R.: How to Teach Pivotal Behaviors to Children with Autism: A Training Manual (1988)

12. Koegel, R., et al.: Improving question-asking initiations in young children with autism using pivotal response treatment. J. Autism Dev. Disord. **44**(4), 816–827 (2014)

13. Koegel, R., et al.: Parent education for families of children with autism living in geographically distant areas. J. Posit. Behav. Interv. **4**(2), 88–103 (2002)

14. Lecavalier, L., et al.: Moderators of parent training for disruptive behaviors in young children with autism spectrum disorder. J. Abnorm. Child Psychol. **45**(6), 1235–1245 (2017)

15. Lewis, C., Rieman, J.: Task-centered user interface design. A practical introduction (1993)

16. Machalicek, W., et al.: Training teachers to assess the challenging behaviors of students with autism using video tele-conferencing. Educ. Train. Autism Dev. Disabil. **45**, 203–215 (2010)

17. Nefdt, N., et al.: The use of a self-directed learning program to provide introductory training in pivotal response treatment to parents of children with autism. J. Posit. Behav. Interv. **12**(1), 23–32 (2010)

18. Rudovic, O., et al.: Personalized machine learning for robot perception of affect and engagement in autism therapy. Sci. Robot. **3**, 19 (2018)

19. Smith, I.M., Flanagan, H.E., Garon, N., Bryson, S.E.: Effectiveness of community-based early intervention based on pivotal response treatment. J. Autism Dev. Disord. **45**(6), 1858–1872 (2015)

20. Steiner, A., et al.: Pivotal response treatment for infants at-risk for autism spectrum disorders: a pilot study. J. Autism Dev. Disord. **43**(1), 91–102 (2013)

21. Suhrheinrich, J., Chan, J.: Exploring the effect of immediate video feedback on coaching. J. Spec. Educ. Technol. **32**(1), 47–53 (2017)

22. Urbieta, M., Torres, N., Rivero, J.M., Rossi, G., Dominguez-Mayo, F.J.: Improving mockup-based requirement specification with end-user annotations. In: Garbajosa, J., Wang, X., Aguiar, A. (eds.) XP 2018. LNBIP, vol. 314, pp. 19–34. Springer, Cham (2018). https://doi.org/10.1007/978-3-319-91602-6_2

23. Ventola, P., et al.: Improvements in social and adaptive functioning following short-duration PRT program: a clinical replication. J. Autism Dev. Disord. **44**(11), 2862–2870 (2014)

24. Pivotal response treatment PRT example. https://www.youtube.com/watch?v=vZOSaYRVOI. Accessed 6 June 2019
25. Vismara, L., et al.: Preliminary findings of a telehealth approach to parent training in autism. J. Autism Dev. Disord. **43**(12), 2953–2969 (2013)
26. Winne, P.: A cognitive and metacognitive analysis of self-regulated learning. In: Schunk, D.H., Zimmerman, B. (eds.) Handbook of Self-regulation of Learning and Performance, pp. 29–46. Routledge, London (2011)

Robot-Assisted Composite Manufacturing Based on Machine Learning Applied to Multi-view Computer Vision

Abtin Djavadifar[1], John Brandon Graham-Knight[2], Kashish Gupta[1],
Marian Körber[3], Patricia Lasserre[2], and Homayoun Najjaran[1(✉)]

[1] School of Engineering, University of British Columbia, Vancouver, Canada
homayoun.najjaran@ubc.ca
[2] Department of Computer Science, University of British Columbia,
Vancouver, Canada
[3] Center for Lightweight-Production-Technology, German Aerospace Center,
Augsburg, Germany

Abstract. This paper introduces an automated wrinkle detection method on semi-finished fiber products in the aerospace manufacturing industry. Machine learning, computer vision techniques, and evidential reasoning are combined to detect wrinkles during the draping process of fibre-reinforced materials with an industrial robot. A well-performing Deep Convolutional Neural Network (DCNN) was developed based on a preliminary, hand-labelled dataset captured on a functioning robotic system used in a composite manufacturing facility. Generalization of this model to different, unlearned wrinkle features naturally compromises detection accuracy. To alleviate this problem, the proposed method employs computer vision techniques and belief functions to enhance defect detection accuracy. Co-temporal views of the same fabric are extracted, and individual detection results obtained from the DCNN are fused using the Dempster-Shafer Theory (DST). By the application of the DST rule of combination, the overall wrinkle detection accuracy for the generalized case is greatly improved in this composite manufacturing facility.

Keywords: Computer vision · Composite manufacturing · Wrinkle detection · Process automation · Machine learning · Deep neural network · Belief functions · Data fusion · Classification

1 Introduction

Fibre-reinforced materials are becoming increasingly important in the modern aviation industry. However, the automated handling of these materials in the manufacturing process of carbon-fiber reinforced plastic (CFRP) components is still challenging. The process investigated in this paper aims at improving the automated production of a preform created from 25 dry carbon fiber cut

© Springer Nature Switzerland AG 2020
T. McDaniel et al. (Eds.): ICSM 2019, LNCS 12015, pp. 199–211, 2020.
https://doi.org/10.1007/978-3-030-54407-2_17

pieces. The complexity of this handling process lies in the double-curved target geometry. The cut pieces are gripped in the flat state and transferred to the target geometry during the deformation process, also known as draping. For this purpose, an end-effector system was developed in the AZIMUT project, which is able to deform its gripper surface to a double curved geometry with the aid of a rib-spine design. The spine consists of two glass fiber rods connected to the gripper structure by three linear actuators. The rods are bent by shortening the linear axes, causing an inhomogeneous curvature of the suction surface. The 15 ribs are able to create independent curvatures; together, ribs and spine produce a double curvature. The suction surface consists of 127 suction units that are individually adjustable in their suction intensity [19]. The ribs and spine are deformed to selectively manipulate the carbon fiber fabric so that the cut-pieces show the predefined boundary edge geometry as well as the predefined fiber orientation. During deformation, undesired wrinkles can form, which need to be identified and removed.

The Center for Lightweight Production Technologies (ZLP) in Augsburg, Germany, developed an optical sensor system which provides information on relative movement between the suction surfaces and the fabric during the draping process [9]. However, this setup is limited in its ability to detect boundary geometry and wrinkles. A multi-view camera setup, designed at University of British Columbia (UBC), was mounted in front of the form-variable end-effector at the ZLP. Figure 1 is an image captured by one such camera, showing the fabric, gripper, and linear wrinkles which appeared during the draping process.

Fig. 1. Fabric on gripper

The complicated shear stresses involved when draping a flexible fabric material on a curvature can lead to wrinkling of the fabric. Wrinkles greatly affect the manufacturing process and reduce the quality of the final product. The aerospace industry, having little tolerance for error, requires a high product quality. Manual handling of such materials is time consuming, and can lead to delays in manufacturing. This makes it imperative to establish an automated method to identify wrinkles if and when they form on the fabric throughout the manufacturing process.

The primary contribution of this paper is a method for combining multiple, co-temporal views of a fabric with defects into a single representation. This combined view can then be mapped back to each of the original views, providing increased defect detection accuracy. To facilitate this multi-view inferencing, a method of extracting components and detecting defects using traditional computer vision techniques is presented; a technique for combining these views is also developed and presented.

2   Objective and Approach

This paper presents a wrinkle detection method on a semi-finished dry fiber product. This method currently has minimal interaction from an operator in selecting keypoints used in perspective correction; future work will remove this need and produce a fully automated solution. For practical applicability, automated detection is expected to be independent of the fabric's shape, orientation, size and even visually dominant characteristics such as color. Furthermore, detection performance should be robust to change in experimental conditions such as lighting and location of the fabric with respect to the gripper. To accommodate such design requirements, the proposed solution enhances a data-driven, automated wrinkle detection module, developed independent of the hand-crafted features as presented in [6].

The work in this paper is executed in 3 phases:

1. Model development, training and evaluation (Sect. 3).
2. Evaluation of the algorithm's ability to generalize (Sect. 4).
3. Development and evaluation of an approach for combining co-temporal views to improve the algorithm's accuracy in various conditions (Sect. 5).

In phase 1, a convolutional neural network was designed and trained for the task of wrinkle detection. The training and test datasets were generated by acquiring images during the draping process. Each image was divided into smaller regions to facilitate efficient hand-labeling of data. Supervised learning was employed on the generated sub-images to train an image classifier. Three different sizes of training dataset were evaluated and it was observed that, past a point, increased size offered diminishing returns. The results of Phase I can be seen in Table 1. The best trained network could successfully identify a wrinkle with an accuracy of 95.5%.

In phase 2, an unlabelled complementary dataset was generated with altering lighting conditions, different wrinkle shapes and sizes, fabric shapes, and significantly varying distance and location of the camera with respect to the scene. The pre-trained network from Phase 1 was evaluated on this dataset to test the ability of the model to generalize; results are presented in Table 2. Notably, classification accuracy of wrinkles decreased to 66.6%.

The observed loss of detection accuracy while testing in new situations motivated Phase 3. Multiple views of the scene are combined to create a robust algorithm. The dataset created in phase 2, consisting of co-temporal views of the same fabric, was re-used. The pre-trained neural network model from Phase 1 was used to label each view of the scene separately. To combine multiple views, an algorithm using traditional computer vision techniques was developed to extract and overlap fabrics from multiple images corresponding to different view-points on a stationary scene. The Dempster-Shafer combination rule [5,18] was then applied to find the most probable label of each pixel in the anchor image based on individual view probability. Finally, the combined labels were mapped back to each original view. Detection accuracy was improved considerably when compared with phase 2, achieving 85.9% success in wrinkle detection (Table 3). This was accomplished without the need for any re-training or fine-tuning of the pre-trained model.

3   Phase 1 - Model Development

3.1   Convolutional Neural Networks

The roots of Convolutional Neural Networks for image classification started in the 1980s; this early work focused on identification of hand-written digits, specifically as related to automated zip code detection [11–13]. This work continued through the late 1990s, but with little adoption [14]. The method worked well, but suffered from lack of parallel compute power available at the time [16].

Advancement in GPU computation and increased availability of datasets led to a renewal of interest in 2006, and led to technological advances such as the first application of maximum pooling for dimensionality reduction [1,4,7,8,15].

The current enthusiasm for Deep Convolutional Neural Networks (DCNN) was sparked by the ImageNet Large Scale Visual Recognition Challenge (ILSVRC), where in 2012 the winning entry was a DCNN [10]. DCNNs have since dominated the ILSVRC, and specifically the image classification component [17].

The network developed was motivated by the current dominance of Convolutional Neural Network image classifiers and modelled on these recent advances.

3.2   Network and Training

The network used for training can be broadly classified into two major parts. The first part consists of convolutional neural network layers along with batch normalization and max pooling which together act as a feature extractor. This part of the network extracts meaningful information and presents it in a feature latent space to the rest of the network to map the extracted features to a particular label. The second part of the network consists of fully connected layers which complete the extracted latent space by matching it to a label.

The input mechanism and the data-set itself consist of highly sequential information from the camera. As such, the network tends to learn only the local features of each segment while driving itself to a local minima. To break the self-correlation in the input stream and the dataset, the training is executed on a mini dataset, consisting of randomly sampled input-output pairs from the original dataset. The mini dataset is created in batches and sent to the network until the learning gradient starts to disappear.

The training network employs a data loading mechanism that inputs data from the mini dataset and performs a random transformation before feeding it to the network. The random transformation consist of a random resize, flip and crop with a mean and standard normalization. The data loader then converts the input to a tensor for the network.

The input is fed through 14 units of neural net with each unit consisting of a convolution layer, batch normalization and a ReLU[1]. Max pooling is executed every 3 to 4 units and finally an average pooling at the end of 14th unit. The output of average pooling is fed through a fully connected layer that outputs the classification probability of each class. Adam optimizer is used for training and optimization with learning rate decaying from 1e-4 to 1e-9 with respect to the number of epochs. Each image input is fed through a series of convolutional layers with the $kernel\_size = 3$, $stride = 1$ and $padding = 1$. The detection was conducted with $batch\_size = 32$ and 4 CPU workers for data loading. The units (consisting of a CNN, a Normalizer and an activation layer) incremented from 32 to 128 output features before forming the input for the fully connected layer.

3.3 Development of the Dataset

To train the deep neural network, a dataset of approximately sixteen thousand images was created. A stereo imaging module developed using two IDS XS Cameras was used to capture movements of the robot holding the gripper with differently sized and shaped fabrics. The image pair (Left & Right) from the imaging module was recorded in 14 different scenarios, each at 14 fps (the duration of each video was around 40 s). Then, each frame of the image pair was divided into 128 (64 for Left and 64 for Right) smaller images to enhance the features local to the area. Each acquired frame from the stereo imaging module was 1280 × 720 pixels in size, which was then subjected to a grid of 8 × 8 to facilitate hand labelling. The process yielded 64 smaller images per frame of size 160 × 90 pixels.

Hand labelling sixteen thousand images is a challenge in itself. To accelerate this process, slow movement of the experimental setup was exploited; images were batched into groups where little movement had occurred between frames and thus labels were expected to be similar. The first image was labelled manually (see Fig. 2), and those labels copied to every other image in the batch. The batch was then visually inspected for errors. In the Fig. 2, an image frame is shown before and after the manual labelling process. The image is divided into 64 units, each indexed based on its position in the image matrix. The indexed

---

[1] Rectified Linear Units.

images are labelled as "Background", "Gripper", "Fabric" or "Wrinkle," with each label shown in a different color for visual inspection.

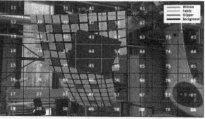

Fig. 2. A frame before and after the hand-labelling process, with the colored grids in the second image coded to represent the different classification categories of detection: Wrinkle (Cyan), Gripper (Green), Fabric (Yellow) and Background (Black) (Color figure online)

3.4   Phase 1 Results and Accuracy

The neural network achieved 95.5% accuracy in detecting wrinkles. Accuracy for other classes was even higher, as presented in Table 1. The slightly lower level of accuracy in wrinkle detection can be explained by the fact that, at a very small scale (32 * 32), it is hard to distinguish between a fabric and a wrinkle.

The network was trained on three datasets with different sizes to evaluate the effect of training set's size on accuracy of detection. The small, medium, and large training sets contained 750, 1500 and 3000 images respectively. Results show diminishing returns between the medium and large training sets. It is noteworthy that cross validation technique was used by splitting the dataset into training and testing sets, including 80% and 20% of the entire dataset, respectively.

Table 1. Accuracy of detection on initial dataset

	Accuracy of detection (%)		
Label	Small	Medium	Large
Wrinkle	92.5	95.5	95.5
Fabric	94.5	98.5	99.5
Background	95.5	97.5	98.5
Gripper	94.5	97.5	97.5
Overall	92.5	95.5	95.5

4 Phase 2 - Model Generalization

The neural network created in Sect. 3 was applied to a new fabric shape with different wrinkle properties. The same gripper was used to grasp the fabric, and all labels exhibited similar properties to the images in the first dataset. The new images were hand-labelled as explained in Sect. 3.3. This information was used strictly for evaluation; the neural network was not re-trained with these new labels (Fig. 3).

Fig. 3. Example of: Wrinkles used for training (left); Wrinkles in new data set (right)

4.1 Phase 2 Results and Accuracy

Wrinkle detection accuracy in this phase was evaluated to be 66.6% (Table 2), which is considerably less than the 95.5% accuracy obtained in Phase 1. The significant difference in the two results indicates that the model had some difficulty in generalizing to the new dataset. Gripper and fabric detection rates were down significantly; however, this was not explored, as the primary goal of the project was detection of fabric and wrinkles, and fabric detection is possible using traditional computer vision techniques as shown in Sect. 5.1.

Visual inspection of failed cases showed that this is largely due to wrinkle occlusion combined with poor lighting and shadow effects in failed cases. These occlusion and lighting issues changed for different views of the multi-view setup, which led to certain wrinkles being highly visible, and thus detectable, in one view while missed in another.

Table 2. Accuracy of detection against new dataset

	Accuracy of detection (%)
Wrinkle	66.6
Fabric	12.3
Background	85.5
Gripper	37.6
Overall	76.3

5   Phase 3 - Multi-view Inferencing

An approach was devised to increase accuracy when generalizing the model through correlation of multiple co-temporal views of the same fabric. View correlation consists of detecting the fabric using traditional computer vision techniques, and overlaying those fabrics as closely as possible to allow inference across multiple views. Once the fabrics are overlaid, the Dempster-Shafer Theory of Evidence [5,18] is applied to combine votes on each pixel from each view.

5.1   Fabric Detection

Fabric detection is facilitated by the observation that the gripper forms a nice frame, reliably separating the fabric from the background. Fabric detection, therefore, begins with locating and closing the gripper; the largest hole in the gripper mask is then the presence of fabric. An example of the initial input to this process can be seen in Fig. 1. Values such as intensity threshold and morphological structuring elements were selected manually through trial-and-error. Such a method presents problems in finding values which generalize to various images; the values which produced good results for the largest number of images in the sample set are presented here. The same values are used for all images and all views.

The contour of the gripper was found by combining three methods:

1. Identification of white gripper squares.
2. Identification of green gripper squares.
3. Edge detection to supplement boundary detection.

Item (1) is accomplished by thresholding in the CIE L*a*b color space. By accepting low color values, only white/gray pixels are retained. High values of lightness are retained to separate white pixels from gray. Good results were achieved by rejecting all pixels where either color channel is greater than 140, and rejecting lightness values below 180.

Item (2) is accomplished by thresholding in the HSV color space. Since the goal is to retain only green colors, hue values outside of the range 60–100 are rejected, and very low saturations (less than 80) or very high saturations (greater than 200) are also rejected.

Item (3) is accomplished by first denoising using the non-local means method [2] with an aggressive h value of 10. Canny edge detection [3] is then employed to identify significant edges in the image.

These three masks are combined, where any pixel which is retained in any mask is overall retained.

The gripper squares are joined through an alternating series of morphological closing with a disk structuring element of radius 3, and morphological dilation with a disk of radius 1. A general solution for the number of iterations is difficult; for the sample dataset, 35 iterations were performed on all images.

The gripper mask is inverted such that the fabric is kept and the gripper rejected. The main component is then separated from the other components and retained. All connected components are identified, and components not meeting specific requirements are discarded. These requirements are:

- An area of at least 150,000 pixels
- A maximum distance between the image center and the nearest non-zero pixel in the component
- A density less than 0.4 (number of white pixels in the bounding box, normalized by bounding box area)
- A height span or width span greater than 0.7, where the span is the dimension of the bounding box divided by the dimension of the image.

This filtration removes excessively large or small components. The components are then ranked by score, and the highest scoring component is deemed to be the fabric. The score combines closeness to the center of the image and area; if the component overlaps the center of the image, it is given maximum score so that it is always retained.

The morphological closing to connect the gripper squares is then reversed: multiple iterations of morphological opening with a disk of radius 3 and erosion with a disk of radius 1 are performed. One fewer iterations than the number of closings are performed, which gives a nice edge to the fabric.

Finally, any holes in the mask are filled by tracing the contour and then flood filling at the centroid.

5.2   Centering and Rotating the Image

The orientation and position of the gripper in the image relative to the camera changes across images, so the fabric mask is of non-uniform position and non-uniform rotation in the final images. To normalize these differences, the centroid of the mask is found and translated to the center of the image. The image is then rotated in the range -90 to $90°$, and the best orientation is used. An orientation is preferred if it maximizes the non-zero pixels in the center column of the image, plus the maximum number of non-zero pixels in any row of the image. The image is cropped to the rectangle with minimum bounds which contains non-zero pixels.

5.3   Correlating Multiple Views

Perspective correction is performed to normalize, as much as possible, non-uniform fabric orientation between images. Since the end-result is highly susceptible to small changes in perspective correction keypoints, human intervention is required to make identification as accurate as possible. The user is first presented with all camera views available for a time period (shown in Fig. 4), and must select the one with the least skewing and curvature. Control points are collected by having the user select four points on each image (top left of the fabric, top right of the fabric, bottom left of the fabric, and bottom right of the fabric). These points are then used to create a perspective warp transform for each image (Fig. 5).

Fig. 4. Five co-temporal masks of the same fabric

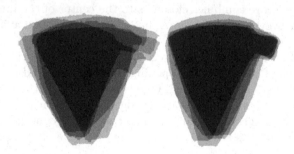

Fig. 5. Five overlaid, co-temporal fabric masks before correction (left) and after (right)

Some views are insufficient to be included in processing. That is, sometimes the fabric is too small, too skewed, or has some other unacceptable features which prevents inclusion; in such a case, the image is blacklisted and not included in results.

Fabric size is normalized by resizing each image to the maximum dimension (height and width) in all images. The aspect ratio is preserved in this resizing, and each image is then zero-padded as required to make absolute dimension match for all images; padding is done evenly from all sides so as to keep the fabric centered.

5.4   Re-labelling

Every acquired view consists of a tensor of probabilities mapping each pixel to a certain class. Once multiple views are overlapped, each pixel consists of multiple class probability tensors ($\vec{m}_{ij}$) coming from different views.

$$\vec{m}_{ij} = \begin{bmatrix} m_{ij}(Gripper) \\ m_{ij}(Fabric) \\ m_{ij}(Wrinkle) \\ m_{ij}(Background) \end{bmatrix} \tag{1}$$

Where i is the camera id, $i \in \{1, 2, ..., 5\}$, and j is the pixel location in the image, $j \in (2592 \times 1944)$. These probabilities are combined using the Dempster-Shafer rule of combination.

$$\vec{m}_j = \vec{m}_{1j} \oplus \vec{m}_{2j} \oplus \cdots \oplus \vec{m}_{5j} \tag{2}$$

Where $\oplus$ is the orthogonal sum. This produces a single tensor of classification probability ($\vec{m}_j$), which is mapped back to each source view by reversing the processing steps described above. Each source image is relabelled based on these new probabilities.

5.5   Phase 3 Results and Accuracy

Wrinkle detection accuracy is 85.9%, a significant increase over the Phase 2 results. Since wrinkle detection accuracy is the main goal, Gripper and Background labels were not preserved in Phase 3 and are combined in the Other label.

Results of this process are shown in Table 3. As in Phase 2, fabric detection accuracy is very low; however, as can be seen above, this problem can be solved by traditional computer vision techniques.

Table 3. Accuracy of detection after multi-view inferencing

	Accuracy of detection (%)
Wrinkle	85.9
Fabric	8.6
Other	89.7
Overall	83.9

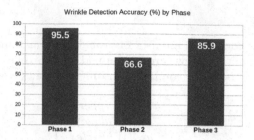

Fig. 6. Wrinkle detection results by phase

6   Conclusion

Wrinkle detection in the generalized inferencing case was 85.9% when evidential reasoning was used to fuse multi-view information (Fig. 6). This is an increase of 19.3% compared to the base case established in Phase 2.

The result is very promising, and shows that introducing a combination of computer vision and evidential reasoning can be used to help increase feature detection accuracy when a Deep Convolutional Neural Network (DCNN) is generalized to previously unseen, but similar, images.

7   Future Work

Inference on images with new features using a pre-trained neural network led to an expected decrease in accuracy. The neural network had learned the features which existed in both data sets, but not features exhibited only in the new data set. However, the certainty of classification was increased by combining multiple votes from several observations of the weaker classifier. It was shown that this method was able to produce good results. A logical extension of this possibility would be re-training the neural network on the new dataset, allowing it to learn the new features.

The arbitrary orientation and position of the gripper relative to the camera necessitated a process to overlap fabrics. Keypoint detection for perspective correction was performed by hand, which is obviously not desired in an automated process. Moreover, arbitrary geometries result in images with rotation occlusion, small fabric size, or other undesirable properties which can affect results. A fixed configuration of gripper and camera geometry could maximize lighting effects while minimizing warping, perspective and occlusion issues. Homography could then be used in transformations, making the overall process automatable, faster, and more robust.

The machine learning model could also be trained on a wider variety of wrinkles to allow greater generalization accuracy. However, the hand-labelling process used to create the supervised learning dataset is time consuming, and it would be desirable to create a faster alternative.

References

1. Bengio, Y., Lamblin, P., Popovici, D., Larochelle, H.: Greedy layer-wise training of deep networks. In: Advances in Neural Information Processing Systems, pp. 153–160 (2007)
2. Buades, A., Coll, B., Morel, J.M.: Non-local means denoising. Image Process. On Line **1**, 208–212 (2011). https://doi.org/10.5201/ipol.2011.bcm_nlm
3. Canny, J.: A computational approach to edge detection. IEEE Trans. Pattern Anal. Mach. Intell. **PAMI–8**(6), 679–698 (1986). https://doi.org/10.1109/TPAMI.1986. 4767851
4. Chellapilla, K., Puri, S., Simard, P.: High performance convolutional neural networks for document processing. In: Lorette, G. (ed.) Tenth International Workshop on Frontiers in Handwriting Recognition. Université de Rennes 1, Suvisoft, La Baule, France, October 2006. https://hal.inria.fr/inria-00112631, http://www. suvisoft.com
5. Dempster, A.P.: Upper and lower probabilities induced by a multivalued mapping. Ann. Math. Stat. **38**(2), 325–339 (1967). https://doi.org/10.1214/aoms/ 1177698950
6. Gupta, K., Körber, M., Krebs, F., Najjaran, H.: Vision-based deformation and wrinkle detection for semi-finished fiber products on curved surfaces. In: 2018 IEEE 14th International Conference on Automation Science and Engineering (CASE), pp. 618–623, August 2018. https://doi.org/10.1109/COASE.2018.8560559
7. Hinton, G.E., Osindero, S., Teh, Y.W.: A fast learning algorithm for deep belief nets. Neural Comput. **18**(7), 1527–1554 (2006)
8. Hinton, G.E., Salakhutdinov, R.R.: Reducing the dimensionality of data with neural networks. Science **313**(5786), 504–507 (2006)
9. Körber, M., Frommell, C.: Sensor-supported gripper surfaces for optical monitoring of draping processes. In: SAMPE (2017)
10. Krizhevsky, A., Sutskever, I., Hinton, G.E.: ImageNet classification with deep convolutional neural networks. In: Advances in Neural Information Processing Systems, pp. 1097–1105 (2012)
11. Lecun, Y.: Generalization and network design strategies. Elsevier (1989)
12. Lecun, Y., et al.: Backpropagation applied to handwritten zip code recognition. Neural Comput. **1**(4), 541–551 (1989)
13. Lecun, Y., et al.: Handwritten digit recognition with a back-propagation network. In: Advances in Neural Information Processing Systems, pp. 396–404 (1990)
14. Lecun, Y., et al.: Handwritten digit recognition with a back-propagation network. Neural Inf. Process. Syst. **2** (1997)
15. Ranzato, M., Huang, F.J., Boureau, Y., LeCun, Y.: Unsupervised learning of invariant feature hierarchies with applications to object recognition. In: 2007 IEEE Conference on Computer Vision and Pattern Recognition, pp. 1–8, June 2007. https:// doi.org/10.1109/CVPR.2007.383157
16. Rawat, W., Wang, Z.: Deep convolutional neural networks for image classification: a comprehensive review. Neural Comput. **29**(9), 2352–2449 (2017). https://doi. org/10.1162/neco_a_00990. pMID: 28599112
17. Russakovsky, O., et al.: Imagenet large scale visual recognition challenge. Int. J. Comput. Vis. **115**(3), 211–252 (2015)
18. Shafer, G.: A Mathematical Theory of Evidence, vol. 42. Princeton University Press, Princeton (1976)
19. Voggenreiter, H., Nieberl, D.: AZIMUT Abschlussbericht. TIB (2015)

Tile Priorities in Adaptive 360-Degree Video Streaming

Igor D. D. Curcio[1]([✉]) [iD], Dmitrii Monakhov[2], Ari Hourunranta[1],
and Emre Baris Aksu[1]

[1] Nokia Technologies, Tampere, Finland
{igor.curcio,ari.hourunranta,emre.aksu}@nokia.com
[2] Department of Signal Processing, Tampere University, Tampere, Finland
dimitrii.monakhov@tuni.fi

Abstract. For video applications, tiled streaming is a popular way to deliver viewport dependent 360-degree video. Unfortunately, dynamic adaptation to network bandwidth fluctuations of such video streams is still a challenge. This paper proposes a method for managing in a controlled way the graceful quality degradation in DASH-based streaming systems to deliver omnidirectional video. The method is enabled by the signaling of tile priority maps in order to reduce the impact of graceful degradation on the users' Quality of Experience (QoE). Simulation results show that this method allows degrading the system by over 10% of minor bandwidth usage during Viewport Dependent Streaming, without sacrificing the user QoE so much compared to the case that does not make use of this technique. Furthermore, the presented method improves flexibility from the service provider's standpoint.

Keywords: Video streaming · 360-degree video · Tiled streaming · Omnidirectional video · Bandwidth adaptation

1 Introduction

Within the video applications domain, 360-degree video is lately becoming more and more popular. This content allows users to experience an omnidirectional scene and increase the sense of immersion within the media. One way to experience 360-degree video is by using a Head Mounted Display (HMD), which enables a Virtual Reality (VR) immersive experience. Despite upcoming HMDs may have a large Field of View (FoV) (e.g., more than 180° horizontally), the user is capable of watching only a small portion of the whole omnidirectional space at a given time instant.

Streaming the whole 360-degree FoV is highly bandwidth demanding, although it provides a constant video quality for any possible user view orientation. In the last few years the research and industrial effort have concentrated on optimizing the bandwidth usage, by taking advantage of the partial FoV (i.e., *viewport*) seen by the users at any given time instant. Ideally, if a part of the content is not seen, then it does not need to be streamed, or it may be streamed only at lower quality, while the viewport content

© Springer Nature Switzerland AG 2020
T. McDaniel et al. (Eds.): ICSM 2019, LNCS 12015, pp. 212–223, 2020.
https://doi.org/10.1007/978-3-030-54407-2_18

is always streamed at high quality. This is the conceptual basis of what is known as *Viewport Dependent Streaming (VDS)* [1], as opposed to streaming the full 360-degree content at high quality (*Viewport Independent Streaming (VIS)*) [1]. VDS allows saving a considerable amount of bandwidth, in the order of more than 40% [2].

To increase efficiency and take advantage of current widely deployed video codecs features (such as HEVC), each 360-degree video frame (in equirectangular projection) is partitioned into tiles (i.e., sub-pictures) of smaller size which are independently decodable. The video data in the user viewport is, therefore, typically made of a tile grid of a given size. Common tile grids are horizontally and vertically organized into a grid, for example a 6 × 4 or 8 × 6 grid or even finer granularity grids [3].

The tile-based streaming problem is then reduced to streaming the minimum sufficient number of tiles to cover the viewport area, such that the user is guaranteed with continuous media rendering and display. Upon the user's change of orientation, a new set of tiles (corresponding to the new orientation) will have to be streamed, trying to minimize the *motion-to-high-quality (MTHQ) delay* which is perceived by the user [4].

To foster the deployment of a standardized solution for 360-degree streaming, the Motion Pictures Expert Group (MPEG) has been working and releasing the first version of the *Omnidirectional MediA Format (OMAF)* [5] specification, which uses DASH as delivery protocol and the ISO Base Media File Format as storage format for omnidirectional video streaming. MPEG is currently finalizing the second version of the OMAF standard, which includes new advanced features [6].

OMAF defines a mechanism to request tiles of different qualities independently. Therefore, there may be many tiles encoded at different qualities visible in the viewport at a given time instance. In a bandwidth-limited streaming session, the challenge for the player is to decide which tiles in the viewport to stream first, which ones may be streamed later (because its delayed rendering does not likely impair the QoE), and at which "higher" quality. This paper contributes to addressing this challenge, by enabling a mechanism to assign priorities to each of the tiles, so that the player has a deterministic way to gracefully degrade the video quality during VDS [7]. Our simulation results show that this technique efficiently allows degrading the system by over 10% of minor bandwidth usage during VDS, without sacrificing the user QoE so much compared to the case that does not make use of this technique.

The work is organized as follows: Sect. 2 introduces the usage of tile priorities; Sect. 3 shows simulation results of our experiments; Sect. 4 concludes the work.

2 Tile Priorities

2.1 The Method

A content creator is typically in the best position to decide, during VDS operations, what areas (within the omnidirectional space) are to be displayed at the highest quality, what areas may be displayed at a slightly lower quality within the viewport, and what areas may be displayed with a certain MTHQ delay within the viewport. This may be due to some prior knowledge or assumption that these degradations would not impair the subjective quality of the degraded parts.

The content creator may produce a priority map such as the one depicted in Fig. 1. This map can be obtained also using the users' collected watching pattern statistics, or other automatic semantic scene segmentation-based algorithms. The map could be defined based on the complexity of the content of each tile (e.g., number of objects in the scene), motion in the scene, saliency map estimation, hot spots, size of the tiles, etc. The server makes the map available to the player prior to the presentation time of each tile.

3	3	2	2	2	2	2	3	3	3
3	3	2	1	1	1	2	3	3	2
2	3	2	1	1	1	2	3	1	1
2	3	2	2	2	2	2	3	1	1
3	3	3	3	3	3	3	3	3	3

Fig. 1. Example of priority map.

In the above figure, each cell represents a tile within the equirectangular representation. If there are M × N tiles in a picture, there will be M × N priority values for a picture. In a DASH-based implementation, the priority values may be assigned on a segment-by-segment (or sub-segment) granularity level and be communicated from the server to the client (player) in advance. The server keeps a number of DASH video representations (e.g., encoded at different SNR qualities or resolutions) according to the number of priority levels defined in the system. The priority map value assigned by the content creator to each tile may have two possible usage modes:

1. A **relative quality** of the tile when this is displayed in a viewport. For example, if quality = 1 is defined as the highest quality level, then quality = 2 indicates that it is still visually acceptable to stream that given tile at that lower quality for the purpose of graceful degradation. During non-graceful degradation periods, all tiles within a viewport are streamed with quality = 1.
2. A **relative order** of the tile when it is streamed for display within a viewport. For example, if order = 1 is defined as the highest order level, then the tiles with order = 2 are streamed after all tiles with order = 1, for display within the viewport. This means that in case of lack of bandwidth, the relative order defines the streaming order, and such order determines what tiles are displayed first and which are displayed later, for a given fixed quality. This may produce a higher MTHQ delay for the tiles with order > 1, since those tiles will stay displayed at lower quality for a longer period of time. However, being this effect under the content creator control, there is a reasonable assurance that this strategy is the best for preserving the user's QoE. During non-graceful degradation periods, all tiles within a viewport are streamed with order = 1.

A DASH player with VDS capability can select the proper qualities for the tiles to stream based on the user's viewing direction. Typically, this would result in two quality levels: foreground and background. The priority map enables dividing the foreground quality level further. The priority map in Fig. 1 may be static or dynamic. A *static* one is a map that does not change over time, so it is fixed for the whole duration of a streaming session. A *dynamic* one is such that it changes over time, for example because the content has changed and shows different hot spots. Finally, a player may perform bandwidth adaptation based on two criteria:

A. **"Instantaneous" streaming** of the tiles based on the priority map. All tiles in a viewport are streamed at a quality calculated based on the available network bit rate and the graceful degradation to be achieved.
B. **Order-based streaming** of the tiles based on the priority map. All tiles in a viewport are streamed according to an order and progressively displayed at different time instances, based on the available bit rate and the graceful degradation to be achieved.

2.2 Example

Figure 2 illustrates an example usage for the order-based streaming (option B above). Given a 5 × 10 tile structure, the tiles are numbered sequentially from 1 onwards (as indicated in the top left corner of each grid element with a small number). The tile priority rank values at time T0 are indicated with a large number in Fig. 2, with a lower number indicating a higher priority. The current viewport at time T0 is depicted in red color. The client streams the current (and future) tiles priority map information prior to the presentation time of the tile segments (i.e., time T0). Based on the viewport, the client requests tile segments in the following order:

15, 16, 25, 26, 17, 27, 5, 6, 7, 35, 36, 37, 8, 18, 28, 38.

The player may perform simultaneous streaming requests of the same priority ranked tile segments. By analyzing the current available network throughput, the client may perform graceful degradation operations or bandwidth management to avoid bit rate spikes during a streaming session.

¹ 3	² 3	2	2	⁵ 2	⁶ 2	⁷ 2	⁸ 3	3	3
3	3	2	1	¹⁵ 1	¹⁶ 1	¹⁷ 2	¹⁸ 3	3	2
2	3	2	1	²⁵ 1	²⁶ 1	²⁷ 2	²⁸ 3	1	1
2	3	2	2	³⁵ 2	³⁶ 2	³⁷ 2	³⁸ 3	1	1
3	3	3	3	3	3	3	3	3	3

Fig. 2. Example of priority map usage (priority-based, adaptation criteria B. Time T0). (Color figure online)

In case of dynamic priority map, if the user watches the same viewport, but the tiles priority values change at time T1 > T0 (see Fig. 3), then the player requests tile segments in the following order for the next media segment duration:

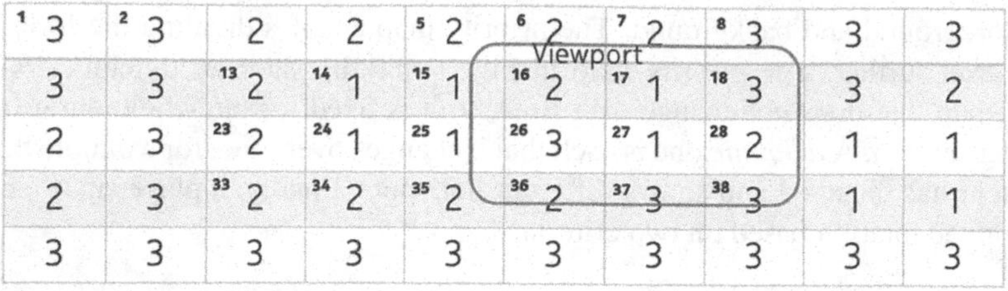

¹ 3	² 3	2	2	⁵ 2	⁶ 2	⁷ 2	⁸ 3	3	3
3	3	¹³ 2	¹⁴ 1	¹⁵ 1	¹⁶ 2	¹⁷ 1	¹⁸ 3	3	2
2	3	²³ 2	²⁴ 1	²⁵ 1	²⁶ 3	²⁷ 1	²⁸ 2	1	1
2	3	³³ 2	³⁴ 2	³⁵ 2	³⁶ 2	³⁷ 3	³⁸ 3	1	1
3	3	3	3	3	3	3	3	3	3

(Viewport spans columns 6–8, rows 1–4.)

Fig. 3. Example of priority map usage (priority-based, adaptation criteria B. Time T1 > T0 with tile priorities changed).

17, 27, 15, 25, 16, 28, 35, 36, 5, 6, 7, 8, 18, 26, 37, 38.

If the available network bandwidth is not sufficient, the player may, for example, only request the tiles with order = 1, i.e., 17, 27, 15 and 25 in high quality and leave the other tiles to be at low quality or delay their streaming and display at high quality. This increases the MHTQ delay for some tiles, but this operation is well controlled since it is recommended by the content creator via the usage of the priority maps.

If the user changes the viewport as depicted in Fig. 4 (i.e., the old viewport at time T0 is the one with dotted lines, and the new viewport at time T1 is the one with solid lines), then the player requests the tiles segments in the following order:

14, 24, 13, 23, 33, 34 (assuming 15, 16, 25, 26, 35 and 36 were already requested as high quality already before time T0).

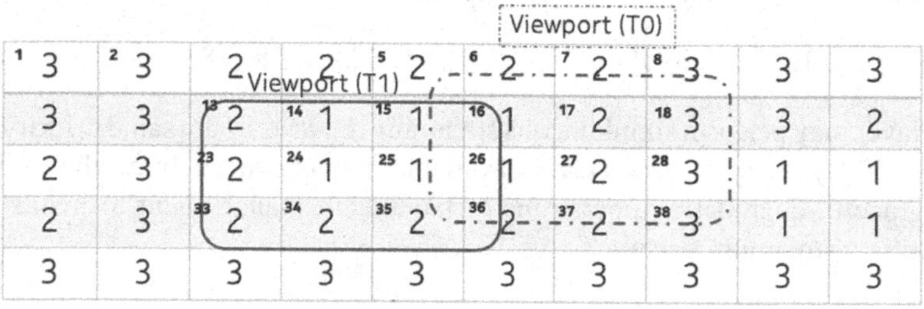

¹ 3	² 3	2	2	⁵ 2	⁶ 2	⁷ 2	⁸ 3	3	3
3	3	¹³ 2	¹⁴ 1	¹⁵ 1	¹⁶ 1	¹⁷ 2	¹⁸ 3	3	2
2	3	²³ 2	²⁴ 1	²⁵ 1	²⁶ 1	²⁷ 2	²⁸ 3	1	1
2	3	³³ 2	³⁴ 2	³⁵ 2	³⁶ 2	³⁷ 2	³⁸ 3	1	1
3	3	3	3	3	3	3	3	3	3

(Viewport (T0) shown with dotted lines spanning columns 6–8; Viewport (T1) shown with solid lines spanning columns 3–6.)

Fig. 4. Viewport change at time T1 > T0.

3 Simulation Results

This section shows simulation results based on the relative quality value (option 1 in Sect. 2.1) assigned to each tile, and the adaptation follows the option A described in the Sect. 2.1 ("Instantaneous" streaming). We selected five different video sequences as reported in Table 1. The number of users was 10, and the users watching patterns were free (no special guidance was given) for these sequences. We defined a static priority map for each of these clips, and the tile structure was 4 × 6 in horizontal and vertical directions, respectively. Two different experiments were run, and these are described in the following sections.

Table 1. Video clips used in the experiments.

Name	Resolution (pixels)	Duration (seconds)	Reference
360° Wife Carrying I 100 Moods From Finland (Wife Carry)	4 K (3840 × 1920)	49	[8]
360° Barn Dance I 100 Moods From Finland (Barn Dance)	4 K (3840 × 1920)	49	[9]
String quartet in Turku - 360 - Spatial Audio (Turku Street)	4 K (3840 × 1920)	49	[10]
Australia-Twelve-Apostles-Lookout (Apostles)	6 K (5760 × 2880)	61	[11]
Harbor	6 K (6144 × 3072)	60	[12]

The total video streams bit rate is calculated by summing up the sizes of the streamed DASH segments for the clips that make use of the tile priority maps. To compare it with the non-mapped (fixed) high quality levels, we used the following approximation:

1. Set the fixed quality level L;
2. Calculate the total number of DASH segments in a video clip;
3. Calculate the size S of all the streamed DASH segments for a given tile at quality level L;
4. Calculate the number N of DASH segments streamed at high quality for a tile;
5. Calculate the ratio R between N and the total number of DASH segments for a given tile;
6. The product R × S will give an approximation of how much data is streamed for the viewport tile at quality level L, i.e., the streamed tile data size across all DASH segments;
7. Finally, sum up the tile DASH segments sizes to get the total amount of streamed data for a clip with a given quality level L.

Note that in order to calculate the total streaming data size, the procedure above is performed for both low- and high-quality tiles, since there are two quality levels: high quality L, and low-quality X, the sizes of both a summed up. This procedure has been applied to both the following experiments described in Sects. 3.1 and 3.2.

3.1 QP-Based

In this experiment, the relative quality value was assigned to the priority map based on the encoding quantization parameter (QP) levels, as shown below in Figs. 5, 6, 7, 8 and 9. The mapping between the QP and the quality value for the 4 K sequences was as follows:

- QP 20 -> Quality value 0 (highest quality);
- QP 22 -> Quality value 1;
- QP 24 -> Quality value 2;

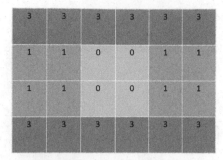

Fig. 5. Wife Carry priority map.

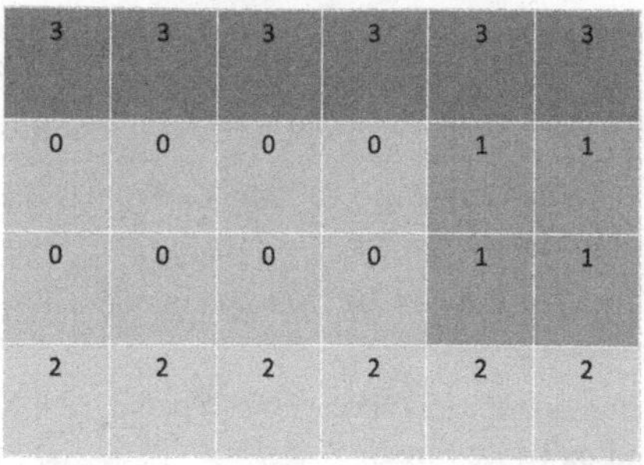

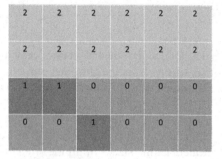

Fig. 6. Barn Dance priority map.

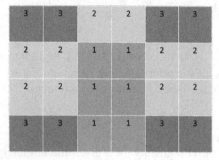

Fig. 7. Turku Street priority map.

Fig. 8. Apostles priority map.

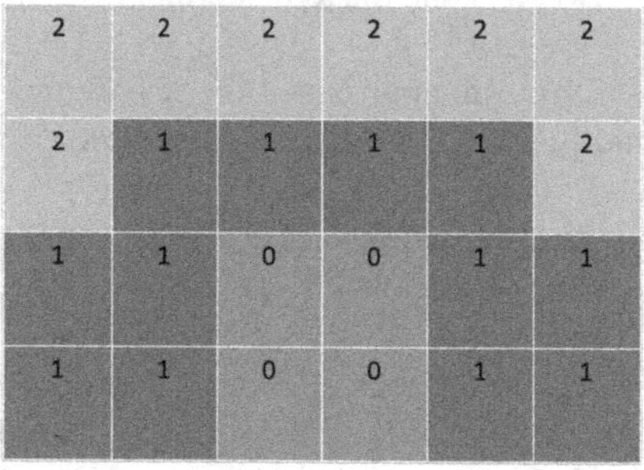

Fig. 9. Harbor priority map.

- QP 26 -> Quality value 3 (lowest quality).

The mapping between the QP and the quality value for the 6 K sequences follows:

- QP 23 -> Quality value 0 (highest quality);
- QP 26 -> Quality value 1;
- QP 30 -> Quality value 2 (lowest quality).

The criteria for assigning the QP levels to each tile was based on manual inspection of the interesting areas of the content.

Table 2. Bit rate savings for average watching patterns for the different video clips.

Clip	Viewport QP (no map)	Total bit rate without map (Mbps)	Total bit rate with map (Mbps)	Mode viewport QP (with map)	Bit rate saving (%)
Wife Carry	20	6.18	5.47	26	−11.41
Barn Dance	20	10.18	9.44	20	−7.30
Turku Street	22	11.18	10.44	24	−6.60
Apostles	23	59.71	53.24	30	−10.83
Harbor	23	30.84	26.58	26	−13.82
Average bit rate saving					**−9.99**

The column labeled with "Viewport QP (no map)" indicates the constant maximum quality level that the user would be watching in the viewport without using this method, whereas the column labeled as "Mode Viewport QP (with map)" indicates the most frequent quality level related to the viewport trajectories for the users' watching sessions. The columns "Total Bit Rate without map" and "Total Bit Rate with map" indicate respectively the total video streams bit rate (including viewport + non viewport areas) without and with priority map usage. The average bit rate saving across all video clips is 10%, showing that the usage of the priority maps is useful, and serves the purpose of graceful degradation when lacking sufficient bandwidth during VDS. In particular, for the Apostles sequence (6 K sequence), we show in Fig. 10 the bit rate plots for the different video clips representations. Here, the X axis denotes the QP value of the high-quality tiles in different video representations used in the experiment, whereas the Y axis denotes the total average bit rate of the videos when the viewport tiles are streamed only at that level, averaged across the users.

From the result in figure, the following observations can be done:

1. The usage of the priority map representation shows clearly a bit rate reduction of about 11%, compared to the next higher quality representation (QP23), offering an effective method for graceful degradation, whenever needed. For this 6 K sequence, the bit rate saving is over 6 Mbps, which is of significance.
2. The video representation using the priority map offers a higher quality on graceful degradation periods, compared to switching to the next available lower quality representation (i.e., switching drastically from QP23 down to QP26), since the bit rate of the representation using priority map is 53.24 Mbps, i.e., 39% higher than the QP26 representation (which has a total bit rate of 38.43 Mbps).
3. In a graceful degradation scenario, priority maps offer a way to "create" on-the-fly mixed quality representations, without the need of pre-encoding a large number of

representations for handling multiple bit rate cases. This gives a great flexibility to content creators, since a mixed quality representation can be formed during a streaming session based on the available network bandwidth, greatly reducing the number of needed representations, saving time and money for a content provider.

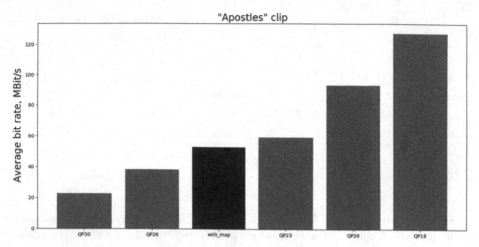

Fig. 10. Bit rates for the different representations of the Apostles (6 K) clip.

3.2 Average Bit Rate-Based

The second experiment was run with the same setup and parameters as described in the previous experiment. The only difference was in the way how the relative priority levels were assigned. In the experiment shown in Sect. 3.1 where a fixed QP (i.e., quality) was assigned, a variable bit rate stream was produced. In this experiment, the average bit rate for each quality level was fixed. The encoder [13] then divided the bits budget to different tiles according to its rate control algorithm [14, 15]. This produced a variable quality stream. The priority maps of the five test sequences were the same as we used for the first experiment (Figs. 5, 6, 7, 8 and 9). The mapping between the encoded bit rate and the quality value for the 4 K sequences was as follows:

- 13.3 Mbps -> Quality value 0 (highest quality);
- 11.4 Mbps -> Quality value 1;
- 9.5 Mbps -> Quality value 2;
- 7.6 Mbps -> Quality value 3 (lowest quality).

The mapping between the QP and the quality value for the 6 K sequences was as follows:

- 100 Mbps -> Quality value 0 (highest quality);

- 60 Mbps -> Quality value 1;
- 30 Mbps -> Quality value 2 (lowest quality).

Table 3. Bit rate savings for average watching patterns for the different video clips.

Clip	Total bit rate without map (Mbps)	Total bit rate with map (Mbps) A	Standard deviation of A (Mbps and %)	Bit rate saving (%)
Wife Carry	9.33	8.15	0.38 (4.7%)	−12.70
Barn Dance	10.04	9.38	0.53 (5.7%)	−6.60
Turku Street	8.84	8.10	0.45 (5.6%)	−8.40
Apostles	68.33	61.53	4.36 (7.1%)	−10.00
Harbor	61.83	43.45	2.98 (6.9%)	−29.70
Average bit rate saving				**−13.48**

The results were collected in the same way as it was done for the those presented in Sect. 3.1. We averaged the results over the test subjects, and these are shown in Table 3. The target bit rates were selected to provide roughly the same visual quality than in the first experiment. However, for simplicity, we used the same target bit rates for all sequences of the same resolution, which resulted to some differences in the column "Bit Rate without Map" between Tables 2 and 3 due to different complexities of the sequences. For example, Harbor is much simpler than Apostles, and hence the bit rate for it in the first experiment is significantly lower than in the second experiment.

In Table 3 we also included the standard deviation (the maximum is about 7%) of the calculated total bit rates with priority map across the 10 test subjects. The average bit rate saving is 13.5%, showing that the usage of the priority maps is useful also in this second experiment and it serves the purpose of graceful degradation when lacking sufficient bandwidth during VDS. Harbor is a sequence recorded with a moving camera, and this is the reason why the bit rate savings are considerably different than the other video clips. As already done in Sect. 3.1, for the Apostles sequence (which is a 6 K sequence), we show in Fig. 11 the bit rate plots for the different representations. Also in this case, the X axis denotes the bit rate of the high quality tiles in different video representations used in the experiment, whereas the Y axis denotes the total average bit rate of the videos when the viewport tiles are streamed only at that level, averaged across the users.

As done for the previous experiment, also for this experiment similar observations hold for the results in Fig. 11:

1. The priority map shows a bit rate reduction of 10% compared to the representation at 68.33 Mbps, offering an effective method for graceful degradation, whenever

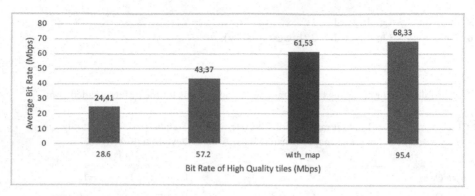

Fig. 11. Bit rates for the different representations of the Apostles (6 K) clip.

needed. For this 6 K sequence, the saving would be in the order of 7 Mbps, which is (again) non-negligible for a service provider.

2. The priority map offers a higher quality on graceful degradation periods, compared to switching to the next available lower quality representation, i.e., the bit rate of the priority map representation is about 42% higher than the bit rate of the next lower quality representation at 43.37 Mbps.

3. Priority maps offer a way to "create" on-the-fly mixed quality representations, as already stated in the previous experiment.

4   Conclusions

In viewport dependent streaming of omnidirectional video, adaptation to network bandwidth fluctuation can be eased thanks to the usage of the priority maps described in this work. With this solution, each video tile has an assigned priority that is used in case of bandwidth adaptation. Results of two different experiments show that the system may be degraded up to over 10% of minor bandwidth usage during VDS, without a drastic impact on the user's QoE. We used static priority maps in our experiments. Dynamic priority maps, which are time-based priority maps, may offer even improved results, since they could change based on the actual content in the videos. We also note that a content-based fine tuning of the priority values could give even further improvements in the results, especially for the cases of moving camera content (e.g., the Harbor sequence). We also note that while it was possible to calculate the average bit rate savings, the measurements of change in quality perception should be performed in a separate subjective evaluation test. In theory, for the users, the areas of lower quality in the priority maps should not be as interesting as the areas of higher quality. So, for those lower quality areas, the quality perception should be higher than what the objective metric would suggest.

References

1. Naik, D., Curcio, I.D.D., Toukomaa, H.: Optimized viewport dependent streaming of stereoscopic omnidirectional video. In: Proceedings of the 23rd ACM Packet Video Workshop (Within the ACM Multimedia Systems Conference), Amsterdam, The Netherlands (2018)

2. Curcio, I.D.D., Toukomaa, H., Naik, D.: Bandwidth reduction of omnidirectional viewport-dependent video streaming via subjective quality assessment. In: Proceedings of the ACM International Workshop on Multimedia and Alternate Realities (Within the Multimedia Conference), Mountain View, CA, U.S.A. (2017)
3. Monakhov, D., Curcio, I.D.D., Mate, S.: On data wastage in viewport-dependent streaming. In Proceedings of the 21th IEEE Multimedia Signal Processing Workshop, Kuala Lumpur, Malaysia (2019)
4. Curcio, I.D.D., Toukomaa, H., Naik, D.: 360-degree video streaming and its subjective quality. SMPTE Motion Imaging J. **127**(7), 28–38 (2018)
5. ISO/IEC: Information technology — Coded representation of immersive media (MPEG-I) — Part 2: Omnidirectional media format, FDIS (2018)
6. ISO/IEC: Text of ISO/IEC DIS 23090-2 2nd edition OMAF, w19042 (2020)
7. Curcio, I.D.D., Hourunranta, A., Monakhov, D., Aksu, E.B.: [OMAF] Update on sub-picture segment priority ranks for graceful degradation: simulation results and signaling. In: MPEG #127 Meeting, Göteborg, Sweden, m49411 (2019)
8. https://www.youtube.com/watch?v=E2dOKkg0ozY
9. https://www.youtube.com/watch?v=skUHYb7FqK4
10. https://www.youtube.com/watch?v=gkh4yW3WVn0
11. https://stock.atmosphaeres.com/video/350/Twelve+Apostles+Lookout
12. http://phenix.it-sudparis.eu/jvet/doc_end_user/current_document.php?id=4113
13. https://github.com/ultravideo/kvazaar
14. Ylä-Outinen, A.: Coding efficiency and complexity optimization of Kvazaar HEVC encoder. M.Sc. thesis, Tampere University of Technology (2018)
15. Li, B., Li, H., Li, L., Zhang, J.: λ domain rate control algorithm for high efficiency video coding. IEEE Trans. Image Process. **23**(9), 3841–3854 (2014)

Improving Temporal Stability in Inverse Tone-Mapped High Dynamic Range Video

Neeraj J. Gadgil$^{(\boxtimes)}$ and Guan-Ming Su

Dolby Laboratories Inc., 432 Lakeside Dr., Sunnyvale, CA 94085, USA
njgadg@dolby.com, guanmingsu@ieee.org

Abstract. Inverse tone mapping (ITM) is widely used to convert a standard dynamic range (SDR) image to its high dynamic range (HDR) version. While using frame-specific ITMs for a video sequence, temporal stability needs to be maintained not to cause visual artifacts such as flashing, flickering and delayed intensity-change. In this paper, we propose a weighted temporal filtering method to smooth look-up table (LUT)-based ITM to avoid such artifacts. Our proposed method uses a LUT-similarity measure and a histogram-based content-aware weighing for filtering LUTs in the time-domain. Our method is highly portable and can be applied to any set of LUT-based ITMs, agnostic to the way of their generation. Experiments exhibit effectiveness of our method.

Keywords: Visual artifact removal · Temporal filtering · Inverse tone mapping · High dynamic range

1 Introduction

High dynamic range (HDR) technology is becoming increasingly popular due to the superior viewing experience it offers, mainly in terms of increased contrast, brightness and richer colors [1, 2]. Tone mapping operation is used to convert HDR content to its SDR version which can be transmitted using existing video communication infrastructure [3, 4]. At the display side, an inverse of the tone mapping operation known as inverse tone mapping (ITM) is generally used to convert the standard dynamic range (SDR) signal into its HDR version. A 1D discrete-valued function such as a look-up-table (LUT)-based ITM is an efficient way to reconstruct HDR images, especially in real-time systems [7]. The LUT is generally computed for each frame of a video, such that it closely estimates the SDR-to-HDR transfer characteristics for that image.

Converting successive frames of a video scene into HDR using the ITM, poses a major challenge in terms of maintaining temporal stability. Naïve methods addressing the time-domain filtering can result in significant temporal visual artifacts. These artifacts are mainly of two types. Firstly, visual flashing or flickering i.e. a sudden change or fluctuations of signal intensity is observed in the mapped HDR video. We call a sudden increase or decrease of luminance at two nearby time instances as flashing. Such flashing is annoying to common viewers when there is no apparent indication of change of content e.g. scene, and more so to the content creators/colorists. Flickering is due to frequent

© Springer Nature Switzerland AG 2020
T. McDaniel et al. (Eds.): ICSM 2019, LNCS 12015, pp. 224–233, 2020.
https://doi.org/10.1007/978-3-030-54407-2_19

changes in luminance seen for a perceivable duration of time e.g. 5 s. These temporal artifacts occur mainly due to each frame using a significantly different ITM, resultantly constructing successive HDR frames that differ in the level of luminance. Secondly, a delay in the change of luminance is observed due to the lack of crisp transition, especially at the scene boundary. This means, the luminance-change is not where it should be, causing the delayed response to viewers. Temporal smoothing methods that rely on the scene-cut information also often fail mainly in real-time processing systems, due to the lack of a perfect on-the-fly scene-cut detector.

A time-domain filtering of the LUT-based ITM can be used to smooth the successive frame's overall luminance levels, reducing the temporal fluctuations as perceived by viewers. Our main idea is to use a different *weight* for each frame in the filtering process. Firstly, it is useful to decide the weight of a neighboring frame based on how close the LUT is to that of the frame under consideration. We call it the LUT-similarity measure which can be quantified based on the difference between the LUTs. Another important consideration is the image statistics such as the distribution of pixels (histogram) to their codewords. The histogram can identify the codewords that are deemed important due to a heavy representation in terms of a large number of pixels. We consider these two factors namely, the LUT-similarity and image histogram to determine smoothing weight in the filtering process.

In this paper, we propose a weighted filtering of the LUT-based ITM to address the temporal instability issues. We use a content-dependent LUT-similarity measure for improving temporal stability of the mapped HDR video. The main contributions of this paper are:

- A LUT-similarity measure that can sufficiently differentiate between similar and different LUTs in consecutive frames is described
- Image histogram is used as a measure of content-dependency for each frame
- We propose a weighted temporal filter, using the LUT-similarity measure and the content dependent factor to mitigate visual artifacts
- Our method is suited for a fixed maximum-delay system such as *linear* encoding i.e. broadcasting one-frame-in, one-frame-out/real-time scenario
- Our method is agnostic to the way LUT-based ITM is generated and is portable to any LUT-based HDR video communication system

We present key related works in terms of a brief summary of the state-of-the-art in the following section.

2 Related Works

HDR technology has been studied largely in terms of new color spaces, electro-optical transfer functions (EOTF), contrast enhancement mechanisms and end-to-end codec systems by many academic and industrial setups [1–4, 12]. In the past few years, there has been a considerable interest in proposing single image range extension methods with and without the use of ITM [5–7]. Pixel-based SDR-to-HDR transfer generally does not require an ITM. However, due to a high amount of computations involved, the pixel-based approach is not practicable where the conversion needs to happen on-the-fly and often in real-time. The current hardware support prefers a level of computational complexity to afford only simple ITMs e.g. a 1D/3D LUT for HDR reconstruction.

There have been many methods to design the ITM for doing the SDR-to-HDR transfer for images [5–12]. In [6], a high quality tone mapping algorithm is designed for wide range of exposure images, but it is used independently on each individual frame in a video. Our previous work from [7] also uses a dynamic ITM algorithm for single images. Only a few approaches have addressed the temporal stability issues in handling the HDR video. The method from [8] addresses temporal coherency only by fixing the display parameters such as black levels, white points irrespective of image content. This leads to a conservative and static quality enhancement. In other work [9], temporal stability is addressed by having the range expansion map that is extended temporally using a "median-cut" method. The work in [10] uses samples from backward and forward frames while rendering a video. However, these methods do not use a 1D ITM curve, but instead rely on a pixel-level map, which adds to data rate in video transmission and increases heavy load on the computational resources. Furthermore, such specific methods cannot be applied to a general LUT-based ITM. In [11], piecewise polynomials are used to design the ITM that efficiently converts an SDR image to HDR. A LUT can be easily derived by evaluating the polynomial for all SDR codewords. But this work does not address the temporal stability aspect.

To apply LUT-based ITM for HDR videos, a method that is dependent on the neighboring LUTs is needed for the temporal smoothing. It is also important that the smoothing method is aware of the image content along with the ITM.

3   Proposed Method

We improve the state-of-the-art solutions by proposing a new method to temporally filter framewise LUTs to avoid flickering in the resulting HDR video. There can be several cases of intensity fluctuations in time-domain:

- The framewise LUT changes for successive frames in a single scene that needs to be temporally stabilized
- The framewise LUT changes for successive frames on a scene-boundary and needs to maintain the crisp transition (due to scene-cut)
- A scene-cut detection method can falsely indicate a scene-boundary, thus cannot be used reliably to filter framewise LUTs

3.1   The Key Concept: Weighted Temporal Filtering of LUTs

Considering above key cases, we employ a weighted LUT-smoothing approach that considers a symmetric window of M frames around the central frame. The weights of the temporal LUT filter are designed based on the following principles:

- A LUT-similarity measure to indicate how "similar" the current frame's LUT is to the LUT of its temporal neighbors. A significantly different LUT suggests the tone-mapped HDR values of temporal neighbors are much different from that of the current frame. Hence, such temporal neighbors should carry lower influence in temporal smoothing.

- A content-dependent weight is determined by the SDR luminance (Y-channel in YCbCr image). It generally gives a higher influence on those codewords having a large number of pixels.

The weight of a LUT is computed based on the above two influence-factors. Using the weight of each LUT in the window, the filtering is done to compute the central frame's output LUT. Thus, our proposed method ensures that the LUT smoothing process is based on temporally-local LUT similarity, content-adaptive and independent of any external scene-cut detection method.

3.2 Notations and Preliminaries

Let T_j be the non-smoothed LUT computed as ITM for the jth frame of a video sequence and T_j^b be the normalized HDR codeword value between [0 1] at the b'th SDR luma codeword for frame j. Denote N^S as the total number of SDR codewords $N^S = 2^{B_S}$, where B_S is the SDR bit-depth. An example LUT for $B_S = 10$ is shown in Fig. 1.

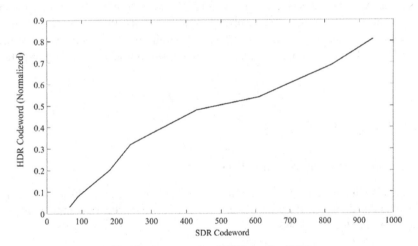

Fig. 1. An example of LUT used as ITM

There are total $N^S = 1024$ SDR codewords. Each SDR codeword is mapped to an HDR codeword on a scale of 0 to 1. Next, we show an example of non-smoothed LUTs for consecutive frames: $j - 1$, j and $j + 1$ in Fig. 2. It can be observed that the LUTs differ in the highlight part. When they are used to reconstruct successive HDR images as a part of a video scene, the highlight part of the images has considerable intensity changes due to the differences in LUTs. Temporal smoothing becomes necessary.

To do the weighted smoothing of LUTs, we consider a symmetric window of M frames on each side (total $2M + 1$ frames) of the center-frame j, i.e. $[j - M, j + M]$, for smoothing T_j. The smoothed output LUT for the frame j is $\tilde{T}_j$.

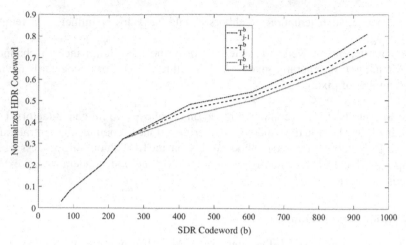

Fig. 2. Examples of LUTs of consecutive frames

3.3 LUT Similarity

LUT similarity is measured for the mapped HDR values from each SDR codeword b between central frame j and each temporal neighbor frame $m \in [j - M, j + M]$, in terms of normalized squared-difference. The LUT similarity ($\beta_{j,m}^b$) at the b'th codeword for the LUT of the m'th frame, with respect to the center frame at j, can be computed as

$$\beta_{j,m}^b = \left(T_j^b - T_m^b \right)^2 \tag{1}$$

Note that $\beta_{j,j}^b = 0$.

3.4 Content-Dependent Weighing Factor

Let α_j^b be the content-dependent weighing factor that is used as a multiplier to the LUT similarity and is determined for each b'th SDR codeword by the SDR image histogram of the j'th frame: h_j^b, as follows:

$$\alpha_j^b = \frac{\log\left(h_j^b + 1\right)}{\left(\sum_{k=0}^{N^S-1} \log\left(h_j^k + 1\right)\right)} \tag{2}$$

Taking the logarithm of histogram reduces the unbalanced impact from extreme large and small pixel distribution of some codeword. We add 1 while taking the logarithm to ensure that the weighing factor is 0 for a codeword that is not represented in the image by any pixel.

3.5 Temporal Smoothing

To smooth the LUT of the j'th frame, the weight for each m'th frame LUT where m is from its temporal neighborhood: $[j - M, j + M]$, is used. The weight is computed as exponential term involving contributions from both histogram and LUT difference. Using Eqs. (1) and (2), the weight for the j'th frame ($w_{j,m}$) LUT for smoothing the j'th frame LUT is computed as:

$$w_{j,m} = \exp\left(-\gamma \frac{1}{N^S} \sum_{b=0}^{N^S-1} \alpha_j^b \beta_{j,m}^b\right), \tag{3}$$

where γ is a constant determined empirically, such that the smoothing acts reasonably based on test content and observations. Thus, our weight is specific to a frame and same for all codewords in that frame.

Using the weight $w_{j,m}$ from Eq. (3) as the multiplier to each T_m^b for $m \in [j - M, j + M]$, we compute the smooth LUT for the center frame j (i.e., $\tilde{T}_j$) as follows:

$$\tilde{T}_j^b = \frac{\sum\limits_{m=-M}^{M} w_{j,m} T_m^b}{\sum\limits_{m=-M}^{M} w_{j,m}} \tag{4}$$

We use $M = 12$ (i.e. 12 frames on each side) for LUT smoothing for 24 frame per second (fps) content. The resulting LUT for the j'th frame, $\tilde{T}_j$ is used as a transfer function to convert SDR frame to HDR.

4   Results and Discussion

A total of 352 clips in our database with a variety of content such as movies, sport, animations etc., and of various spatial, temporal resolution and time durations were tested on several HDR displays such as reference monitors, TVs. The proposed method eliminated all visual artifacts and improved the temporal stability of the resulting HDR content considerably.

Figure 3 shows example (I) of comparison among different LUT smoothing methods: (a) No Filter (dashed magenta), (b) No scene-cut (dotted black), (c) Scene-cut aware filter (dashed green) and (d) Our proposed method (blue). The X-axis is temporal frame index, the Y-axis is the 16-bit HDR codeword normalized on [0, 1] corresponding to the 10-bit SDR codeword of 750. Thus, the plot shows for successive frames, the corresponding HDR codewords of a fixed SDR codeword. The dashed vertical lines indicate the scene-cut frames as detected by an external scene-cut detector.

Note the second scene from the above figure is zoomed for clarity in Fig. 4. It can be observed that the LUT with no filtering i.e. (a) in magenta line has a lot of fluctuations within a scene. The difference of 0.01 on the Y-axis, i.e. the range of plot shown in Fig. 5, means more than 650 in 16-bit codeword domain or 55 nits of linear light which

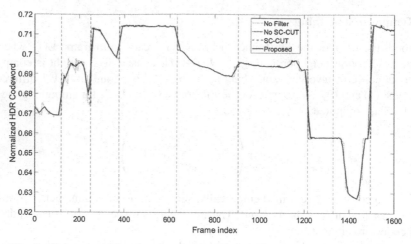

Fig. 3. Comparison of various temporal LUT smoothing methods for example (I)

is significantly noticeable on an HDR display. It can be visually observed as the change in brightness levels, causing annoying flickering effect. Our proposed method i.e. (d) in blue curve is able to produce a smooth-valued temporal curve that removes the visual flickering. The other two curves (b) and (c) are also able to reasonably avoid the flickering by smoothing the curve.

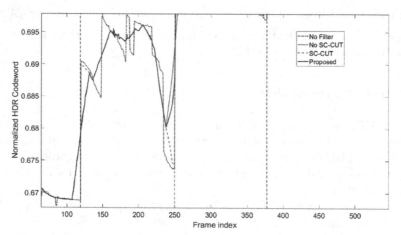

Fig. 4. Enlarged plot emphasizing scene # 2 of the clip in example (I)

Figure 5 shows example (II). Here, the Y-axis is the 16-bit HDR codeword normalized on [0, 1] corresponding to the 10-bit SDR codeword of 800. For this clip, (c) has produced a jump in intensity (indicated by the vertical arrow) between two successive frames from a single scene (indicated by **Q**) due to a false detection of scene-cut. Based on the codeword values, this amounts to 5 nits of light, but is noticeable to common viewers since it is a relatively darker scene as compared with example (I). This false scene-cut is

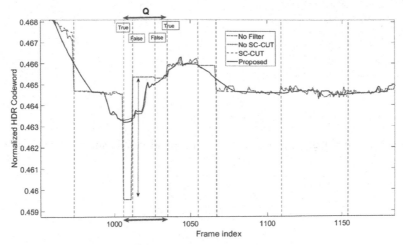

Fig. 5. Comparison of various temporal LUT smoothing methods in example (II)

due to a bright burn-in subtitle disappearance from the scene, causing overall intensity going down, hence falsely detecting as scene-cut. The difference in the resulting HDR intensity causes visual flashing in both cases i.e. (a) No smoothing and (c) Smoothing with scene-cut. Whereas, our proposed smoothing method (blue) is able to provide a relatively smoother curve by disregarding the binary scene-cut data and relying more on the LUT-similarity information. Method (b) disregards the scene-cut data and uses equal weights, hence for example (II) method (b) is free of flashing.

However, in a true scene-cut scenario where the scenes have totally different contents, we obviously see the delayed scene-brightness transition by (b). Our proposed method has a quicker transition and does not produce any visible delay in brightness change from scene-to-scene due to a low LUT-similarity weight for those unrelated frames.

Figure 6 shows final LUTs by methods (a), (b) and (d) of 10 frames, 5 frames in each of the two neighboring scenes, as example (III). Thus, there is a true scene-cut after 5 frames. With two different scenes, we expect to see two well separated groups of LUTs in the plot. From Fig. 6, method (a) produces an artifact-free video due to LUT separation indicated by arrows, same as (c) in this case. Despite having a true scene-cut, method (b) produces LUTs closer to each other, not distinguishing two different scenes, thus causing slow brightness change in the resulting HDR images. Our proposed method is able to keep the separation reasonably well, indicated by arrows. The HDR codeword difference at the scene-cut occurrence in (d) is smaller as compared to (a) or (c), but the separation is sufficient to maintain a crisp transition from one scene to other, not causing any visual artifacts.

Thus, for the key representative examples (I), (II) and (III), each with a different temporal stability challenge, overall our method is considerably better than any other LUT-smoothing method.

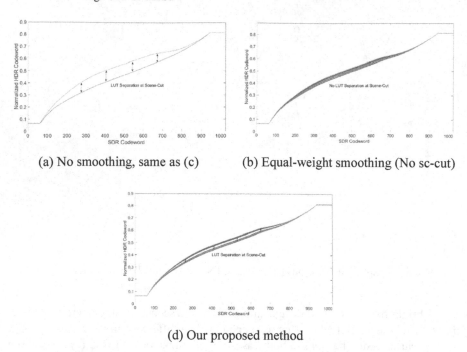

(a) No smoothing, same as (c)   (b) Equal-weight smoothing (No sc-cut)

(d) Our proposed method

Fig. 6. Comparison of various temporal LUT smoothing methods in example (III)

5 Conclusion

In this paper, we proposed a LUT-smoothing method for achieving temporal stability for the mapped HDR video. Our proposed method uses LUT-similarity and content-dependent ITM-smoothing weights for filtering. Experimental results indicate that our method is able to mitigate the visual artifacts such as temporal flashing, flickering and delayed luminance change. Our method does not rely on a perfect scene-cut detector and is highly portable such that is can be applied for any ITM-generation method.

References

1. Reinhard, E., Heidrich, W., Debevec, P., Pattanaik, S., Ward, G., Myszkowski, K.: High Dynamic Range Imaging: Acquisition, Display, and Image-Based Lighting. Morgan Kaufmann, Burlington (2010)
2. Borer, T., Cotton, A.: A display Independent high dynamic range television system, Research & Development White Paper-WHP 309, British Broadcasting Corporation (2015)
3. Gadgil, N., Song, Q., Su, G.-M., Hulyalkar, S.: The technology behind the exceptional visual experience via high dynamic range. APSIPA Trans. Sig. Inf. Process. **7**, e17 (2018)
4. Konstantinides, K., Su, G.M., Gadgil, N.: High dynamic range video coding. In: Bhattacharyya, S., Deprettere, E., Leupers, R., Takala, J. (eds.) Handbook of Signal Processing Systems, pp. 165–191. Springer, Cham (2019). https://doi.org/10.1007/978-3-319-91734-4_5
5. Banterle, F., Ledda, P., Debattista, K., Chalmers, A.: Inverse tone mapping. In: Proceedings of the 4th International Conference on Computer graphics and Interactive Techniques in Australasia and Southeast Asia, pp. 349–356. ACM (2006)

6. Kovaleski, R., Oliveira, M.: High-quality reverse tone mapping for a wide range of exposures. In: 2014 27th SIBGRAPI Conference on Graphics, Patterns and Images, pp. 49–56. IEEE (2014)
7. Kadu, H., Gadgil, N., Su, G.-M.: Reverse tone mapping of high dynamic range video using Gaussian process regression. In: IEEE International Conference on Multimedia Information Processing and Retrieval, San Jose, CA, March 2019, pp. 409–414. IEEE
8. Rempel, A., et al.: Ldr2hdr: on-the-fly reverse tone mapping of legacy video and photographs. ACM Trans. Graphics (TOG) **26**, 39 (2007)
9. Banterle, F., Ledda, P., Debattista, K., Chalmers, A.: Expanding low dynamic range videos for high dynamic range applications.: In: Proceedings of the 24th Spring Conference on Computer Graphics, pp. 33–41. ACM (2008)
10. Banterle, F., Chalmers, A., Scopingo, R.: Real-time high fidelity inverse tone mapping for low dynamic range content. In: Eurographics (Short Papers), pp. 41–44 (2013)
11. Chen, Q., Su, G.-M., Yin, P.: Near constant-time optimal piecewise LDR to HDR inverse tone mapping. In: Proceedings of SPIE, vol. 9404, pp. 9404.1–11 (2015)
12. Kadu, H., Song, Q., Su, G.-M.: Single layer progressive coding for high dynamic range videos. In: IEEE Picture Coding Symposium, San Francisco, CA, June 2018

Multimedia in Medicine

Assessing the Capability of Deep-Learning Models in Parkinson's Disease Diagnosis

Christopher West$^{(\boxtimes)}$, Sara Soltaninejad , and Irene Cheng

Department of Computing Science, University of Alberta, Edmonton, AB, Canada
chrisjwest99@gmail.com, {soltanin,locheng}@ualberta.ca

Abstract. Parkinson's Disease is one of the leading age-related neurological disorders affecting the general population. Current diagnostic techniques rely on patient symptoms rather than biomarkers. Symptomatic diagnoses are subjective and can vary highly. Our work aims to remedy this by presenting a novel approach to Parkinson's Disease diagnosis. We propose and assess four deep-learning based models that classify patients based on biomarkers found in structural magnetic resonance images, and find that our 3D-Convolution-Neural-Network model demonstrates high efficacy in the task of diagnosing Parkinson's disease, with an accuracy of 75% and 76% sensitivity. As well, our work highlights potential biomarkers for the disease found in the cerebellum and occipital lobe.

Keywords: Deep-learning · Parkinson's Disease · Biomarkers

1 Introduction

Parkinson's Disease (PD) is a progressive neurodegenerative disease that primarily affects the ability of an individual to perform basic motor movements. Common symptoms include bradykinesia (slow movement), difficulty in speaking and an unsteady gait. PD ranks as the second most common neurological disease after Alzheimer's disease, with a prevalence of 6.2 million affected globally [1]. The disease is particularly prevalent in the aging community, affecting 1% of those above age 60 [2]. Despite this, the underlying pathology of the disease is not well understood [3].

In general, PD is diagnosed when motor symptoms begin to manifest. However, a patient may have lost 50–70% of their dopaminergic neurons before these symptoms appear [4]. With this in mind, diagnostic methods such as MRI are of particular interest. This is because a pre-symptomatic diagnosis may prove crucial in stopping or slowing the disease before it progresses to a debilitating stage. Although PD is ostensibly incurable, promising new treatments such as Exenatide [5] may be effective if used at an early stage.

For the most part, structural MRI (sMRI) is not currently used in PD diagnosis. This is due to a traditionally poor ability for sMRI to detect subtle physiological changes in areas associated with PD (i.e. Basal Ganglia) [6]. However,

© Springer Nature Switzerland AG 2020
T. McDaniel et al. (Eds.): ICSM 2019, LNCS 12015, pp. 237–247, 2020.
https://doi.org/10.1007/978-3-030-54407-2_20

our approach seeks to circumvent this through the computational sensitivity of deep-learning based methods. As well, unlike CT or x-ray imaging, sMRI does not subject the patient to high levels of ionizing radiation [7].

When discussing diagnosis, it is important to consider the severity of the disease. A treatment that is helpful in early stage PD may become ineffective if applied only at a later stage. To classify severity, clinicians commonly use two metrics: Hoehn and Yahr (H&Y) Score [8] or the Unified Parkinson's Disease Rating Scale (UPDRS) [9]. These metrics provide a useful method for doctors to quantify and evaluate patient outcomes. Primarily, our work focuses on binary classification between PD and Healthy control (HC) patients, but could be extended to fit these metrics.

Our work presents a novel approach to diagnosis of PD based on deep-learning frameworks. Specifically, we construct multiple models to classify patients strictly from sMRI data. Similar approaches with computer-aided diagnosis have been taken in the past for conditions such as Alzheimer's disease [10] and Attention Deficit Hyperactivity disorder [11].

We will now touch on some of the related work done in deep-learning based PD diagnosis, followed by an explanation of our data and preprocessing. Then, we explain our methods and their results, with a final discussion on the findings of this work.

2   Related Work

In the case of deep-learning-based classification of PD, it is important to consider several distinct elements of the problem. The first and arguably most important of these elements is the overall accuracy of the method. Regardless of the elegance or apparent efficacy of a model, one which yields poor results is ultimately not useful in a practical setting. Along with accuracy comes the simplicity of the method, as well as the availability of the data. These two points are of particular importance in this task, as the domain of PD classification is largely medical rather than computational. Data is often not abundant, and any tool built to assist clinicians must be readily applicable. It is important to remember that a clinician is not a data scientist. With this in mind, we will assess new work in the field of deep-learning-based PD classification.

Choi et al. propose a model to classify PD patients based on Convolutional-neural-networks (CNN) and SPECT imaging [12]. SPECT imaging is highly specialized, and requires an injection of a radioactive isotope to monitor its uptake in different areas of the body. This specialization is reflected in the fact that over a one year period of England's NHS imaging operations, there were approximately 100 times more MRI scans performed than SPECT [13]. As well, because of the injection of a tracer, the technique may be considered somewhat invasive. This suggests that a model based on SPECT imaging may lack applicability in common medical use. Despite this, the model achieves a 96.0% accuracy with 100% sensitivity. This is coupled with a relatively large dataset (in medical terms) of 624 preprocessed samples, which suggests a relatively robust model.

It is important to consider that there is a significant class imbalance, with 431 PD to 193 HC samples. Class imbalance in the training set is detrimental to the performance of CNNs because they tend to over-classify the majority class [14]. The authors do no upsampling or downsampling to correct this class imbalance, but they perform data-augmentation in the form of L-R flipping to increase the total training sample size. In summation, Choi et al. put forward a promising but somewhat niche deep-learning based model to classify PD.

Long et al. [16] propose a machine-learning based approach to classification of PD from resting-state functional MRI (rsf-MRI). What makes rsf-MRI different from sMRI is that it detects subtle changes in blood-flow between areas of the brain, effectively allowing one to observe areas of activity due to higher metabolism. Meanwhile, sMRI only detects general anatomical features in the brain, while ignoring activity. The researchers segment into separate grey-matter, white-matter and cerebrospinal fluid maps, and then extract 116 features for classification. The actual classification process is done with a hyperbolic tangent kernel, and the researchers achieve 87% classification accuracy. These results are quite good, although it's important to consider that the experiment was done with very small number of samples (17 PD and 27 HC). This is not as much of a problem for rsf-MRI, because the data is rich and one can extract many features from very few scans. They discover several regions-of-interest, some of which are supported from previous clinical findings and it would be of significant interest to explore further research in rsf-MRI-based PD detection.

3   Data and Preprocessing

3.1   Data Acquisition

In our work, subject data is obtained from the Parkinson's Progression Markers Initiative (PPMI) public dataset. The dataset consists of T1-weighted sMRI scans for 568 PD and HC subjects. From this, 445 subjects are selected, with the rest omitted due to structural abnormalities during preprocessing. There exists a large class imbalance among the remaining data, with 299 PD to 146 HC subjects. This class imbalance is resolved with the supplementation of 153 HC T1-weighted sMRI scans from the publicly available IXI dataset, with a resulting total of 598 class-balanced patients. Demographic data is also collected and shown in Table 1.

Table 1. Demographic data

	PD	HC	Total
Age (years)	62.0 ± 9.54	49.2 ± 16.9	55.6 ± 15.1
Sex (male/female)	189/110	172/127	361/237

3.2 Preprocessing

Due to morphological and dimensional differences between scans, the samples must be standardized to a common format so that they are comparable. We initially resize all scans to the same dimensions so that they will fit in our model. Then, we must perform an intensity normalization. MRI intensity is measured in arbitrary units, and as such, there is a large discrepancy in inter-subject intensity values. We correct this by standardizing intensity on a per-patient basis, fixing all values to the range $[0, 1]$. After this, more complex preprocessing operations are performed with the use of the FSL toolkit [17], as explained below.

A pipeline is constructed to preprocess the dataset using the Anatomical Processing Script (fsl_anat). Firstly, the data is reoriented to MNI orientation (fslreorient2std) such that all scans face the same direction. Then we perform a bias-field correction (FAST) [18] to remove general intensity non-uniformities. Following this, the brain is extracted from the scan (FNIRT/BET) [19] and linearly registered to the standard MNI152 format (FLIRT) [20,21]. Non-linear registration (FNIRT) was omitted because of a tendency to have unpredictable deformation corrections with regard to a standard template [22]. At this point, artifacts created in the preprocessing step, namely erroneous voxel intensity values higher than the global max of 1, are corrected to be within the normal range of $[0, 1]$. Note that scans are zero-padded from a size of $91 \times 109 \times 91$ to a size of $96 \times 112 \times 96$ when they are inputted into the model, since these dimensions are repeatedly divisible by 2 and thus lead to cleaner convolution (Fig. 1).

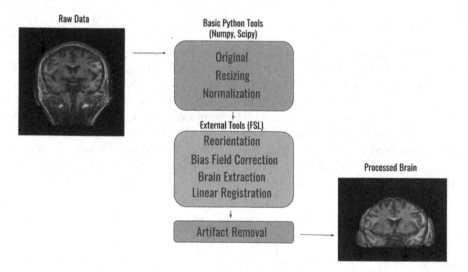

Fig. 1. Preprocessing pipeline

4   Proposed Method

We take two distinct approaches to classification for deep-learning based models. The first approach is based on three-dimensional analysis, while the second is two-dimensional. All models are built using TensorFlow.

4.1   Three-Dimensional Models

(M1: 3D-CNN). In the three-dimensional approach, we test three models. The first of these is a generic $3D$ Convolutional Neural Network, with 3 sets of $3D$ Convolution + Max Pooling Layers. Kernel Size is $[3, 3, 3]$ and stride is $[2, 2, 2]$. Leaky ReLU units are used at each layer to introduce non-linearity to the data. We flatten the output of the final pooling layer, and use it as the input of a small 4 layer neural network. The flat layer is passed into the first dense layer of 512 neurons. Dropout with 30% loss is introduced after the first dense layer to minimize over-fitting. Following this, we enter a 128 neuron layer, and then the final 2 class-logit layer. The output is the computed softmax of the two class probabilities. We train using cross-entropy loss and ADAM optimizer with a learning rate of 0.00001. Model architecture is shown in Fig. 2(a).

(M2: 3D-DAE). The second model is a $3D$ Denoising Convolutional Autoencoder followed by a classifying neural network. The autoencoder is under-complete, and the input is purposely corrupted. The corruption is done by masking between 20–30% of the input pixels to zeros before passing into the autoencoder. Both the corruption and under-completeness force the autoencoder to obtain an efficient latent-space-representation of the voxel data. We allow the autoencoder to train unsupervised for some time, using mean-squared-error and ADAM optimizer. Once it can recreate input scans with high accuracy, we take the compressed latent space representation of our "encoder" and pass it to the neural network. This is a form of feature reduction for our data. The classifying neural network has the same structure as the one used in the 3D-CNN, starting with a flat layer and ending in a softmax between the PD and HC logit. See Fig. 2(b) for the detailed structure. Note that we tried stacking autoencoders, but the results were generally poor and are not included in this paper.

4.2   Two-Dimensional Models

sMRI data is represented as a $3D$ matrix of voxel intensities, in which case it may be parsed into a series of $2D$ frames. In this sense, we can consider 3D-sMRI scans as a series of 96 2D-slices. This allows us to classify on a per-slice basis rather than from an entire 3D scan. This presents some unique facets to our task.

Classification on a per-slice basis means that for any given scan, some slices may be identified as Parkinsonian, while others are marked as healthy. Ultimately, a decision must be made for the entire 3D scan. In general, we simply

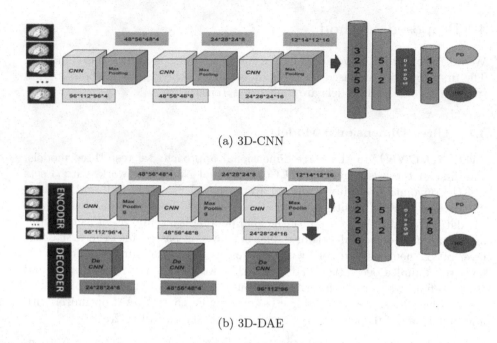

(a) 3D-CNN

(b) 3D-DAE

Fig. 2. 3D model architecture

take the mode of the class "votes" as the final decision, as seen in Fig. 3. However, not all 96 slices are relevant to a diagnosis. If PD mostly affects the inner brain (Basal Ganglia), then it may be best to ignore slices on the boundary of the brain in our diagnosis.

(M3: 2D-CNN). The first $2D$ model we test is a basic two-dimensional CNN, which follows the same general structure as the $3D$-CNN. We stack three units one after another, in which one unit consists of a $2D$ convolutional layer followed by a max-pooling layer. Convolutional kernel size is $[5, 5]$ and stride is $[2, 2]$. ReLU is used at each step, and the final output is flattened and passed as the input to the neural network. This network follows the same structure as the $3D$ neural network, and the resulting output is the softmax of the class logits. Note that we use a batch-size of 96 both because it allows our 2D model to train more efficiently, and because it allows us to calculate statistics with the same dimensions as our 3D models. We calculate loss with cross-entropy, and use ADAM optimizer on a per-slice basis with a learning rate of 0.0003. Final classification is done by taking the mode of the class votes for each slice. Detailed architecture is shown in Fig. 4(a).

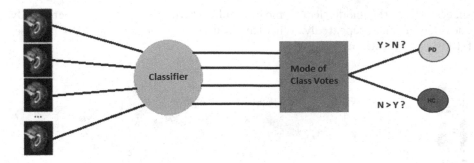

Fig. 3. 2D voting system

(M4: 2D-DAE). The next model is a 2D Denoising Autoencoder and neural network classifier. This model follows the same basic structure as the 3D equivalent. Kernel and stride are the same as the 2D-CNN. The autoencoder is trained with mean-squared error and ADAM optimizer with a learning rate of 0.00003. All other aspects are the same. See Fig. 4(b) for clarification.

5 Results

The results of the 4 models are shown in Table 2. Although no model performs exceptionally well, all models perform better than the baseline class-distribution (50%).

Interestingly, the 2D models generally have very high sensitivity but less than satisfactory specificity. This would suggest that they mainly accumulate error from false-positive diagnoses. In this sense, the 2D models over-diagnose PD. It's likely that this stems from the small filter-space of our 2D models, which must learn to detect very small features in only a few frames. Many of the frames we pass into the model would not seem to contain meaningful information in detecting PD.

Table 2. Model results

	Sensitivity	Specificity	Precision	Accuracy
M1: 3D-CNN	0.76	0.74	0.74	0.75
M2: 3D-DAE	0.72	0.57	0.62	0.64
M3: 2D-CNN	1.00	0.54	0.58	0.69
M4: 2D-DAE	0.92	0.53	0.65	0.70

The best performing 3D model was the 3D-CNN, with 75% accuracy and balanced metrics in sensitivity, specificity and precision. It almost equally misdiagnoses with false-positives and false-negatives. This is promising because it suggests that the model learns meaningful features rather than preferentially guessing one class repeatedly. With this in mind, we consider the 3D-CNN useful for generalization.

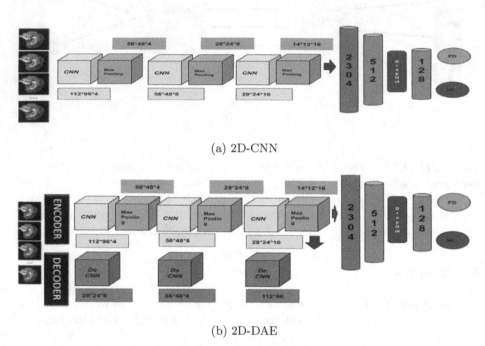

(a) 2D-CNN

(b) 2D-DAE

Fig. 4. 2D model architecture

We perform an occlusion sensitivity analysis using our best model, the 3D-CNN. In the analysis, we allow the model to fully train, and then obtain the test sample which maximally activates the PD-positive logit. We occlude a small $4 \times 4 \times 4$ section of the sMRI sample by masking with zeros, and then obtain the new PD-positive logit value. This occlusion process is done for each block in the sample. We introduce a minimum threshold so that we can find the blocks which maximally activate the logit, which is necessary because all blocks activate it to some degree. Those blocks which when occluded, lowered the logit value the most, are overlayed a sample brain as seen in Fig. 5. The sample brain has the mean intensity values of the entire preprocessed dataset. In general terms, the red boxes shown in Fig. 5 are the areas our model finds most important in making its diagnosis.

It follows from the occlusion sensitivity analysis that PD diagnosis is strongly correlated with voxel intensity in both the cerebellum and occipital lobe regions. As shown in the symmetry between the right and left sagittal (side) views in Fig. 5, this relationship is bilateral. These findings are supported in literature, with significant atrophy in the cerebellum [24] and the occipital lobe [25] associated with Parkinson's disease.

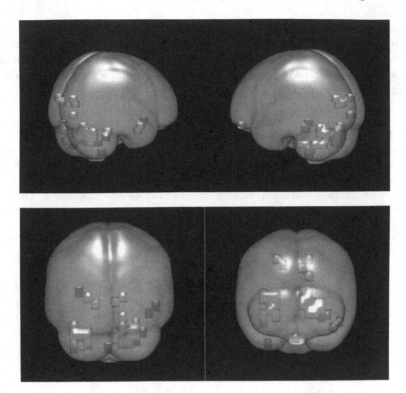

Fig. 5. Occlusion sensitivity analysis

6   Discussion and Future Work

In general, no model tested is yet applicable in a clinical setting. Symptomatic diagnosis and medical history analysis are still the gold-standard in PD diagnosis for the time being. Despite this, our deep-learning model assessment demonstrates competency in the task of PD diagnosis, as well as highlighting potential biomarkers in PD progression. With improved accuracy, the proposed method could certainly be applied in a practical situation.

There is significant potential for future research in the task at hand. An area of consideration is deep-learning based classification with segmented subcortical structures. In the case of our research, classification models could be built based only on voxel intensities in the segmented cerebellum and occipital lobe regions. Furthermore, our models could be expanded to a categorical classification metric, such as UPDRS, rather than the current binary classification for more precise diagnosis.

7   Conclusion

We have demonstrated a deep-learning based approach to diagnose Parkinson's Disease from T1-weighted structural MRI images. The proposed method (3D-

CNN) shows promising results in autonomous detection, which is an important field in modern medical applications. The work also highlights potential biomarkers of the disease in the cerebellum and occipital lobe. To summarize, the work suggests that structural MRI can provide useful and complementary information in the diagnosis of Parkinson's disease.

Acknowledgments. Special thanks to PPMI for supporting Parkinson's disease research by maintaining and updating their clinical dataset.

Data used in the preparation of this article were obtained from the Parkinson's Progression Markers Initiative (PPMI) database (www.ppmi-info.org/data). For up-to-date information on the study, visit www.ppmi-info.org.

PPMI – a public-private partnership – is funded by the Michael J. Fox Foundation for Parkinson's Research and funding partners found at www.ppmi-info.org/fundingpartners.

We acknowledge the support of the Natural Sciences and Engineering Research Council of Canada (NSERC).

References

1. Vos, T., et al.: Global, regional, and national incidence, prevalence, and years lived with disability for 310 diseases and injuries, 1990–2015: a systematic analysis for the Global Burden of Disease Study 2015. Lancet **388**(10053), 1545–1602 (2016)
2. Reeve, A., Simcox, E., Turnbull, D.: Ageing and Parkinson's disease: why is advancing age the biggest risk factor? Ageing Res. Rev. **14**, 19–30 (2014)
3. Lang, A.E., Espay, A.J.: Disease modification in Parkinson's disease: current approaches, challenges, and future considerations. Mov. Disord. **33**(5), 660–677 (2018)
4. Cheng, H.-C., Ulane, C.M., Burke, R.E.: Clinical progression in Parkinson disease and the neurobiology of axons. Ann. Neurol. **67**(6), 715–725 (2010)
5. Athauda, D., et al.: Exenatide once weekly versus placebo in Parkinson's disease: a randomised, double-blind, placebo-controlled trial. Lancet **390**(10103), 1664–1675 (2017)
6. Ziegler, D.A., Corkin, S.: New magnetic resonance imaging biomarkers advance the characterisation of Parkinson's disease. Eur. Neurol. Rev. **8**(2), 85 (2013)
7. Brown, N., Jones, L.: Knowledge of medical imaging radiation dose and risk among doctors. J. Med. Imaging Radiat. Oncol. **57**(1), 8–14 (2012)
8. Hoehn, M.M., Yahr, M.D.: Parkinsonism: onset, progression, and mortality. Neurology **17**(5), 427–442 (1967)
9. Movement Disorder Society Task Force on Rating Scales for Parkinson's Disease: The Unified Parkinson's Disease Rating Scale (UPDRS): status and recommendations. Mov. Disord. **18**(7), 738–750 (2003)
10. Wang, S.-H., Phillips, P., Sui, Y., Liu, B., Yang, M., Cheng, H.: Classification of Alzheimer's disease based on eight-layer convolutional neural network with leaky rectified linear unit and max pooling. J. Med. Syst. **42**(5), 85 (2018)

11. Zou, L., Zheng, J., Miao, C., Mckeown, M.J., Wang, Z.J.: 3D CNN based automatic diagnosis of attention deficit hyperactivity disorder using functional and structural MRI. IEEE Access **5**, 23626–23636 (2017)
12. Choi, H., Ha, S., Im, H.J., Paek, S.H., Lee, D.S.: Refining diagnosis of Parkinson's disease with deep learning-based interpretation of dopamine transporter imaging. NeuroImage Clin. **16**, 586–594 (2017)
13. Diagnostic Imaging Dataset Statistical Release, 27 October 2016. Internet: https://www.england.nhs.uk/statistics. Accessed 10 Aug 2018
14. Buda, M., Maki, A., Mazurowski, M.A.: A systematic study of the class imbalance problem in convolutional neural networks. Neural Netw. **106**, 249–259 (2018)
15. Pereira, C.R., Weber, S.A.T., Hook, C., Rosa, G.H., Papa, J.P.: Deep learning-aided Parkinson's disease diagnosis from handwritten dynamics. In: 2016 29th SIBGRAPI Conference on Graphics, Patterns and Images (SIBGRAPI) (2016)
16. Long, D., et al.: Automatic classification of early Parkinson's disease with multi-modal MR imaging. PLoS ONE **7**(11), e47714 (2012)
17. Woolrich, M.W., et al.: Bayesian analysis of neuroimaging data in FSL. NeuroImage **45**(1), S173–S186 (2009)
18. Zhang, Y., Brady, M., Smith, S.: Segmentation of brain MR images through a hidden Markov random field model and the expectation-maximization algorithm. IEEE Trans. Med. Imaging **20**(1), 45–57 (2001)
19. Jenkinson, M., Pechaud, M., Smith, S.: BET2: MR-based estimation of brain, skull and scalp surfaces. In: Eleventh Annual Meeting of the Organization for Human Brain Mapping (2005)
20. Jenkinson, M., Smith, S.: A global optimisation method for robust affine registration of brain images. Med. Image Anal. **5**(2), 143–156 (2001)
21. Jenkinson, M., Bannister, P., Brady, M., Smith, S.: Improved optimization for the robust and accurate linear registration and motion correction of brain images. NeuroImage **17**(2), 825–841 (2002)
22. Allen, J.S., Bruss, J., Mehta, S., Grabowski, T., Brown, C.K., Damasio, H.: Effects of spatial transformation on regional brain volume estimates. NeuroImage **42**(2), 535–547 (2008)
23. Damien, A.: recurrent_network.py. github.com, 29 August 2017. https://github.com/aymericdamien/TensorFlow. Accessed 6 Aug 2018
24. Borghammer, P., et al.: A deformation-based morphometry study of patients with early-stage Parkinson's disease. Eur. J. Neurol. **17**(2), 314–320 (2009)
25. Burton, E.J.: Cerebral atrophy in Parkinson's disease with and without dementia: a comparison with Alzheimer's disease, dementia with Lewy bodies and controls. Brain **127**(4), 791–800 (2004)

Remote Photoplethysmography (rPPG) for Contactless Heart Rate Monitoring Using a Single Monochrome and Color Camera

Xiaocong Ma[1]([✉]) [ID], Diana P. Tobón[2][ID], and Abdulmotaleb El Saddik[1][ID]

[1] Multimedia Communications Research Laboratory, University of Ottawa,
Ottawa, Canada
{xma064,elsaddik}@uottawa.ca
[2] Universidad de Medellin, Medellin, Colombia
dptvallejo@gmail.com
http://www.mcrlab.net

Abstract. Human vital signs are essential information that are closely related to both physical cardiac assessments and psychological emotion studies. One of the most important data is the heart rate, which is closely connected to the clinical state of the human body. Modern image processing technologies, such as Remote Photoplethysmography (rPPG), have enabled us to collect and extract the heart rate data from the body by just using an optical sensor and not making any physical contact. In this paper, we propose a real-time camera-based heart rate detector system using computer vision and signal processing techniques. The software of the system is designed to be compatible with both an ordinary built-in color webcam and an industry grade grayscale camera. In addition, we conduct an analysis based on the experimental results collected from a combination of test subjects varying in genders, races, and ages, followed by a quick performance comparison between the color webcam and an industry grayscale camera. The final calculations on percentage error have shown interesting results as the built-in color webcam with the digital spatial filter and the grayscale camera with optical filter achieved relatively similar accuracy under both still and exercising conditions. However, the correlation calculations, on the other hand, have shown that compared to the webcam, the industry grade camera is superior in stability when facial artifacts are presented.

Keywords: Computer vision · Heart rate · Photoplethysmography · rPPG · Signal processing

1 Introduction and Related Works

Human heart rate and heart rate variability are the crucial parameters corresponding to the functions of the heart. The speed and volume of the blood pulse

© Springer Nature Switzerland AG 2020
T. McDaniel et al. (Eds.): ICSM 2019, LNCS 12015, pp. 248–262, 2020.
https://doi.org/10.1007/978-3-030-54407-2_21

can explicitly indicate various physical conditions of one's body such as emotions, cardio activity levels, stress, fatigue, and heart diseases [1], and thus these parameters are usually measured for quick clinical diagnostics in the first place when necessary. On the other hand, long-term heart rate monitoring is undertaken when abnormal symptoms such as palpitation and extra systole need to be in check on a regular basis. Traditional wearable heart rate monitors, such as Fitbit^{TM} and smart watches can measure heart rate and give accurate results, but they are usually dedicated to just one user and need to be placed close against the skin of the user. Impressively, the rPPG technology has taken another approach; by examining the intensity change of a reflective light caused by the change of blood flow on a person's face and applying adequate computer vision and signal processing techniques, determining an approximate value of the heart rate from a distance using a video camera system has been made possible. Due to the nature of video signals, the rPPG method can acquire multi-model vital signs including heart rate, respiratory rate, and facial expression both in real-time and offline. Therefore, it is ideal for the rPPG to become a cost-efficient and user-friendly solution in real-world applications.

Academically, computer vision-based methodologies for front face remote heart rate measurement have already become popular in recent researches. C. Wang in his paper [2] has conducted a survey on multiple rPPG methods that can be classified into either intensity-based methods, which focus on facial light reluctance [3], or motion-based methods, which focus on head movements [4], and he concluded that intensity-based methods are still much more effective in terms of speed and accuracy. In [3,5], the authors have compared Signal to Noise Ratios (SNRs) of the blood pulse in the Red-Green-Blue (RGB) color space model and have shown that the green channel is the best pick for rPPG heart rate detection. In [6], an rPPG heart rate detector on the iOS platform using offline videos had been developed and sufficient usable results were obtained; however, the author did not mention its real-time performance.

It is also noteworthy that rPPG methods can be tailored at various stages of the entire process, such as pre-processing, signal extraction, and post-processing [2]. At the pre-processing stage, Po and his colleagues [7] implemented their system with an adaptive Region of Interest (ROI) selection method based on the detected signal qualities and concluded with improved accuracy at a cost of computational expense in real-time. In [8,9], Rahman's team proposed real-time rPPG systems using Independent Component Analysis (ICA) to combat motion artifacts, but in [10], Demirezen claimed that their work with the nonlinear mode decomposition method achieved better results than ICA. In terms of optical modeling, Sanyal in [11] took another approach by using hue parameters from the Hue-Saturation-Value (HSV) color space model instead of green in the RGB before applying ICA and also summarized a higher accuracy in the performance outcomes. In the post-processing stage, the time domain peak-detection or frequency domain algorithms were the most commonly applied methods used in the past [2], but machine learning and modeling techniques are trending among most recent research. The types of supervised learning methods can include kNN-based modeling [12], cNN-based modeling [13,14], spatial-temporal modeling [15], adaptive neural network model selection [16], etc. However, obtaining a dataset with appropriate ground truth can be a crucial factor for training accurate models, and real-time performance reduction needs to be addressed considering the complexity of the model trained [2].

The structure of this paper is as follows. Section 2 describes the used methods and materials in this study, Sect. 2.10 presents detailed steps to obtain the final data, Sect. 3 conducts an analysis on the final results, and Sect. 4 draws an open conclusion for future work.

2   Materials and Methods

This work has been implemented as a hybrid system in which either a regular built-in color webcam or a FILR^{TM} industrial grade grayscale camera can be utilized as its image input sensor based on the detection of the connected hardware. The captured facial image frames were converted to grayscale for further signal extraction and heart rate detection in later stages, and the heart rate results were updated on the screen rapidly in real-time. In addition, a BTChoic^{TM} blood oxygen and dynamic heart rate bracelet was used as a skin attached device for providing the ground truth to our results. Subsection 2.1 provides details regarding our hardware environment, subsection 2.2 describes how the data was collected for our work, subsection 2.3 explains the selection of color space and channel input, subsection 2.4 gives a quick overview of the highlighted signal processing techniques used in our implementation, and subsections 2.5 to 2.10 go through more details on the multiple stages of the entire signal processing process.

2.1   Hardware Setup

The implementation and tests of this project were performed on a PC with an Intel^{TM} i5-8250U processor under Microsoft^{TM} Windows 10 operating system and Python 3.5 environment. The sensors used for image and data collections were the BTChoic^{TM} skin contact smart wear bracelet, FLIR^{TM} Blackfly S BW industrial camera with Rainbow^{TM} H3.5 mm 1:1.6 fixed lens and 500–555 nm light green band-pass filter, and a laptop with a built-in Asus^{TM} USB2.0 HD webcam.

2.2   Data Collection Setup

Data tests were conducted by a group of 20 volunteers aged between 25–40 years with mixed races, skin tones, genders, and various amount of facial hair. Each person was asked to wear the BTChoic^{TM} bracelet to obtain the ground truth heart rate, and was then told to sit still and breathe normally in front of the camera at about 0.5 meters away. Three camera hardware setups were used in our rPPG data collections: a FLIR^{TM} industrial grayscale camera with an optical green filter; a FLIR^{TM} industrial grayscale camera without an optical filter; an Asus^{TM} HD built-in webcam by itself. Approximately 30 s of data reading was then performed on both the camera and the BTChoic^{TM} bracelet a under controlled light environment in the lab as shown in Fig. 1. The output display seemed to be more stabilized over time, thus we took a visually averaged output as our test result approximately 20 s after the program started. The test subject was then asked to perform a light exercise such as jogging or push-ups for approximately 20 s, and then immediately sit back in front of the camera to take another set of readings.

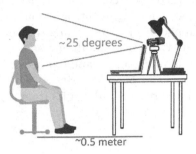

Fig. 1. Data collection setup.

2.3   Selection of Color Space and Channel

Our original plan was to initially implement and pass raw images, a.k.a. data in all RGB channels through an ICA stage for selecting the best signal, and then pass the resulting independent components through the follow-up stages. According to our previous researches, the signals related to the absorption bands for oxy- and deoxyhemoglobin on the facial skin have the strongest signal-to-noise ratio in the yellow and green light color spectrum [2], and even though many other methods have been explored, the green color data in the RGB color space remains to be the most popularly used channel for extracting HR [17]. Our implementation using FastICA agreed with the research results by showing that the projection highly weighted towards the green channel, with fewer contributions from red, and almost none from blue. Thus, with this less significant improvement on accuracy, we decided to reduce the computation expense for better performance in real-time by replacing ICA and applying only the green channel as the selected input in our implementation.

The FLIR^{TM} grayscale camera filters out non-green color spectrum using the equipped optical filter in the analog domain, while the built-in color webcam produces all color channels, from which the green channel was selected in the digital domain. Thus, it was necessary to perform a comparative analysis between these optical and digital filters later in this paper.

2.4 Applied Key Techniques

To perform feature extraction together with signal processing in real-time, the overall system needs to be optimized so that the image data collection performance will satisfy the demand of correct heart rate determination within the reasonable frequency spectrum. According to the Nyquist Theory, to correctly determine a 3 Hz or 180 beats per minute (bpm) heart rate, a video frame rate of at least 6 frames per seconds (fps) is needed. To increase the accuracy and efficiency of the detection, we had utilized OpenCV face detection together with the Dlib facial landmark prediction engine for a fast and accurate facial ROI image extraction. Next, the facial alignment, value outlier correction, and Gaussian average filter were applied at pre-processing to combat lens distortion and motion movement artifact. Once a signal data was extracted, it was then fed through a multi-stage conditioning and shaping process. Finally, temporal filtering, Fast Fourier Transform, and power density selection techniques were used to accelerate calculation and produce end results from the frequency domain, as described in Fig. 2.

Fig. 2. Signal processing flow chart diagram for heat rate calculation.

2.5 Feature Extraction

The key feature we aimed to extract in our proposed method was the time-series data obtained from spatially averaged grayscale values in multiple ROIs that could represent the slight intensity changes of reluctant light caused by facial blood volume changes, particularly in the green color spectrum.

2.6   Face Detection and Facial Landmark Prediction

The OpenCV library is widely accepted for its fast face detection using Haar Cascade classifier [18]. We have combined this classifier together with a Dlib pre-trained 68-points facial landmark prediction engine to efficiently detect facial bounding boxes and to also crop out selected ROI regions from raw video frames. To speed up the face detection process, the image was downsized to only a quarter of its original size. Once the position of the face box was determined, a face image frame was cropped from the original video frame to retain high resolution, and it was then resized to a 256 by 256 pixels matrix to equalize the size of the input data. Next, to correct the face pose for the landmarks' prediction and minimize the artifacts caused by body movement, a facial alignment process using Imutils library [19] was followed to straighten up the face if the detected face pose was tilted or rotated.

2.7   ROI Selection and Data Collection

To find rich blood vessels, uniformly distributed skin tone, and minimal facial expression movements on the face, three ROIs were selected using rectangular boxes for achieving better signal to noise ratio (SNR) at the following locations: two on the cheeks from each side and one on top of the forehead just above the eyebrows (See Fig. 3). All the selected ROI image data were then cropped and stored for further processing; the ROI image data collected from the FLIR^{TM} camera output was directly reformatted into an 8-bit grayscale data array, while the green channel data from the built-in webcam had to be extracted from the RGB color space before doing so. The formatted data was also filtered through an outlier filter, which replaces any high contrast pixel with the mean value of the array if the standard deviation is 1.5 times higher or lower than the mean value, and was then smoothed by a Gaussian filter for further noise reduction.

An average value for each ROI data was then continuously calculated and fed into a corresponding buffer with a total size of 75. Once 75 useful rPPG frames were collected and calculated, the buffer was filled up and ready for the next process.

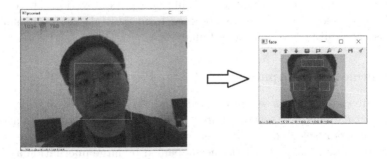

Fig. 3. Face detection, landmarks prediction, and face pose alignment.

2.8   Data Buffer Shaping and Conditioning

The data buffer was detrended to avoid the interference of light change during processing, and interpolated by 1 to smooth the change. It was then fed through a hamming filter to become more periodic for spectral leakage prevention, and was eventually normalized according to its average value. Next, the normalized data were amplified by a factor of 10 for boosting small temporal changes according to a pre-designed gain from Eulerian Video Magnification [20], and another Gaussian filter was applied here to further smoothen the data fluctuation.

2.9   FIR Band-Pass Filtering and Power Spectrum Density Selection

The Fast Fourier Transform is utilized to transfer the conditioned data in the buffer from the time domain into the frequency-power density spectrum. Here a 6th order FIR Butterworth filter with a low cut-off at 0.667 Hz and high cut-off at 3 Hz is applied to remove any data from outside the corresponding reasonable spectrum of the human heart rate frequencies, i.e. 40 bpm to 180 bpm. Finally, within the pass band range, the frequency indexes for the highest power density are picked to represent the desired heart rate on each ROI.

2.10   Heart Rate Calculation

The heart rate calculated from each ROI can be slightly different due to the varying SNRs and facial light conditions. The average of the final results was obtained by using a moving average filter with a window size of 20 values. According to our lab test feedback, among all the three results, the one with the least standard deviation over time seemed to have the closest value compared to our ground truth data, and thus, we selected this as the final output on the screen. In real-time, the screen will usually be updated approximately every 2 to 3 s.

3   Results Evaluation and Discussion

In this section, we have provided intermediate outputs at various stages of the entire data process, the end results obtained from multiple voluntary subjects, as well as our limited observation and analysis.

3.1   Intermediate Outputs

Intermediate data outputs were obtained from the FLIR^{TM} grayscale camera with an optical green filter setup. Figure 4 shows a one-minute raw data averaged by the ROI region selected on the forehead of the test subject. From the data, we could see some clear ECG ripples accompanied by large fluctuation and noise DC trends. Next, Fig. 5 shows conditioned data with 8 clear heartbeat peaks in a data buffer filled by a 75-frames window. The detected frame rate was about 10 fps during the test, thus approximately 7 s was required to fill the buffer window, yielding a heart rate of 68.5 bpm. Furthermore, in Fig. 6, the spectrum power density chart, calculated using the same data from the buffer window, indicates a peak of strong signal at close to 70 bpm. Both bpms estimated from Fig. 5 and Fig. 6 are close to the ground truth result, 67 bpm, obtained from the contact hand bracket in Fig. 7. In addition, the plot in Fig. 8 gives a continuous bpm output for a length of roughly 50 s after 10 s of the start of the test. The relatively flat line shows a stable reading across the entire testing period. In short, the above figures have shown the capability of our system to produce a reasonable accuracy within 5% as compared to our skin-contacted ground truth.

3.2 Group Test Observation and Results

Table 1 and Table 2 show the detected heart rate results from both the sitting still and exercising conditions. Table 3 compares the percentage error with respect to the hand brace ground truth reading under each condition. Table 4 compares the overall correlation values with respect to the hand brace ground truth reading under each camera setup.

3.3 Evaluation: Sit Still vs. After Exercise

The calculated percentage error values with respect to our ground truth data for the FLIR^{TM} camera with filter, without filter, and Webcam detection under sitting still conditions were 4.9%, 6.0%, and 4.2%, respectively, whereas the values were 9.9%, 10.0%, and 12.4% right after light exercise. The percentage error calculation formula is given by:

$$Percentage\ Error = |\frac{Camera\ Reading\ -\ Ground\ Truth\ Reading}{Ground\ Truth\ Reading}| \times 100\%$$

By purely examining the numbers, it can be observed that the results from the three setups are fairly close to each other, and the slightly larger deviation after exercise is possibly due to motion artifacts such as heavy breathing. Interestingly, even the built-in color webcam achieved accurate results regardless of having a smaller number of effective pixels, and the difference between the optically filtered grayscale camera and the webcam was negligible at times. This is contradictory to our original thoughts—we expected a higher accuracy output from the grayscale camera since it comes with a high resolution and a more sensitive image sensor. In fact, we found the reduced resolution on selected ROIs to be a contributing factor in stabilizing the output reading because the image output at the data acquisition stage was already heavily compressed and averaged by the camera's internal processor. Since the experiments were conducted under an indoor artificial light environment and each detection result was marked down by visual inspection over a period of roughly 30 s, this did not fully represent the actual performance of the system.

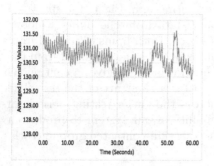

Fig. 4. A 60-s window: averaged intensity values obtained by one ROI Area vs. Time.

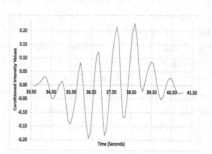

Fig. 5. An 8-s window: Normalized and Conditioned Intensity Values vs. Time.

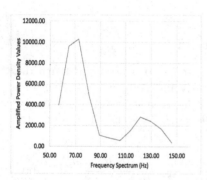

Fig. 6. Frequency spectrum from 50 Hz to 150 Hz: Amplified Power Density Values vs. Heart Rate.

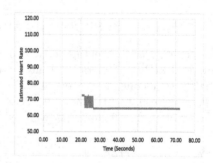

Fig. 7. A 72-s window: Estimated Heart Rate vs. Time.

Fig. 8. Reference data: skin contact hand brace for ground truth heart rate detection.

Table 1. Sit still test results (all units are in bpm).

Test subjects	FLIR^{TM} with filter	FLIR^{TM} without filter	Webcam	Hand brace
Subject #1	66	60	62	64
Subject #2*	84	87 (unstable)	87 (unstable)	90
Subject #3	65	60	70	74
Subject #4***	71	71 (unstable)	70	79
Subject #5**	66	63	67 (unstable)	68
Subject #6	72	59 (unstable)	71	71
Subject #7	72	68 (unstable)	72	71
Subject #8	72	78	75	74
Subject #9	74	70	70	71
Subject #10*	60	63	62	62
Subject #11	76	69	72	80
Subject #12	70	71	68	71
Subject #13	88	88	87	84
Subject #14	96	95	96	93
Subject #15	72	78	74	75
Subject #16	72	74	76	75
Subject #17	64	64	68	64
Subject #18	60	64	65	70
Subject #19*	81 (unstable)	82 (unstable)	80 (unstable)	74
Subject #20	76	73	80	73

*with sunscreen and makeups **large amount of facial hair ***failed reference reading

Table 2. Light exercise test results (all units are in bpm).

Test subjects	FLIR^{TM} with filter	FLIR^{TM} without filter	Webcam	Hand brace
Subject #1	95	90	88	91
Subject #2*	98	90	105	74
Subject #3	96	92	92	96
Subject #4***	96	90	93	No reading
Subject #5**	100 (unstable)	58 (incorrect)	55 (incorrect)	86
Subject #6	90	78 (unstable)	90	88
Subject #7	83	84	96	95
Subject #8	90	107	102	96
Subject #9	80	85	80	90
Subject #10*	80 (unstable)	75 (incorrect)	76	110
Subject #11	93	88	85	87
Subject #12	100	94	65 (incorrect)	90
Subject #13	94	97	99	95
Subject #14	106	108	85 (incorrect)	100

(*continued*)

Table 2. (*continued*)

Test subjects	FLIR^{TM} with filter	FLIR^{TM} without filter	Webcam	Hand brace
Subject #15	108	110	102	95
Subject #16	90	88	85	95
Subject #17	96	95	101	95
Subject #18	91	88	82	83
Subject #19*	93 (unstable)	72 (unstable)	100 (unstable)	82
Subject #20	80	88	88	86

*with sunscreen and makeups **large amount of facial hair ***failed reference reading

Table 3. Percentage error comparison table.

	Percentage error with respect to reference		
	FLIR^{TM} with Filter	FLIR^{TM} without filter	Webcam
Sit still	4.9%	6.0%	4.2%
After exercise	9.9%	10.0%	12.4%

3.4 Evaluation: Correlation for Each Camera Setup

Figure 9, 10, 11, 12, 13 and 14 show the scatter plots for comparison with linear regression lines and the correlation values calculated based on the result data selection and camera setup. The red dots and lines represent the results by the FLIR^{TM} camera with a filter on, blue represents results by FLIR^{TM} without a filter, and pink represents results from the webcam. It may be hard to distinguish which setup would have an advantage in accuracy as compared to the reference by simply looking at the plot at the first place, however, by a closer examination, one can see that the correlation values give the information about which comparison is the best, and this confirms that the webcam performs less accurately compared to the FLIR^{TM} camera.

The test results from subjects with heavy facial artifacts, makeup, sunscreen, and failed reference readings are treated as data outliers due to their instability in this experiment. In Table 4, we calculated the Pearson Correlation coefficient values in two groups, either using all test results or using results without outliers. The Pearson Correlation coefficient lies within the range of +1 to −1, with a number 0 considered to have no association between the two data sets. The readings from the FLIR^{TM} camera with optical filter generated the highest correlation value of 0.75, which indicates a strong accuracy as compared to the

Table 4. Calculated correlation values with respect to hand brace ground truth.

	Correlation values with respect to reference		
	FLIR^{TM} with Filter	FLIR^{TM} without Filter	Webcam
All data	0.7517	0.7286	0.5934
Data outliers excluded	0.8871	0.8870	0.8102

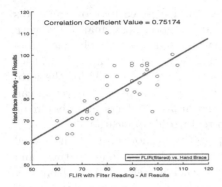

Fig. 9. Scatter plot - FLIR^{TM} with filter (All Data).

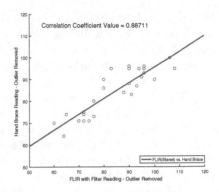

Fig. 10. Scatter plot - FLIR^{TM} with filter (Outliers Removed).

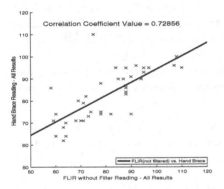

Fig. 11. Scatter plot - FLIR^{TM} without filter (All Data).

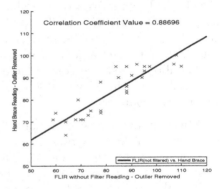

Fig. 12. Scatter plot - FLIR^{TM} without filter (Outliers Removed).

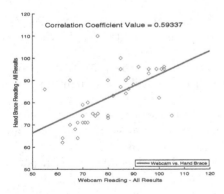

Fig. 13. Scatter plot - webcam (All Data).

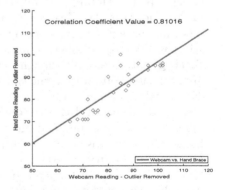

Fig. 14. Scatter plot - webcam (Outliers Removed).

reference reading among all the three setups. The lowest correlation value was 0.59 from the color webcam, which still indicates a good performance but with relatively large deviations. Interestingly, once we exclude the data obtained from the outliers, the correlation values increased to a much stronger level: 0.8871 for FLIR™ with filter, 0.8870 for FLIR™ without filter, and 0.8102 for the webcam. This would be an indication that the accuracy of the proposed system can be heavily reduced due to the presence of the above artifacts and should be properly dealt with while incorporating it in real-world applications.

In reality, when the optical filter was equipped, we noticed that the actual heart rate outputs had more stable readings and less fluctuation over time, and this was reasonable because the camera was receiving signals only from the green color spectrum where the signal for blood volume intensity change was strong. The results color webcam and the unfiltered grayscale camera appeared to be more unstable most of the time, and sometimes even incorrect due to the heavy noise inside the selected spectrum band. Additionally, it was obvious that the webcam struggled to produce stable results when we dimmed the light output in the room. The smaller aperture on the webcam with less effective pixels contributed much more noise as compared to the industrial FLIR™ camera, thus making this setup less desirable in a darker environment.

We also noticed that several factors could affect and reduce the accuracy of the results, and these should be taken into consideration in both laboratory and real-life environments:

- **Makeup and sunscreen:** Large fluctuations or even incorrect readings were observed in the heart rate of people wearing heavy makeup and sunscreen on their faces, due to the block of the reflective light change on blood oxygen saturation that was received by the camera.
- **Facial hair:** The heart rate of people with large amounts of facial hair can sometimes be hard to detect.
- **Length of the face:** People belonging to different races may have distinct facial length variations, and this may contribute to size variation of the ROIs selected by the Dlib facial landmarks engine.
- **Head movements:** Heads with regular horizontal movements introduced more fluctuation as compared to that of vertical movements. People who sat still had the most stable readings.
- **Sitting distance:** Even though the subjects were asked to sit at a distance of approximately 50 cm from the camera, this distance could vary slightly upon the actual execution during the tests.
- **Physical heart condition:** People with stronger heart conditions could have more blood volume pumped into their facial blood vessels, thus creating a higher signal to noise ratio, resulting in more stable detection.
- **Exercise intensity:** Exercises conducted by subjects depended on their personal preferences and the load to each of their hearts can also be different.
- **Speed of rest recovering:** Some people are able to calm down quickly after exercise, while others may take more time for it. Usually, heart rate readings gradually decrease after exercise, but the time to take a measurement could vary from person to person.

As future work, we will explore how to overcome the limitation of why the lightness of skin tone affects the accuracy of the system.

4 Conclusion

Multimedia in medicine has gone a long way in providing efficient clinical assistance. While a single image can provide rich information for a physical exam [21], a series of video sequences has proven to be much more useful for an in-depth clinical analysis [22]. In this paper, we have proposed a real-time rPPG system that is capable of detecting the vital signals of the heart rate by using either an optically filtered grayscale camera or a digitally filtered color camera sequentially from a distance. Then, we compared the experimental results on several subjects under a pre-setup indoor environment with the help of data collected by a skin-contact reference device. The obtained results show that while the built-in color camera can be great for handy heart rate detection given enough luminance on a sit still subject, the pre-optically filtered grayscale camera is more robust to facial and motion artifacts and can outperform a regular camera under less ideally lighted condition. In addition, we have also identified several factors that may reduce the accuracy of our proposed rPPG system, such as makeup and sunscreen, which heavily block light reflection from the face. Therefore, our future work will be focused on improving the accuracy of this study, dealing with more difficult reading scenarios such as sunscreen and heavy makeup, as well as combining other approaches possibly in machine learning fields for achieving better results.

Acknowledgments. Our work is fully supported by the Multimedia Communication Lab at the University of Ottawa and the ICSM2019 conference committee. We would also like to sincerely appreciate and express our gratitude to every participant for the time and effort they invested in conducting our tests.

References

1. Monfredi, O., et al.: Biophysical characterization of the underappreciated and important relationship between heart rate variability and heart rate. Hypertension **64**(6), 1334–1343 (2014)
2. Wang, C., Pun, T., Chanel, G.: A comparative survey of methods for remote heart rate detection from frontal face videos. Front. Bioeng. Biotechnol. **6**, 33 (2018)
3. Verkruysse, W., Svaasand, L.O., Nelson, J.S.: Remote plethysmographic imaging using ambient light. Opt. Express **16**(26), 21434 (2008)
4. He, D.D., Winokur, E.S., Sodini, C.G.: A continuous, wearable, and wireless heart monitor using head ballistocardiogram (BCG) and head electrocardiogram (ECG). In: 2011 Annual International Conference of the IEEE Engineering in Medicine and Biology Society (2011)
5. Freitas, U.S.: Remote Camera-Based Pulse Oximetry. eTELEMED (2014)
6. Kwon, S., Kim, H., Park, K.S.: Validation of heart rate extraction using video imaging on a built-in camera system of a smartphone. In: 2012 Annual International Conference of the IEEE Engineering in Medicine and Biology Society (2012)

7. Po, L.-M., Feng, L., Li, Y., Xu, X., Cheung, T.C.-H., Cheung, K.-W.: Block-based adaptive ROI for remote photoplethysmography. Multimedia Tools Appl. **77**(6), 6503–6529 (2017). https://doi.org/10.1007/s11042-017-4563-7

8. Rahman, H., Ahmed, M., Begum, S., Funk, P.: Real time heart rate monitoring from facial RGB color video using webcam. In: The 29th Annual Workshop of the Swedish Artificial Intelligence Society (SAIS) (2016)

9. Fan, Q., Li, K.: Non-contact remote estimation of cardiovascular parameters. Biomed. Signal Process. Control **40**, 192–203 (2018)

10. Demirezen, H., Erdem, C.E.: Remote photoplethysmography using nonlinear mode decomposition. In: 2018 IEEE International Conference on Acoustics, Speech and Signal Processing (ICASSP) (2018)

11. Sanyal, S., Nundy, K.K.: Algorithms for monitoring heart rate and respiratory rate from the video of a user's face. IEEE J. Transl. Eng. Health Med. **6**, 1–11 (2018)

12. Monkaresi, H., Calvo, R.A., Yan, H.: A machine learning approach to improve contactless heart rate monitoring using a webcam. IEEE J. Biomed. Health Inform. **18**(4), 1153–1160 (2014)

13. Qiu, Y., Liu, Y., Arteaga-Falconi, J., Dong, H., Saddik, A.E.: EVM-CNN: real-time contactless heart rate estimation from facial video. IEEE Trans. Multimedia **21**(7), 1778–1787 (2019)

14. Tang, C., Lu, J., Liu, J.: Non-contact heart rate monitoring by combining convolutional neural network skin detection and remote photoplethysmography via a low-cost camera. In: 2018 IEEE/CVF Conference on Computer Vision and Pattern Recognition Workshops (CVPRW) (2018)

15. Niu, X., et al.: Robust remote heart rate estimation from face utilizing spatial-temporal attention. In: 2019 14th IEEE International Conference on Automatic Face & Gesture Recognition (FG 2019) (2019)

16. Wu, B.-F., Chu, Y.-W., Huang, P.-W., Chung, M.-L.: Neural network based luminance variation resistant remote-photoplethysmography for driver's heart rate monitoring. IEEE Access **7**, 57210–57225 (2019)

17. Chen, D.-Y., et al.: Image sensor-based heart rate evaluation from face reflectance using Hilbert-Huang transform. IEEE Sens. J. **15**(1), 618–627 (2015)

18. Kaehler, A., Bradski, G.R.: Learning OpenCV 3: Computer Vision in C with the OpenCV Library. O'Reilly Media, Sebastopol (2017)

19. Ucar, M., Hsieh, S.-J.: Board 137: MAKER: facial feature detection library for teaching algorithm basics in Python. In: 2018 ASEE Annual Conference & Exposition, Salt Lake City, Utah, June 2018. ASEE Conferences (2018). https://peer.asee.org/29934Internet. Accessed 31 Jul 2019

20. Wu, H.-Y., Rubinstein, M., Shih, E., Guttag, J.V., Durand, F., Freeman, W.T.: Eulerian video magnification for revealing subtle changes in the world. ACM Trans. Graph. **31**(4), 1–8 (2012)

21. Cai, J., Wang, X., Jiang, X., Gao, S., Peng, J.: Research on low-quality finger vein image recognition algorithm. In: 2019 International Conference on SmartMultimedia (2019)

22. West, C., Soltaninejad, S., Cheng, I.: Assessing the capability of deep-learning models in Parkinson's disease diagnosis. In: 2019 International Conference on SmartMultimedia (2019)

Haptics and Applications

A Simulation Platform for Early Haptic Training in Surgical and Medical Education

Sylvain Bouchigny[1]([✉]), Julien Davrou[1,3], Christine Mégard[1], Laurent Eck[1], Elie Cattan[2], Matthieu Nesme[2], François Faure[2], and Bernard Devauchelle[3]

[1] CEA, LIST, Gif-sur-Yvette, France
sylvain.bouchigny@cea.fr
[2] Anatoscope, 38330 Montbonnot-Saint-Martin, France
faure@anatoscope.com
[3] IFF - Facing Faces Institute, Amiens, France
devauchelle.bernard@chu-amiens.fr

Abstract. Haptic training in simulation is a rising pedagogical trend in medical education. It is a rather new field that appeared partly because the adage "see one, do one, teach one", from a mentoring standpoint, is undesirable due to public consideration for patient safety. Teaching strength management for a given procedure is a difficult task. This is not a skill one can retrieve from books or by only "seeing" the procedure. It needs to be experienced by the trainee. For this matter, haptic training on virtual patients offers a good opportunity to tackle this problem at the price of a constant trade-off between what technology can do and the expectation of realism. The technology is expensive, complex to maintain and very specific. Many simulators on the market use low-end devices to maintain the cost and are therefore unable to simulate proper interactions with the virtual patient. The platform presented here is an ecosystem which aims to study how to extend haptic simulations on a broader range of applications. We present an approach using innovative mechatronics, based on purely resistive force, to reach better haptic feedback at lower cost. The system is designed to be compact and safe. It allows strong and high resolution feedback as well as easy integration in existing devices. This technology will help to extend haptic simulations earlier in the curriculum where the resident requires basic hands-on experience.

Keywords: Simulation · Education · Haptic · Magneto-rheological mechatronics · Biomechanics

Supported by ANR SimUSanté and EQUIPEX FIGURES - We thank Az-Eddine Djebara for the organization of the evaluation as well as Pr. Patrick Mertl, the Amiens orthopaedic unit and the Chimère research team.

T. McDaniel et al. (Eds.): ICSM 2019, LNCS 12015, pp. 265–273, 2020.
https://doi.org/10.1007/978-3-030-54407-2_22

1   Training Haptics in Medicine

1.1   Historical Background

The platform presented here originates from the European project SKILLS (FP6) that lasted from 2006 to 2011 in which a surgical platform was specifically designed to provide high fidelity haptic feedback [1]. For this purpose, a 6 dof (degrees of freedom) haptic feedback interface was developed for applications in bone surgery procedures [2]. The platform was tested in several hospitals through a training program on maxillofacial surgery [3]. Since the first prototype, a second version of the platform was developed and delivered to the Facing Faces Institute at the University hospital of Amiens, France. The objective was to integrate the system in a real medical environment to reach a large population of students.

Our investigations showed that providing high fidelity haptic rendering is a key asset to reach stakeholder approbation. There is indeed a strong demand for haptic simulation in medicine but with great expectation on feedback fidelity. However, the price of such robotic systems, like the one developed during the SKILLS project, is very high and the question of the economical model must be addressed either by broadening the range of application or by lowering the cost. The platform had to evolve toward a cheaper and more versatile system while maintaining a high degree of realism. To achieve this goal, it is necessary to open the technology of the platform and to think of the platform as a global research tool in a broader ecosystem.

In order to find a solution to the difficult question of expectation versus cost, we have started investigating the use of a novel haptic technology based on magneto-rheological (MR) fluids. The main idea is to replace a standard electric motor by a purely resistive system to reduce size, cost, and improve security by removing instabilities in the control loop. Such systems may not be applicable to all simulations but are suitable to many of them. Our research program starts with a simple case of only 1 dof : the clinical examination of a knee joint. In the following, we introduce this orthopaedic simulation in Sect. 1.2, hardware in Sect. 2, and we describe the biomechanical simulation of the knee in Sect. 3. A first evaluation of the system was performed in Amiens Hospital and is presented in Sect. 4. Finally, in Sect. 5, we conclude on how the platform will be extended and used in the future.

1.2   Orthopaedic Simulation

Educational resources in the orthopaedic curriculum include lecture courses, academic books, experience in the clinical setting, and experience in the operating theater. Additional knowledge is gained from reading scientific literature in texts and journals, performing dissections on cadavers in the anatomy labs, and from web-based resources. Residency programs have opted to develop 'skills labs' where techniques and skills are taught and practised on simulators, bench models, and serious games. The potential benefit these labs offer is increased opportunities for residents to gain familiarity with their working environment and the basic skills, procedures, and techniques in a low-risk, low-cost and easily accessible environments [4,5]. Simulation in medicine can be defined as "any technology or process that recreates a contextual background in a way that allows a learner to experience mistakes and receive feedback in a safe environment" [6]. The advantages of simulation extend beyond simple technical and procedural skills. Simulation allows trainees to engage with a multi-disciplinary team and focus on individual and team-based cognitive skills including problem solving, decision-making, and team behavior skills [7,8]. Technological advances in VR immersive environments allow the creation of new learning modalities including 3D vision and haptic (tactile and force) feedback, which are essential in skill learning, retention, and transfer of information to the real world. The anatomy can be re-discovered by learning an active dynamic anatomy, which is much more informative and detailed on osteo-articular displacements in normal and pathological situations [9–11], but the literature to date is scarce in this field. Many research programs are oriented in procedural surgical simulation, but very few are involved in the visuo-haptic understanding of the clinical examination of a knee joint.

Finally, it is important to draw together the knowledge and quantitative findings that help to explain why certain types of skills are difficult to learn. One of the most important functional features of a simulation training device is the capacity to emulate the procedure to be learned and give detailed, reliable, and valid quantitative measures of performance, i.e. metrics. A simulator without these metric attributes is nothing more than a fancy video game [12].

2   Hardware for Dynamic Anatomy

At this stage, applications are limited to two clinical examinations called the Lachman and Drawer test, consisting in testing the laxity of the cruciate ligaments. Previous studies have already investigated the clinical examination of a knee joint [13] with good results as a pedagogical tool but the phantom-based interaction was using a robot to render the force. Cost is however still a major limitation for the market penetration of these technologies. Heavy robotic systems needed for simulation in orthopaedics where large forces must be managed is neither practical nor economically viable. It is therefore important to investigate alternative technologies in order to make dynamic anatomy for education a reality.

For applications like the Lachman test where the movement is in one direction, applying a force in the opposite direction of the movement is usually enough. This can be achieved using a brake instead of a motor. Haptic feedback applications in virtual reality, especially in medicine, usually require stronger resistive force than driving force. Many papers can be found that use brakes for haptic [14,15] or prosthetic applications [16], some with hybrid technologies combine an electric motor and a brake [17]. To achieve the required performance in terms of reliability, form factor, range of torque and haptic fidelity, we have chosen a technology based on MR fluid. It provides high torque/weight ratio, low response times and low power. The counter force can be precisely controlled with good linearity and passivity [17, 18]. The device was specifically engineered in our lab for haptic rendering [19, 20]. The MR brake works in rotation with a torque from 10 mN.m to 1.5 N.m and response time below 8 ms. The movement is then transformed into a translation with a pulley and a belt providing a force up to 160 N.

From a mechanical point of view, the movement of the leg is performed with a rotation situated 25 cm below the knee. During the clinical examination, the movement of the knee is neither a translation nor a rotation. Combining the two was considered too expensive to implement and the movement depends too much on the patient physiology. Rotation was a better choice from a mechanical perspective leading to a lighter and more reliable system.

The coupling between the knee and the simulation is done via a USB connection : sensors on the knee send the position of the tibia relative to the femur to the simulation and the simulation returns the force that the brake has to apply. The prototype is shown in Fig. 1.

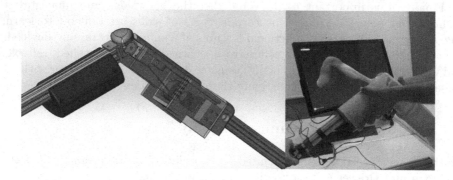

Fig. 1. First prototype of the dynamic anatomy simulator

3   Simulation of the Knee Biomechanics

3.1   Physical Model of the Knee Joint

We simulate the biomechanics of the knee using the SOFA framework [21]. The focus of our simulation is to emphasize the differences between a healthy knee compared to a knee with a broken ligament. The physics of our simulation is thus centered on the ligaments elongation and resistance.

The femur and the duo tibia/fibula are the two articulated rigid bodies of our simulation with a mass and an inertia computed from the shape of our 3D models of the bones. The tibia can move relative to the femur with six degrees of freedom and contacts between the bones are computed as repulsive forces when the two meshes intersect. However, we are mainly interested in two dimensions: the angle of flexion and the translation forward when pulling the tibia during a Lachman test.

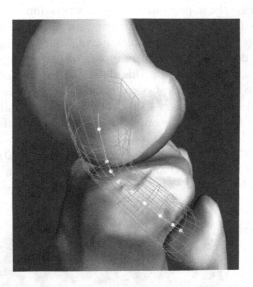

Fig. 2. Simulation of the fibular collateral ligament. The chain of springs (yellow) is following the deformation of the ligament (orange wireframe) attaching the femur and the fibula (gray) (Color figure online).

The two rigid systems are attached by ligaments, whose strength is modeled as a chain of springs. Only the main ligaments assuring the stability of the knee joints are kept: the anterior cruciate, the posterior cruciate, the tibial collateral and the fibular collateral. When the knee moves, the 3D meshes of these ligaments deforms according to an animation skinning based on the bones position and orientation. The intermediate points of the spring chains are constrained by this skinning and deform accordingly (Fig. 2). A constraint is put on the total length of each chain which creates a pulling force when the ligaments are stretched. In the case of a broken ligament simulation, we simply remove this constraint. The power of the constraint can also be modulated to simulate a partial tear of the ligament.

When the tibia is pulled forward for the Lachman test, we can, at each time step of the simulation, note the force applying on the tibia in the axis of its translation. To this force, we add a global affine force, only depending on the tibia translation, to simulate the resistance of all the other tissues (muscles, skin...) to the pulling gesture. The parameters of this affine function are computed so that the total force pulling back the tibia matches the order of magnitude of force measurements made with a GNRB arthrometer [22].

3.2   Mapping of the Simulation

Haptic simulation needs high frame rate and low latency to
experience, and running a live physical simulation could slow
Since the input sent by the haptic interface is only two dimensi
translation of the tibia), it is possible to create a discretizati
inputs in the range of anatomical limitations, while keeping
precision. We thus decided to make a mapping of precomputed
simulation and then interpolate into this data. Hence, the haptic
longer bound to the speed of the physical simulation which is exp

We automatized the simulation to be launched sequentially with
different inputs and to register the output force on the tibia depending
starting conditions. The tibia angle was sampled between 0° (strai
90° with a step of 10° and its translation between 0 mm and 50 mm with
1.00 mm. Two maps were created and used by the application, one for
knee, another for a broken anterior cruciate ligament.

Fig. 3. Testing the prototype at the orthopaedic department of the CHU Amiens,
France.

4   First Evaluation

In the user-centered design methodology, a first evaluation of the prototype was
organized at the orthopaedic department of the CHU Amiens, France (Fig. 3).
The evaluation was performed with a group of 10 orthopaedic surgeons. The
panel of expertise was heterogeneous with expert surgeons, interns and medical
students.

The evaluation started with a presentation of the purpose of the development
and the methodology used for the evaluation. The group was informed that the
design followed a user-centered methodology and that the aim was to gather any
remarks that would help to improve the design. The methodology was in two
sections : one was to gather remarks on the fly during the test of the prototype

and the second one was a questionnaire about the quality of the simulator. As some participants did not give their consents relative to the audio and video recording of the evaluation session, the video was restricted to the orthopaedics who gave their consent. Other feedback was gathered through the answers to the questionnaire.

The dynamic haptic simulator of the knee was introduced. The simulation allowed the surgeons to experience two different states of the knee, with cruciate ligament being either broken or healthy. The visual rendering was then presented on a screen. It showed, on demand, the knee and leg according to different viewpoints : whole leg/knee with or without skin, muscles, bones, or ligaments. The visual rendering was linked to the haptic model of the knee.

The prototype was tested by the participants. All feedback converged on the interest of dynamic knee simulation for learning the diagnosis of knee pathology. The need is relative to the Lachman test for the diagnosis of cruciate ligament rupture, but other tests have been mentioned, such as drawer test and the rotational jump test. The interviews indicated the importance of the position, the movements of the hands during the test hands and the feeling of the knee reaction. The latter is described as "feeling the sensation of hard stop" (no ligament rupture) and soft stop (cruciate ligament rupture). The analogy that seems most representative of the feeling of experts is that of a "string being stretched".

The dynamic simulator of the knee is considered very accurate for the anterior drawer test when the knee is bent at 90°. However, the haptic simulator is judged too "lax" for the Lachman test when the Knee is bent at 20° and experts do not feel any "hard stop" which indicates the end of the course of the ligament. At the stage of the evaluation, the prototype could not provide the ideal metaphor of a "string being stretched". The difference may be explained from the fact that the arthrometer used in the definition of the model does not provide a good insight in the clinical examination. The arthrometer explores the joint with a quasi-static displacement and constrains the knee in a strict translation while, for the Lachman test, the surgeons in our studies applied a fast movement, combining a translation and a rotation. Surgeons were not evaluating the overall stiffness but were looking for this feeling of a "hard stop". However, for the drawer test the movement they applied was actually very similar to what the arthrometer does and they were indeed evaluating the stiffness. This knowledge will be used to refine the model in future works in order to distinguish between the two possible approaches of the examination.

Another interesting fact is that the graphic model is not considered useful by the experts. They indicate that they base their diagnosis solely on the haptic sensation of the behavior of the knee and that they do not rely on vision, which gives them very few diagnostic elements. Young medical students did not express their opinions about the interest of the visual model, but we will have to consider how the visual model could become a pedagogical and evaluation resource.

The answers to the questionnaire indicate that many factors can impact the diagnostic and could be considered in the future versions of the dynamic simulator. Stressed patients may induce wrong diagnostics; athletes are difficult to examine because developed muscles make the leg difficult to examine (heavy and difficult to move); the laxity is also a factor that contributes to make the diagnostics difficult with a risk of false positive.

5   Conclusion

In this document, we presented a first attempt to simulate the haptic clinical examination of the knee with purely resistive actuators. This approach may be a good solution to extend the range of applications of simulation in medical education. The surgeons involved in our first evaluation never mentioned any problems with the fact that the actuation was not dynamic, leading to the conclusion that the omission of motors is a viable solution for this kind of procedure.

The evaluation conducted with the device provided key feedback and gave us better insight of the clinical aspect of the examination. The device turns out to be indeed a great tool to help the surgeon talk about their practice. They all have a different way to do the examination and testing the simulation helps a great deal in defining the common ground of their unsaid sensations.

The second step of our research program is already in the works. It aims at extending the use of the MR brakes to a more complex therapeutic procedure: the reduction of mandibular dislocation. Three brakes will be used to simulate the dynamics of this procedure. At this stage, we will use the platform as a complete research ecosystem. The 6 dof SKILLS platform will be used to evaluate and test the model of the mandible and pedagogical protocol will benefit from both the robotic and the MR based systems leading to a thorough comparison between different technologies.

There is a real benefit in bringing force management training earlier in curriculum. Procedures like the one studied here are often performed in the Emergency Room with young residents. Such simulators will help them practice before having access to the patient. This is important especially for complex, rare, and potentially painful procedures like mandibular dislocation. This is the reason why we introduce the idea of dynamic anatomy as a means to improve the overall expertise of students all along their curriculum.

References

1. Bouchigny, S., Mégard, C., Gosselin, F., Hoffmann, P., Korman, K.: Designing a VR training platform for surgeons: theoretical framework, technological solutions and results. In: Bergamasco, M., Bardy, B., Gopher, D., (eds.) Skill Training in Multimodal Virtual Environments, p. 199. Taylor and Francis, Bergamasco (2013)
2. Gosselin F., Ferlay F., Bouchigny S., Mégard C., Taha F.: Specification and design of a new haptic interface for maxillo facial surgery. In: IEEE International Conference on Robotics and Automation, Shanghai, pp. 737–744 (2011)
3. Gosselin, F., Bouchigny, S., Mégard, C., Taha, F., Delcampe, P., d'Hauthuille, C.: Haptic systems for training sensorimotor skills: a use case in surgery. Robot. Autonomous Syst. 61(4), 380–389 (2013)

4. Wolf, B.R., Britton, C.L.: How orthopaedic residents perceive educational resources. Iowa Orthop. J. **33**, 185–190 (2013)
5. Aggarwal, R., et al.: Training and simulation for patient safety. Qual. Saf. Health Care **19**(Suppl 2), i34–43 (2010)
6. Gaba, D.M.: The future vision of simulation in health care. Qual. Saf. Health Care **13**(Suppl 1), i2–10 (2004)
7. Stirling, E.R.B., Lewis, T.L., Ferran, N.A.: Surgical skills simulation in trauma and orthopaedic training. J. Orthop. Surg. Res. **9**, 126 (2014). https://doi.org/10.1186/s13018-014-0126-z
8. Ruikar, D.D., Hegadi, R.S., Santosh, K.C.: A systematic review on orthopedic simulators for psycho-motor skill and surgical procedure training. J. Med. Syst. **42**(9), 1–21 (2018). https://doi.org/10.1007/s10916-018-1019-1
9. Popescu, D., Iacob, R., Laptoiu, D.: Virtual reality in orthopedic surgeons training. Key Eng. Mater. **638**, 344–351 (2015)
10. Lazennec, J., Laudet, C., Guérin-Surville, H., Roy-Camille, R., Saillant, G.: Dynamic anatomy of the acetabulum: an experimental approach and surgical implications. Surg. Radiol. Anat. **19**(1), 23–30 (1997). https://doi.org/10.1007/BF01627730
11. Grow, D.I., Wu, M., Locastro, M.J., Arora, S.K., Bastian, A.J., Okamura, A.M.: Haptic simulation of elbow joint spasticity. In: Symposium on Haptic Interfaces for Virtual Environment and Teleoperator Systems. Reno, NE, vol. 2008, pp. 475–476 (2008)
12. Gallagher, A.G., O'Sullivan, G.C.: Fundamentals of Surgical Simulation, p. 31. Springer, London (2012). https://doi.org/10.1007/978-0-85729-763-1
13. Riener, R., Frey, M., Proll, T., Regenfelder, F., Burgkart, R.: Phantom-based multimodal interactions for medical education and training: the Munich knee joint simulator. IEEE Trans. Inf Technol. Biomed. **8**(2), 208–216 (2004)
14. Senkal, D., Gurocak, H.: Serpentine flux path for high torque MRF brakes in haptics applications. Mechatronics **20**(3), 377–383 (2010)
15. Cinq-Mars, M., Gurocak, H.: Pneumatic actuator with embedded MR-brake for haptics. In: IEEE World Haptics Conference (WHC), Munich, pp. 322–327 (2017)
16. Bulea, T.C., Kobetic, R., To, C.S., Audu, M.L., Schnellenberger, J.R., Triolo, R.J.: A variable impedance knee mechanism for controlled stance flexion during pathological Gait. IEEE/ASME Trans. Mechatron. **17**(5), 822–832 (2012)
17. Rossa, C., Lozada, J., Micaelli, A.: Design and control of a dual unidirectional brake hybrid actuation system for haptic devices. IEEE Trans. Haptics **7**(4), 442–453 (2014)
18. Rossa, C., Jaegy, A., Lozada, J., Micaelli, A.: Design considerations for magnetorheological brakes. IEEE/ASME Trans. Mechatron. **19**(5), 1669–1680 (2014)
19. Hafez, M., Lozada, J., ECK, L., Changeon, G.: Fluid haptic interface with improved haptic rendering using a torque or load sensor. Patent US9898032B2
20. Eck, L., Lozada, J., Changeon, G., Hafez, M.: Interface haptique prenant en compte l'intention d'action de l'utilisateur". Patent FR14 59187
21. Allard, J., Cotin, S., Faure, F., Bensoussan, P.J., Poyer, F., Duriez, C., Grisoni, L.: Sofa-an open source framework for medical simulation. In: MMVR 15-Medicine Meets Virtual Reality, vol. 125, pp. 13–18. IOP Press, February 2007
22. Robert, H., Nouveau, S., Gageot, S., Gagniere, B.: A new knee arthrometer, the GNRB®: experience in ACL complete and partial tears. Orthop. Traumatol. Surg. & Res. **95**(3), 171–176 (2009)

Tissue Discrimination Through Force-Feedback from Impedance Spectroscopy in Robot-Assisted Surgery

Brayden Kent[(✉)], Angelica Cusipag, and Carlos Rossa

Faculty of Engineering and Applied Science, Ontario Tech University,
Oshawa, ON, Canada
{brayden.kent,angelica.cusipag,carlos.rossa}@uoit.ca

Abstract. Haptic force feedback in teleoperated robot-assisted minimally invasive surgery is difficult to implement with traditional force sensors at the tool tip. A novel approach to displaying forces to the user is explored using electric impedance spectroscopy with an electrode embedded needle. To give substance to the proposed method, user trials were conducted to compare the accuracy of inserting needles by hand and through electric impedance based haptic teleoperation. The results of the experiment suggest that, when compared to the control scenario, novice operators could accurately locate the phantom tumour with a high degree of accuracy and repeatability using force feedback derived from electric impedance spectroscopy.

Keywords: Robot-assisted minimally invasive surgery · Electric impedance spectroscopy · Haptics

1 Introduction

Robot-assisted minimally invasive surgery (RMIS) has shown increasing promise in improving the quality of treatment in the operating room. Typically, the goal of teleoperated RMIS systems is to enhance the dexterity and precision of the surgeon rather than have robots replace them in the operating room. Through a remote console, the surgeon controls a robotic manipulator that operates on the patient. However, the lack of force feedback in the commercially available systems presents a steep learning curve for novice surgeons to become proficient in RMIS and achieve the desired levels of performance. In some minimally invasive procedures, the surgeon can rely on other forms of sensory feedback such

We acknowledge the support of the Natural Sciences and Engineering Research Council of Canada (NSERC), the Canadian Institutes of Health Research (CIHR), and the Social Sciences and Humanities Research Council of Canada (SSHRC), [funding reference number NFRFE-2018-01986]. Cette recherche a été financée par le Conseil de recherches en sciences naturelles et en génie du Canada (CRSNG), par les Instituts de recherche en santé du Canada (IRSC), et par le Conseil de recherches en sciences humaines du Canada (CRSH), [numéro de référence NFRFE-2018-01986].

T. McDaniel et al. (Eds.): ICSM 2019, LNCS 12015, pp. 274–285, 2020.
https://doi.org/10.1007/978-3-030-54407-2_23

as laparoscopic cameras to visualize the surgical site. Yet, this is not always a feasible solution for percutaneous procedures such as brachytherapy.

Alternatively, haptic feedback systems for RMIS can recreate the tool-tissue interaction contact force as a displayable force to the surgeon since it is an intuitive leap. In developing such haptic feedback, one tends to relate a physical property, such as tissue stiffness or contact force, to render the haptic force. Traditionally, there are two ways of developing the haptic force: measuring tool-tissue interaction forces directly or inferring them from measurements of the mechanical properties of the tissue. For needle based procedures, one can implement a force sensor at the base of the needle, outside of the body, to estimate the tissue composition during insertion. Unfortunately, friction along the needle shaft can obscure the data and consequently compromise the force feedback. To solve this, one can attempt to implement a force sensor at the tip of the needle. The challenge in integrating a force sensor at the tip is due to the constraints posed by the surgical environment, namely limited size and degrees of freedom [17].

However, tissues do need to be characterized solely on their mechanical properties, as organic tissues also have unique electric and dielectric properties. In the current state of the art, several instruments have been developed to differentiate healthy and cancerous cells through their electrical characteristics. NASA and BioLuminate Inc. developed a biopsy probe to identify breast cancer through electric impedance [1]. Yun et al. utilized an electrode embedded needle to identify thyroid cancer [21]. Park et al. integrated a microelectrode array onto a biopsy needle for liver cancer discrimination [19]. Measuring a tissue's response to electric stimulus at the tip of an electrode embedded needle can provide an alternative way to develop force feedback.

In this paper, an electrode embedded needle was developed to measure a tissue's electrical impedance through impedance spectroscopy, see Fig. 1(c). As a robot manipulator inserts the needle into the tissue, the robot's operator can feel forces through a haptic device. Using a rudimentary model, the haptic force is developed from the tissue's electric impedance at the tip. The paper culminates with the proposed technique tested in user trials with gelatin phantoms to address its potential usability for future surgical procedures. The users were to find the gelatin layer that represented a cancerous tumour in two scenarios: inserting a needle by hand, and with an RMIS setup with haptic force feedback derived from the electric impedance model. While this paper has been written with a specific focus on differentiating cancer cells from healthy tissue in needle based RMIS, the proposed method could potentially be adapted to other tissue types and surgical procedures including fat in percutaneous liposuction, struvite crystals in nephrolithotomy and arterial plaque in angioplasty.

2   Electric Impedance Spectroscopy

The act of applying a spectrum of alternating current to an object to determine its composition is coined electric impedance spectroscopy (EIS) [2]. For decades, researchers have endeavoured to classify tissues based on their response to a spectrum of electric stimuli. Notably, as shown in [3], tissues exhibit unique and distinct electrical conductivities when exposed to various frequencies of alternating current. Halter *et al.* have shown that in a prostate; glandular tissue, stroma, carcinoma and benign hyperplasia have distinct ranges of conductivity and relative permittivity [7]. Furthermore, cancerous breast tissue have significantly different impedivity modulus and phase angle than healthy breast tissues [8]. Typically, the instruments used in EIS resemble one of the configurations shown in Fig. 1. With a current source based device, it is possible to limit the amount of current seen by the tissue, making it a safer choice for biomedical applications.

Classification of electric parameters for biological tissue is a vast and challenging field of research. Over the past few decades, researchers have been exploring new models for bioimpedance measurements. For the extent of this paper it is sufficient to recognize the following: The first, that a given tissue has a frequency dependent electric impedance and can be determined using EIS. Secondly, that two different tissues can be discriminated by their respective regions of electric impedance.

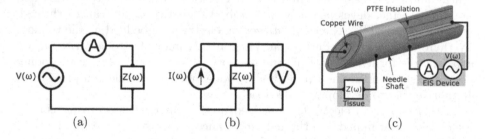

Fig. 1. A simplified bipolar spectroscopy measurement (a): two electrodes are attached to an object with unknown, frequency dependent impedance $Z(\omega)$ where a voltage is applied and current is measured in line. A simplified tetrapolar spectroscopy measurement (b): the applied signal electrodes are separate from the measurement electrodes, requiring four electrodes attached to the object. (c) An example of a bipolar electrode arrangement with an electrode embedded needle.

In traditional circuit analysis, one can determine the resistance of a circuit element through Ohm's Law by applying an electric signal (voltage or current) and measuring the corresponding property (current or voltage). If an alternating current with frequency ω is applied, the impedance $Z(\omega)$ of the element, a combination of resistance R and reactance $X(\omega)$, can be evaluated as

$$Z(\omega) = R + jX(\omega) \tag{1}$$

It is well recognized that tissues exhibit behaviour of resistance and capacitive elements. To truly capture the behaviour, one must look at the electrochemical behaviours of the cells that comprise the tissue. In gist, cell structures react to an electric field through polar molecule alignment and relaxation. This behaviour is encompassed in a popular electrochemical model proposed by Debye and adapted by Cole [4,15],

$$Z(\omega) = \frac{R + (R_o - R_\infty)}{1 + (j\omega/\omega_o)^\alpha} \tag{2}$$

where R_o and R_∞ correspond to the low and high frequency intercepts of the complex impedance plane, see Fig. 2(a), respectively. ω_o represents "turnover" frequency [15]. The constant $0 < \alpha \leq 1$ defines the angle between the complex impedance locus arc and the intercepts [15]. The model in (2) can be fitted to an equivalent circuit of which is comprised of two resistors and a constant phase element (CPE), see Fig. 2(b).

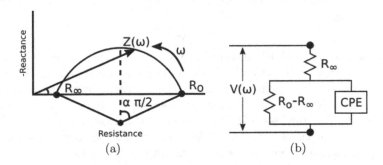

Fig. 2. (a) A typical Cole-Cole plot in the complex impedance plane that represents how a biological tissues electric impedance can change with an applied alternating current of frequency ω. (b) An equivalent circuit model for biological tissue with Cole parameters [4,15].

Provided that one can now differentiate two tissues given their electric impedance the following section derives how this property can be used in haptic force feedback.

3   Developing Force Feedback

Alas, there is no known direct correlation between the electrical and mechanical properties for organic tissue. When comparing malignant to healthy cells in glandular organs, such as breast or prostate, malignant cells are generally more stiff and have greater electric impedance [6,8,10,13]. However, cancerous cells can offer better electrical conductivity relative to healthy tissue, as seen in liver cancer [11]. Thus, the model proposed here should be adapted accordingly depending on the application. A crude model can be made, where the mechanical stiffness K is proportional to the electrical impedance $Z(\omega)$ of a given tissue,

$$K = \gamma_1 Z(\omega) \tag{3}$$

where γ_1 is a conversion factor. The conversion factor will differ for any given tissue and should be calibrated for the specific situation.

It has been shown elsewhere that for needle-tissue interaction that the force at the base of the needle is comprised of three parts: puncturing, cutting and friction. [9,20] To simplify the model, assume that the needle has already punctured the tissue. Furthermore, eliminating the friction component will improve the haptic feedback for tissue discrimination. Thus, only cutting forces are presented where the force at the base of the needle F is proportional to the tissue stiffness K through a factor γ_2,

$$F = \gamma_2 K \tag{4}$$

In combining (3) and (4) a lumped conversion factor $\gamma = \gamma_1 \gamma_2$ relates electric impedance to force,

$$F = \gamma Z(\omega) \tag{5}$$

Consider a needle with EIS electrodes at the tip that has punctured an organ which is comprised of healthy cells with a tumor at an unknown depth. The electric impedance of the tissue at the tip can be evaluated by averaging n electric impedance measurements. To discriminate between the two tissues, the electric impedance data is compensated to be relative to the measurement immediately after puncturing the tissue. The initial electric impedance $Z(\omega, 0)$ is consequently removed from measurements at needle tip depth d. The haptic force can then be estimated as,

$$F(d) = \gamma \left(\frac{\sum_{i=1}^{n} Z_i(\omega, d)}{n} - Z(\omega, 0) \right) \tag{6}$$

In summary, using EIS, one can determine the local electric impedance at the tip of the needle and render that as a force F to the user. The haptic force can be adjusted through a tunable parameter γ.

With the relationship between the electric impedance and haptic force now developed, the following section describes the RMIS setup and phantom tissues used to test the proposed force feedback model.

4   Experimental Setup

The experimental setup used to validate the concept is shown in Fig. 3.

The Meca500 6-DOF serial robot arm (Mecademic, Québec, Canada) inserts an electrode embedded needle as controlled by the operator with the Novint Falcon 3-DOF parallel manipulator haptic joystick (Novint Technologies, New Mexico, USA). The impedance data gathered by a spectroscopy system is then used in the force feedback model to display a force to the user through the haptic device.

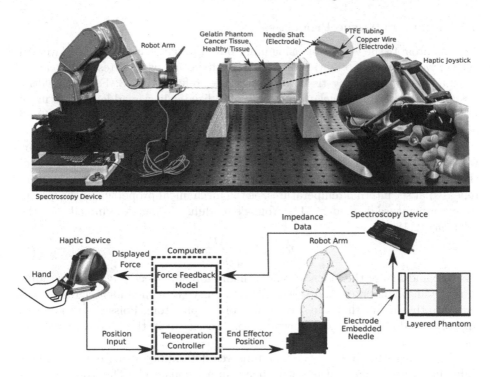

Fig. 3. The experimental setup: the haptic device controls the needle insertion depth as the robotic arm inserts the needle into the phantom tissue. The electrode at the tip of the needle is used by the spectroscopy device to determine the local electric impedance of the phantom. The impedance is converted to a force and displayed to the user as haptic feedback.

The electrode embedded needle was fabricated following the design shown in Fig. 1(c), see Fig. 3. An 18 gauge brachytherapy needle (Eckert & Ziegler, New York, USA) was modified for the experiment. Enamelled copper wire was fed through the shaft and served as the primary electrode. The needle shaft itself acted as the secondary electrode. A PTFE sleeve was used as an additional means of insulation between the primary and secondary electrode. Cyanoacrylate was used to bond the assembly. Fine grit sandpaper was used to strip the enamel of the copper wire and expose the tip of the electrode. While the developed electrode embedded needle is primitive and impedes its ability to deposit radiation for brachytherapy, further refinement of the design can be done to miniaturize the electrodes as seen in [19].

Using the electrode embedded needle the Quadra electric impedance spectroscopy device (Eliko, Tallin, Estonia) [16] was used to measure the electric impedance of a phantom tissue. The analogue front end of the module was connected to the electrode embedded needle to form a bipolar EIS measurement scheme.

4.1 Phantom Tissue Properties

The phantom tissue was made using unflavoured porcine gelatin. Three layers of gelatin were created to fabricate one of the phantoms used in testing: a cancer layer adjacent to healthy tissue on either side, refer to Fig. 3. For the healthy tissue, a ratio of 25 g of gelatin with 5 g of iodized salt was added to 240 ml of water. To make the cancerous layer, the ratio used was 40 g of gelatin to 240 ml of water.

The healthy and cancerous phantom types were prepared such that they would acquire unique mechanical and electrical properties. The stiffness of the gelatin phantoms was measured through indentation tests. The tests were repeated at set internal temperatures, as the mechanical properties of the gelatin were temperature dependent. The Young's modulus K was determined with the relation [12, 18],

$$K = \frac{(1 - v^2)F_k}{2ax\kappa} \tag{7}$$

where x and F_k are the indentation depth and force, respectively, a is the radius of the cylinder indenter, and κ was taken as unity since the indenter radius was significantly smaller than the surface area of the phantom. Poisson's ratio v was approximated as 0.45, a value between the those seen in the literature, 0.4 [14] and 0.495 [5].

The Young's modulus of the phantom was determined using data from four different internal temperatures with five compressions each. The Young's modulus for the healthy tissue gelatin phantom and the cancerous gelatin phantom were determined to be 6.88 ± 0.10 kPa and 12.0 ± 0.17 kPa respectively at 14 °C. These values are comparable to those obtained for gelatin phantoms in other publications [5]. The created phantoms are less stiff than actual human organs but do mirror the behaviour of prostate cancer, which has nearly twice the elastic modulus of healthy tissue [10].

5 Experiment Results

The model formulated in (6) is integrated in the system shown in Fig. 3. The complete results of the experiment are in shown in Fig. 4.

An unmodified 18 gauge brachytherapy needle was attached to a load cell to determine the axial insertion force, see Fig. 4 (b). This plot is representative of the force the surgeon would feel by inserting the needle by hand. The three components of the needle-tissue interaction are clearly visible: cutting, friction and puncturing. Noticeably, the slope of the force increases while transitioning into the cancer phantom. This is a result of the increased stiffness created by altering the water to gelatin ratio in the phantom fabrication for the respective layers. The overall difference in force seen along the needle depth is relatively inappreciable, which would make it difficult to distinguish between the tissue types while inserting by hand. Thus, for the haptic feedback RMIS scenario, it is prudent that the force be more discernible for the transition into the cancer layer.

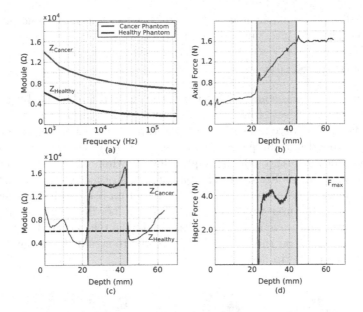

Fig. 4. Experimental results: differentiating the phantom layers.

Figure 4(a) showcases the difference in electric impedance of the gelatin layers with respect to an alternating frequency ω through EIS measurements. The addition of salt in the healthy gelatin resulted in a distinctly different conductivity compared to the cancerous layer. The impedance data shown in Fig. 4(a) is not compensated for the impedance of the electrode embedded needle. It is reasonable to expect that the needle would introduce both resistance and capacitance and consequently have an impact on the measured values. However, in this application we are not attempting to classify the composition of the phantom, rather, the application is to distinguish between the layers that compose it. Since the properties of the needle do not change through the insertion, its effect is considered negligible.

In the RMIS control loop the magnitude of the phantom's electric impedance at the needle tip was determined by averaging $n = 10$ spectra samples. The electric impedance at lower frequencies provided the greatest relative difference in the tissue types as shown in Figure 4(a), thus the electric impedance at $\omega = 1$ kHz was used in calculating the displayed force in (6).

The electrode embedded needle was inserted into the tissue and the impedance at a given depth was recorded, see Fig. 4(c). These impedance values are evaluated as a force to be displayed to the user as shown in Fig. 4(d). For any $F(d) < 0$ was taken as $F(d) = 0$, otherwise the haptic device would pull the user in rather than impede their insertion. Furthermore, to provide a safe limit to the displayable force any $F(d) > F_{max}$ was set such that $F(d) = F_{max}$. In comparison to (b), the force is significantly more noticeable during the transition into the cancer phantom.

The results of the experiment suggested that the haptic feedback would be more detectable than inserting the needle manually.

6   User Trial Study

An additional study was conducted to test if the method was applicable to a more pragmatic scenario. A set of user trials were designed to mimic a surgeon inserting a needle during percutaneous brachytherapy. First, the user would insert the needle by hand into unique phantoms, see Fig. 5(a). Second, the user would control the robot arm through the haptic device, where they would detect the force based on EIS, see Fig. 5(b). The participant's objective was to determine where the cancer layer existed in the gelatin phantom using only force feedback. In the hand trial the user would stop inserting the needle when they perceived the cancer layer, and leave it within the tissue. In the teleoperated test, the user would press a button on the haptic device handle to signal the change in tissue and record the needle tip depth.

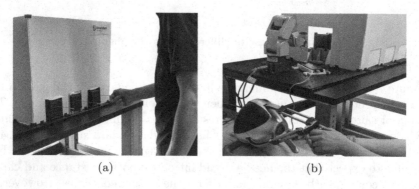

(a)   (b)

Fig. 5. The two stages of the user trials. (a) The test participant would first insert the needle by hand to determine the depth of the cancer layer in three unique phantoms. (b) The participant would then determine the depths using haptic feedback in the teleoperated scenario.

Three different phantoms were used, with the cancer layer at different depths. The test participant was unable to view any of the phantoms, similar to a black box problem. The participant would insert the electrode embedded needle into the phantom through a grid template.

The user trials consisted of N = 16 participants. All participants were given the same set of written instructions prior to the start of the test. Each participant was shown an example gelatin phantom that they could practice with hand insertion to familiarize themselves with the needle force associated with the healthy and cancerous layers of the gelatin. Additionally, a simulated force was presented to the user in the haptic device such that they could recognize the haptic force they were to expect in the actual trials. Each participant was only permitted to one insertion per phantom.

6.1   User Study Test Results

Figure 6 shows the final depths that the user perceived the cancer for both tests in each of the three phantoms.

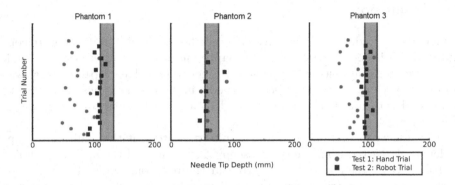

Fig. 6. Results of the user trials in each of the three phantoms. The shaded region represents the cancer layer of the phantom.

Noticeably, the teleoperated trials performed significantly better than the hand trials overall. The hand trials were more successful at finding the cancer layer in Phantom 2, where the layer was at a shallow depth. It is speculated that the users had more difficulty in Phantom 1 and Phantom 3 hand trials due to the amount of friction experienced. In the teleoperation scenario, friction is eliminated, since the haptic device only displayed a force from the electric properties of the phantom, which may explain the increase in performance.

Many of the teleoperated results show final depths recorded before the transition line. This is a result of two circumstances. First, while the gelatin layers were prepared separately, when combined in the phantom, the salt ions diffuse gradually into the non-salinated layer which alters the local conductivity near the layer transition. Second, the haptic force pushes against the user, causing them to unintentionally move the joystick handle slightly outward and consequently move the needle out of the cancer. For the latter it can be seen in the Phantom 2 and Phantom 3 results that the users more readily anticipate the haptic force and become more consistent in stopping within the cancer layer.

Table 1. User trial statistics (Units are in [mm])

	Phantom 1		**Phantom 2**		**Phantom 3**	
	Cancer Start:	112.5	Cancer Start:	56.0	Cancer Start:	94.5
	Cancer End:	134.5	Cancer End:	78.0	Cancer End:	116.5
	Avg Depth	**Success**	**Avg Depth**	**Success**	**Avg Depth**	**Success**
Test 1: Hand	74.9 ± 18.5	0%	61.7 ± 11.1	78%	72.5 ± 15.5	6%
Test 2: Robot	109.1 ± 9.1	25%	59.9 ± 11.3	75%	96.6 ± 4.3	81%

The average depth with standard deviation for each of the phantoms in the two test scenarios are listed in Table 1 along with the percentage of trials that successfully finished within the cancer layer.

7   Conclusion

Implementing traditional force sensors on needles for haptic feedback in teleoperated RMIS is not a trivial task. This paper introduces an alternative through analysis of a tissue's electric impedance. Electric impedance spectroscopy was performed with an electrode embedded needle in gelatin phantoms. The method was tested with user trials and compared to a control scenario to evaluate its effectiveness.

The user trials and experimental results indicate that the addition of haptic feedback derived from the spectroscopy data improved the operators ability to detect where the cancer layer started in the phantom tissue. The proposed method of using electric impedance to display haptic feedback may hold new possibilities in several medical procedures including percutaneous brachytherapy, nephrolithotomy and angioplasty. At a minimum, it is worthwhile to further explore and develop this new avenue of providing haptic feedback as a substitute or supplement to conventional methods of sensory feedback.

References

1. Andrews, R.J., Mah, R.W.: The NASA smart probe project for real-time multiple microsensor tissue recognition. Stereotact. Funct. Neurosurg. **80**(1–4), 114–119 (2003)
2. Barsoukov, E., Macdonald, J.R.: Impedance Spectroscopy: Theory, Experiment, and Applications. Wiley, Hoboken (2018)
3. Brown, B.H.: Electrical impedance tomography (EIT): a review. J. Med. Eng. Technol. **27**(3), 97–108 (2003)
4. Cole, K.: Dispersion and absorption in dielectrics. J. Chem. Phys **9**, 341 (1941)
5. Hall, T.J., Bilgen, M., Insana, M.F., Krouskop, T.A.: Phantom materials for elastography. IEEE Trans. Ultrason. Ferroelectr. Freq. Control **44**(6), 1355–1365 (1997)
6. Halter, R.J., Schned, A., Heaney, J., Hartov, A., Paulsen, K.D.: Electrical properties of prostatic tissues: I. Single frequency admittivity properties. J. Urol. **182**(4), 1600–1607 (2009)
7. Halter, R.J., Schned, A., Heaney, J., Hartov, A., Schutz, S., Paulsen, K.D.: Electrical impedance spectroscopy of benign and malignant prostatic tissues. J. Urol. **179**(4), 1580–1586 (2008)
8. Jossinet, J.: The impedivity of freshly excised human breast tissue. Physiol. Meas. **19**(1), 61 (1998)
9. Khadem, M., Rossa, C., Usmani, N., Sloboda, R.S., Tavakoli, M.: A two-body rigid/flexible model of needle steering dynamics in soft tissue. IEEE/ASME Trans. Mechatron. **21**(5), 2352–2364 (2016)
10. Krouskop, T., Wheeler, T., Kallel, F., Garra, B., Hall, T.: Elastic moduli of breast and prostate tissues under compression. Ultrason. Imaging **20**(4), 260–274 (1998)

11. Laufer, S., Ivorra, A., Reuter, V.E., Rubinsky, B., Solomon, S.B.: Electrical impedance characterization of normal and cancerous human hepatic tissue. Physiol. Meas. **31**(7), 995 (2010)
12. Lehmann, T., Rossa, C., Usmani, N., Sloboda, R.S., Tavakoli, M.: Intraoperative tissue young's modulus identification during needle insertion using a laterally actuated needle. IEEE Trans. Instrum. Meas. **67**(2), 371–381 (2017)
13. Li, Q., Lee, G.Y., Ong, C.N., Lim, C.T.: AFM indentation study of breast cancer cells. Biochem. Biophys. Res. Commun. **374**(4), 609–613 (2008)
14. Markidou, A., Shih, W.Y., Shih, W.H.: Soft-materials elastic and shear moduli measurement using piezoelectric cantilevers. Rev. Sci. Instrum. **76**(6), 064302 (2005)
15. McAdams, E., Jossinet, J.: Tissue impedance: a historical overview. Physiol. Meas. **16**(3A), A1 (1995)
16. Min, M., Lehti-Polojärvi, M., Hyttinen, J., Rist, M., Land, R., Annus, P.: Bioimpedance spectro-tomography system using binary multifrequency excitation. Int. J. Bioelectromagnetism **209**, 76–79 (2018). https://doi.org/10.18154/RWTH-CONV-224930
17. Okamura, A.M.: Haptic feedback in robot-assisted minimally invasive surgery. Curr. Opin. Urol. **19**(1), 102 (2009)
18. Ottensmeyer, M.P., Salisbury, J.K.: In vivo data acquisition instrument for solid organ mechanical property measurement. In: Niessen, W.J., Viergever, M.A. (eds.) MICCAI 2001. LNCS, vol. 2208, pp. 975–982. Springer, Heidelberg (2001). https://doi.org/10.1007/3-540-45468-3_116
19. Park, J., Choi, W.M., Kim, K., Jeong, W.I., Seo, J.B., Park, I.: Biopsy needle integrated with electrical impedance sensing microelectrode array towards real-time needle guidance and tissue discrimination. Sci. rep. **8**(1), 264 (2018)
20. Rossa, C., Tavakoli, M.: Issues in closed-loop needle steering. Control Eng. Pract. **62**, 55–69 (2017). https://doi.org/10.1016/j.conengprac.2017.03.004
21. Yun, J., Hong, Y.T., Hong, K.H., Lee, J.H.: Ex vivo identification of thyroid cancer tissue using electrical impedance spectroscopy on a needle. Sens. Actuators, B Chem. **261**, 537–544 (2018)

Towards a Dual-User Haptic Training System User Feedback Setup

Angel Ricardo Licona, Guillermo Zamora de la Pena, Oscar Diaz Cruz,
Arnaud Lelevé(✉) ⓘD, Damien Ebérard, and Minh Tu Pham

Univ Lyon, INSA Lyon, Ampère (UMR 5005), 69621 Lyon, France
arnaud.leleve@insa-lyon.fr
http://www.ampere-lab.fr

Abstract. This paper introduces preliminary works on building an
experimental end-user evaluation for dual-user haptic systems for hands-
on training. Such systems bring together the advantages of haptic
computer-based training systems and those of supervised training where
an expert trainer actively helps in the learning process. The first results
mainly permitted to highlight several technical and organizational issues
to overcome in a close future. The objective of this project is to test
other architectures such as those listed in the state-of-the-art section, to
provide comparative conclusions about the pros and cons of each one.

Keywords: Computer simulation · Dual-user system · Hands-on
training · Haptic interfaces · Shared control

1 Introduction

In many gesture-based professions, dexterous manipulation is necessary. Staff
then requires initial and continuing hands-on training on regularly evolving
methods. In Medicine, simulators such as cadavers and animals have been a
convenient way to learn by trial for decades in universities. However, due to
the growing cost of providing them and ethical issues, phantoms are increasingly
used. Yet, phantoms provide a limited set of common cases to practice on. Nowadays, medical trainees are still offered too few opportunities to perform hands-
on training during their curriculum, due to limited access to hands-on training
resources. For instance, epidural anesthesia requires at least eighty attempts to
be mastered enough to practice it on a real patient [14] but only a few of them
are performed during the studies. Therefore, cost-efficient solutions to be used
during supervised sessions but also autonomously are necessary for sufficient
hands-on training during their curriculum.

Over the last decade, Computer-Based Simulators (CBS) have been designed
to overcome the aforementioned drawbacks [15]. Virtual patients, parameterized
on-demand, provide an infinite set of medical cases with various difficulty levels. Such simulators have progressively improved to provide trainees with more

© Springer Nature Switzerland AG 2020
T. McDaniel et al. (Eds.): ICSM 2019, LNCS 12015, pp. 286–297, 2020.
https://doi.org/10.1007/978-3-030-54407-2_24

realistic environments, in 2D and more recently in 3D [2]. In haptic training simulators, the additional force feedback provides a realistic tool behavior, which
leads to efficient training for advanced tasks such as suturing [13]. These systems
feature a haptic interface (i.e. a device by which tool-environment interaction
forces are transmitted back to a human operator based on their hand motion)
which acts as a master and a software architecture which connects the master
to the slave (a software simulating a virtual tool inside a virtual environment,
or a real robot handling a real tool).

Common training simulators provide only solutions to train oneself. But,
for some difficult cases, the implication of a trainer remains necessary. He/she
can guide the trainees' motions to accomplish accurate and efficient gestures.
Traditionally, he/she directly guides the hands of a trainee but this "four-hand
fellowship" does not permit the trainee to feel and dose the correct level of
force to apply on their tool. Dual-user systems are a practicable solution to
this problem, as they can reproduce this important force information to both
users, each one interacting with their haptic interface. These systems extend the
aforementioned master-slave architecture by adding a second master, as shown in
Fig. 1. Users share the slave control according to a dominance factor ($\alpha \in [0,1]$).
When $\alpha = 1$ (respectively 0), the trainer (respectively trainee) has full control
over the slave, and the trainee's (respectively trainer's) device follows the slave
motions. When $0 < \alpha < 1$, both users share the slave control with dominance
(over the other user) which is a function of α. According to the architectures
found in the literature, the effect of α on the force feedback provided to the users
differs. These differences are highlighted in Sect. 2. It has been stated [7] that the
existing solutions did not fit all the requirements for efficient hands-on training
where interaction forces have to be learned through the haptic architecture.
Thus, a dual-user control architecture had been first introduced: the *Energy-
based Shared Control* (ESC) [5]. It reuses the robust control approach introduced
by Stramigioli [12], which ensures passivity even in presence of robot model
uncertainties, limited bandwidth, or non-linearities (saturation). It thus provides
robust passive and compliant interfaces. We reuse in this paper a n degree-of-
freedom (dof) version, for haptic devices with the same kinematics and with an
adaptive dominance mechanism [7].

The objective of this paper is to introduce the development of end-user
experiments aiming at evaluating the performance of dual-user architectures
for hands-on training. It is applied to the ESC aforementioned architecture. In
this system, trainers and trainees manipulate their haptic interface. They share
the same slave robot. They are all located in the same room.

This paper is organized as follows. Section 2 describes the dual-user concept
in the literature. Section 3 introduces the method used for this experimentation,
and Sects. 4 and 5 the preliminary results and conclusions.

2   Related Works

Various architectures have been proposed for the control of dual-user haptic
systems. The "shared control" concept has been introduced by Nudehi *et al.* in

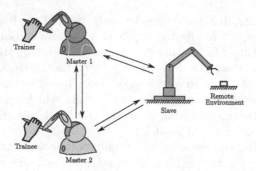

Fig. 1. Architecture of a dual-user system

[8] for Minimal Invasive Telesurgical Training purpose, i.e. to "allow experienced surgeons mentor trainee surgeons through shared control of a surgical robot". Unfortunately, each user is provided with feedback forces proportional to the difference of position of their device, according to α: this dual-user architecture can only be used to train users on motions, not on tool-interaction forces.

Khademian *et al.* introduced two distinct architectures [4]. The first one is the "Complementary Linear Combination" (CLC) architecture which provides feedback forces combining the environment and the other user forces. The desired position and force commands for each device are a complementary weighted sum of positions and forces of the other two devices. Therefore, when trying to perform a mentoring (resp. evaluation) session, the trainee (resp. trainer) has no direct force feedback from the environment, only from the other user. This is why the authors advise using this system with values of $\alpha \in \{0.2, 0.5, 0.8\}$ to get the best transparency. Yet, in these cases, both users influence the slave trajectory, which may lead to inaccurate motions, not compliant with mentoring (resp. evaluation) modes. In the second architecture, based on "Masters Correspondence with Environment Transfer" (MCET) [4], both user devices follow the motion of each other and the effort fed back to both users is half the force applied by the environment on the slave tool. Yet, according to the authors, this architecture transmits a distorted environment force to both users.

Ghorbanian *et al.* defined two dominance factors α and β [3]. α determines the balance of authority between the trainer and the trainee, while β indicates the supremacy of both trainer and trainee over the slave robot. They set a nonlinear relation between α and β to adjust the authority of the leader (the user for which $\alpha > 0.5$) over the slave. It also supports users located at distance with uncertain communication channels. However, when $\alpha = 1$, the desired Master 2 force is only linked to the position of Master 1, not to the tool-environment interaction force.

An interesting work has been introduced by Shamaei *et al.* [11] where two dominance factors are used. They experimentally evaluated, in terms of impedance matching between trainer and trainee during soft and hard interactions, an architecture which tracks the positions of all three devices. Yet, no information about force tracking error is provided. Also, the authors specify that this approach is limited in terms of control freedom as derivative operators may destabilize it.

In [10] the users' haptic feedback is a weighted (with α) sum of the virtual tool-environment interaction force and the other user interaction (with their master device) force. Experiments show that when $\alpha = 0.5$ and both users follow very close trajectories, they feel very close force feedback, in presence of time delays between each master and the slave. This is an interesting result but only limited to cooperative mode. We also need this kind of behavior in the demonstration and evaluation modes.

Furthermore, in a dual-user hands-on training system, the authority factor α should be switched anytime by the trainer. The architectures should guarantee that fast changes of α may not destabilize the system. Every LTI-based models do not inherently guarantee the stability of a variable parameter. At best, a LMI approach can ensure that the system is stable for every value of α. Only a few architectures guarantee some robustness versus α variations, employing a Lyapunov function [3,10] or through an unconditional stability approach based on Llewellyn's criterion [11]. This short review shows that different approaches have been introduced in the literature but it remains difficult to compare them from a user point of view on their capability to train users on gestures requiring precision guiding and correct force level transmission. This motivates the work illustrated in this paper, for a generic experimental setup able to provide such comparative information.

3 Proposed Method

3.1 Typical Scenario to Test

The following typical use case helps determine the main requirements of the system. Suppose, at first, that the trainer (an experienced surgeon) aims at demonstrating the right trajectories of their surgical tool to perform a task featuring free motions and some tool–environment contacts. This implies that they require realistic force feedback to dose their force, as in a bilateral teleoperation context. The trainer manually sets $\alpha = 1$ to become the **leader** (the trainee becomes the **follower**): it is a **mentoring mode**. They then get full force feedback from the slave to perform their task as if they were handling the real instruments. Meanwhile, the trainee's device follows the trajectory of the leader one. If the trainee deviates from this reference trajectory when in free motion, the compliance of the device brings them back to the right position. In case of interaction between the tool and its environment, the trainee can also feel in their hands the right level of effort to provide to the tool, through a display that guides them to set their device in the right position with the right applied force. Afterward, the functioning can be inverted by reversing α so that the trainee manipulates and the trainer follows and evaluates trainee's motions and applied forces: it is an **evaluation mode**.

3.2   Tested Dual-User Architecture

In a first approach, we reused the ESC [7] architecture, which guarantees, by means of a Time-Domain Passivity Controller (TDPC), the passivity of the system (and then its stability) even for nonlinear models and active users and the environment. We already showed in simulation [6] that ESC had equivalent performance in terms of low-level tracking functions compared to CLC and MCET architectures. For space reasons, ESC is not recalled in this paper. It is detailed in a recent paper [7].

In the future, other architectures such as those listed in the previous section will be used to provide comparative studies. For a comparative study between different architectures, a virtual slave should be preferred as it permits to obtain more repeatable experiments. Some virtual fixtures can help limit the trajectories and then objectively compare them.

3.3   Objectives and Requirements

The main objective of this setup is to provide end-user evaluation of such dual-user architectures for teaching (from the trainer point of view) and learning (from the trainee's point of view) experiences, on simple gestures which require haptic feedback.

It is necessary, as prerequisites, that each user context (typically their previous experience on haptic systems) be known. The setup requires recording objective user gesture performance information (feedback forces, positions, timing, and potentially undesired collisions). We also need to get comfort feedback from the users (their subjective opinion) on completion. Users must be proposed simple exercises to avoid any fatigue as these kinds of devices requires much concentration. We have to train them a minimum on using such haptic devices to avoid mixing this learning with real gesture learning. In practice, we had to take into account the limited work volume of the Geomagic 3D Touch haptic devices and over-all their limited maximum force ($\approx$3N).

3.4   Protocol

To rapidly create a simple setup, we chose a real slave (the same haptic device as for masters). It has the advantage of being tangible, easier for us to set up and to be understood by users, and more realistic than a virtual one. The main drawback is that the repeatability is lower and variables (forces, positions, ...) are easier to record in a virtual world. Eight propositions of exercises were studied: surgical game, tying a knot, dictating dimensions, cutting something, following a path, building a Jenga, writing, and stitching. These proposals were evaluated on their capacity of being performed with the provided haptic devices, taking into account various technical, feasibility and didactic criteria. The best scores belonged to *writing* and *stitching* exercises. However, after a few trials, it was concluded that it was not feasible with this hardware. Stitching could not be done because the device did not permit it and the development of a virtual device would have been risky and time-consuming in comparison to other options. We concluded that the two most suitable exercises were "pushing an object a certain distance" and "pulling a spring a certain distance". They were respectively called PUSH and PULL. Their characteristics are summed up in Table 1 and the corresponding installation is visible in Fig. 2.

Table 1. Description of the motions

	Push	Pull
Description	Pushing a block up a slope up to a specific line	Pulling a spring in a designated direction with a designated force (1N)
Objective metrics	Distance between the final block location and the target location (mm)	Final force vector magnitude and angle
Time required per individual motion	10 s	10 s
Installation	Block on an inclined plane	A spring meter fixed on an horizontal plane
Target value	X cm	1.8 N

Fig. 2. Push (on the ramp) and Pull (with the spring meter, on the left) exercises

These exercises were chosen as they do not require rare experts. We used an "artificial trainer" who was this person previously trained on the exercises and installed in an advantageous position concerning the trainee. The trainer with a plain view of the working area with clear goal indicators had greater instantaneous knowledge and could easily perform correct and precise gestures. In the case of the PULL exercice, the indicator was the force scale indicated on the side of the spring scale. In the case of the PUSH exercise, the indicator was a drawn line that indicated the final position.

Although the participants could see these two markers on screen, the optical distortion of the webcam made these markers unreliable and ultimately less valuable than the trainer's instructions. For instance, the angle between the camera lens and the mass-spring was small acute and this distorted the view.

In the case of the block, as the objected passed a certain height in the ramp the object itself blocked the view of the reference line. The participants did not have clear goal indicators and thus had to rely on haptic guidance the trainer provided – they were obliged to use their kinaesthetic abilities.

3.5   Setup

The setup is composed of three Geomagic 3D Touch haptic devices (see Figs. 3 and 4). The devices' kinematic and dynamic parameters are available in [9]. These devices are six d.o.f. systems but only three d.o.f. are actuated. The control software was implemented in Matlab Simulink. Concerning the software connection with the devices, the Open Haptics software library was used along with the Phantorque block [1] and extended to simultaneously work with three devices.

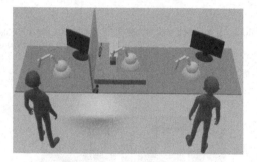

Fig. 3. The global setup organization

The slave device is located in-between the trainee's device and the trainer's device. A wall separates the participants from the slave, blocking visibility. On the other side of the wall, the teacher has a full view. A camera is located on the table 5 cm away from the platform. Another one was added to surveillance the entire procedure. The camera has an overview of what was happening during the experiment (see Fig. 5) and records a separate video for the development each participant undertook during the experiment. The videos are references for outliers in the data collected.

3.6   User Interface

As explained in the previous scenario, the *following* user needs to position his/her tool at the exact position as the leaders'. To help him/her, we developed a specific software to display an intuitive help on screen. As the control of the whole dual-user system is performed by Simulink in real-time, three alternatives were considered:

Fig. 4. Experiment set up (in laboratory)

Fig. 5. Distorted view the participants had throughout the experiment

- generating C code from the Simulink control model, and enriching this code with the desired HMI functions;
- manually coding the control law in C++ accompanied by the desired HMI functions;
- developing a communication module between Simulink and a standalone HMI program.

The first option required the Simulink Coder software which we did not have. The second option required too much time to write in C++ a stable real-time controller running the ESC model. These two options also required to manage the communication with the three haptic devices, through Chaid 3D API[1] for instance. Their complexity and their high risk of incompatibility during the integration of each part convinced us to choose the third option. For this option, three ways to communicate between Simulink and a standalone HMI home-made software were considered:

- a TCP/IP local connection (both software running on the same computer);
- *SendMessage* mechanisms, which provide functions to communicate between Microsoft Windows applications;
- a Memory Mapped File, which is a fake file, located in RAM and shared by two Windows applications.

The "Memory Mapped File" (MMF) solution was chosen, as it provided the best performance with a low implementation complexity. As Simulink does

---

[1] See https://www.chai3d.org/.

not provide Memory Mapped File blocks, a MEX Function was programmed in C++ to send data vectors out of the Simulink model in real-time. This function retrieves these data and stores them in the MMF utilizing the Boost library[2]. The HMI software, written with Visual Basic .Net, retrieves these data from the MMF and display it on screen. It featured a 3D and a camera view to help users interact and perform their tasks. Two spherical objects were displayed in the view, corresponding each one to the tip of the tools of the trainer and the trainee. Initially, we also displayed the position of the slave robot but it disturbed the users. Note that the 3D world displayed on screen is oriented so that the motions of the tip of both user devices coincided with the directions on screen. It was written using HelixToolKit[3] (Fig. 6).

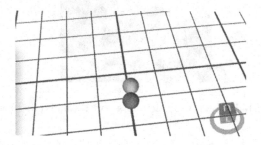

Fig. 6. The HMI software 3D view

4 Preliminary Results

18 participants, divided into two groups, were invited:

- Group 1: 8 participants successively used the system in the demonstration, **guidance** [7] and evaluation modes.
  For each exercise, the participants had 3 demonstrations, 3 attempts with guidance and 3 evaluations.
- Group 2: 8 participants tested demonstration and evaluation modes.
  For each exercise, the participants had 3 demonstrations and 6 evaluations. The first 3 evaluations were not analyzed and were only there to remove any advantage group-1 participants might have had due to the higher number of attempts (the three guided attempts).

Finally, since the two groups had the same exercises, practiced the same number of times and had the same haptic interfaces, the only difference between the two groups comes down to the haptic guidance (guidance mode). Thus, their improvement (or lack thereof) can be attributed to the help brought by the training system.

---

[2] See https://www.boost.org/.
[3] See http://helix-toolkit.github.io/.

The evaluation took approximately 15 min per participant. Each motion took approximately 1 min. In total, the number of attempted motions was that of 9 min. The survey took 5 min, which amounts to a total of 14 min. We recorded the evolution of the positions and the actuation forces for the Master 1, the master 2 and the slave, and α. For the PUSH exercise, the angle between the effective force vector and the reference force vector was calculated. Participants 10 and 16 were eliminated (inconsistent angle values).

5 Discussion

We faced a few issues. Initially, the pens of the Phantom devices were not fixed sufficiently solidly and precisely, so that the position and force measures provided by the devices were not accurate enough. To counter this, a band was later placed around each pen so that all pens were fixed in the same position. Also, whenever any of the masters overpassed the 3N limit, the overshoot affected the calibration between the slave and the masters. The guidance mode could be interpreted as a disagreement between two masters and this might have caused calibration problems and may account for Group 1's poor performance.

In terms of objective measures, the precision in the performance of the exercises obtained by the participants of group 1 was nearly the same as for group 2. With the error tolerance, it was not possible to differentiate the users of group 1 who were guided during their training, compared to the others. These results lead to several conclusions: the guidance mode is not efficient in hands-on training, the exercises are not sufficiently probative, the power range (3N) of the haptic device is not sufficient to get valuable data (and generates disturbing calibration issues), and, in any case, the number of participants was too low. Concerning subjective feedback, it was noted that some participants were shy to grab the haptic device. These participants were nervous and might have performed below their abilities. On the other hand, some participants with previous experience (participant 14 for instance) may prove to have significantly higher skills than other participants. To go around this, we propose a warm-up exercise.

For future experiments, we recommend the trainer subjectively assessing the gestures performed by the trainees on each exercise completion, through participants' performance grades. This should permit to tune objective assessment according to a subjective one, performed by an expert on a first panel of participants. We would then test it on another panel of users which level is known in advance to determine with which level of precision, the system can situate trainees in their learning curve.

6 Conclusion

This paper introduced preliminary works on building an experimental end-user evaluation for dual-user haptic systems for hands-on training. Such systems bring together the advantages of haptic computer-based training systems and those of supervised training where an expert trainer actively helps in the learning process.

It was tested with the ESC architecture. The first results were not convincing but they mainly permitted to highlight several technical and organizational issues to overcome in a close future. The objective of this project is to test other architectures such as those listed in the state-of-the-art section, to provide comparative conclusions about the pros and cons of each one.

Acknowledgments. The authors acknowledge the financial support of the China Scholarship Council (CSC) and the Consejo Nacional de Ciencia y Tecnologia (CONA-CyT) in Mexico.

References

1. Aldana, C.I., Nuño, E., Basañez, L., Romero, E.: Operational space consensus of multiple heterogeneous robots without velocity measurements. J. Franklin Inst. **351**(3), 1517–1539 (2014)
2. Delorme, S., Laroche, D., DiRaddo, R., Del Maestro, R.F.: Neurotouch: a physics-based virtual simulator for cranial microneurosurgery training. Neurosurgery **71**, 32–42 (2012)
3. Ghorbanian, A., Rezaei, S., Khoogar, A., Zareinejad, M., Baghestan, K.: A novel control framework for nonlinear time-delayed dual-master/single-slave teleoperation. ISA Trans. **52**(2), 268–277 (2013)
4. Khademian, B., Hashtrudi-Zaad, K.: Shared control architectures for haptic training: performance and coupled stability analysis. Int. J. Rob. Res. **30**(13), 1627–1642 (2011)
5. Liu, F., Lelevé, A., Eberard, D., Redarce, T.: A dual-user teleoperation system with online authority adjustment for haptic training. In Proceedings of the 37th Annual International Conference of the IEEE Engineering in Medicine and Biology Society (EMBC15), Milano, Italy (2015)
6. Liu, F., Lelevé, A., Eberard, D., Redarce, T.:. An energy based approach for passive dual-user haptic training systems. In Proceedings of the IEEE International Conference on Intelligent Robots and Systems (IROS 2016), Daejeon, South Korea (2016)
7. Liu, F., Licona, A.R., Lelevé, A., Ebérard, D., Pham, M.T., Redarce, T.: An energy-based approach for n-d.o.f. passive dual-user haptic training systems. Robotica **38**(7), 1–21 (2019). Revision majeur
8. Nudehi, S., Mukherjee, R., Ghodoussi, M.: A shared-control approach to haptic interface design for minimally invasive telesurgical training. IEEE Trans. Control Syst. Technol. **13**(4), 588–592 (2005)
9. Sansanayuth, T., Nilkhamhang, I., Tungpimolrat, K.: Teleoperation with inverse dynamics control for phantom omni haptic device. In: Proceedings of SICE Annual Conference (SICE 2012), pp. 2121–2126 (2012)
10. Shahbazi, M., Talebi, H., Atashzar, S., Towhidkhah, F., Patel, R., Shojaei, S.: A new set of desired objectives for dual-user systems in the presence of unknown communication delay. In: 2011 IEEE/ASME International Conference on Advanced Intelligent Mechatronics (AIM), pp. 146–151 (2011)
11. Shamaei, K., Kim, L., Okamura, A.: Design and evaluation of a trilateral shared-control architecture for teleoperated training robots. In: 2015 37th Annual International Conference of the IEEE Engineering in Medicine and Biology Society (EMBC), pp. 4887–4893 (2015)

12. Stramigioli, S.: Modeling and IPC Control of Interactive Mechanical Systems: A Coordinate-Free Approach. Springer, Heidelberg (2001). https://doi.org/10.1007/BFb0110400
13. Talasaz, A., Trejos, A.L., Patel, R.V.: The role of direct and visual force feedback in suturing using a 7-dof dual-arm teleoperated system. IEEE Trans. Haptics **10**(2), 276–287 (2017)
14. Vaughan, N., Dubey, V.N., Wee, M.Y., Isaacs, R.: A review of epidural simulators: where are we today? Med. Eng. Phys. **35**(9), 1235–1250 (2013)
15. Yiannakopoulou, E., Nikiteas, N., Perrea, D., Tsigris, C.: Virtual reality simulators and training in laparoscopic surgery. Int. J. Surg. **13**(9), 60–64 (2014)

Smart Multimedia Beyond the Visible Spectrum

Cascaded Region Proposal Networks for Proposal-Based Tracking

Ximing Zhang[1][✉], Xuewu Fan[1], and Shujuan Luo[2]

[1] Institute of Optics and Precision Mechanics of CAS, Xi'an 710119, China
zhangximing@opt.ac.cn
[2] School of Astronautics, Northwestern Polytechnical University, Xi'an 710072, China

Abstract. There still remains some problems which have not been solved in RPN-based trackers, including data imbalance, inappropriate proposals and poor robustness to spatial rotation even scale variation. We propose a cascaded region proposal network framework for visual tracking based on region proposal networks, spatial transformer networks and proposal selection strategy. We first to extract the features from deep and shallow layers via cascaded region proposal network to ensure the spatial information and semantic cue of the appearance model. Then, the feature extraction model based on spatial transformer networks is performed to calculate the parameters of spatial transformer and obtain the fused features. During the tracking and testing of proposed networks, the proposals are generated and re-ranked by formulating the proposals selection strategy to ensure the localization and scale of the estimated target. We extensively prove the effectiveness of the proposed method though the ablation studies of the tracking benchmark which include OTB2015, VOT2016 and UAV123. The experimental results perform that the accuracy and robustness of the proposed method as the real-time tracker and the long-term tracker as well. In the meantime, the test on the benchmark UAV123 shows that the tracker can be employed to some engineering area.

Keywords: Visual tracking · Spatial cascaded networks · Multi-features · Region proposals networks · Spatial transformer networks

1 Introduction

Visual tracking is aiming at solving the accurate and fast estimation of target localization, scale and rotation, when offering the ground-truth of such target in the first frame. To this end, visual tracking plays the key role in the application of drone auto-tracking, medical host markers tracking, space non-cooperative visual tracking, automatic driving and so on. However, visual tracking may fail to track the target when suffering heavy occlusion, rotation, deformation, motion blur and illumination variation. In engineering applications, the visual tracking should meet the demand of real-time tracking and long-term robust tracking. Therefore, it is still a challenge to propose the real-time and robust trackers in the complex scenarios.

© Springer Nature Switzerland AG 2020
T. McDaniel et al. (Eds.): ICSM 2019, LNCS 12015, pp. 301–314, 2020.
https://doi.org/10.1007/978-3-030-54407-2_25

Visual tracking based on region proposal networks (RPN) have currently made a great progress. Among them, the methods combine region proposal networks (RPN) [1] with Siamese networks (SN) [2] perform well. Firstly, the target template and searching area are transferred into the model which combines region proposals networks and Siamese network to obtain the similarity response map and corresponding regression coordinates of the tracking target, and the new target localization is updated by where the localization with the highest similarity to the target template. Li et al. proposes SiamRNN [3] which combines these two kinds of networks and accomplishes the end-to-end training and testing. Zhu et al. proposes the DaSiamRPN [4] which designs the attention model in order to get rid of the easy samples and ensure the discriminative power of such model. The other framework treats visual tracking problem as tracking-by-detection problem. The networks are firstly employed to generate the proposals in the searching image in which the object are localized, and then employ the proposals selection strategy to obtain the proposals with the highest similarity scores through the classifier to adopt the tracking bounding box. Guo et al.[5] proposes to utilize the EdgeBox method to generate the proposals in the searching image, and then complete the visual tracking process through the method of proposals selection. Zhu et al. [6] also used EdgeBox to generate proposals, and then perform the SVM classifier though the positives and negatives from proposals set to accomplish tracking results.

The methods based on region proposals networks have drawn the attention of researchers for its characteristic of simple and clear. However, the one-stage region proposal networks employs the extraction of semantic features to complete the training procedure which cannot guarantee the tracking accuracy of the method. Moreover, the one-stage bounding box regression based on the predefined anchor cannot ensure the accurate estimation of the scale change. However, most methods pay attention to the easy samples which reduces accuracy and robustness.

Deep convolutional features such as semantic features helps to improve the robustness of tracking methods, while shallow convolutional features such as spatial features do well to improving the accuracy of tracking methods. The visual trackers which combine two types of features can extremely improve the performance. Ma et al. [7] proposes a hierarchical convolution tracking method (HCT), which extracts deep and shallow convolutional features using pre-trained network models and fused hierarchical convolutional feature to predict target localization based on correlation filter. Qi et al. [8] proposes a multi-layer convolutional correlation filter tracking method (HDT), which employs multi-layer convolutional features for tracking in the framework of correlation filter tracking framework. Danelljan et al. [9] proposes continuous convolution tracking method (CCOT), which integrates convolutional feature, HOG and CN to train multiple filters for tracking with high tracking accuracy.

By means of multi-layer feature fusion and end-to-end network training, the visual tracking method improves the accuracy, robustness and speed. However, in the process of sample processing, the existing methods still have data imbalance issue. When suffering from a rotation, scale change and long-term tracking, the track will drift away which will affect the performance of visual tracking method. In this paper, we further come up with the visual tracking method from three aspects: multi-stage network feature fusion, spatial transformer network and proposal selection strategy. The main work is as follows: 1) we design the structure of cascaded region proposals networks and offer the training method and proposal selection method based on the network, so as to obtain high-quality samples; 2) we propose the feature extraction model based on spatial transformer network to improve the robustness of tracking method for spatial rotation and scale transformation; 3) we utilize the proposals selection and re-ranking strategy to remove the easy anchor through the method of center localization filter and scale change penalty, and effectively estimate the localization and scale of the tracked target. The comparison between our proposed method, RPN-based method [3] and the groundtruth is shown in Fig. 1.

Ground Truth ▬▬▬   RPN-based Method ▬▬▬   Cascaded RPN Method ▬▬▬

Fig. 1. Comparison between the ground truth, RPN-based method and our proposed method

2 Cascaded Region Proposals Networks

This section mainly introduces cascaded region proposals networks for visual tracking method, including the one-stage region proposals networks, the cascaded region proposals networks and the feature extraction model based on spatial transformer network. The main component and flow framework of visual tracking method based on cascaded region proposals networks is shown in Fig. 2.

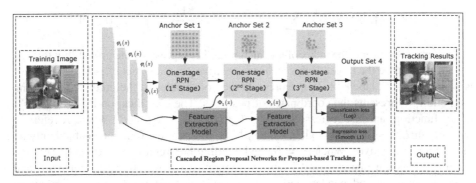

Fig. 2. Main component and framework flow of the proposes cascaded region proposal networks based visual tracker

2.1 One-Stage Region Proposals Networks

This section mainly introduces the one-stage region proposals networks [1], which consists of two independent branch including the classification branch and the bounding box regression branch aimed at the anchor which is shown in Fig. 3.

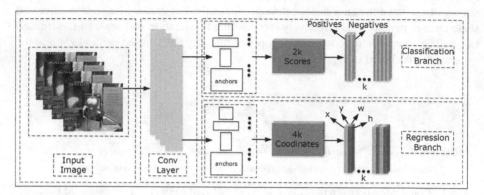

Fig. 3. Schematic diagram of the one-stage region proposal networks

In the training procedure of the one-stage region proposals networks, all anchors are assigned to a binary classification label (target/non-target). Positives consist of two categories: one is the anchor within the groundtruth bounding box; the other is the anchor whose Intersection-over-union (IoU) overlap with the groundtruth bounding box is larger than 0.7. The negatives means that the anchors whose overlap with the groundtruth bounding box is lower than the 0.3.

By minimizing the multi-task loss function, the classification score $\{p_i\}$ and regression coordinate $\{t_i\}$ of each anchor can be obtained, where the loss function is shown as follows,

$$L(\{p_i\}, \{t_i\}) = \frac{1}{N_{cls}} \sum_i L_{cls}(p_i, p_i^*) + \lambda \frac{1}{N_{reg}} \sum_i p_i^* L_{reg}(t_i, t_i^*) \qquad (1)$$

Where, i represents the index of the anchor, and p_i represents the probability that the anchor turns to be the target. If the anchor is positive, then its label p_i^* is 1, if the anchor is negative, its p_i^* labeled is 0. t_i represents the coordinates of the predicted bounding box, and t_i^* represents the coordinates of positives. The classification loss $L_{cls}(p_i, p_i^*)$ is log function, and the regression loss is $L_{reg}(t_i, t_i^*) = R(t_i - t_i^*)$ where R refers to the smooth-L_1 loss defined in [10], where $p_i^* L_{reg}$ refers to the function enabled only by the anchor of positives. When $p_i^* = 0$, the bounding box regression term is 0. Through training procedure, one-stage RPN network generates proposals for target detection, and these proposals are independent and diverse enough with priori information. The visual tracking task can be accomplished efficiently by proposals selection strategy.

2.2 Cascaded Region Proposals Networks

Most visual tracking methods based on one-stage region proposals networks are designed without considering the problem of data imbalance, the tracking results will drift when there is distracter similar to the target appearance in the tracking process. In addition, the one-stage RPN network only employs the semantic features in the process of training and testing which does not fully utilize the advantages of combining multi-layer features. In order to solve the problems, several one-stage region proposals networks $L(L \leq N)$ can be connected to form a multi-stage framework by feature extraction model. The implementation process is described as follows:

Assuming that, RPN_l represents the $l^{th} (1 < l \leq L)$ cascaded region proposals networks, its input layer is the feature extraction model (FEM) to extract feature of convolution layer Conv-l layer and high level Extraction Feature $\Phi_l(x)$ which is different from that extracted from a single convolution layer $\varphi_l(x)$. The feature representation $\Phi_l(x)$ of the input layer is shown in Eq. (2).

$$\Phi_l(x) = FEM\left(\Phi_{l-1}(x), \varphi_l(x)\right) \tag{2}$$

The feature extraction model $FEM(\cdot, \cdot)$ is described in detail in Sect. 2.3. For the one-stage region proposals networks RPN_l, satisfy $\Phi_1(x) = \varphi_1(x)$. Therefore, the classification score $\{p_i^l\}$ and coordinates regression $\{t_i^l\}$ of stage l are shown as follow,

$$\begin{aligned} \{p_i^l\} &= L_{cls}(\Phi_l(x)) \\ \{t_i^l\} &= L_{reg}(\Phi_l(x)) \end{aligned} \tag{3}$$

As for loss function, the classification loss $L_{cls}(\Phi_l(x))$ and the bounding box regression loss $L_{reg}(\Phi_l(x))$ are respectively the log loss and smooth L_1 loss.

Let A_l denotes the anchor set of stage l. With the classification score $\{p_i^l\}$, we can filter out anchors in A_l whose negative confidence score is greater than the threshold θ, and filter out the samples whose distance from the center of the target estimated localization is greater than the threshold η in the previous frame. The filtered samples form a new set A_{l+1} of anchors for further training. For RPN_l, A_1 of predefined. Besides, in order to provide a better initialization for regression of RPN_{l+1}, we refine the center locations and sizes of anchors in A_{l+1}, using the regression results $\{t_i^l\}$ in RPN_l, thus generate more accurate localization compared to a single step regression in one-stage network. The schematic diagram of Cascaded Region Proposal Networks (CRPN) structure is shown in Fig. 2, and RPN_l the loss function ℓ_{RPN_l} is shown as follows.

$$\ell_{RPN_l}\left(\{p_i^l\}, \{t_i^l\}\right) = \sum_i L_{cls}\left(p_i^l, p_i^{l*}\right) + \lambda \sum_i p_i^{l*} L_{loc}\left(t_i^l, t_i^{l*}\right) \tag{4}$$

Where i is the anchor index in A_l of stage l, λ a weight to balance losses, p_i^{l*} the label of anchor i, and t_i^{l*} the true distance between anchor i and groundtruth. $t_i^{l*} = \left(t_{i(x)}^{l*}, t_{i(y)}^{l*}, t_{i(w)}^{l*}, t_{i(h)}^{l*}\right)$ is a 4d vector, such that

$$\begin{aligned} t_{i(x)}^{l*} &= (x^* - x_a^l)/w_a^l & t_{i(y)}^{l*} &= (y^* - y_a^l)/h_a^l \\ t_{i(w)}^{l*} &= \log(w^*/w_a^l) & t_{i(h)}^{l*} &= \log(y^*/h_a^l) \end{aligned} \tag{5}$$

where x, y, w and h are center coordinates of a box and its width and height. Variables x^* and x_a^l are for groundtruth and anchor of stage l (likewise for y, w and h). It is worth noting that, different from using fixed anchors, the anchors in our proposed method are progressively adjusted by the regressor in the previous stage, and computed as,

$$x_a^l = x_a^l + w_a^{l-1} t_{i(x)}^{l-1} \quad y_a^l = y_a^l + h_a^{l-1} t_{i(y)}^{l-1}$$

$$w_a^l = w_a^{l-1} \exp\left(t_{i(w)}^{l-1}\right) \quad h_a^l = h_a^{l-1} \exp\left(t_{i(h)}^{l-1}\right) \tag{6}$$

For the anchor in the first stage, x_a^1, y_a^1, w_a^1 and h_a^1 are predefined.

By using the method of filtering the easy samples in the network training process, we keep the balance of the training samples in each stage region proposals networks. Therefore, the trained network can generate high quality proposals in the testing process which is convenient for the proposals selection in visual tracking. It also improves the classification ability of the network. In addition, multi-stage feature fusion method is used to improve the discrimination ability of visual tracking method in complex scenarios. In the testing experiment, three-stage region proposals networks are adopted. The detection response map and appearance representation capability of each stage are shown in Fig. 4. From left to right, they are the original image, one-stage, two-stage and three-stage, respectively.

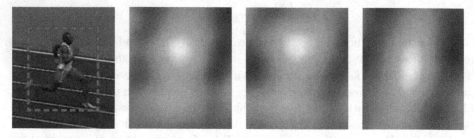

Fig. 4. Detection response map and their appearance representation capability of each stage

The loss function ℓ_{CRPN} of cascaded region proposals networks is composed of the loss function of each stage, the total loss is shown as follows,

$$\ell_{CRPN} = \sum_{l=1}^{L} \ell_{RPN_l} \tag{7}$$

2.3 Feature Extraction Model Based on Spatial Transformer Networks

The main component of feature extraction model is Spatial Transformer Networks (STN) [11]. Jaderberg et al. proposes spatial transformer network to solve the recognition problem by calculating the translation, rotation and scale of the target. In order to ensure that the extracted features of each stage can be fused with each other and applied to network training. The features of target also perform robustness of spatial transformation, the spatial transformer network is adopted to complete feature extraction.

Spatial transformer network consists of three essential components including localization network, grid generator and sampler. The localization network is used to estimate spatial transformer parameters (translation, rotation, and scale) based on feature maps. These parameters are transferred to the grid generator and sampler to generate the grid and spatial transformed feature map. The advantage of certain network is that it can be inserted into the existing network as an independent module in series and parallel.

In order to effectively extract the features from multi-stage networks, feature extraction model is adopted to combine high-level semantic features and low-level spatial features and spatial transformation features to ensure the accuracy and robustness. The schematic diagram of feature extraction model is shown in Fig. 5. The deconvolution layer is used to match the feature dimensions of different inputs. The features of different stages are fused by element-wise summation. The ReLU layer is added to prevent the disappearance of gradient and effectively prevent overfitting.

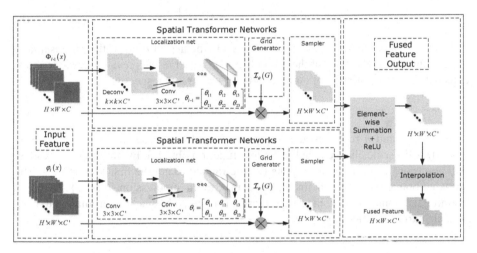

Fig. 5. Schematic diagram of the feature extraction model

The rotation parameters of spatial transformer network in the feature extraction model should be strictly limited through network training. Otherwise, too many easy samples will be generated due to the appearance change of samples, and the training process may barely converge which cannot meet the requirements of detection and recognition. Therefore, the rotation parameters of spatial transformation parameters are limited to 10° clockwise and anti-clockwise.

3 Tracking Strategy

3.1 Proposals Selection Strategy

The visual tracking estimates the localization of target based on the groundtruth in the previous frame. Therefore, after obtaining the proposals generated by the network, it is necessary to filter the proposals through prior information. Therefore, the visual tracking strategy employs the following two steps to filter out the proposals generated by the network to determine the localization of the tracking target.

In the first step, we propose to remove the anchor which is too far away from the center of target in the previous frame. Because the anchor obtained in the cascaded region proposals networks is gradually converged to the center. In most tracking sequences, the target will not be far away from the original localization, so the anchor with more than 7 pixels from the center of the visual tracking results in the previous frame can be effectively complete the proposals selection strategy.

In the second step, Cosine Window (CW) and Scale Change Penalty (SCP) are adopted to re-rank the proposals, and the proposals are sorted by the score. After removing the anchor that is too far away from the center, cosine window can be used to limit the large movement of the anchors, and the scale and aspect ratio variation of the anchor can be restricted by the scale change penalty which is shown as follows,

$$penalty = e^{k*\max\left(\frac{r}{r'},\frac{r'}{r}\right)*\max\left(\frac{s}{s'},\frac{s'}{s}\right)} \tag{8}$$

Where, k is the hyper-parameter, r represents the aspect ratio of the proposal, and r' represents the aspect ratio of the groundtruth proposal in the previous frame. s and s' represent the scale variation of current and previous frame respectively.

$$(w + p) \times (h + p) = s^2 \tag{9}$$

Where, w and h represent the width and height of the target, respectively. $p = (w + h)/2$. By scale change penalty, the loss function obtained by multiplying the classification score and scale change penalty is re-ranked to get the first K proposals. The estimated bounding box is obtained by non-maximum-suppression (NMS) [12]. When obtaining the bounding box, the scale of target is updated by linear interpolation to keep the scale variation smoothly.

3.2 Training Procedure

The training method of cascaded region proposals networks is to extract images by random interval sampling in the same image sequence. Each image generates up to 64 samples. The loss function of network training adopts the total loss of cascaded region proposals networks. In most cases, the localization and scale of the target between two adjacent frames will not change significantly. Therefore, the scale of the anchor [3] is selected as [0.33, 0.5, 1, 2, 3]. The filtering threshold of anchor θ and η are 0.9 and 10, respectively, where the overlap threshold of positives is set to be greater than θ_{pos}, and the overlap threshold of negatives is set to be less than θ_{neg}.

3.3 Tracking Procedure

The benchmarks of visual tracking include OTB2015 [13], VOT2016 [14] and UAV123 [15]. The above benchmarks can effectively evaluate the accuracy, robustness, running speed and tracking ability of complex scenarios of visual tracking method.

Method 1: Cascaded Region Proposal Networks for Proposal-based Tracking

Input: Image sequences $\{X_t\}_{t=1}^T$; GroundTruth b_1 of First frame X_1 ;Pre-trained networks

Output: Tracking Results $\{b_t\}_{t=2}^T$;

Initialized anchors A_1 ;

For $t = 2$ to T do

Feature extraction $\{\varphi_l(x)\}_{l=1}^L$ based on the input image x and pre-trained networks;

For $l = 1$ to L do

If l is equal to 1 **then**

$\quad \Phi(x) = \varphi_1(x)$;

Else

$\quad \Phi_l(x) = FEM(\varphi_{l-1}(x), \varphi_l(x))$;

End

Proposals calculation based on classification score and bounding box regression according to equation(3);

Coarse refining anchors i from proposals set A_l according to equation(6);

End

Proposals Selection Strategy to obtain the estimated target bounding box b_s ;

End

The visual tracking process is similar to multi-stage detection. Firstly, the pre-trained network is used to extract features from the first frame of the image. For each stage of the network, the feature extraction model is used to extract and transfer features, and to calculate the classification and bounding box regression scores. Then, coarse refining anchor is used at each stage. In the end, the coordinates of the highest score proposal are obtained by using the method of proposal selection strategy. The final tracking result is obtained by the method which is described in details in Sect. 3.1. The method flow is shown in method 1.

4 Experimental Results and Analysis

4.1 Implementation Details

In experiments, the backbone networks adopts the AlexNet [16] by reserving Conv layers to extract the features of images. The networks framework is introduced in details in Sect. 2.2. The networks we combined includes AlexNet, spatial transformer networks and region proposal networks. We implement the whole training and tracking process using MatConvNet [17] on single NVidia GTX1080Ti with 16 GB Memory. The pre-trained parameters are directly come from the existing model on ImageNet [18]. Our proposed method is end-to-end trained with stochastic gradient descent (SGD) by 40 epochs. We employ a warm-up learning rate of 0.001 for first 5 epochs to train the RPN braches. For the last 15 epochs, the whole network is end-to-end trained with learning rate exponentially decayed from 0.001 to 0.00001. We set the stage number L to 3. We also assign the IOU of the positives and negatives to 0.7 and 0.3 respectively. The training loss is illustrated in Eq. (7).

4.2 Reliability Ablation Study

In this paper, our proposed method improves the accuracy and robustness mainly based on three key components including multi-stage, feature extraction model and proposal selection strategy. Therefore, we need to do the reliability ablation study to test the influence of each component to our proposed method. We perform the experiment in VOT2016 benchmark mainly on four measurement metrics including tracking accuracy A_{av}, robustness R_{av}, expected average overlap EAO and frames per second FPS_{av}. These metrics help to evaluate the method on accuracy of estimated bounding box, long-term tracking, tracking ability in complex scenarios and tracking speed [14].

Number of Stage? We propose to test the number of stage evolving to the networks in the VOT2016 benchmark. The comparison results are shown in Table 1. Among them, three-stage networks get better results than one-stage and two-stage networks in terms of A_{av}, R_{av} and EAO with the FPS_{av} 17 fps. However, it can be concluded that the gain from two-stage network to three-stage network is not as high as the gain from the one-stage to two-stage. Therefore, when considering of the higher real-time requirements, three-stage network can be replaced by the two-stage network.

Table 1. The effect on the number of the stages of cascaded region proposal network

Stage	One-stage	Two-stage	Three-stage
A_{av}	0.523	0.565	0.577
R_{av}	1.23	1.02	0.97
EAO	0.321	0.356	0.361
FPS_{av}	39	30	17

Feature Extraction Model. We mainly test the spatial transformer networks in the feature extraction model in three-stage cascaded region proposal network. The comparison results are shown in Table 2. Compared with the results without spatial transformer network, the tracking accuracy A_{av} gains are not that obvious. However, as for R_{av} and EAO, the FEM with STN performs better than that without STN. Because of STN, the extracted feature from FEM is more robust to spatial transformation and scale variation. The robustness of overall tracking method is improved by FEM.

Scale Change Penalty. We propose to test the influence of SCP in proposal selection strategy. The comparison results are shown in Table 3. The scale change penalty has a great influence to proposal selection strategy. The measurement metrics decrease significantly without scale changes penalty which is shown as follows.

Table 2. The effect on the feature extraction model (FEM)

FEM	STN	Non-STN
A_{av}	0.577	0.563
R_{av}	0.97	1.19
EAO	0.361	0.355
FPS_{av}	17	24

Table 3. The effect on the scale change penalty (SCP)

SCP	Scale penalty	Non-scale penalty
A_{av}	0.577	0.517
R_{av}	0.97	1.29
EAO	0.361	0.323

4.3   Comparison with State-of-the-Art Methods

In order to further verify the overall performance of our proposed method, we employ 9 state-of-the-art methods including SiamFC [2], SiamRPN [3], EBT [6], HCFT [7], DeepSRDCF [17], Staple [19], ECO [20], CFNet [21] and MDNet [22]. Among them, HCFT, ECO, CFNet and MDNet are methods based on deep convolutional network. Staple is an online update method using correlation filter; SiamFC and SiamRPN are RPN-based network methods. EBT and SiamRPN are methods using proposals. ECO and DeepSRDCF are methods based on the combination of deep feature and correlation filter. The state-of-the-art methods contain almost all advanced tracking frameworks.

OTB2015. The main metrics to evaluate methods in OTB2015 benchmark contains precision and success rate. We performs our proposed method with 9 state-of-the-art methods using OPE in Fig. 6. Overall, the proposed method ranks the third in accuracy and success rate. The method which combines deep convolutional network and correlation filter ranks the top. The method which employs the pre-trained model training by object tracking dataset. Compared with the Siamese region proposals networks, the proposed method improves the accuracy and robustness by 3.7% and 4.2% respectively, and greatly improves the visual tracking method based on the deep network.

VOT2016. The experimental evaluation results of the compared method in VOT2016 benchmark are shown in Table 4. The number ranked first is highlighted in red and the number ranked second is highlighted in blue. Our proposed method ranks first in EAO and accuracy, and second in robustness. It can be concluded that the method of extracting deep and shallow features by cascaded region proposal networks improves the accuracy and expected overlap of visual tracking results. The methods based on deep feature extraction such as SiamRPN, DeepSRDCF and HCFT have better overall performance than that based on original feature such as EBT and Staple. The performance

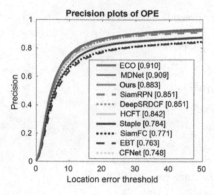 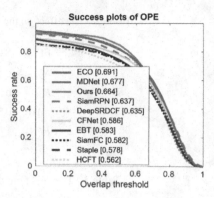

Fig. 6. Distance precision & overlap success plots using OPE on OTB2015 by compared method

of DeepSRDCF shows the effectiveness of background suppression method in solving the problem of data imbalance. Our proposed method still has room for improvement.

Table 4. The performance evaluation on the VOT2016 benchmark by compared methods

Tracker	Ours	HCFT	EBT	Staple	SiamRPN	DeepSRDCF
A_{av}	**0.57**	0.50	0.45	0.54	**0.56**	**0.56**
R_{av}	**1.03**	1.17	1.02	1.2	1.12	1.0
EAO	0.363	0.293	0.313	0.295	**0.344**	0.318

UAV123. UAV123 benchmark contains 123 video sequences, many of them are suffering fast motion, camera movement, similar distractors, scale variation and full occlusion which provide great challenge to visual tracking method. The overall precision and success rate of compared methods in UAV123 benchmark are shown in Fig. 7. Our proposed method ranks first in precision and robustness compared with other methods. The method based on region proposals networks is more suitable for long-term tracking task. When the target is suffering partial occlusion or even full occlusion in the image sequence, the proposals generated by region proposal networks can also be used to re-locate the estimated target. The feature extraction model of our method aims at the feature extracting of spatial rotation and scale variation which improves the robustness of the tracking method and makes the method perform well in complex scenarios. The average running speed of our proposed method in UAV123 benchmark is 13 fps which meets the requirements of real-time processing.

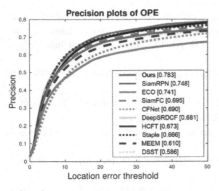
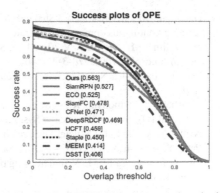

Fig. 7. Distance precision & overlap success plots using OPE on UAV123 by compared method

5 Conclusion

In this paper, we propose to cascaded region proposal networks which combines multi-stage region proposal network based on one-stage RPN and spatial transformer network. The cascaded region proposal network make full use of the semantic and spatial features, the STN-based feature extraction model improves the robustness of spatial rotation and scale variation simultaneously. The proposal selection strategy guarantee to provide the high-quality anchors for tracking procedure based on scale change penalty which improves the tracking accuracy and speed. The compared experiments in the benchmark of OTB2015, VOT2016 and UAV123 proves the effectiveness of our proposed method.

References

1. Ren, S., He, K., Ross, G., et al.: Faster R-CNN: towards real-time object detection with region proposal networks. In: NIPS (2015)
2. Bertinetto, L., Valmadre, J., Henriques, J., et al.: Fully convolutional Siamese networks for visual tracking. In: Proceedings of the European Conference on Computer Vision, pp. 3376–3383 (2016)
3. Li, B., Yan, J., Wu, W., et al.: High performance visual tracking with Siamese region proposal network. In: CVPR (2018)
4. Zhu, Z., Wang, Q., Li, B., et al.: Distractor-aware Siamese networks for visual tracking. In: ECCV (2018)
5. Guo, G., Wang, H., Yan, Y., et al.: A new target-specific object proposal generation method for visual tracking (2018)
6. Zhu, G., Porikli, F., Li, H.: Beyond local search: tracking objects everywhere with proposal-specific proposals. In: Proceedings of the IEEE Conference on Computer Vision and Pattern Recognition (CVPR), Las Vegas, USA, 26–31 June 2016, pp. 943–951 (2016)
7. Ma, C., Huang, J., Yang, X., et al.: Hierarchical convolutional features for visual tracking. In: IEEE International Conference on Computer Vision (ICCV), Los Alamitos, Washington, DC, pp. 3074–3082. IEEE Computer Society Press (2015)
8. Qi, Y., Zhang, S., Qin, L., et al.: Hedged deep tracking. In: IEEE Conference on Computer Vision and Pattern Recognition, Los Alamitos, Washington, DC, pp. 4303–4311. IEEE Computer Society Press (2016)

9. Danelljan, M., Robinson, A., Shahbaz Khan, F., Felsberg, M.: Beyond correlation filters: learning continuous convolution operators for visual tracking. In: Leibe, B., Matas, J., Sebe, N., Welling, M. (eds.) ECCV 2016. LNCS, vol. 9909, pp. 472–488. Springer, Cham (2016). https://doi.org/10.1007/978-3-319-46454-1_29

10. Ross, G.: Fast R-CNN. In: IEEE International Conference on Computer Vision, pp. 3293–3302 (2015)

11. Jaderberg, M., Simonyan, K., Zisserman, A., et al.: Spatial transformer networks. In: Advances in Neural Information Processing Systems, pp. 2017–2025 (2015)

12. Neubeck, A., Gool, L.: Efficient non-maximum suppression. In: International Conference on Pattern Recognition, pp. 1453–1467 (2006)

13. Wu, Y., Lim, J., Yang, M.: Visual tracking benchmark. IEEE Trans. Pattern Anal. Mach. Intell. **37**(9), 1834–1848 (2015)

14. Matej, K., Ales, L., Jiri, M., et al.: The sixth visual visual tracking VOT2016 challenge results. In: ECCV Workshops (2018)

15. Mueller, M., Smith, N., Ghanem, B.: A benchmark and simulator for UAV tracking. In: Leibe, B., Matas, J., Sebe, N., Welling, M. (eds.) ECCV 2016. LNCS, vol. 9905, pp. 445–461. Springer, Cham (2016). https://doi.org/10.1007/978-3-319-46448-0_27

16. Krizhevsky, A., Sutskeverl, I., Hinton, G.: ImageNet classification with deep convolutional neural networks. In: NIPS (2012)

17. Vedaldi, A., Lenc, K.: MatConvNet: convolutional neural networks for MATLAB. In: Proceedings of the ACM International Conference on Multimedia, Brisbane, Australia, 26–30 June 2015, pp. 689–692 (2015)

18. Deng, J., Dong, W., Socher, R., et al.: ImageNet: a large-scale hierarchical image benchmark. In: CVPR (2009)

19. Bertinetto, L., Valmadre, J., et al.: Staple: complementary learners for real-time tracking. In: Proceedings of the Conference on Computer Vision and Pattern Recognition, pp. 1354–1378 (2016)

20. Danelljan, M., Khan, S., et al.: ECO: efficient convolution operators for tracking. In: Proceedings of the IEEE Conference on Computer Vision and Pattern Recognition, pp. 6931–6939 (2017)

21. Valmadre, J., Bertinetto, L., Henriques, J., et al.: End-to-end representation learning for correlation filter based tracking. In: Proceedings of the IEEE Conference on Computer Vision and Pattern Recognition, pp. 5000–5008 (2017)

22. Nam, H., Han, B.: Learning multi-domain convolutional neural networks for visual tracking. In: Proceedings of the IEEE Conference on Computer Vision and Pattern Recognition, pp. 4293–4302 (2016)

Low-Rank & Sparse Matrix Decomposition and Support Vector Machine for Hyperspectral Anomaly Detection

Shangzhen Song, Huixin Zhou, Zhe Zhang, Yixin Yang, Pei Xiang, Juan Du, and Jiajia Zhang[✉]

School of Physics and Optoelectronic Engineering, Xidian University, Xi'an, China
1131303762@qq.com

Abstract. Due to the limited resolution of hyperspectral sensors, anomalous targets expressed with subpixels are often mixed with nonhomogeneous backgrounds. This fact makes anomalies difficult to be distinguished from the surrounding background. From this perspective, we propose a novel hyperspectral anomaly detection (AD) algorithm based on low-rank & sparse matrix decomposition (LRaSMD) and support vector machine (SVM). First, based on the LRaSMD technique, the Go decomposition (GoDec) model is utilized to decompose the original image into three components: background, anomalies and noise. In this way, the robust background can be obtained. Subsequently, a clustering algorithm is employed to pick some obvious anomalies. Accordingly, we use both samples of background and anomaly to train an SVM model. The original dataset is sent into the SVM model and both anomalous components and background components can be classified. Experiments on a synthetic hyperspectral image validate the performance of the proposed method.

Keywords: Hyperspectral imagery (HSI) · Support vector machine (SVM) · Low rank and sparse matrix decomposition · Anomaly detection (AD)

1 Introduction

In recent years, with the rapid development of remote sensing technology, target detection has aroused extensive attention because more feature information is hidden in the multiple spectral bands of hyperspectral images (HSI) compared with traditional images and this feature information can be used to detect the targets [1]. In real situations, it is difficult to obtain the prior knowledge of objects, hence it is not simple to detect targets by the only known radiation information of objects in an HSI. Therefore, anomaly detection (AD), which does not require the prior knowledge of objects, has become much more popular. AD does not need to know the spectral samples of any object in advance, and it can effectively separate all pixels of an image into two categories, of which a small number of high-intensity pixels are considered as anomalies. Because anomaly detection assumes that the spectral feature information of the interested targets is less than that of the background, we can distinguish the background and anomaly pixels by

© Springer Nature Switzerland AG 2020
T. McDaniel et al. (Eds.): ICSM 2019, LNCS 12015, pp. 315–321, 2020.
https://doi.org/10.1007/978-3-030-54407-2_26

solving the statistical characteristics of the background on the HSIs. Anomaly detection has been applied in many fields, such as battlefield investigation, pollution monitoring, mineral exploration, food detection, etc.

Over the past twenty years, plenty of popular hyperspectral AD algorithms have been proposed. For instance, the GRX detector [2] is one of the most popular statistical approaches. It considers that the background obeys a multivariate normal distribution. Under this assumption, the generalized likelihood ratio test (GLRT) formula is derived, and the RX operator with a constant false alarm rate (CFAR) property is obtained. The false alarm rate of the RX algorithm obeys a fixed probability distribution. As long as the decision threshold does not change, the false alarm rate will not change. However, in practice, the noise and background components in a real HSI are usually nonuniform. They cannot be simply modeled by a Gaussian distribution. Therefore, to overcome these drawbacks, researchers have proposed several improved algorithms based on GRX, including the subspace RX (SSRX) [3] and the local RX (LRX) [4]. Local approaches are able to improve the detection rate, but the isolated noise pixels are still retained in the results, which will increase the false alarm rate dramatically. Therefore, RX-based methods are insufficient to meet the requirements of detection performance. Other algorithms have also made rapid progress. Recently, some low-rank-based AD algorithms have also been the focus of researchers. Among them, the most representative one called the low rank and sparse matrix decomposition (LRaSMD)-based anomaly detection method [5, 6] became popular. The Euclidean distance between pixels is first calculated and the mean vector also needs to be solved from the sparse part. Compared with other traditional detectors, the LRaSMD-based methods can generate superior detection performance.

Generally, there are three common models for LRaSMD-based methods: Robust PCA (RPCA) [7], low rank representation (LRR) [8] and GoDec [9]. In the GoDec model, the original image can be decomposed into three components: background, anomalies and noise. After decomposition, many anomalous components are still hidden in the background, meanwhile some background pixels are also mixed in the anomalies. In the subsequent procedures, it is necessary to eliminate redundant background and retain as many anomalous components as possible. From this perspective, machine learning is one of the best technologies because it can obtain the characteristics of all pixels by constructing a model and learning from known samples. As one of the most popular statistical learning algorithms, SVM has become an attractive and popular tool in pattern recognition and machine learning. In this paper, we propose a novel hyperspectral AD algorithm based on LRaSMD and SVM. First, the original dataset is decomposed by the GoDec model. Principle component analysis (PCA) is then performed to obtain the principle components (PCs). The first few PCs are picked as the background samples. Secondly, the k-means clustering algorithm is utilized to separate the anomaly matrix into several categories. We choose the category with the largest number of elements as anomaly samples. Both kinds of samples are utilized to construct the SVM model. After the model is accomplished, the original dataset is sent into the SVM procedure to train and obtain the classification result. The final detection result can be obtained as well.

The rest of this paper is organized as follows. Section 2 describes the proposed algorithm in detail. Section 3 evaluates the algorithm using a synthetic dataset. Conclusion is drawn in Sect. 4.

2 Proposed Algorithms

2.1 GoDec Model for HSI Dataset

We assume that the matrix $\mathbf{D} \in \mathbf{R}^{P \times B}$ is used to represent an HSI dataset, where P denotes the number of image pixels in one band and B denotes the number of spectral bands. In practice, the original data obtained by a sensor is always contaminated by the independent and identically distributed Gaussian noise. Therefore, the dataset can be decomposed into three components, which are defined as:

$$\mathbf{D} = \mathbf{B} + \mathbf{A} + \mathbf{N} \tag{1}$$

where $\mathbf{B}$ is the background matrix, $\mathbf{A}$ is the anomaly matrix and $\mathbf{N}$ is the noise matrix. The background matrix can be expressed as a linear combination of some independent background endmembers. Hence, we can consider that $\mathbf{B}$ lies in a low-dimension subspace. In addition, for the anomalies of an image, the separated anomaly matrix $\mathbf{A}$ can be considered as sparse since the number of anomalies is very small. By using LRaSMD, the HSI dataset $\mathbf{D}$ can be decomposed as Eq. (1). So far, many effective methods have been proposed to solve the problem of LRaSMD. In this paper, we utilize the Go Decomposition (GoDec) algorithm. In the GoDec algorithm, the bilateral random projection (BRP) is applied to replace the singular-value decomposition (SVD) in the traditional model. Therefore, it provides a fast and effective way to solve the problem of LRaSMD.

The main object of the GoDec algorithm is to minimize the decomposition error in Eq. (1):

$$\min_{\mathbf{B},\mathbf{A}} \|\mathbf{D} - \mathbf{B} - \mathbf{A}\|_F^2 \ \ s.t. \ rank(\mathbf{B}) \leq r, \ card(\mathbf{A}) \leq kN \tag{2}$$

where $\|\cdot\|_F^2$ is the Frobenius norm, which means that the square sum of the absolute values of all elements in the matrix is first solved, and then the square root of the sum is taken. r is the upper bound of the rank of $\mathbf{B}$ and k represents the sparsity level of $\mathbf{A}$. To solve Eq. (2), we take it apart and solve the optimization problems of $\mathbf{B}$ and $\mathbf{A}$ respectively. The equation is written as follows:

$$\begin{cases} \mathbf{B}_t = \arg \min_{rank(\mathbf{B}) \leq r} \|\mathbf{D} - \mathbf{B} - \mathbf{A}_{t-1}\|_F^2 \\ \mathbf{A}_t = \arg \min_{card(\mathbf{A}) \leq kN} \|\mathbf{D} - \mathbf{B}_{t-1} - \mathbf{A}\|_F^2 \end{cases} \tag{3}$$

where t is the iteration time. Compared with the SVD in traditional model, Eq. (3) can be solved by the BRP-based low-rank approximation to improve the efficiency. Then $\mathbf{B}_t$ is updated as:

$$\mathbf{B}_t = \mathbf{X}_1 (\mathbf{M}_2^T \mathbf{X}_1)^{-1} \mathbf{X}_2^T \tag{4}$$

where $\mathbf{X}_1 = \mathbf{H}\mathbf{M}_1$ and $\mathbf{X}_2 = \mathbf{H}^T\mathbf{M}_2$, wherein $\mathbf{M}_1 \in \mathbf{R}^{B \times r}$ and $\mathbf{M}_2 \in \mathbf{R}^{N \times r}$ are random matrices.

During the process of iteration, $\mathbf{A}_t$ is updated as follows:

$$\mathbf{A}_t = P_\Omega(\mathbf{D} - \mathbf{B}_{t-1}), \quad \Omega : \left|(\mathbf{D} - \mathbf{B}_{t-1})_{i,j \in \Omega}\right| \neq 0$$

$$and \geq \left|(\mathbf{D} - \mathbf{B}_{t-1})_{i,j \in \Omega}\right|, \quad |\Omega| \leq kN \tag{5}$$

where Ω is the nonzero subset, and $P_\Omega\left(\cdot\right)$ refers to the projection of a matrix to an entry set Ω. Finally, the three component matrices can be solved.

2.2 Hyperspectral Anomaly Detection Based on LRaSMD and SVM

For the tested HSI dataset $\mathbf{D} \in \mathbf{R}^{N \times B}$, the GoDec algorithm is executed and the three decomposed components in Eq. (1) are obtained. However, for $\mathbf{B}$ and $\mathbf{A}$, the background and anomaly components cannot be completely separated. Similar to the background pixels in $\mathbf{A}$, there are quite a few anomalous elements hidden in $\mathbf{B}$. Accordingly, a subsequent procedure is necessary to eliminate redundant background and retain as many anomalous components as possible. For the background matrix $\mathbf{B}$, the PCA method is employed to obtain the PCs according to the eigenvalues and eigenvectors by singular value decomposition (SVD) of the covariance matrix. We select the PCs corresponding to the first few largest eigenvalues as the robust background. For the anomaly matrix $\mathbf{A}$, it is sparse in space, which means that most of the elements in $\mathbf{A}$ are zero. The non-zero elements in $\mathbf{A}$ are mainly anomalies, although a small number of background pixels are also contained. To make a further separation, the clustering algorithm is an effective approach that can separate the matrix into different categories. Here we use the k-means clustering algorithm. After clustering, the obvious anomalies are clustered. The SVM model is then constructed to train the original dataset.

To make the SVM binary classification more accurate, reasonable selection of training samples is a key issue. In this paper, we randomly select two thirds of the obvious anomaly pixels from $\mathbf{A}$ as the training samples T_a of the anomaly targets and select one-half of the robust background pixels from $\mathbf{B}$ as the training samples T_b of the background.

Through the aforementioned training samples T_a and T_b, the SVM model can be trained and the original HSI can be classified. The radial basis function (RBF) is selected as the kernel function of the model. Accordingly, there are two important parameters C and δ in the SVM model, where C is the penalty coefficient and δ is a parameter of RBF. The optimal parameters C and δ are determined by the five-fold cross validation [10] with known training samples T_a and T_b. In this case, the anomaly probability results $R_{SVM} \in R_{m \times n}$ can be obtained by the SVM classification.

Finally, the anomaly detection results $R_{final} \in R_{m \times n}$ are obtained by fusing the anomaly detection results R_{Go} from GoDec and R_{SVM}.

$$R_{final} = R_{Go} + R_{SVM} \tag{6}$$

The design flowchart is shown in Fig. 1.

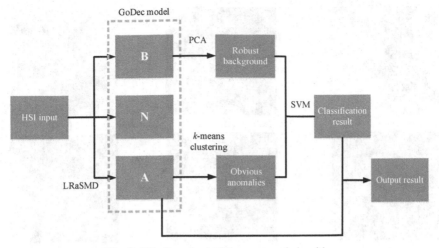

Fig. 1. The flowchart of the proposed algorithm

3 Experimental Results and Analysis

In this section, our proposed algorithm is evaluated with a synthetic hyperspectral image dataset. The dataset was generated based on the Jasper Ridge hyperspectral imagery, covering a riverbank area with a size of 100×100 pixels. The original imagery consists of 224 spectral channels spanning the wavelength range of 380 to 2500 nm. After removing the channels affected by water vapor and atmosphere, 198 channels were retained in our experiment, as shown in Fig. 2. Sixteen anomalous targets (four rows and four columns) are embedded into some certain pixels through the target implantation method [11].

$$\mathbf{z} = f \cdot \mathbf{t} + (1 - f) \cdot \mathbf{b} \tag{7}$$

where $\mathbf{t}$ is a desired target spectrum from another region of the image. $\mathbf{b}$ is a given pixel of the background spectrum in this image. Thus, a synthetic anomaly target pixel with spectrum $\mathbf{z}$ can be generated by implanting $\mathbf{t}$ into $\mathbf{b}$. The abundance fractions f are 0.05, 0.1, 0.2, and 0.4 for different columns respectively.

In the experiment, we compare the proposed approach with three representative approaches, including Global RX (GRX), Local RX (LRX) and SSRX. Color detection maps of all methods for the dataset are provided in Fig. 2. Intuitively, it is obvious that the proposed algorithm shows a better detection performance than other algorithms.

For quantitative comparison, the receiver operating characteristic (ROC) curve is used as one of the most popular tools in signal processing and target detection. Here the measuring results of ROC curves are shown in Fig. 3. The proposed method has a higher probability of detection (PD) than other methods under the same false alarm rate (FAR).

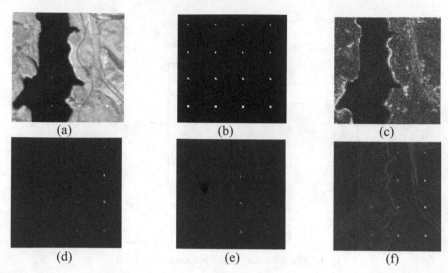

Fig. 2. Color detection maps for the Jasper Ridge dataset (synthetic images). (a) Image scene. (b) Reference. (c) GRX. (d) LRX. (e) SSRX. (f) Proposed method.

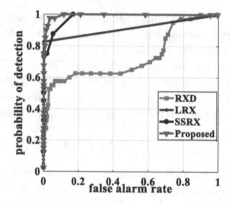

Fig. 3. ROC curves of the compared algorithms for synthetic images.

4   Conclusion

In this paper, we first discuss the advantages and drawbacks of existing anomaly detection algorithms. Then we find that in most current AD approaches, the noise cannot be eliminated clearly and is usually confused with anomalies. From this perspective, a novel method based on LRaSMD and SVM is proposed. Experimental results show that our proposed algorithm can successfully detect the anomalous targets and remove the noise from the data at the same time. In the future, our work is mainly to add more experiments and improve the computational efficiency of our proposed algorithm.

References

1. Landgrebe, D.: Hyperspectral image data analysis. IEEE Sig. Process. Mag. **19**, 17–28 (2002)
2. Reed, I.S., Yu, X.: Adaptive multiple-band CFAR detection of an optical pattern with unknown spectral distribution. IEEE Trans. Acoust. Speech Sig. Process. **38**, 1760–1770 (1990)
3. Schaum, A.: Joint subspace detection of hyperspectral targets. In: Proceedings of the IEEE Aerospace Conference, vol. 3, pp. 1824 (2004)
4. Molero, J.M., Garzón, E.M., García, I., Plaza, A.: Analysis and optimizations of global and local versions of the RX algorithm for anomaly detection in hyperspectral data. IEEE J. Sel. Top. Appl. Earth Observ. Remote Sens. **6**(2), 801–814 (2013)
5. Sun, W., Liu, C., Li, J., Lai, Y.M., Li, W.: Low-rank and sparse matrix decomposition-based anomaly detection for hyperspectral imagery. J. Appl. Remote Sens. **8**, 083641 (2014)
6. Zhang, Y., Du, B., Zhang, L., Wang, S.: A low-rank and sparse matrix decomposition-based mahalanobis distance method for hyperspectral anomaly detection. IEEE Trans. Geosci. Remote Sens. **54**, 1376–1389 (2016)
7. Candès, E.J., Li, X., Ma, Y., Wright, J.: Robust principal component analysis? ACM **3**, 11 (2011)
8. Liu, G., Lin, Z., Yu, Y.: Robust subspace segmentation by low-rank representation. In: Proceedings of the 27th International Conference on Machine Learning (ICML), pp. 663–670 (2010)
9. Zhou, T.; Tao, D.: GoDec: Randomized low-rank & sparse matrix decomposition in noisy case. In: Proceedings of the International Conference Machine Learning, pp. 33–40 (2011)
10. Melgani, F., Bruzzone, L.: Classification of hyperspectral remote sensing images with support vector machines. IEEE Trans. Geosci. Remote Sens. **42**(8), 1778–1790 (2004)
11. Stefanou, M.S., Kerekes, J.P.: A method for assessing spectral image utility. IEEE Trans. Geosci. Remote Sens. **47**(6), 1698–1706 (2009)

Infrared and Visual Image Fusion via Multi-modal Decomposition and PCNN in Gradient Domain Fusion Measure

Wei Tan[1,2]([✉]), Jiajia Zhang[1], Kun Qian[3,4], Juan Du[1], Pei Xiang[1], and Huixin Zhou[1]

[1] School of Physics and Optoelectronic Engineering, Xidian University, Xi'an 710071, China
twtanwei1992@163.com
[2] Department of Computer Science, University of Copenhagen, Copenhagen 2100, Denmark
[3] Shanghai Institute of Spaceflight Control Technology, Shanghai 201109, China
[4] Infrared Detection Technology Research and Development Center of CASC, Shanghai 201109, China

Abstract. Infrared and visual image fusion aims to obtain a complex image which contains more recognizable information. To obtain the complex image, a fusion algorithm via multi-modal decomposition and pulse-coupled neural network (PCNN) in gradient domain fusion measure is proposed. Firstly, the source images are decomposed into three layers through the decomposition model. Then, a gradient domain PCNN fusion measure is employed in the three layers. Finally, the fused image is reconstructed through the three fused layers. Experimental results demonstrate that the proposed algorithm performs effectively in both qualitative and quantitative measures.

Keywords: Infrared and visual image fusion · Pulse-coupled neural network · Multi-level Gaussian curvature filtering · Multi-scale morphological gradient

1 Introduction

The infrared (IR) and visual (VIS) images of the same scene could contain more information. But more redundant information might be created. Moreover, the IR sensor acquires the thermal information, while the VIS sensor is focused on obtaining clear texture and high spatial information [1]. Therefore, the scene can be described completely through combining the IR and VIS information into one complex image. Furthermore, due to its superior integration capability, image fusion technology is also widely employed in object surveillance [2, 3], remote sensing detection [4–7], and medical diagnosis [8].

Generally, IR and VIS image fusion methods are mainly divided into two categories: transform domain method and spatial domain method [9]. The transform domain method is a type of technique which process the image in the transform domain. The most widely applied method is the multi-scale transform (MST) method. In this method, source images are decomposed into high-frequency and low-frequency sub-images. Then, the

© Springer Nature Switzerland AG 2020
T. McDaniel et al. (Eds.): ICSM 2019, LNCS 12015, pp. 322–329, 2020.
https://doi.org/10.1007/978-3-030-54407-2_27

sub-images are fused according to some fusion rules in different sub-band frequencies. Finally, the fused image is reconstructed through the corresponding inverse transform. Traditional MST methods include discrete wavelet transform (DWT) [10], non-subsampled contourlet transform (NSCT) [11], and non-subsampled shearlet transform (NSST) [12]. However, once the source images are misregistered, the fusion images may lose useful information in local blocks. In addition, these MST methods may consume a lot of time when executing the program.

The spatial domain method is another widely used method. It contains two main categories: pixel-based method and region-based method [13]. In the pixel-based method, once the source images are misregistered, it may cause undesirable artefacts in the fused image. In the region method, the fusion executes in the light of some fusion measure, such as spatial frequency (SF), local variance (LV), and energy of image gradient (EOG). However, although these measures have good performance, the fused image may still suffer from blocking artefacts. This is caused by information asymmetry in the source images.

Recently, pulse-coupled neural network (PCNN), a simplified model capable of realizing synchronous pulse excitation behavior, has been widely applied in image fusion [14, 15]. The parameters of PCNN are modulated by the SF measure, which provides a good solution for the precise performing.

In this paper, a method combining transform domain and spatial domain is proposed. In this method, a multi-level Gaussian curvature filtering (MLGCF) method is presented. This MLGCF framework is similar to the MST, but it performs better than MST. The source images are first decomposed into three layers via the MLGCF decomposition model. Then, a PCNN whose parameters are modulated by the multi-scale morphological gradient (MSMG) fusion measure is used to merge different layers. Finally, the fused image is reconstructed by summing the three fused layers.

The rest of the paper is organized as follows. The theory of the proposed method is introduced in Sect. 2. The experiments and results are shown in Sect. 3. Finally, the conclusion is given in Sect. 4.

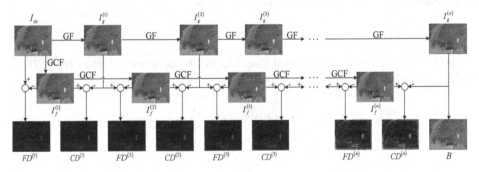

Fig. 1. Structure diagram of MLGCF.

2 Proposed Algorithm

2.1 MLGCF-Based Image Decomposition

The Gaussian curvature filtering (GCF) is an effective edge-preserving filtering (EPF). It has the advantage of retaining the fine-scale structure. The concrete theory of GCF can be found in [16]. This article focuses on the multi-level GCF (MLGCF). It has been proposed in our previous result [1]. This paper is further research.

For convenience, we define $GF(\bullet)$ and $GCF(\bullet)$ as Gaussian filtering operation and Gaussian curvature filtering operation, respectively. The structure of MLGCF is shown in Fig. 1. In Fig. 1, I_{in} is the input image, $I_g^{(i)}(i = 1, 2, \ldots, n)$ is the filtered result of the i-th GF, B is base layer, $FD^{(i)}$ and $CD^{(i)}(i = 1, 2, \ldots, n)$ represent i-th fine-detail and coarse-detail layers, respectively. Constant n indicates the number of decomposition layers. The three types of layers $FD^{(i)}$, $CD^{(i)}$ and B are computed as

$$FD^{(i)} = \begin{cases} I_{in} - I_f^{(1)}, \ i = 1 \\ I_g^{(i-1)} - I_f^{(i)}, \ i = 2, 3, \ldots, n \end{cases}, \tag{1}$$

$$CD^{(i)} = I_f^{(i)} - I_g^{(i)}, \ (i = 1, 2, \ldots, n), \tag{2}$$

where $I_g^{(i)}$ and $I_f^{(i)}$ are formulated as

$$I_g^{(i)} = \begin{cases} GF(I_{in}, \mu_g, \sigma_g), \ i = 1 \\ GF(I_g^{(i-1)}, \mu_g, \sigma_g), i = 2, 3, \ldots, n \end{cases}, \tag{3}$$

$$I_f^{(i)} = \begin{cases} GCF(I_{in}, m), \ i = 1 \\ GCF(I_f^{(i-1)}, m), i = 2, 3, \ldots, n \end{cases}, \tag{4}$$

where μ_g and σ_g denote the mean and variance of GF operation; and m is the number of GCF iterations. The base layer B is represented as

$$B = I_g^{(n)}, \tag{5}$$

After the decomposition, the input image I_{in} will be decomposed into $FD^{(i)}$, $CD^{(i)}$, and B. I_{in} can be reconstructed as

$$I_{in} = \sum_{i=1}^{n} \left(FD^{(i)} + CD^{(i)}\right) + B. \tag{6}$$

2.2 MSMG-PCNN Fusion Strategy

Multi-Scale Morphological Gradient (MSMG). MSMG is an operator which can easily and well extract gradient information from an image. It is operated as follow:

First, a multi-scale structure element is defined as

$$SE_j = \underbrace{SE_1 \oplus SE_1 \oplus \cdots \oplus SE_1}_{j}, j \in \{1, 2, \ldots, N\}, \tag{7}$$

where SE_1 denotes a basic structuring element, and N represents the number of scales.

Then, the gradient feature G_j are extracted from the image f through the morphological gradient operator.

$$G_j(x, y) = f(x, y) \oplus SE_j - f(x, y) \ominus SE_j, j \in \{1, 2, \ldots, N\}, \tag{8}$$

where $\oplus$ and $\ominus$ denote the morphological dilation and erosion operators, respectively.

Finally, MSMG can be obtained by weighted sum

$$MSMG(x, y) = \sum_{j=1}^{N} w_j \cdot G_j(x, y), \tag{9}$$

where w_j represents the weight of gradients in j-th scale, and it can be computed as

$$w_j = \frac{1}{2j + 1}. \tag{10}$$

Pulse-Coupled Neural Network (PCNN). PCNN has been widely used in image fusion. The theory of PCNN can be found in [14]. In this paper, we focus on the fusion measure combined by MSMG and PCNN.

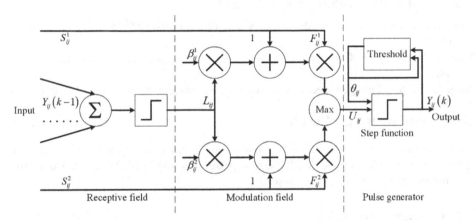

Fig. 2. Diagram of PCNN.

The diagram of PCNN is shown in Fig. 2, where S_{ij}^1 and S_{ij}^2 denote the pixel value of two source images; L_{ij} represents the linking parameter; β_{ij}^1 and β_{ij}^2 denote the linking strength; F_{ij}^1 and F_{ij}^2 represent the feedback of inputs. U_{ij} is the output of the dual-channel, and θ_{ij} is the threshold of step function. $Y_{ij}(k)$ is the k-th output of PCNN.

$$F_{ij}^1(k) = S_{ij}^1(k), \tag{11}$$

$$F_{ij}^2(k) = S_{ij}^2(k), \tag{12}$$

$$L_{ij}(k) = \begin{cases} 1, & \text{if } \sum_{r,t \in S} Y_{rt}(k-1) > 0 \\ 0, & \text{otherwise} \end{cases}, \tag{13}$$

$$U_{ij}(k) = \max \left\{ \begin{array}{l} F_{ij}^1(k)\left(1 + \beta_{ij}^1 L_{ij}(k)\right), \\ F_{ij}^2(k)\left(1 + \beta_{ij}^2 L_{ij}(k)\right) \end{array} \right\}, \tag{14}$$

$$Y_{ij}(k) = \begin{cases} 1, & \text{if } U_{ij}(k) \geq \theta_{ij}(k-1) \\ 0, & \text{otherwise} \end{cases}, \tag{15}$$

$$\theta_{ij}(k) = \theta_{ij}(k-1) - \Delta + V_\theta Y_{ij}(k), \tag{16}$$

$$T_{ij} = \begin{cases} k, & \text{if } U_{ij}(k) \geq \theta_{ij}(k-1) \\ T_{ij}(k-1), & \text{otherwise} \end{cases}, \tag{17}$$

In this paper, the MSMG is applied to modulate the linking strength

$$\beta_{ij}^1 = M_1, \tag{18}$$

$$\beta_{ij}^2 = M_2, \tag{19}$$

where M_1 and M_2 are the MSMG of input.

2.3 MLGCF-MSMG-PCNN Fusion Method

Step 1. The source images are decomposed into three layers, $FD^{(i)}$, $CD^{(i)}$, and B, where i values 3.
Step 2. The MSMG-PCNN fusion measure is used in each layer to obtain three fused layers.
Step 3. The fused image is reconstructed through summing the three fused layers.

3   Experiments and Results

To demonstrate the performance of the proposed method, several methods, NSCT, guided filter fusion (GFF) [17] and MST-sparse representation (MST-SR) [18] are used for qualitative and quantitative comparison.

3.1   Qualitative Evaluation

Figures 3 and 4 show the experiments. It can be seen that the fused result of NSCT method looks like averaging the IR and VIS images, and some of the details are blurred (the cloud in Fig. 3(c) and the fine-details in Fig. 4(c)). The GFF method performs worse than NSCT. The cloud in Fig. 3(d) is completely blurred, and the building in Fig. 4(d) is blocked. The MST-SR method performs better than the two methods. However, the car window displays like IR, not the clear VIS information, and the fine-details are also not enough clear. The proposed method (denoted as MLGCF-MSMG-PCNN) outperforms other state-of-the-art methods in visual effect.

Fig. 3. Experiments in "Jeep" image pair. (a) IR, (b) VIS, (c) NSCT, (d) GFF, (e) MST-SR, (f) Proposed.

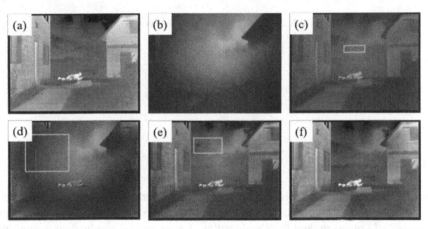

Fig. 4. Experiments in "Soldier" image pair. (a) IR, (b) VIS, (c) NSCT, (d) GFF, (e) MST-SR, (f) Proposed.

3.2 Quantitative Evaluation

Moreover, in order to evaluate the fusion effect more objective, some evaluation indices should be employed. The entropy (H) [19], mutual information (MI) [20] and total fusion metrics ($Q^{AB/F}$) [21] are used in this paper.

Table 1 shows the evaluation indices of the experiments. It can be seen that the proposed MLGCF-MSMG-PCNN performs the best in most cases.

3.3 Time Consumption

Time consumption is also an important parameter to decide whether the algorithm could be operated in real-life. All the experiments are implemented in MATLAB R2018b on a

Table 1. Quantitative evaluation of experiments.

Group	Index	NSCT	GFF	MST-SR	Proposed
Jeep	H	6.422	6.9342	7.0837	**7.6140**
	MI	1.9296	2.6654	3.1818	**3.7653**
	$Q^{AB/F}$	0.3329	0.5892	**0.5967**	0.5823
Soldier	H	6.6106	7.1325	**7.2546**	7.2057
	MI	1.7342	3.4215	3.1854	**3.7805**
	$Q^{AB/F}$	0.3021	0.5073	0.5228	**0.5457**

PC with 2.3 GHz CPU and 8G RAM. Table 2 shows the time consumption of different methods. It can be seen that the proposed MLGCF-MSMG-PCNN consumes much more time. Therefore, the method needs further optimization.

Table 2. Time consumption in seconds.

Group	NSCT	GFF	MST-SR	Proposed
Jeep	19.336	1.761	13.428	14.066
Soldier	9.776	0.757	9.072	7.537

4   Conclusion

In this paper, an MLGCF-MSMG-PCNN image fusion method is proposed. It is a further extension of our previous algorithm. This method combines MLGCF decomposition model, MSMG measure, and PCNN algorithm. Experimental results demonstrate that the proposed method performs best in most cases in qualitative and quantitative measures.

Acknowledgement. The authors are grateful to the anonymous reviews for their valuable comments and suggestion. This paper is supported by National Natural Science Foundation of China (61675160); 111 Project (B17035), China Scholarship Council (CSC201906960047). We thank TNO providing their dataset freely [22].

References

1. Tan, W., Zhou, H., Song, J., Li, H., Du, J.: Infrared and visible image perceptive fusion through multi-level Gaussian curvature filtering image decomposition. Appl. Opt. **58**(12), 3064–3073 (2019)
2. Qian, K., Zhou, H., Qin, H., Rong, S., Zhao, D., Du, J.: Guided filter and convolutional network based tracking for infrared dim moving target. Infrared Phys. Technol. **85**, 431–442 (2017)

3. Lai, R., Guan, J., Yang, Y., Xiong, A.: Spatiotemporal adaptive nonuniformity correction based on btv regularization. IEEE Access **7**, 753–762 (2018)
4. Song, S., Zhou, H., Yang, Y., Song, J.: Hyperspectral anomaly detection via convolutional neural network and low rank with density-based clustering. IEEE J. Sel. Top. Appl. Earth Obs. Remote Sens. **12**(9), 3637–3649 (2019)
5. Song, S., Zhou, H., Zhou, J., Qian, K., Cheng, K., Zhang, Z.: Hyperspectral anomaly detection based on anomalous component extraction framework. Infrared Phys. Technol. **96**, 340–350 (2019)
6. Xiang, P., et al.: Hyperspectral anomaly detection by local joint subspace process and support vector machine. Int. J. Remote Sens. **41**(10), 3798–3819 (2020)
7. Song, S., Zhou, H., Yang, Y., Qian, K., Du, J., Xiang, P.: A graphical estimation and multiple-sparse representation strategy for hyperspectral anomaly detection. Infrared Phys. Technol. **99**, 212–221 (2019)
8. Du, J., Li, W., Lu, K., Xiao, B.: An overview of multi-modal medical image fusion. Neurocomputing **215**, 3–20 (2016)
9. Tan, W., Zhou, H., Rong, S., Qian, K., Yu, Y.: Fusion of multi-focus images via a Gaussian curvature filter and synthetic focusing degree criterion. Appl. Opt. **57**(35), 10092–10101 (2018)
10. Lewis, J., O'Callaghan, R.: Pixel- and region-based image fusion with complex wavelets. Inf. Fusion **8**(2), 119–130 (2007)
11. Zhao, C., Guo, Y., Wang, Y.: A fast fusion scheme for infrared and visible light images in NSCT domain. Infrared Phys. Technol. **72**, 266–275 (2015)
12. Yin, M., Duan, P., Liu, W., Shen, Q.: A novel infrared and visible image fusion algorithm based on shift-invariant dual-tree complex shearlet transform and sparse representation. Neurocomputing **226**, 182–191 (2017)
13. Tan, W., et al.: Multi-focus image fusion using spatial frequency and discrete wavelet transform. In: AOPC 2017: Optical Sensing and Imaging Technology and Applications, vol. 10462, pp. 104624K. SPIE, Beijing (2017)
14. Kong, W., Zhang, L., Lei, Y.: Novel fusion method for visible light and infrared images based on NSST-SF-PCNN. Infrared Phys. Technol. **65**, 103–112 (2014)
15. Lai, R., Li, Y., Guan, J., Xiong, A.: Multi-scale visual attention deep convolutional neural network for multi-focus image fusion. IEEE Access **7**, 114385–114399 (2019)
16. Gong, Y., Sbalzarini, I.: Curvature filters efficiently reduce certain variational energies. IEEE Trans. Image Process. **26**(4), 1786–1798 (2017)
17. Li, S., Kang, X., Hu, J.: Image fusion with guided filtering. IEEE Trans. Image Process. **22**(7), 2864–2875 (2013)
18. Liu, Y., Liu, S., Wang, Z.: A general framework for image fusion based on multi-scale transform and sparse representation. Inf. Fusion **24**, 147–164 (2015)
19. Roberts, J., Ahmed, J.: Assessment of image fusion procedures using entropy, image quality, and multispectral classification. J. Appl. Remote Sens. **2**(1), 023522 (2008)
20. Qu, G., Zhang, D., Yan, P.: Information measure for performance of image fusion. Electron. Lett. **38**(7), 313–315 (2002)
21. Petrovic, V., Xydeas, C.: Objective image fusion performance characterisation. In: IEEE International Conference on Computer Vision, vol. 2, pp. 1866–1871. IEEE, Beijing
22. TNO Dataset. https://figshare.com/articles/TNO_Image_Fusion_Dataset/1008029. Accessed 22 Oct 2019

RCA-NET: Image Recovery Network with Channel Attention Group for Image Dehazing

Juan Du[✉], Jiajia Zhang, Zhe Zhang, Wei Tan, Shangzhen Song, and Huixin Zhou

School of Physics and Optoelectronic Engineering, Xidian University, Xi'an 710071, China
juandu_xidian1107@outlook.com

Abstract. In this paper, we propose an image dehazing network with a channel attention model. Most existing methods try to resolve the dehazing problem through an atmospheric transmission model, but always fail to get promising results since the real-world physical imaging system is of high complexity. Therefore, we propose recovering a fog-free image from its foggy image using an end-to-end pipeline which can produce more realistic results. We apply a channel-wise attention model into our network and also employ the perceptual loss for supervision. Experimental results indicate that our method performs better than several state-of-the-art algorithms.

Keywords: Image dehazing · Image recovery network · Channel attention group · Transmission matrix · Atmospheric scattering model

1 Introduction

The existence of haze degrades the quality of the image captured by the surveillance system. Therefore, haze removal has become one of the hotspots in image processing; it can provide promising solutions for various tasks such as remote sensing, surveillance systems, and aerospace.

Originally, image dehazing was performed via enhancing image contrast to reduce the effects of haze on images. [1, 2] introduced a method to resolve the haze problem by maximizing local contrast of input images. A fast image defogging method was refined to estimate the amount of fog in an image using a locally adaptive wiener filter [3]. Subsequently, more algorithms were proposed based on the atmospheric scattering model theory. In [4], the albedo of a scene is estimated to aid in haze removal. [5–8] apply the dark channel prior to the atmospheric scattering model to calculate the transmission map. Further, algorithms have been proposed to improve the defogging by: enforcing the boundary constraint and contextual regularization [9], minimizing the nonconvex potential in the random field [10], enriching contextual information [11], or automating the defogging algorithm [12]. Recently, the prior information has been applied in dehazing to recover haze-free images. [13] proposed a method to dehaze in the same, or different, scale images using internal patches. [14] built a haze removal

© Springer Nature Switzerland AG 2020
T. McDaniel et al. (Eds.): ICSM 2019, LNCS 12015, pp. 330–337, 2020.
https://doi.org/10.1007/978-3-030-54407-2_28

model of scene depth, then trained this model with a color attenuation prior. The above algorithms reduce the image blur to some extent, but the restored image still has color distortion.

Recently, a deep convolutional neural network (CNN) method has become a hotspot for image dehazing [15, 16]. [17] introduced a strategy which generated first a coarse transmission matrix and then tried to obtain an accurate transmission matrix through refinement. The Dehazenet uses hazy images to train the network for the medium trans-mission matrix and then uses the atmospheric scattering model to recover haze-free images [18]. Most methods are based on the transmission matrix estimation which, unfortunately, cannot generate the defogging image directly. Furthermore, existing CNN-based networks usually treat each channel function equally, and hence varing information features and important details are missing [19–22].

To resolve these problems, we consider using channel-wise information as a weight in the normal convolution layer for excellent feature extraction. In this paper, we propose an image recovery network with channel attention (RCA-Net) to extract, adaptively, channel-wise features. Firstly, the transmission model $M(x)$ is drawn from an end-to-end network by minimizing the reconstruction errors. Secondly, the $M(x)$ is gradually optimized through an image recovery network with channel attention. Finally, more realistic color and structural details can be drawn from the recovery network.

The remainder of this paper is organized as follows: the proposed algorithm is described in Sect. 2. The experimental results and analysis are reported in Sect. 3. Finally, the conclusion is given in Sect. 4.

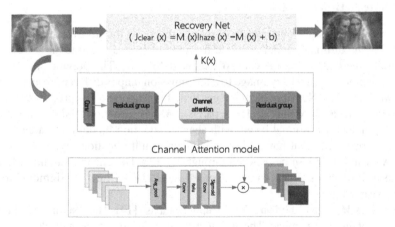

Fig. 1. Structure of recovery network with channel attention model.

2 Proposed Algorithm

In this paper, an end-to-end network with channel attention is proposed to achieve a high-level restoration of foggy images. Specifically, the atmospheric scattering model in RCA-Net has been simplified during the image restoration process. Furthermore, the channel attention model focuses on more significant information to improve haze removal.

2.1 Physical Model

An atmospheric scattering model is a foundation of defogging algorithms. The atmospheric scattering model can be expressed as

$$I_{haze}(x) = J_{clear}(x)t(x) + A(1 - t(x)) \tag{1}$$

$$J_{clear}(x) = \frac{1}{t(x)}I_{haze}(x) - \frac{A}{t(x)} + A \tag{2}$$

$$J_{clear}(x) = M(x)I_{haze}(x) - M(x) + b \tag{3}$$

where, $I_{haze}(x)$ denotes observed foggy image, $J_{clear}(x)$ is the fog-free image needed to be recovered.

According to the atmospheric scattering model, the final expression of $M(x)$ is

$$M(x) = \frac{\frac{1}{t(x)}(I_{haze}(x) - A) + B}{I_{haze}(x) - 1} \tag{4}$$

wherein the $M(x)$ parameter is a parameter that combines A and $t(x)$, B is the value of A-b, and the final value depends only on the model input $I_{haze}(x)$. A and $t(x)$ represent the global atmospheric light and the transmission matrix, respectively.

2.2 Dehaze Network Architecture

The previous models are obtained from a hazy image to the transmission matrix, but RCA-Net is the ultimate model acquired from the hazy image to the hazy-free image, which trains the end-to-end network to achieve defogging. The previous model of the defogging method from a hazy image to a transmission map is different from an end-to-end network of RCA-Net from hazy images to no hazy images. The proposed RCA-Net contains two parts as shown in Fig. 1: one part is an $M(x)$ estimation module that estimates $M(x)$ using five convolutional layers with channel attention model integrated. Another part is a recovery net that has 21 layers including multiplication layers and addition layers; A clean image can be restored through Eq. (3). The channel attention function is obtained through "Average pool $\rightarrow$ Conv $\rightarrow$ ReLU $\rightarrow$ Conv $\rightarrow$ Sigmoid" to get a channel-wise feature.

The matrix $M(x)$ is trained on NYU2 Depth Database [14]. The test image is then used as input to obtain a clear image. The architecture includes five steps in model parameters estimation, that is, the output of RCA-Net can be reconstructed in sequence through convolution feature extraction, a residual group, a channel attention model, and a residual group to the recovery image. The foggy image $I_{haze}(x)$ and the clear image $J_{clear}(x)$ is the input and output of RCA-Net model respectively and the network parameters are optimized by minimizing the loss. The image processing goes through three operations, which is shown in the following equations:

$$F_{con}(x) \rightarrow H_{\_conv}(I_{haze}(x)) \tag{5}$$

$$F_{rd}(x) \rightarrow H_{\_Residual}(F_{con}(x)) \tag{6}$$

$$F_{ca}(x) \rightarrow H_{\_channel}(F_{rd}(x)) \tag{7}$$

where $H_{\_Conv}$ represents the convolution operation, and $F_{con}(x)$ is then used for deep feature extraction; $H_{\_Residual}$ denotes a deep convolution group with a long skip connection, $F_{rd}(x)$ is the furthest feature from the residual group; $H_{\_channel}$, the operation of channel attention function, which includes three steps: global average pooling, the sigmoid function, and ReLU function. $F_{ca}(x)$ is the feature map obtained from the channel attention model, which is multiplied by the channel attention feature, and then added to $F_{rd}(x)$.

The next part is the estimation of $M(x)$, which can be given by

$$M(x) \rightarrow H_{\_Residual}(F_{ca}(x)) \tag{8}$$

$$J_{clear}(x) = M(x) * I_{haze}(x) - M(x) + b = H_{\_Recovery}(I_{haze}(x)) \tag{9}$$

The loss function minimizes the error between the target image and the input image used to achieve network optimization. The common loss function in deep networks are the L1 loss and the L2 loss, or a combination of L1 loss and L2 loss. This is closely related to Mean Squared Error (MSE), but the visual effect is not good enough. To resolve this problem, a perceptual loss is introduced in RCA-Net for the purpose of making the feature extraction level of SR consistent with that of the original image. In this way, we can achieve perfect visual effects and more details close to the target image.

3 Preliminary Results

3.1 Experimental Setup

The Training Process: The weights are initialized using random numbers; the channel attention convolution group is more effective for a deep network; the decay parameter in model training is set to 0.0001;

The Database: We use the NYU2 Depth Database [14] which includes ground-truth images and depth meta-data. We set the atmospheric light A $\in$ [0.6, 1.0], and $\beta \in \{0.4, 0.6, 0.8, 1.0, 1.2, 1.4, 1.6\}$. For the NYU2 database, 27, 256 images are the training set and 3,170 images are the non-overlapping, called TestSet A.

3.2 Experiments and Results

To test the performance of the proposed algorithm, our method is compared with the traditional algorithms Boundary Constrained Context Regularization (BCCR) [9], Color Attenuation Prior (CAP) [14], Fast Visibility Restoration (FVR) [23], Gradient Residual Minimization (GRM) [24], Dark-Channel Prior (DCP) [4] and MSCNN [8].

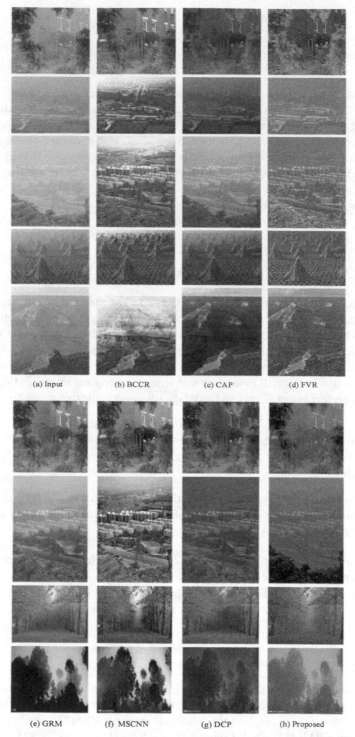

(a) Input   (b) BCCR   (c) CAP   (d) FVR

(e) GRM   (f) MSCNN   (g) DCP   (h) Proposed

Fig. 2. Comparison of BCCR, CAP, FVR, GRM, MSCNN, DCP, and proposed RCA-Net

Figure 2 shows the defogging results of eight sets of images. The CNN-based algorithm is better than BCCR (0.9569), CAP (0.9757), FVR (0.9622), GRM (0.9249), and DCP (0.9449). The MSCNN and the proposed method, however, have higher SSIM, which are 0.9689 and 0.9792, respectively. Figure 3 shows the PSNR of the above defogging methods. The PSNR values of ATM, BCCR, FVR, NLD are between 15 dB and 20 dB. The PSNR of MSCNN, Dehazenet and the proposed method are higher than 20 dB. Compared with other methods, RCA-Net has perfect visual performance and a little higher PSNR.

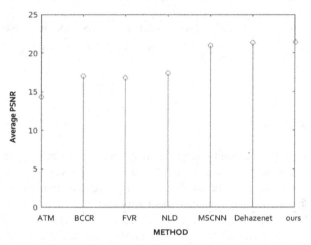

Fig. 3. Comparison of BCCR, ATM, FVR, NLD, MSCNN, DehazeNet and proposed RCA-Net on dehazing 800 synthetic images from the Middlebury stereo database.

Among to previous experiments, few quantitative results about the restoration quality were reported. Table 1 displays the average PSNR and SSIM results on TestSet A.

Table 1. Average PSNR and SSIM results on TestSet A.

Metrics	BCCR	CAP	FVR	GRM	DCP	MSCNN	**RCA-Net**
PSNR	15.751	19.630	15.031	18.974	18.387	19.121	**20.054**
SSIM	0.771	0.837	0.743	0.823	0.833	0.829	**0.841**

To further compare the results, the PSNR of each method is shown in Fig. 3 on the same image. It can be seen that RCA-Net greatly improves the PSNR, which is about 1 dB higher than BCCR, ATM, FVR, and NLD. Therefore, the dehazing strategy in an appropriate model is confirmed to be more effective than other networks.

3.3 Time Consumption

The light-weight structure of RCA-Net leads to faster dehazing. We select 100 images from TestSet A to test all algorithms. All experiments are implemented in Matlab 2016a on a PC with GPU Titan V, 12 GB RAM in an Ubuntu 16.04 system. We crop each input image into patches with a size of 256 * 256 for running time comparison. The per-image average running times of all models are shown in Table 2.

Table 2. Comparison of average running time (seconds).

Metrics	BCCR	CAP	FVR	GRM	DCP	MSCNN	**RCA-Net**
Time	0.523	0.446	3.02	2.18	9.87	0.920	**0.471**

4 Conclusion

In this paper, we propose an end-to-end dehazing network from hazy images to clean images using the channel attention model. Through giving a weight to normal convolution, the channel attention model contributes to further feature extraction. This approach simplifies the dehazing network and can effectively keep more realistic colors and structural details. Ultimately, this network can fully retain real details from the test image, which enables a state-of-art comparison of dehazing, both quantitatively and visually.

Acknowledgement. The authors are grateful to the anonymous reviews for their valuable comments and suggestion. This paper is supported by National Natural Science Foundation of China (61675160); 111 Project (B17035).

References

1. Tan, R.T.: Visibility in bad weather from a single image. In: 2008 Computer Vision and Pattern Recognition, pp. 1–8. IEEE, Anchorage (2008)
2. Guo, D., Liu, P., She, Y., Yang, H., Liu, D.: Ultrasonic imaging contrast enhancement using modified dehaze image model. Electron. Lett. **49**(19), 1209 (2013)
3. Gibson, K.B., Nguyen, T.Q.: Fast single image fog removal using the adaptive wiener filter. In: 2013 IEEE International Conference on Image Processing, pp. 714–718 (2013)
4. Fattal, R.: Single image dehazing. ACM Trans. Graph. (TOG) **27**(3), 72 (2008)
5. Du, Y., Li, X.: Recursive deep residual learning for single image dehazing. In: Proceedings of the IEEE Conference on Computer Vision and Pattern Recognition Workshops, pp. 730–737 (2018)
6. Zhang, H., Sindagi, V., Patel, V.M.: Joint transmission map estimation and dehazing using deep networks. arXiv preprint arXiv:1708.00581 (2017)
7. Tang, K., Yang, J., Wang, J.: Investigating haze-relevant features in a learning framework for image dehazing. In: Proceedings of the IEEE Conference on Computer Vision and Pattern Recognition, pp. 2995–3000 (2014)

8. Diao, Y., Zhang, H., Yadong, W., Chen, M.: Real-time image/video haze removal algorithm with color restoration. J. Comput. Appl. **34**(9), 2702–2707 (2014)
9. Meng, G., Wang, Y., Duan, J., Xiang, S., Pan, C.: Efficient image dehazing with boundary constraint and contextual regularization. In: Proceedings of the IEEE International Conference on Computer Vision, pp. 617–624 (2013)
10. Wang, Y.K., Fan, C.T.: Single image defogging by multiscale depth fusion. IEEE Trans. Image Process. **23**(11), 4826–4837 (2014)
11. Song, W., Deng, B., Zhang, H., Xiao, Q., Peng, S.: An adaptive real-time video defogging method based on context-sensitiveness. In: 2016 IEEE International Conference on Real-Time Computing and Robotics (RCAR), pp. 406–410 (2016)
12. Sulami, M., Glatzer, I., Fattal, R., Werman, M.: Automatic recovery of the atmospheric light in hazy images. In: 2014 IEEE International Conference on Computational Photography (ICCP), pp. 1–11 (2014)
13. Bahat, Y., Irani, M.: Blind dehazing using internal patch recurrence. In: 2016 IEEE International Conference on Computational Photography (ICCP), pp. 1–9 (2016)
14. Zhu, Q., Mai, J., Shao, L.: A fast single image haze removal algorithm using color attenuation prior. IEEE Trans. Image Process. **24**(11), 3522–3533 (2015)
15. Guan, J., Lai, R., Xiong, A.: Wavelet deep neural network for stripe noise removal. IEEE Access. **7**, 44544–44554 (2019)
16. Guan, J., Lai, R., Xiong, A.: Learning spatiotemporal features for single image stripe noise removal. IEEE Access. **7**, 144489–144499 (2019)
17. Ren, W., Liu, S., Zhang, H., Pan, J., Cao, X., Yang, M.-H.: Single image dehazing via multiscale convolutional neural networks. In: Leibe, B., Matas, J., Sebe, N., Welling, M. (eds.) ECCV 2016. LNCS, vol. 9906, pp. 154–169. Springer, Cham (2016). https://doi.org/10.1007/978-3-319-46475-6_10
18. Cai, B., Xu, X., Jia, K., Qing, C., Tao, D.: Dehazenet: an end-to-end system for single image haze removal. IEEE Trans. Image Process. **25**(11), 5187–5198 (2016)
19. Yang, D., Sun, J.: Proximal dehaze-net: a prior learning-based deep network for single image dehazing. In: Ferrari, V., Hebert, M., Sminchisescu, C., Weiss, Y. (eds.) ECCV 2018. LNCS, vol. 11211, pp. 729–746. Springer, Cham (2018). https://doi.org/10.1007/978-3-030-01234-2_43
20. Tao, L., Zhu, C., Song, J., Lu, T., Jia, H., Xie, X.: Low-light image enhancement using CNN and bright channel prior. In: 2017 IEEE International Conference on Image Processing (ICIP), pp. 3215–3219 (2017)
21. Li, J., Li, G., Fan, H.: Image dehazing using residual-based deep CNN. IEEE Access **6**, 26831–26842 (2018)
22. Zhang, Y., et al.: An end-to-end image dehazing method based on deep learning. J. Phys. Conf. Ser. **1169**(1), 012046 (2019)
23. Tarel, J.P., Hautiere, N.: Fast visibility restoration from a single color or gray level image. In: 2009 IEEE 12th International Conference on Computer Vision, pp. 2201–2208 (2009)
24. Chen, C., Do, M.N., Wang, J.: Robust image and video dehazing with visual artifact suppression via gradient residual minimization. In: Leibe, B., Matas, J., Sebe, N., Welling, M. (eds.) ECCV 2016. LNCS, vol. 9906, pp. 576–591. Springer, Cham (2016). https://doi.org/10.1007/978-3-319-46475-6_36

Machine Learning for Multimedia

Certain and Consistent Domain Adaptation

Bhadrinath Nagabandi[(✉)], Andrew Dudley, Hemanth Venkateswara,
and Sethuraman Panchanathan

Arizona State University, Tempe, AZ 85281, USA
{bnagaban,addudley,hemanthv,panch}@asu.edu

Abstract. Unsupervised domain adaptation algorithms seek to transfer
knowledge from labeled source datasets in order to predict the labels for
target datasets in the presence of domain-shift. In this paper we propose the Certain and Consistent Domain Adaptation (CCDA) model
for unsupervised domain adaptation. The CCDA aligns the source and
target domains using adversarial training and reduces the domain adaptation problem to a semi supervised learning (SSL) problem. We estimate
the target labels using consistency regularization and entropy minimization on the domain-aligned target samples whose predictions are consistent across multiple stochastic perturbations. We evaluate the CCDA on
benchmark datasets and demonstrate that it outperforms competitive
baselines from domain adaptation literature.

Keywords: Domain adaptation · Semi supervised learning · Entropy
regularization · Consistency regularization

1 Introduction

Deep neural networks have shown impressive performance on computer vision
tasks when trained with abundant labeled data. In practice, it is not always
possible to collect and annotate large amounts of data to sufficiently train a
model for the required task. Also, the algorithms trained on one task do not
generalize well to a relevant but new task owing to domain shift [1]. Domain
adaptation algorithms overcome domain-shift to transfer knowledge from one
domain (source) to another domain (target) to learn robust models across both
the domains. When the source domain is fully labeled and the target domain is
unlabeled the problem is termed as Unsupervised Domain Adaptation (UDA).

The challenge in domain adaptation is to develop machine learning models
that are invariant to domain shift. In this work we introduce a domain adaptation
algorithm that uses adversarial training [10] to align the features of the source
and the target domains. We hypothesize that when the source and the target
domains are aligned, domain adaptation is similar to semi supervised learning.
In the paradigm of semi supervised learning we have a small labeled dataset and
a large unlabeled dataset from the same distribution. In domain adaptation,

© Springer Nature Switzerland AG 2020
T. McDaniel et al. (Eds.): ICSM 2019, LNCS 12015, pp. 341–356, 2020.
https://doi.org/10.1007/978-3-030-54407-2_29

when the domains are aligned, the labeled source domain and unlabeled target domain can be compared to labeled and unlabeled data as encountered in semi supervised learning.

Semi supervised learning (SSL) techniques leverage the unlabeled data in a transductive manner and use it for training while simultaneously learning from the labeled data [5]. Deep learning based SSL approaches fall under two categories, *Consistency Regularization* and *Entropy Minimization*. The basic assumption in consistency regularization is that a classifier is expected to output the same class distribution even after it is augmented or deformed by modifying the pixel content in the input image. This is inline with the *smoothness* assumption which constraints decision boundaries to vary smoothly. Entropy minimization approaches force the decision boundaries to pass through low density regions in the input space so that the model can effectively discriminate between the categories. This is based on the *cluster* assumption which is complementary to the smoothness assumption. We propose a model to incorporate both these assumptions when predicting target labels.

To align the source and target domains we propose adversarial training [10]. With the domains aligned, we take inspiration from the Mean Teacher model [30] and propose a couple network pair - `Rapid-Smooth` - to perform consistency regularization. Enforcing consistency regularization when the network parameters are nascent can lead to negative transfer. We implement a strategy to select samples that our model is 'certain' about by measuring the variance in predictions across stochastic perturbations of the input data [17]. We enforce consistency loss on these 'certain' samples along with entropy minimization. We term our approach Certain and Consistent Domain Adaptation (CCDA).

Our contributions in this work are two fold. (1) We align the features of the source and target domains thereby reducing the domain adaptation problem to a semi supervised learning (SSL) problem allowing us to avail a rich set of solutions from SSL literature. (2) We develop the CCDA model using principles of adversarial learning, entropy regularization, consistency regularization and prediction certainty. We evaluate the CCDA on popular benchmark datasets (*Office-31* [24] and *Office-Home* [34]) and demonstrate that the CCDA outperforms competitive baselines from unsupervised domain adaptation literature.

2   Related Work

In this section we discuss the literature which is most relevant to our model relating to unsupervised domain adaptation and semi supervised learning.

2.1   Unsupervised Domain Adaptation

We provide a brief survey of statistical and adversarial approaches to domain adaptation that are relevant to our work. For a detailed survey of domain adaptation, we direct the reader to [7,33].

A standard procedure to aligning the data distributions of the source and target is reducing the Maximum Mean Discrepancy (MMD) between source and target features after projecting them onto a high (infinite) dimensional space [18,20,34]. The MMD is a non-parametric measure of the difference between two distributions. A variation of the MMD criterion is deployed by Long et al., where they develop a joint MMD using both input features and labels [21]. Distribution alignment is also achieved by reducing the Wasserstein's distance or Earth Mover's distance between distributions [2,6,26].

The most popular approach to reduce domain disparity is through adversarial training. Adversarial training was introduced through the Generative Adversarial Networks by Goodfellow et al. [12]. Adversarial training in domain adaptation is a two-network min-max game in which one network tries to differentiate between the source and target data and the second network tries to align the two distributions of the datasets. The Domain Adversarial Neural Network (DANN) [10] is a seminal approach that applied adversarial training to domain adaptation. The DANN has a feature extractor network attempting to extract domain-aligned features and an auxiliary network called the discriminator that is trained to discriminate between the features of the source and the target. The feature extractor is trained to make the discriminator perform poorly by negating the gradient of the discriminator using a gradient reversal layer (GRL). There have been multiple variations of adversarial training in domain adaptation literature; maximal domain confusion loss [31], untied feature extractor and discriminator (ADDA) [32] and multiple domain discriminators to enable fine-grained discrimination of data distributions (MADA) [23], to name a few. These approaches apply the adversarial training principle to align feature spaces between domains.

Apart from aligning feature spaces, adversarial training has also been applied to align image spaces. Image translation based domain adaptation approaches convert images from the source domain to the target domain (or vice versa) using adversarial training [3,8,15]. The popular DIRT-T model utilizes adversarial training along with enforcing a cluster assumption with conditional entropy minimization to estimate target labels [27]. More recent approaches that consider the challenge of differences in label space between the source and the target also take recourse to adversarial training to align the domains [4,25,36]. In this work, we apply the standard version of the DANN [10] to reduce domain disparity.

2.2 Semi Supervised Learning

In the semi supervised learning paradigm we have a small set of labeled data and a large set of unlabeled data from the same distribution. The goal in SSL is to train a transductive model that can effectively predict the labels of the target. Recent literature in SSL focuses on *Consistency Regularization* or *Entropy minimization*.

Under Consistency Regularization the network is expected to maintain consistent predictions for an image under different augmentations. This is also called the *smoothness assumption*. The augmentations can be either in the input space with different stochastic transformations of the input or in the parameter space as in Dropout [28]. An ensemble of perturbations is usually applied to implement consistency regularization and has shown promising performance [16,30]. Laine et al. [16], introduced two different models implementing consistency regularization. In the Π-model the unlabeled data is passed through the network twice with different perturbations and a mean square error between the two predictions is minimized to maintain consistency. In Temporal Ensembling, a moving average of predictions is maintained and these are considered as training targets for the unlabeled input.

The Mean-Teacher model [30], defines a pair of coupled identical networks, a Student and a Teacher, where the parameters of the Teacher are a moving average of the Student's parameters. The Student network is trained using a consistency measure (mean-squared loss) between the predictions of the Teacher and the Student. Other measures like consistent attention [37] and feature correlation using Gram matrix [11] have also been developed for the Mean Teacher setup.

Entropy minimization is the other popular technique which forces the decision boundary to cut through low density regions of the target and thus generate confident target predictions [13]. The popular DIRT-T approach applies entropy minimization along with adversarial training for domain adaptation [27]. In the proposed Certain and Consistent Domain Adaptation (CCDA), we train a pair of networks, `Rapid-Smooth`, to output consistent predictions over the target along the lines of Mean-Teacher [30]. In addition the CCDA also ensures certainty in label predictions by minimizing the variance in predictions across multiple augmentations of a data point [17].

3   Certain and Consistent Domain Adaptation

In the unsupervised domain adaptation set up we consider a data set from the source domain, $\mathcal{D}_s = \{x_i^s, y_i^s\}_{i=1}^{n_s}$ with n_s sample pairs where $x_i^s \in X$ are images sampled from a space X and $y_i^s \in Y$ are their corresponding labels from a discrete label space $Y = \{1, \ldots, C\}$. Likewise, we have a dataset from the target domain, $\mathcal{D}_t = \{x_i^t\}_{i=1}^{n_t}$ with only images and no labels. Under the assumption that the label spaces of the domains are identical, i.e., $y^t \in Y$, the goal of unsupervised domain adaptation is to predict the target labels $\{\hat{y}_i^t\}_{i=1}^{n_t}$ for every image in $\mathcal{D}_t$. An additional constraint to the problem is that the joint distributions of the source and target are different with $P_s(X, Y) \neq P_t(X, Y)$.

To solve this problem we develop the Certain and Consistent Domain Adaptation (CCDA) model - a deep neural network that is trained to predict labels for the target by gradually improving their certainty and consistency over multiple iterations of training. The CCDA takes source and target images as input and extracts image features by ameliorating the domain discrepancy. The CCDA is a coupled network system that is modeled after the Mean Teacher [30]. We term them `Rapid-Smooth` networks to denote their training strategies. The `Rapid-Smooth` networks are used to identify the data samples that have high

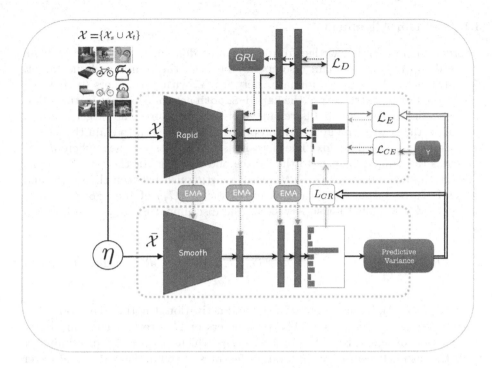

Fig. 1. The Certain and Consistent Domain Adaptation (CCDA) model. The coupled Rapid-Smooth networks have identical architecture based on ResNet-50. The Rapid network is trained using loss terms $\mathcal{L}_D$ (discriminator), $\mathcal{L}_E$ (entropy), $\mathcal{L}_{CE}$ (cross-entropy) and $\mathcal{L}_{CR}$ (consistency). The parameters of Smooth are an exponential moving average (EMA) of Rapid. Random augmentations of the input $\eta(\mathcal{X})$ are used to identify input samples with 'Certain' predictions using predictive variance. The indices of these samples are used to estimate consistency loss (source+target) and entropy loss (target only).

certainty in their label predictions. These certain data points are used to drive a consistency loss for training the coupled networks. In addition, the source data is used to train the CCDA with a cross-entropy loss and the target data is used to determine the unsupervised entropy loss.

The Rapid network has parameters $\{\theta_f, \theta_y\}$ and the Smooth network has parameters $\{\bar{\theta}_f, \bar{\theta}_y\}$, where θ_f and $\bar{\theta}_f$ are the parameters of the feature extractor and θ_y and $\bar{\theta}_y$ are the classifier parameters. The CCDA model has a discriminator network with parameters θ_d. We train the CCDA using mini-batches of source and target data where each mini-batch consists of source samples $\mathcal{X}_s = \{x_i^s\}_{i=1}^B$ and corresponding labels $\mathcal{Y}_s = \{y_i^s\}_{i=1}^B$ and target samples $\mathcal{X}_t = \{x_i^t\}_{i=1}^B$. The mini-batch size is $2B$ and the number of mini-batches goes from $\tau = 0$ to $\mathcal{T}$. In this section we will introduce the different components of the CCDA and discuss them in greater detail. The CCDA model is depicted in Fig. 1.

3.1 Domain Alignment

In order to transfer knowledge from the source domain to the target domain we need to overcome domain discrepancy between the source and the target. We introduce a domain discriminator network G_d with parameters θ_d that will ensure the feature extractors of the Rapid-Smooth networks output features that have very little to no domain discrepancy between the source and target features. We follow the adversarial approach proposed in DANN [10], to train the CCDA to align the feature domains. The data is assigned domain labels where $d = 1$ indicates the sample belongs to the source and $d = 0$ is for the target sample. The discriminator network G_d is trained to distinguish between the source and target features output from the feature extractor (G_f) of the Rapid network using the domain label for supervision. The discriminator's objective function is,

$$\mathcal{L}_D(\theta_d, \theta_f) = -\frac{1}{n_s + n_t} \sum_{x \in \{\mathcal{X}_s \cup \mathcal{X}_t\}} d\log[G_d(G_f(\boldsymbol{x}))] + (1-d)(1-\log[G_d(G_f(\boldsymbol{x}))]),$$

(1)

where $G_d(G_f(\boldsymbol{x}))$, is the output of a sigmoid activation denoting the probability that $\boldsymbol{x}$ belongs to the source. The parameters of G_d are trained using back-propagation by minimizing the objective $\mathcal{L}_D$ which enables the discriminator to distinguish between source and target features. The Gradient Reversal Layer (GRL) reverses the gradient $-\frac{\partial \mathcal{L}_D}{\partial \theta_f}$ when modifying the parameters of the feature extractor G_f (see Fig. 1). This form of adversarial training ensures the source and target features output from the feature extractor are indistinguishable to the discriminator thereby assuring domain alignment.

3.2 Certainty and Consistency

When the distributions of the feature vectors from the source and target are aligned the data can be viewed as coming from a single distribution. The source data can be considered as the labeled set and the target data as the unlabeled dataset and semi supervised learning approaches are applicable in this setting. We plan to incorporate the unlabeled target data into the training process by estimating their labels. In the absence of supervision, self ensembling approaches have led the way in skillfully utilizing unlabeled data to evaluate robust labels for the target with transductive training [16,30]. The core idea in these approaches is smoother estimates and consistent predictions across an ensemble induced by multiple random perturbations. We model a coupled network pair along the lines of [30], and induce random perturbations to estimate certain and consistent predictions for the target data. In this section we introduce the Rapid-Smooth coupled network followed by the predictive variance procedure to identify data points with certain and consistent predictions. We then introduce a consistency loss over the coupled-network predictions of these data points.

Rapid-Smooth Coupled Network: The Rapid-Smooth network pair is illustrated in Fig. 1. The model has two parallel networks, Rapid and Smooth, similar to the Student and Teacher networks in [30]. The networks are so named based on their training strategies. The Rapid network updates its weights (θ_f, θ_y) across every mini-batch of source and target data. This leads to a noisy weight update when the target labels are incorrect. On the other hand, the Smooth network only updates its weights $(\bar{\theta}_f, \bar{\theta}_y)$ using an exponential moving average (EMA) of the Rapid network weights. This results in a relatively smoother weight update which yields significantly better results [30]. If τ denotes the mini-batch index, then the weights of the Smooth network are updated using,

$$\bar{\theta}_{f,\tau} = \alpha\bar{\theta}_{f,\tau-1} + (1-\alpha)\theta_{f,\tau}, \quad \text{and} \tag{2}$$

$$\bar{\theta}_{y,\tau} = \alpha\bar{\theta}_{y,\tau-1} + (1-\alpha)\theta_{y,\tau}, \tag{3}$$

where, α is the momentum hyper parameter for the EMA and the Rapid and Smooth networks are initialized with the same values, i.e., $\bar{\theta}_{f,\tau=0} := \theta_{f,\tau=0}$ and $\bar{\theta}_{y,\tau=0} := \theta_{y,\tau=0}$.

In our bid to deploy target data for training, the Rapid network could be misguided with incorrect target labels leading to a confirmation bias - a hazard caused by over-reliance on the target predictions that are incorrect. In order to mitigate this effect we propose the Certain and Consistent loss where we penalize the inconsistency in prediction over only those samples on which the model is certain. In the following we outline a procedure to identify data samples the Smooth network is certain about.

Measure of Certainty: Usually, ensemble methods consider the outputs of the Smooth (Teacher) network to be sufficiently accurate and apply them to penalize the Rapid (Student) network for inconsistencies in their outputs when compared to the Smooth network [9,16,30]. At the beginning of the training procedure, when the network parameters are still close to their random initialization points, we fear that the Smooth network is not completely certain about its predictions. In view of that, we introduce an uncertainty measure to identify the samples the Smooth network is certain about. We propose using predictive variance as a metric to estimate the uncertainty and distinguish between the certain and uncertain samples in the mini-batch [17]. We define *Certainty* as the ability of the network to output similar predictions for a data point x under stochastic data augmentations. We consider T stochastic augmentations of a data point x denoted by $\{\eta_t(x)\}_{t=1}^T$ during a forward pass through the Smooth network. The T augmentations for each image are chosen from random flips, crops, rotation, Gaussian noise addition and occlusion by removing an image patch. The output of the network for each augmentation t is a softmax probability vector $\bar{G}_f(\bar{G}_y(x)) = [p(y = 1|\eta_t(x), \bar{\theta}_f, \bar{\theta}_y), \ldots, p(y = C|\eta_t(x), \bar{\theta}_f, \bar{\theta}_y)]^\top$. Our goal is to identify samples with consistent predictions across the T random augmentations. We therefore gather the T predictions for the sample and estimate the uncertainty of prediction using variance which is calculated as,

$$\mu_c = \frac{1}{T} \sum_{t=1}^{T} p(y = c | \eta_t(\boldsymbol{x}), \bar{\theta}_f, \bar{\theta}_y), \tag{4}$$

$$PV = \sum_{c=1}^{C} \left(\frac{1}{T} \sum_{t=1}^{T} \left(p(y = c | \eta_t(\boldsymbol{x}), \bar{\theta}_f, \bar{\theta}_y) - \mu_c \right)^2 \right). \tag{5}$$

Here, PV stands for predictive variance. With PV as the criteria, we sort all the data samples in the mini-batch (consisting of both source and target data samples) in an ascending order. The data sample the Smooth network is most 'certain' about comes first and the least certain data sample comes last in this sorted list. The output of the predictive variance procedure is a set of indices $\mathcal{I}(\{\mathcal{X}_s \cup \mathcal{X}_t\}, PV, \tau)$ identifying the source ($\mathcal{X}_s$) and target ($\mathcal{X}_t$) samples that the Smooth network is certain about. Here, $\mathcal{I}(\mathcal{X}, PV, \tau)$ is the set of indices chosen from dataset $\mathcal{X}$ based on the predictive variance PV and mini-batch index τ. Rather than filtering the list with a threshold certainty value, we use a sigmoid ramp-up strategy based on the mini-batch number τ to incrementally identify the samples from the sorted list. These indices are used to determine the Consistency regularization and the Entropy loss which is outlined in the following.

Consistency Regularization: Consistency regularization is very crucial to leverage the unlabeled target data. It is applied to ensure the Rapid classifier outputs similar probability distribution compared to the Smooth classifier under different transformations. This is implemented by penalizing the Rapid network with a consistency regularization term for deviations in the predictions compared to the Smooth network. In order to avoid the rapid network trying to be consistent with smooth network's uncertain predictions at the beginning of training, we apply the consistency loss across the predictions of only those samples the Smooth network is certain about. The certain samples indices are given by $\mathcal{I}_\tau = \mathcal{I}(\{\mathcal{X}_s \cup \mathcal{X}_t\}, PV, \tau)$. More formally, the consistency regularization term is expressed as,

$$\mathcal{L}_{CR}(\theta_f, \theta_y) = \frac{1}{|\mathcal{I}_\tau|} \sum_{i \in \mathcal{I}_\tau} \left|\left| G_y(G_f(\eta(\boldsymbol{x}_i))) - \bar{G}_y(\bar{G}_f(\eta(\boldsymbol{x}_i))) \right|\right|_2^2, \tag{6}$$

where $\eta(\boldsymbol{x})$ is a random perturbation of the input image.

3.3   Entropy Regularization

Existing literature demonstrates that a model trained using only source data tends to be highly confident on source like samples and less confident on target like samples [35]. In addition, when the model has not explored the target data space there is a high probability that the decision boundary of the model passes through high density regions of the target space which implies target data classification is incorrect. In order to ensure a low-density separation between target classes and to utilize the target data for training, we deploy entropy minimization [13,20,27]. For a given image $\boldsymbol{x}$, the softmax output of the Rapid network is $G_f(G_y(\boldsymbol{x})) = [f_1(\boldsymbol{x}), \ldots, f_C(\boldsymbol{x})]^\top$, where $f_j(\boldsymbol{x}) = p(y = j|\boldsymbol{x}, \theta_f, \theta_y)$ - the probability that image $\boldsymbol{x}$ belongs to class j. The output $G_f(G_y(\boldsymbol{x}))$ is a probability vector whose components sum to 1. When the network has high confidence in prediction the output is similar to a one-hot vector where all the components of the probability vector are zeros except for one component. Such a prediction has zero (low) entropy. When the network predicts that the input image $\boldsymbol{x}$ belongs to all classes with equal probability, such a prediction has the highest entropy - the network is not confident about the label. By minimizing entropy we are forcing the Rapid network to have confident predictions over the target data. In early stages of training the model usually has random predictions on a target sample. Rather than forcing the model to be confident on random predictions, we identify the target samples the network is certain about using our certainty measures outlined earlier. Let $\mathcal{I}_{t,\tau} = I(\mathcal{X}_t, PV, \tau)$ be the indices of the target samples for which the Smooth network has high certainty predictions for mini-batch index τ. The entropy regularization loss is then given by,

$$\mathcal{L}_E(\theta_f, \theta_y) = -\frac{1}{|\mathcal{I}_{t,\tau}|} \sum_{i \in \mathcal{I}_{t,\tau}} \sum_{j=1}^{C} f_j(\boldsymbol{x}_i) \log f_j(\boldsymbol{x}_i). \tag{7}$$

3.4 Cross Entropy Loss

Cross entropy is the standard supervised classification loss for multi-class classification. Rapid network uses the source data in the mini-batch to minimize the cross-entropy loss over the known labels. If the source images and their corresponding labels in a mini-batch are represented as $\{\mathcal{X}_s, \mathcal{Y}_s\}$, the cross entropy loss is given by,

$$\mathcal{L}_{CE}(\theta_f, \theta_y) = -\frac{1}{|\mathcal{X}_s|} \sum_{\boldsymbol{x} \in \mathcal{X}_s, y \in \mathcal{Y}_s} \sum_{j=1}^{C} 1\{y = j\} \log f_j(\boldsymbol{x}), \tag{8}$$

where, $1\{\text{cond}\}$ is an indicator function which is true if the cond is true.

3.5 CCDA Objective Functions

The Rapid network is trained with an objective function that brings together multiple loss terms. The overall objective function brings together the discriminator loss Eq. (1), the consistency regularization Eq. (6), the entropy loss Eq. (7) and the cross-entropy loss Eq. (8). The parameters of the Rapid network are modified using,

$$\{\theta_f^*, \theta_y^*\} = \arg\min_{\theta_f, \theta_y} \left[\mathcal{L}_{CE} + \gamma \mathcal{L}_{CR} + \beta \mathcal{L}_E - \lambda \mathcal{L}_D \right] \quad \text{and} \tag{9}$$

$$\{\theta_d^*\} = \arg\min_{\theta_d} \left[\lambda \mathcal{L}_D \right], \tag{10}$$

where, γ, β and λ are hyper parameters that control the importance of individual loss terms. While Eqs. (9) and (10) update the parameters of the Rapid network and the adversarial discriminator, the parameters of the Smooth network are updated using the exponential moving average (EMA) as outlined in Eqs. (2), (3).

4   Experiments

We evaluate the performance of our model on two benchmark datasets and compare the results with competitive domain adaptation algorithms. Code will be made available at github.com/hypothesis2304 upon publication.

4.1   Datasets

Office-31 [24] is the common benchmark dataset used to evaluate domain adaptation algorithms. The dataset consists of about 4650 images from 31 categories of everyday objects. It has 3 domains: *Amazon*(**A**), *DSLR*(**D**) and *Webcam*(**W**). The Amazon domain has 2817 images whereas Webcam and DSLR have only 795 and 498 images respectively. We evaluate the model on the 6 transfer tasks **A → W, D → W, W → D, A → D, D → A** and **W → A** across all the domains. Here **A → W** implies, **A** is the source and **W** is the target.

Office-Home [34] is a more challenging dataset with more than 15,500 images from 65 categories belonging to the following four domains: *Art* (**Ar**), *Clipart* (**Cl**), *Product* (**Pr**) and *Real-World* (**Rw**). The image categories are everyday objects from office and home settings. Similar to the *Office-31* experiments, we evaluate the performance of our model on all the 12 transfer tasks **Ar → Cl, Ar → Pr, Ar → Rw, Cl → Ar, Cl → Pr, Cl → Rw, Pr → Ar, Pr → Cl, Pr → Rw, Rw → Ar, Rw → Cl** and **Rw → Pr** across all the domains.

4.2   Implementation Details

We use the pre-trained Resnet-50 [14] model from PyTorch [22] as our base neural network. We remove the original classifier and add a bottleneck layer of 256 dimensions after the global average pooling layer. Similar to [19], we define a classifier and domain discriminator (dimensions 1024-1024-1) after the bottleneck layer. As the classifier and discriminator are trained from scratch we use 10 times the learning rate that is used to fine-tune the feature extractor. We use the same learning rate strategy implemented in [10]: with $\eta_p = \frac{\eta_0}{(1+\alpha p)^\gamma}$, where p is the training progress varying between $[0, 1]$, while η_0, α and γ are optimized with importance-weighted cross-validation [29]. We use the default values provided from [10] without further fine tuning. To update the weights, we use mini-batch stochastic gradient descent with Nesterov as the optimizer. Similar to [19], we use a weight decay of $5e - 4$ with momentum = 0.9 in the optimizer. For the Rapid-Smooth network, momentum α for EMA = 0.999 [30]. Also, we follow a sigmoid ramp-up strategy from [30] to filter the confident samples.

Table 1. Accuracy of CCDA on *Office-31* (ResNet-50)

Method	A → W	D → W	W → D	A → D	D → A	W → A	Avg
ResNet [14]	68.4	96.7	99.3	68.9	62.5	60.7	76.1
DAN [18]	80.5	97.1	99.6	78.6	63.6	62.8	80.4
RTN [20]	84.5	96.8	99.4	77.5	66.2	64.8	81.6
DANN [10]	82	96.9	99.1	79.7	68.2	67.4	82.2
ADDA [32]	86.2	96.2	98.4	77.8	69.5	68.9	82.9
JAN [21]	85.4	97.4	**99.8**	84.7	68.6	**70.0**	84.3
MADA [23]	**90**	97.4	99.6	87.8	**70.3**	66.4	85.2
CCDA(w/o (Ent+PV))	83.6	97.4	99.6	80.8	68.1	67.6	82.8
CCDA(w/o PV)	88.1	**98.9**	99.3	88.1	66.8	66.5	84.6
CCDA	89.5	**98.9**	99.7	**91.4**	66.7	66.4	**85.4**

Table 2. Accuracy of CCDA on *Office-Home* (ResNet-50)

Method	Ar→Cl	Ar→Pr	Ar→Rw	Cl→Ar	Cl→Pr	Cl→Rw	Pr→Ar	Pr→Cl	Pr→Rw	Rw→Ar	Rw→Cl	Rw→Pr	Avg
ResNet [14]	34.9	50	58	37.4	41.9	46.2	38.5	31.2	60.4	53.9	41.2	59.9	46.1
DAN [18]	43.6	57	67.9	45.8	56.5	60.4	44.0	43.6	67.7	63.1	51.5	74.3	56.3
DANN [10]	45.6	59.3	70.1	47.0	58.5	60.9	46.1	43.7	68.5	63.2	51.5	76.8	57.60
JAN [21]	45.9	61.2	68.9	50.4	59.7	61.0	45.8	43.4	70.3	63.9	52.4	76.8	58.31
CCDA(w/o (Ent+PV))	46.3	61.2	70.8	48.3	59.6	60.4	47.2	43.1	68.8	64.7	53.6	77.6	58.5
CCDA(w/o PV)	47.1	**67.2**	74.1	54.6	68.9	66.9	53.1	**49.1**	73.6	68.1	57.8	80.6	63.4
CCDA	**48.2**	67.1	**74.6**	**55.6**	**71.4**	**69.3**	**54.5**	48.3	**76.5**	**68.7**	**58.8**	**82.5**	**64.6**

4.3 Results

The results of Certain and Consistent Domain Adaptation model on *Office-31* and *Office-Home* are shown in Table 1 and Table 2 respectively. All the reported scores are the classification accuracies for different tasks. We note that only the baselines relevant to our work and also reported results are compared. For fair comparison, the accuracies for baselines are directly reported from their original papers. In addition to comparing with competitive baselines, we compare the full model (CCDA)'s performance with CCDA-without-predictive-variance (CCDA w/o PV) and CCDA-without-entropy-and-predictive-variance (CCDA w/o (Ent+PV)). As reported in Table 1, our model outperforms other methods in most of the tasks. The average performance of our model across all the tasks is also better than the other approaches. Particularly, in tasks like **A → D** and **D → W**, our model has the highest accuracy. Experiments **D → A** and **W → A** have low accuracies across all methods. This can be attributed to the data imbalance between the source and target datasets.

Office-Home is a more difficult challenge with more number of domains and categories. From Table 2, it can be seen that our method outperforms the baselines with a significant margin. Particularly in the transfer tasks **Cl → Pr** and **Pr → Ar**, the improvement is around 10%. In the following transfer learning tasks $\mathbf{Ar} \rightarrow \mathbf{Pr}$, $\mathbf{Cl} \rightarrow \mathbf{Rw}$, $\mathbf{Rw} \rightarrow \mathbf{Ar}$ and $\mathbf{Rw} \rightarrow \mathbf{Pr}$, the CCDA improves over the best-reported method by a margin of 6%.

4.4   Analysis

Ablation Study: In the CCDA, the parameters of the Smooth network are an exponential moving average (EMA) of the weights of the Rapid network. We conduct a study to evaluate the advantage of an EMA weight update. We train the Rapid-Smooth network without the consistency loss $\mathcal{L}_{CR}$ and without the entropy regularization $\mathcal{L}_E$, i.e., the Smooth network is merely an EMA version of the Rapid while the Rapid is trained with cross-entropy $\mathcal{L}_{CE}$ and domain discrimination $\mathcal{L}_D$. These results are depicted in the row CCDA(w/o (Ent+PV)). Note that without the consistency and entropy regularization, the Rapid network is similar to the DANN. From both the tables we can observe that the Smooth network performs consistently better than the DANN leading us to conclude that an ensemble update of the parameters of a network using EMA is a better update than a regular update. We also want to highlight the fact that the Rapid-Smooth model does not incur any significant computation cost as the Smooth network is only an exponential moving average of the Rapid network.

In Sect. 3.3, we discussed that a classifier trained only on source data is likely to misclassify target data as there is a high probability that the decision boundaries cut through high density regions of the target distribution. To validate this hypothesis we conduct another set of experiments by introducing a penalty over the target classification using entropy regularization. We expect a low entropy penalty on the target samples to improve the confidence of the model on target predictions and force the decision boundaries to pass through low density regions in the target space. The results obtained by including entropy are in row CCDA(w/o PV). The effect of entropy regularization significantly boosts the accuracies as seen in both Table 1 and Table 2.

The results of introducing consistency regularization $\mathcal{L}_{CR}$, entropy regularization $\mathcal{L}_E$ along with predictive variance (PV) gives us the entire CCDA. The Smooth network can be uncertain on the target predictions at the early stages of training. The $\mathcal{L}_{CR}$ with Certainty ensures that the Rapid network is updated using samples the Smooth network is 'certain' about. The effect of selectively penalizing consistency between the Rapid and the Smooth network pays rich dividends as seen in the CCDA row of the tables. We further evaluate the effect of penalizing only certain samples by comparing the CCDA model to CCDA-without-Certainty (CCDA w/o Certainty), where we penalize all the samples for consistency. We compare the test accuracies of $\mathbf{A} \rightarrow \mathbf{D}$ transfer learning task from *Office-31* dataset in Fig. 3. We observe that the performance of the model with Certainty measure is always smooth and largely monotonic, whereas the performance of (CCDA w/o Certainty) model is noisy and converges rapidly with relatively lower accuracy.

Feature Visualization: We visualize the feature space of $\mathbf{A} \rightarrow \mathbf{D}$ transfer learning task from the *Office-31* dataset. We use t-SNE Embeddings to visualize

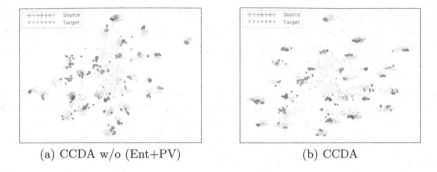

| (a) CCDA w/o (Ent+PV) | (b) CCDA |

Fig. 2. The t-SNE visualizations of CCDA w/o (Ent+PV) and CCDA features for **A** → **D** from *Office-31* with different classes labeled in different colors.

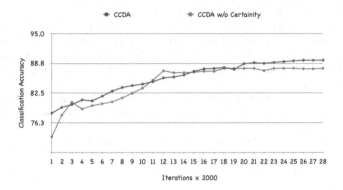

Fig. 3. Classification accuracies on **A** → **D** comparing CCDA and CCDA w/o Certainty vs training iterations.

the features taken from the output of the feature extractor. In Fig. 2, we show the cluster formations of both the source and target domain with (CCDA w/o (Ent+PV)) and our final CCDA model. As expected, our CCDA model forms compact well-defined clusters compared to the baseline. We also observe that the clusters in CCDA are wide spread with samples of the same class held together and samples of other categories spread farther apart.

5   Conclusions

In this paper we develop the Certain and Consistent Domain Adaptation model. The core of the model is based on reducing the domain adaptation problem to a semi supervised learning problem through adversarial domain alignment. We introduce consistency regularization and entropy regularization with a Certainty measure to transductively estimate target labels. We empirically show that our model produces competitive results and outperforms state-of-the-art results in a number of transfer learning tasks across benchmark datasets. We also note that in some transfer learning tasks, due to domain imbalance (number of source samples ≪ number of target samples), our model performs poorly. We hope that by re-weighting instances we can improve the performance in such tasks and we leave it for the future work.

Acknowledgements. The authors thank ASU, and the National Science Foundation for their funding support. This material is partially based upon work supported by the National Science Foundation under Grant No. 1828010.

References

1. Ben-David, S., Blitzer, J., Crammer, K., Kulesza, A., Pereira, F., Vaughan, J.W.: A theory of learning from different domains. Mach. Learn. **79**(1), 151–175 (2009). https://doi.org/10.1007/s10994-009-5152-4
2. Damodaran, B.B., Kellenberger, B., Flamary, R., Tuia, D., Courty, N.: DeepJDOT: deep joint distribution optimal transport for unsupervised domain adaptation. In: Ferrari, V., Hebert, M., Sminchisescu, C., Weiss, Y. (eds.) ECCV 2018. LNCS, vol. 11208, pp. 467–483. Springer, Cham (2018). https://doi.org/10.1007/978-3-030-01225-0_28
3. Bousmalis, K., Silberman, N., Dohan, D., Erhan, D., Krishnan, D.: Unsupervised pixel-level domain adaptation with generative adversarial networks. In: CVPR, pp. 3722–3731 (2017)
4. Cao, Z., Ma, L., Long, M., Wang, J.: Partial adversarial domain adaptation. In: Ferrari, V., Hebert, M., Sminchisescu, C., Weiss, Y. (eds.) ECCV 2018. LNCS, vol. 11212, pp. 139–155. Springer, Cham (2018). https://doi.org/10.1007/978-3-030-01237-3_9
5. Chapelle, O., Scholkopf, B., Zien, A.: Semi-supervised learning (Chapelle, O. et al., eds.; 2006). IEEE Trans. Neural Networks **20**(3), 542 (2009)
6. Courty, N., Flamary, R., Habrard, A., Rakotomamonjy, A.: Joint distribution optimal transportation for domain adaptation. In: NeurIPS, pp. 3730–3739 (2017)
7. Csurka, G.: A comprehensive survey on domain adaptation for visual applications. In: Csurka, G. (ed.) Domain Adaptation in Computer Vision Applications. Advances in Computer Vision and Pattern Recognition, pp. 1–35. Springer, Cham (2017). https://doi.org/10.1007/978-3-319-58347-1_1
8. Deng, W., Zheng, L., Ye, Q., Kang, G., Yang, Y., Jiao, J.: Image-image domain adaptation with preserved self-similarity and domain-dissimilarity for person re-identification. In: The IEEE Conference on CVPR, June 2018
9. French, G., Mackiewicz, M., Fisher, M.: Self-ensembling for visual domain adaptation. arXiv preprint arXiv:1706.05208 (2017)
10. Ganin, Y., et al.: Domain-adversarial training of neural networks. J. Mach. Learn. Res. **17**(1), 2096–2030 (2016)
11. Gatys, L.A., Ecker, A.S., Bethge, M.: A neural algorithm of artistic style. arXiv preprint arXiv:1508.06576 (2015)
12. Goodfellow, I., et al.: Generative adversarial nets. In: Advances in NeurIPS, pp. 2672–2680 (2014)
13. Grandvalet, Y., Bengio, Y.: Semi-supervised learning by entropy minimization. In: Advances in NeurIPS, pp. 529–536 (2005)
14. He, K., Zhang, X., Ren, S., Sun, J.: Deep residual learning for image recognition. In: Proceedings of the IEEE Conference on CVPR, pp. 770–778 (2016)

15. Hoffman, J., et al.: CyCADA: cycle-consistent adversarial domain adaptation. In: Proceedings of the 35th ICML, vol. 80, pp. 1989–1998 (2018)
16. Laine, S., Aila, T.: Temporal ensembling for semi-supervised learning. arXiv preprint arXiv:1610.02242 (2016)
17. Li, Y., Liu, L., Tan, R.T.: Certainty-driven consistency loss for semi-supervised learning. arXiv preprint arXiv:1901.05657 (2019)
18. Long, M., Cao, Y., Wang, J., Jordan, M.I.: Learning transferable features with deep adaptation networks. arXiv preprint arXiv:1502.02791 (2015)
19. Long, M., Cao, Z., Wang, J., Jordan, M.I.: Domain adaptation with randomized multilinear adversarial networks. CoRR abs/1705.10667 (2017)
20. Long, M., Zhu, H., Wang, J., Jordan, M.I.: Unsupervised domain adaptation with residual transfer networks. In: Advances in NeurIPS, pp. 136–144 (2016)
21. Long, M., Zhu, H., Wang, J., Jordan, M.I.: Deep transfer learning with joint adaptation networks. In: ICML-Volume 70, pp. 2208–2217 (2017)
22. Paszke, A., et al.: Automatic differentiation in PyTorch. In: NIPS Autodiff Workshop (2017)
23. Pei, Z., Cao, Z., Long, M., Wang, J.: Multi-adversarial domain adaptation. CoRR abs/1809.02176 (2018). http://arxiv.org/abs/1809.02176
24. Saenko, K., Kulis, B., Fritz, M., Darrell, T.: Adapting visual category models to new domains. In: Daniilidis, K., Maragos, P., Paragios, N. (eds.) ECCV 2010. LNCS, vol. 6314, pp. 213–226. Springer, Heidelberg (2010). https://doi.org/10.1007/978-3-642-15561-1_16
25. Saito, K., Yamamoto, S., Ushiku, Y., Harada, T.: Open set domain adaptation by backpropagation. In: Ferrari, V., Hebert, M., Sminchisescu, C., Weiss, Y. (eds.) ECCV 2018. LNCS, vol. 11209, pp. 156–171. Springer, Cham (2018). https://doi.org/10.1007/978-3-030-01228-1_10
26. Shen, J., Qu, Y., Zhang, W., Yu, Y.: Wasserstein distance guided representation learning for domain adaptation. In: Proceedings of the Thirty-Second AAAI Conference on Artificial Intelligence 2018, pp. 4058–4065 (2018)
27. Shu, R., Bui, H.H., Narui, H., Ermon, S.: A DIRT-T approach to unsupervised domain adaptation. arXiv preprint arXiv:1802.08735 (2018)
28. Srivastava, N., Hinton, G., Krizhevsky, A., Sutskever, I., Salakhutdinov, R.: Dropout: a simple way to prevent neural networks from overfitting. J. Mach. Learn. Res. 15, 1929–1958 (2014)
29. Sugiyama, M., Krauledat, M., MĂžller, K.R.: Covariate shift adaptation by importance weighted cross validation. JMLR 8, 985–1005 (2007)
30. Tarvainen, A., Valpola, H.: Mean teachers are better role models: weight-averaged consistency targets improve semi-supervised deep learning results. In: Advances in NeurIPS, pp. 1195–1204 (2017)
31. Tzeng, E., Hoffman, J., Darrell, T., Saenko, K.: Simultaneous deep transfer across domains and tasks. In: Proceedings of the IEEE ICCV, pp. 4068–4076 (2015)
32. Tzeng, E., Hoffman, J., Saenko, K., Darrell, T.: Adversarial discriminative domain adaptation. In: IEEE CVPR, pp. 7167–7176 (2017)
33. Venkateswara, H., Chakraborty, S., Panchanathan, S.: Deep-learning systems for domain adaptation in computer vision: learning transferable feature representations. IEEE Signal Process. Mag. 34(6), 117–129 (2017)
34. Venkateswara, H., Eusebio, J., Chakraborty, S., Panchanathan, S.: Deep hashing network for unsupervised domain adaptation. In: CVPR, pp. 5018–5027 (2017)
35. Vu, T.H., Jain, H., Bucher, M., Cord, M., Pérez, P.: Advent: adversarial entropy minimization for domain adaptation in semantic segmentation. In: CVPR, pp. 2517–2526 (2019)

36. You, K., Long, M., Cao, Z., Wang, J., Jordan, M.: Universal domain adaptation. In: The IEEE Conference on CVPR, June 2019
37. Zagoruyko, S., Komodakis, N.: Paying more attention to attention: improving the performance of convolutional neural networks via attention transfer. arXiv preprint arXiv:1612.03928 (2016)

Domain Adaptive Fusion for Adaptive Image Classification

Andrew Dudley, Bhadrinath Nagabandi[(✉)], Hemanth Venkateswara,
and Sethuraman Panchanathan

Arizona State University, Tempe, AZ 85281, USA
{addudley,bnagaban,hemanthv,panch}@asu.edu

Abstract. Recent works in the development of deep adaptation networks have yielded progressive improvement on unsupervised domain adaptive classification tasks by reducing the distribution discrepancy between source and target domains. In parallel, the unification of dominant semi-supervised learning techniques has illustrated the unprecedented potential for utilizing unlabeled data to train a classification model in defiance of a discouragingly meager labeled dataset. In this paper, we propose Domain Adaptive Fusion (DAF), a novel domain adaptation algorithm that encourages a domain-invariant linear relationship between the pixel-space of different domains and the prediction-space while being trained under a domain adversarial signal. The thoughtful combination of key components in unsupervised domain adaptation and semi-supervised learning enable DAF to effectively bridge the gap between source and target domains. Experiments performed on computer vision benchmark datasets for domain adaptation endorse the efficacy of our hybrid approach, outperforming all of the baseline architectures on most of the transfer tasks.

Keywords: Domain adaptation · Semi supervised learning · Entropy regularization · Domain-shift

1 Introduction

Supervised learning methods used to train deep neural networks have enabled the development of models with exceptional performance on a wide array of computer vision tasks; however, the performance of such a model can suffer from rapid degradation when they are applied to target domains that differ from the domains on which they were trained. For example, a machine learning model trained to perform lung segmentation on chest x-rays using images from one x-ray machine may fail to generalize well on x-rays taken at a different hospital using a different machine [3]. One solution to this problem would be to fine-tune the model after collecting new labels from the target domain, but doing so is often prohibitively expensive and in many cases impossible. Instead, unsupervised domain adaptation approaches seek to improve the overall performance of

© Springer Nature Switzerland AG 2020
T. McDaniel et al. (Eds.): ICSM 2019, LNCS 12015, pp. 357–371, 2020.
https://doi.org/10.1007/978-3-030-54407-2_30

the model without needing to collect any additional labels by utilizing both the labeled data in the source domain *and* the unlabeled data in the target domain.

The crux of domain adaptation problems is generally seen to lie in the assumption that there is a domain gap between the source and target distributions. By bridging this domain gap, the source distribution becomes aligned with the target distribution and machine learning models trained on the source domain can be extended and adapted to the target domain. Deep neural networks have demonstrated excellent feature learning capabilities that yield generalized and transferable features that help reduce the domain gap [38].

Merely aligning the feature distributions of the domains isn't the end of the problem. Once aligned, a transductive approach utilizing the labeled source data and the unlabeled data together to inform a joint model for both the domains must still be found. We hypothesize that when the domain distributions are aligned, the domain adaptation problem is identical to a semi supervised learning (SSL) problem. The labeled data and the unlabeled data in the SSL problem are similar to the source data and the target data respectively. In other words, ameliorating the domain gap can be seen as reducing a domain adaptation problem to a semi supervised learning (SSL) problem, allowing us to apply SSL based algorithms to solve the domain adaptation problem.

In this paper, we propose the Domain Adaptive Fusion (DAF) model – a deep neural network that aligns feature distributions of the source and target and applies a fusion method to combine source and target data to estimate robust solutions for the target. The DAF architecture has a feature extractor driven by a domain adversarial network that reduces domain discrepancy between the source and the target [7]. DAF fuses images from the source and target creating a convex linear combination and trains the network to predict a fusion of the corresponding labels. Training the DAF on fused data helps the model to gradually transition from being able to classify source data to being able to classify target data.

The contributions in this work are as follows; (1) we align the features of the source and target and reduce the domain adaptation problem to a semi supervised learning (SSL) problem thereby allowing us to deploy a rich array of transductive algorithms from SSL literature, (2) we introduce a domain fusion model that further reduces the domain discrepancy by training on fused samples from the source and target domains. We evaluate the performance of our model on image classification tasks using two popular datasets; Office-31 [27] and Office-Home [34]. The Domain Adaptive Fusion network produces admirable results, outperforming the state-of-the-art techniques across multiple experiments even without tuning the hyperparameters for each domain.

2   Related Work

2.1   Unsupervised Domain Adaptation

A variety of different methods have been explored towards learning to align the feature spaces between a source and target domain, the majority of which fall under two categories: *adversarial training* [6,31,32] and *moment matching* [18,20,21,33].

Adversarial Training. GANs [10] first introduced the idea of using a discriminative module to adversarially train a generative network in order to improve its ability to produce realistic, fake data samples. This was accomplished by training a discriminator D to accurately predict the label for real and fake samples, while simultaneously training a generator G to minimize $\log(1 - D(G))$ and thus to generate fake samples that will fool D into thinking they're real.

Inspired by the discriminative mechanism used for measuring the distribution discrepancy in GANs, Domain Adversarial Neural Networks (DANN) [6] introduced a similar mechanism with the goal of minimizing the discrepancy for domain adaptation by training a feature extractor to instead confuse a domain discriminator. The simplicity and effectiveness of the DANN architecture has resulted in extensive utilization of this technique in domain adaptation literature, including: class-level predictions using multiple domain discriminators conditioned on the softmax predictions of the classifier [4]; combinations of global feature domain discriminators augmented with domain-specific loss functions for learning semantic details of the domains [3,30]; leveraging multiple local domain discriminators and a global discriminator as attention mechanisms for fine-grained transfer [37]; and using the output of domain discriminators as sample-level weighting mechanisms in various domain adaptation settings [2,39,41].

2.2   Semi Supervised Learning

The semi supervised learning (SSL) paradigm consists of a labeled training set $\mathcal{X}_l = \{(\boldsymbol{x}_i, \boldsymbol{y}_i)\}_{i=1}^n$ and an unlabeled training set $\mathcal{X}_u = \{\boldsymbol{x}_i\}_{i=1}^n$. The goal is then to use all of the training data available to learn a model that can either predict the labels for the entire feature space (as in *inductive* learning), or in some cases to only predict the labels of the unlabeled data $\mathcal{X}_u$ (as in *transductive* learning). Domain adaptation is closely related to SSL, with one key distinction: SSL assumes all of the data points are sampled under the same distribution, whereas domain adaptation assumes that the features of the source and target datasets are governed by different probability distributions. This similarity between the two areas of machine-learning research makes many SSL techniques naturally suitable for domain adaptive settings.

Entropy Minimization: When no labeled data is available, assumptions about the structure of the data distribution or geometry must be made in order to identify meaningful patterns within it. A common assumption in classification tasks is that data from the same class will form clusters within the feature space, and is aptly known as the *cluster assumption*. The entropy minimization principle [11] is often used to coax deep neural networks into producing such clusters by noting that the classification of unlabeled samples should be confident, and confident predictions lead to lower entropy on the prediction vector. Minimizing the entropy of the unlabeled data predictions therefore encourages low-density separation of the of the feature embeddings.

In SSL, entropy minimization can be implemented explicitly by adding the entropy of the prediction vector for the unlabeled data to the loss function [11]. Pseudo-labelling [16] – a method of supervised learning on unlabeled data by treating the highest probability prediction as the true label – can be seen as an equivalent, implicit implementation of entropy minimization. Similarly, by taking the average prediction of multiple augmentations of the same unlabeled input, a sharpening function can be applied to that prediction in order to produce a soft pseudo-label with lower entropy [1]. Training with these sharpened pseudo-labels also implicitly minimizes the entropy.

Consistency Regularization: Consistency-based learning methods exploit the smoothness assumption of SSL by ensuring that an input sample is consistently mapped to the same point in the feature space or label space. In the π-model [15], each input is passed through the model twice with different dropout initializations, and the mean squared difference of the predictions is penalized. The Mean-Teacher model [29] asserts consistency on the weights of the network by materializing a "Teacher" network whose weights are the exponential moving average (EMA) of the "Student's". In [17], certainty-driven consistency loss (CCL) is proposed for Mean-Teacher models to either filter or weight the impact of consistency training at the instance-level by measuring the predictive variance of each sample with different augmentations. For the Domain Adaptive Fusion network, multiple augmentations of each unlabeled sample are evaluated and then assigned the averaged, sharpened prediction for that sample as a label to encourage consistent predictions.

Standard Regularization: Machine learning algorithms generally seek to learn a generalized function from the dataset they're trained on. Regularization penalties are often imposed in order to avoid overfitting to the data and thus to improve the generalizability of the learned model. The expansive number of weights in large neural networks make them particularly prone to memorization of the data when effective regularization is not employed. A simple and effective method of moderating the complexity of a model is by penalizing the magnitude of the weights by including the sum of the squared weights in the loss function – a procedure called $\mathcal{L}_2$ regularization [14,23]. Mixup [40] – a data augmentation-based regularization technique – was proposed to compel models to learn a linear continuity between convex combinations of the input features and their corresponding classification labels. The usefulness of Mixup regularization has since been studied in the realm of semi supervised learning problems, including in the recently developed MixMatch algorithm [1], which uses a combination of mixup, label sharpening, and entropy minimization principles to produce a holistic objective function for utilizing unlabeled data. The outstanding results of MixMatch inspired our interest in exploring the combined efficacy of these techniques when applied to various settings of domain adaptation, where discrepancies between the marginal distributions of the labeled and unlabeled datasets introduce challenges not faced by the preceding studies. Domain Adaptive Fusion – the result of this exploration – is discussed in the following sections.

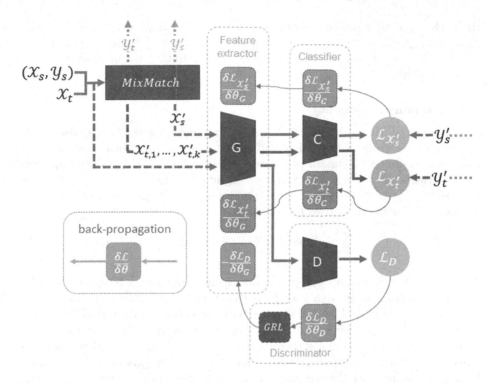

Fig. 1. The Domain Adaptive Fusion architecture. The neural network modules for the feature extractor G, classifier C and domain discriminator D. GRL is the gradient reversal layer. `MixMatch` outputs: **(1)** the domain-fused source batch $(\mathcal{X}'_s, \mathcal{Y}'_s)$ used for the supervised learning task (light blue) and **(2)** K domain-fused target batches with pseudolabels $(\{\mathcal{X}'_{t,1}, \ldots, \mathcal{X}'_{t,k}\}, \mathcal{Y}'_t)$ used for the semi supervised learning task (green). The original source and target batches $\mathcal{X}_s, \mathcal{X}_t$ are used for domain alignment (orange). (Color figure online)

3   Domain Adaptive Fusion

In unsupervised domain adaptation we have labeled data from the source domain; $\mathcal{D}_s = \{x_i^s, y_i^s\}_{i=1}^{n_s}$, and unlabeled data from the target domain; $\mathcal{D}_t = \{x_i^t\}_{i=1}^{n_t}$. The data points x_i^* belong to an input space denoted by X and the labels belong to a discrete space $y_i^* \in Y := \{1, \ldots, \mathcal{C}\}$. The goal is to determine the unknown target data labels given the constraint that the source and target data joint distributions are different, i.e., $P_s(X, Y) \neq P_t(X, Y)$. We introduce Domain Adaptive Fusion (DAF), a deep neural network which performs domain alignment and domain fusion to achieve domain adaptation. The DAF has parameters $\theta := \{\theta_G, \theta_D, \theta_C\}$, where θ_G are the parameters for the base feature extractor component G, θ_D are the parameters for the domain alignment component D and θ_C are the parameters for the classifier C. The different components of the DAF and the gradient paths are illustrated in Fig. 1. In the following section we outline the different components of the DAF network. When training the DAF, we deploy mini-batches of size $2B$ with B samples $\mathcal{X}_s = \{x_i^s\}_{i=1}^B$ and $\mathcal{Y}_s = \{y_i^s\}_{i=1}^B$ from source and B samples $\mathcal{X}_t = \{x_i^t\}_{i=1}^B$ from the target. We describe the model in terms of mini-batches and note that it can be extended to the entire dataset.

3.1 Domain Alignment

In order to reduce the domain adaptation problem to a semi supervised one, we align the features of the source and target. For G to output domain-aligned features we adopt the domain confusion model from DaNN [7], to train an auxiliary network D to align the features output from G. If $d \in \{1,0\}$ are the domain labels where $d = 1$ for source samples and $d = 0$ for target samples, the discriminator network D tries to minimize,

$$\mathcal{L}_D = -\frac{1}{2B} \sum_{x \in \{\mathcal{X}_s \cup \mathcal{X}_t\}} d\log[D(G(x))] + (1-d)(1 - \log[D(G(x))]), \qquad (1)$$

where $D(G(x))$, is the output probability from a sigmoid activation. The discriminator is trained through back propagation to minimize $\mathcal{L}_D$, i.e., distinguish between the source and target samples. On the other hand, a gradient reversal (GRL in Fig. 1) is applied to modify the parameters of G in an adversarial manner in order to align the source and target features and make them indistinguishable to the discriminator. This involves reversing the gradient $-\frac{\partial \mathcal{L}_D}{\partial \theta_G}$ during back propagation over the parameters in G. The domain alignment component ensures that the source and target features output from $G(.)$ have no little to no domain discrepancy.

3.2 Domain Fusion

With domain alignment in place, the G network plays the role of a feature extractor that aligns the source and target data features. This reduces the domain adaptation problem to a semi supervised learning problem with the source data being treated as the labeled set and the target data becoming the unlabeled set. In the following we outline the steps to implement domain fusion.

Data Augmentation. As is common with semi supervised learning procedures, we estimate artificial labels for the target data using consistency regularization techniques [22,29,42]. We augment the training data with multiple stochastic transformations of the input x to yield different versions of the input that have the same label. Data augmentation is performed on the input vectors for both the source and target batches using an $\texttt{Augment}(x)$ function, which performs random flips and crops on the input image x. The source inputs are augmented once, and the target inputs are augmented K times to produce K different augmentations of the target batch:

$$\hat{\mathcal{X}}_s = \{\texttt{Augment}(x_i^s)\}_{i=1}^B \qquad \hat{\mathcal{X}}_t = \{\texttt{Augment}(x_i^t)_k\}_{i=1,k=1}^{B,K} \qquad (2)$$

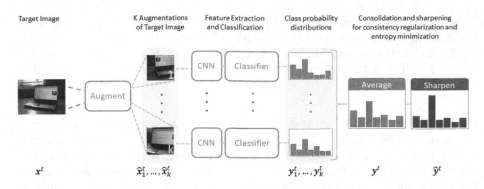

Fig. 2. Soft pseudo labels for the target. We apply K augmentations and estimate the predictions $y_1^t, \ldots, y_K^t$. These are consolidated and sharpened to produce a single soft pseudo label $\hat{y}^t$.

Soft Pseudo Labeling. We perform consistency regularization on the unlabeled data by ensuring that the same pseudo-label is assigned to each of the K augmented versions of an input image x. These pseudo-labels are generated by first predicting a soft label $y_{i,k}^t$ for each $x_{i,k}^t \in \hat{\mathcal{X}}_t$, with,

$$y_{i,k}^t = C(G(x_{i,k}^t)) \quad \forall i \in \{1, \ldots, B\}, k \in \{1, \ldots, K\}, \tag{3}$$

where $C(.)$ is the classifier network and $C(G(x))$ gives the softmax output from the classifier network - a probability vector $y_{i,k}^t = [p_{i,k}^{1,t}, \ldots, p_{i,k}^{C,t}]^\top$ over C classes, where $p_{i,k}^{c,t}$ is the probability $p(y_{i,k}^t = c | x_{i,k}^t)$. To arrive at a consistent prediction for the unlabeled data, we average over the K predictions and estimate a common label for each of the augmented input images $\{x_{i,1}^t, \ldots, x_{i,K}^t\}$:

$$y_i^t = \frac{1}{K} \sum_{k=1}^{K} y_{i,k}^t \quad \forall i \in \{1, \ldots, B\}. \tag{4}$$

Following the approach proposed in MixMatch [1], we encourage the low-density separation of class assignments to target data samples by implicitly exploiting the minimum entropy criterion using a sharpening function on y_i^t. Specifically,

$$\hat{y}_{i,k}^t = \frac{(y_i^t)^{1/T}}{\sum_{c=1}^{C}(y_i^{c,t})^{1/T}} \quad \forall i \in \{1, \ldots, B\}, k \in \{1, \ldots, K\}, \tag{5}$$

where the hyperparameter T controls the *temperature* of the distribution [9]. As $T \to 0$, $\hat{y}_{i,k}^t$ approaches the Dirac-delta function, which will produce one-hot labels. The pseudo labels $\hat{y}_{i,k}^t$ are then assigned to their corresponding input vectors in $\hat{\mathcal{X}}_t$, with all the K augmentations of $x_{i,k}^t$ for $k \in \{1, \ldots, K\}$ assigned the same pseudo label $\hat{y}_{i,k}^t$ for $k \in \{1, \ldots, K\}$. The data augmentation for the source results in the modified datasets, $\hat{\mathcal{X}}_s$ (Eq. 2) with one-hot labels $\hat{\mathcal{Y}}_s$ where

$\hat{\mathcal{Y}}_s$ is one-hot vector representation of source data labels $\mathcal{Y}_s = \{y_i^s\}_{i=1}^B$. Likewise, the data augmentation followed by pseudo labeling for the target dataset yields $\hat{\mathcal{X}}_t$ (Eq. 2) and the corresponding labels $\hat{\mathcal{Y}}_s$ where $\hat{\mathcal{Y}}_s = \{\hat{\boldsymbol{y}}_{i,k}^t\} \forall i \in \{1, \ldots, B\}, k \in \{1, \ldots, K\}$. The data augmentation and pseudo label generation is depicted in Fig. 2.

Data Fusion. The DAF network is trained on data generated from the fusion of source and target samples. Our hypothesis is that a model with linear behavior across domains will be an effective classifier for data from both the domains. Once the domains are aligned, DAF is trained using a convex combination of data from both the domains along with a convex combination of their corresponding labels. We employ the `MixUp` procedure [40] to enforce a linear behavior between data from the two domains. We constrain the DAF model output for a convex combination of inputs to be similar to the convex combination of the DAF model outputs over the individual inputs. We create a unified set of augmented data samples, $\hat{\mathcal{X}}_M = \{\hat{\mathcal{X}}_s \cup \hat{\mathcal{X}}_t\}$ by concatenating and shuffling the augmented source and target datasets. Likewise, we create the unified label set $\hat{\mathcal{Y}}_M = \{\hat{\mathcal{Y}}_s \cup \hat{\mathcal{Y}}_t\}$ all the while maintaining the order between data in $\hat{\mathcal{X}}_M$ and their labels in $\hat{\mathcal{Y}}_M$. The fusion dataset is created using the *MixUp* procedure,

$$\mathcal{X}_s' = \text{MixUp}(\hat{\mathcal{X}}_s, \{\hat{\mathcal{X}}_{M,i}\}_{i=1}^B, \alpha) \qquad \mathcal{Y}_s' = \text{MixUp}(\hat{\mathcal{Y}}_s, \{\hat{\mathcal{Y}}_{M,i}\}_{i=1}^B, \alpha) \qquad (6)$$

$$\mathcal{X}_t' = \text{MixUp}(\hat{\mathcal{X}}_t, \{\hat{\mathcal{X}}_{M,i}\}_{i=B+1}^{|\hat{\mathcal{X}}_M|}, \alpha) \qquad \mathcal{Y}_t' = \text{MixUp}(\hat{\mathcal{Y}}_t, \{\hat{\mathcal{Y}}_{M,i}\}_{i=B+1}^{|\hat{\mathcal{Y}}_M|}, \alpha). \qquad (7)$$

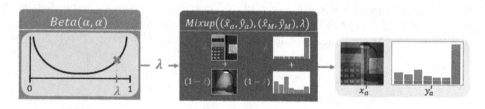

Fig. 3. Illustration of the mixup function, where $(\hat{\boldsymbol{x}}_a, \hat{\boldsymbol{y}}_a) \in (\hat{\mathcal{X}}_s \| \hat{\mathcal{X}}_t, \hat{\mathcal{Y}}_s \| \hat{\mathcal{Y}}_t)$, and $(\hat{\boldsymbol{x}}_M, \hat{\boldsymbol{y}}_M) \in (\hat{\mathcal{X}}_M, \hat{\mathcal{Y}}_M)$. $(\boldsymbol{x}_a', \boldsymbol{y}_a')$ represents an augmented, mixed-up, labeled datum that will be used during the training phase of Domain Adaptive Fusion.

The `Mixup`(X_1, X_2, α), takes two equal sized sets as input along with hyperparameter α. It then performs a linear combination of elements from X_1 and X_2 to create a fused dataset of the same size as X_1. Mixup samples a mixing value λ from the U-shaped $Beta(\alpha, \alpha)$ distribution, where $0 < \alpha < 1$. As alpha approaches 0, $Beta(\alpha, \alpha)$ approaches the Bernoulli distribution. We illustrate `MixUp`() with an example. Let $\boldsymbol{x}_1^i \in X_1$ and $\boldsymbol{x}_2^i \in X_2$ be the ith elements of X_1 and X_2. Let Y_1 and Y_2 be the labels corresponding to X_1 and X_2. If $\boldsymbol{y}_1^i \in Y_1$ and $\boldsymbol{y}_2^i \in Y_2$ are the ith elements of Y_1 and Y_2. Then, the fusion of `MixUp`$(\{\boldsymbol{x}_1^i\}, \{\boldsymbol{x}_2^i\}, alpha)$ and `MixUp`$(\{\boldsymbol{y}_1^i\}, \{\boldsymbol{y}_2^i\}, alpha)$, would yield,

$$x_i' = \lambda x_1^i + (1 - \lambda)x_2^i \tag{8}$$

$$y_i' = \lambda y_1^i + (1 - \lambda)y_2^i \tag{9}$$

In practice we set $\lambda = \lambda_{max} = \max(\lambda, (1 - \lambda))$. This is in order to ensure that the majority of the mixing weight is given to the original sample of the batch being mixed (samples from the first argument of the mixup function). The data fusion procedure is illustrated in Fig. 3. The data fusion component creates fused samples from domain-aligned source and target samples and trains the DAF model to predict their fused labels. In practice, the data augmentation procedure is treated as auxiliary to the training process. This is accomplished by detaching the augmented batches $\mathcal{X}_s'$ and $\mathcal{X}_t'$ from the network to prevent the flow of the gradient through the augmentation steps during backpropagation.

3.3   Objective Function

The DAF network is guided by the following objectives functions. The fused source batch $(\mathcal{X}_s', \mathcal{Y}_s')$ is used to minimize the cross-entropy objective,

$$\mathcal{L}_s = \frac{1}{|\mathcal{X}_s'|} \sum_{x_i'^s \in \mathcal{X}_s', y_i'^s \in \mathcal{Y}_s'} \mathrm{KL}(y_i'^s \| C(G(x_i'^s))), \tag{10}$$

where KL stands for Kullback-Leibler divergence, which estimates the cross-entropy between labels $y_i'^s$ and DAF prediction $C(G(x_i'^s))$. Where $\mathcal{Y}_s'$ is guaranteed to be a fusion predominantly of ground-truth knowledge, the pseudo-labels for the target batch $\mathcal{Y}_t'$ are predominantly artificial, and are therefore assumed to be less confident. In view of these less confident labels, we apply the Brier score [1], which is less sensitive to outliers and is bounded. This is a standard loss function for unlabeled data in semi-supervised learning literature [15]. The objective function for the unlabeled data is given by,

$$\mathcal{L}_t = \frac{1}{|\mathcal{X}_t'|} \sum_{x_{i,k}'^t \in \mathcal{X}_t', y_{i,k}'^t \in \mathcal{Y}_t'} \left\| y_{i,k}'^s - C(G(x_{i,k}'^s)) \right\|_2^2, \tag{11}$$

Finally, to discourage DAF from overfitting to the training data, the $L2$ regularization loss is applied across the layer of the network's parameters,

$$\mathcal{L}_2 = \sum_{\theta_i \in \theta} \|\theta_i\|_2^2. \tag{12}$$

DAF Objective Function. The objective for the DAF model is estimated from Eqs. (1), (10), (11) and (12). In each iteration the DAF objective is determined by a two-player, minimax game,

$$(\theta_G, \theta_C) = \arg \min_{\theta_G, \theta_C} [\mathcal{L}_s - \lambda \mathcal{L}_D + \gamma \mathcal{L}_t + \eta \mathcal{L}_2] \tag{13}$$

$$(\theta_D) = \arg \max_{\theta_D} [-\lambda \mathcal{L}_D - \eta \mathcal{L}_2] \tag{14}$$

where, λ, γ and η are hyerparameters that control the importance of the corresponding terms in the DAF objective.

4   Experiments

In this section, we describe the datasets and implementation details used to evaluate Domain Adaptive Fusion.

4.1   Datasets

Office-31: The *Office-31* dataset [27] is a de-facto standard in computer vision for benchmarking domain adaptation techniques. It consists of three domains – Amazon (**A**), Webcam (**W**), and DSLR (**D**) – with 31 categories of images in each domain, and 4,652 images in total. Images in the Amazon dataset were collected from amazon.com, while the images from Webcam and DSLR are taken with a webcam and digital SLR camera, respectively.

Office-Home: The *Office-Home* dataset [34] consists of approximately 15,500 images of common household and office objects. With 65 categories and four unique domains, this dataset constitutes a more challenging set of domain adaptation tasks as compared to *Office-31*. The domains include Art (**Ar**), Clipart (**Cl**), Product (**Pr**), and Real World (**Rw**).

4.2   Implementation

The network architecture and training procedures of DAF were implemented in PyTorch. The feature extractor is comprised of a Resnet50 model [12] with weights pre-trained on the ImageNet dataset [5], which is fine-tuned during the training process. The domain adversarial discriminator is implemented using a gradient reversal layer with a ramp-up coefficient calculated at each iteration of the training process. Our DAF model was built on top of the `CDAN codebase`[1] for loading image datasets and training parameters, and utilizes network class definitions provided by the `easydl`[2] deep learning utilities library.

An Adam optimizer [13] is used for weight updates, where η is provided as the weight decay parameter for implementing the $\mathcal{L}_2$ regularization. All experiments were conducted with a batch size of 16 on a single Tesla V100 or Titan X using the following hyperparameter values: $\alpha = 0.75, \gamma = 30, \lambda = 1.5, \eta = 0.04$. The learning rate was initialized at 0.001 for the classifier, domain discriminator, and bottleneck layer, and to 0.0001 for the ResNet50 model.

5   Results

The results of DAF on the domain adaptive computer vision classification tasks for the *Office-31* and *Office-Home* datasets are reported in Tables 1 and 2, respectively. The average reported performance values for each of the baseline models are compared against a single complete training run of DAF for each experimental setting.

---

[1] https://github.com/thuml/CDAN.
[2] https://github.com/thuml/easydl.

Table 1. Accuracy of domain adaptation tasks on *Office-31*

Method	A→W	D→W	W→D	A→D	D→A	W→A	Avg
ResNet [12]	68.4	96.7	99.3	68.9	62.5	60.7	76.08
TCA [24]	72.7	96.7	99.6	74.1	61.7	60.9	77.62
GFK [8]	72.8	95.0	98.2	74.5	63.4	61.0	77.48
DAN [18]	80.5	97.1	99.6	78.6	63.6	62.8	80.37
RTN [20]	84.5	96.8	99.4	77.5	66.2	64.8	81.53
DANN [7]	82.0	96.9	99.1	79.7	68.2	67.4	82.22
ADDA [32]	86.2	96.2	98.4	77.8	69.5	68.9	82.83
JAN [21]	85.4	97.4	99.8	84.7	68.6	70.0	84.32
MADA [25]	90.0	97.4	99.6	87.8	70.3	66.4	85.25
SimNet [26]	88.6	98.2	99.7	85.3	**73.4**	**71.6**	86.13
GTA [28]	89.5	97.9	99.8	87.7	72.8	71.4	**86.52**
CGAA [36]	75.2	95.7	99.6	72.3	57.2	57.5	76.25
DAF	**92.33**	**99.25**	**100.0**	**88.35**	68.12	70.22	86.38

On the *Office-31* dataset, DAF outperformed all baselines on the **A → W, D → W, A → D**, and **W → D** adaptive transfer tasks. Compared to DANN, DAF obtained a 10.3% performance improvement on **A → W** and an average 4.2% increase across all Office-31 experiments, indicating that the learning signal provided by the joint semi supervised learning techniques on unlabeled target data significantly improves the model's effectiveness on the target domain. On the more challenging dataset of *Office-Home*, the performance of DAF exceeds all domain adaptation baseline methods on most of the transfer tasks.

5.1   Feature Visualization

To analyze the combined effects of our hybrid regularization techniques, two-dimensional t-SNE embeddings for the features extracted from ResNet-50,

Table 2. Accuracy of domain adaptation tasks on *Office-Home*

Method	Ar→Cl	Ar→Pr	Ar→Rw	Cl→Ar	Cl→Pr	Cl→Rw	Pr→Ar	Pr→Cl	Pr→Rw	Rw→Ar	Rw→Cl	Rw→Pr	Avg
ResNet [12]	34.9	50.0	58.0	37.4	41.9	46.2	38.5	31.2	60.4	53.9	41.2	59.9	46.13
DAN [18]	43.6	57.0	67.9	45.8	56.5	60.4	44.0	43.6	67.7	63.1	51.5	74.3	56.28
DANN [7]	45.6	59.3	70.1	47.0	58.5	60.9	46.1	43.7	68.5	63.2	51.5	76.8	57.60
JAN [21]	45.9	61.2	68.9	50.4	59.7	61.0	45.8	43.4	70.3	63.9	52.4	76.8	58.31
CGAA [36]	43.4	57.1	67.6	49.9	57.7	58.3	51.7	43.5	66.2	59.9	51.7	74.9	56.83
CDAN [19]	49.0	69.3	**74.5**	54.4	66.0	**68.4**	55.6	48.3	75.9	**68.4**	55.4	80.5	63.81
EasyTL [35]	**52.8**	**72.1**	75.9	55.0	65.9	67.6	54.5	46.9	74.7	63.8	52.3	78.0	63.30
DAF	48.8	66.1	73.5	**57.9**	**68.9**	67.9	**55.7**	**49.5**	**79.9**	68.3	**58.8**	**82.2**	**64.79**

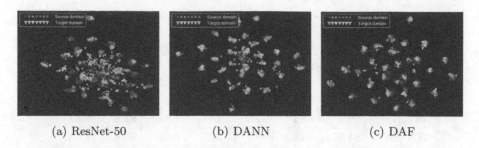

(a) ResNet-50   (b) DANN   (c) DAF

Fig. 4. t-SNE visualizations of the learned features from (a) ResNet-50, (b) DANN, and (c) DAF on the **A**→**W** transfer task. (circles: **A**, triangles: **W**). *Best viewed in color.*

DANN, and DAF are visualized in Figs. 4(a) to 4(c) for the **A**→**W** transfer task. The feature representations of the source and target domains are made increasingly less distinguishable, with DAF producing more defined clusters. The improved visualization of DAF suggests that it successfully reduced the domain discrepancy by learning to bridge the gap between source and target distributions.

6   Conclusions and Future Work

Domain Adaptive Fusion was proposed to demonstrate the efficacy of fusing data from different domains to perform domain adaptation. In the DAF model we align the data from different domains and randomly sample data points along lines connecting two samples and train a deep neural network to predict the combined. We find that the DAF model trained using semi supervised techniques produces competitive results compared to the state-of-the-art techniques and in some cases outperforms them. The DAF model validates our assumption that domain adaptation problems can be reduced to semi supervised learning problems by aligning the domains. This enables us to apply a rich suite of algorithms from SSL literature to solve domain adaptation problems. We hope to further explore the potential of this unified architecture, including the application of various attention- and confidence weighting-based methods to the fusion and training of samples from different domains, as well as the implications of this cross-domain mixup strategy when applied to different levels of the learned feature representations.

Acknowledgements. The authors thank ASU, Adidas, and the National Science Foundation for their funding support. This material is partially based upon work supported by Adidas and by the National Science Foundation under Grant No. 1828010.

References

1. Berthelot, D., Carlini, N., Goodfellow, I., Papernot, N., Oliver, A., Raffel, C.: Mixmatch: a holistic approach to semi-supervised learning. arXiv preprint arXiv:1905.02249 (2019)
2. Cao, Z., You, K., Long, M., Wang, J., Yang, Q.: Learning to transfer examples for partial domain adaptation. arXiv preprint arXiv:1903.12230 (2019)
3. Chen, C., Dou, Q., Chen, H., Heng, P.-A.: Semantic-aware generative adversarial nets for unsupervised domain adaptation in chest X-Ray segmentation. In: Shi, Y., Suk, H.-I., Liu, M. (eds.) MLMI 2018. LNCS, vol. 11046, pp. 143–151. Springer, Cham (2018). https://doi.org/10.1007/978-3-030-00919-9_17
4. Chen, Y.H., et al.: No more discrimination: cross city adaptation of road scene segmenters. In: Proceedings of the IEEE International Conference on Computer Vision, pp. 1992–2001 (2017)
5. Deng, J., Dong, W., Socher, R., Li, L.J., Li, K., Fei-Fei, L.: ImageNet: a large-scale hierarchical image database. In: CVPR09 (2009)
6. Ganin, Y., Lempitsky, V.: Unsupervised domain adaptation by backpropagation. arXiv preprint arXiv:1409.7495 (2014)
7. Ganin, Y., et al.: Domain-adversarial training of neural networks. J. Mach. Learn. Res. **17**(1), 2096–2330 (2016)
8. Gong, B., Shi, Y., Sha, F., Grauman, K.: Geodesic flow kernel for unsupervised domain adaptation. In: 2012 IEEE Conference on Computer Vision and Pattern Recognition, pp. 2066–2073. IEEE (2012)
9. Goodfellow, I., Bengio, Y., Courville, A.: Deep Learning. MIT Press (2016)
10. Goodfellow, I., et al.: Generative adversarial nets. In: Advances in Neural Information Processing Systems, pp. 2672–2680 (2014)
11. Grandvalet, Y., Bengio, Y.: Semi-supervised learning by entropy minimization. In: Advances in Neural Information Processing Systems, pp. 529–536 (2005)
12. He, K., Zhang, X., Ren, S., Sun, J.: Deep residual learning for image recognition. In: Proceedings of the IEEE Conference on Computer Vision and Pattern Recognition, pp. 770–778 (2016)
13. Kingma, D.P., Ba, J.: Adam: A method for stochastic optimization. arXiv preprint arXiv:1412.6980 (2014)
14. Krogh, A., Hertz, J.A.: A simple weight decay can improve generalization. In: Advances in Neural Information Processing Systems, pp. 950–957 (1992)
15. Laine, S., Aila, T.: Temporal ensembling for semi-supervised learning. arXiv preprint arXiv:1610.02242 (2016)
16. Lee, D.H.: Pseudo-label: the simple and efficient semi-supervised learning method for deep neural networks. In: Workshop on Challenges in Representation Learning, ICML, vol. 3, p. 2 (2013)
17. Li, Y., Liu, L., Tan, R.T.: Certainty-driven consistency loss for semi-supervised learning. arXiv preprint arXiv:1901.05657 (2019)
18. Long, M., Cao, Y., Wang, J., Jordan, M.I.: Learning transferable features with deep adaptation networks. arXiv preprint arXiv:1502.02791 (2015)
19. Long, M., Cao, Z., Wang, J., Jordan, M.I.: Conditional adversarial domain adaptation. In: Advances in Neural Information Processing Systems, pp. 1640–1650 (2018)
20. Long, M., Zhu, H., Wang, J., Jordan, M.I.: Unsupervised domain adaptation with residual transfer networks. In: Advances in Neural Information Processing Systems, pp. 136–144 (2016)

21. Long, M., Zhu, H., Wang, J., Jordan, M.I.: Deep transfer learning with joint adaptation networks. In: Proceedings of the 34th International Conference on Machine Learning-Volume 70, pp. 2208–2217. JMLR. org (2017)
22. Miyato, T., Maeda, S.i., Koyama, M., Nakae, K., Ishii, S.: Distributional smoothing with virtual adversarial training. arXiv preprint arXiv:1507.00677 (2015)
23. Ng, A.Y.: Feature selection, l 1 vs. l 2 regularization, and rotational invariance. In: Proceedings of the Twenty-First International Conference on Machine Learning, p. 78. ACM (2004)
24. Pan, S.J., Yang, Q.: A survey on transfer learning. IEEE Trans. Knowl. Data Eng. **22**(10), 1345–1359 (2009)
25. Pei, Z., Cao, Z., Long, M., Wang, J.: Multi-adversarial domain adaptation. In: Thirty-Second AAAI Conference on Artificial Intelligence (2018)
26. Pinheiro, P.O.: Unsupervised domain adaptation with similarity learning. In: Proceedings of the IEEE Conference on Computer Vision and Pattern Recognition, pp. 8004–8013 (2018)
27. Saenko, K., Kulis, B., Fritz, M., Darrell, T.: Adapting visual category models to new domains. In: Daniilidis, K., Maragos, P., Paragios, N. (eds.) ECCV 2010. LNCS, vol. 6314, pp. 213–226. Springer, Heidelberg (2010). https://doi.org/10. 1007/978-3-642-15561-1_16
28. Sankaranarayanan, S., Balaji, Y., Castillo, C.D., Chellappa, R.: Generate to adapt: aligning domains using generative adversarial networks. In: Proceedings of the IEEE Conference on Computer Vision and Pattern Recognition, pp. 8503–8512 (2018)
29. Tarvainen, A., Valpola, H.: Mean teachers are better role models: weight-averaged consistency targets improve semi-supervised deep learning results. In: Advances in Neural Information Processing Systems, pp. 1195–1204 (2017)
30. Tsai, Y.H., Hung, W.C., Schulter, S., Sohn, K., Yang, M.H., Chandraker, M.: Learning to adapt structured output space for semantic segmentation. In: Proceedings of the IEEE Conference on Computer Vision and Pattern Recognition, pp. 7472–7481 (2018)
31. Tzeng, E., Hoffman, J., Darrell, T., Saenko, K.: Simultaneous deep transfer across domains and tasks. In: Proceedings of the IEEE International Conference on Computer Vision, pp. 4068–4076 (2015)
32. Tzeng, E., Hoffman, J., Saenko, K., Darrell, T.: Adversarial discriminative domain adaptation. In: Proceedings of the IEEE Conference on Computer Vision and Pattern Recognition, pp. 7167–7176 (2017)
33. Tzeng, E., Hoffman, J., Zhang, N., Saenko, K., Darrell, T.: Deep domain confusion: maximizing for domain invariance. arXiv preprint arXiv:1412.3474 (2014)
34. Venkateswara, H., Eusebio, J., Chakraborty, S., Panchanathan, S.: Deep hashing network for unsupervised domain adaptation. In: Proceedings of the IEEE Conference on Computer Vision and Pattern Recognition, pp. 5018–5027 (2017)
35. Wang, J., Chen, Y., Yu, H., Huang, M., Yang, Q.: Easy transfer learning by exploiting intra-domain structures. In: IEEE International Conference on Multimedia & Expo (ICME) (2019)
36. Wang, X., Wang, X.: Unsupervised domain adaptation with coupled generative adversarial autoencoders. Appl. Sci. **8**(12), 2529 (2018)
37. Wang, X., Li, L., Ye, W., Long, M., Wang, J.: Transferable attention for domain adaptation (2019)
38. Yosinski, J., Clune, J., Bengio, Y., Lipson, H.: How transferable are features in deep neural networks? In: Advances in Neural Information Processing Systems, pp. 3320–3328 (2014)

39. You, K., Long, M., Cao, Z., Wang, J., Jordan, M.I.: Universal domain adaptation. In: The IEEE Conference on Computer Vision and Pattern Recognition (CVPR) (June 2019)
40. Zhang, H., Cisse, M., Dauphin, Y.N., Lopez-Paz, D.: mixup: beyond empirical risk minimization. arXiv preprint arXiv:1710.09412 (2017)
41. Zhang, J., Ding, Z., Li, W., Ogunbona, P.: Importance weighted adversarial nets for partial domain adaptation. In: Proceedings of the IEEE Conference on Computer Vision and Pattern Recognition, pp. 8156–8164 (2018)
42. Zhou, D., Bousquet, O., Lal, T.N., Weston, J., Schölkopf, B.: Learning with local and global consistency. In: Advances in Neural Information Processing Systems, pp. 321–328 (2004)

Human Body Fall Recognition System

Jannatul Mourey, Ava Sehat Niaki$^{(\boxtimes)}$, Priyanka Kaplish, and Rupali Gupta

Department of Computing Science, University of Alberta, Edmonton, Canada
mourey@ualberta.com,
{asehatni,kaplish,rupali1}@ualberta.ca

Abstract. Falling is one of the major risks for elderly people, kids and people with disabilities. The situation worsens when the victim suffers from serious injuries and is unable to get help on time. In this paper, we propose a method to detect a fall in real-time. The proposed detection method consists of three stages: Video analysis, Body Recognition and Trigger Alert. In this recognition system, human detection algorithms using OpenCV have been implemented. The application accuracy has been tested under different lighting settings and in different environment settings.

Keywords: Fall detection · Video Analysis · Human body recognition · Background subtraction · OpenCV

1 Introduction

Activity recognition and classification is one of the top research topics in computer vision. Automated systems can be developed to store and analyze human activities. The gathered information can be used to capture a fall and report it. Late fall identification may cause some serious and long term injuries. As a result, there is a clear need to develop new technologies to ensure the safety of people suffering from fall-related injuries. Surveillance technologies can help detect falls and mitigate injuries, this can be achieved through three procedures: Video Acquisition, Video Analysis and Notification. This video-based system detects human activity from the streaming video by analyzing each frame to distinguish the moving object from the background. Consequently, the behaviour of the moving object-in this case, the human-is classified as a fall or non-fall motion. This recognition system is designed to perform in real-time. In addition to the video-based fall recognition method, there are various sensor-based techniques that have been developed using pressure, acceleration and sound sensors to detect a fall. However, the major advantage of vision-based systems over sensor-based systems is that the subject is not required to wear gadgets at all times. The sensor-based systems are especially at a disadvantage if the test subject forgets to wear the sensor. A camera, however, is not dependent on the test subjects. Another advantage of a vision-based system is the considerable data that can be gathered from the subjects. In addition to recognizing a fall, the

© Springer Nature Switzerland AG 2020
T. McDaniel et al. (Eds.): ICSM 2019, LNCS 12015, pp. 372–380, 2020.
https://doi.org/10.1007/978-3-030-54407-2_31

detection algorithm can analyze the severity of a fall by calculating how much time the subject took to rise to a stable condition if he/she was able to get up at all. Besides detecting falls, this vision-based technology can be expanded to recognize other human activities using a camera and data processing.

2 Related Work

The majority of fall detection systems can be classified into three categories: Wearable and Ambient Sensor-based, Machine Learning-based and Vision-based methods. We will analyze each of these methods.

- Sensor-based Method: In this method, external sensors are placed on the subject of interest (SOI). A Wearable Sensor-based method uses an accelerometer sensor that is attached to the subject's body to capture the motion. The wearable sensor approach infers the detection based on embedded sensors which sense the movement and position of the object. The Ambient Sensor-based method uses external sensors including pressure sensors and acoustic sensors to classify human actions [1].
- Vision-based Method (Moment Functions and Depth Image): The most common moment functions used in computer vision applications are Shape Analysis, Shape Deformation, and Postures Estimation. Moment functions can be used to describe the human shape which is approximated by an ellipse. Ellipse Approximation and Bounding Box both can be adapted for best results under different environments. The Support Vector Machine (OCSVM) Method and the Multi-class SVM Classification can also be used to classify the normal daily postures and other human activities or falls [2–7].
- Machine Learning Method (Classification): The classification of a fall is based on the fall definition. It is used to distinguish between falling and other human activities like bending, sitting, tripping, etc. The collected data is distinguished based on feature extraction and selection. Decision Trees (DTs) are one of the oldest algorithms used for pattern classification. Artificial Neural Networks (ANNs) are also used to classify falls from daily activities. Support Vector Machine (SVM) can also be used to classify different postures to identify falls. A Bayesian Belief Network (BBS) can be used to model the causality of slip or fall events compared to other events.

3 Implementation Details

The proposed approach takes into account various measures derived by the environment and by the activities of the human body. Based on the environmental factors of the tested data-sets, we have preprocessed the data-set to get a better understanding of human positions in different surroundings. Following that, we have studied behavioural elements of the human body to predict a fall based on the human body responses to a sudden movement. To develop and test this approach, we carried out our research by implementing the Le2i data-set [8].

3.1   Data-Set

The Le2I data-set is created specifically for assessing human falls in different surroundings. This data-set includes various scenarios of human activities that are not limited to a simple fall such as sitting, resting and bending. In addition to assorted activities, the above-mentioned data-set incorporates various environments with a myriad of challenges. In this project, we have tested our method on two environments, Office and Home. These specific environments cover distinguished illumination and motion interference trials in more than 30 videos per environment.

The proposed approach has been developed for accurate classification of activities in the Le2i videos and identification of falls. This method consists of five stages: Video Analysis, Human Body Approximation, Fall Definition, Fall Detection, and Notification. Following the proposed architecture (Fig. 1), each stage is elaborated further below.

- Video Analysis: The first step is to convert the video into frames. An illumination rate for the initial captured-frame is calculated based on the average frame pixel value of the grey-scale conversion of the video which is used to threshold the illumination of the video itself. To ensure the best results for background subtraction, we have used two methods: GMG and MOG2.
  - The GMG algorithm uses the first few frames for background modelling. It employs a probabilistic foreground segmentation algorithm that identifies possible foreground objects using Bayesian inference. This algorithm combines statistical background image estimation and per-pixel Bayesian segmentation.
  - MOG2 is a Gaussian Mixture-based Background/Foreground Segmentation Algorithm. The weights of the mixture represent the time in which colours stay in the scene and select the appropriate number of Gaussian distribution for each pixel.

  An optimal method is selected based on the motion and illumination rate and MOG2 and GMG background subtractors are triggered based on the motion estimation and illumination threshold. To reduce unwanted noise in each frame, a series of filters such as blur and averaging filters are applied. By the end of this step, the algorithm creates a binary mask frame of the moving object in the video.
- Human body approximation: After pre-processing the frame and carefully selecting the Region of Interest (ROI), the human body is approximated with a bounding box and an ellipse. The shape measurements are analyzed and compared with the defined threshold to differentiate between the human body and other objects (Fig. 2).

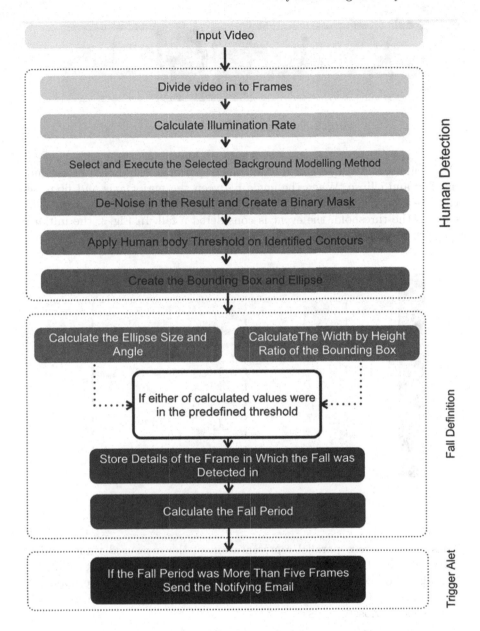

Fig. 1. System architecture

Fig. 2. Frame processing step by step

– Fall Definition: A fall is defined based on the parameter updates of the bounding box and ellipse. When the angle between the major axis and floor, and the size of the ellipse or the ratio of width to height of the bounding box exceeds the threshold, the event is considered a fall. In Fig. 3, the initiation and period of the fall are represented in three sample videos.

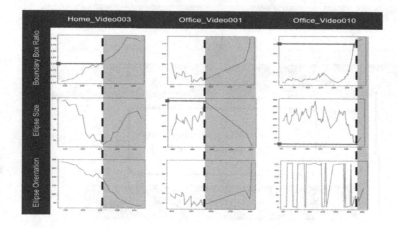

Fig. 3. Fall detection by value analysis

These graphs are a parallel representation of the measured values and the ways in which they change when a fall occurs. By studying the changes in boundary box ratio (w/h), ellipse orientation (θ) and size of the major axis of the ellipse (f), we set thresholds for defining the fall. A fall can be detected in three scenarios:

- Change of w/h: In this case as the size of the human body approximation changes from vertical to horizontal (w/h greater than 1), the fall is detected. This method is most viable when a person falls to either sides. The ellipse size in this method is a discriminating approach to identifying the fall.
- Change of θ and f: As θ gets closer to π or 0 degrees, the change in the angle is used to detect the fall. It can also be used in case the subject falls towards the camera.

• In some scenarios, both methods can be used to define the fall.
- Fall detection: Leveraging the mentioned measures, the proposed algorithm is set to record the frame details, and the absolute values of θ, f and w/h. The contained data is consequently used for measuring the period and intensity of the fall. For visual readability, the shape of the human body approximation is assigned a different colour as the fall is detected (Fig. 4).

Fig. 4. Detected fall

- Notification: After the fall has been defined and detected, we capture the frame details in which the fall occurred and register the fall period. Subsequently, a notification is sent if the fall period is more than 5 frames.

3.2 Results

The accuracy of the proposed system is measured based on two methods:

- Method 1: This method categorizes based on categorizing the test outcomes into four types. The precision of the method is measured using the mAP (mean Average Precision) for the Object Detection technique. Precision measures the accuracy of predictions and calculates the percentage of positive predictions (Table 1).

Table 1. Accuracy method 1

Accuracy calculation method 1				
	True - Positive	False - Negative	False - Positive	True - Negative
Action	Fall and detected	No Fall and not detected	No fall but fall detected	Fall and not detected

- Method 2: This method relies on the potential of the selected data-set. An annotation file is provided with the data-set which contains the information of the fall detected. By comparing our results with the details provided in the file, we calculate the accuracy of our approach.

$$Precision = \frac{TP}{TP + FP} \tag{1}$$

Based on the above-mentioned methods, our approach was able to successfully distinguish between a fall and fall-resembling action in the tested videos
successfully. The current accuracy rate of the proposed approach is 85% (accuracy method 1) and 86.6% (accuracy method 2) (Table 2).

Table 2. Accuracy results

Approach accuracy						
	Average accuracy (Method 1)	Average accuracy (Method 2)	Office (Method 1)	Office (Method 2)	Home (Method 1)	Home (Method 2)
Accuracy	83.33%	86.67%	83.33%	86.6%	86.67%	N/A

3.3   Limitations and Challenges

During the development of the method, we encountered various challenges which
can be categorized in three areas: a) true detection of the human, b) differentiating between human activities to define a fall and c) creating an up-to-date
informative notification system.

- Identification of the Human Body: To ensure accurate fall detection, the first
  step is to identify the proper segmented foreground/background. Challenges
  in identifying the accurate foreground/background can be categorized into
  four areas:
  - Changes in Illumination: Illumination rates are the key factor in concise
    contouring of the human body; in a very dark or light environment defin-
    ing the measurements of the human silhouette can be challenging and
    can lead to misidentification. To achieve an accurate identification algo-
    rithm for environments with variable illumination, our approach follows
    an elimination path to select the best background subtractor amongst the
    above-mentioned models for a specific environment.
  - Other Moving Objects: In frames that include shadows, processing a real-
    time scenario is more challenging than a simulated environment, such as
    Le2i. Multiple moving objects such as pets, furniture or shadows mod-
    ulate the accuracy of the system. The accuracy of the method can be
    compromised if more False-Positives (detecting a false fall)are detected
    than True-Positives. Our approach addresses this problem by pre- pro-
    cessing each frame of the input video and applying de-noising filters in
    addition to converting it to grayscale in order to simplify the frame before
    applying contours.
  - Distance from the Camera: In the proposed approach, we identify a human
    body based on its proportion and bounding area. The predefined thresh-
    old, however, could not be as accurate in videos with a higher depth
    of view (the size of a human in proportion to the frame changes signif-
    icantly). One solution to overcome this issue is to include other back-

ground subtraction methods in the preprocessing stage which extracts specific human features for recognition. In the scope of this project, we have implemented and tested the HOG (feature-based object identification model) in the development phase. However, this model is still limited to certain human shapes and angles.

- Occlusion: Another challenge is when the human body subject to detection is covered by other objects. The measures taken in previous challenges can be used to detect a human in this feature limitation.

– Challenges in Fall Detection: A limitation in defining a fall can arise either from the activity casting conditions or the activity itself. The position of a human body with respect to the camera while falling or activities resulting in sudden and intensive changes in human proportion, are a few examples that limit the capabilities of a detection system.

- Other Human Activities Resembling Fall: Activities such as sitting, lying down and bending to pick up objects mimics a human body fall. The proposed method for fall detection is based on the combination of the mentioned measures, and therefore optimizes the process of differentiating between these activities.

- Challenging Fall Angles: When a person falls down at a certain angle with respect to the camera, the change in orientation of the body is not often detected by many fall detection systems. Even though the proposed model takes into account changes in the ratio of human body, the use of a 3D images can provide better grounds for assessing body position in real world [1]; we can take this research forward by investigating the 3D images to optimize the current model.

Notification Following accurate fall detection: A responsive and operational notification system is required to ensure the safety of the targets. The limitations of such a system include the following:

- False Notification: Even by embedding various measures and methods for detecting the fall and defining a fall, a false notification can result in a false alarm. In order to avoid such situations, we have added time, a third measure for defining a fall more precisely and avoiding false notifications.

- Late Notification: Late notifications can also hinder the accuracy of the model. In many cases, the earlier the person suffering a serious fall is detected, the higher the chances of recovering. Sending an alert email is one example of how the proposed fall detection system can communicate a fall. Notification alerts could also be replaced by more convenient systems according to the target's environment; for instance in a hospital or a care facility, employing a beeper could replace the current email system.

4   Conclusion

To conclude, this system has been developed while considering major factors affecting the human body fall. We used the Gaussian mixture model to remove any unwanted noise from the environment. We implemented two background subtraction methods (MOG2 and GMG) to extract the foreground and background frame. After receiving the processed frame, the features of the human body fall were detected, using the physics of the bounding box and ellipse surrounding the target object. The purpose of using multiple geometrical figures is to get better accuracy without neglecting any external factors. We also categorized the fall based on its severity. The accuracy of this system is being calculated based on two different strategies which have successfully achieved 83.33% (Method 1) and 86.67% (Method 2) accuracy in its results. All the external factors presented in the data-set were considered during this process. The last phase of this system is the notification system in which a notification is sent to the concerned person (guardian/caregiver) whenever the fall is detected. This application can be very useful in developing industrial applications for health care, construction sites and smart homes.

References

1. Yang, L., Ren, Y., Zhang, W.: 3D depth image analysis for indoor fall detection of elderly people. Digit. Commun. Netw. **2**(1), 24–34 (2016)
2. Alaliyat, S.: Video - based fall detection in elderly's houses (2008)
3. Gaikwad, K., Patil, D.: Human activity detection and recognition algorithm from video surveillances. Int. J. Technol. Explor. Learn. **2**(5), 198–202 (2013)
4. Salmi, K.: Improving safety for home care patients with a low-cost computer vision solution (2016). https://doi.org/10.13140/RG.2.2.35833.06242
5. Schrader, N.: Detecting falls and poses in image silhouettes (2011)
6. Skolan, V., et al.: A method for real-time detection of human fall from video (2012)
7. Van Tuan, P., Le Uyen Thuc, H.: An effective video based system for human fall detection. Int. J. Adv. Res. Comput. Eng. Technol. **3**(8), 2820–2826 (2014)
8. Le2i.cnrs.fr.: Fall detection dataset - Le2i - laboratoire electronique, informatique et image (2018)

Image Segmentation and Processing

Race Classification Based Iris Image Segmentation

Xianting Ke[1], Lingling An[1(✉)] [iD], Qingqi Pei[2] [iD], and Xuyu Wang[3] [iD]

[1] School of Computer Science and Technology, Xidian University, Xi'an, China
an.lingling@gmail.com
[2] School of Telecommunications Engineering, Xidian University, Xi'an, China
[3] Department of Computer Science, California State University, Sacramento, USA

Abstract. Iris segmentation is an essential precondition for biometric authentication systems based on iris recognition and dramatically affects the accuracy of personal identification. Due to various noises during iris acquisition, iris images from different databases exhibit different texture characteristics. Existing works mostly design segmentation schemes for specific iris images and thus restrain much room for performance improvement. Therefore, this paper proposes a race classification based iris image segmentation method. Compared with conventional methods, the proposed method firstly exploits the merits of local Gabor binary pattern (LGBP) with support vector machine (SVM) and builds an efficient classifier, LGBP-SVM, to partition iris images into the human eye and non-human eye images. Following this, these two kinds of iris images are segmented by different strategies based on circular Hough transform with the active contour model. Extensive experiments demonstrate the proposed LGBP-SVM outperforms existing works in terms of accuracy of iris race classification. Furthermore, the race classification based iris segmentation method improves the segmentation accuracy and correct segmentation rates for various iris image databases.

Keywords: Iris segmentation · Race classification · Local Gabor binary pattern · Support vector machine

1 Introduction

Iris recognition as an extremely reliable research topic has been applied widely in various fields of identification, e.g., assess control, national ID card, border crossing, and welfare distribution [1,2]. The specificity of iris pattern is from abundant texture details in iris images, which makes it impossible to find two same iris pattern. Usually, iris recognition is made up of four procedures: segmentation, normalization, feature extraction/encoding, and similarity matching. Iris segmentation serves as an essential process when building such a system [3,4], which refers to the process of localizing both interior and exterior boundaries of iris regions in iris images. Iris segmentation has to be performed rigorously to

© Springer Nature Switzerland AG 2020
T. McDaniel et al. (Eds.): ICSM 2019, LNCS 12015, pp. 383–393, 2020.
https://doi.org/10.1007/978-3-030-54407-2_32

avoid wrong feature extraction, which may lead to a failure of personal identification. Meanwhile, due to the variety of acquisition devices, iris images from different databases are corrupted by diverse noises such as eyelid occlusions, eyeglass reflections, and light spots. The noises in iris images make accurate iris segmentation more challenging.

In the recent past, researchers have developed amounts of methods to segment iris regions. Daugman stated the integrodifferential operator(IDO) to locate the circular iris and pupil regions [5]. In Wildes's method [6], a histogram-based voting scheme is utilized to approximate iris boundaries from the enhanced iris image by a series of filtering operations. Masek [7] developed an open-source iris recognition system with a circular Hough transform to detect both iris and pupil boundaries to verify the uniqueness of the human iris. Arvacheh et al. considered that an actual pupil boundary is a near-circular contour rather than a perfect circle and thus applied the active contour model into iris segmentation [8]. A robust iris location method using an active contour model with the Hough transform was designed by Koh et al. [9]. Chen et al. proposed an iris segmentation algorithm by incorporating adaptive mean shift with an active contour model for non-cooperative recognition systems [10]. Radman et al. adopted a circular Gabor filter and IDO in iris segmentation and presented a fast iris segmentation algorithm [11]. Although existing studies have shown the promising performance in addressing the iris segmentation problem, the segmentation performance for iris images from different datasets is still not satisfactory. To enhance the segmentation accuracy, An et al. presented to segment heterogeneous iris images with active contour model and prior noise characteristics [12]. Unfortunately, such prior noise characteristics have to be manually evaluated in this method, which limits its practical application. Therefore, it is highly demanded to design an automatic iris classifier to distinguish iris images from different datasets and thus develop an efficient iris segmentation method to improve the segmentation performance.

To target the problems as mentioned above, we propose a race classification based iris image segmentation method. Our work dedicates to achieve iris race classification for iris images from diverse databases and thus improve the performance of iris segmentation. Specifically, a novel iris race classifier is designed via local Gabor binary pattern (LGBP) and support vector machine (SVM), termed as LGBP-SVM. The LGBP-SVM extracts texture features in iris images and classifies these images into two groups, i.e., human eye and non-human eye iris images. After that, the localizing region-based active contour model and circular Hough transform are separately employed to localize iris regions with different strategies. Extensive experimental results demonstrate that the proposed LGBP-SVM offers a higher correct classification rate (CCR) and low equal error rate (EER). Also, the iris segmentation method based on race classification further improves the segmentation accuracy and correct segmentation rate (CSR).

The remainder of this paper is organized as follows. Section 2 details the proposed race classification based iris image segmentation method. In Sect. 3, extensive experiments are conducted to show the effectiveness and efficiency of the designed iris race classifier LGBP-SVM. Section 4 introduces additional experimental results to demonstrate the segmentation performance in terms of segmentation accuracy and correct segmentation rate. Finally, Sect. 5 concludes this paper.

2 Proposed Method

In this section, we introduce the proposed race classification based iris image segmentation method. As shown in Fig. 1, the proposed method mainly includes two steps: 1) feature extraction and classification, and 2) iris image segmentation. The first step utilizes LGBP [13] to extract texture features from iris images and then feeds such features into SVM for iris image classification. Since iris images are subject to disturbances caused by occlusions, reflections, and light spots, they exhibit various texture characteristics. Based on this, our first step classifies input iris images into two groups: human eye and non-human eye iris images. Thereafter, the second step employs the localizing region-based active contour model and circular Hough transform to segment iris images and localize their interior and exterior boundaries. The details of these two steps are discussed in the following subsections.

2.1 Feature Extraction and Classification

Due to acquisition conditions, iris images from different databases may be corrupted by various noises. As discussed in [12], different noises can affect the localization of the interior and exterior boundaries of iris regions. For example, eyelid and eyelash occlusions in human eye iris images may impede the localization of interior boundary of iris regions, while light spots in non-human eye iris images may impede the segmentation of exterior boundary. Because of this, we build an effective classifier, LGBP-SVM, for iris race classification before segmentation.

Given an input iris image $I(x,y)$, we firstly apply Gabor filters with five scales and eight orientations to generate Gabor feature images $G_{\mu,\nu}(z)$ [14]

$$G_{\mu,\nu}(z) = I(x,y) * \varphi_{\mu,\nu}(z) \tag{1}$$

and

$$\varphi_{\mu,\nu}(z) = \frac{\|\kappa_{\mu,\nu}\|^2}{\sigma^2} e^{\frac{-\|\kappa_{\mu,\nu}\|^2\|z\|^2}{2\sigma^2}} [e^{i\kappa_{\mu,\nu}z} - e^{\frac{-\sigma^2}{2}}] \tag{2}$$

$$\kappa_{\mu,\nu} = \kappa_\nu e^{i\theta}, \kappa_\nu = 2^{-\frac{\nu+2}{2}}, \theta = \mu\frac{\pi}{8}$$

where $\nu = 0, ..., 5$ and $\mu = 0, ..., 7$ are the scale and orientation of Gabor wavelets, respectively. Following this, the information in Gabor feature images is enhanced by local binary pattern to form the LGBP, defined as

$$LGBP_{\mu,\nu}(z_c) = \sum_{p=0}^{7} S(a = \beta_{\mu,\nu}(z_p) - \beta_{\mu,\nu}(z_c))2^p \tag{3}$$

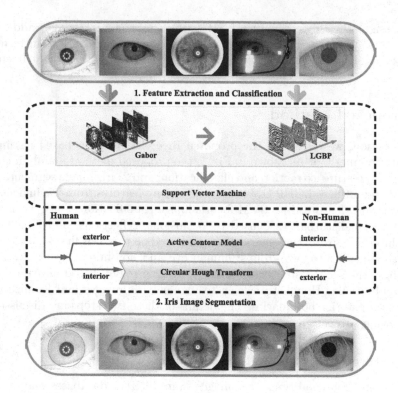

Fig. 1. Framework of race classification based iris image segmentation

where $z = (x, y)$, $\beta_{\mu,\nu}(z_i)$ is the ith element of $G_{\mu,\nu}(z)$, z_p means eight neighbors of the center pixel located at z_c, and $S(a) = 1$ if $a \geq 0$, otherwise $S(a) = 0$.

After features extraction, we perform classification with SVM to partition the input iris image $I(x, y)$ into the human eye or non-human eye iris images. Hereafter, the next subsection will segment the iris image according to its classification label.

2.2   Iris Image Segmentation

Iris image segmentation includes the localization of interior and exterior boundaries of iris regions, but it receives interference from noises caused by occlusions and reflections. Inspired by the idea in [12], we utilize different strategies to target the iris segmentation according to classification labels. As shown in Fig. 1, for human eye iris images, we employ a circular Hough transform to segment the interior boundary and use the localizing region-based active contour model to localize the exterior boundary. To be specific, we first compute the edge-map of $I(x, y)$ via the gradient-based edge detection algorithm, defined as

$$|\nabla L(x, y) * I(x, y)| \tag{4}$$

$$L(x, y) = \frac{1}{2\pi\sigma^2} e^{-\frac{(x-x_0)^2 + (y-y_0)^2}{2\sigma^2}} \tag{5}$$

where $\nabla \equiv \left(\frac{\partial}{\partial x}, \frac{\partial}{\partial y}\right)$, $L(x, y)$ is a 2D Gaussian with center (x_0, y_0) and standard deviation σ. Secondly, the circles passing through each edge point $(x_j, y_j), j = 1, ...n$, are produced by Hough transform [6]

$$H(x_c, y_c, r) = \sum_{j=1}^{n} h(x_j, y_j, x_c, y_c, r) \tag{6}$$

where

$$h(x_j, y_j, x_c, y_c, r) = \begin{cases} 1, (x_j - x_c)^2 + (y_j - y_c)^2 = r^2 \\ 0, otherwise \end{cases} \tag{7}$$

and the iris interior boundary can be determined by the maximum number of votes. Finally, we use the localizing region-based active contour model [15] to localize the exterior boundary of iris region, and its energy function is defined as:

$$M(\phi) = \int_{\Omega_x} \int_{\Omega_y} \delta\phi(x) \mathcal{P}(x, y) \cdot F(I(x, y), \phi(y)) \, dx dy$$
$$+ \lambda \int_{\Omega_x} \delta\phi(x) \|\nabla\phi(x)\| dx. \tag{8}$$

where $\delta\phi(x)$ is the Dirac delta, F is a generic internal energy measure, λ is a weight parameter, $\mathcal{P}(x, y)$ is a characteristic function in terms of a radius parameter r, and $\mathcal{P}(x, y) = 1$ if $\|x - y\| < r$, else $\mathcal{P}(x, y) = 0$. Refer to Fig. 1, similar procedures are conducted to localize iris regions for non-human eye iris images.

3 Experiments for Race Classification

In this section, we conduct extensive experiments to verify the effectiveness and efficiency of the proposed iris race classifier, i.e., LGBP-SVM. The experimental setup is first introduced, which is followed by two iris race classification applications, Human vs. Lions and Asian vs. White, respectively.

3.1 Experimental Setup

In the experiments, several public iris databases [16–18] shown in Fig. 2 are employed to build synthetic data sets for performance evaluation, including (i) CASIA-Iris-Thousand, (ii) CASIA-Iris-Lamp, (iii) CASIA-Iris-Syn, CASIA-Iris-Twins, and CASIA-Iris-Interval, (iv) UPOL database and (v) CASIA-Iris-RACE. As shown in Table 1, Synthetic-A, B, and C are used for the classification of Human vs. Lions, while Synthetic-D is used for Asian vs. White. We randomly select samples from each synthetic dataset as training sets and keep the rest as test sets, and employ CCR and EER for classification performance evaluation. All experiments are conducted on the same computer with Intel Core i5-6500M, 3.2 GHZ CPU, 4 GB RAM, WIN7 64bits System, and Python 3.6.

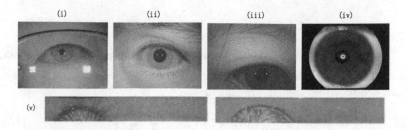

Fig. 2. Examples of iris images from different iris databases

Table 1. Synthetic data sets for performance evaluation

Human vs. Lions			Asian vs. White
Synthetic-A	Synthetic-B	Synthetic-C	Synthetic-D
CASIA-Iris-Thousand	CASIA-Iris-Lamp	CASIA-Iris-Syn	CASIA-Iris-Race
		CASIA-Iris-Twins	
		CASIA-Iris-Interval	
UPOL	UPOL	UPOL	

3.2 Experimental Results for Humans vs. Lions

In this section, the proposed LGBP-SVM is first applied to three synthetic datasets to classify human and lions. The experimental results are shown in Fig. 3, wherein two typical classifiers, i.e., k-nearest neighbors (KNN) and latent Dirichlet allocation (LDA), are employed for comparison. It can be seen that the proposed LGBP-SVM outperforms LGBP-KNN and LGBP-LDA with higher CCR over different training sets. Even when the number of training samples is small, e.g., 8000 in Fig. 3, the classification accuracy of LGBP-SVM is still higher than 0.96, which is better than LGBP-KNN and LGBP-LDA. Also, the CCRs of LGBP-SVM gradually improve with training samples increasing and reach 1.0 when the number of training samples is 20000.

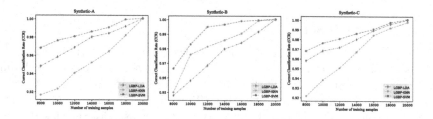

Fig. 3. CCR comparison for different classifiers

Moreover, we compare LGBP with gray level co-occurrence matrix (GLCM) and provide the classification performance for Human vs. Lions, shown in Table 2.

For the same dataset, we can see that the LGBP is superior to GLCM for different classifiers. Because we integrate the merits of LGBP and SVM, the proposed LGBP-SVM classifier achieves the highest CCR and lowest EER over all three synthetic datasets, even when iris images are interfered by occlusion, reflection, and light spots.

3.3   Experimental Results for Asian vs. White

To further demonstrate the superiority of the proposed LGBP-SVM for race classification, we applied LGBP-SVM to the Synthetic-D dataset, i.e., CASIA-Iris-RACE to classify Asian vs. White. Table 3 shows the results of CCR and EER, in which several conventional classification methods listed in [18] are compared. In this experiment, we randomly select 700 Asian and 700 White iris images as the training set and the rest as the test set for LGBP-SVM, LGBP-KNN, and LGBP-LDA. From Table 3, we can conclude that the proposed LGBP-SVM can extract iris features efficiently and achieves higher classification accuracy in comparison with its rivals. To be specific, LGBP-SVM gains the highest CCR, 99.92%, with the EER of zero.

Table 2. Classification performance comparison for Human vs. Lions

Classifier		Synthetic-A		Synthetic-B		Synthetic-C	
		CCR	EER	CCR	EER	CCR	EER
LDA	LGBP	1.0	0.0	0.9999	0.0	0.9996	0.0
	GLCM	0.9998	0.0	0.9998	0.0	0.9993	0.0
KNN	LGBP	0.9999	0.0	1.0	0.0	0.9970	0.0
	GLCM	0.9998	0.0	0.9999	0.0	0.9950	0.0
SVM	**LGBP**	**1.0**	**0.0**	**1.0**	**0.0**	**0.9997**	**0.0**
	GLCM	0.9979	0.0	0.9995	0.0	0.9996	0.0

Table 3. Classification performance comparison for Human vs. White

Method	CCR	EER
Learned iris texton	0.8207	0.1814
Gabor and HVC	0.8650	0.1357
LBP and HVC	0.7486	0.2550
SIFT and LLC	0.9814	0.0157
SIFT and LLC with SPM	0.9986	0.0014
SIFT and HVC	0.9986	0.0014
LGBP with LDA	0.9867	0.1325
LGBP with KNN	0.9960	0.0
LGBP with SVM	**0.9992**	**0.0**

4   Experiments for Iris Segmentation

In this section, we utilize three typical iris segmentation datasets, i.e., CASIA-IrisV1, CASIA-Iris-Thousand [16] and UPOL database [17], to illustrate the effectiveness of the proposed race classification based iris segmentation method. In our experiments, SØrensen-Dice coefficient (DICE) is adopted to evaluate the segmentation accuracy of iris regions, defined as:

$$DICE = \frac{2T_0}{T_M + T_A} \tag{9}$$

where T_M means the manually segmented ground-truth, T_A is the segmented results by our method, and T_0 is the overlapped region of T_M and T_A. For the sake of simplicity, Fig. 4 shows the segmentation results of example iris images,

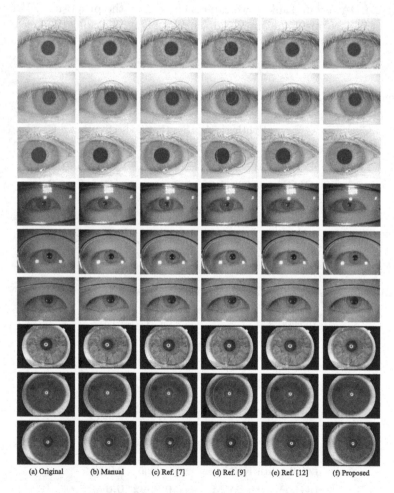

(a) Original   (b) Manual   (c) Ref. [7]   (d) Ref. [9]   (e) Ref. [12]   (f) Proposed

Fig. 4. Segmentation results of examples iris images for CASIA-IrisV1 (1–3 rows), CASIA-Iris-Thousand (4–6 rows) and UPOL (7–9 rows) databases.

and Table 4 gives the average segmentation accuracy based on DICE. Due to the existence of reflection spots in iris images, both DICEs of Refs. [7] and [9] are low for the CASIA-Iris-Thousand database. By contrast, our DICE is 48.71% and 68.48% greater than the results of Ref. [7] and [9] when segmenting interior boundaries, and 47.3% and 28.61% higher when segmenting exterior boundaries, respectively. In a word, our method eliminates the influence of noises caused by occlusions, reflections, and light spots, and thus achieves a higher segmentation accuracy.

Table 4. Average segmentation accuracy for different iris databases

Method	Interior boundary			Exterior boundary		
	CASIA-IrisV1	CASIA-Iris-Thousand	UPOL	CASIA-IrisV1	CASIA-Iris-Thousand	UPOL
Ref. [7]	0.9343	0.5081	0.2916	0.9188	0.4429	0.9463
Ref. [9]	0.4114	0.3104	0.2831	0.8979	0.6298	0.9364
Ref. [12]	0.9462	0.8555	0.8917	0.9459	0.9079	0.9582
Proposed	**0.9627**	**0.9952**	**0.8997**	**0.9675**	**0.9159**	**0.9885**

In addition, we adopt CSR to evaluate the segmentation adaptability. Given the kth iris image, CSR is defined as

$$CSR = \frac{\sum_{k=1}^{N} F_k}{N} \tag{10}$$

$$F_k = \begin{cases} 0, mean\left(DICE_{in}^k, DICE_{ex}^k\right) < T \\ 1, mean\left(DICE_{in}^k, DICE_{ex}^k\right) \geq T \end{cases} \tag{11}$$

wherein N is the number of iris images, T is a threshold, F_k is the segmentation indicator, $DICE_{in}^k$ and $DICE_{ex}^k$ are the segmentation results of interior and exterior boundaries, respectively. Figure 5 shows CSR experimental results, from which we can see that our method achieves more than 85% correct segmentation rate for all test dataset even when the threshold is up to 0.9. Particularly, our CSRs are more than 46% higher than the results in [7] and [9] for CASIA-Iris-Thousand and UPOL databases, which indicates that it can be better applied to the segmentation of various iris image databases.

Moreover, we compute the average execution time of the proposed method to show its adaptability in real scenarios. First, we randomly pick up 30 iris images from each segmentation dataset. Secondly, we employ two steps shown in Fig. 1 to localize iris regions in these images. Table 5 reports the average execution times for three iris databases, in which the classification and segmentation times are separately computed. Average speaking, our proposed method can meet the time requirements in practical applications.

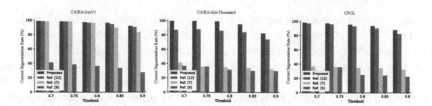

Fig. 5. Correct segmentation rate comparison for different datasets

Table 5. Average execution time for different iris databases

Time (s)	CASIA-IrisV1	CASIA-Iris-Thousand	UPOL
Classification	1.9534	1.9460	1.9751
Segmentation	0.8200	0.7438	1.2093

5 Conclusions

This paper designs a novel race classifier, LGBP-SVM, for iris image classification and thus propose a race classification based iris segmentation method. The LGBP-SVM effectively extracts texture features in iris images and partitions iris images into the human eye and non-human eye groups. Based on this, we adopt different segmentation strategies to localize iris regions by using the circular Hough transform and localizing region-based active contour model. As documented in the experimental results, our LGBP-SVM is superior to typical classifiers in dealing with iris race classification. Also, the iris segmentation method based on race classification can boost the segmentation accuracy and correct segmentation rate. Future efforts will be focused on the multi-race iris classification and design of an effective and efficient iris recognition system. Meanwhile, we will further investigate iris fingerprints for multimedia watermarking systems [19, 20].

Acknowledgments. This work is supported by the Key Program of NSFC-Tongyong Union Foundation (Grant No. U1636209), the National Natural Science Foundation of China (Grant No. 61902292), the Key Research and Development Programs of Shaanxi (Grant Nos. 2019ZDLGY13-07 and 2019ZDLGY13-04), and the Science and Technology Projects of Xi'an, China (Grant No. 201809170CX11JC12).

References

1. Sun, Z., Tan, T.: Ordinal measures for Iris recognition. IEEE Trans. Pattern Anal. Mach. Intell. **31**(12), 2211–2226 (2009)
2. Zhao, Z., Kumar, A.: A deep learning based unified framework to detect, segment and recognize irises using spatially corresponding features. Pattern Recognit. **93**, 546–557 (2019)

3. Badrinarayanan, V., Kendall, A., Cipolla, R.: Segnet: a deep convolutional encoder-decoder architecture for image segmentation. IEEE Trans. Pattern Anal. Mach. Intell. **39**(12), 2481–2495 (2017)
4. Arsalan, M., Naqvi, R.A., Kim, D.S., Nguyen, P.H., Owais, M., Park, K.R.: Iris-DenseNet: robust iris segmentation using densely connected fully convolutional networks in the images by visible light and near-infrared light camera sensors. Sensors **18**(5), 1501 (2018)
5. Daugman, J.: How iris recognition works. In: The Essential Guide to Image Processing, 2nd edn. Academic Press, pp. 715–739 (2009)
6. Wildes, R.P.: Iris recognition: an emerging biometric technology. Proc. IEEE **85**(9), 1348–1363 (1997)
7. Masek, L.: Recognition of human iris patterns for biometric identification. Master's thesis, The University of Western Australia, Perth (2003)
8. Arvacheh, E.M., Tizhoosh, H.R.: Iris segmentation: detecting pupil, limbus and eyelids. In: 2006 International Conference on Image Processing, pp. 2453–2456. IEEE, Atlanta, GA (2006)
9. Koh, J., Govindaraju, V., Chaudhary, V.: A robust iris localization method using an active contour model and hough transform. In: 20th International Conference on Pattern Recognition, pp. 2852–2856. IEEE, Istanbul (2010)
10. Chen, R., Lin, X.R., Ding, T.H.: Iris segmentation for non-cooperative recognition systems. IET Image Process. **5**(5), 448–456 (2011)
11. Radman, A., Jumari, K., Zainal, N.: Fast and reliable iris segmentation algorithm. IET Image Process. **7**(1), 42–49 (2013)
12. An, L., Yan, Y., Wang, Q.: Heterogeneous iris segmentation based on active contour model and prior noise characteristics. In: International Conference on Internet Multimedia Computing and Service, pp. 298–301. ACM, Xi'an (2016)
13. Zhang, W., Shan, S., Gao, W., Chen, X., Zhang, H.: Local Gabor binary pattern histogram sequence (LGBPHS): a novel non-statistical model for face representation and recognition. In: Proceedings of the Tenth IEEE International Conference on Computer Vision, vol. 1, pp. 786–791. IEEE, Beijing (2005)
14. Ma, B., Zhang, W., Shan, S.: Robust head pose estimation using LGBP. In: 18th International Conference on Pattern Recognition, pp. 512–515. IEEE, Hong Kong (2006)
15. Lankton, S., Tannenbaum, A.: Localizing region-based active contours. IEEE Trans. Image Process. **17**(11), 2029–2039 (2008)
16. CASIA Iris Image Database. http://biometrics.idealtest.org/findTotalDbByMode.do?mode=Iris
17. Iris Database. http://phoenix.inf.upol.cz/iris/
18. Sun, Z., Zhang, H., Tan, T., Wang, J.: Iris image classification based on hierarchical visual codebook. IEEE Trans. Pattern Anal. Mach. Intell. **36**(6), 1120–1123 (2014)
19. An, L., Gao, X., Li, X., Tao, D., Deng, C., Li, J.: Robust reversible watermarking via clustering and enhanced pixel-wise masking. IEEE Trans.Image Process. **21**(8), 3598–3611 (2012)
20. Gao, X., An, L., Yuan, Y., Tao, D., Li, X.: Lossless data embedding using generalized statistical quantity histogram. IEEE Trans. Circ. Syst. Video Technol. **21**(8), 1061–1070 (2011)

Level Sets Driven by Adaptive Hybrid Region-Based Energy for Medical Image Segmentation

Bin Han[1,2(✉)]

[1] College of Electronic and Information Engineering,
Nanjing University of Aeronautics and Astronautics, Nanjing, China
bhan4@ualberta.ca
[2] Department of Computing Science, University of Alberta, Edmonton, AB, Canada

Abstract. Medical image segmentation has a great significance for medical diagnosis. In this article, a new level set method (LSM) driven by adaptive hybrid region-based energy is proposed to achieve accurate medical image segmentation. First, new median region intensity descriptions are computed using the filtered input image and combined with traditional mean region intensity descriptions to design a novel global region-based signed pressure force (GRSPF). Then, the global region-based energy is defined using this GRSPF. Second, a similar new local region-based SPF (LRSPF) is also designed and the local region-based energy is defined using this LRSPF, which enhances the model's versatility. Furthermore, an adaptive weight for controlling the roles of the global and local region-based energies is introduced to construct the hybrid region-based energy, which drives the level set more appropriately. Segmentation results for medical images show that the proposed LSM can segment medical images more accurately than existing LSMs.

Keywords: Medical image segmentation · Level sets · Adaptive hybrid region-based energy · GRSPF · LRSPF

1 Introduction

In modern medicine, the use of imaging technology for medical diagnosis has become one of the principal means. Image segmentation is an important link of the above medical diagnosis, however, the captured images always suffer from intensity inhomogeneities, making it difficult to get accurate segmentation results. In the latest years, level set methods (LSMs) have achieved some success in coping with intensity inhomogeneities in medical images [1–10]. The most related works are briefly introduced as below.

1.1 The GRSPF Based LSM

Zhang et al. [11] designed a novel global region-based SPF (GRSPF) to drive the level set, which is constructed by computing the difference between the pixel intensity and

© Springer Nature Switzerland AG 2020
T. McDaniel et al. (Eds.): ICSM 2019, LNCS 12015, pp. 394–402, 2020.
https://doi.org/10.1007/978-3-030-54407-2_33

the average of the global region intensity descriptions inside and outside the level set. Thus, this GRSPF can be formulated as:

$$grspf(u(x)) = \frac{u(x) - \frac{c_1 + c_2}{2}}{\max\left(\left|u(x) - \frac{c_1 + c_2}{2}\right|\right)} \tag{1}$$

where $u(x)$ denotes the pixel intensity, c_1 and c_2 denote the mean global region intensity descriptions inside and outside the level set.

After this, the GRSPF is introduced as a replacement of the edge-detection-function in the geodesic-based LSM. Hence, the partial differential equation of the GRSPF based LSM can be described as:

$$\frac{\partial \varphi}{\partial t} = grspf(u(x)) \cdot \left(\text{div}\left(\frac{\nabla \varphi}{|\nabla \varphi|}\right) + \alpha\right) \cdot |\nabla \varphi| + \nabla grspf(u(x)) \cdot \nabla \varphi \tag{2}$$

To decrease the model calculation, Zhang et al. use the Gaussian kernel function to smooth the level set after each evolution and additionally remove some unneeded terms. Therefore, the above equation can be deformed as:

$$\frac{\partial \varphi}{\partial t} = grspf(u(x)) \cdot \alpha \cdot |\nabla \varphi| \tag{3}$$

The GRSPF based LSM exploits global image features to control the level set and succeeds in coping with intensity homogeneities. However, it is incapable of processing images with intensity inhomogeneities.

1.2 The LRSPF Based LSM

Aiming at handling intensity inhomogeneities in images, Dong et al. [12] designed a local region-based SPF (LRSPF). It employs the local image features through computing the difference between the pixel intensity and the average of the local region intensity descriptions inside and outside the level set. Thus, the energy function of the LRSPF based LSM can be described as:

$$E_{\text{LRSPF}}(\varphi) = -\int_{\Omega} \frac{u(x) - \frac{l_1 + l_2}{2}}{l_1 - l_2} H(\varphi) \mathrm{d}x \tag{4}$$

where l_1 and l_2 denote the mean local region intensity descriptions inside and outside the level set.

Next, l_1 and l_2 are considered as fixed constants and Eq. (4) can be solved using the gradient-descent-method. Therefore, its partial differential equation can be described as:

$$\frac{\partial \varphi}{\partial t} = \frac{u(x) - \frac{l_1 + l_2}{2}}{l_1 - l_2} \delta(\varphi) \tag{5}$$

The LRSPF based LSM draws on local image features to drive the level set and is able to process images with intensity inhomogeneities. However, it can not cope with complex intensity features and depends on the level set initialization greatly.

2 Proposed Method

2.1 The Global Region-Based Energy Term

Note that the above region-based SPFs are constructed using traditional region intensity descriptions inside and outside the level set which are computed in the input images. However, there always exist outlier pixels such as the noise and interference pixels in the input image, making region intensity descriptions inaccurate. To tackle this issue, we design novel median region intensity descriptions. More precisely, the input image is firstly filtered by a Gaussian-filter function, which removes some noises. Then, we compute the medians of pixel intensities inside and outside the level set as region intensity descriptions, which can repress the influence of interference pixels to some extent [13]. On the above basis, a new GRSPF is designed as:

$$grspf_m(u(x)) = \left(2 \cdot u(x) - \left(\frac{c_1 + m_{G1}}{2} + \frac{c_2 + m_{G2}}{2} \right) \right) \cdot |c_1 - c_2| \qquad (6)$$

where m_{G1} and m_{G2} represent the median global region intensity descriptions inside and outside the level set and they can be calculated by:

$$\begin{cases} m_{G1} = \text{med}\left(u_F(x) \cdot H(\varphi)\right) \\ m_{G2} = \text{med}\left(u_F(x) \cdot (1 - H(\varphi))\right) \\ u_F(x) = u(x) * G \end{cases} \qquad (7)$$

where G represents the Gaussian-filer function.

Thereafter, the above GRSPF is used to define a global region-based energy term, which is described as:

$$\begin{aligned} E_G(\varphi) &= - \int_\Omega grspf_m(u(x)) \cdot H(\varphi)dx \\ &= - \int_\Omega \left(2 \cdot u(x) - \left(\frac{c_1 + m_{G1}}{2} + \frac{c_2 + m_{G2}}{2} \right) \right) \cdot |c_1 - c_2| \cdot H(\varphi)dx \end{aligned} \qquad (8)$$

This GRSPF based energy term is explained as follows. We first make $2 \cdot I_{SPF} = \frac{c_1 + m_{G1}}{2} + \frac{c_2 + m_{G2}}{2}$. It can be known that E_G drives the level set to enclose pixels with

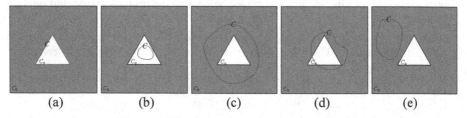

(a)	(b)	(c)	(d)	(e)

Fig. 1. Level sets in different positions. (a) the level set stops at object boundaries; (b) the level set is located in the object; (c) the level set contains the object; (d) the level set intersects both the object and background; (e) the level set is located in the background.

intensities larger than $2 \cdot I_{SPF}$. The specific analysis is divided into five cases shown in Fig. 1. In addition, the image domain is formed of the object and background. An arbitrary level set C is given and c_o and c_b represent region intensity descriptions of the object and background ($c_o > c_b$).

In Fig. 1(a), it is intuitive that $c_1 = m_{G1} = c_o$ and $c_2 = m_{G2} = c_b$, thus we have $I_{SPF} = \frac{c_o + c_b}{2}$. In Fig. 1(b), it can be found that $c_1 = m_{G1} = c_o$ and $c_2 > m_{G2} = c_b$, we derive that $c_b < \frac{c_o + c_b}{2} < I_{SPF} = \frac{c_1 + c_2}{2} < c_o$. Then, Eq. (6) will control the level set to expand to the background. In Fig. 1(c), it can be found that $c_1 < c_o$, $m_{G1} \leq c_o$ and $c_2 = m_{G2} = c_b$, we derive that $c_b < I_{SPF} \leq \frac{c_1 + c_2}{2} < \frac{c_o + c_b}{2} < c_o$. Then, Eq. (6) will control the level set to contract to the object. In Fig. 1(d), this case is similar to that of Fig. 1(c), we no longer discuss it. In Fig. 1(e), it can be found that $c_2 < c_o$, $m_{G2} \leq c_o$ and $c_1 = m_{G1} = c_b$, we derive that $c_b < I_{SPF} \leq \frac{c_1 + c_2}{2} < \frac{c_o + c_b}{2} < c_o$. Then, Eq. (6) will control the level set to enclose the object. Consequently, the new GRSPF based energy term is able to drive the level set towards the object boundaries.

2.2 The Local Region-Based Energy Term

To improve the model's versatility, we similarly design a new LRSPF to cope with images in the presence of intensity inhomogeneities, which can be described as:

$$lrspf_m(u(x)) = \left(2 \cdot u(x) - \left(\frac{l_1 + m_{L1}}{2} + \frac{l_2 + m_{L2}}{2}\right)\right) \cdot |l_1 - l_2| \qquad (9)$$

where m_{L1} and m_{L2} represent the median local region intensity descriptions inside and outside the level set and they can be calculated by:

$$\begin{cases} m_{L1} = \text{med}\left(K * (u_F(x) \cdot H(\varphi))\right) \\ m_{L2} = \text{med}\left(K * (u_F(x) \cdot (1 - H(\varphi)))\right) \end{cases} \qquad (10)$$

where K represents the local window function.

Next, the above LRSPF is utilized to define a local region-based energy term, which is described as:

$$E_L(\varphi) = -\int_{\Omega} lrspf_m(u(x)) \cdot H(\varphi) dx$$

$$= -\int_{\Omega} \left(2 \cdot u(x) - \left(\frac{l_1 + m_{L1}}{2} + \frac{l_2 + m_{L2}}{2}\right)\right) \cdot |l_1 - l_2| \cdot H(\varphi) dx \qquad (11)$$

The explanation of the new LRSPF based energy term is similar to the new GRSPF based energy term. However, unlike it, this LRSPF based energy term is capable of processing intensity inhomogeneities in images.

2.3 Adaptive Hybrid Region-Based Energy Term

To produce desired segmentation results, we integrate the above global and local region-based energy terms to construct the hybrid region-based energy term. However, the main problem is how to control the roles of the above two energy terms. Thus, we design an adaptive weight to automatically adjust their functions. The specific analysis is as below. In regions where pixel intensities vary slight, local region intensity descriptions inside and outside the level set are almost the same and the difference of the local region energies inside and outside the level set is small, making the level set difficult to move toward desired object boundaries. Therefore, we should enhance the role of the global region-based energy to make it being the chief energy, which drives the level set toward desired object boundaries. Contrarily, in regions where pixel intensities vary dramatically, local region intensity descriptions inside and outside the level set differ from each other obviously and the difference of the local region energies inside and outside the level set is adequate to drive the level set toward desired object boundaries. Therefore, we should enhance the role of the local region-based energy, which results in the accurate object boundaries. Consequently, an adaptive weight for controlling the roles of the global and local region-based energy terms is designed based on the local intensity features and is described as:

$$\rho(x) = \beta \cdot \text{average}(C_L) \cdot (1 - C_L) \tag{12}$$

where β is a positive constant, C_L denotes the local intensity contrast of an image which can be computed by:

$$C_L(x) = \frac{M_{AMax} + M_{AMin}}{M_E} \tag{13}$$

where L represents the size of the local region, M_{AMax} and M_{AMin} represent the averages of the highest and lowest two pixel intensities in this local region, respectively, M_E is the maximal intensity-level of an image.

Following this, the adaptive hybrid region-based energy term is constructed as:

$$
\begin{aligned}
E_{AH}(\varphi) =\ & \rho(x) \cdot E_G(\varphi) + (1 - \rho(x)) \cdot E_L(\varphi) + E_R(\varphi) \\
=\ & -\rho(x) \int_{\Omega} \left(2 \cdot u(x) - \left(\frac{c_1 + m_{G1}}{2} + \frac{c_2 + m_{G2}}{2} \right) \right) \cdot |c_1 - c_2| \cdot H(\varphi)dx - \\
& (1 - \rho(x)) \int_{\Omega} \left(2 \cdot u(x) - \left(\frac{l_1 + m_{L1}}{2} + \frac{l_2 + m_{L2}}{2} \right) \right) \cdot |l_1 - l_2| \cdot H(\varphi)dx + \\
& \gamma \cdot \delta(\varphi) \cdot \text{div}\left(\frac{\nabla\varphi}{|\nabla\varphi|} \right) + \mu \cdot \left(\nabla^2\varphi - \text{div}\left(\frac{\nabla\varphi}{|\nabla\varphi|} \right) \right)
\end{aligned}
\tag{14}
$$

where E_R is the regularized energy term [14], namely the last two terms.

Now, we explain the above adaptive hybrid region-based energy term how to automatically regulate the functions of the global and local region-based energies. When the local region is inhomogeneous, i.e. its intensities vary dramatically, therefore C_L of this region is large and further $\rho(x)$ is small. Hence, the local region-based energy term serves as the chief energy. Contrarily, when the local region is homogeneous, i.e. its intensities vary slightly, therefore C_L of this region is small and further $\rho(x)$ is large. Hence, the global region-based energy term serves as the chief energy. Consequently, the proposed LSM can produce the desired segmentation results.

3   Experimental Results and Analysis

To validate the effectiveness of the proposed LSM, we test it on different kinds of images and its results are compared to the GRSPF and LRSPF based LSMs, and the LSM in Ref. [5]. The implementation of the proposed LSM is carried out a PC with AMD Ryzen 5 2400G 3.6 GHz, 16 GB RAM, MATLAB R2017a, Windows 10. Moreover, the related

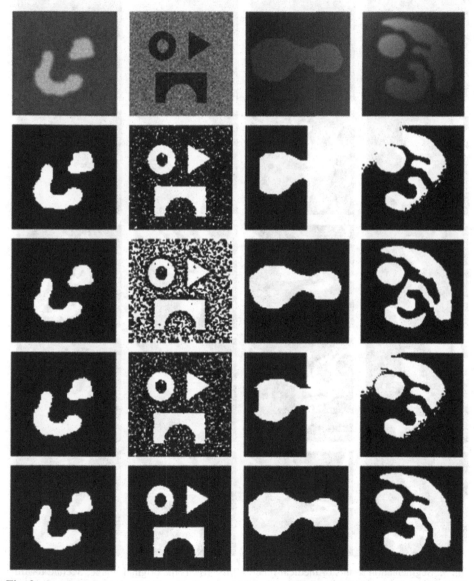

Fig. 2. Segmentation results of synthetic images. First row is the original image; Second to fifth rows represent the results of the GRSPF and LRSFP based LSMs, the LSM in Ref. [5], and the proposed LSM.

parameters are set as: $\beta = 10$, $\gamma = 0.01 \times 255^2$, $\mu = 0.5$, $\Delta t = 0.1$, $\varepsilon = 1$ (unless otherwise specified).

Figure 2 shows the results of synthetic images of four LSMs. Therein, the former two images are homogeneous and the latter two images are inhomogeneous. We find that the GRSPF based LSM can segment homogeneous images, but fail to deal with

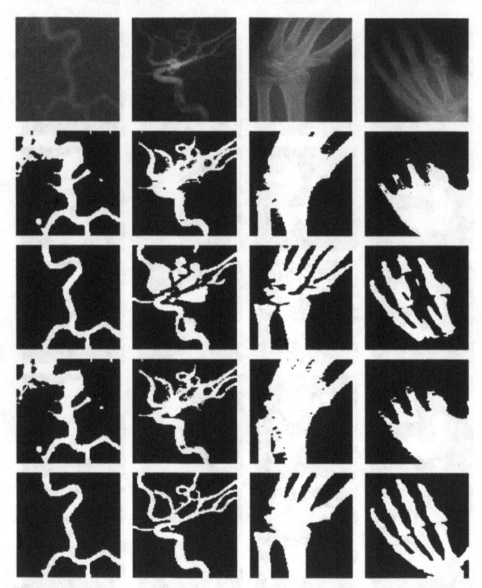

Fig. 3. Segmentation results of medical images. First row is the original image; Second to fifth rows represent the results of the GRSPF and LRSFP based LSMs, the LSM in Ref. [5], and the proposed LSM.

inhomogeneous images. Comparatively, the LRSPF based LSM is better at processing inhomogeneous images. The LSM in Ref. [5] exploits both global and local intensity features to guide the level set, however, its segmentation results are not satisfying. The proposed LSM is capable of coping with both homogeneous and inhomogeneous images and obtains desired segmentation results.

Figure 3 illustrates the segmentation results of medical images. Obviously, the GRSPF based LSM is ineffective to segment medical images and its results are bad. Different from the GRSPF based LSM, the LRSPF based LSM is able to process medical images. Unfortunately, it encounters the boundary leakage due to falling in the local minimum. The LSM in Ref. [5] combines the global and local intensity features to segment medical images, however, its segmentation effect is not satisfying. The proposed LSM succeeds in processing medical images and achieves the accurate segmentation results.

4 Conclusion

In this article, we propose a novel LSM driven by adaptive hybrid region-based energy to achieve accurate segmentation results of medical images. First, we design a new GRSPF based on mean and median region intensity descriptions and construct the global region-based energy using this GRSPF. Second, to improve the model's generality, we similarly design a new LRSPF and construct the local region-based energy this LRSPF. Furthermore, a hybrid region-based energy is built by introducing an adaptive weight which can automatically control the roles of the global and local region-based energies. Experimental results illustrate that the proposed LSM outperforms some existing LSMs in segmentation accuracy.

References

1. Rodtook, A., Kirimasthong, K., Lohitvisate, W., et al.: Automatic initialization of active contours and level set method in ultrasound images of breast abnormalities. Pattern Recogn. **79**, 172–182 (2018)
2. Selvathi, D., Bama, S.: Phase based distance regularized level set for the segmentation of ultrasound kidney images. Pattern Recogn. Lett. **86**, 9–17 (2017)
3. Sun, W., Dong, E.: Kullback-Leibler distance and graph cuts based active contour model for local segmentation. Biomed. Signal Process. Control **52**, 120–127 (2019)
4. Sun, L., Meng, X., Xu, J., et al.: An image segmentation method using an active contour model based on improved SPF and LIF. Appl. Sci. **8**(12), 2576 (2018)
5. Karn, P.K., Biswal, B., Samantaray, S.R.: Robust retinal blood vessel segmentation using hybrid active contour model. IET Image Proc. **13**(3), 440–450 (2019)
6. Zhang, L., Peng, X., Li, G., et al.: A novel active contour model for image segmentation using local and global region-based information. Mach. Vis. Appl. **28**, 75–89 (2017)
7. Xu, H., Jiang, G., Yu, M.: A local Gaussian distribution fitting energy-based active contour model for image segmentation. Comput. Electr. Eng. **70**, 317–333 (2018)
8. Liu, S., Peng, Y.: A local region-based Chan-Vese model for image segmentation. Pattern Recogn. **45**, 2769–2779 (2012)
9. Khadidos, A., Sanchez, V., Li, C.: Weighted level set evolution based on local edge features for medical image segmentation. IEEE Trans. Image Process. **26**(4), 1979–1991 (2017)

10. Fouladivanda, M., Kazemi, K., Helfroush, M.S., et al.: Morphological active contour driven by local and global intensity fitting for spinal cord segmentation from MR images. J. Neurosci. Methods **308**, 116–128 (2018)
11. Zhang, K., Zhang, L., Song, H., et al.: Active contours with selective local or global segmentation: a new formulation and level set method. Image Vis. Comput. **28**(4), 668–676 (2010)
12. Dong, F., Chen, Z., Wang, J.: A new level set method for inhomogeneous image segmentation. Image Vis. Comput. **31**(10), 809–822 (2013)
13. Han, B., Wu, Y.: A novel active contour model based on modified symmetric cross entropy for remote sensing river image segmentation. Pattern Recogn. **67**, 396–409 (2017)
14. Li, C., Xu, C., Gui, C., et al.: Distance regularized level set evolution and its application to image segmentation. IEEE Trans. Image Process. **19**(12), 3243–3254 (2010)

Traffic Image Dehazing Based on Wavelength Related Physical Imaging Model

Yibin Wang[1,2(✉)], Shibai Yin[2,3], and Jia Zheng[1]

[1] Sichuan Normal University, Chengdu 610068, China
[2] University of Alberta, Edmonton T6G1H7, Canada
{yibin4,shibai}@ualberta.ca
[3] Southwestern University of Finance and Economics, Chengdu 610074, China

Abstract. Fog concentration is of crucial importance for traffic image dehazing. However, existing methods neglect it, resulting in inferior dehazing results. To tackle this problem, we propose a dehazing method based on the wavelength related physical imaging model. First, we present a wavelength related physical imaging model for traffic imaging. Then, according to the prior that colors of objects in an image are decided based the reflection of different wavelengths, we design a transmission estimation strategy based on the maximal fuzzy correlation and graph cut result. To be specific, the segmentation can be obtained by the maximal fuzzy correlation and the graph cut algorithm, and then it can be used as the guided image in the guided filter for getting a transmission map with continuous scene information. Such a segmentation design can take advantage of both threshold-based segmentation methods, *e.g.*, maximal fuzzy correlation, and spatial-based segmentation methods, *e.g.*, graph cut. Furthermore, the proposed iterative algorithm also improves the computational efficiency of image dehazing. Finally, the atmospheric light is predicted by the sky region in the segmentation result, and a haze-free image is obtained via the wavelength related physical imaging model. Experiments conducted on 500 synthetic images and real-world images have demonstrated that our algorithm can improve dehazing precision by at least 7% and shorten running time by roughly 15% compared to existing dehazing methods. Hence, the proposed method can be used for image dehazing in the traffic monitoring system.

Keywords: Image dehazing · Traffic image · Graph cut · Maximal fuzzy correlation

1 Introduction

Traffic images captured in the outdoor environment are an important information source for traffic monitoring systems. However, due to the suspended particles in the atmosphere, *e.g.*, water drops and dust [9,11], the light reflected from

Supported by General Project of Sichuan Education Department (No.18ZB0484), National Natural Science Foundation of China (No. 61502396).

an object is usually scattered or absorbed before it reaches the cameras, resulting in degraded hazy images. Traffic image dehazing acts as a pre-processing step to facilitate traffic image analysis in the traffic monitoring system. Hence, the accuracy of dehazing results has an important impact on subsequent analysis and decision, e.g., vehicle tracking [10], accident judgement and obstacle recognition [5], etc. [6]. Although a great deal of progress has been achieved, it is still a challenging task to develop effective methods for handling a complicated outdoor scene.

Generally speaking, two kinds of methods have been previously proposed for traffic image dehazing. The first one is the classical image enhancement techniques, such as retinex theory [4], wavelet transform [13] and histogram equalization [14], which improve the visual appeal of hazy images by enhancing contrast and correcting color. However, existing image enhancement techniques cannot remove the heavy haze. The second one is the dehazing method based on the atmospheric light scattering model [8]:

$$I(x) = J(x)t(x) + A(1 - t(x)), \tag{1}$$

where x denotes the pixel location in the traffic image, I represents the observed hazy image, J denotes the unknown clear image, A corresponds to the atmospheric light, and t denotes the scene transmission map. Assuming that the haze is homogeneous, we can further denote the transmission map $t(x)$ as $e^{-\beta d(x)}$, where d represents the scene depth and β is the scattered coefficient of the atmospheric light. Since only the observed image I is known, estimating J from Eq. (1) becomes an ill-posed problem.

Most methods utilize physical priors and constraints to capture statistical properties of hazy images for estimating the transmission maps and atmospheric lights. For example, the classical Dark Channel Prior (DCP), which asserts that the local minimum of the dark channel of a haze-free image is close to zero, can be used for estimating the transmission map [12]. Road environment constraints proposed based on the Weighted Least Squares (WLS) framework are used for predicting the clear image [15]. Although these methods can achieve promising results, there remains one limitation: the above methods all assume that the haze concentration is even which cannot adequately describe a real situation. To solve this problem, Yoon et al. [16] propose the wavelength related physical imaging model for aerial image dehazing. By exploring the relationship between the haze concentration and light wavelength, the assumption of even haze concentration can be avoided effectively. Then the transmission map is calculated by the proposed geometric classes and dynamic merging strategy. Specifically, the authors [16] propose the color histogram and the transmission map prediction method with the help of geometric classes. However, this method is applicable to aerial image dehazing and cannot be used for traffic image dehazing directly since the geometric classes produced by the histogram fusion strategy would not consider the spatial correlation of scenes, resulting in misclassification.

Inspired by the above discussion, we propose a novel traffic image dehazing method based on the wavelength related physical imaging model. First, we propose a wavelength related physical imaging model and verify its feasibility on the traffic imaging process. Then, according to the relationship between the light wavelength and color, we design the transmission map prediction method by using fuzzy correlation segmentation and graph cut optimization. This segmentation and optimization scheme not only considers the fuzzy characteristics of scene objects, but also takes the spatial correlations into account. Hence, the predicted transmission maps have higher accuracy. In addition, we propose an iterative scheme to accelerate the computation of fuzzy correlation segmentation. Initial experiments have demonstrated that our algorithm can improve dehazing precision by at least 7% and shorten running time by roughly 15% compared to existing dehazing algorithms.

2   The Wavelength Related Physical Imaging Model

According to the Rayleigh's law of atmospheric scattering principle [7], the scattering coefficient β is related to the wavelength λ, and can be defined as:

$$\beta(\lambda) \propto \frac{1}{\lambda^{\gamma}}, \tag{2}$$

where γ represents the size of the suspended particle in the atmosphere. When $\gamma = 1$, the size of the particle is smaller than the wavelength of the light and haze is heavy. Otherwise, $\gamma = 4$, the haze is light. Hence, we can conclude that the concentration of haze is related to the wavelength of light. That also means the concentration of haze is related to the colors of objects in the scene. Figure 1 displays the clear traffic image and its corresponding synthetic images with weak haze, medium haze and heavy haze. The color alignment measures (CAM) [1] of the white region enclosed by the red rectangles are marked under each image. From that, we find that as the amount of haze increases, the corresponding score marked under each image declines, indicating that the concentration of fog and color (wavelength of light) are mutually restricted. Hence, we propose the wavelength related physical imaging model:

$$J(\lambda) = f(\lambda)T(\lambda) + A(\lambda)(1 - T(\lambda)), \tag{3}$$

where $J(\lambda)$ is the hazy image with wavelength; $\lambda \in \{\lambda_{red}, \lambda_{green}, \lambda_{blue}\}$, $f(\lambda)$ denotes the clear image; $A(\lambda)$ and $T(\lambda)$ are the atmospheric light and transmission map with parameter λ. This model can estimate the transmission map and clear image correctly, due to avoiding the assumption of even haze concentration in a traditional model.

3   Traffic Image Dehazing Based on the Wavelength Related Physical Imaging Model

Inspired by the mapping relation between pixel x and $e^{-\beta d(x)}$ in the traditional atmospheric light scattering model, we design the $T(\lambda)$ as:

(a) The haze-free (b) The weak haze (c) The medium (d) The heavy haze
image(0.0047)   image(0.0031)   haze image(0.0025)   image(0.0021)

Fig. 1. Traffic images under different haze concentration. (Color figure online)

$$T(\lambda) = e^{-\alpha J_s(\lambda)^{-\varphi}}, \tag{4}$$

where $J_s(\lambda)$ is the segmentation result of the hazy image $J(\lambda)$. Hence, the $J_s(\lambda)$ can be further expressed as $J_s(\lambda) = [J_s^R(\lambda); J_s^G(\lambda); J_s^B(\lambda)]$. $J_s^R(\lambda), J_s^G(\lambda)$ and $J_s^B(\lambda)$ are the segmentation results of the hazy image in the red, green and blue channel, respectively. α and φ are the wavelength classification coefficient and wavelength index, respectively.

3.1 The Fuzzy Correlation Segmentation by an Iterative Computation Scheme

In this work, we use fuzzy correlation segmentation and graph cut optimization [2] to segment a hazy image in RGB channels. Take J^R as an example. Fuzzy correlation segmentation can divide the image into 3 classes: sky regions U_s, building regions U_V and ground regions U_g. First, we choose the S function and its corresponding opposite Z function to design the membership functions of sets U_s, U_v and U_g.

$$M_v(k) = F(k, m_1, n_1), \tag{5}$$

$$M_g(k) = \begin{cases} F(k, m_1, n_1) & k \leq n_1 \\ G(k, m_2, n_2) & k > n_1, \end{cases} \tag{6}$$

$$M_s(k) = G(k, m_2, n_2), \tag{7}$$

where, k is the pixel in the image J^R. m_1, n_1, m_2 and n_2 are the shape parameters of membership functions, meeting $0 \leq m_1 < n_1 < m_2 < n_2 \leq 255$.

The fuzzy partition probabilities are:

$$\begin{cases} P_v = \sum_{k=0}^{255} M_v(k)h(k) \\ P_g = \sum_{k=0}^{255} M_g(k)h(k), \\ P_s = \sum_{k=0}^{255} M_s(k)h(k) \end{cases} \tag{8}$$

where P_v, P_g and P_s are the fuzzy partition probabilities of the sets U_s, U_v and U_g. $h(\cdot)$ is the normalized histogram. k is the gray level.

The total fuzzy entropy of traffic image is defined as:

$$C(m_1, n_1, m_2, n_2) = -ln\left[\sum_{k=0}^{255}\left(\frac{M_v(k)h(k)}{P_v}\right)^2\right] - ln\left[\sum_{k=0}^{255}\left(\frac{M_g(k)h(k)}{P_g}\right)^2\right]$$
$$- ln\left[\sum_{k=0}^{255}\left(\frac{M_s(k)h(k)}{P_s}\right)^2\right], \tag{9}$$

To obtain the optimal segmentation results, we aim to find the best parameters m_1, n_1, m_2, n_2 which make $C(m_1, n_1, m_2, n_2)$ reach the maximal value. For accelerating the computation process, we propose an iterative computation scheme.

First, we rewrite the Eq. (9) as:

$$C(m_1, n_1, m_2, n_2) = -ln(P_A P_B P_C) + 2ln(P_s P_g(1 - P_s - P_g)), \tag{10}$$

where

$$\begin{cases} P_A = \sum_{k=0}^{255}\left(M_s(k)h(k)\right)^2 \\ P_B = \sum_{k=0}^{255}\left(M_v(k)h(k)\right)^2, \\ P_C = \sum_{k=0}^{255}\left(M_g(k)h(k)\right)^2 \end{cases} \tag{11}$$

Now we try to compute P_A, P_B and P_C in an iterative scheme. P_A, P_B and P_C can be rewritten as:

$$P_A = \frac{1}{(m_1 - n_1)^2}\sum_{k=m_1+1}^{n_1}(k - n_1)^2 h^2(k) + \sum_{k=0}^{m_1} h^2(k), \tag{12}$$

$$P_B = \frac{1}{(n_1 - m_1)^2}\sum_{k=m_1+1}^{n_1}(k - m_1)^2 h^2(k) + \sum_{k=n_1+1}^{m_2} h^2(k)$$
$$+ \frac{1}{(m_2 - n_2)^2}\sum_{k=m_2+1}^{n_2}(k - n_2)^2 h^2(k), \tag{13}$$

$$P_C = \frac{1}{(n_2 - m_2)^2}\sum_{k=m_2+1}^{n_2}(k - m_2)^2 h^2(k) + \sum_{k=n_2+1}^{255} h^2(k), \tag{14}$$

where $G(y, z) = \sum_{k=y+1}^{z}(k-y)^2 h^2(k)$, $H(y, z) = \sum_{k=y+1}^{z}(k-z)^2 h^2(k)$ and $I(y, z) = \sum_{k=y}^{z} h^2(k)$.

Let the value of $G(y, z)$ change with z; then the iterative process can be obtained by:

$$\begin{cases} G(y, z) = G(y, z - 1) + (z - y)^2 h^2(z) \\ G(y, y + 1) = h^2(y + 1), z = y + 2, \cdots, 255, \end{cases} \tag{15}$$

In a similar way, we can get the iterative process for $H(y, z)$:

$$\begin{cases} H(y, z) = H(y + 1, z) + (y + 1 - z)^2 h^2(y + 1) \\ H(z - 1, z) = 0, y = 0, \cdots, z - 1, \end{cases} \tag{16}$$

Finally, the iterative process for $I(y, z)$ is:

$$I(y, z) = I(y, z - 1) + h^2(z), \tag{17}$$

Since the P_s, P_g can be expanded as:

$$P_s = \sum_{k=0}^{m_1} p(k) + \frac{1}{m_1 - n_1} \sum_{m_1+1}^{n_1} (k - n_1) h(k), \tag{18}$$

$$P_g = \sum_{k=n_2+1}^{255} h(k) + \frac{1}{n_2 - m_2} \sum_{m_2+1}^{n_2} (k - m_2) h(k), \tag{19}$$

The sum items in Eq. (18) and Eq. (19) are recorded as:

$$\begin{cases} S(y, z) = \sum\limits_{k=y+1}^{z} (k - y) h(k) \\ T(y, z) = \sum\limits_{k=y+1}^{z} (k - y) h(k), \\ R(y, z) = \sum\limits_{k=y}^{z} h(k) \end{cases} \tag{20}$$

And the iterative processes for $S(y, z)$, $T(y, z)$ and $R(y, z)$ can be expressed as:

$$\begin{cases} S(y, z) = S(y, z - 1) + (z - y) h(z) \\ S(y, y + 1) = h(y + 1), z = y + 2, \cdots, 255, \end{cases} \tag{21}$$

$$\begin{cases} T(y, z) = T(y + 1, z) + (y + 1 - z) h(y + 1) \\ T(z - 1, z) = 0, y = 0, \cdots, z - 1, \end{cases} \tag{22}$$

$$R(y, z) = R(y, z - 1) + h(z) \tag{23}$$

3.2 Graph Cut Optimization Based on Fuzzy Correlation Segmentation

To be precise, we further use graph cut to optimize the segmentation results. First, the membership functions M_v, M_g and M_g from Sect. 3.1 are used to define the data term E_{data} of graph cut:

$$
E_{data} = \begin{cases}
-log \sum_{k=0}^{255} h(k)M_g(k) & l_x =' g' \\
-log \sum_{k=0}^{255} h(k)M_v(k) & l_x =' v', \\
-log \sum_{k=0}^{255} h(k)M_s(k) & l_x =' s'
\end{cases}
\tag{24}
$$

where l_x is the label of a pixel which can be marked as sky $'s'$, buildings $'v'$ or ground $'g'$.

The smooth term E_{data} in graph cut is defined based on the one proposed by Boykov and Jolly:

$$
E_{data} = exp(-\frac{(I_x - I_{x'})^2}{2\sigma^2}) \times \frac{1}{dist(x,x')},
\tag{25}
$$

where I_x and I'_x are the intensities of adjacent pixels x and x', $dist(x,x')$ is the average distance between the pixels x and x', and σ is related to the level of variation between neighboring pixels within J^R. We set σ to 1 in our experiment. After setting the data term and the smooth term for all the pixels, the optimal label assignment for different pixels is computed by the maximum flow minimum cut algorithm [17]. Then the final segmentation result J_s^R from J^R can be obtained. The segmentation results $J_s(\lambda) = [J_s^R(\lambda); J_s^G(\lambda); J_s^B(\lambda)]$ can be calculated in a similar way.

3.3 Estimation of Transmission Map

Instead of substituting $J_s(\lambda)$ into Eq. (4) directly, we estimate the transmission map by implementing the guided filter on $J_s(\lambda)$ first. This operation can generate the context adaptive image $J_G(\lambda)$ which has smooth edges. Hence, the final transmission is estimated by

$$
T(\lambda) = e^{-\alpha J_G(\lambda)^{-\varphi}},
\tag{26}
$$

Where α and φ are set to 0.34 and 1.5, respectively.

3.4 Estimation of Atmospheric Light

In this section, we estimate the atmospheric light using the sky regions in $J_s(\lambda)$. As a result, the atmospheric light is estimated as:

$$
A(\lambda) = max\big(J(\lambda) \cap J_{S(U_g)}(\lambda)\big),
\tag{27}
$$

where $J_{S(U_g)}(\lambda)$ is the sky region in the $J_s(\lambda)$.

Given the atmospheric light $A(\lambda)$ and transmission map $T(\lambda)$, the haze free image can be obtained as:

$$f(\lambda) = \frac{J(\lambda) - A(\lambda)}{T(\lambda)} + A(\lambda), \tag{28}$$

4   Experiment Results

In this section, we quantitatively evaluate the proposed approach on both synthetic images and real world images with comparisons to several state-of-the-art methods, including DCP method proposed by Wang [12], WLS method proposed by Yao [15] and wavelength related physical imaging model (WRPIM) proposed by Yoon [16].

4.1   Testing on the Synthetic Images

We randomly select 500 synthetic images from the public RESIDE dataset [3] for testing the accuracy of transmission maps. From Fig. 2, we find that compared methods such as DCP, WLS, WRPIM can estimate the transmission map with structural details, but they also tend to generate errors. For example, the results displayed in Fig. 2(b)–Fig. 2(d) show that the vehicles have similar colors in the sky region, since these methods view all white objects as atmospheric light. In comparison, our method can deal with the white object properly and the results shown in Fig. 2(e) are much closer to the ground truths. The quantitative PSNR and SSIM evaluated on 500 test images are tabulated in Table 1 which further demonstrate that our method can improve dehazing precision by 7%.

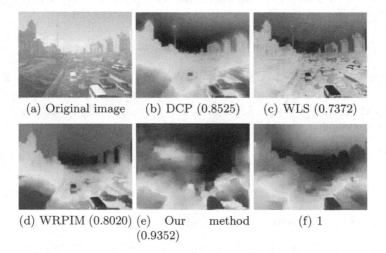

(a) Original image   (b) DCP (0.8525)   (c) WLS (0.7372)

(d) WRPIM (0.8020) (e) Our method   (f) 1
(0.9352)

Fig. 2. Comparisons of transmission maps on synthetic images.

Table 1. Quantitative SSIM results for the transmission map and SSIM/PSNR results for dehazing results based on the synthetic testing dataset.

Methods	DCP [12]	WLS [15]	WRPIM [16]	Our method
Transmission	0.854	0.892	0.886	0.9742
Image	19.13/0.895	21.45/0.932	20.35/0.922	23.12/0.961

4.2 Testing on the Real World Images

To further investigate the generalization ability of the proposed method, we conduct visual comparisons on real-world images (see Fig. 3). As displayed in Fig. 3(b)–Fig. 3(d), the results from compared methods are either too dark or too white, which demonstrates that these methods fail to recover the real color. Comparatively, our results displayed in Fig. 3(e) can remove haze with fine details and realistic color shifts.

(a) Input   (b) DCP   (c) WLS   (d) WRPIM   (e) Our method

Fig. 3. Comparisons of transmittance maps on synthetic images.

4.3 Comparisons of Running Time

To test the efficiency of the proposed method, Table 2 reports the average run-times of different algorithms on 500 synthetic images. As we expected, our method which uses an iterative scheme to accelerate computation can improve the run-time sharply. Compared with existing methods, the running time is shortened by roughly 15%.

Table 2. Comparisons of running time of different algorithms. (seconds)

Methods	DCP [12]	WLS [15]	WRPIM [16]	Our method
Running time	1.15 s	2.79 s	2.21 s	1.88 s

5   Conclusions

In this work, we propose a traffic image dehazing based on the wavelength related physical imaging model. First, we present a wavelength related physical imaging model for a traffic imaging process, in terms of the correlation between wavelength and fog concentration. Then, according to the prior that colors of objects in the image are decided based the reflection of different wavelengths, we design a transmission estimation strategy by using fuzzy correlation segmentation and graph cut optimization. Such a segmentation design can take advantage of the threshold-based segmentation method and spatial-based segmentation method, avoiding misclassification of scene objects. Furthermore, the proposed iterative algorithm also improves the computational efficiency of the fuzzy correlation segmentation. Finally, the atmospheric light can be predicted by the sky region in the segmentation result, and the haze-free image can be obtained via the wavelength related physical imaging model. Compared with existing dehazing methods, our algorithm can improve dehazing precision by at least 7% and shorten running time by roughly 15%.

Acknowledgments. This work is supported by the National Natural Science Foundation of China (No. 61502396), the Central Universities-Yong Scholar Development Project (No. JBK1801076), the Education Department Foundation of Sichuan Province (No. 18ZB0484). In addition, this work is also supported by the Key Laboratory of Financial Intelligence and Financial Engineering of Sichuan Province and the Multimedia Research Centre at the University of Alberta.

References

1. Bando, Y., Chen, B.Y., Nishita, T.: Extracting depth and matte using a color-filtered aperture. In: ACM Transactions on Graphics (TOG), vol. 27, p. 134. ACM (2008)
2. El-Azab, M., Shokry, M., et al.: Correlation measure for fuzzy multisets. J. Egypt. Math. Soc. **25**(3), 263–267 (2017)
3. Li, B., et al.: Benchmarking single-image dehazing and beyond. IEEE Trans. Image Process. **28**(1), 492–505 (2018)
4. Li, M., Liu, J., Yang, W., Sun, X., Guo, Z.: Structure-revealing low-light image enhancement via robust retinex model. IEEE Trans. Image Process. **27**(6), 2828–2841 (2018)
5. Liu, C., Cheng, I., Basu, A.: Synthetic vision assisted real-time runway detection for infrared aerial images. In: Basu, A., Berretti, S. (eds.) ICSM 2018. LNCS, vol. 11010, pp. 274–281. Springer, Cham (2018). https://doi.org/10.1007/978-3-030-04375-9_23
6. Liu, Y., Shang, J., Pan, L., Wang, A., Wang, M.: A unified variational model for single image dehazing. IEEE Access **7**, 15722–15736 (2019)
7. Narasimhan, S.G., Nayar, S.K.: Vision and the atmosphere. Int. J. Comput. Vision **48**(3), 233–254 (2002)
8. Narasimhan, S.G., Nayar, S.K.: Contrast restoration of weather degraded images. IEEE Trans. Pattern Anal. Mach. Intell. **6**, 713–724 (2003)

9. Nigam, J., Sharma, K., Rameshan, R.M.: Detection-Based online multi-target tracking via adaptive subspace learning. In: Basu, A., Berretti, S. (eds.) ICSM 2018. LNCS, vol. 11010, pp. 285–295. Springer, Cham (2018). https://doi.org/10. 1007/978-3-030-04375-9_24

10. Ruixing, Y., Bing, Z., Meng, C., Xiao, Z., Jiawen, W.: Research on path planning method of an unmanned vehicle in urban road environments. In: Basu, A., Berretti, S. (eds.) ICSM 2018. LNCS, vol. 11010, pp. 235–247. Springer, Cham (2018). https://doi.org/10.1007/978-3-030-04375-9_20

11. Sun, X., Kottayil, N.K., Mukherjee, S., Cheng, I.: Adversarial training for dual-stage image denoising enhanced with feature matching. In: Basu, A., Berretti, S. (eds.) ICSM 2018. LNCS, vol. 11010, pp. 357–366. Springer, Cham (2018). https:// doi.org/10.1007/978-3-030-04375-9_30

12. Wang, J.B., He, N., Zhang, L.L., Lu, K.: Single image dehazing with a physical model and dark channel prior. Neurocomputing **149**, 718–728 (2015)

13. Wang, W., Yuan, X., Wu, X., Liu, Y.: Fast image dehazing method based on linear transformation. IEEE Trans. Multimedia **19**(6), 1142–1155 (2017)

14. Xu, Y., Wen, J., Fei, L., Zhang, Z.: Review of video and image defogging algorithms and related studies on image restoration and enhancement. IEEE Access **4**, 165–188 (2015)

15. Yao, D.N.L., Bade, A., Suaib, N.M., Sulaiman, H.A.B.: Digital image enhancement using enhanced detail and dehaze technique (dde). Adv. Sci. Lett. **24**(3), 1559–1561 (2018)

16. Yoon, I., Jeong, S., Jeong, J., Seo, D., Paik, J.: Wavelength-adaptive dehazing using histogram merging-based classification for uav images. Sensors **15**(3), 6633–6651 (2015)

17. Yuan, J., Bae, E., Tai, X.-C., Boykov, Y.: A spatially continuous max-flow and min-cut framework for binary labeling problems. Numer. Math. **126**(3), 559–587 (2013). https://doi.org/10.1007/s00211-013-0569-x

Biometrics

Fingerprint Liveness Detection Based on Multi-modal Fine-Grained Feature Fusion

Chengsheng Yuan[1,2](✉) and Q. M. Jonathan Wu[2]

[1] School of Computer and Software,
Nanjing University of Information Science and Technology, Nanjing, China
ycs_nuist@163.com
[2] Department of Electrical and Computer Engineering, University of Windsor, Windsor, Canada
wuw888@gmail.com

Abstract. Recently, fingerprint recognition systems are widely deployed in our daily life. However, spoofing via using special materials such as silica, gelatin, Play-Doh, clay, etc., is one of the most common methods of attacking fingerprint recognition systems. To handle the above defects, a fingerprint liveness detection (FLD) technique is proposed. In this paper, we propose a novel structure to discriminate genuine or fake fingerprints. First, to describe the subtle differences between them and make full use of each algorithm, this paper extracts three types of different fine-grained texture features, such as SIFT, LBP, HOG. Next, we developed a feature fusion rule, including five fusion operations, to better integrate the above features. Finally, those fused features are fed into an SVM classifier for the subsequent classification. Experimental results on the benchmark LivDet 2013 fingerprints indicate that the classification performance of our method outperforms other FLD methods proposed in recent literature.

Keywords: Fingerprint liveness detection · Feature fusion · SIFT · LBP · HOG · SVM

1 Introduction

With the rapid development of multimedia and digital imaging technology, it is recently possible to collect large amounts of high-resolution images using sophisticated digital cameras or other high-resolution sensors. Because of the convenience and security of biometrics, biometric recognition techniques have a broad application prospect in the field of identity authentication and network security. There are a variety of biometric authentication methods, including fingerprint, face, and iris, among which fingerprint recognition is the most common. Fingerprints are characterized by uniqueness, stability, and invariability. Moreover, compared with traditional authentication methods, fingerprint recognition requires no password to be remembered. Accordingly, personal identities can be associated with a fingerprint [1]. Afterward, we can verify the authenticity of a user's identity by comparing his or her fingerprint features with pre-saved features in a database. Fingerprints are claimed to be safe and hard to steal and copy. However, with

© Springer Nature Switzerland AG 2020
T. McDaniel et al. (Eds.): ICSM 2019, LNCS 12015, pp. 417–428, 2020.
https://doi.org/10.1007/978-3-030-54407-2_35

the increasing demand for high-level security in some smart devices, research points out that these fingerprint authentication devices are unsafe and easily spoofed by some artificial replicas made from wax, moldable plastic, Play-Doh, clay or gelatin [2] when the simulation performance is high enough and the texture is clear enough. Thus, the security of fingerprint recognition systems is threatened. To cope with the above issues, a fingerprint liveness detection (FLD) [3] method has been proposed.

SIFT [4] (Scale-Invariant Feature transform) has the characteristics of invariant rotation, invariant scale and invariant brightness, which are conducive to the effective and efficient expression of target texture information. However, it fails to extract those features from smoothing targets. LBP [5] (Local Binary Pattern) has the advantages of invariant rotation and invariant gray to some extent. However, it does not meet invariant scale. HOG [6] (Histogram of Oriented Gradient) can represent the structural texture information of an edge (gradient), and it can reflect the local shape information. Because of the neglect of the influence of light brightness in the image, the extracted feature adopting HOG contains a lot of noise. In addition, due to the use of block and unit processing ideas, the relationship between the center and adjacent pixels is well represented. In order to describe the subtle differences between genuine or fake fingerprints and take advantage of each feature algorithm, this paper proposes a novel structure for fingerprint liveness detection.

The remainder of this paper is organized as follows. Section 2 describes the related work to FLD in recent years. Section 3 presents the Methodology. Experiments are given in Sect. 4. Finally, conclusions are drawn in Sect. 5.

2 Related Work

In modern times, fingerprint recognition systems are widely deployed in mobile devices, such as tablets, laptops, and smart cellphones. However, one of the common problems with these devices is that they neglect to verify the authenticity of fingerprints before identification. Namely, they do not have the ability to distinguish between genuine and fake fingerprint images [7], which has led to the emergence of FLD technology to solve the problems of spoofing attacks. Researchers and scholars have devoted considerable effort to differentiating genuine fingerprints from fake ones during the past several years by analyzing different physical or psychological traits [7]. Through the research of FLD methods at home and abroad, we note that the existing FLD methods fall into two categories: hardware-based FLD methods and software-based FLD methods. Some recent studies have depicted that anti-spoofing FLD methods based on hardware can discriminate those genuine fingerprints from fake ones only by measuring physiological characteristics, such as pulse oximetry, skin resistance, blood oxygen, temperature, electrocardiogram, etc. Although the above biometrics can recognize genuine and fake fingerprints, the drawback is that these instruments are bulky, expensive and require trained professionals to perform measurements [8]. Hence, to save costs and simplify operations, an ideal anti-spoofing detection method is to exploit as few additional hardware devices as possible and assign all the work to the computer, and some novel software based FLD methods without any additional sensors are proposed. Moreover, late maintenance based on a software detection strategy is also very convenient only via a simple software upgrade.

Texture is an important visual trait that describes the homogeneity phenomenon of the image, and it reflects the arrangement property of the surface structure with slow change. It can reflect different texture phenomenon for those genuine and fake fingerprints, such as morphology, smoothness, and orientation; hence, the texture representation has been used in FLD and is the main content of this paper. At present, how to better represent the texture pattern of the fingerprints and achieve a higher classification accuracy is the hotspot of FLD. Recently, Abhyankar et al. [9] proposed a novel FLD method by combining the multiresolution texture analysis and the interring frequency analysis. They attempted to use different texture information to quantify how the pixel value distribution of the fingerprints change when the physical structure changes. Next, two feature extraction methods, including a multiresolution texture analysis and a ridge-frequency analysis, are utilized. Finally, they exploit the Fuzzy C-means classifier for those combined features to distinguish genuine fingers from fake ones. In 2012, Yuan [10] assessed the recently introduced Local Phase Quantization (LPQ) algorithm and applied it to FLD. A series of experiments based on several common feature extraction algorithms were performed, including LPQ, LBP, LBP's variants [11], and results also demonstrated that LPQ based detection performance was optimal.

3 Methodology

3.1 Feature Extraction

In order to distinguish the genuine fingerprints from the fake ones, the key is to extract the differentiable features between them. Accordingly, this paper designs a novel fingerprint liveness detection structure analyzing three epidemic feature extractors, including SIFT, LBP, and HOG, to extract subtle differences between them. On one hand, the above three methods can extract some different fine-grained (local) texture features of fingerprints; On the other hand, after feature fusion, the advantages of each algorithm can be fully utilized to make up for the detailed information that cannot be observed by a single feature. Experimental results also demonstrate that the performance of feature fusion is better than that of a single feature extractor.

SIFT: Scale-invariant feature transform, which is a kind of local feature descriptor, can detect the key subtle information between genuine and fake fingerprints. As a stable local feature descriptor, SIFT remains unchanged when these images are rotated and zoomed, even when the intensity changes. First, the image scale is reconstructed using the gray-scale transformation to gain the multi-scale space representation sequences of images, and the main contour of the scale space is extracted from these sequences, which are regarded as a feature vector to realize the extraction of key points in edge and corner detection at different resolutions. Then, to ensure that the detected key points are local extremum points in the scale space and two-dimensional image space, each pixel point is compared with its adjacent pixel points. In addition, the stable extremum points are extracted in different scale space to guarantee the scale invariance of the key points. Moreover, to make the key points invariable to the image angle and rotation, the direction assignment is operated by finding the gradient of each extremum. Finally, the key point descriptor is to generate a unique vector by dividing the pixel area around the key point into blocks, calculating the gradient histogram within the key point. This vector is an abstract representation of the image (Fig. 1).

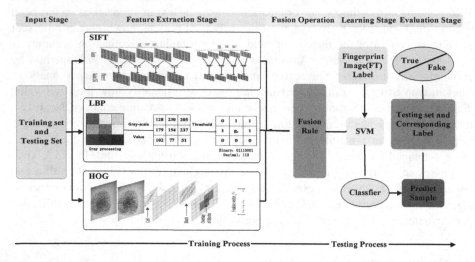

Fig. 1. Flow chart of fingerprint liveness detection based on multi-modal fine-grained feature fusion.

During the above calculation, the scale space L(x, y, σ) denotes convolutional operation between an original image I(x, y) and a variable-scale 2D Gauss function G(x, y, σ). The two-dimensional Gaussian distribution formula is as follows:

$$G(x_i, y_i) = \frac{1}{2\pi\sigma^2}\exp\left(-\frac{(x-x_i)^2 + (y-y_i)^2}{2\sigma^2}\right) \tag{1}$$

The scale space of the image is the calculation of convolution operation using two-dimensional Gaussian distribution and the original image. The scale space expression is as follows:

$$L(x, y, \sigma) = G(x, y, \sigma) * I(x, y) \tag{2}$$

LBP: LBP [12, 13] is an operator used to describe local texture features of images, and it has the obvious advantages of rotation invariance and gray invariance. The goal is to measure the local contrast of the fingerprints and describe the local texture information of the image.

Before constructing the local texture, we need to preprocess the given image, then transform the image into grey-scale image and analyze the relationship between central pixel and adjacent pixels. The LBP operator is defined in the window of size 3 × 3, and the threshold is the central pixel in the window. Next, the central pixel is compared with its adjacent 8 pixels. If the adjacent pixel is larger than the central pixel, the position of the pixel is marked as 1; otherwise it is marked as 0. In this way, an 8-bit binary number has been generated by comparing with the adjacent 8 points in a window of size 3 × 3 and arranging them in sequence to form a binary number. Take this value as the new value of the pixel in the center of the window to reflect the texture information. It worth nothing that there are 256 kinds of LBP values and each value can represent a different texture.

Because LBP records the difference between the central pixel and its adjacent pixel, when the light changes cause the gray value of the pixel to increase and decrease at the same time, the change in LBP is not obvious. Therefore, it can be considered that LBP is not sensitive to the change of illumination. LBP only detects the texture information of images, so it can further make histogram statistics of LBP which are used as the feature operator of texture analysis. Generally, the image after LBP operation is divided into many square regions, such as 4×4, 10×10 or 16×16, and we can get 16, 100, 256 histograms representing the feature of fingerprint images by means of the above regions.

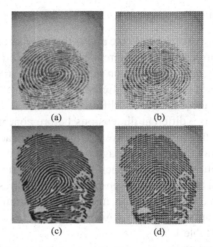

(a)   (b)

(c)   (d)

Fig. 2. True, fake fingerprints and their visualizations using HOG. (a) True fingerprint. (b) True fingerprint visualization. (c) Fake fingerprint. (d) Fake fingerprint visualization.

HOG [14] is short for histogram of oriented gradient, and it consists of local features formed by calculating the gradient histogram of the given images. Since HOG denotes the structural feature of an edge (gradient), it can describe the local shape information; thus, it is a commonly used feature descriptor. The quantization of position and direction space can restrain the influence of translation and rotation to some extent. Moreover, after normalizing the histogram in the local region, the influence of illumination change can be partially offset.

The detailed implementation steps are as follows:

Step 1: Before calculation, grayscale and gamma correction are carried on reducing the influence of local shadow and light changes in the image. Meanwhile, to some extent, the interference of noise is suppressed;

Step 2: To obtain a histogram of gradient, the horizontal and the vertical gradients of the image by the convolution of the filter and the image are calculated;

Step 3: Next, the magnitude and direction of each pixel are calculated;

Step 4: After that, each cell consists of 4×4 pixels, and the histogram of gradients is computed for each pixel in the cell;

Step 5: Before feature generation, to make the generated feature robust to light, shadow and edge changes, it is necessary to normalize the HOG features of the block. Finally, make 4×4 cells denote a block and concatenate the features of the block to get the final feature of image, which is employed for subsequent classification.

As shown in Fig. 2, visual images of the genuine and fake feature fingerprints using the HOG method are listed. Among them, the genuine fingerprint features are evenly distributed, the fake fingerprints are damaged more, and there are stains and other fuzzy states.

3.2 Feature Fusion Rule

By analyzing the features extracted using the above three algorithms, the ways of feature fusion are diverse. Thus, to describe the difference between genuine and fake fingerprints, in this paper, we develop a new feature fusion rule to fuse the extracted features. Because the dimensions of extracted features are different, it is difficult to directly splice them. Hence, to piece together these features of different dimensions, we need to make up 0 for the features of the above different dimensions before concatenation. In this paper, five types of different feature fusion rules are set, including an addition operation, maximum operation, minimum operation, average operation and concatenation operation. Table 1 reports the specific operation for each feature fusion rule, where F denotes the feature, the SIFT, LBP and HOG in the subscript are the corresponding features, and the addition operation, maximum operation, minimum operation, average operation and concatenation operation are abbreviated as Add, Max, Min, Ave and Con. The detailed operations are shown in Table 1.

Table 1. Feature fusion rules of different fusion operations.

Operation	Addition	Maximum	Minimum	Average	Concatenation
Rule	$[Add(F_{SIFT} + F_{LBP} + F_{HOG})]$	$[Max(F_{SIFT}, F_{LBP}, F_{HOG})]$	$[Min(F_{SIFT}, F_{LBP}, F_{HOG})]$	$[Ave(F_{SIFT} + F_{LBP} + F_{HOG})]$	$[Con(F_{SIFT}, F_{LBP}, F_{HOG})]$

3.3 Parameter Optimization

After fusing the features using our proposed rule, the generated features will be fed into an SVM (Support Vector Machine) classifier for the subsequent training and testing. However, in order to obtain a better model classifier, it is necessary to perform parameter optimization before model training.

SVM is a learning method based on the criterion of structural risk minimization, which is divided into two categories: linear SVM and nonlinear SVM, depending on the nuclear function used. To eliminate the influence of outliers between features and limit the features to a certain range, a standardization operation should be performed first so as to eliminate the adverse effects caused by outliers' samples and dimensions. Then, to gain a robust and effective model classifier, optimization of the parameters C and gamma (that is <C, g>) for the fused features, which are constructed via our proposed fusion rule, is necessary. Figure 3 gives the result images of parameter optimization in the Biometrika dataset, and we can obtain the optimal parameter pair (<C, g>) from each figure. Finally, these fused features are trained via an SVM classifier with the optimal parameter pair <C, g>.

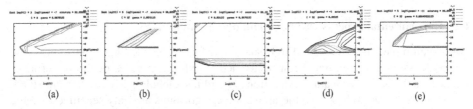

    (a)   (b)   (c)   (d)   (e)

Fig. 3. Parameter optimization figures under different feature fusion operation in the Biometrika data set. (a) addition operation; (b) maximum operation; (c) minimum operation; (d) average operation; (e) concatenation operation.

Table 2. The image distribution of the LivDet2013 data set.

Dataset ID	Sensor	Size	Samples in training set		Samples in testing set	
			Live	Spoof	Live	Spoof
Liv2013-1	Biometrika	352 × 384	1000	1000	1000	1000
Liv2013-2	CrossMatch	800 × 750	1250	1000	1250	1000
Liv2013-3	Italdata	480 × 640	1000	1000	1000	1000
Liv2013-4	Swipe	1500 × 208	1221	979	1153	1000

4 Experiments

4.1 Database

The detection performance of our proposed schema is verified using the benchmark fingerprint image set LivDet2013 [1], which consists of a total of 16853 genuine and fake fingerprints and constructed via adoption of four different flat optical sensors, including Biometrika, CrossMatch, Italdata and Swipe. In addition, two types of fingerprints are included: A training dataset with a total of 8450 images and a testing dataset with a total of 8403 images. The training image set is used to learn and obtain a model classifier, and the performance evaluation of the model classifier is evaluated using the testing dataset. Note that it is hard to observe the slight difference between the real fingerprints and the fake ones by the naked eye. The detailed distribution of the LivDet 2013 dataset is shown in Table 2. From Table 2, we can find that the ratio of genuine fingerprints and fake fingerprints is 1:1 approximately, and the sizes/scales of given fingerprints are varied from 315×372 to 1500×208.

4.2 Experimental Process and Performance Evaluation

First, to eliminate the influence of light and other factors for the fingerprints, an image gray processing operation has been performed. Next, the features of the fingerprints are extracted using three feature extraction algorithms, including SIFT, LBP and HOG. The features extracted based on the above three algorithms are only sensitive to some feature changes, but not to other features. Hence, the classification performance of the fingerprint liveness detection adopting a single feature method is unsatisfactory, and the experimental results confirm this point in this paper. To solve the problem, one possible solution is to fuse the features to make up for the shortcomings of a single feature method. Thus, the feature fusion operation, combined with the strengths of each algorithm, can reach the goal of complementary weaknesses. In addition, feature fusion for multiple different algorithms can also enhance final performance.

The specific feature fusion rules involved in this paper are classified into five types: addition operation, maximum operation, minimum operation, average operation and concatenation operation. Due to the difference between the above three algorithms, the dimensions of the feature extracted are inconsistent. To perform successfully the above five feature fusion operations, insufficient parts need to be filled with 0.

Since the distribution and range of each feature are different, it is necessary to map these features extracted to the same interval by normalization operations to make the components of features consistent. Moreover, rescaling to the appropriate range can make training and testing faster. Before gaining a robust model classifier, parameter optimization needs to be carried out to find the optimal parameter pair $<C, g>$; the optimal parameter is then exploited for the subsequent model training and testing. Finally, the classification result is obtained by using a trained model classifier.

In order to verify the performance of the feature extraction algorithm in the paper, we adopt average classification error (ACE) [15–17] as a metric. The formula is defined as follows:

$$ACE = \frac{FAR + FRR}{2} \tag{3}$$

In formula 3, FAR denotes the probability that a fake fingerprint is mistaken as the genuine fingerprint, and FRR is the probability that a genuine fingerprint is mistaken as the fake one. The outcome of fingerprint liveness detection may be any value between 0 and 100. Suppose that the given threshold is 50, and the value of a detected image is more than 50. This image can be recognized as a genuine fingerprint. If not, it will be recognized as a fake fingerprint. Finally, we can obtain the performance of our proposed algorithm by using formula 3.

4.3 Results

First, we analyze and evaluate the performance of our method on the LivDet 2013 dataset when adopting different feature fusion rules, including addition operation, maximum operation, minimum operation, average operation and concatenation operation. The results are reported in Table 3. From Table 3, we can find that, in general, the detection performance after feature fusion is better than that of a single feature algorithm. For example, in the Biometrika dataset, the classification accuracies of SIFT, LBP and HOG are 86.7, 94.0 and 93.8 respectively. After performing the feature fusion operation, the classification accuracy of LBP+HOG is 99.9. Namely, feature fusion can improve the detection performance of genuine and fake fingerprints. In the CrossMatch dataset, the classification results of SIFT, LBP and HOG are 88.8, 90.6 and 90.5, respectively. After performing the feature fusion operation, the classification accuracy of SIFT+LBP is 93.6, and the FLD performance has been further improved. In addition, the time after testing all datasets is also listed in Table 3, and is quite acceptable. Moreover, the task of testing a fingerprint is basically done without our even knowing it, showing that our method is also applicable to real life.

Table 3. Average classification accuracy and testing time of different feature fusions in the LivDet2013 fingerprint set.

Feature fusion	Average classification correct accuracy				Testing time(s)			
	Biometrika	Crossmatch	Italdata	Swipe	Biometrika	Crossmatch	Italdata	Swipe
SIFT	86.7	88.8	85.2	91.2	9	19	15	12
LBP	94.0	90.6	90.6	93.3	23	10	73	43
HOG	93.8	90.5	96.6	92.3	42	9	37	59
SIFT+LBP	84.9	93.6	95.6	97.9	33	45	62	25
SIFT+HOG	78.4	86.4	85.9	95.7	13	25	33	11
LBP+HOG	99.9	84.0	91.5	96.2	20	34	54	15
Add(SIFT, LBP, HOG)	99.6	92.4	94.3	96.5	12	22	25	10
Max(SIFT, LBP, HOG)	98.8	83.9	95.0	96.6	3	21	24	9
Min(SIFT, LBP, HOG)	98.1	56.5	72.3	79.3	15	7	10	80
Ave(SIFT, LBP, HOG)	95.4	94.2	94.7	93.7	14	17	17	14
Con(SIFT, LBP, HOG)	99.9	94.0	94.9	97.3	19	51	45	12

Table 4 lists the detailed comparison results when adopting different concatenation operations. In Table 4, the ACEs of our proposed method are the lowest. To compare the performance of different algorithms, the optimal results for each sensor are all highlighted in bold in each row. The result of the Biometrika sensor in LivDet 2013 is close to 0, and the ACE of our method is 0.02 lower than the second result of [21]. The FLD method based on convolutional neural networks (CNN) achieves the state-of-the-art performance in Crossmatch, but it has some drawbacks. For example, the training time of the model is long, the interpretability of the features based on CNN is weak, a large number of training samples are required, and it relies on high-performance computers. However, the texture feature algorithms, which can capture these subtle differences between genuine and fake fingerprints, are used to solve those shortcomings of CNN. In addition, our results of Italdata and Crossmatch are 2.75 and 2.8 higher than the two results of [20, 21] in Table 4, respectively; however, the results of Biometrika and Swipe sensors are 0.7 and 2.55, respectively, lower than that of [20, 21]. Table 3 shows that different feature fusion methods should be used to obtain a better detection performance when the types of fingerprint scanners are known.

Table 4. The comparisons of the ACE of different algorithms in LivDet 2013.

Algorithm name	Average classification error rate *ACE* in (%)				
	Biometrika	Crossmatch	Italdata	Swipe	Average
Our method	**0.1**	6.0	5.1	**2.7**	**3.48**
ULBP [19]	10.68	46.09	13.7	14.35	21.21
Winner [1]	4.7	31.2	3.5	14.07	13.37
HIG-MC [18]	4.3	39.96	10.6	32.41	21.92
UniNap [1]	4.7	31.2	3.5	14.07	13.37
HIG-BP [18]	3.9	34.13	8.3	14.44	15.19
PHOG [20]	3.87	9.92	6.7	9.05	7.24
MSDCM [20]	3.55	20.84	**2.35**	5.25	7.59
CNN-Rand [21]	0.8	**3.2**	2.4	7.6	3.5

5   Conclusion

It is well known that the SIFT feature descriptor is characterized by invariant rotation, scale and brightness; The HOG feature descriptor ignored the influence of light on the image, reducing the dimension of the feature for the image; The LBP feature descriptor is insensitive to light and fast to operate. Combining the advantages of SIFT features,

LBP features, and HOG features can make up for the shortcomings of each algorithm and improve the final detection performance. Finally, these fused features are fed into the SVM classifier for the subsequent training and testing. Contrasted by experiment, the classification performance based on fused features by using SIFT, HOG and LBP is better than other FLD methods, and our method is more suitable for fingerprint liveness detection to prevent spoof attacks related to these artificial replicas.

Acknowledgements. The authors are grateful for the anonymous reviewers who made valuable comments and improvements. Furthermore, many thanks to Xinting Li and Weijin Cheng for helping us polish the article and make suggestions. This research was funded by the Canada Research Chair Program and the NSERC Discovery Grant; by the Startup Foundation for Introducing Talent of NUIST (2020r015); by the Priority Academic Program Development of Jiangsu Higher Education Institutions (PAPD) fund; by the Collaborative Innovation Center of Atmospheric Environment and Equipment Technology (CICAEET) fund, China.

References

1. Ghiani, L., et al.: Livdet 2013 fingerprint liveness detection competition 2013. International Conference on Biometrics (ICB), pp. 1–6, Madrid, Spain (2013)
2. Yuan, C., Xia, Z., Sun, X., Sun, D., Lv, R.: Fingerprint liveness detection using multiscale difference co-occurrence matrix. Opt. Eng. **55**(6), 1–10 (2016)
3. Zhang, Y., Tian, J., Chen, X., Yang, X., Shi, P.: Fake finger detection based on thin-plate spline distortion model. In: Lee, S.-W., Li, S.Z. (eds.) ICB 2007. LNCS, vol. 4642, pp. 742–749. Springer, Heidelberg (2007). https://doi.org/10.1007//978-3-540-74549 5_78
4. Lowe, D.G.: Object recognition from local scale-invariant features. In: International Conference on Computer Vision, Corfu, Greece, pp. 1150–1157 (1999)
5. Ojala, T., Pietikäinen, M., Mäenpää, T.: Multiresolution gray-scale and rotation invariant texture classification with local binary patterns. IEEE Trans. Pattern Anal. Mach. Intell. **24**(7), 971–987 (2002)
6. Dalal, N., Triggs, B.: Histograms of oriented gradients for human detection. In: Proceedings of IEEE Conference CVPR, San Diego, United States, pp. 886–893 (2005)
7. Maltoni, D., Maio, D., Jain, A., Prabhakar, S.: Synthetic fingerprint generation. In: Handbook of Fingerprint Recognition, vol. 33, no. 5, p. 1314 (2005)
8. Marasco, E., Sansone, C.: Combining perspiration- and morphology-based static features for fingerprint liveness detection. Pattern Recogn. Lett. **33**(9), 1148–1156 (2012)
9. Abhyankar, A., Schuckers, S.: Fingerprint liveness detection using local ridge frequencies and multiresolution texture analysis techniques. In: International Conference on Image Processing. Atlanta, GA, USA (2007)
10. Yuan, C., Sun, X., Lv, R.: Fingerprint liveness detection based on multi-scale LPQ and PCA. China Commun. **13**(7), 60–65 (2016)
11. Nogueira, R.F., Lotufo, R.D.A., Machado, R.C.: Evaluating software-based fingerprint liveness detection using convolutional networks and local binary patterns. In: Biometric Measurements and Systems for Security and Medical Applications, pp. 22–29 (2014)
12. Beamer, L.J., Carroll, S.F., Eisenberg, D.: The BPI/LBP family of proteins: a structural analysis of conserved regions. Protein Sci. **7**(4), 906–914 (2010)
13. Tan, X., Triggs, B.: Fusing Gabor and LBP feature sets for Kernel-based face recognition. In: Zhou, S.K., Zhao, W., Tang, X., Gong, S. (eds.) AMFG 2007. LNCS, vol. 4778, pp. 235–249. Springer, Heidelberg (2007). https://doi.org/10.1007/978-3-540-75690-3_18

14. Saito, H., Tatebayashi, K.: Regulation of the osmoregulatory HOG MAPK cascade in yeast. J. Biochem. **136**(3), 267–272 (2004)
15. Lee, H.-S., Maeng, H.-J., Bae, Y.-S.: Fake finger detection using the fractional Fourier transform. In: Fierrez, J., Ortega-Garcia, J., Esposito, A., Drygajlo, A., Faundez-Zanuy, M. (eds.) BioID 2009. LNCS, vol. 5707, pp. 318–324. Springer, Heidelberg (2009). https://doi.org/10.1007/978-3-642-04391-8_41
16. Nogueira, R.F., Lotufo, R.D.A., Machado, R.C.: Evaluating software-based fingerprint liveness detection using convolutional networks and local binary patterns. In: IEEE Workshop on Biometric Measurements & Systems for Security & Medical Applications, Rome, Italy. IEEE (2014)
17. Yuan, C., Sun, X., Wu, Q.M.J.: Difference co-occurrence matrix using BP neural network for fingerprint liveness detection. Soft. Comput. **23**(13), 5157–5169 (2018). https://doi.org/10.1007/s00500-018-3182-1
18. Gottschlich, C., Marasco, E., Yang, A., Cuick, B.: Fingerprint liveness detection based on histograms of invariant gradients. In: IEEE International Joint Conference on Biometrics, Clearwater, FL, USA, pp. 1–7 (2014)
19. Jiang Y., Liu, X.: Uniform local binary pattern for fingerprint liveness detection in the Gaussian pyramid. J. Electr. Comput. Eng., 1–9 (2018)
20. Yuan, C., Xia, Z., Sun, X., Wu, Q.M.J.: Deep residual network with adaptive learning framework for fingerprint liveness detection. IEEE Trans. Cogn. Dev. Syst., 1–13 (2019)
21. Nogueira, R.F., Lotufo, R.D.A., Machado, R.C.: Fingerprint liveness detection using convolutional neural networks. IEEE Trans. Inf. Forensics Secur. **11**(6), 1206–1213 (2016)

Synthetic Aerial Image Generation and Runway Segmentation

Harsh Sharma[1], Changjiang Liu[2(✉)], and Irene Cheng[1]

[1] Department of Computing Science, University of Alberta,
Edmonton, AB T6G 2R3, Canada
{hsharma,locheng}@ualberta.ca
[2] Sichuan Province University Key Laboratory of Bridge Nondestruction Detecting
and Engineering Computing, Sichuan University of Science and Engineering,
Zigong 643000, China
liuchangjiang@189.cn

Abstract. Vision assisted navigation is an active area of research to assist pilots during bad weather conditions. However, these systems are not completely accurate. We propose 3D models to synthesize accurate 2D representations of the airport and the runway. A synthesized image sequence obtained from a 3D model of a view would be effective in conveying 3-D characteristics of the vanishing point (intersection between the horizon line and runway axis) and the beginning of the runway to the pilot. This can help to improve the pilot's visual perception of the surroundings under adverse weather conditions, leading to a safer landing. We propose a system to generate 2D images of runway captured during takeoff and landing to provide better tracking. We analyze the results by segmenting the runway and comparing it with actual data captured by the aircraft.

Keywords: Vision assisted navigation · Image synthesis · 3D projection · Image segmentation

1 Introduction

The Flight Safety Foundation (FSF) data shows that almost 60% of all commercial aircraft crashes occur during the approach and landing phase of the flight [1]. Vision assisted navigation systems can help prevent a lot of these accidents by providing the pilots with a better understanding of the scene and conveying the details about key points like the vanishing point and the beginning of the

Supported in part by Sichuan Science and Technology Program under Grant No. 2019YJ0541, the Open Project of Sichuan Province University Key Laboratory of Bridge Non-destruction Detecting and Engineering Computing under Grant No. 2019QZJ03 and Natural Science Foundation of Sichuan University of Science and Engineering (SUSE) under Grant No. 2019RC09, 2020RC28.

T. McDaniel et al. (Eds.): ICSM 2019, LNCS 12015, pp. 429–438, 2020.
https://doi.org/10.1007/978-3-030-54407-2_36

runway. However, to improve these systems we need a better understanding and representation of the scene.

The use of artificial data to gain a better understanding of all the scenarios is gaining traction in recent years. It has been successfully used for tasks like object classification [2], pedestrian identification [3], self-driving car training [4,5], etc. In this paper, we focus on generating artificial data to improve assisted landing and navigation of aircraft. We develop an approach to generate accurate 2D representations of a flight sequence rendered in a virtual world using 3D models. We simulate a flight sequence using an aircraft's onboard GPS and AHRS data and then project the taking off and landing sequences as 2D images. We also analyze them for accuracy by segmenting the runway and comparing it with the actual data collected. We aim to provide a dataset of image sequences for the airport and runway that can be used for improving the visual perception of the pilot.

The developed algorithm relies on the GPS and AHRS data from an aircraft along with the 3D models discussed in detail in the upcoming sections. We demonstrate the approach developed for Xinjin airport in China but it can be extended to other airports. As will be visible from our results, our approach is an improvement over the results of [6] in terms of accuracy.

2 Image Generation

There are several ways in which virtual images can be synthesized. Broadly, it can be classified into two categories: using video games or simulators and using 3D CAD models. Both approaches have been used widely in the past and have their pros and cons. Gaidon et al. [7], Shafaei, Little and Schmidt [8] and Ros et al. [9] showcase the use of artificial worlds to generate synthetic data. In all these papers, the authors were able to generate high-quality data by playing around in the game/simulator. However, it must be noted that, in this approach, to capture meaningful data for generating the images a certain level of expertise is required in playing the game/simulation. Without the availability of good 3D data, it is not possible to get accurate representations for use in real-world problems.

On the other hand, Marin et al. [3], Sun and Saenko [10], Jiang et al. [11], and Bhandari [5] leverage 3D models to generate virtual data. They rely on models generated using CAD tools, like blender, to generate photorealistic images. The models can be configured to modify the characteristics and easily obtain a huge dataset. The downside of using this approach is the availability of good 3D models. In our proposed approach we have used a 3D Model of the earth enhanced by a 3D model of just the airport. As shown in Fig. 1 (a), we use this hybrid model in conjunction with data captured from the attitude and heading reference system (AHRS) of an airplane to create our dataset.

2.1 3D Model

To generate photorealistic images, a photorealistic model is required. This is possible by enhancing the DEM data with a high-quality image as a texture.

The DEM data used during our testing is from Xinjin Airport in China and we used satellite image data from Google Earth to render the texture. Since our main focus is on the airport and the runway, to improve the quality we use a high precision model of just the airport.

Once the model is ready, we use OpenSceneGraph to navigate across the model. The data obtained from the onboard GPS and AHRS of the aircraft is used to manipulate the camera and with the help of OpenSceneGraph APIs we simulate a flight sequence. We then define the projection matrix, discussed in detail below, to calculate the projection coordinates in two dimensions and obtain the representation of the scene.

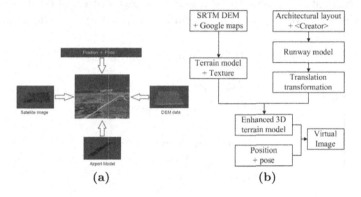

(a)   **(b)**

Fig. 1. Virtual image synthesis: **(a)** Components of the 3D model used [6] **(b)** Flow diagram [6]

2.2 Projection Matrix

As mentioned above, we project the 3D coordinates at a given moment to the corresponding 2D environment using a projection matrix. To obtain an accurate representation, we use the homogeneous coordinate system. The data available from the GPS and AHRS of the aircraft contains the details for the latitude, longitude, altitude, heading, pitch and roll at a given moment. We first calculate the translation parameters for the latitude, longitude, and altitude of the simulated sequence and then calculate the rotation matrices corresponding to each of the three axes (heading, pitch, and roll) and then taking the translation (delta change in latitude, longitude, and altitude) into consideration, we obtain the 4×4 transformation matrix defined by Eq. (1). We then use this matrix to convert 3D homogeneous coordinates to the corresponding 2D representation.

$$\begin{pmatrix} cos\alpha cos\beta & cos\alpha sin\beta sin\gamma - sin\alpha cos\gamma & cos\alpha sin\beta cos\gamma + sin\alpha sin\gamma & x_t \\ sin\alpha cos\beta & sin\alpha sin\beta sin\gamma + cos\alpha cos\gamma & sin\alpha sin\beta cos\gamma - cos\alpha sin\gamma & y_t \\ -sin\beta & cos\beta sin\gamma & cos\beta cos\gamma & z_t \\ 0 & 0 & 0 & 1 \end{pmatrix} \quad (1)$$

The order of operation for obtaining Eq. (1) is critical. In Eq. (1) the order followed is 1) Roll by γ, 2) Pitch by β, 3) Heading by α and then 4) translation by (x_t, y_t, z_t). We calculate the 2D coordinates by multiplying the 3D homogeneous coordinates with the projection matrix and generate the virtual images. The flow diagram for the entire process is shown in Fig. 1 (b).

2.3   Error Analysis

GPS and AHRS are common instruments aboard an aircraft, however, they are prone to measurement error. As discussed, the virtual image generation requires the position and pose values along with the model. The error in measurement leads to a mismatch between the synthetic and real data and must be analyzed and corrected. The various parameters and their precisions are listed in Table 1.

Table 1. Device parameters and precision

Parameter	Precision
Heading	0.1° (baseline >1 m)
Attitude	0.5°
Position	Horizontal < 2 m
	Vertical < 4 m
Velocity	0.1 m/s

If we assume that the camera has a focal length f and is located at the origin $(0,0,0)$ and the object is located at $\mathbf{X} = (X, Y, Z)^T$, according to the pinhole imaging model, the coordinates s_x and s_y in the image plane are

$$s_x = \frac{fX}{Z}, \quad s_y = \frac{fY}{Z} \tag{2}$$

We analyze the error in the GPS and AHRS using this equation and assume the aircraft carrying the camera as the origin and the airport location at point $P(x, y, z)^T$. Errors in GPS will produce errors in position $\Delta T = (\Delta x, \Delta y, \Delta z)^T$ and AHRS will lead to angular errors $(\Delta\alpha, \Delta\beta, \Delta\gamma)$ which leads the final position in camera coordinates to be

$$P' = R_z R_y R_x P = \begin{bmatrix} cos\Delta\gamma & -sin\Delta\gamma & 0 \\ sin\Delta\gamma & cos\Delta\gamma & 0 \\ 0 & 0 & 1 \end{bmatrix} \times \begin{bmatrix} cos\Delta\beta & 0 & sin\Delta\beta \\ 0 & 1 & 0 \\ sin\Delta\beta & 0 & cos\Delta\beta \end{bmatrix} \times$$
$$\begin{bmatrix} 1 & 0 & 0 \\ 0 & cos\Delta\alpha & sin\Delta\alpha \\ 0 & sin\Delta\alpha & cos\Delta\alpha \end{bmatrix} \times \begin{bmatrix} x + \Delta x \\ y + \Delta y \\ z + \Delta z \end{bmatrix} \tag{3}$$

Since the error for AHRS is small ($< 0.5°$), we can assume that $sin\theta \approx 0$ and $cos\theta \approx 1$ (for $\theta = \alpha, \beta, \gamma$). Using this assumption and Eq. 2, the image coordinates can be simplified to

$$s'_x = \frac{f(x + \Delta x)}{z + \Delta z}, \quad s'_y = \frac{f(y + \Delta y)}{z + \Delta z} \tag{4}$$

which can be used to calculate $\Delta s_x = s'_x - s_x$ and $\Delta s_y = s'_y - s_y$ as,

$$\Delta s_x = \frac{f(z\Delta x - x\Delta z)}{z(z + \Delta z)}, \quad \Delta s_y = \frac{f(z\Delta y - y\Delta z)}{z(z + \Delta z)} \tag{5}$$

$\Delta x, \Delta y$ and Δz are position precision and their maximum values are 2m, 2m and 4m respectively. For each frame, Δs_x and Δs_y were solved by substituting current location (x, y, z) and $\Delta x, \Delta y$, Δz into Eq. 5.

3   Runway Segmentation and Fusion with Real Images

The primary objective of creating the new dataset is to improve the accuracy of vision assisted navigation, particularly during the taking off and landing sequence. If the virtual images are an accurate representation of the airport, it would help in increasing the accuracy of such systems. To test the accuracy of the synthesized images, we tried out two different approaches

1. Using image segmentation
2. Use image fusion

Both approaches are extremely fast and help in enhancing the quality of the data obtained by the onboard cameras. This enhanced data can be used to identify finer details and subsequently used for improving the navigation systems.

3.1   Segmentation

From the histograms in Fig. 2 it can be easily deciphered that the generated images have only one peak (grayscale). We leverage this fact and apply a binary thresholding procedure to segment the brighter parts of the image, in this case, the runway. After applying morphological operations, we plot the image on top of the actual images to compare the results. The virtual image along with the mask and the enhanced images are shown in Fig. 3.

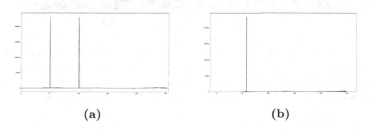

(a)   (b)

Fig. 2. Histograms for the generated images. **(a)** RGB Mode. **(b)** Grayscale mode.

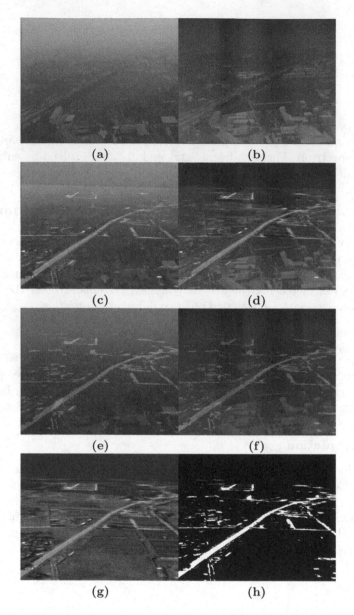

Fig. 3. Landing sequence images - (**a**) Visible spectrum image from aircraft. (**b**) IR image. (**c**) Visible image enhanced via fusion (**d**) IR image enhanced via fusion (**e**) Visible image overlapped with segmented runway. (**f**) IR image overlapped with segmented runway. (**g**) Generated virtual image (**h**) Binary image for (g)

3.2   Image Fusion

Image fusion is the process of creating enhanced images by combining images of the same scene which differ on certain aspects like exposure, focus, etc. Since, the virtual image is a representation of the image captured by the onboard camera, we combine the two images using wavelet transforms [12, 13]. The approach followed is similar to [14], we first calculate the wavelet transform for each image using 'db1' wavelets, and then merge these two approximations by choosing the maximum of the two elements. In the next step we apply inverse transform followed by integer normalization on the merged data to get back the image. The results are shown in Fig. 3.

4   Registration of Misaligned Virtual and Real Images

Automated registration of virtual and real images using the methods described in Sect. 3 result in an enhanced image in most scenarios, however as seen in Fig. 4 (d), there can be cases with misalignment. These can be resolved by manually selecting points in the virtual image and doing a registration with the real images. Since the runway is the most important part of the image for our study, we segment the runway out and manually select key points along the corners before performing the registration. The resulting images are shown in Fig. 4 (e) and (f).

The registration is done using a 2D projective geometric transformation. If the point $(u, v, 1)$ in one image corresponds to point $(x, y, 1)$ in the other image, then using a project matrix M, we can define

$$[x\ y\ 1] = M \times [u\ v\ 1] \tag{6}$$

where M is a 3×3 matrix of the form,

$$M = \begin{bmatrix} a & b & c \\ d & e & f \\ g & h & i \end{bmatrix} \tag{7}$$

Using 4 unique pairs of points across the images, we can solve for M by following steps similar to those described in Sect. 2.3.

5   Results, Analysis and Limitations

As discussed before, the outcome of the approach can be analyzed based on two metrics, first, the visual quality of the images and second, the accuracy. The visual quality of the images depends on a lot of factor like the lighting, and the texture used among others. The generated images are shown in Fig. 5. In our case, as mentioned earlier, we obtained the texture data from Google Earth. Due to the scale of the 3D model, the image saved from Google Earth corresponds to a scale level of approximately 280000 (4.5 miles to 1 in.). Due to such a high scale the finer details in the map are lost. We have tried to compensate for this by

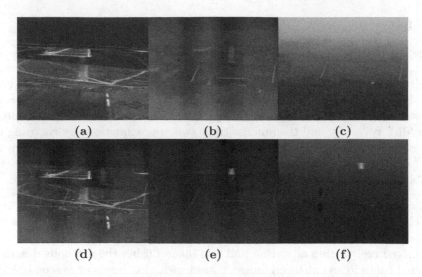

Fig. 4. Mismatch and registration with manual keypoints - **(a)** Generated virtual image. **(b)** IR image from the aircraft. **(c)** Visible spectrum image from the aircraft. **(d)** Mismatched IR image enhanced via fusion **(e)** IR image registered with the runway from virtual image **(f)** Visible image registered with the runway from virtual image

Fig. 5. Comparison **(a)** New virtual Images. **(b)** Image from aircraft **(c)** Result from [6]

overlaying an airport model which has helped increase the quality considerably while still leaving a scope for improvement.

As discussed in the previous section, to analyze the accuracy we employed segmentation and image fusion techniques. As visible from Fig. 5, our approach has a visible improvement in the accuracy of generated images over the previous work by Liu et. al. However, due to the scaling issues the representations are not 100% accurate. To get better accuracies, we need to improve the airport model that was overlayed on top of the actual Digital Elevation Map (DEM).

6   Conclusion and Future Work

The proposed approach relies only on the availability of the GPS+AHRS data and the 3D model and produces output with a good visual quality and accuracy comparable to the actual images captured by the aircraft. We demonstrated that the generated dataset can be successfully used to segment the runway from the image and enhance the captured infrared and visible images. Since the segmentation and enhancement processes do not use any intensive learning-based techniques, both of them are extremely fast. Once the virtual images have been generated, they can be merged with data from the optical camera or the IR camera in real-time. This would help pilots have a better view of the runway and can also be used to improve the accuracy of assisted navigation systems.

The accuracy of our system can be further increased by considering a smaller 3D model so that a higher quality image from Google Earth can be used as a texture. For a 3D model covering a larger area, images from Google Earth can be captured at a better scale and then stitched together to get better outputs. For segmentation, we tried multiple supervised approaches and got the best results using simple thresholding. Other thresholding approaches can provide better results but at the expense of increased processing time which is undesirable in current scenarios. Image fusion helps in highlighting the finer details in the picture but is limited by the details present in the virtual images.

References

1. Liu, C., Cheng, I., Zhang, Y., Basu, A.: Enhancement of low visibility aerial images using histogram truncation and an explicit retinex representation for balancing contrast and color consistency. ISPRS J. Photogrammetry Remote Sens. **128**, 16–26 (2017)
2. Christie, G., et al.: Training object detectors with synthetic data for autonomous uav sampling applications. In: 2018 International Conference on Unmanned Aircraft Systems (ICUAS), pp. 352–357. IEEE (2018)
3. Marin, J., Vazquez, D., Geronimo, D., Lopez, A.M.: Learning appearance in virtual scenarios for pedestrian detection. In: 2010 IEEE Computer Society Conference on Computer Vision and Pattern Recognition, pp. 137–144, June 2010
4. Tsirikoglou, A., Kronander, J., Wrenninge, M., Unger, J.: Procedural modeling and physically based rendering for synthetic data generation in automotive applications. CoRR abs/1710.06270 (2017)
5. Bhandari, N.: Procedural synthetic data for self-driving cars using 3D graphics. Ph.D. thesis, Massachusetts Institute of Technology (2018)
6. Liu, C., Cheng, I., Basu, A.: Synthetic vision assisted real-time runway detection for infrared aerial images. In: Basu, A., Berretti, S. (eds.) ICSM 2018. LNCS, vol. 11010, pp. 274–281. Springer, Cham (2018). https://doi.org/10.1007/978-3-030-04375-9_23
7. Gaidon, A., Wang, Q., Cabon, Y., Vig, E.: Virtual worlds as proxy for multi-object tracking analysis. CoRR abs/1605.06457 (2016)
8. Shafaei, A., Little, J.J., Schmidt, M.: Play and learn: Using video games to train computer vision models. CoRR abs/1608.01745 (2016)

9. Ros, G., Sellart, L., Materzynska, J., Vazquez, D., Lopez, A.: The SYNTHIA Dataset: a large collection of synthetic images for semantic segmentation of urban scenes. In: CVPR (2016)

10. Sun, B., Saenko, K.: From virtual to reality: fast adaptation of virtual object detectors to real domains. In: Proceedings of the British Machine Vision Conference 2014 (2014)

11. Jiang, C., et al.: Configurable, photorealistic image rendering and ground truth synthesis by sampling stochastic grammars representing indoor scenes. CoRR abs/1704.00112 (2017)

12. Pajares, G., De La Cruz, J.M.: A wavelet-based image fusion tutorial. Pattern Recognit. **37**(9), 1855–1872 (2004)

13. Naidu, V., Raol, J.R.: Pixel-level image fusion using wavelets and principal component analysis. Defence Sci. J. **58**(3), 338–352 (2008)

14. Li, H., Manjunath, B., Mitra, S.K.: Multisensor image fusion using the wavelet transform. Graph. Models Image Process. **57**(3), 235–245 (1995)

ProDeblurGAN: Progressive Growing of GANs for Blind Motion Deblurring in Face Recognition

Kushal Mahalingaiah[1] and Bruce Matichuk[2(✉)]

[1] University of Alberta, Edmonton, Canada
[2] Aidant Intelligent Technology Inc., Edmonton, Canada
bruce.matichuk@aidant.ai

Abstract. Elimination of motion blur is one of the key challenges in face recognition, especially from the video feed of low quality surveillance cameras. We present ProDeblurGAN, a progressively growing Generative Adversarial Nets (GAN) for single photograph motion deblurring. The current state-of-the-art DeblurGAN network performs well in structural similarity and visual appearance. However, the discriminator's inability in distinguishing real and fake images concerning to finer or lower-level details result in the generator synthesizing low quality deblurred image. With recent advances in the progressive growing of GANs, we propose a motion deblurring model to utilize the advantages of such progressive adversarial training and generate a high quality deblurred image. The approach to gradually increase layers in training instead of initializing all at once facilitates the generation of higher resolution images. Also, at higher resolution, the finer details like the facial hair, moles, freckles and so on, are considered as features and used in the learning process. The proposed generator takes the blurred image as input as opposed to random noise in the case of traditional GAN networks. Implementation of the proposed method in face recognition systems will enhance the quality of the captured image and the accuracy of recognition of the face. The quality of the deblurred image generated by ProDeblurGAN is evaluated using state-of-the-art metrics.

1 Introduction

Face recognition through surveillance cameras suffers from real-world motion blur problems due to the subjects' movement and the shutter speed. Many image processing and machine learning approaches have been proposed to address this issue. One of the most popular image processing techniques to remove motion blur is to deconvolute the image by studying the point spread function (PSF) of the image. PSF is an energy density function where each pixel position (x, y) in the image detector is exposed to a light from a single point. Some of the popular algorithms implemented to study the motion of the object by learning PSF are discussed in [1,2]. Although image processing techniques output good results,

© Springer Nature Switzerland AG 2020
T. McDaniel et al. (Eds.): ICSM 2019, LNCS 12015, pp. 439–450, 2020.
https://doi.org/10.1007/978-3-030-54407-2_37

they are not feasible to implement in a real-time system due to their computational cost. Step forward deep learning models that study the features of specific image content, in our case a human face, and perform probability estimation on the test image. The next Sect. 2 discusses some of the most pertaining and recent approaches in brief, with most approaches co-relating the latent information in the blurred image and learned features to deblur the image.

Since Ian Goodfellow came up with GANs in 2014, [3], various researchers have experimented with it to generate random high-quality images of various objects. In 2017, NVidia introduced progressively growing GAN (ProGAN) [4] to address some of the issues in stabilizing the GAN training and produce high-resolution images up to 1024×1024 resolution. In this regard, we propose ProDeblurGAN, a novel progressively growing GAN approach to deblur a blurred image without estimating the blur kernel. ProDeblurGAN is an expansion of the ProGAN, improvised and tailor-made to perform deblurring of a single image. Section 3 discusses our proposed approach in detail. The motion blur introduced in the captured frame of a person through surveillance cameras causes loss of identifiable features and makes it difficult for face recognition systems to re-identify the same person. With our approach, we plan to perform blind motion deblurring of a human face image to improve the accuracy of face recognition in a real-time surveillance system.

2   Related Work

DeblurGAN. In 2017 Kupyn et al.'s work [5] introduced DeblurGAN, a conditional GAN optimized using multi-component loss function, learns from the observed image and a random noise vector for blind motion deblurring. The deblurring is done by the trained Generator, which estimates a sharp image (termed as a fake) for every blurred image. Also, during the training phase, a critic network, Discriminator, is introduced as an adversary to the generator. The discriminator takes a random sharp image from the training dataset along with the generated image and distinguishes the real from the fake by approximating the distance between the samples.

Deep-Deblur. Nah [6] introduced Deep Multi-scale Convolutional Neural Network for Dynamic Scene Deblurring, a deep convolutional neural network (CNN) that uses a kernel-free multi-scale approach to directly deblur the image. A discriminator network is used to classify the ground truth sharp image and the generated finest scale output image as a deblurred image or a sharp image. The model is trained using the combined multi-scale content loss and the adversarial loss in a coarse-to-fine approach.

Blur-Invariant Deep Learning for Blind-Deblurring. Nimisha et al. [7], introduced a blind motion deblurring architecture that consists of an autoencoder and a GAN. The autoencoder which learns from the clean image for the task of data learning then guides the deblurring process. The GAN is trained to obtain a generator that can produce blur-invariant features from the blurred input image and relate them to clean image features that are fed to a decoder to output the final deblurred image.

Scale-Recurrent Network for Deep Image Deblurring, in short SRN-Deblur, [8] introduced by Tao et al., is a single image "coarse-to-fine" deblurring scheme. In this work, the authors gradually restore the sharp image of different resolutions in a pyramid. The generation of a sharp latent image at each scale is considered a sub-problem of the image deblurring task, which takes a blurred image and an initial deblurring result (upsampled from the previous scale) as input, and estimates the sharp image at this scale.

Deep Generative Filter for Motion Deblurring introduced by Ramakrishnan et al. [9] utilizes a deep filter based on Generative Adversarial Network (GAN) architecture integrated with global skip connection and a dense convolutional architecture. This work consists of a densely connected generator and a discriminator. The task of the generator is to recycle features spanning across multiple receptive scales to generate an image that fools the discriminator.

Other work includes the **Blind Motion Deblurring with Cycle Generative Adversarial Networks**,[10], by Yaun et al. 2019, which uses an encoder-decoder architecture to learn the mapping function between the blurred and sharp domain of an image. This architecture is coupled with a PatchGAN architecture, [11], to classify each image patch from the whole image using perceptual loss [12] in the discriminator.

2.1   Preliminary Test Results

Experiments are conducted on the DeblurGAN model [5], using weights obtained by training the model on GoPRO Large dataset [13], VGG Face 2 dataset [14], and the Flickr High Quality (FFHQ) dataset [15]. The qualitative results of the experiments conducted on the VGG Face 2 test dataset, as shown in Figs. 1, 2, 3, confirm the need to use a progressive upgrade to generate high quality images closer to ground truth. The DeblurGAN [5] training of the FFHQ dataset was done for 182 epochs with around 10,000 pairs of blurred and sharp Portable Network Graphics (PNG) quality images. The training of the VGG Face2 dataset was done for 400 epochs with around 37,000 pairs of blurred and sharp Joint Photographic Experts Group (JPEG) quality images. Gaussian kernel-based blur was applied to all the sharp images to prepare the dataset. The generated results were JPEG quality images at 256×256 resolution.

Fig. 1. DeblurGAN results, for GAN trained on generic scenery images in GOPRO dataset - blurred image on the left, deblurred image on the right

Fig. 2. DeblurGAN results, for GAN trained on high quality face images in FFHQ dataset - blurred image on the left, deblurred image on the right

Fig. 3. DeblurGAN results, for GAN trained on low quality face images in VGGFACE2 dataset - blurred image on the left, deblurred image on the right

3   ProDeblurGAN Approach

The proposed approach is a progressive growing of GAN, trained in an adversarial manner. A burred-sharp image pair is given to the network as input, where the generator uses the blurred image to generate a prediction of appearance of the sharp image. The discriminator then reviews the generated sample as real or fake. Discriminator uses semantic information from the input blur-image pair against the generated sample to calculate a loss.

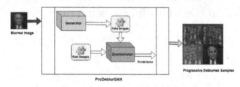

Fig. 4. Progressive deblur GAN

The progressive approach facilitates the generator to produce fine details, resulting in a high-quality image, up to 1024×1024 resolution. The adversarial training is performed at different resolutions of the input image pair, starting from 4×4. The optimization of the generator is performed using the calculated loss between the generated samples and the input sharp image. However, the optimization of discriminator takes the input blurred-sharp image pair into consideration, giving it more control on the quality of the generated image. Also, our proposed architecture is developed using PyTorch, [16] implementation of ProGAN [4] as the base framework.

3.1   Architecture

Progressive Growing GAN, introduced by Karras et al. [4], involves using a generator and discriminator model with the same general structure and starting with very small images, such as 4×4 pixels, as depicted in Fig. 5. During training, new blocks of convolutional layers are systematically added to both the generator model and the discriminator models. The proposed architecture uses the latent space information in the blurred image as input to the generator instead of random code, as illustrated in Fig. 4. The incremental addition of the layers allows the models to effectively learn coarse-level detail and later learn finer detail, both on the generator and discriminator side. A skip connection is used to connect the new block to the input of the discriminator or output of the generator, during the phasing in of a new block of layers. This block is added to the existing input or output layer with a weighting. The weighting controls the influence of the new block and is achieved using a parameter alpha α that starts at zero or a very small number and linearly increases to 1.0 over training iterations. Figure 6 shows a generator that outputs a 16×16 image and a discriminator that takes a 16×16 pixel image and the models are grown to the size of 32×32.

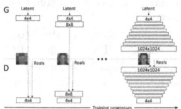

Fig. 5. Progressive growing of GANs

Fig. 6. Phasing in the addition of new layers to the generator and discriminator models

Growing the Generator. A new block of convolutional layers is added that outputs a 32×32 image. The output of this new layer is combined with the output of the 16×16 layer that is upsampled using nearest-neighbor interpolation to 32×32. Traditional GAN generators use a transpose convolutional layer. The contribution of the upsampled 16×16 layer is weighted by $(1 - \alpha)$, whereas the contribution of the new 32×32 layer is weighted by α. α is small initially, giving the most weight to the scaled-up version of the 16×16 image, although slowly transitions to giving more weight and then all weight to the new 32×32 output layers over training iterations. During the transition, we treat the layers that operate on the higher resolution like a residual block, whose weight alpha increases linearly from 0 to 1.

Growing the Discriminator. A new block of convolutional layers is added for the input of the model to support image sizes with 32×32 pixels. The input image is downsampled to 16×16 using average pooling so that it can pass through the existing 16×16 convolutional layers. The output of the new 32×32 block of layers is also downsampled using average pooling so that it can be provided as input to the existing 16×16 block. This is different from most GAN models that use a 2×2 stride in the convolutional layers to downsample. The two downsampled versions of the input are combined in a weighted manner, starting with a full weighting to the downsampled raw input and linearly transitioning to a full weighting for the interpreted output of the new input layer block. Spectral normalization, explained in the next section, is performed n each convolutional layer of the discriminator network to control the Lipschitz constant of the discriminator function.

Figure 7 shows the general configuration of a Generator and Discriminator in a progressive adversarial generative network. It used an output layer with a 1×1-sized filters and a linear activation function, instead of the more common hyperbolic tangent activation function (tanh). The discriminator also used an output layer with 1×1-sized filters and a linear activation function. The models start with a 4×4 input image and grow until they reach the 1024×1024 target. The standard deviation of activation across images in the mini-batch is added as a new channel before the last block of convolutional layers in the discriminator model. This is referred to as "Minibatch standard deviation." A pixel-wise normalization is performed in the generator after each convolutional layer that normalizes each pixel value in the activation map across the channels to a unit length. This is a type of activation constraint that is more generally referred to as "local response normalization." The bias for all layers is initialized as zero and model weights are initialized as a random Gaussian rescaled using the He weight initialization method.

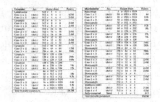

Fig. 7. Generator and discriminator configuration

3.2 Spectral Normalization

Spectral normalization, introduced by Miyato et al. [17], controls the Lipschitz constant of the discriminator function f by literally constraining the spectral norm of each layer $g :_{in} \mapsto_{out}$. Lipschitz norm $\|g\|_{\text{Lip}}$ is equal to $\sup_\sigma(\nabla g())$, where $\sigma(A)$ is the spectral norm of the matrix A (L_2 matrix norm of A)

$$\sigma(A) := \max_{:\neq 0} \frac{\|A\|_2}{\|\|_2} = \max_{\|\|_2 \leq 1} \|A\|_2, \tag{1}$$

which is equivalent to the largest singular value of A. Therefore, for a linear layer $g() = W$, the norm is given by $\|g\|_{\text{Lip}} = \sup_\sigma(\nabla g()) = \sup_\sigma(W) = \sigma(W)$. Spectral norm "regularization" introduced by [18], imposes sample data *independent* regularization on the cost function, just like L2 regularization and Lasso which is different from Spectral Normalization [17].

3.3 Loss Function

The discriminator network employed a general adversarial loss while the generator network loss function is a summation of adversarial loss and perceptual loss, explained below.

Adversarial Loss: Our model uses WGAN-GP [19] as the critic function, which is shown to be robust to the choice of generator architecture [20]. The loss is calculated as follows:

$$\mathcal{L}_{GAN} = \sum_{n=1}^{N} -D_{\theta_D}(G_{\theta_G}(I^B)) \tag{2}$$

where, L_{GAN} is the adversarial loss D and G are discriminator and generator networks with training parameters θ_D and θ_G respectively. I^B is the blurred image input.

The Lipschitz constraint is enforced using Gradient Penalty. A differentiable function is referred as 1-Lipschtiz if and only if it has gradients with the norm at most 1 everywhere, so we consider directly constraining the gradient norm of the critic's output concerning its input. Recently [21] provided an alternative way of using least square GAN [22] which is more stable and generates higher quality results. More details about WGAN-GP is explained in [19].

Perceptual Loss: We adopted recently proposed Perceptual loss [12]. Perceptual loss is a simple L2-loss but based on the difference of the generated feature maps and target image convoluted neural net feature maps. The perceptual loss is the difference between the VGG-19 [23] conv3.3 feature maps of the sharp and restored images. It is defined as follows:

$$\mathcal{L}_X = \frac{1}{W_{i,j}H_{i,j}} \sum_{x=1}^{W_{i,j}} \sum_{y=1}^{H_{i,j}} (\phi_{i,j}(I^S)_{x,y} - \phi_{i,j}(G_{\theta_G}(I^B))_{x,y})^2$$

where $\phi_{i,j}$ is the activated feature map obtained by the j-th convolution before the i-th maxpooling layer within the VGG19 network, pretrained on ImageNet [24], $W_{i,j}$ and $H_{i,j}$ are the dimensions of the feature maps. The perceptual loss focuses on restoring general content while adversarial loss focuses on restoring texture details.

Relativistic GAN Loss: We also experimented with the Relativistic discriminator, introduced by Alexia et al. [25], which estimates the probability of real data being more realistic than randomly sampled fake data. We have adopted the Relativistic average GAN (RaGAN) loss, for both discriminator and generator, proposed in [25] at each resolution progressively. The general loss functions of RaGAN can be summarised using the below equation.

$$L_D = \mathbb{E}_{x_r \sim \mathbb{P}} \left[f_1 \left(C(x_r) - \mathbb{E}_{x_f \sim \mathbb{Q}} C(x_f) \right) \right) \right] + \mathbb{E}_{x_f \sim \mathbb{Q}} \left[f_2 \left(C(x_f) - \mathbb{E}_{x_r \sim \mathbb{P}} C(x_r) \right) \right].$$
(3)

$$L_G = \mathbb{E}_{x_r \sim \mathbb{P}} \left[g_1 \left(C(x_r) - \mathbb{E}_{x_f \sim \mathbb{Q}} C(x_f) \right) \right) \right] + \mathbb{E}_{x_f \sim \mathbb{Q}} \left[g_2 \left(C(x_f) - \mathbb{E}_{x_r \sim \mathbb{P}} C(x_r) \right) \right].$$
(4)

where $\tilde{f}_1, \tilde{f}_2, \tilde{g}_1, \tilde{g}_2$ are scalar-to-scalar functions, $\mathbb{P}$ is the distribution of real data, $D(x)$ is the discriminator evaluated at x, $\mathbb{Q}$ is the distribution of fake data. Real data is referred as x_r and fake data as x_f. As per general assumption both L_D and L_G are loss functions to be minimized. $C(x)$ is the non-transformed discriminator output called the *critic* as per [20]).

4   Experiments and Results

4.1   Circles and Squares Experiment

Initial experiments are conducted on the proposed approach, to generate a varied set of circles and squares images. The Fig. 8 shows samples of the circle of circles and circle of squares images for the experiment. The generator network uses random noise to generate perfect replicas of the original input images, as seen in Fig. 8. The PNG circle and square images were generated using Matplotlib [26], at 256×256 resolution and dots per inch (dpi) set to 32. The proposed network's ability to generate perfect fake samples is the ground study for further evaluation of more complex data like human faces. Feeding more information to the generator about what the generated data should look like, using blurred images, should result in higher quality images compared to using random noise as input. The generated results were PNG images at 256×256 resolution.

Fig. 8. Circle and square experiment - from left, three input samples, last image is the generated result samples

Fig. 9. Single blur face experiment - from left to right, blur input face, sharp input face, generator output

4.2 Single Blurred Face Experiment

We trained the proposed ProDeblurGAN network with 512 samples of the same pair of the blur-sharp images of a human face (taken from the VGG Face2 dataset [14]). The blurred image is given as the seed or key to the generator which performs image-to-image translation between the generated image and the batch sample from the training set. The generator loss is a summation of perceptual loss and adversarial loss between the fake sample and the real sample (sharp image). The discriminator loss is the traditional adversarial loss between the fake sample and the real sample. The network is trained for 120–180 epochs per resolution, from 4×4 to 256×256, with n_critic = 5. Figure 9 shows the input images in the training set and the four generator output samples at the end of the training. The generated results were PNG images at 256×256 resolution.

4.3 Multiple Blurred Faces Experiment

We conducted several experiments on faces from the VGG Face 2 dataset [14]. The most notable one is the experiment with the Gaussian motion blur applied on 3129 sharp images from [14]. The model was trained in google cloud with single Tesla T4 for 5 days, iteration details are: 120, 120, 120, 150, 150, 180, 180 number of epochs at 4×4, 8×8, 16×16, 32×32, 64×64, 128×128, 256×256 resolutions respectively. The loss function used for this

Fig. 10. Results of multiple blur face experiment

particular experiment is the Relativistic loss [25] discussed earlier in Sect. 3.3. The final result at the 256×256 resolution layer is as shown in the Fig. 10. The generated results were PNG images at 256×256 resolution. The results, although not desirable, gave insight into how to stabilize the training and generate quality images for further research. Improving the loss function for the discriminator and providing more information about the blurred image to the adversarial training is the next research direction. Training the model using better GPUs, with more computations to a higher resolution will result in better results.

4.4   Training Parameters

For the optimizer, we have used Adam optimizer with $\alpha = 0.001$, $\beta1 = 0$, $\beta2 = 0.99$, while using WGAN-GP and Perceptual loss as the loss functions. For WGAN-GP the n_critic value was set to be 5, even though Progressive GAN only required n_critic = 1, which increased the stability of this training method and the discriminator performance but slowed down the training. Also the drift penalty rate was set to 0.001 for the discriminator loss. For training, we used 3129 images of low resolution faces at 256×256 to 512×512 from the state-of-the-art face dataset, VGG Face2 [14]. The training was carried out on a Ubuntu operating system equipped with Nvidia RTX 2070 graphic cards along with experiments on the Google Colab Research program equipped with Tesla K80 GPU and the Google Cloud computing instance equipped with a single Tesla T4 GPU.

4.5   Quantitative Evaluation

Comparative evaluation was done using state of the art metrics PSNR (Peak Signal to Noise Ratio), SSIM (Structural Similarity Measure) and MSE (Mean Squared Error) between the sharp image and the deblurred image output. The considered architectures for the evaluation are: SRN deblur [8] base model with pre-trained weights on GoPRO Large dataset [13], Deep Generative Filter for Motion Deblurring [9] model with trained weights on single face dataset, mentioned in Sect. 4.2, and the proposed ProDeblurGAN model trained on the single face dataset. The quantitative results for the above comparisons are mentioned in Table 1, which also has the corresponding dataset on which the model was trained. For a fair evaluation, the same or similar dataset and blurring using similar Gaussian Kernel are considered.

Table 1. Peak signal-to-noise ratio, structural similarity measure and Mean Squared Error, of the test image. All models were tested on the test image (sharp) from [14]. The second row indicate the training dataset for the model.

	Ram [9]	Tao [8]	Kupyn [5]		ProDeblurGAN
Metric	*Single*	*GOPRO*	*GoPRO*	*VGGFace2*	*Single*
PSNR	23.29	13.69	18.00	18.72	**23.41**
SSIM	0.79	0.52	0.58	0.57	**0.79**
MSE	913	8349	3089	2621	**890**

4.6 Qualitative Evaluation

The qualitative results for the conducted experiments considered for the evaluation are shown in Fig. 11. As seen in Fig. 11, ProDeblurGAN nearly generates the complete sharp image, while other models barely deblur the blurred image. In particular, state-of-the-art model [9] generates impressive output, very close to proposed work but just falling short. But [9] tends to over-saturate the image and reproduced colors are off in comparison. Also, [9] final output at the last epoch (10) is completely saturated, the trained model with singe face dataset converged at epoch 5 and discriminator loss became 0 after epoch 6.

Fig. 11. Qualitative results for the single face experiment in relation to Table 1. From left to right, original sharp image, blurred image input, deblurred image using SRN (result after 10 epoch), deblurred image using SRN (best result after 5 epoch), deblurred image using DeblurGAN GoPRO, debluured image using DeblurGAN VGG Face2, deblurred image using ProDeblurGAN

5 Discussion and Future Work

In this paper, we proposed the ProDeblurGAN - a progressively growing motion deblur network, specifically designed for human faces. We also conducted several experiments, with circle-squares, single faces, and multiple faces, to support our theory that the latent information in the blurred image should help a generator to reproduce a better quality deblurred image. Furthermore, we experimented with spectral normalization of discriminator layers and several loss functions to stabilize the training and avoid mode of collapse. The qualitative and quantitative results prove our proposed model performs better than state-of-the-art models on a single image and should improve the accuracy of face recognition.

However, for multiple faces, the results are still not favorable as the model is incompletely trained due to the lack of computational power.

Future research is needed to fully grow the network and output images at 1024×1024 resolution, which requires higher computational power as with a progressively growing GAN network. Another research area would be to use a facial recognition network to create embedding of faces and compute the perceptual loss instead of the used VGG-19 network [23] which is pre-trained on a broader imagenet database [24]. [27] redesigned generator normalization to improve training performance and enhance image quality, could be incorporated to stabilize our model for multiple faces. We greatly encourage researchers and machine learning enthusiasts with better computing power to experiment with our approach.

References

1. Jansson, P.A.: Deconvolution of images and spectra. Courier Corporation (2014)
2. Yitzhaky, Y., Mor, I., Lantzman, A., Kopeika, N.: Direct method for restoration of motion-blurred images. JOSA A **15**(6), 1512–1519 (1998)
3. Goodfellow, I., et al.: Generative adversarial nets. In: Advances in Neural Information Processing Systems, pp. 2672–2680 (2014)
4. Karras, T., Aila, T., Laine, S., Lehtinen, J.: Progressive growing of GANs for improved quality, stability, and variation. arXiv preprint arXiv:1710.10196 (2017)
5. Kupyn, O., Budzan, V., Mykhailych, M., Mishkin, D., Matas, J.: DeblurGAN: blind motion deblurring using conditional adversarial networks. In: The IEEE Conference on Computer Vision and Pattern Recognition (CVPR), June 2018
6. Nah, S., Hyun Kim, T., Mu Lee, K.: Deep multi-scale convolutional neural network for dynamic scene deblurring. In: Proceedings of the IEEE Conference on Computer Vision and Pattern Recognition, pp. 3883–3891 (2017)
7. Nimisha, T.M., Kumar Singh, A., Rajagopalan, A.N.: Blur-invariant deep learning for blind-deblurring. In: The IEEE International Conference on Computer Vision (ICCV), October 2017
8. Tao, X., Gao, H., Shen, X., Wang, J., Jia, J.: Scale-recurrent network for deep image deblurring. In: IEEE Conference on Computer Vision and Pattern Recognition (CVPR) (2018)
9. Ramakrishnan, S., Pachori, S., Gangopadhyay, A., Raman, S.: Deep generative filter for motion deblurring. In: Proceedings of the IEEE International Conference on Computer Vision, pp. 2993–3000 (2017)
10. Yuan, Q., Li, J., Zhang, L., Wu, Z., Liu, G.: Blind motion deblurring with cycle generative adversarial networks. arXiv preprint arXiv:1901.01641 (2019)
11. Isola, P., Zhu, J.Y., Zhou, T., Efros, A.A.: Image-to-image translation with conditional adversarial networks. In: Proceedings of the IEEE Conference on Computer Vision and Pattern Recognition, pp. 1125–1134 (2017)
12. Johnson, J., Alahi, A., Fei-Fei, L.: Perceptual losses for real-time style transfer and super-resolution. In: Leibe, B., Matas, J., Sebe, N., Welling, M. (eds.) ECCV 2016. LNCS, vol. 9906, pp. 694–711. Springer, Cham (2016). https://doi.org/10.1007/978-3-319-46475-6_43
13. Gopro large dataset. https://github.com/SeungjunNah/DeepDeblur_release

14. Cao, Q., Shen, L., Xie, W., Parkhi, O.M., Zisserman, A.: VGGFace2: a dataset for recognising faces across pose and age. In: International Conference on Automatic Face and Gesture Recognition (2018)
15. Karras, T., Laine, S., Aila, T.: A style-based generator architecture for generative adversarial networks. In: Proceedings of the IEEE Conference on Computer Vision and Pattern Recognition, pp. 4401–4410 (2019)
16. Paszke, A., et al.: Automatic differentiation in PyTorch (2017)
17. Miyato, T., Kataoka, T., Koyama, M., Yoshida, Y.: Spectral normalization for generative adversarial networks. arXiv preprint arXiv:1802.05957 (2018)
18. Yoshida, Y., Miyato, T.: Spectral norm regularization for improving the generalizability of deep learning. arXiv preprint arXiv:1705.10941 (2017)
19. Gulrajani, I., Ahmed, F., Arjovsky, M., Dumoulin, V., Courville, A.C.: Improved training of Wasserstein GANs. In: Advances in Neural Information Processing Systems, pp. 5767–5777 (2017)
20. Arjovsky, M., Chintala, S., Bottou, L.: Wasserstein GAN. arXiv preprint arXiv:1701.07875 (2017)
21. Zhu, J.Y., Park, T., Isola, P., Efros, A.A.: Unpaired image-to-image translation using cycle-consistent adversarial networks. In: Proceedings of the IEEE International Conference on Computer Vision, pp. 2223–2232 (2017)
22. Mao, X., Li, Q., Xie, H., Lau, R.Y., Wang, Z., Paul Smolley, S.: Least squares generative adversarial networks. In: Proceedings of the IEEE International Conference on Computer Vision, pp. 2794–2802 (2017)
23. Simonyan, K., Zisserman, A.: Very deep convolutional networks for large-scale image recognition. arXiv preprint arXiv:1409.1556 (2014)
24. Deng, J., Dong, W., Socher, R., Li, L.J., Li, K., Fei-Fei, L.: ImageNet: a large-scale hierarchical image database. In: IEEE Conference on Computer Vision and Pattern Recognition, pp. 248–255. IEEE (2009)
25. Jolicoeur-Martineau, A.: The relativistic discriminator: a key element missing from standard GAN. arXiv preprint arXiv:1807.00734 (2018)
26. Hunter, J.D.: Matplotlib: a 2D graphics environment. Comput. Sci. Eng. 9(3), 90–95 (2007)
27. Karras, T., Laine, S., Aittala, M., Hellsten, J., Lehtinen, J., Aila, T.: Analyzing and improving the image quality of StyleGan. arXiv preprint arXiv:1912.04958 (2019)

3D and Image Processing

3D Object Classification Using 2D Perspectives of Point Clouds

Leland Jansen[1], Nathan Liebrecht[1], Sara Soltaninejad[2(✉)], and Anup Basu[1]

[1] Departments of Electrical Engineering and Computing Science, University of
Alberta, Edmonton, Canada
{ljjansen,liebrech}@ualberta.ca
[2] Department of Computing Science, University of Alberta, Edmonton, Canada
soltanin@ualberta.ca

Abstract. As three-dimensional point clouds become an increasingly
popular for representing spatial data, with it comes a need to classify
objects represented in this form. This paper proposes an image feature
representation technique which classifies 3D point clouds by using several 2D perspectives, and then using YOLO (v3) as object classification
tool to classify the rasters. Existing works have had limited success using
this technique with only one perspective, likely due to the considerable
information loss during the projection. We hypothesize that multiple
projections mitigate these effects by capturing lost data in other perspective projections. Our method is effective in classifying pedestrians
and vehicles in the Sydney Urban Objects data set, where our technique
has achieved a classification accuracy of 98.42% and an f1 score of 0.9843,
which are considerably higher than existing methods.

1 Introduction

Point clouds are a common, primitive representation of three-dimensional (3D)
data. Creating these point clouds can be achieved using a variety of technologies, such as LiDAR imaging systems. As 3D capture technologies becomes more
ubiquitous, there emerges a growing need to quickly and accurately extract features from these data to perform tasks such as object recognition. Point cloud
object recognition is especially relevant in autonomous vehicle research to detect
other cars, pedestrians, road signs, etc. and makes real-time decisions. Classifying objects represented by 3D point clouds is therefore a very important problem
to solve. Furthermore, solutions for self-driving cars must run in real-time and
must be very high accuracy. Both accuracy and performance are essential to
have a safe and reliable vehicle that responds in real-time.

Our research proposes representing 3D point clouds as a series of 2D rasterized images generated from different perspectives. These images can then be
integrated into a single raster and fed into a one-shot detection network. This
maintains high efficiency while providing semi-redundant perspectives of the
original point cloud. You Only Look Once (YOLO) is a state-of-the-art, real-
time object detection algorithm which was proposed by Joseph et al. [1] in 2016.

© Springer Nature Switzerland AG 2020
T. McDaniel et al. (Eds.): ICSM 2019, LNCS 12015, pp. 453–462, 2020.
https://doi.org/10.1007/978-3-030-54407-2_38

The published model recognizes 80 different objects in images and videos, but most importantly it is fast and accurate. Recently, the new version of YOLO (v3) [2] significantly improves the performance of object detection. However, it comes at the cost of increasing model complexity. In this paper, YOLO (v3) is used for object detection in a 3D point cloud dataset.

The remainder of the paper is organized as follows: related work is summarized in Sect. 2. In Sect. 3 we present the methodology, followed by experimental results in Sect. 4. Finally, future work and conclusion are presented in Sect. 5 and Sect. 6 respectively.

2   Related Work

Substantial research has been performed to classify objects through 2D images. This technique opens up the possibility of using any of the many existing image classification algorithms, possibly leading to gains i classification accuracy. Huang and You [3] mention that a simple 2D representation of a point-cloud can lead to a loss in 3D structural representation. We hope to avoid this loss of information by adding additional rotation to the scene and utilizing many instances during the classification process. Landrieu and Simonovsky [4] represented the state-of-the-art for point-cloud semantic segmentation. This paper uses a technique dubbed "super-point graph" which works in a way similar to super-pixels; that is, by grouping neighboring similar clusters of points into larger objects, which simplifies further processing by reducing the amount of data. In a similar way we propose reducing the total amount of data by flattening the 3D space into a more convenient 2D representation.

Substantial research has been performed in the domain of 2D image object recognition. Early techniques included feature detectors such as SIFT [5] and SURF [6] which extracted invariant features from images that were then used to feed into a model, such as a database of features or an SVM [7]. Recently, deep learning has been the de-facto standard for 2D image object classification. Techniques such as convolutional networks are often used. Since AlexNet became popular in the ImageNet [8] Large-Scale Visual Recognition Challenge (ILSVRC), deep learning has become the go-to method for image recognition tasks, surpassing traditional computer vision methods used in the literature. In 2016, Lie et al. [9] proposed the Single Shot MultiBox Detector (SSD) network which is a popular algorithm in object detection. SSD discretizes the output space of bounding boxes into a set of default boxes over different aspect ratios and scales per feature map location. The network generates scores for the presence of each object category in each default box at prediction time, and produces adjustments to the box to better match the object shape.

Research has also been performed in the domain of 3D point cloud feature recognition. Early research employed techniques such as surface reconstruction and feature extraction. Recent research has explored promising techniques, such as directly deploying 3D point clouds into deep neural networks using a voxelized structure. However, this approach can be challenging to implement efficiently in hardware, since the 3D space is quite sparse and points exist in continuous space rather than in a discrete grid like traditional images. Ali et al. [10] proposed an end-to-end real-time 3D oriented object bounding box detection system for Automated Driving (AD). In this paper, they used the success of one shot regression meta-architecture in the 2D perspective image space with YOLO (v2). The output of the 2D space was extended to generate oriented 3D object bounding boxes from LiDAR point cloud.

We improve current techniques by combining the rich 3D representation of objects using point clouds with the efficiency of processing 2D images. By using a one-shot detection network such as YOLO, we can maintain high efficiency while adding semi-redundant rotated 2D perspectives of the point-clouds. We may also increase information density by encoding point depth information in a color channel. For example, farther pixels could be darker. We expect this shaded depth representation will achieve greater edge discrimination. Maturana and Scherer [11] reported an average F1 classification score of 0.73 using a convolutional neural network. Their methods also take around 6 ms to classify an object using a Tesla K40 GPU. We will investigate the accuracy and performance differences using our perspective rasterization technique coupled with a one-shot classifier.

3   Methodology

The proposed method has three general steps which are preprocessing, training and inference which the last two steps are done using YOLO (v3). The framework of the proposed object detection system is shown in Fig. 1.

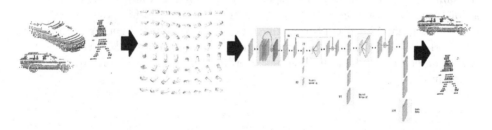

Fig. 1. Overview of the proposed object detection for 3D point cloud with 2D perspectives and using YOLO (v3).

3.1   Data Set

The Sydney Urban Objects data set is selected due to its size and the variety of objects it contains. This data set contains a variety of common urban road objects scanned with a Velodyne HDL-64E LIDAR, collected in the CBD of Sydney, Australia. There are 631 individual scans of objects across classes of vehicles, pedestrians, signs and trees. Figure 2 shows sample point clouds from this data set.

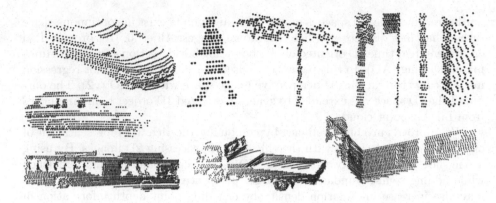

Fig. 2. Example objects in our data set.

3.2 Preprocessing

Our proposed technique involves pre-processing as the first step. The data set is loaded into memory by parsing the raw data file. After that, the scene properties are set such as background color, point color, etc. Then, the geometric centre of the point clouds needs to be determined. The "camera" should be positioned such that it is facing the centre of the point cloud. Presently, the radius is manually determined and hard-coded such that the entire point cloud is visible by the camera. Future work could involve automatically adjusting the radius. In the next step the camera is moved around the center of the point cloud (maintaining the same radius) to capture 64 perspectives of the point cloud. At each iteration, a "picture" is taken and saved to a temporary file on the file system. After all perspectives have been captured, the images are stitched together following a 8×8 grid. We also reduce the image size to get more reasonable results at the end. A label file with 64 bounding box coordinates is generated, one around each image in our grid.

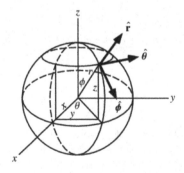

Fig. 3. Polar and Cartesian coordinates

To move the camera around the image, we translate the camera's position from Cartesian to polar coordinates as described in Eqs. 1–3 and visualized in Fig. 3. Additionally, we ensure that the camera is "pointing" at the origin.

$$r = \sqrt{x^2 + y^2 + z^2} \tag{1}$$

$$\theta = \tan\left(\frac{y}{x}\right) \tag{2}$$

$$\phi = \cos\left(\frac{z}{r}\right) \tag{3}$$

An example result of a car's point cloud after preprocessing is shown in Fig. 4. Note that we have inverted the colors for greater visibility when printed.

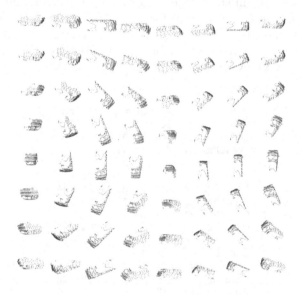

Fig. 4. Example objects in our chosen data set

3.3   Training

As mentioned before, YOLO does the classification and localization of the object in only one step which results in determining the position and category of the object directly at the output layer [12]. Object detection is treated as a regression problem in the YOLO algorithm, which greatly improves the operation speed by meeting real-time requirements. First, the input image is divided into an $S \times S$ grid of cells. Each grid cell is said to be "responsible" for predicting each object that is present in the image. Each grid cell predicts B bounding boxes as well as C class probabilities. The bounding box prediction has 5 components: $(x, y, w, h, confidence)$. The (x, y) coordinates represent the center of the box relative to the grid cell location. These coordinates are normalized to fall between 0 and 1. The (w, h) box dimensions are also normalized to $[0, 1]$, relative to the image size. If no object exists in that cell, the confidence score should be zero. Otherwise we want the confidence score to equal the intersection over union (IOU) between the predicted box and the ground truth. The YOLO (v2) [1] adds anchor boxes on the basis of the YOLO and trains the bounding boxes to find better dimensions of boxes automatically using the K-means [13], which makes it easier and more accurate to predict the object location. However, since less information on small objects is saved in the high-level feature map, when there are too many adjacent objects, the detection result is not satisfactory. The YOLO (v3) [2] uses the network adapting features on the basis of Darknet-53, and the softmax loss in the YOLO (v2) is replaced by a logistic loss, which has obvious advantages in small object detection. The architecture of Darknet-53 is displayed in Fig. 5. YOLO (v3) uses a variant of Darknet-53 for the task of detection, 53 more layers are stacked onto it, giving us a 106 layer fully convolutional underlying architecture for YOLO (v3). This is the reason behind the slower speed of YOLO (v3) compared to YOLO (v2).

	Type	Filters	Size	Output
	Convolutional	32	3 × 3	256 × 256
	Convolutional	64	3 × 3 / 2	128 × 128
	Convolutional	32	1 × 1	
1×	Convolutional	64	3 × 3	
	Residual			128 × 128
	Convolutional	128	3 × 3 / 2	64 × 64
	Convolutional	64	1 × 1	
2×	Convolutional	128	3 × 3	
	Residual			64 × 64
	Convolutional	256	3 × 3 / 2	32 × 32
	Convolutional	128	1 × 1	
8×	Convolutional	256	3 × 3	
	Residual			32 × 32
	Convolutional	512	3 × 3 / 2	16 × 16
	Convolutional	256	1 × 1	
8×	Convolutional	512	3 × 3	
	Residual			16 × 16
	Convolutional	1024	3 × 3 / 2	8 × 8
	Convolutional	512	1 × 1	
4×	Convolutional	1024	3 × 3	
	Residual			8 × 8
	Avgpool		Global	
	Connected		1000	
	Softmax			

Fig. 5. Darknet 53 network architecture which is the base structure for YOLO (v3) network for object detection.

We train our preprocessed images on the YOLO (v3) network [2] which has is known for high performance and accurate object detection. We add 64 bounding boxes, one for each perspective, and feed this ground truth data to the network. Figure 6 shows the progression of training on a 1080 Ti GPU over a span of around 6 h.

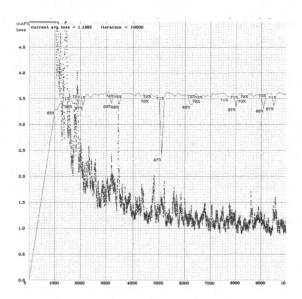

Fig. 6. Training with data set of 630 images (70/30 training/testing split.)

3.4   Inference

After preprocessing the point cloud and arranging it into an image grid, we perform inference on this image using the YOLO (v3) network. The result of this inference step is a list of classes and bounding boxes. To make sense of these detected objects, we first sort the list of detected classes. We then count the number of objects for the most detected class and apply a configurable threshold to this number. If the number of detected objects equals or exceeds the given threshold, we consider this class to be the final classification. Using this voting mechanism we are able to add redundancy through multiple perspectives.

4   Experimental Results

We perform a standard classification evaluation which consists of finding the precision, recall, and f1 values for each class, and the weighted average of these values over each class. Our results are shown in the following table:

		Precision	Recall	f1-score	Support
Class	Car	0.9839	1.0000	0.9919	61
	Pedestrian	1.0000	0.9688	0.9841	96
	None	0.9429	1.0000	0.9706	33
Average	Micro avg	0.9842	0.9842	0.9842	190
	Macro avg	0.9756	0.9896	0.9822	190
	Weighted avg	0.9849	0.9842	0.9843	190

As seen in the "Training" section, the mAP is around 0.70 which is rather low. However by using our voting mechanism we are able to achieve a far greater aggregate result. With this voting technique we achieve a classification accuracy of 98.42% on the Sydney Urban Objects data set.

As mentioned in the "Inference" section, an important parameter to tune is the threshold at which we consider the object to be classified. We perform an empirical study to gauge the most effective value and find that the optimal value is 58. Figure 7 shows the relation between the threshold value and accuracy.

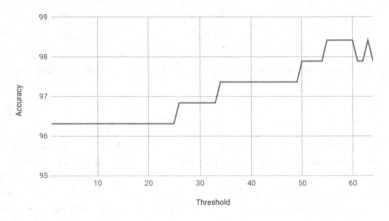

Fig. 7. Accuracy vs threshold plot.

In order to evaluate the run-time of our system, we simply take the total run-time of the inference step and divide by the number of images. Using a 1080 Ti we are able to get inference time of approximately 10 milliseconds per object. Because an optimized preprocessing step (rasterization of simple points) would be almost immediate using modern graphics acceleration hardware, we can assume that the majority of the time will be spent in the inference step and that this time measure is a good estimate of the end-to-end time spent for lidar point-cloud classification.

There are two papers that attempt to classify the point cloud data in our chosen data set. De Deuge et al. [14], achieve a maximum f1 score of 0.671.

In Quadros [15] the f1 score is 0.7. The average f1 score of 0.9843 that we attained indicates a significantly higher performance than these recent methods. Since the Sydney data set is quite small and deep learning techniques thrive on abundant data, we expect that a richer data set would further increase the accuracy of our method.

In terms of runtime, previous papers are more efficient (6ms vs our 10ms per image). However, this comes at the expense of accuracy.

5 Future Work

We presently draw the image label bounding box around the entire perspective raster which includes a considerable amount of "empty" space (i.e. black background). We might see better classification results with a tighter bounding box around each image. Right now each point in the point cloud is a single, white dot. We might see accuracy improvements by encoding additional information into the color of each point. For example, depth information such as distance from the camera could be encoded into one color channel, curvature into another channel, etc. All perspective rasters are presently captured using a single, fixed radius from the geometric center of the point cloud. Varying the radius of the camera from the point cloud's center might make our classifier more robust to scale.

6 Conclusion

In this paper, we effectively classified vehicles and pedestrians from 3D point-clouds by using multiple 2D perspectives for feature representation. Rasterized 2D perspectives are used for training and inference through the state-of-the-art object detection method called YOLO (v3). Furthermore, a voting mechanism for object classification is introduced. We were able to preserve depth information and increase accuracy while maintaining efficiency. The Sydney Urban Objects data set was used for evaluation of the proposed method. Experimental results show that the 3D point cloud classification algorithm proposed in this paper has high accuracy. In future work we will be using tighter bounding box, encode additional information through colour for getting better classification results and scale robustness with multiple radii for the camera.

References

1. Redmon, J., Divvala, S., Girshick, R., Farhadi, A.: You only look once: unified, real-time object detection. In: Proceedings of the IEEE Conference on Computer Vision and Pattern Recognition, pp. 779–788 (2016)
2. Redmon, J., Farhadi, A.: YOLOv3: an incremental improvement. arXiv preprint arXiv:1804.02767 (2018)

3. Huang, J., You, S.: Point cloud labeling using 3D convolutional neural network. In: 2016 23rd International Conference on Pattern Recognition (ICPR), pp. 2670–2675. IEEE (2016)
4. Landrieu, L., Simonovsky, M.: Large-scale point cloud semantic segmentation with superpoint graphs. In: Proceedings of the IEEE Conference on Computer Vision and Pattern Recognition, pp. 4558–4567 (2018)
5. Bay, H., Tuytelaars, T., Van Gool, L.: SURF: speeded up robust features. In: Leonardis, A., Bischof, H., Pinz, A. (eds.) ECCV 2006. LNCS, vol. 3951, pp. 404–417. Springer, Heidelberg (2006). https://doi.org/10.1007/11744023_32
6. Lowe, D.G., et al.: Object recognition from local scale-invariant features. In: ICCV, vol. 99, pp. 1150–1157 (1999)
7. Malisiewicz, T., Gupta, A., Efros, A.A., et al.: Ensemble of exemplar-SVMs for object detection and beyond. In: ICCV, vol. 1, p. 6. Citeseer (2011)
8. Krizhevsky, A., Sutskever, I., Hinton, G.E.: ImageNet classification with deep convolutional neural networks. In: Pereira, F., Burges, C.J.C., Bottou, L., Weinberger, K.Q. (eds.) Advances in Neural Information Processing Systems 25, pp. 1097–1105. Curran Associates, Inc. (2012)
9. Liu, W., et al.: SSD: single shot MultiBox detector. In: Leibe, B., Matas, J., Sebe, N., Welling, M. (eds.) ECCV 2016. LNCS, vol. 9905, pp. 21–37. Springer, Cham (2016). https://doi.org/10.1007/978-3-319-46448-0_2
10. Ali, W., Abdelkarim, S., Zidan, M., Zahran, M., Sallab, A.E.: YOLO3D: end-to-end real-time 3D oriented object bounding box detection from LiDAR point cloud. In: Leal-Taixé, L., Roth, S. (eds.) ECCV 2018. LNCS, vol. 11131, pp. 716–728. Springer, Cham (2019). https://doi.org/10.1007/978-3-030-11015-4_54
11. Maturana, D., Scherer, S.: VoxNet: a 3D convolutional neural network for real-time object recognition. In: 2015 IEEE/RSJ International Conference on Intelligent Robots and Systems (IROS), pp. 922–928. IEEE (2015)
12. Zhang, X., Yang, W., Tang, X., Liu, J.: A fast learning method for accurate and robust lane detection using two-stage feature extraction with YOLO v3. Sensors **18**, 4308 (2018)
13. Tang, X., Yang, W., Hu, X., Zhang, D.: A novel simplified model for torsional vibration analysis of a series-parallel hybrid electric vehicle. Mech. Syst. Signal Process. **85**, 329–338 (2017)
14. De Deuge, M., Quadros, A., Hung, C., Douillard, B.: Unsupervised feature learning for classification of outdoor 3D scans. In: Australasian Conference on Robitics and Automation, vol. 2, p. 1 (2013)
15. Quadros, A.J.: Representing 3D shape in sparse range images for urban object classification. Ph.D. thesis, The school of the thesis, October 2013. http://hdl.handle.net/2123/10515

Poisson Surface Reconstruction from LIDAR for Buttress Root Volume Estimation

Jianfei Ma, Ruoyang Song, Tao Han, Arturo Sanchez-Azofeifa,
and Anup Basu[✉]

Departments of Computing Science and Earth and Atmospheric Science,
University of Alberta, Edmonton, Canada
basu@ualberta.ca

Abstract. Tree buttress volumes are significant in analyzing bioinformation of a forest. However, forestry researchers have no accurate method for estimating the volume of complex tree buttress roots. Light Detection and Ranging (LiDAR) scanning can be used to scan large multi-hectare areas of forests with thousands of trees. In this paper, we introduce a new method for accurate tree buttress volumes estimation based on the LiDAR system and the Poisson Surface Reconstruction algorithm.

1 Introduction

Accurate estimation of forest structure attributes such as diameter at breast height, tree height and canopy structure are important to a number of applications including forest management, global warming and carbon management [1]. Wood volume contained in the stem of a tree is one of the most crucial measurements in forests, because it is an important attribute to determine tree biomass. It is predicted that biomass represents 50% of the total carbon stocked in forests. Therefore, accurate estimation of tree volume can provide important information for carbon changes, thereby estimating climate change on earth [2]. Buttress trees are very common for many old-growth forests, a relatively small number of very tall trees make considerable contributions to the stand basal area and biomass [3]. Such trees are easy to distinguish from others as they have buttress roots with irregular non-convex shapes. Buttress roots are large, wide roots on all sides of a shallowly rooted tree, and they always account for relatively large percent of the total volume of the trees. Quantifying their components in the whole stem will improve the estimation of the total biomass [4]. Traditionally, tree volume is directly measured by harvesting and weighing whole forest plots, which is costly and has a negative influence on the forests [5]. Instead, allometric equations based on the indirect relationships between destructive tree samples and easily measured tree metrics such as diameter at breast height (DBH), tree height and wood density are widely used [6]. These methods can be useful for specific species and plots. However, they may lead to greater uncertainty for

© Springer Nature Switzerland AG 2020
T. McDaniel et al. (Eds.): ICSM 2019, LNCS 12015, pp. 463–471, 2020.
https://doi.org/10.1007/978-3-030-54407-2_39

trees with buttresses, because of their irregular shapes. Terrestrial laser scanning (TLS), also named terrestrial LiDAR, is an active remote sensing method that uses laser light to measure the distance between the sensor and objects. It can retrieve the 3D vegetation structure with a high level of accuracy, thus giving it a broad spectrum of uses in ecological and environmental studies during the last decades. This equipment is widely used to measure forests characteristics including above ground biomass, forest vertical profile, canopy gap fraction and plant area index (Fig. 1).

Fig. 1. Complex tree buttress roots.

In this paper, we propose a new method for accurate tree buttress volumes estimation based on the LiDAR scanner and the Poisson Surface Reconstruction algorithm. The general steps of the proposed method include scanning and collecting Point Cloud data, computing normals of point clouds, applying the Poisson Surface Reconstruction algorithm to point clouds, and calculating the mesh volume.

The remaining sections of this paper are structured as follows: Sect. 2 provides details on the dataset used. Section 3 outlines some previous work related to our topic. Section 4 covers the proposed method. Section 5 presents the comparison between ground truth and experimental results. Concluding remarks are given in Sect. 6.

2   Data Set

The data used in this article was collected by scanning two small potted miniature trees, bought from a home improvement store, using a Lidar camera. As shown in Fig. 2, the first tree has a straight branch whose volume can be measured using cyliners with existing segmentation technologies, while the other tree has a complicated irregular shaped buttress structure as shown in Fig. 3. The volume estimation for this tree is difficult following existing techniques. Thus, we use this miniature tree to verify our theory through experiments.

3   Related Work

Vosselman et al. introduced various techniques for recognizing structure in point clouds in 2004 [7]. Using these methods, we can extract planar surfaces and specific shapes in point clouds. While this method performs well in recognizing tree branches and simple tree roots, the shapes of buttress roots are quite random and cannot be represented simply by composing several surfaces, spheres or cylinders. For a complex tree buttress shown below, this method may lead to a wrong segmentation of the point cloud.

Fig. 2. Regular shaped branch.

Fig. 3. Irregular shaped buttress.

For volume calculation, the Convex Hull algorithm [8] is useful for simple geometric shapes. This algorithm was later generalized to 3D in 1996 [9]. The Convex Hull algorithm connects all the points in a point cloud. The result of applying the Convex Hull on our sample buttress roots is shown in Fig. 5. From the figure we can see that there is a large deviation from the actual model after applying the Convex Hull algorithm on a complex buttress root (Fig. 4).

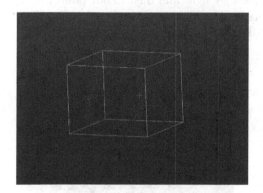

Fig. 4. A sample tree buttress.

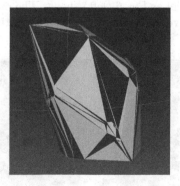

Fig. 5. Sample buttress with Convex Hull.

4 Proposed Method

We propose a new method with the following components: (1) scanning and collecting point cloud data; (2) computing normals of the point clouds; (3) applying the Poisson Surface Reconstruction algorithm to the point clouds; (4) segmenting the buttress part and closing holes; and, (5) calculating the mesh volume. Next, each step is explained in detail.

4.1 Scanning and Collecting Point Cloud Data

We used the RIEGL vz-400 LIDAR to scan and export the buttress data. The data collected was stored in TXT format. We converted the data into PCD (point cloud data) format for the following reasons [10]:

1. The ability to store and process organized point cloud datasets is important for real time applications;
2. Binary mmap/munmap data types are the fastest for loading and saving data to a disk;
3. Storing different data types (all primitives supported: char, short, int, float, double) allows the point cloud data to be flexible and efficient with respect to storage and processing; and,
4. n-D histograms for feature descriptors are important for 3D perception/computer vision applications.

The point cloud data gathered from Laser scans has varying point densities. Also, there are many situations, such as insects and falling leaves that lead to outliers in a real forest environment. Even for the data scanned in a laboratory, we can observe some visible outliers caused by light and dust in our point cloud model as Fig. 6 (left) shows. The outliers lead to bias; the densities do not affect the volume, but the varying densities will make subsequent steps such as normal

Fig. 6. Comparison between the point clouds before and after removing the outliers.

calculation complicated. Hence, we apply a Statistical Outlier Removal Filter on our point clouds. We can see the bias points are removed in the right part of Fig. 6.

Our sparse outlier removal is based on computing the distribution of point to neighbors distances in the input dataset. For each point, we compute the mean distance from it to all of its neighbors. Assuming that the resulting distribution is Gaussian, all points whose mean distances are outside an interval defined by the global mean and standard deviation are considered to be outliers and trimmed from the dataset [11]. After we convert our point cloud into the PCD format, we remove noise in the point cloud to generate a meticulous mesh in the next step. We can see the comparison before and after removing the outliers from Fig. 6. All the outliers floating outside of the main object are removed and the result is ready for generating a mesh.

4.2   Computing Normals of the Point Clouds

The problem of determining the normal at a point on the surface is approximated by the problem of estimating the normal of a plane tangent to the surface, which in turn is a least-square plane fitting estimation problem [12]. The solution for estimating the surface normal is therefore reduced to an analysis of the eigenvectors and eigenvalues (or PCA – Principal Component Analysis) of a covariance matrix created from the nearest neighbors of the query point. More specifically, for each point p_i, we compute the covariance matrix C as follows:

$$C = \frac{1}{k} \sum_{i=1}^{k} \cdot (p_i - \bar{p}) \cdot (p_i - \bar{p})^T, C \cdot \overrightarrow{V_j} = \lambda_j \cdot \overrightarrow{V_j}, j \in \{0, 1, 2\} \tag{1}$$

Where k is the number of point neighbors considered in the neighborhood of p_i, $\bar{p}$ represents the 3D centroid of the nearest neighbors, λ_j is the j-th eigenvalue of the covariance matrix, and v_j is the j-th eigenvector. For our irregular shaped tree model, Fig. 7 shows the result of estimating the normals.

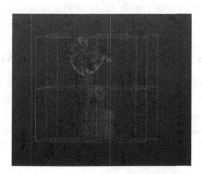

Fig. 7. Result of estimating normals.

4.3 Using Poisson Reconstruction to Generate a Mesh

In this step, we will implement a surface reconstruction procedure whose input is the points with normal, assuming the outliers have been removed by the SOR filter. The output is a surface mesh, generated by extracting an isosurface of a surface contouring algorithm [13]. The result of poisson reconstruction can be seen in Fig. 8.

Fig. 8. Result of poisson reconstruction.

4.4 Segmenting the Buttress Part and Closing Holes

Using our approach, we can also calculate volume of the whole tree. If we only want to calculate the volume of the buttress part we can segment the buttress part from the original mesh. Note that if redundant parts are included, we can apply a second level of segmentation on the initial segmentation result. Figure 9 compares the meshes before and after segmentation. Note that in Fig. 10 there are two significant holes in our mesh after segmentation. There will be a large error if the mesh has holes. This problem can be fixed using the Meshlab software.

4.5 Calculating the Volume from the Buttress Mesh

After having an accurate mesh of the buttress, we use a polyhedron volume calculation algorithm to calculate the volume [14]. The mesh surfaces consist of many triangles. We connect the vertices of triangles with the origin at (0,0,0). Then, we can get a tetrahedron whose volume can be calculated as:

$$V = \frac{1}{6}(v_1 \times v_2) \cdot v_3 \tag{2}$$

We add up the volumes of all the tetrahedrons to obtain the volume of the whole mesh. Note that each tetrahedron's volume has a sign so that the overlapping parts are subtracted and only the inner part is left.

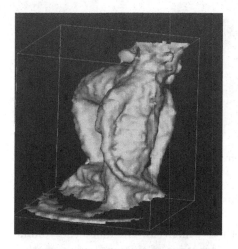 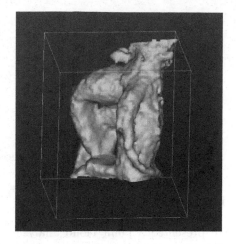

Fig. 9. Comparison between the meshes before and after segmentation.

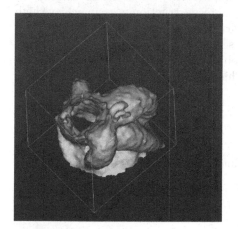 

Fig. 10. Comparison between the meshes with and without holes.

5 Experimental Results

Our algorithm computes the volume of the buttress root to be $191.5\,cm^3$. To obtain the actual volume of the buttress, we used a 3D printer to create an exact 3D model of the same buttress root. The volume of this 3D model was measured by observing the volume of water it displaces in a measuring container (Fig. 11).

The 3D-printing model's volume is about $202\,cm^3$. Thus, the accuracy of our method is around 94.5%. The tree model we used is small, and the 3D printed model contains rough edges which over-estimates the actual volume. Thus, the actual accuracy of our method should be higher. Also, our method should have higher accuracy for real trees with larger buttress.

Fig. 11. Tools (left) and procedure used to measure volume.

6   Conclusion

We presented a point cloud analysis method which can calculate the volume of any irregular-shaped buttress root. The advantage of this method over other volume estimation methods is that it has high accuracy for buttresses of different shapes. Since this method is based on Poisson reconstruction, we can achieve high accuracy applying this method on irregularly shaped buttress. The drawback of the method is that it requires a precisely scanned point cloud.

In future work, we will estimate the volume of buttress roots for a collection of tree in a region of a real rainforest. This will be a step towards monitoring carbon changes in forests.

References

1. Liang, X., et al.: Terrestrial laser scanning in forest inventories. ISPRS J. Photogram. Rem. Sens. **115**, 63–77 (2016)
2. Astrup, R., Ducey, M.J., Granhus, A., Ritter, T., von Lüpke, N.: Approaches for estimating stand-level volume using terrestrial laser scanning in a single-scan mode. Can. J. For. Res. **44**, 666–676 (2014)
3. Momo Takoudjou, S.: Using terrestrial laser scanning data to estimate large tropical trees biomass and calibrate allometric models: A comparison with traditional destructive approach. Methods Ecol. Evol. **9**, 905–916 (2018)
4. Gonzalez, J., de Tanago, A., Lau, H.B., Herold, M.: Estimation of above-ground biomass of large tropical trees with Terrestrial LiDAR. Methods Ecol. Evol. **9**, 223–234 (2018)
5. David, B.C., James, R.K.: Tropical forest biomass estimation and the fallacy of misplaced concreteness. J. Veg. Sci. **23**, 1191–1196 (2012)
6. Chave, J., et al.: Tree allometry and improved estimation of carbon stocks and balance in tropical forests. Oecologia **145**, 87–99 (2005)
7. Vosselman, G., et al.: Recognising Structure in Laser Scanner Point Clouds (2004). https://www.researchgate.net/
8. Chand, D.R., Kapur, S.S.: An algorithm for convex polytopes. J. ACM (JACM) **17**(1), 78–86 (1970)
9. Chan, T.M.: Optimal output-sensitive convex hull algorithms in two and three dimensions. Discrete Comput. Geom. **16**(4), 361–368 (1996). https://doi.org/10.1007/BF02712873

10. PCD Documentation. https://pointclouds.org/
11. Removing outliers using a StatisticalOutlierRemoval filter. https://pointclouds.org/documentation/tutorials/
12. Estimating Surface Normals in a PointCloud. http://pointclouds.org/documentation/tutorials/normal_estimation.php
13. Michael, K., et al.: Poisson Surface Reconstruction (2006). https://www.cs.jhu.edu/misha/MyPapers/SGP06.pdf
14. Lien, S.-L., Kajiya, J.T.: A symbolic method for calculating the integral properties of arbitrary nonconvex polyhedra. IEEE Comput. Graph. Appl. 4(10), 35–42 (1984)

Fog Removal of Aerial Image Based on Gamma Correction and Guided Filtering

Xinggang Liu[1], Changjiang Liu[1,2(✉)] [ID], and Hengyou Lan[1,2,3]

[1] College of Automation and Information Engineering, Sichuan University of Science and Engineering, Zigong 643000, China
hengyoulan@163.com
[2] College of Mathematics and Statistics,
Sichuan University of Science and Engineering, Zigong 643000, China
liuchangjiang@189.cn
[3] Sichuan Province University Key Laboratory of Bridge Nondestruction Detecting and Engineering Computing,
Sichuan University of Science and Engineering, Zigong 643000, China

Abstract. In order to improve the pilots' perception of the runway and the surrounding things in foggy days and improve the visual effect of aerial images, a combination of Gamma correction and Retinex defogging algorithm is proposed for aerial foggy images. First of all, the original image is corrected by Gamma as the guided map, and the light intensity of the aerial image is estimated by the guided filter, and the preliminary fog removal image is obtained by Retinex. In combination with the histogram truncation technique, the output of the image is mapped to between 0 and 255, then a de-fogging enhanced image is achieved. Compared with other de-fogging algorithms, this algorithm has higher contrast and color consistency.

Keywords: Aerial image · Gamma correction · Guided filtering · Retinex algorithm

1 Introduction

Aircraft take-off and near-earth landings have been an important factor affecting aviation safety, especially near-earth landings. It is especially important to improve pilots' acceptance of the runway information. Image defogging is a means of removing undesirable factors in an image due to inclement weather or blurring incurred by the camera. Removing severe weather effects such as rain, snow [9], haze [13], etc., which leads to images with severe images, some

Supported in part by Sichuan Science and Technology Program under Grant No. 2019YJ0541, the Open Project of Sichuan Province University Key Laboratory of Bridge Non-destruction Detecting and Engineering Computing under Grant No. 2019QZJ03 and Natural Science Foundation of Sichuan University of Science and Engineering (SUSE) under Grant No. 2019RC09, 2020RC28.

T. McDaniel et al. (Eds.): ICSM 2019, LNCS 12015, pp. 472–479, 2020.
https://doi.org/10.1007/978-3-030-54407-2_40

of the researchers studied the causes of image degradation by using the physical model [1]. He [3] proposed a method based on dark channel prior image dehazing. Huang [5] used the wavelet threshold to estimate the atmospheric light, then employed the atmospheric light to recover the image. Kapoor [7] introduced a guided filter to refine the transmission map based on dark channel defogging. Contrast-limited finite adaptive histogram equalization (CLAHE) has been used to improve visibility and effectively reduce halo. Other researchers have analyzed the foggy image by image enhancement [19]. Early image enhancement was dominated by histogram equalization [16]. Land and McCann [8] proposed retinal theory. Variant Retinex models were put into use including single-scale Retinex (SSR) [6], multi-scale Retinex (MSR) [14] and Multi-Scale Retinex with Color Restore(MSRCR) [12]. In previous work, we [10] improved the MSR algorithm of more than 3 scales by mathematical derivation, which has a better effect on balancing dynamic range and color consistency. Pu [15] proposed a fractional variational frame theory on the Retinex framework, which improved the texture details of the image. Neural network based dehazing has also appeared. Among them, the anti-fog algorithm based on anti-neural network defogging [17] excels in the defogging effect, but the data is not easy to access. However, different algorithms perform somewhat differently on foggy images. Based on the dark channel prior, the block effect and color inconsistency are shown in the defogging of aerial image, while the typical Retinex algorithm is hard to remove the fog effect entirely. The enhanced images via aforementioned algorithms lack contrast and abundant details. In this paper, on the basis of the SSR model, the gamma transform is used to adjust the image contrast. Subsequently, the images with different contrasts are used as the guide map for guided filtering. As a result, the proposed Retinex algorithm is implemented to defogg aerial images.

2 Related Works

2.1 Retinex Algorithm

Retinex is an image dehazing enhancement algorithm proposed by the American physicist Edwin Land. The expression of the Retinex algorithm is:

$$S(x, y) = R(x, y) \times L(x, y), \tag{1}$$

where $S(x, y)$ is a foggy image, which consists of two parts, the incident light component $L(x, y)$ and $R(x, y)$, the reflected light component. Since the essence of the image is the $L(x, y)$, Eq. (1) is converted to the logarithmic domain, given by:

$$lnR(x, y) = lnS(x, y) - lnL(x, y). \tag{2}$$

The core of traditional Retinex is to estimate the incident light component. Generally, it is estimated by the convolution of input image $S(x, y)$ and Gaussian filter function $F(x, y)$, which is defined by:

$$F(x, y) = \lambda e^{\frac{-(x^2 + y^2)}{\sigma^2}}, \tag{3}$$

where λ is the normalization constant such that:

$$\int\int F(x,y)dxdy = 1. \tag{4}$$

σ is the scale of the Gaussian convolution function. The larger the σ is, the smoother image is, at the cost of losing edge details; Similarly, the smaller the σ is, the edge information is more prominent, however with color deviation.

2.2   Guided Filter

Guided filtering is an image filtering algorithm based on local linear model proposed by He [2, 4, 11]. Guided filtering framework is modeled as linear expression:

$$q_i = a_k I_i + b_k, \forall i \in \omega_k. \tag{5}$$

where I_i is a guided image, ω_k is a filter window of the k-th pixel. Employing least square method to minimize the difference between the output q and input image p, the coefficients of linear fitting in Eq. (5) are calculated as:

$$\begin{cases} a_k = \dfrac{\frac{1}{|\omega_k|}\sum\limits_{i\in\omega_k} I_i p_i - \mu_k \overline{p_k}}{\sigma_k^2 + \varepsilon} \\ b_k = \overline{p_k} - a_k \mu_k \end{cases} \tag{6}$$

where $|\omega_k|$ is the number of pixels in the window ω_k, μ_k and σ_k^2 are the mean and variance of the guided graph I in the filter window respectively, p_k is the mean of input image p in the filter window.

3   Improved Retinex Algorithm

In this paper, according to the Retinex algorithm, the details are lost, the color is distorted, and so on. Before the image is defogged, Gamma correction is performed to correct the contrast and brightness of the original image, and then the different Gamma corrected images are subjected to three-scale guided filtering processing. The scale is divided into three filtering radii of large, medium and small. The filtered image is weighted and fused, and the fused filtered image is introduced in the single scale Retinex model to defog aerial images. Finally, Weighted fusion is implemented to finally enhance aerial images.

Considering the low contrast and brightness of aerial imagery under low visibilities, when the highlighted area, such as runway, is enhanced directly by Retienx algorithm, the exposure phenomenon occurs. And enhanced dark area is insufficient to reflect the image detail. Therefore, the Gamma transform is performed on the image ahead of the Retienx enhancement. Thus, the highlighted and dark areas are stretched, thereby improving the image contrast and enhancing the brightness of the dark areas. Aerial images are enhanced by Gamma correction, and the correction factors of $\gamma > 1$ and $\gamma < 1$ are selected. And corrected images are presented by:

$$\begin{cases} R_1(x,y) = I_i^{\gamma_1}(x,y), \gamma_1 > 1 \\ R_2(x,y) = I_i^{\gamma_2}(x,y), \gamma_2 < 1 \end{cases} \tag{7}$$

The gamma-corrected images are used as a guide map to perform the filtering process. Three scales are employed to filter different gamma corrected images. The mathematical form is:

$$\begin{cases} q_i^1 = a_{k_1} I_i^{\gamma_1} + b_{k_1} \\ q_i^2 = a_{k_2} I_i^{\gamma_1} + b_{k_2} \\ q_i^3 = a_{k_3} I_i^{\gamma_1} + b_{k_3} \end{cases} \begin{cases} q_i^4 = a_{k_4} I_i^{\gamma_2} + b_{k_4} \\ q_i^5 = a_{k_5} I_i^{\gamma_2} + b_{k_5} \\ q_i^6 = a_{k_6} I_i^{\gamma_2} + b_{k_6} \end{cases} \tag{8}$$

wherein, q_i^j is a filter map after different boot maps and different filter window sizes are imposed. The a_{k_i} and b_{k_i} can be calculated according to Eq. (6).

The guided filtered images with variant scale r are fused. To be detailed, the $\gamma 1$ guided filter has a bigger weight on the large scale, which can smooth the image and ensure effective defogging. The $\gamma 2$ guided filter has a bigger weight on the small scale, which preserves image details and original texture features. After filtering, the merged image is shown in Fig. 1. Fusion strategy is depicted as:

$$\begin{cases} q_i^{\gamma_1} = \lambda_1 q_i^1 + \lambda_2 q_i^2 + \lambda_3 q_i^3, 0 < \lambda_i < 1 \\ q_i^{\gamma_2} = \lambda_4 q_i^4 + \lambda_5 q_i^5 + \lambda_6 q_i^6, 0 < \lambda_i < 1 \end{cases} \tag{9}$$

The $q_i^{\gamma_j}$ is the fusion result of filter map with different weights, and λ_i is the weight of the multi-scale filters for large, medium and small scale respectively. Repeated trials indicate that the λ_1, λ_2, and λ_3 takes 1/4, 1/4, and 1/2, respectively, and λ_4, λ_5, and λ_6 takes 1/2, 1/4, and 1/4 respectively, and results on different experimental images are preferable.

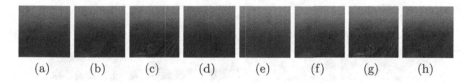

| (a) | (b) | (c) | (d) | (e) | (f) | (g) | (h) |

Fig. 1. Different scale filtered images with (a)(e) $r = 3$ (b)(f) $r = 31$ (c)(g) $r = 131$ and (d)(h) fusion result.

The incident light component obtained by the guided filtering is brought into the Retinex model to recover a the light component, therefore a defogged image is described in mathematics:

$$R^{SSR}(x,y) = lnI(x,y) - lnq_i^\gamma. \tag{10}$$

Inspired by the MSR theory, two single scale Retinex enhancement are incorporated balancing contrast and details, presented by:

$$R^{MSR}(x,y) = \alpha R^{SSR1}(x,y) + (1-\alpha)R^{SSR2}(x,y), 0 < \alpha < 1. \quad (11)$$

where α is a weighting factor, and the effect of enhancing the image is adjusted by different weights.

In this paper, the histogram truncation method is used to count the gray level of the MSR domain, and the two continuous lower level gray-scale parts at two ends, denoted by R_{min} and R_{max}, are truncated, and then the retained part is linearly mapped to [0, 255] to adapt to display domain. Its process is seen below:

$$R^{OUT}_{MSR} = 255 * \frac{R_{MSR} - R_{min}}{R_{max} - R_{min}} \quad (12)$$

4   Experimental Result

Proposed algorithm is implemented on Microsoft Visual Studio 2015 development platform and Open CV three-party library. The configuration of the computer is memory: 4GB, operating system: Windows 10 (64 bit). Different aerial images are experimented for verification. Results demonstrate that proposed method can achieve high contrast and color consistency.

4.1   Experimental Results of Proposed Algorithm

The image in the aerial video is intercepted for testing. It can be seen visually that after defogging, the image has better visual effects in detail and contrast, shown in Fig. 2. It is noted that enhanced image can assist pilots to improved surroundings perception, as the runway is highlighted in red rectangle.

(a)   (b)   (c)   (d)

Fig. 2. Proposed enhancement (a)(c) original image (b)(d) enhanced image.

It also shows a good dehazing effect on a general foggy image. As shown in Fig. 3.

Fig. 3. Proposed enhancement (a)(c) original image (b)(d) enhanced image.

4.2 Comparison with Existing Algorithms

In recent years, defogging research has matured, but there are few studies on defogging of aerial imagery. The comparison is based on dark channel dehazing, traditional MSRCR algorithm and the proposed algorithm. The proposed method in this paper achieves high contrast and high color reproduction, as shown in Fig. 4.

Comparing to the dark channel dehazing and standard MSRCR algorithm, the proposed method has higher contrast and color consistency, especially the sky region.

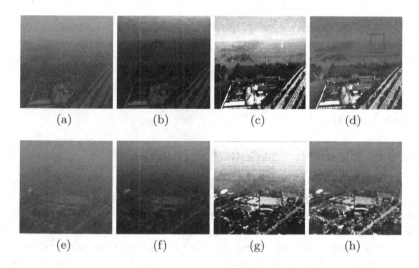

Fig. 4. Comparisons with standard dark channel prior and MSRCR. (a)(e) original image (b)(f) dark channel prior enhanced image (c)(g) MSRCR enhanced image (d)(h) our method's enhanced image.

5   Image Quality Evaluation

In this paper, AMBE (Absolute mean brightness error), entropy, PSNR (Peak signal-to-noise ratio) are used as objective evaluation factors [18]. Among them, the smaller the AMBE value is, the higher the entropy value is, the higher the PSNR is, then the higher the image quality is. The assessment indexes are shown in Table 1, where V_e, V_P, and V_A represents entropy, PSNR and AMBE respectively. It is worth pointing out that the proposed method prevails in all assessment indexes. The quality has improved significantly. The objective images of different algorithms in Fig. 4 are objectively evaluated. The results are shown in Table 1. In Table 1, ♣, ★, ♦ represent the optimal index of the tested images.

Table 1. Entropy, PSNR and AMBE of tested images Fig. 4 in this paper.

Image number	Original image and different defogging methods	V_e	V_A	V_P
Fig. 4 first group (a,b,c,d)	Original image(a)	6.871	–	–
	Dark Channel Prior(b)	7.271	46.466	32.480
	MSRCR(c)	7.374	36.666	29.019
	Our methods(d)	**♣7.429**	**★27.299**	**♦32.824**
Fig. 4 second group (e,f,g,h)	Original image(e)	6.721	–	–
	Dark Channel Prior(f)	7.248	55.384	25.280
	MSRCR(g)	7.365	32.044	27.992
	Our methods(h)	**♣7.522**	**★26.940**	**♦34.838**

6   Conclusion

For harsh weather aerial images, low visibility, low contrast and gray color, greatly affects pilots' judgment during landing in the near-field. Therefore, it is necessary to provide a clearer and higher contrast auxiliary vision system. According to the characteristics of aerial image, this paper proposes an improved Retinex algorithm to elevate contrast. According to the analysis and comparison of the experimental results, the improved method proposed in this paper can effectively remove the aerial fog, improve the image contrast, and maintain consistency in color. The algorithm in this paper can help pilots or machines to effectively identify flight paths. In the future work, we will use other methods to increase the processing speed for practical purposes.

References

1. Fattal, R.: Single image dehazing. ACM Trans. Graph. (TOG) **27**(3), 72 (2008)

2. He, K., Sun, J., Tang, X.: Guided image filtering. In: Daniilidis, K., Maragos, P., Paragios, N. (eds.) ECCV 2010. LNCS, vol. 6311, pp. 1–14. Springer, Heidelberg (2010). https://doi.org/10.1007/978-3-642-15549-9_1

3. He, K., Sun, J., Tang, X.: Single image haze removal using dark channel prior. IEEE Trans. Pattern Anal. Mach. Intell. **33**(12), 2341–2353 (2010)

4. He, K., Sun, J., Tang, X.: Guided image filtering. IEEE Trans. Pattern Anal. Mach. Intell. **35**(6), 1397–1409 (2012)

5. Huang, D., Fang, Z., Zhao, L., Chu, X.: An improved image clearness algorithm based on dark channel prior. In: Proceedings of the 33rd Chinese Control Conference, pp. 7350–7355. IEEE (2014)

6. Jobson, D.J., Rahman, Z.U., Woodell, G.A.: Properties and performance of a center/surround retinex. IEEE Trans. Image Process. **6**(3), 451–462 (1997)

7. Kapoor, R., Gupta, R., Son, L.H., Kumar, R., Jha, S.: Fog removal in images using improved dark channel prior and contrast limited adaptive histogram equalization. Multimed. Tools Appl. **78**(16), 23281–23307 (2019). https://doi.org/10.1007/s11042-019-7574-8

8. Land, E.H., McCann, J.: Lightness and retinex theory. J. Opt. Soc. Am. **61**(1), 1–11 (1971)

9. Li, S., Ren, W., Zhang, J., Yu, J., Guo, X.: Single image rain removal via a deep decomposition–composition network. In: Computer Vision and Image Understanding (2019)

10. Liu, C., Cheng, I., Zhang, Y., Basu, A.: Enhancement of low visibility aerial images using histogram truncation and an explicit retinex representation for balancing contrast and color consistency. ISPRS J. Photogram. Remote Sens. **128**, 16–26 (2017)

11. Liu, P., Wang, M., Wang, L., Han, W.: Remote-sensing image denoising with multi-sourced information. IEEE J. Sel. Top. Appl. Earth Observ. Remote Sens. **12**(2), 660–674 (2019)

12. Livingston, M.A., Garrett, C.R., Ai, Z.: Image processing for human understanding in low-visibility. Techical report, Naval Research Lab Washington DC Information Technology Div (2011)

13. Lu, H., Li, Y., Nakashima, S., Serikawa, S.: Single image dehazing through improved atmospheric light estimation. Multimed. Tools Appl. **75**(24), 17081–17096 (2015). https://doi.org/10.1007/s11042-015-2977-7

14. Patil, M.D., Sutar, M.S., Mulla, M.A.: Automatic image enhancement for better visualization using retinex technique. Int. J. Sci. Res. Publ. **3**(6), 1–4 (2013)

15. Pu, Y.F., et al.: A fractional-order variational framework for retinex: fractional-order partial differential equation-based formulation for multi-scale nonlocal contrast enhancement with texture preserving. IEEE Trans. Image Process. **27**(3), 1214–1229 (2017)

16. Sahu, S., Singh, A.K., Ghrera, S., Elhoseny, M., et al.: An approach for de-noising and contrast enhancement of retinal fundus image using clahe. Optics Laser Technol. **110**, 87–98 (2019)

17. Suarez, P.L., Sappa, A.D., Vintimilla, B.X., Hammoud, R.I.: Deep learning based single image dehazing. In: 2018 IEEE/CVF Conference on Computer Vision and Pattern Recognition Workshops (CVPRW) (2018)

18. Tanchenko, A.: Visual-psnr measure of image quality. J. Vis. Commun. Image Represent. **25**(5), 874–878 (2014)

19. Wang, W., Yuan, X.: Recent advances in image dehazing. IEEE/CAA J. Automatica Sinica **4**(3), 410–436 (2017)

Smart Social and Connected Household Products

3D Virtual Environments to Support New Product Development: A Mobile Platform Based on an Open Innovation Laboratory Applied in Higher Education

José Martín Molina Espinosa[1], Jhonattan Miranda[1(✉)], Daniel Cortés[1],
Jorge Medina[2], and Arturo Molina[1]

[1] School of Engineering and Sciences, Tecnologico de Monterrey, Mexico City, Mexico
{jose.molina,jhonattan.miranda,armolina}@tec.mx,
a01655708@itesm.mx
[2] Mechanical Engineering Department, Universidad de Los Andes, Bogotá, Colombia
jmedina@uniandes.edu.co

Abstract. Nowadays, it is observed that native digital students demand the use of innovative learning methods, as well as the use of specialized technological equipment that can positively influence their professional training, but at the same time it is observed that there is still a deficit not only in the commitment and interest of students to learn, but also to relate how they can apply the knowledge obtained by proposing solutions to real problems. This paper proposes a mobile platform based on 3D virtual environments to support new product development (NPD) as an alternative to address these issues in the Higher Education sector. This mobile platform is an interactive and learning management system that is used to efficiently gather and manage the tangible/intangible resources necessary in an Open Innovation process for the development of new products in which the co-creation and co-development take place. Therefore, an Open Innovation Laboratory applied in higher education was used as a reference. A case study is presented to demonstrate how the proposed platform can be applied in the higher education context.

Keywords: Multimedia and education · Open innovation · Virtual reality · Augmented reality · Educational innovation · Higher education

1 Introduction

Today, there are still challenges in the higher education sector to improve teaching-learning processes that are mainly related to the deficit in the motivation and interest of students to learn including intrinsic and extrinsic motivations, the link between the acquired knowledge and the labor work, the difficulty in developing desirable competencies in today's student profile, among others [1, 2]. In recent years, there are emerging initiatives related with the concept and vision of Education 4.0 to face these challenges

© Springer Nature Switzerland AG 2020
T. McDaniel et al. (Eds.): ICSM 2019, LNCS 12015, pp. 483–496, 2020.
https://doi.org/10.1007/978-3-030-54407-2_41

since Education 4.0 promotes the implementation of desirable physical/virtual infrastructure by using new learning methods to improve the teaching-learning processes and to develop core competencies in students [3–5].

In this sense, it is observed that some recent platforms involve students into the creation process and promote desirable competencies of Education 4.0 [6]. Different solutions have arisen based on App development (e.g. Balsamiq Mockups, Mockingbid, MockFlow), virtual learning environments (e.g. Com8s, Edmodo, Lectrio, Ude-my), visualization and engagement apps developed through game environments (e.g. Unity, Godot, Unreal Engine 4) but also for product development which lead students into novel education methods. These platforms have been developed by universities, associations or initiatives from makers to promote the competencies people need today. Product Development Platforms (CooL:SLiCE Platform, Creativation Challenge, NovoEd, UCV(a), make-it.io, Snap, Berkely Bridge) make use of emergent technologies, virtual reality (VR) and augmented reality (AR), graphic vision and make use of existing infrastructure of internet of things (IoT) and cloud computing. Observing the behavior of new generations to learn and develop in the student field, interaction with technology becomes evident as an extended method for problem-solving [7, 8]. With this, structuring the stages of product development and providing platforms for students. This article aims at providing a platform to take advantage of technology as a learning enabler to introduce products with a sustainable approach to the market, in a systematic way.

Also, in this paper, the Open Innovation paradigm is addressed. The Open Innovation paradigm assumes that "firms can and should use external ideas as well as internal ideas, and internal and external paths to market" [9]. Therefore, Open Innovation has been used by many organizations during the last years to shorten product development times and shorten the introduction of products in the market. In the education sector, the concept of Open Innovation has been applied to offer an environment to foster innovation and creativity. Consequently, by applying Open Innovation, the participation of internal and external resources (including human mobility, knowledge transfers and infrastructure sharing) for the development of joint projects are prioritized. In this sense, many universities have adopted this paradigm where the collaborative relationship between universities and different organizations such as industries, government, social institutions, and other universities are promoted. Hence, universities are providing mechanisms for improving technology transfer, knowledge transfer and human mobility processes [10, 11]. Another relevant activity that is promoted by using Open Innovation in the educational sector is that students can be immersed in real problems, then they can propose solutions and can implement those solutions in real scenarios.

At Tecnologico de Monterrey University in Mexico, the Open Innovation concept has been applied in an Open Innovation Laboratory where the co-creation and co-development of new products take place. The proposal in this paper is a mobile platform based on 3D virtual environments to support new product development (NPD) used as part of this laboratory. The proposed mobile platform adopts the four key components of Education 4.0 (I- New learning methods, II- Virtual and physical facilities, III- ICTs and IV- Development of core competencies) and has the purpose of providing tools that can improve the interest of students to learn and achieve their engagement in their courses. This platform is based on mobile technologies using VR and AR which are powered by using artificial intelligence (AI). These technologies support decision-making processes in NPD, which will guide students throughout the entire product development lifecycle. Likewise, it will allow them to make use of VR resources and AR. Through AI algorithms, students can be able to rely on the equipment that is found in the laboratories, and that will help them to co-create new products. By implementing the proposed mobile platform, the aim is to verify how the resources used to influence the deficit in the commitment and interest of the student to learn, as well as to check the advantages, improvements and results that the students of specific engineering careers can obtain during its teaching-learning process using the proposed innovation.

2 New Product Development in Education

2.1 The Development of Sensing, Smart and Sustainable Products

NPD has become a relevant activity since it allows designers to propose innovative solutions to face the current problems of different sectors; therefore, several organizations are taking this activity as a strategy to introduce new products and remain competitive in the market. Also, this activity has been considered as an enabler not only to promote entrepreneurship and the development of technology-based products but also to activate the economy in regional and global markets.

In the education sector, NPD is considered as a relevant activity since it promotes the implementation of knowledge and the development of specific skills and competencies throughout the entire product development life cycle. Among the different activities to be carried out during NPD, there are four key components that provide a solid structure during this task that student must know [12]. (i) Material. Know what material is being worked on and the associated manufacturing processes for its transformation. (ii) Information. Knowledge of the target market and the limitations of the product that allow to associate different technologies and make use of them [13]. (iii) Research and development. The transfer of knowledge between multidisciplinary groups, public or private, that allow technologies to be exploited to produce better goods. (iv) Framework. To provide a systematic structure throughout the product development life cycle stages.

Once there are known the four key components, it is very important not to lose sight of where you are working from and if product development is influenced to create a value chain that benefits multiple associated agents. On the other hand, product development is part of a technological development that contributes to the state of the art of technology itself. The challenges that arise in the development of products go hand in hand with the last two dimensions exposed, the development of products to solve a specific problem and, the use of technology for the development of activities and methods that allow extending its use [14]. The first is influenced by the monitoring of methodologies or standards, the second by research and the need to reproduce effective ways of creating products [15, 16]. Thus, the big challenges are i) the creation of products that allow the use of technologies to accelerate the development process and, ii) introduce products that benefit a specific audience in a short period. For this, techniques have been developed that allow us to make use of imagination processes, basic development, detailed development, prototyping, market introduction and life cycle assessment. However, the gap between product development and the use of technology still exists.

Also, the development of technology-based products is another relevant issue that must be addressed in this context, since these types of products provide greater social impacts and better opportunities to be competitive in the market but they also demand the implementation of new skills and competencies that must be trained and developed in today's students. According to the social and technology megatrends, these type of products are taking advantages of sensing and smart systems, and also consider sustainability aspects. Therefore, today, designers are looking for improving sensing, smart and sustainable solutions in products. In this work, authors are promoting the development of new products considering these type of solutions and promoting desirable activities to train and develop desirable skills and competencies that are necessary in today's students.

Sensing solutions improve different product functions where sensing solutions are necessary for monitoring systems, control systems, optimization systems and autonomy applications. Therefore, designers must select from a plurality of different types of sensors such as convectional physical (digital/analogue) sensors, virtual sensors, smart sensors, wireless sensors, among others and also must select between different sensing techniques to be implemented such as sensor fusion, virtual sensors, sensorless, among others.

Smart solutions provide a better performance in products since they are directly applied to the actuation and the control functionalities of products. According to Porter and Heppelmann (2014) smart product can be composed of three main components i) physical components (mechanical and electrical/electronic parts), (ii) smart components (control systems, microprocessors, data storage, software and user interface) and (iii) connectivity components (ports, antennas and wired/wireless communication protocols) [17]. Hence, designers must choose the best smart components to be implemented in new products.

Sustainable solutions, allow designers to make the best decision not only about the type of materials and components to be used but also about the manufacturing processes of the product to be developed. An important consideration when this analysis is done is that designers have to consider the concept of "product life cycle" considering manufacture, use, and end-of-life according to the social, economic and environmental stated design objectives.

Due to the plurality of existing sensing, smart and sustainable solutions, the level of complexity of some products and the multidisciplinary participation for the design of these products, a framework was proposed in 2017 [18]. This framework is based on the new product development life cycle, where four designing stages are carried out (i) product ideation, (ii) concept design and target specification, (iii) detailed design, and (iv) prototyping. By using this reference framework, designers can identify the main functions and propose better solutions and components to be implemented in new products.

At Tecnologico de Monterrey University in Mexico, the theory of "S^3" has been implemented as part of an Open Innovation Laboratory. Consequently, students can be immersed in open innovation environments and can propose solutions to a current problem through the development of new products that provide sensing, smart and sustainable (S^3) solutions [16].

3   3D Virtual Environments: Virtual Reality and Augmented Reality in Education

The use of 3D environments has been widely accepted in the education sector thanks to the advantages offered in the teaching-learning process, which is a faster way of learning and greater motivation for study. 3D environments in the educational sector have been used in various ways such as communication, conversation and sharing platforms to interact in a safer environment. Not only students can interact with the virtual environment, but they also can manage virtual resources, an experiment in a safer platform, manage tools and knowledge and are able to create their own objects to interact and try different concepts [19]. Currently, the use of 3D environments is useful in education, since it allows teachers and students to use a number of resources, make more efficient and productive the educational courses, increasing the possibilities of performing the desired functions in the students, which in another way would be difficult and expensive.

In this sense, the incursion of new visual technologies such as VR and AR have been significant in several sectors. VR is a visual technology that allows users to access environments and objects that have a realistic appearance. This environment is generated using computer technology and systems, which allows the user to feel immersed in it [20]. In the educational sector, technology based on VR has begun to be used, and this allows students to experience learning in immersive scenarios and break down geographical and temporal barriers. Examples of "Travel without leaving classes" to learn new cultures, "Exploration without limits" to travel in Space or geographical areas, "Travel in time", applied to a history course [21], among others.

On the other hand, AR provides the opportunity to create Mixed Learning Environments (MLE) where virtual and real elements are combined. These three-dimensional virtual objects are incorporated into the real context with the objective of complementing, enhancing, enriching, reinforcing and amplifying it to increase learning possibilities [22]. At the end of the 90s AR was considered as the technology that combines real and virtual elements, creating interactive scenarios, in real-time and recorded in 3D [23]. In the education sector, AR has been used to combine real and virtual scenarios and in this way, guide and make the learning process more efficient. Some examples of AR implemented in Education are Human Anatomy Learning [24], Digital Manufacturing and its use for fault diagnosis and corrective maintenance [25], English Language Learning using virtual objects and sounds to mention some outstanding examples [26].

These days, studies and researches have been carried out reflecting the advantage and benefits of these technologies in the educational sector, where technical and aesthetic aspects have been analyzed, ease of use, understanding of the functioning, viability, among others. Furthermore, it has reflected positive evaluations for students in terms of the teaching-learning processes [27]. For this reason, some authors claim that virtual education promotes connections not only with technology but also with several users, thus, allowing greater interconnectivity with the world and with information sources, besides, promoting collaborative learning [28]. Using these emerging technologies in combination with contexts of experiential learning and real environments will make this teaching-learning process a better experience for students.

4   3D Virtual Environments to Support New Product Development

4.1   Proposal: A Mobile Platform Based on an Open Innovation Laboratory Applied in Higher Education

The proposed mobile platform seeks to stimulate the development of specific skills and competencies in students, which would increase their capabilities of creating, designing and proposing solutions to current social challenges. In this way, it seeks to offer new alternatives for content presentation, promoting an active learning method to work dynamically and address the deficit of interest to learn from students.

Besides, the proposed mobile platform aims at allowing students to offer a new teaching-learning experience, efficiently using new learning techniques and technological tools that will allow them to develop desirable competences in the area of engineering, as well as to obtain and maintain attention of the students thanks to the activities and interaction offered by the promoted activities. The proposed mobile platform consists of three main components (i) Learning techniques that allow users getting access to specific learning materials and activities to be carried out during design and development processes, (ii) Methodologies for NPD that provide different design tools, guides and examples of how carry out this process, and (iii) The rapid product realization platform that include links to online resources, virtual tools using AR and VR, 360° virtual lab tours and links to remote labs (See Fig. 1).

Consequently, the proposed mobile platform is based on specific design and development methodologies that will allow guiding students during the process of co-creation and co-development of innovative products throughout the different stages of the product development life cycle. It considers implementations of AI technologies, VR and AR that will allow students to know and explore tools, equipment, laboratories, software platforms, MOOC's (Massive Open Online Courses) and virtual environments that would be used along the development process.

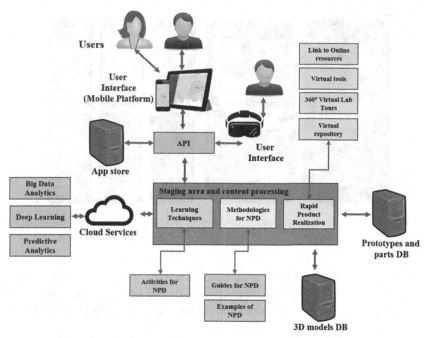

Fig. 1. The architecture of the Open Innovation Laboratory Mobile Platform using Virtual Reality (VR) and Augmented Reality (AR).

During the courses of design and development of engineering projects, students can use as the main tool the Open Innovation Laboratory Mobile Platform as a Virtual Exploration Platform which can be accessed by using smartphones and tablets based on the iOS operating system (See Fig. 2a, b). The functionality of the mobile platform focuses on the creation of a project that aims to create a new product following the scheme of the Open Innovation Laboratory (See Fig. 2c). Each project has a team associated with them; each user can be participating in several projects by being a member of several work teams. Also, this platform has a user profile through which it is possible to store the preferences and progress of each user's activities (See Fig. 2d). The development of the project is done by following a workflow represented by a product development methodology, and each methodology is composed of a set of activities and design tools organized in stages, and also learning content is provided in order to guide students during this process (See Fig. 2e). In order to provide a reference of the product development process dynamic, some examples of projects are provided, then students can see how the design and development process can be carried out (See Fig. 2g). Also, this mobile platform has a forum section where students can post questions, comments or any other topic related to the design and development process, then, the interaction between students and lecturers is promoted (See Fig. 2f). Finally, a help section is provided, then in this section students will find topics related to the use of the proposed mobile platform (See Fig. 2h).

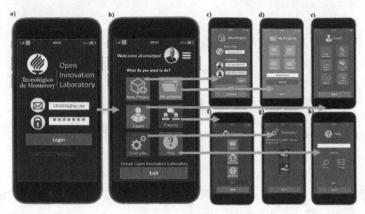

Fig. 2. The user interface of the Open Innovation Laboratory Mobile Platform as a Virtual Exploration Platform.

Each user coordinates with his team to carry out the activities that are marked in each stage of the product development methodology, the delivery dates of the activities are transferred to the device calendar so that the user has a reminder and a To-Do list of activities.

The mobile platform allows the user to navigate through the list of available resources to carry out the activities. Each activity recommends the use of some physical or virtual resource. In this way, the user can navigate between a list of laboratories, facilities, or physical spaces where there is equipment or tools suitable to be used in the creation of a new product or contains hyperlinks to virtual resources. For each physical resource, the mobile platform presents a list of photographs, videos and 3D models associated with that facility. There is also the possibility to explore the physical space in a virtual way through the presentation of photographs or videos in 360° formats. In this way, the user is transported to an AR viewer where the mobile device allows him to explore the appearance of the laboratory. The platform also allows the visualization of 3D objects in the form of AR so that users can discover the equipment or specialized tools found in that laboratory. The user is able to interact with these 3D models through functions such as rotation and resizing of the model. Finally, for each physical space, a descriptive video of the capabilities or ways of using the laboratory is presented, this video is presented through a virtual screen projected as AR. All these features allow the user to explore and interact with the facilities they will be using in a virtual and remote way. The platform presents a map of the place where the laboratory or facility is located and proposes a route to reach from the user's current location.

The mobile platform also has the integration of an image classification model, which was trained with a set of photos of the main equipment of the laboratories. This model can recognize some equipment through the camera of the mobile device. This functionality allows the user to identify the equipment once it is inside one of the laboratories or even it also works when the user is visualizing the laboratory through the VR and AR functionalities (See Fig. 3).

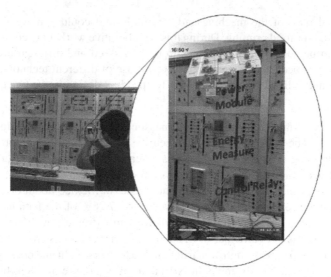

Fig. 3. Students of engineering using the platform to learn about smart-grids– information is displayed using augmented reality systems.

The aim of these functionalities of VR and AR with machine learning algorithms is to create an interactive user experience where users can perform the activities of creating products in a fun and innovative way.

The information used within the mobile platform is obtained through a web service, in this way, it is possible to update the list of laboratories, virtual resources, as well as the information associated with each resource/laboratory such as photos, videos, 360° materials and 3D models. Likewise, from the webserver, the methodologies of product development with their list of phases and activities are obtained. The progress of the activities carried out by the users are recorded in a document-oriented database that resides in the cloud.

The mobile platform has features of gamification, where the user can create an avatar within the mobile platform. The user can customize the appearance of the avatar through the selection of skin color, type, shape and color of hair, shape of the eyes, types of shoes. The objective is to offer a platform with high visual content, friendly and easy to use.

4.2 Case Study: Development of a 3D Food Printer for Customization at Home or Social Institutions

This case study describes how internal actors from the Tecnologico de Monterrey in collaboration with external actors from Universidad de los Andes propose solutions to face current problems related to food security. The binational project aims at developing a machine to produce food using emerging technologies, it must be a machine that could be used in any house, customize food and personalize ingredients for different formulations. Therefore, a multidisciplinary team was required to develop the 3D Food Printer that enables the possibility to achieve the main objective of the project. The development of the machine includes the formulation and design of the machine, it was occupied a technological base of the machine and a module that could achieve the extrusion process required for food printing. During this collaborative work, both countries expose the problem to be solved, the challenges to be addressed and different areas into the open innovation process. It was required to make use of different technologies, virtual environments and following a methodology for product design in the Open Innovation context.

Problem. Food and nutritional security are an issue that falls within the national security agenda [29, 30]. The Food and Nutrition Security Platform (PSAN) reports indicators that reflect alarming data that need to focus research and development efforts which are classified according to the four pillars of food security: availability, access, use and stability. Regarding food expenditure and waste, in Mexico about 88 million tons of wasted food are reported annually, equivalent to 37.26% of the national average of waste; which could feed 27.4 million populations in extreme poverty in the country [31]. This problem is not particular of Mexico, but other countries from Latin America present similarities. There is a nutritional deficit due to overweight and obesity, which has had significant growth. For example, in 2010 there was a figure of 3.8 million children under five years of age with obesity, and in the case of adults, it was found in 2015 that 39% of the total population over the age of 20 suffer from malnutrition because of overweight and obesity. The most relevant factors for which this disease is on the rise are: physical inactivity, low consumption of fruits, vegetables, cereals and legumes, and the replacement of healthy diets with a diet based on foods high in saturated fat, sugar and sodium. Obesity and overweight are the main responsible for the increase in the suffering of chronic noncommunicable diseases (hypertension, cancer, diabetes, among others), and their treatment constitutes a great public health expenditure. Observing the present problems from Latin America, there is an opportunity area that was faced by researchers from Mexico and Colombia in a binational project.

Proposal. Develop 3D printing systems for food as a solution to existing problems in Latin America related to Food Security and Nutrition, particularly from resources available in Mexico and Colombia. Establish and experimentally control the rheological, mechanical, structural, thermal and physical-chemical stability parameters of the food formulas in order to adapt them to 3D printing technologies while determining substances with customizable nutritional values that can be obtained from the Mexican-Colombian environment to avoid waste and that also comply with the characteristics required in 3D printing by extrusion and development of a functional 3D printing prototype for the creation of personalized foods in structure and nutritional value.

Solution. A 3D Food Printer was developed to address binational problems. Different substances were analyzed to determine a feasible formulation with structure and positive nutritional value for those in need, children and elderly people. Different tests related to the structure of the ailment, customization and rheological characteristics were done. The relevant activities and stages of the product development process are shown in Table 1. Development stages were determined from S^3 Product Development methodology in the Open Innovation context, and different technologies were occupied during this project.

Table 1. Case study – development process of a 3D Food Printer

Stages of Product Development Life Cycle	Tools/Techniques	Use of the Mobile Platform	Results
Product Ideation	• Megatrends (agricultural biotechnology, technological health) • Jobs To Be Done (JTBD) and analysis of the outcome expectations (OE) of the customer • Matrix of needs and satisfiers	• Support for generating a new product idea 	 Students participating in the ideation process
Concept Design and Target Specification	• Functional Decomposition and product architecture • Product Model • Product Cost • Conceptual Product	• Provide multimedia materials for learning purposes 	 Definition of the principle of operation and first 3D Models obtained
Detailed Design	• Morphological matrix • CAD-CAE • Component assembly • Prototype 1.0 • Data Sheet	• Display recommend tools/techniques to be used at the detailed design 	 Detailed design of the structure by using CAE analysis
Prototyping	• Functional 3D Food Printer (prototype 2.0) • Tests of extrusion • Test of customization • Evaluation of prototypes and usability	• Display recommend tools/techniques to be used for rapid prototyping • Show 360° Labs tours • Provide VR and AR materials to improve the prototype development 	 Functional prototype of the proposed 3D Food Printer

5 Findings and Conclusions

It is observed that the proposed mobile platform provides useful teaching-learning dynamics for digital-native students. Also, it is noted that this technology is a viable and coherent tool to face current problems in society. In the open innovation context, by using this technology the participation of internal and external actor is promoted to develop new products. Therefore, these participants are taking advantage of emerging physical and virtual resources to improve their experience while learning. Some identified findings by applying this mobile platform in higher education are:

- The students are guided through the complete product development life cycle. Then, according to the type of product to be developed, students receive recommendations about the activity to be performed and the tools to be used.
- The students know about available infrastructure to be used for the development of products. Therefore, the mobile platform shows students the available infrastructure according to each stage of the product development life cycle. This infrastructure can be physical, by using laboratories, tools, books, machines, among others, and can be virtual, by using multimedia material such as videos, online material, MOOCs, 360° virtual tours, among others.
- It is observed that students are proposing technology-based products that consider sensing, smart and sustainable solutions.
- According to surveys filled by about 50 students. Students think that they are training the competencies of creativity and innovation, collaboration, cooperation, communication and critical thinking.

Future work would be centered on comparing traditional courses against those where technology has been implemented to determine which areas would be beneficial for students.

Acknowledgements. This research was supported by the NOVUS program 2018-2019, funded by Tecnologico de Monterrey as part of the project: "Virtual Platform of Exploration of the Open Innovation Laboratory to promote the Development of Sensing, Smart and Sustainable Products/Services S3". Also, the authors would like to acknowledge the financial support of Writing Lab, TecLabs, Tecnologico de Monterrey, Mexico, in the production of this work.

References

1. Alsawaier, R.S.: The effect of gamification on motivation and engagement. Int. J. Inf. Learn. Technol. **35**(1), 56–79 (2018)
2. Barnacle, R., Dall'Alba, G.: Committed to learn: student engagement and care in higher education. High. Educ. Res. Dev. **36**(7), 1326–1338 (2017)
3. Miranda, J., López, C.S., Navarro, S., Bustamante, M.R., Molina, J.M., Molina, A.: Open Innovation Laboratories as enabling resources to reach the vision of Education 4.0. In: 2019 IEEE International Conference on Engineering, Technology and Innovation (ICE/ITMC), pp. 1–7 (2019)

4. Binkley, M., et al.: Defining twenty-first century skills. In: Griffin, P., McGaw, B., Care, E. (eds.) Assessment and Teaching of 21st Century Skills, pp. 17–66. Springer, Dordrecht (2012). https://doi.org/10.1007/978-94-007-2324-5_2

5. Häkkinen, P., Järvelä, S., Mäkitalo-Siegl, K., Ahonen, A., Näykki, P., Valtonen, T.: Preparing teacher-students for twenty-first century learning practices (PREP 21): a framework for enhancing collaborative problem solving and strategic learning skills. Teach. Teach. Theory Pract. **23**(1), 25–41 (2017)

6. Broekhuizen, T.L.J., Emrich, O., Gijsenberg, M.J., Broekhuis, M., Donkers, B., Sloot, L.M.: Digital platform openness: drivers, dimensions and outcomes. J. Bus. Res. (2019)

7. Andersen, A.-L., Rösiö, C.: Investigating the transition towards changeability through platform-based co-development of products and manufacturing systems. Procedia Manuf. **28**, 114–120 (2019)

8. Cenamor, J., Parida, V., Wincent, J.: How entrepreneurial SMEs compete through digital platforms: the roles of digital platform capability, network capability and ambidexterity. J. Bus. Res. **100**, 196–206 (2019)

9. Chesbrough, H.W.: Open Innovation: The New Imperative for Creating and Profiting from Technology. Harvard Business School Press, Harvard (2003)

10. Perkmann, M., Walsh, K.: University–industry relationships and open innovation: towards a research agenda. Int. J. Manag. Rev. **9**(4), 259–280 (2007)

11. Molina Gutiérrez, A., et al.: Open Innovation Laboratory for rapid realisation of sensing, smart and sustainable products: motives, concepts and uses in higher education. In: Camarinha-Matos, L.M., Afsarmanesh, H., Rezgui, Y. (eds.) PRO-VE 2018. IAICT, vol. 534, pp. 156–163. Springer, Cham (2018). https://doi.org/10.1007/978-3-319-99127-6_14

12. Bitzer, M., Vielhaber, M., Dohr, F.: From product development to technology development. Procedia CIRP **21**, 247–251 (2014)

13. Hou, T., Yannou, B., Leroy, Y., Poirson, E.: Mining customer product reviews for product development: a summarization process. Expert Syst. Appl. **132**, 141–150 (2019)

14. Fahmideh, M., Zowghi, D.: An exploration of IoT platform development. Inf. Syst. **87**, 101409 (2020)

15. Müller, R., Hörauf, L., Speicher, C., Obele, J.: Communication and knowledge management platform for concurrent product and assembly system development. Procedia Manuf. **28**, 107–113 (2019)

16. Xu, K., Huang, K.-F., Gao, S.: Technology sourcing, appropriability regimes, and new product development. J. Eng. Tech. Manage. **29**(2), 265–280 (2012)

17. Porter, M.E., Heppelmann, J.E.: How smart, connected products are transforming competition. Harvard Bus. Rev. **92**(11), 64–88 (2014)

18. Miranda, J., Pérez-Rodríguez, R., Borja, V., Wright, P.K., Molina, A.: Sensing, smart and sustainable product development (S3 product) reference framework. Int. J. Prod. Res., 1–22 (2017)

19. Potkonjak, V., et al.: Virtual laboratories for education in science, technology, and engineering: a review. Comput. Educ. **95**, 309–327 (2016)

20. Barker, M., et al.: The global impact of science gateways, virtual research environments and virtual laboratories. Future Gener. Comput. Syst. **95**, 240–248 (2019)

21. Rodríguez-Simon, A.I., López, S.R.: Estrategias de enseñanza en los entornos mediados: resultados de la experiencia de la performance virtual educativa. Revista de Educación a Distancia. Núm. 55. Artíc. 10 (2017)

22. Ke, F., Lee, S., Xu, X.: Teaching training in a mixed-reality integrated learning environment. Comput. Hum. Behav. **62**, 212–220 (2016)

23. Azuma, R.: A survey of augmented reality. Presence Teleop. Virt. Environ. **6**(4), 355–385 (1997)

24. Kurniawan, M.H., Suharjito, D., Witjaksono, G.: Human anatomy learning systems using augmented reality on mobile application. Procedia Comput. Sci. **135**, 80–88 (2018)
25. Qeshmy, D.E., Makdisi, J., Ribeiro da Silva, E.H.D., Angelis, J.: Managing Human Errors: Augmented Reality systems as a tool in the quality journey. Procedia Manuf. **28**, 24–30 (2019)
26. Hsu, T.-C.: Learning English with augmented reality: do learning styles matter? Comput. Educ. **106**, 137–149 (2017)
27. Yip, J., Wong, S.-H., Yick, K.-L., Chan, K., Wong, K.-H.: Improving quality of teaching and learning in classes by using augmented reality video. Comput. Educ. **128**, 88–101 (2019)
28. Martín-Gutiérrez, J., Fabiani, P., Benesova, W., Meneses, M.D., Mora, C.E.: Augmented reality to promote collaborative and autonomous learning in higher education. Comput. Hum. Behav. **51**, 752–761 (2015)
29. Revista Hidroponia: Seguridad Alimentaria en México. http://hidroponia.mx/seguridad-ali mentaria-que-es/. Accessed 03 Mar 2017
30. Urquía-Fernández, N.: Salud pública de México. Salud Pública de México, vol. 44. http:// www.scielo.org.mx/scielo.php?pid=S0036363420020005000011&script=sci_arttext&tln g=pt. Accessed 05 May 2019
31. FAO: Panorama de la Inseguridad Alimentaria en América Latina y El Caribe, Boletín 2 (2015). http://www.fao.org/3/a-i4636s.pdf

Simulation Framework for Load Management and Behavioral Energy Efficiency Analysis in Smart Homes

Manuel Avila$^{(\boxtimes)}$ ⓘ, Pedro Ponce ⓘ, Arturo Molina ⓘ, and Katya Romo

Tecnologico de Monterrey, 14380 Mexico City, Mexico
A01133426@itesm.mx, {pedro.ponce,armolina,kerm}@tec.mx

Abstract. Most of today's technological advances related to electricity consumption boast being intelligent and able to communicate with other smart devices, owners, and suppliers. But regardless of the smart appliances, control interfaces, flexible demand services, and the willingness of the user to save energy, it is challenging to achieve energy efficiency at households due to the lack of synchronization, loss of information, and misuse of devices, as well as the shortage of simulations and models that allow evaluate the human factor. Hence, the efficient management of electrical devices in households and consumption patterns under different conditions must be studied in conjunction, which is possible with simulation tools to emulate decision-making processes of energy management and demand-side management systems, different types of user, and controllers of conventional and smart electrical devices. This paper proposes a simulation framework to efficiently manage a group of home appliances and lighting systems of a smart home, according to the disposition of users to modify their consumption patterns through a multimedia interface, analyzing the behavioral energy efficiency. In this proposal, the probability of using loads in different periods and their features as power and controllability, are taking into account to classify and prioritize them; with fuzzy logic type II, load groups are controlled according to user preferences and managed optimally. There were simulated scenarios with different consumption conditions, price schemes, and types of users, showing reductions in electricity bills, avoiding peak rates and reducing power or time of use.

Keywords: Home energy management system · Behavioral energy efficiency

1 Introduction

The twenty-first-century electrical grid is the result of the social demands and the technological improvements over the years to the old-fashioned grid, which has provided energy to modern society since the end of the eighteenth century, but now concerned with providing clean energy to the growing population in a cheap, efficient way [1]. Technologies such as distributed energy resources (DERs), advanced metering infrastructure (AMI), Internet of Things (IoT), and controllable loads, are changing the electrical grid from a centralized carbon generation network with one-way electricity flow to the consumer

© Springer Nature Switzerland AG 2020
T. McDaniel et al. (Eds.): ICSM 2019, LNCS 12015, pp. 497–508, 2020.
https://doi.org/10.1007/978-3-030-54407-2_42

and no feedback more than total consumption, to a decentralized greener generation network with bidirectional electrical flow among prosumers and energy information flow among stakeholders for an efficient distribution, and controlled consumption [2]. In this new electrical paradigm, energy management systems (EMS) and demand-side management (DSM) systems have been developed to determine the effective operation of electrical generation and transmission facilities to ensure adequate security of energy supply at minimum cost [3], and regulate the energy demand using incentive-based and time-based rates for demand response (DR) techniques based on forecasting models of energy consumed and generated in time-lapses [4], respectively.

On the residential consumer side, the end-user is expected to plan, control, or at least monitor energy use through a home energy management system (HEMS) in order to avoid energy waste, reduce the electricity bills, as well as improve home comfort and security [5]. With the help of the smart home concept, a modern living space equipped with smart appliances, smart plug sensors, remote and intelligent controls, internet, and energy monitoring systems, the householder can automatically manage the interconnected electrical devices according to the electricity market, own preferences, needs, and goals [6]. However, mentioned all of the above, it is challenging to achieve energy efficiency due to the lack of synchronization among electrical devices, negligence on appliance control, lack of user ability to program and use smart devices and resources, and the loss of information to interact correctly with the electricity market [7, 8]. Moreover, the shortage of simulation tools and models to evaluate the human factor on energy management systems impeded analyze the results for DR techniques, related to modifying energy consumption patterns of home appliances in different conditions, operating periods, power rating, and specific duties of the appliances [5]. Thereby, the simulation tools can improve the decision-making process of energy management and demand-side management systems taking into account different types of user and loads' features, to choose the most suitable energy strategy (see Fig. 1).

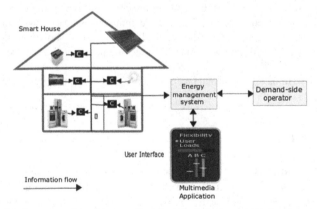

Fig. 1. Interaction between the end-user, the electrical devices, and the demand-side operator through HEMS.

This paper proposes a simulation framework to efficiently manage a group of home appliances and lighting systems of a smart home, according to the disposition of users to modify their energy consumption patterns on flexible appliances to efficiently manage the energy flow between them and achieve behavioral energy efficiency. The probability of using loads in different periods is modeled using Gaussian probability density functions (PDFs); the classification and prioritization of loads is done with a decision tree of their features, as power and controllability, to control them efficiently. User type modelling is done through fuzzy logic type II scheme taking into account the user preferences. The load management avoids peak rates and reduces time of use (TOU) and power.

The organization of the paper is as follows: Sect. 2 presents a review of previous works and researches related to simulation frameworks for HEMS; Sect. 3 provides the methodology to classify home appliances and other energy resources, determination of the type of users, and parameterization of the energy price scheme, as well as the infrastructure of the framework to simulate the electrical flow in a smart home and the user interaction; Sect. 4 presents an implementation case of study, and Sect. 5 concludes the work.

2 Related Work

Several studies have been addressing energy efficiency in households due to the increasing energy demand. According to [9], the energy consumed by the residential sector in 2015 was about 21.9% of global total energy consumption, while in Mexico, the energy consumed by the residential, commercial, and public sectors in 2016 was about 18.1% of the final energy consumption; besides, the energy consumption per capita was 6.1% greater than in 2015 and the Mexican population grew from 121.01 to 122.27 million inhabitants between 2015 and 2016. Here the importance to achieve the prime objective of a HEMS including reducing peak load demand, electricity consumption charge, and emission of greenhouse gases. [10] presents a systematic review of HEMS considering the following pricing techniques: real-time pricing (RTP), time of use (ToU), and critical peak pricing (CPP); moreover, it mentions that energy management schemes are based on forecasting, scheduling and coordinating the activities of home appliances in time slots with different electricity rates, as well as making suggestions for the consumer to start or stop using appliances, avoiding peak hours and energy waste. Stochastic energy scheduling strategies for a smart home are proposed in [11–13], providing an initial framework to estimate the uncertainty and variability of the output power of renewable energy resources, and stochastic models for home load demand and battery storage systems.

In relation to the load analysis in a smart home, the increase in the data collection of load's consumption through smart devices, allows EMS to use machine learning techniques to analyze and classify loads in a continuous load, intermittent load, or phantom load [6]. Furthermore, analyzing consumption data on smart home, the user behavior, defined as the user's preferences to allow appliances participating in DR, can be inferred to calculate the appliance flexibility or the potential of the appliance to participate in DR programs considering appliance characteristic without losing the preferences of appliance usage and appliance controllability [14].

Thereby, as explained in [14], achieving energy efficiency in a smart home not only depends on the optimal management of the electrical devices, but also taking advantage of the flexible demand, which involves the use of communication and control technology to shift electricity demand across time while delivering end-use services. An expected change by end-user from their normal consumption patterns to save energy, in response to changes in the need of power grid through simple, actionable messages, is known as behavioral energy efficiency [7]. Hence the crux in energy systems simulation tools is to consider the human factor as an agent to provide remarkable local intelligence, not only as a disturbance or stochastic variable [4].

3   Methodology and Framework Design

Simulation frameworks can mitigate the complexity of modeling dynamic systems by separating core infrastructure code that supports model and simulation development from specific software applications for model building [15]. The proposed framework is illustrated in Fig. 2, where components define the functionality and behavior of objects in the electrical model in a general manner; on the infrastructure side are defined the relationships between them, the execution of workflows and time-steps by the simulation engine, and the interaction with the user through a graphical user interface (GUI).

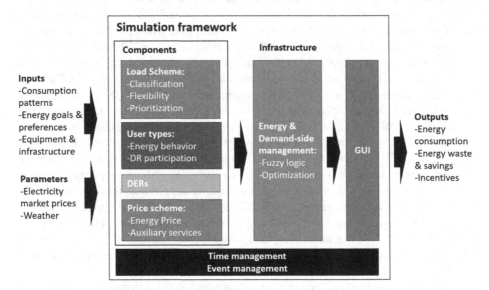

Fig. 2. Components and infrastructure of the simulation framework for HEMS.

Broadly, the framework classifies the loads according to consumption patterns and given features of each appliance, where a flexibility determined here will be useful to manage the load later, along with the type of user, related to the consumption preferences and energy goals of the user. DERs could be distributed generators and batteries modeled with random variables and discrete probability distributions. The partial outputs of each block are inputs to determine the EMS and DSM according to the load scheme, user type, DERs, and price scheme. The GUI shows the energy consumption, energy waste and savings within the selected time slot, as well as possible incentives and comparisons to improve the decision-making related to energy management. Each block is detailed below.

3.1 Load Classification and Prioritization

The first part of the framework is to define the class of load related to an average time of use and the expected initial and final times of use, inferring continuous, intermittent or random patterns when using each appliance (see Fig. 3). A load is considered continuous (cont) if it has one or two defined periods by T_i, T_f, T_i', and T_f', and intermittent (int) if has an uncertain performance patterns in time, both with an average time of use by day θ. Moreover, the features of controllability Co and power consumption P of each load have to be defined (see Table 1). Controllability alludes to the automation or fixed-use of the initial and final time of appliance usage.

Fig. 3. Load scheme diagram.

Table 1. Load scheme proposed.

Appliances	P (W)	Class	Co	T_i	T_f	T_i'	T_f'	θ (hrs)
Interior lightings	60	Int	No	–	–	–	–	6
Exterior lightings	30	Cont	Yes	00:00	07:00	20:00	00:00	11
Refrigerator	100	Cont	Yes	05:00	11:00	17:00	23:00	12
TV	90	Int	No	–	–	–	–	5
Washing machine	1500	Int	Yes	–	–	–	–	1.5
HVAC	300	Cont	Yes	–	–	–	–	6
EWH	600	Int	Yes	06:00	06:15	–	–	1
Microwave	900	Int	No	–	–	–	–	1
Electric stove	800	Int	No	–	–	–	–	2

According to [14], the appliance flexibility is the potential of the appliance to participate in DR programs considering appliance features and user consumption preferences. This range assumes a Gaussian distribution related to the habits of the consumer using their appliances, characterized by the initial and final times, and the average power consumption (see Fig. 4). The larger the area under the curve, the more flexible the device.

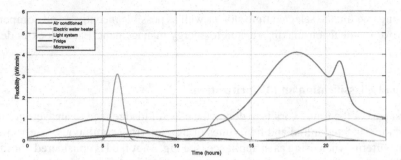

Fig. 4. Flexibility of appliances (taken from [14]).

Loads are classified and grouped by a decision tree algorithm according to their features (see Fig. 5). The decision tree algorithm weights controllable loads using their power and ToU features, e.g. a smart appliance that consumes a considerable amount of power in a peak hour, and also is a flexible one, will be ranked with a high priority to be rescheduled in a mayor range of non-peak time slots that another appliance that consumes less power.

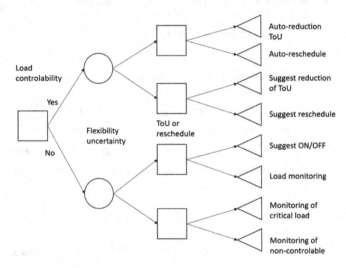

Fig. 5. Decision tree for load management.

3.2 Archetype of Users and Classification

Based on the types of user described in [16], a flexibility user scheme is proposed according to features that the user may have when consuming energy. These features are the environmental commitment, knowledge or interest in the technology field, desired level of comfort, and interest in saving money. Each type of user is described in Table 2.

Each input of the system is ranked between 0 and 1, then the fuzzification stage gives a linguistic value according to the membership functions showed in Fig. 7. If-Then rules determine the output related to the expected user flexibility.

Table 2. Classification user scheme.

Type of user	Description	Environmental commitment	Tech field knowledge	Desired comfort	Save-money interest	Flexible output expected
Green advocate	Show the most positive overall energy-saving behaviors, have the strongest positive environmental sense and high interest in new technologies	High	High	Low	High	**Highest**
Traditionalist cost-focused energy savers	Their energy-saving behavior is motivated by cost savings rather than the environmental impact. Limited interest in new technologies	High	Low	Low	High	**High**
Home-focused selective energy savers	They are concerned about saving energy and interested in home-improvement efforts	Medium	Medium	High	High	**Medium**
Non-green selective energy savers	Selective energy saving behaviors focused on "set and forget" type of interventions. They are not concerned about environmental considerations	Low	Medium	High	Low	**Low**
Disengaged energy savers	Less motivated to save money through energy savings, they are not concerned about environment nor new technologies	Low	Low	High	Low	**Lowest**

The user flexibility is related to the wiliness of the user to participate in DR programs and the change in her/his consumption patterns depends on the equipment and infrastructure to monitor and control the appliances. A smart home is supposed to be equipped with smart appliances and smart plugs, so the consumption patterns can be inferred by monitoring for several weeks the use of appliances [14]. The uncertainty of the user behavior relates a stochastic use of appliances, and EMS tires to minimize this uncertainty when autonomously manage appliances at certain slots times or suggest the user to turn on/off specific appliances. The fuzzy logic type II scheme uses linguistic inputs and rules to assess the flexibility of the user when using flexible electric devices mentioned above (see Fig. 6), the uncertainty is inherent when using fuzzy logic and in the upper and lower membership functions used in the fuzzy logic type II to represent the inputs and the output (see Fig. 7). The more flexible, less total energy consumed is expected; the less flexible, the total energy consumption does not have noteworthy changes.

Fig. 6. User classification diagram.

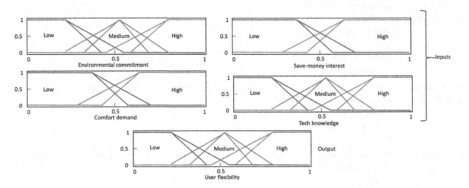

Fig. 7. Membership functions for fuzzification and defuzzification stages.

3.3 Storage and Energy Generation

DERs could be distributed generators and energy storage systems (ESSs). The output of the generator could be deterministic or probabilistic, to represent the model of conventional generators (e.g. diesel generator) or greener generators (e.g. photovoltaic panels or wind turbines) through linear, non-linear function or probability density functions (PDFs), respectively (Fig. 8).

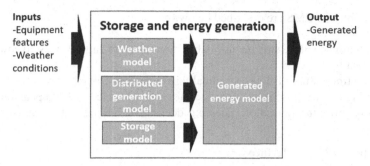

Fig. 8. DERs diagram.

3.4 Price Scheme

The price scheme component is the parameterization of the energy price according to the electricity market fluctuations. It could be static or change between basic, intermediate, and peak rates through time-slots of hours or minutes, taking into account the days of the week and seasons. Also, auxiliary services can be charged at the billing (Fig. 9).

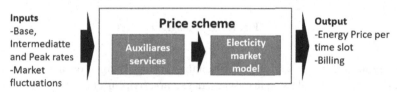

Fig. 9. Membership functions.

3.5 Energy and Demand-Side Management

The range from non-flexible to flexible and the type of load are going to define the management systems which will act in the load using techniques of ToU, rescheduling, suggestion scheme, or power reduction determined in the decision tree algorithm (see Fig. 5) (Fig. 10).

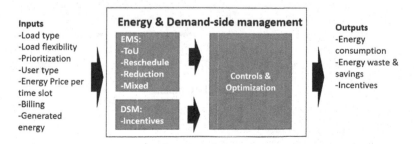

Fig. 10. EMS and DSM diagram.

The options for EMS are described below:

- Rescheduling flexible, smart/controllable devices from higher rates to lower rates automatically.
- Reducing time of use (ToU) automatically in smart/controllable devices.
- Suggesting the user reschedule or reduce ToU by messages to avoid peak rates.
- Reducing power in applicable devices, e.g. decorative lighting systems and light bulbs.

3.6 Graphical User Interface

The user interface shows the energy consumed with and without EMS for the load scheme proposed, along with the incentives proposed for the DSM system for the type of user (See Fig. 11). To model the acceptance of the suggestions made for the DSM, probabilistic functions are used to simulate the reality of the DSM process.

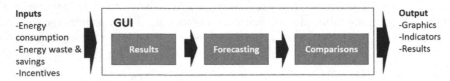

Fig. 11. GUI diagram.

The graphs and results can show the monthly billing, energy consumed per defined time slot (which can be adjusted in minutes, days, months), current energy rate, auxiliary services, group of appliances usage, as shown in Fig. 12.

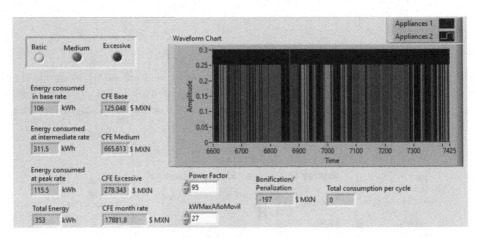

Fig. 12. GUI example.

4 Framework Implementation: Case of Study

For the framework implementation, it was programed each block in LabView based on the load consumption scheme proposed in Table 1 and the flexibility of loads showed in Fig. 3. An EMS was programed to reschedule flexible loads in order to avoid peak rates and reduce TOU controlling the expected initial and final times of the controllable loads. The dynamic price scheme is based on the Mexican tariff with a base, intermediate, and high rates for weekdays in winter season. The base rate is from 00:00 to 06:00, the intermediate rate is from 06:00 to 18:00 and 20:00 to 24:00, and the peak rate is from 18:00 to 20:00.

Within this dynamic pricing scheme, the EMS tries to avoid peak rates in flexible appliances and suggests to the green advocate type of user to shut down appliances when they are not in use. It was showing a reduction from $20.72 MXN to $17.76 MXN per day if the user has the willingness to accept these changes and suggestions or automatically the smart appliances do (Fig. 13).

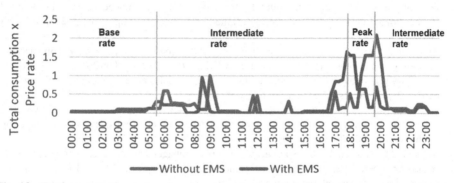

Fig. 13. Total consumption comparison in a smart home with an energy management system and without it.

5 Conclusions

EMS can reduce the TOU of smart appliances and conventional appliances and reschedule them using smart plugs, through monitoring and suggestion scheme to use their appliances in lower rates, and shut them down when they are not in use. Meanwhile, the use of simulation framework can evaluate the effectiveness of EMS and DSM systems taking into account different types of user behavior, showing the economic incentives to the end user and the benefits to the electrical grid, reducing energy consumption and avoiding peak rates.

Acknowledgment. This research is a product of the Project 266632 "Laboratorio Binacional para la Gestión Inteligente de la Sustentabilidad Energética y la Formación Tecnológica" ["Bi-National Laboratory on Smart Sustainable Energy Management and Technology Training"], funded by the CONACYT SENER Fund for Energy Sustainability (Agreement: S0019201401).

References

1. Geels, F.W.: Disruption and low-carbon system transformation: progress and new challenges in socio-technical transitions research and the Multi-Level Perspective. Energy Res. Soc. Sci. **37**, 224–231 (2018)
2. Plociennik, M., et al.: Interoperability and decentralization as key technologies for future smart urban environments. In: 2018 European Conference on Networks and Communications (EuCNC). IEEE (2018)
3. Zia, M.F., Elbouchikhi, E., Benbouzid, M.: Microgrids energy management systems: a critical review on methods, solutions, and prospects. Appl. Energy **222**, 1033–1055 (2018)
4. Palensky, P., Dietrich, D.: Demand side management: demand response, intelligent energy systems, and smart loads. IEEE Trans. Industr. Inf. **7**(3), 381–388 (2011)
5. Alimi, O.A., Ouahada, K.: Smart home appliances scheduling to manage energy usage. In: 2018 IEEE 7th International Conference on Adaptive Science & Technology (ICAST). IEEE (2018)
6. Soe, W.T., Belleudy, C.: Load recognition from smart plug sensor for energy management in a smart home. In: 2019 IEEE Sensors Applications Symposium (SAS). IEEE (2019)
7. de Leon Barido, D.P., et al.: Opportunities for behavioral energy efficiency and flexible demand in data-limited low-carbon resource constrained environments. Appl. Energy **228**, 512–523 (2018)
8. Zipperer, A., et al.: Electric energy management in the smart home: perspectives on enabling technologies and consumer behavior. Proc. IEEE **101**(11), 2397–2408 (2013)
9. https://www.gob.mx/cms/uploads/attachment/file/288692/Balance_Nacional_de_Energ_a_2016__2_.pdf. Accessed 04 Oct 2019
10. Patel, K., Khosla, A.: Home energy management systems in future smart grid networks: a systematic review. In: 2015 1st International Conference on Next Generation Computing Technologies (NGCT). IEEE (2015)
11. Yousefi, M., Hajizadeh, A., Soltani, M.: Energy management strategies for smart home regarding uncertainties: state of the art, trends, and challenges. In: 2018 IEEE International Conference on Industrial Technology (ICIT). IEEE (2018)
12. Alavi, S.A., Ahmadian, A., Aliakbar-Golkar, M.: Optimal probabilistic energy management in a typical micro-grid based-on robust optimization and point estimate method. Energy Convers. Manag. **95**, 314–325 (2015)
13. Hu, M.-C., Lu, S.-Y., Chen, Y.-H.: Stochastic programming and market equilibrium analysis of microgrids energy management systems. Energy **113**, 662–670 (2016)
14. Zhai, S., et al.: Appliance flexibility analysis considering user behavior in home energy management system using smart plugs. IEEE Trans. Industr. Electron. **66**(2), 1391–1401 (2018)
15. King, D.W., Hodson, D.D., Peterson, G.L.: The role of simulation frameworks in relation to experiments. In: 2017 Winter Simulation Conference (WSC). IEEE (2017)
16. Frankel, D., Heck, S., Tai, H.: Using a Consumer Segmentation Approach to Make Energy Efficiency Gains in the Residential Market. McKinsey and Company, New York (2013)

S⁴ Product Design Framework: A Gamification Strategy Based on Type 1 and 2 Fuzzy Logic

J. I. Méndez¹⁽✉⁾ ⓘD, P. Ponce¹ ⓘD, A. Meier² ⓘD, T. Peffer³ ⓘD, O. Mata¹ ⓘD,
and A. Molina¹ ⓘD

¹ School of Engineering and Sciences, Tecnológico de Monterrey, Mexico City, Mexico
A01165549@itesm.mx, {pedro.ponce,omar.mata,armolina}@tec.mx
² Lawrence Berkeley National Laboratory, University of California, Berkeley, CA 94720, USA
akmeier@ucdavis.edu
³ Institute for Energy and Environment, University of California, Berkeley, CA 94720, USA
tpeffer@berkeley.edu

Abstract. Connected thermostats control the HVAC in buildings by adjusting the setpoint temperatures without losing the comfort temperature. These devices consider end user profiles, preferences, and schedules to reduce electrical energy consumption. However, users are reluctant to use connected thermostats due to behavior and usability problems with the interfaces or the product. Typically, users do not use connected thermostats correctly, which can lead to increased rather than decreased electrical consumption. Thus, the S⁴ product concept is emerging as a strategy and framework to design functional prototypes to provide user-friendly sensing, smart, sustainable, and social features. An S⁴ product enables communication between products and between products and end users. Such communication can provide better understanding of the type of consumer who uses the product. Gamification and serious games are emerging as a strategy to shape human behavior to achieve goals; however, such strategies are not applied to product design. Fuzzy logic can be applied to human reasoning and has been used in intelligent systems based on if-then rules. Nevertheless, to the best of our knowledge, applying a gamification strategy based on fuzzy logic to develop an S⁴ connected thermostat has not been studied previously. Therefore, a framework that integrates gamification and serious games elements using fuzzy logic is proposed to develop a tailored gamification human machine interface. Thus, the proposed framework could tackle the behavior and usability problems of connected thermostats to teach, engage, and motivate end users to become energy aware, thereby reducing electrical consumption.

Keywords: Connected thermostat · Gamification · HMI · S⁴ products · Fuzzy logic

1 Introduction

Residential buildings in the United States (U.S.) represents approximately 50% of total peak energy demand, 36% of total electricity consumption, and 20% of total energy

© Springer Nature Switzerland AG 2020
T. McDaniel et al. (Eds.): ICSM 2019, LNCS 12015, pp. 509–524, 2020.
https://doi.org/10.1007/978-3-030-54407-2_43

consumption in the U.S. [1]. Residential buildings contribute significantly to increasing greenhouse gas emissions and energy and electricity consumption in a world that requires the active participation of people to reduce energy consumption. However, due to the increase of the Internet of Things, smart household appliances are increasingly available. Such smart appliances can facilitate routine tasks, adjust visual and thermal comfort, and provide building security [1, 2]. Household appliances, such as televisions, interior lighting, electric stoves, coffee makers, washing machines, geysers, refrigerators, clothes irons, and thermostats, have different energy consumption pattern according to their operating periods, power rating, and the specific characteristics of each appliance [3]. For instance, in "Simulation Framework for Load Management and Behavioral Energy Efficiency Analysis in Smart Homes" is proposed a simulation framework to manage household appliances and lighting systems of a smart home [4].

Table 1. Primary problems with connected thermostats by consumer behavior and usability problems.

Behavior problems	Usability problems
• Users operate the Connected Thermostat (CT) in a manner that differs from how the design engineers intended. • Users do not understand the functions. They feel using the CT is complicated. • Users do not know and/or care about the advantages of the CT. • Users are not aware of the environmental impacts. • User are not primarily focused on energy saving. • Users do not know how to use the HVAC system.	• Visibility of the status • Match between system and real world • User control and freedom • Consistency and standards • Recognize, diagnose, and recover from errors • Error prevention • Recognition rather than recall • Flexibility and minimalism design • Aesthetics • Help and documentation • Skills • Pleasurable and respectful interaction with the user • Privacy

Thermostats are used in 85% of residential buildings [5]. Thermostats control the heating, ventilation, and air condition systems; therefore, they represent an opportunity to optimize high energy and load-demand systems. Relative to energy consumption, connected thermostats can reduce energy consumption from 10% to 35% of the peak load and can reduce occupant energy efficiency by 5% due to behavioral change [1]. Although it is possible to achieve such reductions by interactions between the end user and the connected thermostat, that successful reduction occurs infrequently because users do not entirely accept the connected device, which leads to poor energy behavior. Thus, Miranda et al. [6] proposed a reference framework to design sensing, smart, and sustainable products (S^3 products) to reinforce communication and solve the behavior and usability problems between devices and consumers. Ponce et al. [7] proposed including social factors in the design process by implementing a gamification strategy to send stimuli to change consumer behavior; thus, the end product is an S^4 rather than an S^3 product. The six usability and thirteen behavioral problems that occur when users interact with connected thermostats are listed in Table 1 [8, 9]. Gamification is the development and creation of positive experiences using game mechanics, behavioral economics, and design thinking in non-game contexts to motivate, engage, and educate individuals to solve real-world or productive activities problems [10, 11]. In software development, fuzzy logic is used to represent human thinking to provide a better user experience [12]. In this regard, Romero et al. [13] developed a fuzzy logic model using gamification elements to profile five types of aspirants based on the characteristics of the aspirant behavior.

The remainder of this paper is organized as follows. Section 2 describes the methodology used to gather the behavior models, user types, gamification and serious games in energy saving, fuzzy logic types 1 and 2, and the characteristics of S^4 products. Section 3 presents the proposed three-step framework for a tailored HMI suitable for S4 products. Section 4 presents a mock-up of the connected thermostat framework that could be used in a tablet or mobile phone. In Sect. 5 we describe the scope of the framework and discuss its advantages and disadvantages. Conclusions and suggestions for future work are presented in Sect. 6.

2 Methodology

2.1 Behavior Models

Ponce et al. [7] proposed using a gamification strategy in an HMI to shape consumer behavior. Several behavior theories and models to change user habits and produce real change have been proposed. The transtheoretical model [14] has been applied to change behavior in various areas, such as behavioral medicine, residential customer water use behavior, and residential customer energy-related behavior. The transtheoretical model classifies the process of behavioral change into six stages: pre-contemplation, contemplation, preparation, action, maintenance, and termination. In the Fogg behavior model [15] motivation, ability, and prompt elements must converge simultaneously to produce a behavior change. In the theory of planned behavior (TPB) [16] behavioral intention and a person's attitude toward a specific behavior are determined by being able to understand three pairs of determinants: behavioral belief-attitude, normative beliefs-subjective norm, and control belief-perceived behavioral control.

2.2 Types of Users

For the proposed framework, a variety of research papers, including gamification in households, smart thermostats, and pro-environmental behavior models, were analyzed. Based on the literature review, Tables 2, 3, and 4 represent three categorizations of types of end-users.

1. Five personality traits that cannot be changed but help understand user behavior [17]. These personality traits have demonstrated a close relationship between the individual personalities and their pro-environmental behaviors [16] (Table 2).

Table 2. Personality traits and characteristics [17].

Personality trait	Characteristics
Openness	Tend to have environmental engagement
Conscientiousness	Are somewhat positive regarding environmental engagement
Extraversion	Do not appear to have a significant impact on behavior
Agreeableness	Tend to have environmental engagement
Neuroticism	Experience significant environmental concern

Table 3. Energy end user segments and characteristics [8].

End user segment	Characteristics
Green advocate	Users are interested in technologies and are energy aware
Traditionalist cost-focused	Users have limited interest in new technologies. Energy-saving behavior is motivated by cost-saving
Home focused	Users are interested in home improvement efforts and concerned about saving energy and reducing cost
Non-green selective	Users are selective at energy-saving appliances, focus on set-and-forget inventions, and are not energy aware
Disengaged	Users are not interested in new technologies and are not concerned about the environment

Table 4. Energy target groups and characteristics [18].

Energy target group	Characteristics
Early adopter	They are new technology enthusiasts and participate in social media communities. They are not energy aware
Cost-oriented	They take care of their household and focus on cost-oriented behaviors. They try to adopt a sustainable lifestyle
Energy-conscious	They attempt to lead a sustainable lifestyle. They are energy aware. They use smartphones and are not necessarily active on social media

2. Ponce et al. [8] proposed five energy end user segments (Table 3).
3. Peham, Breitfuss, and Michalczuk [18] proposed three energy target groups (Table 4).

2.3 Gamification and Serious Games in Energy Saving

Based on the self-determination theory, Wee and Choong [19] classified nine-game design elements based on autonomy, competence, and relatedness satisfaction for a gamified energy-saving campaign, i.e., *personal profile, non-fixed structure, challenge, feedback, theme, short cycle time, competition, cooperation, and chat-based social network*. Johnson et al. [20] realized a systematic review of gamification energy applications and proposed propose twelve-game elements, i.e., *feedback, challenges, social sharing, rewards, leaderboards, points, tips, levels, rankings, avatars, badges, and user-generated content*. Stieglitz, Lattemann, and Ro [21] stated that an achievement system structure to engage users in any gamified application requires an identifier (name of the achievement), an achievement unlocking-logic (problem solution), and rewards.

Chou [22] proposed a complete octalysis framework based on extrinsic, intrinsic, positive, and negative motivations to analyze and build strategies to make engaging applications. Schiele [23] reviewed game design elements in 25 gamified energy applications and proposed best practices for a sustainable application. AlSkaif et al. [24] proposed a gamification-based framework to engage end-users in energy applications by shaping their energy behavior using the TTM and the following game design elements: *statistics, messages, tips, electricity bill discounts, virtual currency, prizes, offers and coupons, competition, collaboration, energy community, dashboard, leaderboard, progress bar, message box, notifications, degree of control, points, badges, and levels*. Fijnheer and Oostendorp [25] used gamification elements to design an energy game called Powersaver that influences the reduction of household energy consumption.

1. Powersaver game and dashboard prototypes. The design and effects of similar energy games were reviewed to develop design principles. Energy-saving activities were formulated to identify gamification elements and create energy-saving suggestions in the game.
2. Game evaluation. Potential users evaluated the prototype via questionnaires administered outside gameplay. The aspects that were evaluated included:

   - Knowledge: in-game quizzes
   - Attitude toward saving energy: questionnaires administered before and after playing the game
   - Actual energy usage: real-time monitoring of intelligent devices
   - Engagement: extent to which users continued playing the game and monitoring player behavior during playing

Peham, Breitfuss and Michalczuk [18] proposed a gamified application called ecoGator that support consumer awareness of energy-efficient purchases and everyday use of products through a gamification strategy based on rewarded activities. The application considers three types of end-users to promote a sustainable lifestyle by sending messages, challenges, and tips to make energy-efficient purchase decisions.

Serious games refer to games designed primarily for non-entertainment purposes with an explicit and carefully thought-out educational purpose. In developing these games, it is necessary to strike a balance between entertainment and education such that they are not intrusive or cease to be intrinsically motivating. Therefore, typically, they exhibit characteristics such as a goal-oriented nature with specific rules or a feedback system, competitive comparative elements, and element challenging activities, choices, and fantasy elements. These games are useful because the player is immersed in the gaming experience and receives feedback from the other participants. The games also provide information in a ludic manner so that the players feel active. On a large scale, serious games allow further investigation into the intervention's effectiveness strategy in influencing behavior [20, 26].

The gameful experience questionnaire, i.e., GAMEFULQUEST [27] is a guideline to evaluate user experiences in systems within a gamification context. The questionnaire uses a seven-point Likert scale ranging from "strongly disagree" to "strongly agree".

2.4 Type 1 and 2 Fuzzy Logic

Fuzzy logic proposes to model uncertainty based on linguistic variables related to human reasoning rather than using numerical values. Zadeh [28] proposed this theory in 1965, in which a class of object belongs to a fuzzy set with membership grades from 0 to 1 and inference rules proposed by experts, polls, or consensus-building that do not require a mathematical model of the real system [12]. There are two types of fuzzy logic, i.e., type 1 fuzzy logic (T1FL) and type 2 fuzzy logic (T2FL). T1FL involves three steps.

1. Fuzzification is based on a process where variables have an uncertainty metalinguistic degree and are classified in fuzzy sets, e.g., attitude variable = {High, Low, Medium}, where those values range from 0 to 1 in the membership function.
2. Inference linguistic rules are proposed with the help of experts, and they have an antecedent IF part and a consequent THEN part.
3. Defuzzification determines the optimal values outputs, i.e., the system passes the fuzzy values into crisp outputs throughout fuzzy inference methods. This study uses both the Mamdani inference model and Sugeno inference model to compare if the outputs values have any significant results between them.

T2FL is an extension of T1FL and involves four steps.

1. Fuzzification uses a secondary membership function known as footprint of uncertainty (FOU) with upper and lower membership functions.
2. Inference linguistic rules consider all expert opinions and assign them to that FOU.
3. The type reducer reduces the type 2 output sets to a type 1 set to facilitate the defuzzification process.
4. Defuzzification. This study uses the Sugeno inference model with the IT2-FLS Matlab/Simulink toolbox developed by Taskin and Kumbasar [29].

2.5 S^4 Products

Miranda [6] proposed the S^3 product development reference framework to implement sensing, smart, and sustainable features. In addition, Ponce et al. [7] proposed to include a fourth element, i.e., the social product development process, in the S^3 product.

- Sensing is the capability of a system to detect events, obtain data, and measure changes using sensors that allow monitoring of physical or environmental conditions.
- Smart refers to the incorporation of physical components, smart components, and connectivity complements to make the product intelligent and available to connect to other devices.
- Sustainable includes the social, environmental, and economic factors to produce balanced and optimized performance. The social aspect is related to the contribution of a product to people's quality of life.
- Social *is a product that can observe, register, analyze, and change the consumer behavior or adapt its features online/offline by itself to improve its performance or acceptability in the market* [7]

3 Proposed Framework

The goal of the proposed framework is to shape end user behavior using a connected thermostat to encourage them to reduce electricity consumption. In other words, the goal is to teach end users to take advantages of their S^4 connected thermostat product using an engaging interactive interface that uses game design elements and techniques (gamification and serious games). In the proposed framework, a fuzzy logic system decision determines end user's profile. This system considers user immersion relative to end user knowledge of their product and house, attitude toward saving energy, actual energy usage, and engagement. Thus, it is possible to propose a customized interface for each end user.

To fill the gap between the information provided by the thermostat, the user's expectations, and the environmental impact using a HMI, the proposed framework (Fig. 1) involves the following three steps based on Fijnheer and Oostendorp's energy game design methodology [25] to use the framework in an S^4 connected thermostat product.

1. Knowledge base: analyzes the types of energy end users and personalities proposed by Oliver and Srivastava [17], Ponce el al. [8], and Peham, Breitfuss, and Michalczuk [18], as well as the behavior and usability problems associated with the connected thermostat [8, 9], the effects of the application, and the gamification and serious games elements used for connected thermostat.
2. T1FL or T2FL: This step analyzes the four effects of the game to propose the gamification elements that best fit the user type. The fuzzy systems help the designer determine when T1FL is sufficient to propose a tailored interface or whether a more specific analysis using T2FL is required to propose a more accurate interface.
3. Evaluation: The end user interacts with the HMI. Through the social element of S^4, user engagement with the product and interface can recognized. This phase provides continuous feedback to the user and the knowledge base to determine whether the user is engaged or if adjustments are required.

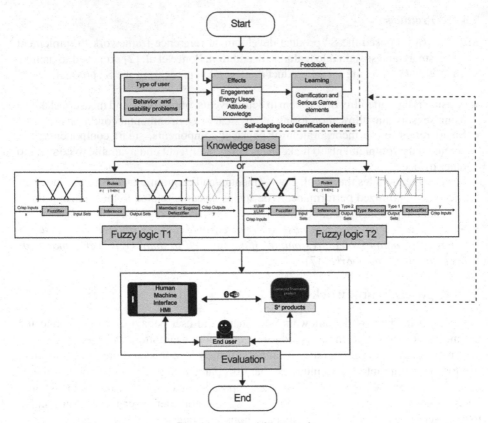

Fig. 1. Proposed framework.

3.1 Knowledge Base Phase

The interface of an interactive system influences user decisions, expectations, and motivations; thus, the interface should be useful, easy to use, and designed to be enjoyable and exciting [18, 24]. In this phase, the gamification and serious games elements of the energy application (Sect. 2.3) play a central role because they help test which elements keep the user interested through the *reward, achievement*, and *interface elements*. It uses the extrinsic elements suggested in energy applications because they are tangible and measurable [24].

3.2 Fuzzy Logic Phase

The fuzzy logic phase uses Mamdani's T1FL and Sugeno's T1FL and T2FL to analyze the most accurate outputs values to propose a customized HMI for each user. Fijnheer and Oostendorp [25] proposed that the effects of engagement, knowledge, attitude, and energy usage elements be measured in percentages as inputs, while the output elements are gamification and serious game elements (Sect. 2.3). Thus, the gamification elements are divided into three groups, i.e., trigger, interface, and reward elements. To shape user energy behaviors, the input values are related to saving money using the engagement and knowledge elements, and saving energy using the energy usage and attitude elements. Figure 2 shows the relationship between the effects and gamification elements used to propose the fuzzy rules and the TPB model used to propose the energy-saving behavior diagram to develop eco-saving and money-saving user behaviors. Thus, a gamification technique is applied to motivate them.

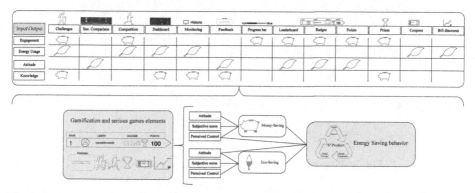

Fig. 2. Relationship between effects and gamification elements used to propose fuzzy rules and energy behavior diagram, which drives end user behaviors

The relationships among the input and output values are summarized as follows.

- Engagement: Challenges, competition, progress bar, leaderboard, points, badges, and prizes are used to monitor the player's behavior when the application is used to determine user engagement [25].
- Energy usage: Challenges, competition, dashboard, monitoring, coupons, and bill discounts to measure whether the user has a reduction in electrical bill [25].
- Attitude: Social comparison, feedback, leaderboard, badges, and points are used to measure whether the user has a change in attitude toward saving energy and money [25].
- Knowledge: Challenges, dashboard, monitoring, feedback, prizes can be measured using in-game quizzes [25].

Figure 3 shows the fuzzy logic proposed for the connected thermostat. Eighty-one rules are used to test the fuzzy system. In addition, the output values are measured using the semantic differential scale to detect behavior changes on a scale from one to seven, where four is considered a neutral pole [30].

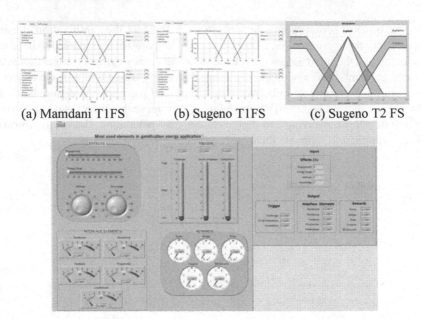

<table>
<tr><td>(a) Mamdani T1FS</td><td>(b) Sugeno T1FS</td><td>(c) Sugeno T2 FS</td></tr>
</table>

Fig. 3. Proposed fuzzy system used to test the application.

3.3 Evaluation Phase

The evaluation phase analyzes the type of user to propose a tailored connected thermostat interface that promotes an energy saving behavior in the user. An example of this phase is described below with the evaluation of an individual who has the following characteristics.

- Neuroticism [17], non-green selective [8], and cost-oriented user [18]
- Behavior problem of a user whose interests are different than saving energy [8].
- Usability problem of the information presented in the HMI is complicated to search because it is not focused on the user's task [9].

The initial input values of this user are low engagement (13.72%), medium energy usage (38.03%) and attitude (39.67%), and high knowledge (79.71%). Table 5 shows the results for each inference model. The T1FL, i.e., the Mamdani inference model (a), is more precise than the Sugeno model (b); however, the difference is not significant for measured outputs. The Mamdami model considers the area of the MF, but the Sugeno model does not; thus, the best option for this fuzzy system is the Mamdani inference model (a). Sugeno T2FL (c) uses an FOU; thus, it yields the more accurate outputs compared to the type 1 inference model. Here, the results consider the semantic differential scale; thus, the Sugeno Type 2 (c) inference model best fits this evaluation.

Table 5. Fuzzy logic inference results running on LabVIEW for Mamdani and Sugeno T1 and on Matlab/Simulink Toolbox for Sugeno T2.

Effects measured		Results		
Engagement		13.7		
Energy Usage		38.0		
Extraversion		39.7		
Agreeableness		79.7		
Gamification elements		Mamdani T1	Sugeno T1	Sugeno T2
Trigger	Challenges	3.1	3.1	4.3
	Social Comparison	3.4	3.4	2.9
	Competition	3.1	3.0	2.6
Interface	Dashboard	3.1	3.1	4.3
	Monitoring	3.1	3.1	4.3
	Feedback	3.9	4.0	3.9
	Progress bar	0.5	0.5	0.5
	Leaderboard	3.1	3.0	2.6
Rewards	Points	3.4	3.4	2.8
	Badges	3.4	3.4	2.8
	Prizes	5.4	5.9	6.2
	Coupons	3.1	3.0	2.7
	Bill discounts	3.1	3.0	2.7

As this user is cost-oriented and has low engagement, the interface must focus on high and medium output values. For example, the application can give the user more rewards based on how much knowledge about the connected thermostat and its economic benefits the user is achieving. In this phase, the S^4 product helps us evaluate the user and its relationship with the interface and the product itself.

4   Results

Based on the result of the evaluation phase, in Fig. 4 it is proposed for the end user three types of dashboard layout that the user can select. Figure 5 shows an example and descriptions of the gamified elements shown in the dashboard. The right part of the dashboard shows the most common elements in an energy gamified application, i.e., the progress bar, leaderboard, points, badges, social comparison, challenges, competition, prizes, coupons, and bill discounts. The interior layout shows information about the connected thermostat in a gamified structure. The feedback rectangle (right side) has the following options.

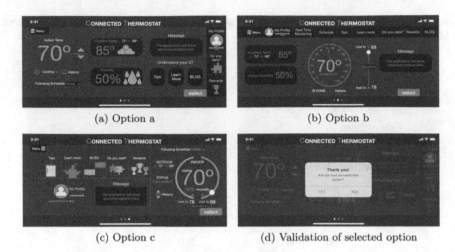

(a) Option a   (b) Option b

(c) Option c   (d) Validation of selected option

Fig. 4. Dashboard options.

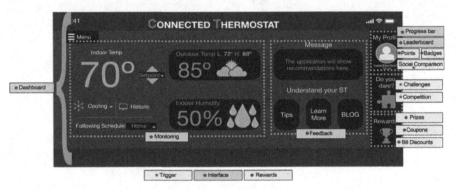

Fig. 5. Dashboard elements.

1. Tips. Here, the HVAC and Dwelling sections provide advice about how to improve the use of the air conditioner and housing.
2. Learn More. Using serious game techniques, e.g., virtual scenarios, this function teaches the user to understand the dashboard features to improve the use of the connected thermostat.
3. BLOG. This button redirects the user to a webpage where they post comments or complaints about the application.

When the user begins to use the application, feedback and adjustment of the evaluation phase are executed to determine whether the proposed dashboard is correct for the target user or whether the gamification functions in the HMI should be updated.

5 Discussion

This paper proposes a three-phase framework based on Fijnheer and Oostendorp's game design methodology [25]. The sensing, smart, and sustainable product prerequisites of the S^4 product are satisfied; thus, the proposed framework is based on social product. Knowledge base phase collects data provided by questionnaires or a database to obtain the end user types. Here, the information was taken from Oliver and Srivastava [17], Ponce et al. [8], and Peham, Breitfuss, and Michalczuk [18]. From the literature review in the energy field, the most common gamification and serious game elements were collected. The initial values of the effects in energy games were obtained through user surveys. The initial values came from the relationship between end user characteristics and each energy game effect. Thus, if the end user is not energy-aware, the energy usage effect is low (and vice versa). In fuzzy logic phase, using T1FL or T2FL, an end user profile is proposed, and the gamified elements are customized for each user type. Finally, in evaluation phase, a dashboard for the HMI is suggested. In addition, feedback and adjustments are provided while the user uses the application. In other words, this step begins the social interaction of the S^4 product, i.e., interaction between the end user and the product, and the interaction between the HMI and the product. The feedback and adjustments in the proposed framework help the user become engaged because the HMI can be adjusted as required. The proposed framework can be improved by automating the knowledge base process using an artificial neural network to gather information to feed the knowledge base in order to propose the most effective gamification and serious game elements. The knowledge base can be improved using the collected information from the automated process to propose multiple usability and behavior solutions. Note that the proposed framework does not consider its interaction with other connected devices; however, in future, it will be possible to make the knowledge base aware of the usability and behavior problems associated with various smart devices. With the proposed framework and interface, the user can be taught to take advantage of connected thermostats. Therefore, the behavior and usability problems found by Ponce et al. [8, 9] can be resolved by providing the user proper gamification and serious games elements. In addition, the feedback can help thermostat designers resolve physical usability problems based on the suggestions made by the proposed framework.

6 Conclusion

In this paper, we have proposed a framework that integrates gamification, serious games, and fuzzy logic to reduce energy for S^4 products. The HMI has the following stages: obtaining input values, profiling the end user, selecting gamification features to promote user engagement reduce electricity consumption, and validating those gamification features into the HMI. In addition, the HMI runs in continuous operation mode to reinforce and update the gamification functions displayed by the interface. According to uncertainty in the selection system, T1FL and T2FL are used to address uncertainty problems effectively. The S^4 concept for products is based on four classification characteristics, i.e., sensing, smart, sustainable, and social; thus, the proposed framework impacts each aspect of S^4 products. As a result, implementing the proposed framework is expected to improve S^4 products acceptability.

Note that some of the authors of this paper have proposed an HMI for thermostats based on usability problems and energy users using fuzzy systems that do not consider gamification and serious games elements. To the best of our knowledge, no existing interface uses gamification and serious game with a fuzzy logic decision system to reduce energy consumption. Thus, the proposed framework was integrated into connected thermostats. However, to promote effective use of products is a complex problem that requires a high-tech HMI, which increases implementation costs. Therefore, we targeted mobile devices, e.g., tablets and smartphones. Finally, by using an adaptable HMI, user can change their behavior by using S^4 products. Thus, the proposed three-phase framework can be used as a guideline for product designers to propose S^4 products that fill the gap between user expectations and usability problems. In addition, users can change their ecological behavior, and adoption of S^4 products would increase. In future, the proposed framework will be evaluated by undergraduate students.

Acknowledgments. Research Project supported by Tecnologico de Monterrey and UC Berkeley under the collaboration ITESM-CITRIS Smart thermostat, deep learning and gamification (https://citris-uc.org/2019-itesm-seed-funding/).

References

1. Cetin, K.S., O'Neill, Z.: Smart meters and smart devices in buildings: a review of recent progress and influence on electricity use and peak demand. Curr. Sustain. Energy Rep. **4**, 1–7 (2017). https://doi.org/10.1007/s40518-017-0063-7
2. Kang, W.M., Moon, S.Y., Park, J.H.: An enhanced security framework for home appliances in smart home. Hum. Centric Comput. Inf. Sci. **7**, 6 (2017). https://doi.org/10.1186/s13673-017-0087-4
3. Alimi, O.A., Ouahada, K.: Smart home appliances scheduling to manage energy usage. In: 2018 IEEE 7th International Conference on Adaptive Science Technology (ICAST), pp. 1–5 (2018). https://doi.org/10.1109/ICASTECH.2018.8507138
4. Avila, M., Ponce, P., Molina, A., Romo, K.: Simulation framework for load management and behavioral energy efficiency analysis in smart homes. In: McDaniel, T., et al. (eds.) ICSM 2019, LNCS, pp 1–12. Springer, Cham (2020). https://doi.org/10.1007/978-3-030-54407-2_42
5. Huchuk, B., O'Brien, W., Sanner, S.: A longitudinal study of thermostat behaviors based on climate, seasonal, and energy price considerations using connected thermostat data. Build. Environ. **139**, 199–210 (2018). https://doi.org/10.1016/j.buildenv.2018.05.003
6. Miranda, J., Pérez-Rodríguez, R., Borja, V., Wright, P.K., Molina, A.: Sensing, smart and sustainable product development (S^3 product) reference framework. Int. J. Prod. Res., 1–22 (2017). https://doi.org/10.1080/00207543.2017.1401237
7. Ponce, P., Meier, A.K., Miranda, J., Molina, A., Peffer, T.: The next generation of social products based on sensing, smart and sustainable (S3) features: a smart thermostat as case study. In: 9th IFAC Conference on Manufacturing Modelling, Management and Control, p. 6 (2019)
8. Ponce, P., Peffer, T., Molina, A.: Framework for communicating with consumers using an expectation interface in smart thermostats. Energy Build. **145**, 44–56 (2017). https://doi.org/10.1016/j.enbuild.2017.03.065

9. Ponce, P., Peffer, T., Molina, A.: Framework for evaluating usability problems: a case study low-cost interfaces for thermostats. Int. J. Interact. Des. Manuf. IJIDeM. **12**, 439–448 (2018). https://doi.org/10.1007/s12008-017-0392-1
10. Huotari, K., Hamari, J.: Defining gamification: a service marketing perspective. In: Proceeding of the 16th International Academic MindTrek Conference, pp. 17–22. ACM, New York (2012). https://doi.org/10.1145/2393132.2393137
11. Baptista, G., Oliveira, T.: Gamification and serious games: a literature meta-analysis and integrative model. Comput. Hum. Behav. **92**, 306–315 (2019). https://doi.org/10.1016/j.chb.2018.11.030
12. Ponce-Cruz, P., Molina, A., MacCleery, B.: Fuzzy Logic Type 1 and Type 2 Based on LabVIEW(TM) FPGA. Springer, Cham (2016). https://doi.org/10.1007/978-3-319-26656-5
13. Romero, J.A., García, P.A.G., Marín, C.E.M., Crespo, R.G., Herrera-Viedma, E.: Fuzzy logic models for non-programmed decision-making in personnel selection processes based on gamification. Inform. Lith Acad Sci. **29**, 1–20 (2018)
14. Prochaska, J.O., Velicer, W.F.: The transtheoretical model of health behavior change. Am. J. Health Promot. **12**, 38–48 (1997). https://doi.org/10.4278/0890-1171-12.1.38
15. Fogg, B.: What causes behavior change? https://www.behaviormodel.org/index.html
16. Greaves, M., Zibarras, L.D., Stride, C.: Using the theory of planned behavior to explore environmental behavioral intentions in the workplace. J. Environ. Psychol. **34**, 109–120 (2013). https://doi.org/10.1016/j.jenvp.2013.02.003
17. Oliver, J., Srivastava, S.: The Big Five Trait Taxonomy: History, Measurement, and Theoretical Perspectives. The Guilford Press, New York (1999)
18. Peham, M., Breitfuss, G., Michalczuk, R.: The ecoGator App: Gamification for enhanced energy efficiency in europe. in: proceedings of the second international conference on technological ecosystems for enhancing multiculturality, pp. 179–183. ACM, New York (2014). https://doi.org/10.1145/2669711.2669897
19. Wee, S.C., Choong, W.W.: Gamification: predicting the effectiveness of variety game design elements to intrinsically motivate users' energy conservation behaviour. J. Environ. Manage. **233**, 97–106 (2019). https://doi.org/10.1016/j.jenvman.2018.11.127
20. Johnson, D., Horton, E., Mulcahy, R., Foth, M.: Gamification and serious games within the domain of domestic energy consumption: a systematic review. Renew. Sustain. Energy Rev. **73**, 249–264 (2017). https://doi.org/10.1016/j.rser.2017.01.134
21. Stieglitz, S., Lattemann, C., Robra-Bissantz, S., Zarnekow, R., Brockmann, T., Ag, S.I.P.: Gamification using game elements in serious contexts (2017). https://doi.org/10.1007/978-3-319-45557-0
22. Chou, Y.-K.: Actionable Gamification: Beyond Points, Badges, and Leaderboards. Octalysis Media, California (2015)
23. Schiele, K.: Utilizing gamification to promote sustainable practices. In: Marques, J. (ed.) Handbook of Engaged Sustainability, pp. 427–444. Springer, Cham (2018). https://doi.org/10.1007/978-3-319-71312-0_16
24. AlSkaif, T., Lampropoulos, I., van den Broek, M., van Sark, W.: Gamification-based framework for engagement of residential customers in energy applications. Energy Res. Soc. Sci. **44**, 187–195 (2018). https://doi.org/10.1016/j.erss.2018.04.043
25. Fijnheer, J.D., van Oostendorp, H.: Steps to design a household energy game. In: De Gloria, A., Veltkamp, R. (eds.) Games and Learning Alliance, pp. 12–22. Springer, Cham (2016). https://doi.org/10.1007/978-3-319-40216-1_2
26. Moloney, J., Globa, A., Wang, R., Roetzel, A.: Serious games for integral sustainable design: level 1. Procedia Eng. **180**, 1744–1753 (2017). https://doi.org/10.1016/j.proeng.2017.04.337
27. Högberg, J., Hamari, J., Wästlund, E.: Gameful experience questionnaire (GAMEFULQUEST): an instrument for measuring the perceived gamefulness of system use. User Model. User Adapt. Interact. (2019). https://doi.org/10.1007/s11257-019-09223-w

28. Zadeh, L.A.: Fuzzy sets. Inf. Control **8**, 338–353 (1965). https://doi.org/10.1016/S0019-995 8(65)90241-X
29. Taskin, A., Kumbasar, T.: An open source Matlab/Simulink toolbox for interval type-2 fuzzy logic systems. In: 2015 IEEE Symposium Series on Computational Intelligence, pp. 1561–1568 (2015). https://doi.org/10.1109/SSCI.2015.220
30. Evans, G.T.: Use of the semantic differential technique to study attitudes during classroom lessons. Interchange **1**, 96–106 (1970). https://doi.org/10.1007/BF02214884

Improving the Attention Span of Elementary School Children in Mexico Through a S4 Technology Platform

Edgar Lopez-Caudana[1]([✉]) [iD], Pedro Ponce[2] [iD], Nancy Mazon[3], Luis Marquez[1], Ivan Mejia[1], and Germán Baltazar[1]

[1] School of Engineering and Sciences, Tecnologico de Monterrey, Mexico City, Mexico
edlopez@tec.mx
[2] Writing Lab, TecLabs, Tecnologico de Monterrey, Monterrey, Mexico
[3] Psychology Faculty, UNAM, Mexico City, Mexico

Abstract. Today's education faces a powerful enemy: lack of interest from students, who, even when attending class, find themselves distracted. This enemy has been in our schools for a long time, where technology has made it worse. This investigation intends to turn technology back to our side by proposing the use of an assistive robot, proving that it is capable of attracting student's attention and increasing their motivation for a Physical Education (PE) class. This paper demonstrates that for the use of this robot, the characteristics of a sensitive, sustainable, intelligent, and social service/product (S^4 products) need to be covered. The obtained data was analyzed from both an engineering and a psychological background. This study concludes that the attention span of children improves while their motivation increases as a result of participating in a robot-assisted PE class.

Keywords: Social robotics · Assistive education · S^4 products · Educational innovation · Higher education

1 Introduction

Nowadays, education professionals are constantly confronted with the fact that their students have a lack of attention and behavioral problems in the classroom. From [1], it was observed that usual outdoor physical education activities are inefficient, and children are quickly discouraged. According to this study, Mexico is the most inactive country in levels of physical-sport activities with a higher dropout rate [2]. Because of this, there is a need to develop open science strategies that guarantee the improvement of educational achievements among the school-age population, without forgetting to emphasize groups at risk of being excluded in opportunities to participate and learn [3, 4]. To improve the learning and cognitive processes (like memory and executive functions), it is critical to stimulate the attentional resources of children during their first years of school [5]. Technology is defined as "the set of scientifically ordered technical knowledge that allows for the design and creation of goods and services" [6]. In this sense, the use of

© Springer Nature Switzerland AG 2020
T. McDaniel et al. (Eds.): ICSM 2019, LNCS 12015, pp. 525–532, 2020.
https://doi.org/10.1007/978-3-030-54407-2_44

robotics in different areas related to the interaction in ordinary tasks with humans has taken great interest. Such interactions are associated with the assistance of the elderly [6, 7] or the education of children in different grades. Educational robotics is a discipline whose objective is the conception, creation, and functionality of robotic prototypes and specialized programs with pedagogic ends [8]. It is necessary to notice that educational robotics in Mexico refers to workshops outside traditional classes or private workshops of the same schools [9]. This robotic platform is conceptualized as a smart, sensing, sustainable product, taking into account social aspects, given its characteristics.

1.1 Juvenile Attention and Its Measurement in the Classroom

Attention is the manner that actively processes a fraction of a vast number of stimuli using our senses and other cognitive processes. It is analyzed by measuring five indicators: the concentration of the person (referring to the precision and memorization of information), the habituation to a stimulus, the dishabituation of such stimulus, the distraction or the neglect of the main activity, and the motivation and enthusiasm showed when working in a specific task [10]. When talking about attention, one of the main challenges is measuring it, and thus, the first step is to create unique observational instruments for a proper methodology [11]. The use of scientific knowledge allows us to study the occurrence of perceptible behaviors in a way that can be adequately registered and quantified [12, 13]. To sufficiently observe them, certain conditions are desirable [14].

1.2 Technological Instrument: NAO Robot

Robots have evolved into a relevant tool with significant achievements in the learning process by being developed as an adequate strategy to motivate children, and increasing their curiosity [15, 16]. Even though there are plenty of studies about the importance of learning robotics [17], most of them are models where the robot itself is a tool to obtain better results in the teaching-learning process, but not an assistive platform for the teaching process per se. A clear example is shown in [18], where a clear and disruptive instance on the use of a robot helps to lower anxiety. Another example of the implementation of a robotic teaching-learning process regarding PE is mentioned in [19], where the authors used a socially assistive robot (SAR) to improve the motivation for physical exercise developed by them. In [20], an NAO robot was used to give dancing lessons to a group of children, where the robot explained the movements, and the children needed to perform and learn a dancing phrase. In [21] can be seen how it can be achieved greater efficiency in children learning, with the proper use of a robot. The work shown in [22] demonstrates that a robotic platform is capable of improving social, supportive behaviors in a language learning application.

In this project, version 4 of SoftBank Robotics NAO robot was used as a teacher's assistant. The NAO has 25 Degrees Of Freedom (DOF), which gives it the capacity to execute a wide range of movements, like walking, sitting, standing up, dancing, evading obstacles, kicking, grabbing, among others. Integrated with WIFI communication, NAO is entirely autonomous and can establish a secure connection to the Internet to download and transmit content. It is also equipped with two speakers and microphones, allowing it to reproduce music, as well as implement voice recognition algorithms that can localize where the sound is coming from so that it can turn its head towards the source. This humanoid robot can be programmed in the visual environment Choregraphe, as well as on Python, depending on the programmed routine [21, 23] (Fig. 1).

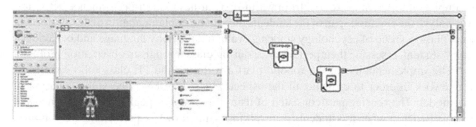

Fig. 1. Example of the Choregraphe programming environment

Referring to the concept of Industry 4.0, the implementation of the robotic platform follows the S^3 framework that evaluates the smart, sensing, and sustainable application of technologies [24]. The objective of this framework is to integrate the use of technological platforms through Concurrent Engineering (CE) and Product Lifecycle Management (PLM) [25].

In [26], the designed projects adopt the S^4 concept, including the NAO robot, by combining the functionalities of the robot with the purposes of the service. Table 1 presents the S^4 solutions of the proposed humanoid robot assistant. A learning environment with educational robotics is an experience that contributes to the development of new skills, concepts, and strengthening children's logical, structural and systematic thought while developing particular problem-solving skills, thus providing an efficient response to the ever-changing environments of the contemporary world [23, 27].

Table 1. Humanoid robot assistant as S^4 technology [19]

Description of main S^4 solutions	
Sensing	• The robot is programmed to recognize faces, emotions, and sounds (infrared sensors, proximity sensors, inertia sensors, sound sensors, touch sensors, and cameras)
Smart	• The robot must be configured according to the required functions to get the desirable movements, communications, and interactions • The robot allows Wi-Fi and Ethernet communication • The robot has some sceneries to choose according to the interactions with students
Sustainable	• Economic: This product/service promotes productivity • Environment: The humanoid robot has a long useful life cycle and was designed to have a low environmental impact
Social	• Social: This platform contributes to the quality of life of people and provides training purposes to support education and work • The robot increases the motivation for students and interaction between them

2 Methodology

This work proposes the implementation of a robotic platform as a supportive tool for the PE professor. During every experimental session, an NAO robot gave the instructions and examples of different exercises, from warm-up routines to high-performance activities. To analyze the attention span of the students during the implementation of the platform in their class, a group of psychology students evaluated the body language and behavior of every student, assessing their performance during class through an observation protocol.

The implementation of the robotic platform during the PE class followed the S^4 framework in order to evaluate all the aspects related to the successful evaluation of the model. The sensing part consisted of using the robot's speakers, microphones and motors to detect when the students were talking with him while performing the routines. The smart aspect of the implementation is based on the fact that the class methodology was designed in collaboration with the PE professor. This approach assured that the movements and explanations given by the platform were appropriate for the class and its population. The sustainable part of this implementation is focused on the fact that one platform is enough for designing and giving the same class methodology to all the different groups of the school. Finally, the fact that the robot asks for the collaboration of the students while the professor makes sure they do the exercises appropriately creates an environment of social communication between the students, the professor, and the robot.

The creation of postures and movements was done with the help of the program Choregraphe, SoftBank Robotics' proprietary programming environment in which programming blocks are used for the robot's routine [28]. Because the robot does not have the same capability as humans regarding movement execution, the exercises were tailored to its capacities. At first, it has been analyzed how a human performs each one of the established exercises, focusing on their speed, sequence of movements, physical wear, among others, to create a lifelike imitation by the robot that children could also execute. Each of the previously established exercises was studied in detail to identify particular points in the movements, critical support points, and changes in the center of mass, to have a better perspective and develop an efficient sequence, capable of being executed by a robot (Fig. 2).

Fig. 2. Examples of Nao's posture and application with students

It is essential to point out that the objective was not to completely reproduce all the exercises proposed. For example, to put the students to jog, it was decided that the NAO would give the instructions, while the teachers accompanied the students.

Also, the sample was taken entirely from two groups selected by the administration of the "Martin Torres Padilla" elementary school, and no restrictions were set as to the gender or academic status to approximate the use of the robotic platform in a regular group. Children were informed of this at every session, which established it as a fair contact point for the sessions.

3   Results and Discussion

The results obtained, in qualitative and quantitative aspects, show that the use of a humanoid robot, with which the students could interact, meant an adequate and efficient way to achieve greater motivation and attention of the children in the classes, which is meant as an improvement in the objectives of the physical education sessions proposed. Both quantitative and qualitative analyses were done with a study of the group (4th and 3rd grade). The quantitative analysis was based on a questionnaire that the observers filled out at every session, indicating whether different factors were present or absent (Yes, No or No Applicant); the observational scale methodology used was created by researcher from UNAM School of Psychology, based in [10]. The qualitative study corresponds to comments made by the observers (mostly psychology students) to note relevant observations with regards to points of interest (motivation and attention). It is necessary to mention that in this work, a non-parametric contrast is introduced, which is usually the method necessary to draw inferential conclusions about nominal or ordinal data.

In Fig. 3 and 4, starting from the first group from left to right, there are the analyzed dimensions: Concentration, Memory, Habituation, Dehabituation, Distraction, Enthusiasm, and Motivation analysis of both groups, respectively. The results showed that children were slightly distracted and occasionally did not pay attention to the indications the teachers gave. In general, the group behaved but showed some distraction if the teacher was not nearby. With the incorporation of the robot, there were a few noticeable changes, such as the case of their concentration, as most of the children would center their attention on the robot and follow its instructions. The exercises were done in a better way, which meant that the activities were done correctly, minimizing the need for the teacher to discipline children. The most remarkable thing about this group was that the children tried to imitate every one of the exercises done by the robot.

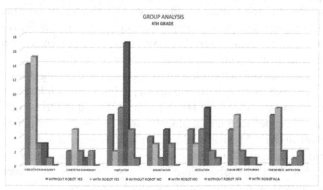

Fig. 3. Group analysis 4th grade

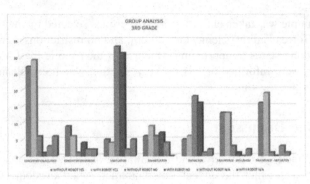

Fig. 4. Group analysis 3rd grade

The interviews made to the students showed that most of them considered that the presence of the robot made the class more interesting. Also, some others assured that the robot helped them comprehend the subjects while denying feeling uncomfortable with the presence of the platform. Although no statistical analysis was made, it has been obtained an 85% reliability inter-judges in the observed behaviors, which represent outstanding results about descriptive statistics with frequency analysis. This idea shows the validation of the obtained results.

Even though the total population that participated during this session is not statistically convincing, it still points to the utility of a robotic platform in environments different than the ones where mathematics and other STEM-related topics are given. Also, the results obtained showed that the group is eager to take a class that uses technological platforms instead of following the same routine in a regular PE session.

4 Conclusions

This study is the starting point for designing and evaluating a robotic platform in a PE class in Mexico. Even though the initial results demonstrate that there is an improvement in the students' attention span, it is still necessary to assess this implementation in the long-term analysis. A further study could also validate if the attention span of the students' group does not decrease because they get familiar with the platform so the robot could not attract the children's attention anymore. Also, the presented strategy could be extended to evaluate different forms of implementing the robotic platform, creating new PE class routines and methodologies. Moreover, this paper presented how an assistive robotic platform can be analyzed and structured as an S^4 product.

The convenience of using a robotic tool to improve the learning process, increasing attention levels, and the motivation of elementary school-aged children, was shown. It was demonstrated an increase in the attention span; thus, it could be inferred that the robotic system is a proper step into a global strategy to widen the perspective on the treatment of this problem in Mexican children. One of the main contributions of this paper is to show how to evaluate its effectiveness in a Mexican elementary school. However, this paper does not argue about all the benefits of technology in education. Therefore, the main contribution is focused on the creation of an interdisciplinary, concise, and conclusive methodology that allows to observe and analyze the attention span of elementary school students during a PE class.

Although the selected platform is not the most efficient one in terms of cost, it still helped demonstrate that the use of a robotic platform as a supportive tool for the professor improves the attention and eagerness of the students in the execution of routinary tasks performed during a regular PE class. It is still necessary to evaluate the same implementation in a larger group to obtain statistical evidence of the utility of the S4 framework in class design and the proper implementation of supportive technological platforms.

Acknowledgment. The authors would like to thank the enthusiastic participation of the personnel and directing body of the Public Elementary School "Martin Torres Padilla" for their collaboration in the development of this project.

The authors would like to acknowledge the financial and technical support of Writing Lab, TecLabs, Tecnologico de Monterrey, Mexico, in the production of this work.

References

1. Conesa, P.V., Juan, F.R.: Clima motivacional en Educación Física y actividad físico-deportiva en el tiempo libre en alumnado de España, Costa Rica y México. In: Federación Española de Asociaciones de Docentes de Educación Física (FEADEF) (ed.) Retos: nuevas tendencias en educación física, deporte y recreación, vol. 29, pp. 195–200 (2016)
2. Administración Federal de Servicios Educativos en el D.F.: El trastorno por déficit de atención con o sin hiperactividad (TDA-TDAH): Atención a la diversidad en escuelas inclusivas. Secretaría de Educación Pública (SEP), Mexico City (2011)
3. World Health Organization: Physical activity: fact sheets. World Health Organization (WHO) (2018)
4. Teixeira Costa, H.J., Abelairas-Gomez, C., Arufe-Giraldez, V., Pazos-Couto, J.M., Barcala-Furelos, R.: Influence of a physical education plan on psychomotor development profiles of preschool children. J. Hum. Sport Exerc. **10**(1), 126–140 (2015)
5. Ghiglion, M., Filippetti, A., Manucci, V., Apaz, A.: Programa de Intervención para Fortalecer Funciones Cognitivas y Lingüísticas, Adaptado al Currículo Escolar en Niños en Riesgo por Pobreza. Interdisciplinaria **28**(1), 17–36 (2011)
6. Ferraro, R.A., Lerch, C.: Qué es qué en Tecnología?, Granica (1997)
7. Werner, F., Krainer, D., Oberzaucher, J., Werner, K.: Evaluation of the acceptance of a social assistive robot for physical training support together with older users and domain experts. In: Assistive Technology: From Research to Practice: AAATE, vol. 33, no. 2013, p. 137 (2013)
8. Krainer, D., Werner, F., Oberzaucher, J.: Performance of a socially assistive robot as trainer for physical exercises for older people. Wohnen–Pflege–Teilhabe–"Besser leben durch Technik" (2014)
9. Heredia, Y.: Incorporación de tecnología educativa en educación básica: dos escenarios escolares en México. In: XI Encuentro Internacional Virtual Educa, Santo Domingo (2010)
10. Sternberg, R.J., Salinas, M.E.O., Julio, E.R., Ponce, L.R.: Psicología Cognoscitiva, 5th edn. Cengage Learning, São Paulo (2010)
11. Sánchez, P.A., Martínez, M.B.: Guía para la observación de los parámetros psicomotores. Revista Interuniversitaria de Formación del Profesorado **37**, 63–85 (2000)
12. Díaz, L.: La observación (2010)

13. Sas, L.G., Fariña, E.F., Ferreiro, M.C., Fernández, J.E.R., Couto, J.P.: Mejora de la autoestima e inteligencia emocional a través de la psicomotricidad y de talleres de habilidades sociales. Sportis **3**(1), 187–205 (2017)
14. Kawulich, B.B.: Participant observation as a data collection method. Forum Qualitative Sozialforschung/Forum Qual. Soc. Res. **6**(2) (2005)
15. Goh, H., Aris, B.: Using robotics in education: lessons learned and learning experiences. In: 1st International Malaysian Educational Technology Convention (2007)
16. Reich-Stiebert, N., Eyssel, F.: Learning with educational companion robots? Toward attitudes on education robots, predictors of attitudes, and application potentials for education robots. Int. J. Social Robot. **7**(5), 875–888 (2015). https://doi.org/10.1007/s12369-015-0308-9
17. Blar, N., Jafar, F.A., Idris, S.A.: Robot and human teacher. In: 2014 International Conference on Computer, Information and Telecommunication Systems (CITS) (2014)
18. Alemi, M., Meghdari, A., Ghazisaedy, M.: The impact of social robotics on L2 learners' anxiety and attitude in English vocabulary acquisition. Int. J. Social Robot. **7**(4), 523–535 (2015). https://doi.org/10.1007/s12369-015-0286-y
19. Fasola, J., Mataric, M.: A socially assistive robot exercise coach for the elderly. J. Hum. Robot. Interact. **2**(2), 3–32 (2013)
20. Ros, R., Baroni, L., Demiris, Y.: Adaptive human-robot interaction in sensorimotor task instruction: from human to robot dance tutors. Robot. Auton. Syst. **62**(6), 707–720 (2014)
21. Shamsuddin, S., et al.: Humanoid robot NAO: review of control and motion exploration. In: 2011 IEEE International Conference on Control System, Computing and Engineering, pp. 511–516. IEEE, November 2011
22. Saerbeck, M., Schut, T., Bartneck, C., Janse, M.D.: Expressive robots in education: varying the degree of social, supportive behavior of a robotic tutor. In: Proceedings of the SIGCHI Conference on Human Factors in Computing Systems (2010)
23. Pot, E., Monceaux, J., Gelin, R., Maisonnier, B.: Choregraphe: a graphical tool for humanoid robot programming. In: RO-MAN 2009 - The 18th IEEE International Symposium on Robot and Human Interactive Communication, pp. 46–51. IEEE, September 2009
24. Chavarría-Barrientos, D., Camarinha-Matos, L.M., Molina, A.: Achieving the sensing, smart and sustainable "everything". In: Camarinha-Matos, L.M., Afsarmanesh, H., Fornasiero, R. (eds.) PRO-VE 2017. IAICT, vol. 506, pp. 575–588. Springer, Cham (2017). https://doi.org/10.1007/978-3-319-65151-4_51
25. Molina Gutiérrez, A., et al.: Open innovation laboratory for rapid realisation of sensing, smart and sustainable products: motives, concepts and uses in higher education. In: Camarinha-Matos, L.M., Afsarmanesh, H., Rezgui, Y. (eds.) PRO-VE 2018. IAICT, vol. 534, pp. 156–163. Springer, Cham (2018). https://doi.org/10.1007/978-3-319-99127-6_14
26. Odorico, A.: Marco teorico para una robotica pedagogica. Rev. Informatica Educ. y Medios Audiovisuales **1**(3), 34–46 (2004)
27. Park, I.-W., Han, J.: Teachers' views on the use of robots and cloud services in education for sustainable development. Cluster Comput. **19**(2), 987–999 (2016). https://doi.org/10.1007/s10586-016-0558-9
28. Miranda, J., Pérez-Rodríguez, R., Borja, V., Wright, P.K., Molina, A.: Sensing, smart and sustainable product development (S^3 product) reference framework. Int. J. Prod. Res., 1–22 (2017)

Short Paper

Evaluation of Human Roughness Perception by Using Tactile MFCC

Masahiro Fukada[1], Taiju Shizuno[1], and Yuichi Kurita[1,2(✉)]

[1] Graduate School of Engineering, Hiroshima University,
1-4-1 Kagamiyama, Higashihiroshima, Hiroshima 739-8527, Japan
{masahirofukada,ykurita}@hiroshima-u.ac.jp
[2] JST PRESTO, 4-1-8, Honmachi Kawaguchi, Saitama 332-0012, Japan

Abstract. In this study, we created a tactile Mel filter bank using the Pacinian corpuscle sensitivity model and proposed tactile Mel frequency cepstrum coefficients (TMFCC), which is an evaluation method that performs the same processing as Mel frequency cepstrum coefficients (MFCC), to calculate roughness perception from fingertip vibration. In the regression analysis of the index calculated from the measured fingertip vibration and the subjective roughness perception, the accuracy was verified using leave-one-subject-out cross-validation. The correlation coefficient, indicating the accuracy, was $r = 0.819$ in the proposed TMFCC.

Keywords: tactile MFCC · MFCC · Roughness perception · Fingertip vibration

1 Summary of Contributions

We propose a tactile MFCC (Mel-Frequency Cepstrum Coefficients) using a tactile Mel filter bank created from the Pacinian corpuscle sensitivity model to evaluate roughness perception from fingertip vibration. Figure 1 shows the results of accuracy verification by using leave-one-subject-out cross-validation, based on the regression analysis of TMFCC features calculated from measured fingertip vibrations and subjective roughness perception. To demonstrate the effectiveness of the proposed method, the comparative index was MFCC. The correlation coefficient between the true and estimated values of roughness perception, indicating the accuracy, was $r = 0.728$ in the conventional MFCC, but $r = 0.819$ in the proposed TMFCC method. Our method enables to quantitatively evaluate the roughness perception from fingertip vibration.

2 Brief Background on State-of-the-Art

We focused on MFCC used in speech recognition as an evaluation method for fingertip vibrations so that the roughness perception of human can be evaluated more quantitatively.

This Research is Partially Supported by the Center of Innovation Program from Japan Science and Technology Agent, JST.

T. McDaniel et al. (Eds.): ICSM 2019, LNCS 12015, pp. 535–537, 2020.
https://doi.org/10.1007/978-3-030-54407-2

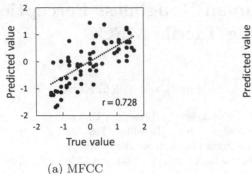
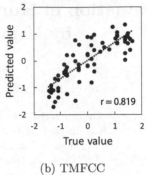

(a) MFCC   (b) TMFCC

Fig. 1. Scatter plot of estimated and true values with Leave-one-subject-out cross validation. $p < 0.001$ for all evaluation methods.

Strese *et al.* [1] calculated the features of MFCC from the measured tactile vibrations and showed that Naive Bayes Classifier could correctly identify 69 textures with a 95% recognition rate. However, as the original MFCC is designed for speech recognition, it does not include the characteristics of tactile receptors and is not suitable as an evaluation index for tactile sensation. Taking a mechanism of human tactile sensation into consideration, better evaluation method of human's roughness perception can be realized.

3   Summary of Improvements

To develop tactile MFCC (TMFCC), we created a tactile Mel filter bank using the Pacinian corpuscle sensitivity model. This model was assumed to have a normal distribution (1):

$$F(x) = -\frac{1}{\sqrt{2\pi\sigma^2}}e^{-\frac{(x-\mu)^2}{2\sigma^2}}. \tag{1}$$

Optimization of Pacinian corpuscle sensitivity model and the tactile filter bank were performed using Sequential Model-Based Global Optimization (the tree-structured Parzen estimator) [2], First, the TMFCC process divided the measured fingertip vibration with frame length F_l of 2048 points and shift length F_s of 512 points, and performed a fast Fourier transform on each part of the data. The created tactile filter bank was superimposed on the calculated frequency spectrum and converted to a power spectrum. The power spectrum is regarded as a time signal, and a discrete cosine transform was performed to obtain the TMFCC features. The average of the obtained feature values over the sum of each section was used as the TMFCC feature value.

4   Preliminary Results

Figure 2(a) shows the frequency characteristics of the previously reported and obtained Pacinian corpuscle sensitivity models. We confirmed that the obtained

Pacinian characteristics have similar tendency to the previously reported characteristics. Based on this model, we created the Mel filter bank. Figure 2(b) shows the created filter bank for tactile perception. In this model, the sensitivity of vibration in the range between 200 and 400 Hz has higher than those less than 200 Hz or more than 400 Hz due to the Pacinian corpuscle's characteristics. By superimposing this tactile filter bank, the proposed TMFCC fingertip vibration evaluation method reflects the sensitivity characteristics of the Pacinian corpuscle. The experimental results to evaluate the performance of the proposed method were described in Sect. 1 and Fig. 1.

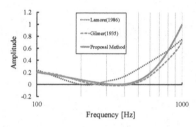
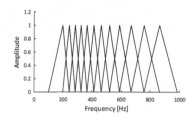

(a) Comparison with conventional Pacinian corpuscle sensitivity[3, 4](normalized).

(b) Tactile filter bank obtained by optimization calculation.

Fig. 2. Comparison of obtained sensitivity model with previous research and tactile filter bank.

References

1. Strese, M., Schuwerk, C., Steinbach, E.: Surface classification using acceleration signals recorded during human freehand movement. In: 2015 IEEE World Haptics Conference (WHC), pp. 214–219. IEEE, Evanston, IL, USA (2015)
2. Bergstra, J., Bardenet, R., Bengio, Y., Kégl, B.: Algorithms for Hyper-parameter Optimization. In: Proceedings of the 24th International Conference on Neural Information Processing Systems, pp. 2546–2554. Curran Associates Inc., (2011)
3. Lamore, P.J.J., Muijser, H., Keemink, C.J.: Envelope detection of amplitude modulated high frequency sinusoidal signals by skin mechanoreceptors. J. Acoust. Soc. Am. **79**(4), 1082–1085 (1986)
4. von Haller Gilmer, B.: The measurement of the sensitivity of the skin to mechanical vibration. J. Gen. Psychol. **13**(1), 42–61 (1935)

Author Index

Printed in the United States
By Bookmasters